THE ENGLISH CASTLE

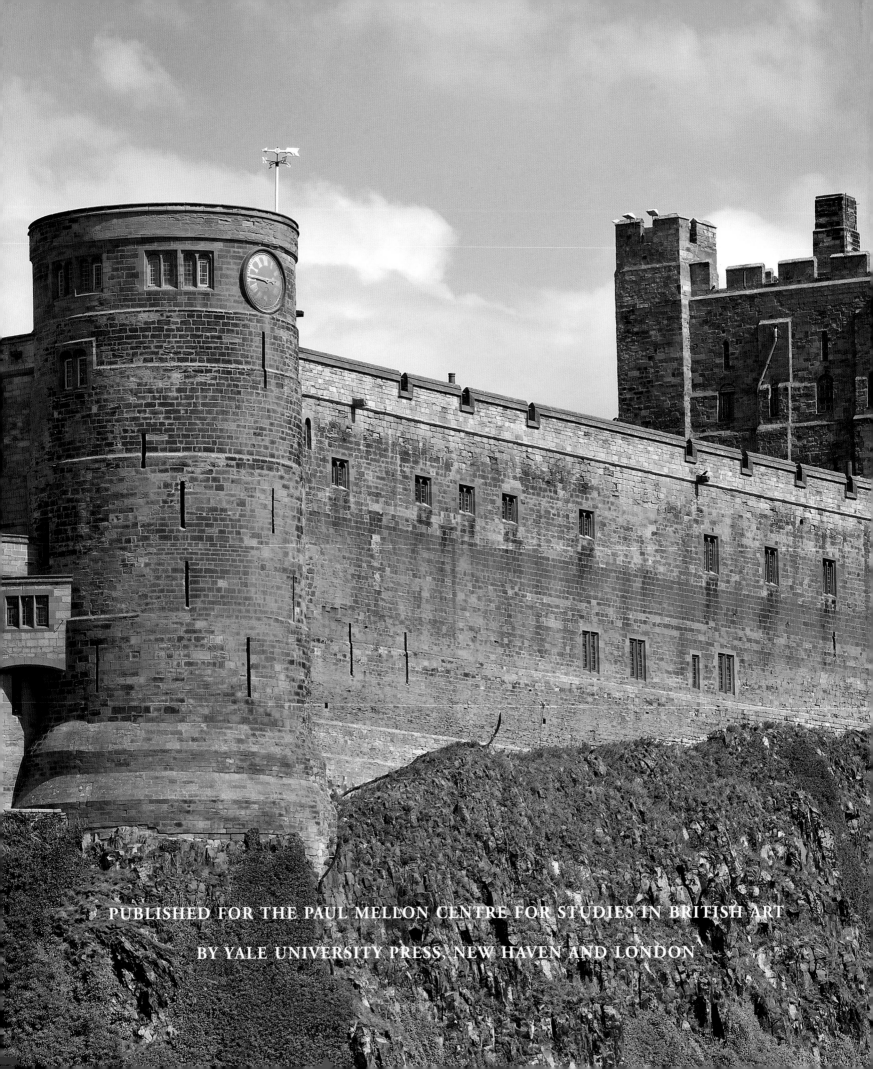

PUBLISHED FOR THE PAUL MELLON CENTRE FOR STUDIES IN BRITISH ART

BY YALE UNIVERSITY PRESS, NEW HAVEN AND LONDON

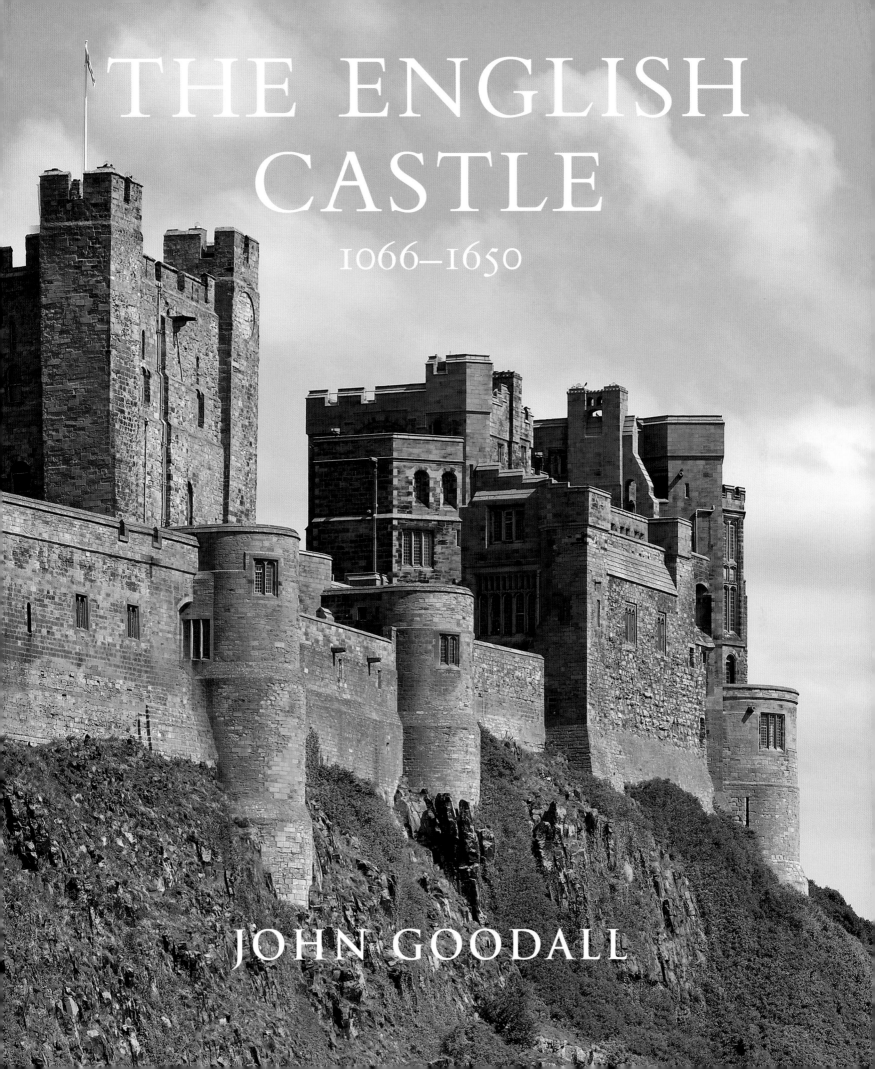

THE ENGLISH CASTLE

1066–1650

JOHN GOODALL

Designed by Sarah Faulks

Printed in China

Library of Congress Cataloging-in-Publication Data
Goodall, John, 1970–
  The English castle, 1066–1650 / John Goodall.
      p. cm.
  Includes bibliographical references and index.
  ISBN 978-0-300-11058-6 (cl : alk. paper)
  1. Castles–England–History. 2. Architecture and
society–England–History. I. Title.
  NA7745.G66 2010
  728.8'10942–DC22

                                                2010045969

A catalogue record for this book is available from The British
Library

Front endpapers: Herstmonceux, Sussex, *circa* 1918.
© Country Life.

Back endpapers: Dover, Kent, 1922.
© A. E. Henson / Country Life.

Pg. ii–iii: Bamburgh, Northumberland.
© Paul Barker / Country Life.

Pg. iv: Grosmont, Monmouthshire.
© John Goodall.

FOR CAROLINE

ACKNOWLEDGEMENTS

I came to write this book by what seems – in retro-spect – a tortuous route. It is one, moreover, that has left me indebted for every variety of kindness to a bewildering number of people.

From 1993, while working on my doctorate at the Courtauld Institute in London, Giles Worsley – then architectural editor of *Country Life* – commissioned me to write several articles on medieval buildings for the magazine. His successor from 1994, Michael Hall, sent back one on Tattershall Castle for redrafting, and the upshot of our discussion was an article on the defi-nition of what a castle was. Research for this latter article led to my spending a stimulating day in 1999 at Bodiam Castle with Charles Coulson, an outspoken critic of the received scholarship on castles. At the time, none of these events seemed very significant, but they came to be so in the light of other work.

Between submitting my doctorate and my viva in 1997 I was appointed a researcher for English Heritage at Dover Castle by the Head of Properties in the south-east, Jonathan Coad. At the time the archaeologist Kevin Booth was involved in recording the fabric of the great tower at Dover, and I had the opportunity through his help, and with the gentle steering of Jonathan Coad, to explore every corner of this immense site over a period of two years. The project

of researching and preparing two exhibitions at Dover, besides the additional invitation to write the new English Heritage guide on Pevensey Castle, gave me for the first time a proper grounding in the study of castles. In the same period I also inherited Nicholas Moore's archive of material on brick architecture, which has been of great help in elucidating the histo-ries of particular sites. I am grateful to the kindness shown to me by both Nicholas and his widow, Dinah.

When my series of short contracts at English Her-itage came to an end in 1999, I decided to put aside some time to publish my doctoral thesis as a book. While I worked on this, I was asked to do other writing and research work and I settled down for the next four years as a freelance. The experience of working on guidebooks, websites and exhibitions, as well as teach-ing at Warwick University and on the British Studies at Oxford course, taught me a great deal. All these tasks made me think hard about the problems of presenting architecture to those less obsessive about it than myself.

Meanwhile, Jeremy Musson, my predecessor as architectural editor at *Country Life*, continued to com-mission articles from me for the magazine. The disci-pline of producing articles for *Country Life* – readable but authoritative treatments of buildings for an inter-ested audience – further widened my experience. In

Facing page: Helmsley, North Yorkshire.

particular, it brought home to me the breathtaking quantity of historic architecture that remains in private ownership and which in many cases waits patiently for engaged scholarly attention.

Over time, my *Country Life* work, through the labours of consecutive editors and subs – including Anne Wright, Bronwen Riley and Polly Chiapetta – helped me find my voice as a writer. It also, thanks to the meticulous and painstaking labours of Paul Barker and June Buck (and more recently Will Pryce), shaped my expectations of architectural photography and helped me understand its possibilities.

It was while working as a freelance, and by now with a developed interest in castles, that I decided to write this book. With the encouragement and advice of Stuart Hay, Jeremy Ashbee and Michael Hall – amongst others – I sent off a proposal to several publishers. The book that Gillian Malpass at Yale agreed to publish on the strength of two generous readers' reports was essentially that which you hold now, but with the important difference that it was meant to be 90,000 words long. In the event – and to paraphrase Gibbon's celebrated excuse for his voluminous *The Decline and Fall of the Roman Empire* – I made it long because I had not the wit to make it short.

Almost as soon as the contract was signed events got in the way of completing the book in the two years that I had initially planned. In 2003 I got a job as a historian at English Heritage. As one strand of this work I was involved in the launch of a new guidebook series known as the Red Guides. My boss at the time, David Robinson, had previously been editor of the CADW series of guidebooks and I learnt a great deal from him about the nuts and bolts of putting together these publications. To my mind they remain highly technical publications for the simple reason that they are created – ideally at least – to be read in a particular place.

The experience of writing for *Country Life* had already made me respect good editing and subbing, but working with the guidebook editors at English Heritage – Susannah Lawson, Katy Carter, Sarah Yates, Jen Nelson, Cat Howitson, Abigail Wheatley and Bronwen Riley (again) – made me, if possible, value it more. Similarly, this work revealed to me the possibilities of understanding and interpreting ruined buildings not only through good photography but also through the medium of artistic reconstructions.

In different projects, four artists – Stephen Conlin, Peter Dunn, Ivan Lapper and Liam Wales – had already initiated me in the processes of producing reconstruction drawings and paintings. Now, working on my first guidebooks as an insider, I became involved in more intense collaborations than ever before. I also worked with other artists including Terry Ball, Chris Jones-Jenkins, Phil Kenning and David Simon. Images by most of these individuals are reproduced in this book.

The accuracy of many of these drawings reflects the technical and architectural knowledge of another colleague, Richard Lea. His computer modelling made it possible to interrogate the surviving physical evidence in far greater detail than I had thought possible. In some cases it also allowed the detailed comparison of historic views of monuments with their extant fabric for the purposes of identifying lost architectural features. Underpinning such analysis was Mark Fenton's knowledge of plans and the history of plan making in English Heritage and its predecessor institutions.

In the meantime, these and other responsibilities involved me in a college-like community comprising my immediate colleagues at English Heritage in which people generously shared information and ideas. Particularly important in this were Jeremy Ashbee, Jonathan Coad, Richard Hewlings, Alastair Oswald, Paul Pattison, David Robinson, Nicola Stacey, Susie West and Susan Greaney. Others at English Heritage who materially contributed in some way to this book were Patrick Adam, Dirk Bennett, Steven Brindle, John Clark, Gordon Higgott, Edward Impey, Louisa Sherman and John Yarker. I am also grateful to Anna Keay and the Properties Presentation Department for several months' unpaid leave to work on this book.

Moving to my present job at *Country Life* has brought fresh experience and many more debts. All my colleagues there deserve thanks, but I must particularly mention the editor, Mark Hedges, who kindly agreed that this book should be illustrated where possible using photographs from the magazine's incomparable archive. Meanwhile, others in this busy office have found time to sort out problems and offer technical advice: Phil Crewdson, Nicola Friend, Susannah Glynn, Heather Lock, Vicky Wilkes and Dominic Walters. Octavia Pollock, who subs the architectural articles, has kept me on my toes and saved me from many errors in my articles (and therefore by extension, unwittingly, in this book). So too have Marianka Swain and Jane Watkins.

My colleague on the architecture desk, Mary Miers, has been a wonderfully stimulating partner. I fear she will lead the field of critics who say this book has far too little about Scottish buildings in it. The office assistants,

Hetty Chidwick and Megan Jenkins, besides several others doing short stints of work experience, have helped facilitate lots of tasks. Justin Hobson, the librarian of the Country Life photographic library, meanwhile, has helped sort out the illustrations and Helen Carey has done the donkey work of pulling pictures.

As architectural editor I necessarily attempt to cover the full spectrum of architecture in the British Isles including historic and modern buildings. This has hugely broadened my understanding of the subject and has helped set my understanding of the English Middle Ages in context. This is particularly true because the house visits I make in preparation for articles all have – thanks to the input of owners and the specialist commissioned writers – something of the character of historical and architectural master classes.

Besides those listed in this rather simplified account are numbers of people who have otherwise contributed in large and small ways to the production of this book: Jenny Alexander, Tim Ayers, Richard Bales, Paul Barnwell, Lawrence Butler, Peter Brears, Sharon Cather, Derek Chivers, Jonathan Clark, Caroline Cliffe, Vivienne Coad, Nicola Coldstream, Nicholas Cooper, Fr Edward Corbould osb, Carol Davidson Cragoe, Paul Crossley, Kathleen Doyle, Anthony Emery, Peter Fergusson, Eric Fernie, Robin Frame, Alexandra Gajewski, David Gardner, Oliver Garnett, Mark Girouard, Duncan Givans, my namesake the late John Goodall, Neil Guy, Stuart Harrison, Cecily Hennessy, Sandy Heslop, Karen Impey, Adrian James, Anna Keay, Laurence Keen, Michael Leslie, Rob Liddiard, Lynne McBean, Tom McNeill, Conleth Manning, Pamela Marshall, Richard Morris, Rachel Moss, Harry Mount, Jeremy Musson, John Nelson, Bernard Nurse, Kevin O'Brien, Zoë Opacic, David Park, Colin Platt, Sue Pratt, Derek Renn, Steven Rickerby, John Martin Robinson, Warwick Rodwell, Lisa Shekede, Jane Spooner, Roger Stalley, Gavin Stamp, Jenny Stratford, Roy Strong, Henry Summerson, Tim Tatton-Brown, Simon Thurley, Charles Tracy, Dennis Turner, Rick Turner, Twigs Way, Pam White, Christopher Wilson, Rita Wood and Bill Woodburn.

In the practical preparation of this book I must thank those who have helped me assemble images, including Duncan Brown and Christine Kenyon. Pete Laurence, Richard Lea, David Robinson and Diane Williams have all contributed to getting the plans generously supplied to me by English Heritage and Cadw as accurate as possible. Drew Smith has likewise worked carefully to create a series of new plans and diagrams specifically for this volume. Meanwhile, amongst those who have generously supplied pictures are Stephen Conlin, Mark Taylor, John Crook, Malcolm Thurlby, Stephen Papworth and Michael Jones. Paul Barker and John Crook have also very kindly taken a few pictures to close gaps.

Those who have read and commented on all or parts of the text deserve special thanks – Alixe Bovey, Alexandrina Buchanan, Anna Eavis, Michael Hall, Gordon Higgott, John Kenyon, John McNeill, Richard Plant, Nigel Saul and Abigail Wheatley. Also, Eric Fernie and two other anonymous readers for Yale made helpful suggestions for improvements to the final draft text and spotted some glaring errors.

Besides reading the text, three friends have additionally been crucial in different ways to imagining and writing this book. Stuart Hay has seen it through every stage of its journey and wrote detailed and unsparing comments on the final draft as an interested reader. Linda Monckton shares with me a fascination – judged by most an eccentricity – with late medieval English architecture, and visiting buildings with her over many years has shaped my understanding of the subject. Lastly, Jeremy Ashbee, whose attention to detail and scholarly generosity is matched only by his self-effacing kindness.

The final thanks for this book are due to my family in its broadest sense. My father, mother, sister and brother have all read and commented on the manuscript, as have my wife and my brother-in-law, Andrew Wareham. In addition, my wife's family – Norman, Jennifer, Lucy, Alastair and Brenda – have indulged my interest and opened my eyes to the architectural riches of Northern Ireland. Finally, Delia Gaze has meticulously copyedited the manuscript, Meg Davies has compiled the index and Sarah Faulks and Gillian Malpass have overseen its publication at Yale. The Paul Mellon Centre for Studies in British Art has also generously subsidised half the cost of the illustrations.

Quite as important, the Goodall and Campbell clans have kept my enthusiasms within reasonable limits and otherwise filled out my life with much happiness. The most ruthless enemies of my work have been my daughter and son, Isobel and Edward. Without them both, the last three years would have been a great deal more professionally productive but inconceivably less pleasurable and rewarding. Meanwhile, particularly to my parents, siblings and wife, I owe a depth of thanks that cannot be properly expressed.

PREFACE

From coast to coast England is still richly studded with the remains of castles, great and small. As living houses, ruins, earthworks or just outlines traced in the street names of modern towns, they may still be discovered within almost every land- and cityscape of the twenty-first century. Today, castles are objects of curiosity, part of the flotsam and jetsam of England's distant past, but for centuries these buildings were great monuments at the heart of its social and political life. As strongholds, centres of government, houses and political showpieces, the story of their use and development is fascinating to trace. Woven into the history of these buildings and reflected in their physical remains is an extraordinary portrait of the changing face of the society that created, fostered and finally destroyed them.

This book is an architectural study that aims to set this legion of buildings in historical context, tracing the development of the castle in England through the Middle Ages and beyond. It is intended to be a provocative work, challenging received opinions and, hopefully, formulating many new ones. In all, it surveys a period of nearly 600 years, from the Norman Conquest in 1066 to the Civil War of the 1640s. It is arranged chronologically, with chapters corresponding to the reigns of monarchs, and has been deliberately structured to give equal emphasis to buildings of every period within its scope. This chronological breadth may in itself come as a surprise to some readers, familiar with castles primarily as medieval buildings. It is one aim of this book, however, to illustrate the continued richness of the castle-building tradition in England far beyond the end of the Middle Ages. In the course of discussion it will touch on numerous subsidiary themes – such as warfare, politics, domestic living and governance – and draw on a wide spectrum of evidence, from chronicles to building accounts and from the fabric of castles themselves to the furniture that filled them.

Covering this huge sweep of time with such an ambitious purpose in a single volume presents numerous difficulties, of which two are perhaps preeminent. First, that this work cannot claim to completeness, and second that it may not pause to mull over details. But these inherent constraints are outweighed by the opportunities such an approach affords. Most importantly, it offers the opportunity for a reappraisal of the history of the castle and its architecture at a moment when this task seems both important and desirable. To understand why, it is

Facing page: Richmond, North Yorkshire.

perhaps best to present a very brief historiography of English castle studies.

Two groups with different but related interests have long been engaged with the analysis of castles and their fabric. The first comprises those professionally involved in maintaining and managing these buildings. In the medieval and early modern period, these were usually surveyors and masons who were charged to assess old structures for a wide variety of practical reasons. These might include the creation of plans in anticipation of alterations and improvements or even rough drawings to record room use. Aside from the buildings themselves, such material commonly constitutes the earliest physical evidence for the appearance and form of English castles.

From the seventeenth century practitioners of architecture continued to be engaged in such work. Whether judged by their writings or the buildings they created, architects such as Nicholas Hawksmoor (d. 1736), John Nash (d. 1835) and Anthony Salvin (d. 1881) – to name but three – had an intimate understanding of medieval castle architecture. They did so, indeed, in exactly the same way that their respective contemporaries Christopher Wren (d. 1723), A. W. N. Pugin (d. 1852) and George Fredrick Bodley (d. 1907) understood Gothic church design. These figures are the pioneers in the technical study of English castle architecture, and their role in this respect remains poorly understood. Where the appreciation of medieval castle and church architecture principally differed was in its public reception. In simplistic terms, castles were understood to represent an order that had passed away. By contrast, church architecture resonated with vigorous contemporary debates about the nature of Christianity and the character of its different denominations.

The scholarly counterparts of these architectural practitioners worked in a long tradition of antiquarian scholarship that focused on history, topography and genealogy. The founding fathers of this tradition were heralds. Their compilations of lists of arms collected on visitations around the country from the sixteenth century onwards are in some cases interspersed with drawings and notes that record important details of buildings including castles.

Heralds were prominent, too, in the burgeoning field of topographic and historical studies that began to be published during the seventeenth century. Perhaps the most celebrated amongst them are William Camden (d. 1623), writer of the voluminous description of Britain and its antiquities entitled *Britannia* (first edition, 1586), and William Dugdale (d. 1686). Other important scholars, such as William Somner (d. 1669), worked under the patronage of noblemen or churchmen, many of whom were themselves scholars and genealogists of ability. In some cases, gentlemen even published books of this kind, such as Richard Carew in his *Survey of Cornwall* (1602).

A number of accomplished artists were involved in illustrating this antiquarian literature for publication. Amongst them were the Bohemian etcher Wenceslaus Hollar (d. 1677) and the engraver Daniel King (d. 1661). Their topographical views, as well as works by much less well-known contemporaries such as William Lodge (d. 1689) and Francis Place (d.1728), constitute an invaluable early source of information about the appearance of many castles. Nearly all their work, unfortunately, post-dates the destruction of the 1640s. In fact, much of their study was inspired by affection for the things that the fighting of the Civil War had swept away and a determination that they should not pass unrecorded.

Following the Civil War, two institutions added impetus to the analysis of England's history and antiquities. The first was the Royal Society, founded in 1660, which brought together figures of every interest and stimulated an extraordinary breadth of scholarship. Fellows such as John Aubrey (d. 1697) rather defy modern categorisation: besides his interests as a naturalist, he drew and described architecture with an antiquarian's attention to detail and history.

Rather more specialist was the Society of Antiquaries, founded in 1707 and established under royal charter a decade later. This forum for discussion amongst enthusiasts fostered a more wide-ranging appreciation of English antiquities. One reflection of this was the project announced in 1726 by Samuel Buck, an artist under the patronage of the society, to illustrate all the historic monuments of England, including its ruined abbeys and castles.

The series of engravings produced by him and his brother into the 1740s – like most English topographical illustrations in this period – are valuable but surprisingly unaccomplished in a techincal sense and a disappointment in comparison with those of the preceding century. Rather more artistically assured was a yet more detailed illustrative survey of monuments with an accompanying textual gloss by the soldier scholar Francis Grose (d. 1791). His work, entitled *The*

Antiquities of England and Wales, began to be published in 1772 and was later followed by volumes on Ireland and Scotland.

While Grose was publishing his survey of English antiquities, his contemporary Edmund King published what can perhaps claim to be the first illustrated monographs on English castles in 1778 and 1782. King's analysis is often difficult to follow, but if modern readers are inclined to mock the hugely eccentric claims he occasionally makes, or to censure his inaccuracies, it is only fair to remember that the ruins he saw were overgrown and largely unvalued except in a romantic sense. His work was also premised on a deeply flawed chronology. Nevertheless, even in his own lifetime his observations were sometimes fiercely criticised.

The eighteenth century witnessed a steady growth of educated interest in medieval buildings. This is clearly reflected in the early history of Gothic revival architecture and the pages of perhaps the most important general-interest publication of the period, the *Gentleman's Magazine*, published from 1731. This included descriptions and engravings of all sorts of curiosities and antiquities. Towards the close of the century the magazine also began to publish articles by the artist and antiquarian John Carter, a pugnacious and outspoken critic of those who damaged historic buildings.

The destruction of medieval buildings and the overthrow of the *ancien régime* in France after the revolution of 1789 were to have important long-term effects on attitudes towards antiquities in England. The French government was forced to take responsibility for ancient monuments and, by natural extension, to study, to analyse and to value them. French ideas and methods of scholarship were to prove a powerful influence in England during the nineteenth-century explosion of interest in medieval architecture.

This interest was initially driven by a romantic fascination with the past and the phenomenal success of Walter Scott's novels, such as *Ivanhoe* (1819) and *Kenilworth* (1821), as well as events such as the Eglinton Tournament (August 1839). These celebrated castles and ideas of medieval chivalry in a way that contemporaries evidently found both captivating and compelling. Something of this popular sensibility is vividly conveyed by the collections of engravings reproduced in *The Mansions of England in the Olden Time* by John Nash, published between 1839 and 1849. This includes numerous carefully observed views of historic buildings all populated by men and women of yore, conversing, playing, idling and wassailing in period costume.

Feeding such popular interest, and developing in parallel with it, national and local antiquarian journals began to be published in growing quantity from the 1840s. In their pages, numerous studies of individual castles or groups of castles started to appear. Outstanding amongst the scholars involved was G. T. Clark, whose articles were printed regularly in the pages of the *Archaeological Journal* from its first publication in 1844. His numerous monographs, illustrated with engraved plans, were eventually published together in 1884.

It was as a product of this growing interest that between 1851 and 1859 the first over-arching study on medieval secular buildings from the Norman Conquest to the reign of Henry VIII was published through the combined labours of T. Hudson Turner and J. H. Parker: *Some Account of Domestic Architecture*. This well-illustrated, multiple-volume work is a landmark in the scholarship of medieval secular architecture in England.

By the middle of the nineteenth century architects were actively informing the scholarly discussion of castles. The celebrated French architect Viollet-le-Duc was particularly influential through his writings in this respect. So too was Anthony Salvin, a prolific builder and restorer. He became a fellow of the Society of Antiquaries in 1824 and was widely acknowledged as an authority on English castle buildings. His approach was further developed by William Burges (d. 1881), another admirer of Viollet-le-Duc, in his astonishing and eclectic restorations of Castell Coch and Cardiff Castle for the marquess of Bute.

As interest in the architectural analysis of castles intensified, so too did the historical discussion that surrounded their creation and development. This culminated in the robust confrontations between the historians J. H. Round and E. A. Freeman over the origins of feudalism and the effect of the Conquest on England. While this thinly veiled political wrangle raged, attitudes towards historic monuments in Britain were undergoing a profound change.

The Ancient Monuments Protection Act of 1882 established the principle that designated antiquities should be maintained by the state if the owner was happy to transfer guardianship of the property to the Commissioners of Works. Immediate inspiration for this change came from the example of France, but the

British imperial experience was probably important too. Following the Indian Mutiny of 1857, the viceroy, Lord Canning, set in place the foundations for the Archaeological Survey of India and established by extension the principles of government responsibility for the protection of monuments.

The antiquarian, archaeological and historical traditions of castle studies were partly reconciled in the early twentieth century by a group of scholars, most of them with much wider interests. Foremost amongst them was A. H. Thompson, a historian, teacher and writer interested in the architecture of the Middle Ages at large. His blend of documentary research and architectural analysis, first applied to ecclesiastical monuments by Professor Robert Willis (d. 1875), was new to the field of castle studies and proved hugely influential.

Similar concerns were also reflected in the work of Thompson's colleague and friend William St John Hope, secretary of the Society of Antiquaries and a prolific excavator and historian of all kinds of medieval remains. St John Hope's voluminous three-volume history of Windsor Castle, published by *Country Life*, remains one of the most lavish and impressive monographs ever compiled by one man on one building.

The outstanding historian of this generation, meanwhile, who built on Round's work, was Ella Armitage. Her brilliant analysis of Norman castles at the Conquest – formulated in response to G. T. Clark's work – was published in 1912, the year after Thompson's principal book on castle architecture. It has shaped the modern understanding of these buildings as essentially the product of the Norman Conquest.

Beside these giant figures it is easy to overlook the generation of scholars who succeeded to their labour in the 1930s and 1940s. Their achievement was to broaden the knowledge of castle buildings through description, photography and the analysis of fabric. Particularly important amongst them was Harold Leask, who inaugurated the modern study of Irish castles in 1941. In England, Sidney Toy and Harold Sands were likewise active at this time. Their plans and elevations of castles on private property – despite their limitations and pitfalls (they often silently reconstruct details) – have in some cases never been superseded

Over the same period and under the direction of a series of eminent architectural editors – Avray Tipping, Christopher Hussey and Arthur Oswald – *Country Life* also contributed to the discussion of castles. Besides its weekly series of architectural fea-

tures, which presented illustrated histories of numerous medieval buildings, the magazine collaborated in the production of a book of aerial castle views written by the prolific castle scholar W. Douglas Simpson, published in 1949. This venture was hardly significant in a scholarly sense, but it reflected the immense popularity that these buildings had come to enjoy.

As a background to the study of architecture in the early twentieth century was the expansion of the Office of Works (from 1943 the Ministry of Works), which steadily grew in strength and sense of purpose. Under its direction archaeological sites began to be systematically cleared in large numbers, their remains surveyed and documentary research undertaken to furnish information for guidebooks. Such intervention was in some cases highly controversial and often shocked those of romantic sensibility. One such dispute over the restoration of the castle at Farleigh Hungerford spilled over onto the pages of *Country Life* in November 1921.

The post of Chief Inspector of Ancient Monuments, the figure responsible for directing such works across England, Wales and Scotland, was consequently occupied by a series of important medievalists. In the field of castles prior to the 1960s, two in particular were of importance: the remarkably long-serving Sir Charles Peers (1910–33) and Bryan H. St John O'Neil (appointed in 1945).

It was under the aegis of the state, too, that one of the definitive reference works in the field of medieval architecture was undertaken. *The History of the King's Works*, published between 1963 and 1982, was a huge project: a chronological survey of all royal architectural projects from the Anglo-Saxon period to the nineteenth century. Its early volumes employed the expertise of three exceptional scholars: Howard Colvin (the editor of the entire series), R. Allen Brown and Arnold Taylor, who was Chief Inspector of Ancient Monuments between 1961 and 1972.

The two medieval volumes of *The History of the King's Works* introduced to English architectural history an authoritative and over-arching chronology of building operations that was based on documentary evidence. So valuable is this work that its limitations have become ingrained in subsequent scholarship. Ireland, for example, was excluded from the survey and our understanding of architecture there has developed slowly in consequence. For a study concerned with architecture, too, these volumes are curiously under-illustrated. The compilers, indeed, were more concerned with grounding their study in documentary research than the remains of the buildings themselves.

Over the next two decades, the analysis of castle architecture was greatly enriched by a series of new surveys of architecture of different periods, notably Derek Renn's gazetteer volume of Norman castles published in 1968 and Anthony Emery's analysis of late medieval secular architecture in his monograph on Dartington Hall two years later. Another important treatment of castle building in the context of church building was provided almost a decade later by John Harvey in his study of the Perpendicular style. Meanwhile, the subject of daily life in great houses was authoritatively examined for the first time by Mark Girouard in his book *Life in the English Country House*, published in 1978.

The early 1980s witnessed a sea change in the field of castle studies. A full list and bibliography of castles in England and Wales by David Cathcart King was published in 1983. The following year the Ministry of Works was superseded by four bodies: the Department of the Environment in Northern Ireland, English Heritage, CADW in Wales and Historic Scotland. Each has taken its guidebook series in decisively different directions, but in every case these publications – updated or rewritten and variable in quality though they are – commonly remain the most authoritative studies of the sites they cover. They have also become one of the most important points of contact between changing ideas about the castle in scholarly circles and the public at large.

Over the last twenty-five years there has been an explosion of publications on castles, which generally fall into one of two categories. On the one hand there has been a steady flow of popular studies that aim to present an overview of the history of castles, and on the other large numbers of scholarly books and articles written by academics, primarily with their own constituency in mind. Gradually, these two bodies of literature have come to offer very different perspectives on the buildings they discuss.

Most of the popular works continue to be informed by a thesis first formulated more than 150 years ago and which may most entertainingly be absorbed from the colourful medieval novels of Sir Walter Scott and Sir Arthur Conan Doyle. According to this, the castle is essentially to be viewed as an instrument of war, used by the Normans as a means of enforcing their conquest and quickly developed to a pitch of architectural sophistication around 1300. Subsequent developments

in military technology rendered it obsolete and the castle gradually declined in importance to meet its death at the close of the Middle Ages. There have, over time, been small changes rung to ornament this story, but in essentials it has remained unvaried.

The recently published scholarly work in the field could not offer a greater contrast to this picture. Some sense of both its extent and diversity is provided by the chronological bibliography to the Preface and the notes to the text. Of particular importance have been studies by literary and political historians and archaeologists into the symbolic importance and the landscape setting of castles. At the same time, the social, economic and military functions castles served have been discussed afresh and a wealth of new excavated material has been made available about them. This has helped clarify the use of these buildings and the realities of life within them. Castles have also been treated in all recent studies of grand English domestic architecture, as well as the three major London exhibitions between 1987 and 2005 that aimed collectively to present an interdisciplinary overview of the art of the Middle Ages in England.

As many individual authors of such works have been at pains to point out, their discoveries in these fields often contradict the received wisdom about the castle as it is popularly represented. In particular, they have emphasised the symbolic importance of the setting and architecture of castles as well as their role in day-to-day-life as centres of administration and aristocratic life. Indeed, most of those involved in the vigorous running discussion on the subject would acknowledge that discoveries and research over the last twenty years, whatever their shortcomings, have reformulated the received understanding of the castle to the point of revolution.

This parting of ways between the public and scholarly communities, as reflected in the literature, is in every way regrettable. The former misses a wealth of information that can only enrich its understanding of the buildings it visits and loves; the latter loses the satisfaction of conveying its ideas to a wide audience, as well as the discipline and perspective imposed by so doing. In the present climate there is an added danger that the division adds ammunition to the contention that public or enthusiastic and academic interests are mutually incompatible. Nowhere are the damaging results of this argument better exposed than in the presentation of some castles by the heritage industry and television. In order to attract audiences, it is only too tempting to jettison scholarship for the sake of popular appeal. When this happens, the resultant products are invariably shallow and often misleading.

The principal object of this book, then, is to offer an accessible, updated overview of the castle in the light of recent research. But in doing this I aim to do much more than simply present the research of others. By its very nature, much of the recent authoritative work on castles has been narrowly focused, looking either at individual sites or at a small sample of buildings over a short period of time. What has been created, in fact, is a kind of scholarly dot-to-dot puzzle in which the points of reference are individual buildings, themes and periods. To make sense of these there remains the important task of setting them in their overall context, that is to say, joining the dots together to create a picture. This book is an attempt at that task. It is undertaken in the firm belief that the picture of the castle that emerges is radically different from that which has so long been popularly accepted.

As well as presenting a new overview of the history of the castle, this book aims to serve a practical purpose that is quite as important. Unquestionably, the single most valuable source of information about castles is the physical remains of the buildings themselves; and it is probably safe to say that for every reader it is these buildings – their architecture, setting and atmosphere – that first fired an enthusiasm for the subject. Nevertheless, the architectural history of the English castle is neither well understood nor well discussed in the current literature on the subject. This lacuna is the ostensible excuse for this book, which is first and foremost an architectural study. If it occasionally seems evangelical in tone about the importance of technical details – masonry, mouldings and mortar – there is a particular reason.

In my experience, when most people visit a castle and are confronted by its earth, stone and timber, they simply do not understand how to engage with the fabric critically and quarry it for information. Yet there is nothing especially complex about analysing a building and anyone with a careful eye, a modicum of knowledge and a little patience can certainly begin to do it for themselves. In the preparation of this book I have sought to present the buildings as directly as possible through photographs, and to explain in the captions what their fabric illustrates. By doing this I hope readers will be encouraged to think independently about the castles that they visit and come to informed opinions of their own about them.

By adopting a narrative structure for this book – as opposed to a thematic one – it is possible to present a great sweep of buildings in their historical context. Dividing the chapters into reigns may appear arbitrary, but it does have three advantages. First, because the political character of different reigns did materially affect the development of castles, these divisions have a natural importance in the story. Second, our knowledge of castles for the greater part of the period discussed is dependent to some extent on royal records, the nature of which varies from reign to reign. This approach, therefore, makes the documentary and architectural evidence easier to match and manage. Finally, there is the incidental advantage that the names of kings and queens should provide readers with a comforting element of familiarity in what is necessarily a complex narrative.

Four well-preserved and important castles are repeatedly referred to in the course of this book: Dover, Windsor, Kenilworth and Durham. Broadly speaking, these might be understood to represent four types of major castle, though their character as such is by no means clear-cut or consistent. They are respectively the great fortress, the royal palace, and the magnate's and the prelate's castle. The development of these buildings serves to illustrate the organic growth typical of the greatest English castles right up to the Civil War. Their architectural evolution also usefully illustrates the wider patterns of change described in this book. Where appropriate, the conclusion to each chapter takes the form of a detailed discussion of a particular building illustrative of the themes typical of the period. This formula is intended to anchor the narrative, giving due emphasis both to change as well as to the continuity of castles and their architecture.

It may be objected, in the light of these points, that by including certain Welsh and Irish castles within the main narrative – as will appear subsequently – I am either guilty of mislabelling this work or, what is worse, of English chauvinism. But the justification for doing this is that there are imperial castles in both Wales and Ireland; that is to say, buildings of exotic design, erected as part of a colonisation process that can be properly understood only in the light of English architectural developments. These buildings not only serve as a useful gloss on the development of contemporary English castles, illustrating admired fashions and new ideas, but in some cases they also informed in return the architectural mainstream in England that is the subject of this book.

NOTE ON COUNTIES

Pre-1970 county boundaries have been used to identify the location of all castles and places mentioned in the text. To all intents and purposes, these county boundaries correspond to those in existence in the Middle Ages. They are, moreover, the divisions that apply to most scholarly surveys, such as The Victoria History of the Counties of England (*VCH*) and the 'Pevsner' *Buildings of England* series. For these reasons – and since they anyway remain familiar – they are much more useful than their modern counterparts in an account of this kind.

NOTE ON PLANS

I had intended to reproduce all the plans in this book at a consistent scale. This proved impossible, however, within the constraints of the layout. Instead, it was decided to make the individual plans as legible as possible. All are provided with scale bars, which should allow for detailed comparisons of size.

INTRODUCTION

Before break of day on Monday, 2 February 1355, the feast of the Purification of the Virgin, the bishop of Salisbury presented himself at the bar of the Court of Common Pleas in the great hall of Westminster Palace. Bishop Wyville had come to the court to settle a long-running legal dispute by the most dramatic of means, a trial by combat, and the court yearbook enthusiastically reports every detail of the preliminaries.[1] To assert his claim the bishop was joined at the bar by his champion, a certain Richard Shawell. The champion was dressed – as convention dictated – not in armour but in a long jerkin of white leather and a red silk surcoat painted with the arms of the bishop. Shawell's battlepick, the weapon conventional in such combats, was carried beside him by a knight, and standing behind the champion was a servant holding a specially shaped shield. As the group stood before the bar the servant raised this shield, which – we are told – was elaborately painted with figures, above the champion's head. This action was probably intended to identify him to the court and the colours under which he fought, in this case almost certainly an image of the Virgin Mary, the patroness of Salisbury Cathedral.

The claim that Bishop Wyville had come to assert through force of arms was the ownership of the castle of Sherborne in Dorset, one of four outstandingly ambitious castles built in the early twelfth century by a predecessor of his, Roger, bishop of Salisbury from 1103 to 1139. The castle had been seized by the crown almost immediately after its construction, Bishop Roger having fallen into disgrace at the end of his life. But two centuries had not effaced the memory of this lost possession. When Edward III granted Sherborne to William Montacute, earl of Salisbury, in 1337, Bishop Wyville immediately took the opportunity of its return into private hands to sue for recovery. The earl, a true tactician, responded by declaring his intention to defend his right by combat. This placed Wyville in an awkward position; as a cleric, combat was hardly an appropriate means for him to settle a lawsuit. But after having been advised by his lawyers that he must either fight or lose the case, he acceded to the challenge. At the same time he mobilised all the spiritual resources at his disposal to offer up devout prayers and Masses for the happy outcome of the encounter.

Next to present himself at the bar was the defendant, the earl of Salisbury. His champion, Nicholas, was also dressed in a white leather jerkin and red surcoat, but this bore the arms of his master, Montacute. As before, the earl's champion was displayed to

the court by having his shield raised above his head. With both parties in attendance the sergeants-at-law then confirmed the determination of their respective clients to pursue the case. Having heard this formal statement of intent, Justice Green, the presiding judge, directed that the arms and harness of the champions be surrendered for inspection. To give time for this to be done properly and also to make enquiry as to whether there was any fraud or deceit in the case, he delayed the combat for a full week. In the meantime it was instructed that accommodation should be found for all concerned within the Palace of Westminster.

The week passed and the champions returned to the bar with their patrons as before. But Justice Green now announced that the king had ordered a stay of the combat for three more days. He also said that there were defects in the harness of the two champions – rumour had it that Shawell had illegally filled his with prayer rolls and charms. So high did feeling now run in the court that neither side would be the first to leave the bar, and Justice Green was forced to threaten the bishop with loss of the case unless he would move away first. And no doubt it was this spirit of brinkmanship that really had control of the proceedings, because before the dispute came to issue three days later the two parties had decided to remove it from the uncertain sphere of combat altogether. Upon receiving payment of the very substantial sum of 2,500 marks, the earl resigned his claim to Sherborne Castle. It must have been with an air of blustering triumph, therefore, that the bishop came to the bar with his champion for the third and last time. The earl was called for to answer his claim, but no one appeared. As the year-book of the court succinctly notes, the default was noted. Sherborne Castle belonged once more to the bishop and see of Salisbury.

Twenty years later Bishop Wyville died in the very castle he had striven to recover. His body was taken to Salisbury Cathedral for burial and there in the middle of the choir it was laid to rest beneath an extraordinary monumental brass (pl. 1). Wyville is depicted on it as a praying figure dressed in full pontifical vestments with a mitre and crosier. But rather than being displayed full-length – as one would expect of such an effigy – his figure is awkwardly enclosed within a symmetrical frame of architecture. This unmistakably evokes a castle with three concentric walls and a high central tower, all busy with the trappings of fortification: towers, turrets, battlements, arrow slits, openings for cannon and machicolis vents for dropping missiles from the wall heads. The gates are shown with portcullises, and barring the main entrance to the building is a bearded figure brandishing a battlepick in the garb of a champion. In a charming but important detail there are also several rabbits emerging from warren runs around the walls of the castle.

The inscription on the monument specifically identifies the castle as that of Sherborne and by extension the champion at the gates as Richard Shawell. It reads:

Here lies Robert Wyville, of happy memory, Bishop of the church of Salisbury, who ruled that church peaceably and laudably for more than forty-five years; he prudently gathered together the dispersed possessions of the church, and they having been collected, he maintained them as a vigilant pastor. And amongst the least of his other gifts he recovered in the manner of an intrepid champion the castle of Sherborne, which for two hundred years or more had been withheld from this church by hand of military might, and he also obtained restitution to the same church of the chase of Bere; who on the 4th day of September in the year of Our Lord 1375 and the 46th year since his consecration, as the Most High pleased, he rendered his debt of human nature in the said castle. May He, in whose power he hoped and believed, have mercy on his soul.[2]

This monument makes a perfect introduction to this book because it clearly sets out some of the complications inherent in understanding castles and their architecture. At the heart of the image is a startling disjunction, easily legible even to a modern audience. By his vestments and marks of office Wyville is an ecclesiastic and a pastor, forbidden by canon law to draw blood or bear arms. Yet he stands in the heart of a castle bristling with fortifications in an architectural celebration of war. The medieval world was fully alive to the contradiction implicit in this juxtaposition and, though it was a widely accepted reality that spiritual authority was inextricably allied to secular power, Wyville's monument would certainly have found contemporary critics. But to read this monument purely as a contradiction would be to miss a crucial point: Wyville stands in a castle, and that meant something very special to a medieval audience.

In this context the castle is not a reflection of Wyville's ambition as a soldier, though it does boast of his determination to defend the rights of the see of Salisbury. Rather, it serves as a symbol of his temporal lordship, technically independent from his office as a

bishop yet – as the inscription emphasises – inherited with it and essential to its prestige. The detail of the rabbit warren too – presumably a reference to his restitution of the chase of Bere to the church – illustrates one of the most prestigious and jealously defended rights of lordship, that of hunting. In effect, Wyville is proclaiming himself on this monument as a prince of both the church and the state, dressed in the robes of the former and presented within the attributes of the latter.

As a whole, this image also articulates what might be understood as the core qualities or characteristics of the castle, a series of inextricably twisted strands of association that confront students of the subject like a Gordian knot. The castle is a symbol: Wyville presents Sherborne as an attribute of lordship and power. But the symbolism of the castle is effectively underwritten by its manifest physical strength: the castle appears imposing, fortified and threatening. Its character in these respects is enhanced by the busy composition of the architectural frame around the figure. The detailing of this both adds to the splendour of the building and accentuates its function. As sports cars are admired for their sleek curves – curves that both suggest and permit driving at speed – so were castle fortifications clearly deemed beautiful for their appearance of deadly impregnability. And Wyville's castle looks marvellously impregnable. Bound up in this is an admiration for warlike attributes. Because medieval and early modern society had a fighting class of noblemen and knights, so the architectural celebration of war evoked their prestige and power. In effect, castles were at once understood as symbolic, magnificent, powerful and prestigious buildings, each quality reinforcing the other.

As a final twist, it is worth making the obvious point that the castle on the monument is not properly a building at all but an image of one. Nor, as a matter of fact, does it bear the slightest physical similarity to the surviving ruins of Sherborne Castle (see pls 60 and 61). This illustrates a crowning and vitally important point that complicates but also enriches the task of this book immeasurably. The castle is an ideal, and one, moreover, that can be easily evoked. That is to say, if you make the right visual references an audience will recognise a castle in almost any object. Delight in this fact is widely apparent in medieval and early modern England, the forms of the castles appearing in everything from the architecture of churches to table centrepieces. This also remains true today, too, as the imagery of films, computer games and any number of other contemporary objects powerfully and colourfully illustrate.

THE CASTLE AND ITS DEFINITION

Books on castles necessarily begin by posing the question 'what is a castle?'. And the response is consistently the same. A castle, we are told, is the private and fortified residence of a lord. By this definition castles seem relatively easy to identify. Their character as fortifications removes them from the sphere of merely domestic building and their role as lordly residences not only distinguishes them from forts or defended settlements but also places them in a specific European historical and social context: the feudal society of the Middle Ages. As conventionally represented, this feudal society was geared for the prosecution of war on horseback. Knights, the soldiery of such a society, were very expensive to equip and their expertise in the saddle the product of long training and experience. In combination, these circumstances conspired to create a professional fighting class maintained on agricultural wealth. Castles were the houses in which this class lived; by which they defended and managed their property; and from which they practised their profession.

It is important to understand that this definition has reinforced a fixed picture of these buildings and their role in English history. In essentials, this picture might be outlined as follows: the castle was introduced by the Normans at the Conquest, who used it to enforce the Norman, feudal political settlement over an unwilling Anglo-Saxon populace. This settlement, however, was inherently unstable, because if royal government failed everyone withdrew to their strongholds to wage private war. Attempts were made to check the construction of private castles, but it was only when new siege techniques rendered earth and wood defences obsolete in the late twelfth century that the sheer cost of stone fortification necessarily limited their construction, with a consequent improvement in law and order.

For the next century the architect laboured in stone for the king and England's greatest magnates to defeat the ingenuity of the siege engineer in a golden age of castle building. But the technology of war gradually overtook the castle and, by the late fourteenth century, they were becoming obsolete. And at this moment something critical happened: in response to their obsolescence castles ceased to be built as truly defensible

structures. As Allen Brown put it in his classic study *English Castles*: 'the unique combination of fortress and personal, lordly residence, which is the castle, falls apart, and when it does so the history of the castle as a living and viable type of building is at an end'.[3] At this moment, therefore, the castle tradition is portrayed as entering into decline, a passage accelerated both by the development of cannon and increasingly centralised government. Moreover, except on its turbulent northern border, England now enjoyed comparative peace, and men and women wanted comfortable houses, not draughty fortresses, to live in. So fortification became divorced from domestic living; the castle was abandoned, and the history of the country house began.

The rights and wrongs of this thesis will be a central concern of this book, but two elements of it are of particular importance to this discussion. Not only does it represent castles throughout as an essentially military phenomenon, but also their whole history is understood in terms of an evolutionary struggle between attacker and attacked for technological superiority in war: the Norman versus the Anglo-Saxon, the siege engineer versus the architect. These ideas have determined that the castle has traditionally been the natural preserve of the military historian, a monopoly that was broken only in the 1980s. Furthermore, its architecture has become the subject of typological study, as if it were susceptible to Darwinian evolutionary explanation. This traces the development of defences in response to changes in warfare from the simple to the more complex and, ultimately, to decadent display in obsolescence.

Nothing could be more appealing than the clarity with which the received definition of the castle presents its material, or the grand cyclical narrative of birth, maturity and dotage that it imposes on its subject. Yet it also raises many difficulties and involves one intellectual sleight of hand. By appropriating 'castle' as a technical term it follows that there is a correct and an improper usage of the word. But this word was not technically applied in medieval and early modern usage; nor was there one single term used to describe the buildings that we understand to be castles today. A twelfth-century selection of words that have been treated by modern scholars, and sometimes selectively, as synonyms for castle might include the Anglo-Norman *chastel* and the Latin *castellum, arx, mota, turris, oppidum, munitiones, firmitas* and *municipium*.[4] Indeed, nearly all these Latin words can be found in

4

one paragraph of a treaty agreed at Westminster in 1153 between King Stephen and the future Henry II to describe a group of buildings that everyone today would simply term castles.[5] To make the point another way, one castle in England whose medieval name has remained in continuous use to the present is in London. Confusingly, this building is not familiar to us as London Castle, but by its medieval name *Turris Londiniensis*, the Tower of London.

Yet rather than acknowledge that the word castle is a useful umbrella term, the conventional solution to the problem of reconciling the difference between the historical and the modern usage of the word has been to create new categories of building. Most popular amongst these has been the 'real' castle, so-called. The Real Castle is an invention of historians and architectural historians and is a term bestowed approvingly upon buildings that conform to the technical requisites of a castle *as it has been defined by them*. That is to say that it is a private, lordly residence that they deem to be truly defensible. Of course, once you have Real Castles – which are the things you are also 'really' interested in – everything else must either be described as something different or demoted to the status of being, in some sense, a fake.

So the Anglo-Saxon chronicler who described Dover as possessing a *castelle* in 1051 – before the introduction of feudalism and the castle at the Conquest – was really, technically speaking about a fortified settlement or *burh*.[6] And when the late medieval nobility built residences that they called castles, some modern scholars have claimed a more profound insight. Without the fortifications of Real Castles they must be politely accorded titles such as 'castles of display' and 'chivalric castles', residences shorn of proper fortifications and caparisoned in crenellations. These are the *castrati* of castle studies: you can admire them for their flamboyant virtuosity but they sing in the wrong register.

This whole process of recategorising castles according to a modern technical vocabulary is both confusing and destructive. Moreover, as applied to different periods it has distorted the study of castles in different ways. During the early Middle Ages it served to reduce the castle, focusing attention narrowly on the buildings and defences at the expense of what they contained and what surrounded them. Indeed, one of the great achievements of recent writers in the field has been to bring the wider physical and social context of castles into proper consideration.[7] With regard to later castles it has generated a huge quantity of highly sub-jective discussion about the relative efficacy of fortifications in an attempt to trace the supposed decline of this tradition of building.

In this latter context the application of a technical vocabulary seems particularly absurd. This cannot be presented as a simple problem, but it seems logical that if someone calls the building they construct a castle, the task of the modern scholar is to explain why they accorded it that title and not to presume to explain why they got it wrong. We are, after all, the students, not the instructors of the past. As a matter of fact, however, even up to the seventeenth century it can be difficult to find unambiguous record of what particular residences were entitled by those who built them. Moreover, just to confuse matters, administrative documentation can refer to all kinds of major residences as 'manors' or 'manor places' simply because they are the seats of lordly authority. This denomination, therefore, does not necessarily prove that a house was a manor as distinct from a castle. In fact, documentation can be openly contradictory on this point. In a survey of Thornbury made in 1521, the duke of Buckingham's splendid new residence is described as 'the manor or castell' for precisely this reason.[8] Similarly, in 1340 the buildings of Oakham Castle were described in an inquisition as being 'likewise called the manor'.[9] On occasion, even the word castle can be left aside: in Sir John Paston's will of 31 October 1477, the great fifteenth-century brick residence of Caister in Norfolk – which is otherwise repeatedly called a castle in this period – is referred to as 'my seid maner and fortresse'.[10]

Such matters aside, satisfaction with the received definition of the castle has been reinforced by two circumstances. First, that interest in the field has always concentrated on the early development of castles – say from the eleventh century to the thirteenth. In this period the application of the word castle as a technical term does much less damage to its subject than it does from the late medieval period onwards. Indeed, it should be emphasised that the terms by which we discuss castles are really formulated in relation to these early buildings. Second, that despite the recent efforts of a small body of scholars, English secular architecture after about 1350 remains astonishingly under-discussed and under-researched. It should be stressed that this lacuna is not restricted to the field of secular architecture. Across the board the discussion of Gothic architecture in England is thin after 1400, but there is not even a published overview of the subject after 1485.[11]

This shortcoming in the literature expresses, and has served to reaffirm, a presumption scored deep into English historiography and the popular consciousness: that the Middle Ages began to die on its feet from the mid-fourteenth century and that life – political, social, religious and artistic – was reinvented by the Tudors at the touch of the Renaissance. One victim of this grotesquely distorted vision has undoubtedly been the castle. However you define the word, the fact remains that the medieval and early modern nobility of England occupied, built and rebuilt buildings that they called castles. It is no exaggeration to say that, whether as a principal residence or as one in a suite of great residences, from 1066 to 1640 a nobleman without a castle was like a knight without a horse. If our understanding of castles cannot accommodate this reality, we need a looser working definition of these buildings lest we do an academic violence to this architectural tradition.

I would advocate the following: a castle is the residence of a lord made imposing through the architectural trappings of fortification.

The advantage of this definition is that it sidesteps the whole issue of defence without denying its importance. Added to this it can, crucially, accommodate the full diversity of castles within England from the Tower of London in the eleventh century to Bolsover in the seventeenth. This book is written in the belief that these buildings do share something in common: Bolsover is not just a pastiche of the Tower but built as part of a continuous and integral tradition of English architecture. Moreover, this tradition was underwritten by the continued existence of a social class: the patrons of these two castles shared, however remotely, what might be termed a knightly vocation. In 1066 William the Conqueror, as the duke of Normandy, famously led his forces to triumph at Hastings. And in 1644 William Cavendish, then the earl of Newcastle, by virtue of his nobility, led a royalist army to catastrophe at Marston Moor. Knighthood and chivalry were not revived as fanciful concepts in early modern England; they had never died as living concerns.

It should be said that these ideas also survived the events of the Civil War, but there are good reasons why this survey does not carry the history of the castle beyond 1650. Most importantly, it is because the Civil War constituted a massive hiatus in the history of English cultural, social and political life. In its events, the last continuities that bound England to the medieval past were decisively severed. Amongst its casualties were numerous of the castles discussed in these pages. In the course of a decade, buildings that had been adapted over centuries as great residences were deliberately demolished and their remains left to ruin. To compound this destruction, following the Civil War patrons and practitioners of architecture took their art in decisively new directions. The history of the castle in England was far from over in 1650; indeed, it is not over today. Nevertheless, the story of the modern English castle, which evolved from the late seventeenth century onwards, is in some important respects totally different from that of its medieval predecessor.

The strands of continuity that lend this narrative between 1066 and 1650 coherence are accompanied by a multitude of important changes in social, artistic, economic and political life, and it is not the intention to belittle these. In artistic terms this survey spans three major periods of artistic change, popularly termed the Romanesque (or Norman), Gothic and Renaissance. For all the continuities between these periods, and whatever may be the limitations of their modern labels, at the inception of each there is apparent a sense of novelty that contemporaries celebrated and del-ighted in. One of the themes of this book will be the manner in which the physical form of the castle responded to the ideas current in each period while retaining an essential integrity.

On a more practical level, over the 600-year period covered by this book there was a real reduction in the number of castles both in active use and being newly founded in England. In purely statistical terms, despite a steady flow of new foundations, from about 1120 the number of castles in England was probably in continuous and more or less rapid decline. This phenomenon is conventionally presented as evidence that the castle was an object of diminishing importance, but it can also be explained in more positive terms and these are worth considering briefly.

PATTERNS OF CASTLE
CONSTRUCTION

The pattern of castle foundation and maintenance has always been closely allied with the material resources and wealth provided by land. It is in direct consequence that more castles were established in the half-century or so following the Norman Conquest than at any other time in English history, when the kingdom was in the process of redistribution amongst its new rulers. Many of the great castle foundations of this period, sustained on vast estates, became the bones of the medieval kingdom of England. Not only did they naturally develop into hubs of administration and justice, but through their attendant estates they also became great inheritances in their own right. Consequently, such castles also became the preserve of the very greatest noble families and were developed by them century after century as fixtures in the English landscape.

Whatever happened to these buildings architecturally across the centuries – however their fortifications were compromised for the sake of fashion and luxurious living – their titles as castles usually remained unchanged. Moreover, they continued to be, quite simply, the grandest residences you could own. In a world where birth and descent were the credentials for power, urgently to be acquired if not already possessed, this enthusiasm for ancient and inherited residences is hardly to be wondered at. Nor is the extraordinary prestige attached to them. Some, of course, such as Windsor Castle, have survived to the present day. Even in the twenty-first century no physical change can compromise the status of this building as a castle or dim its prestige as the principal inherited seat of England's sovereigns. Its medieval estate is still represented by the Little and Great Parks, which in their reconstituted seventeenth-century form comprise a huge, undeveloped swathe of landscape in one of the richest and most densely populated areas of Europe.[12] Such possessions are by definition inheritances, objects far beyond the compass of mere wealth.

To this group of major castles the English nobility never ceased to make occasional additions, usually by upgrading existing manors and residences. But the threshold for membership in both architectural and landed terms was always very high. Even by the late twelfth century new castles were usually smaller than their predecessors. This did not necessarily make them modest buildings, and what they lacked in terms of landed endowment they often made up for in architectural splendour. When new castle foundations of this kind did occur they were usually the product of very particular circumstances, most commonly the elevation of an individual to the peerage. Indeed, the connection between noble title and castle construction will become a familiar theme of this book. Where new foundations were created it was necessary that they stood direct architectural comparison to an established canon of great castles. As we shall see, this could ensure a remarkable degree of conformity in castle design over the six centuries covered by this book.

But if the foundation of major castles became an increasing rarity, their wastage before the events of the Civil War was uncommon too. This usually occurred in direct consequence of some twist in dynastic politics, such as the downfall of a family – either through the extinction of the male line or political disgrace. It also frequently resulted from the passage of a castle into the hands of the crown. Ownership by the crown, it should be said, was a doubtful privilege for a castle throughout the medieval and early modern period. While kings and queens might be very active in maintaining castles at moments of political crisis, at all other times they tended only to invest in those that they used or liked. Added to this, castles in crown ownership were run by men (and occasionally women) primarily interested in exploiting them as a source of income. So the history of most royal buildings, including castles, is of periods of total neglect, sometimes accompanied by the stripping of materials by unscrupulous custodians, punctuated with moments of lavish investment.

Amongst the lesser patrimonies or landed inheritances of England the pattern of castle foundation was rather different. The numbers of castles established on relatively small estates peaked around 1120 and then the numbers declined steeply. This was true to such an extent that after 1400 the establishment of new castles by those of relatively modest means became a distinct rarity. Only on the northern march with Scotland did the small-scale castle survive in the form of the tower house as a vigorous entity into the early modern period. Contrary to what is sometimes supposed, the move away from smaller castles to houses in the kingdom at large had little to do with considerations of safety – as the surviving letters of the Paston family show, life in East Anglia in the late fifteenth century witnessed a good deal of organised violence. Rather it is to be explained in terms of the widening spectrum and growing sophistication of domestic architecture in late medieval and early modern England.

In artistic terms, the driving force behind this development until the Reformation in the 1540s was a determination to apply the dazzling innovations of ecclesiastical architecture, and particularly its window forms, to domestic design. The importance of this phenomenon can scarcely be overstated. As a result, there gradually developed a common vocabulary of architectural forms embracing domestic, castle and ecclesiastical architecture. One outcome of this convergence of traditions, which was largely complete by the early fourteenth century, was that different types of building ceased to be necessarily distinguishable in terms of architectural detail alone: a church and a castle might share identical detailing, such as battlements, buttresses and complex window tracery. Instead, they contrasted with one another by the manner in which their common details were marshalled. Perhaps the only important architectural form specific to domestic buildings was the chimney, an outward sign of domestic comfort and wealth.

The contribution of castle architecture, with its connotations of chivalry and power, to the pool of common architectural details was hugely important. So admired were the architectural trappings of fortification that virtually all major buildings, including churches, in late medieval and early modern Britain in some way made play with them. Moreover, in domestic design the influence of castles is strongly apparent in the organisation and massing of elements. To such an extent, in fact, that almost all residential buildings of any pretension before the 1640s can be read as evocations of castles. The formidable stone walls of towers might dissolve into grids of glass and battlements into elaborate ornament, but the trappings of the castle lived on in grand domestic architecture until the advent of an accomplished and idiomatic classicism by designers such as Inigo Jones. On occasion they even survived beyond this. The sixteenth and seventeenth centuries witnessed not so much the decline of the castle as its universal triumph made possible by the versatility and appeal of its forms.

Yet for all the increasing difficulty of articulating the difference between a castle and other types of domestic architecture, the distinction between them does still apply. More than that, as the architectural distinctions blurred, the decision to call something a castle became much more pointed. And, fascinatingly, the enthusiasm for entitling great residences 'castles' did not wane, though the individuals who chose to do so belonged to an ever more exclusive social circle. Rather in the manner of Old Master paintings today, castles gradually priced themselves out of the market until they were the preserve of the very richest in the kingdom.

THE LICENSING OF FORTIFICATIONS

In 1066 William the Conqueror inherited a royal bureaucracy in England far more complex and sophisticated than the one he was familiar with in Normandy. Indeed, it may be only after the Conquest that he adopted a long-standing English habit of authenticating documents by attaching a wax seal impressed with an image to them. By the twelfth century the professional clerks of this royal bureaucracy had been organised into a department called chancery under the control of the chancellor, who held the principal or great seal of the realm. Throughout the Middle Ages and beyond the royal bureaucracy grew steadily as central government touched the lives of people in ever more varied and complex ways. The whole trend of this bureaucracy, as with all bureaucracies, was to expand and specialise in response to the growing weight of work. From the accession of King John in 1199 its output also came to be systematically enrolled or calendared, copied on long rolls of parchment that would last the passage of time and be available for future reference.[13]

The licensing of fortifications was a royal prerogative (though at different periods there were others in England who enjoyed quasi-regal powers over particular territories and also licensed castle construction within them: the bishop of Durham, the earl of Chester and the earl of Lancaster), and consequently within this huge and varied body of royal documentation are numerous references to fortifications and castles. An early example is the charter issued by Henry I in January 1127 granting custody of Rochester Castle to William de Corbeil, then archbishop of Canterbury, and to his successors in perpetuity. As part of the grant, the king also gave permission for the construction of a fortification (*municionem*) or tower (*turris*), as the archbishop pleased. The grant is universally agreed to refer to the construction of the surviving great tower at Rochester, one of the largest buildings of its kind ever erected in Europe (see pp. 115–18).[14]

It has long been assumed that the king actively used his powers to license fortifications as a means of managing the realm, granting supporters permission to build castles and preventing opponents from creating strongholds that would permit them to resist royal authority.[15] As a result charters regarding fortification have been subject to particular attention by historians. Moreover, those enrolled by chancery from 1200

onwards have been grouped together since the nineteenth century as a specific category of document and collectively dubbed licences to crenellate.[16] This name was chosen because such licences usually permit in specific terms the fortification of buildings by the addition of battlements (or crenellations), walls and towers.

Depending on how you choose to define them, licences to crenellate (pl. 2) continued to be issued until the end of the sixteenth century, as at Mountgrevelle in Warwickshire in 1567.[17] There is also one possible late runner issued in 1622 for Millom in Cumberland, authoritatively cited but untraceable today.[18] Licences can variously refer to towns, monastic sites and private residences, and the number issued peaked in the fourteenth century. In total, approximately five hundred and fifty have been identified over this entire period for sites in England.[19]

Over the last twenty years the subject of royal letters regarding fortifications has been radically reappraised. It has been compellingly argued, notably by Charles Coulson, that English kings did not attempt to condition castle construction through a system of licens-

2   A licence to crenellate: the letter patent issued by Edward IV in 1482 authorising Sir Edmund Bedingfeld to 'build, make, and construct, with stone, lime and sand, towers and walls in and about his manor of Oxburgh in the county of Norfolk, and that manor with such towers and walls to enclose, and those towers and walls to embattle, kernel and machicolate; and that manor so enclosed, and those walls and towers aforesaid so embattled, kernelled and machicolated, built and constructed, to hold for himself and his heirs forever . . . etc.'. It pardons him for work already undertaken to the buildings and goes on in similarly convoluted strains to grant him the right to hold a market.

ing.[20] Instead, that they issued licences to crenellate in response to the demand of petitioners. These individuals, moreover, were primarily interested in getting licences because they gave royal sanction for new building projects that conveyed a message about their social position. In effect, such licences confirmed in an open, royal letter that you were a figure of the requisite social status to occupy a castle. Some authorities have criticised this analysis,[21] but in my opinion, setting aside some niceties, the point stands.

Apart from anything else, this conclusion is amply borne out on many levels by the evidence of the licences themselves, most obviously because the vast majority were issued as 'patent' or public letters under the royal seal. As physical objects, in other words, they comprised a sheet of parchment with a seal attached on a silk cord or vellum strip. This was in contrast to 'close' letters issued by the king, which were physically sealed shut as private correspondence. That patent charters had a demonstrative and symbolic importance is clearly indicated by medieval artistic representations of acts of foundation or endowment. These commonly show a king handing out a charter with a seal appended and a legible text. Such, for example, is the case with the depiction *circa* 1400 of the foundation of the honour of Richmond by William the Conqueror;[22] the lost fifteenth-century panel of glass depicting the foundation of Tamworth Castle, Staffordshire;[23] or the much repainted late medieval panel of St John of Beverley receiving special liberties from King Athelstan on behalf of his minster church (pl. 3).

One unique instance of a patent charter – though in this case not a royal one – being physically set in the context of a castle as an endorsement and explanation of its foundation occurs at Cooling in Kent. Here, a beautifully engraved charter of enamelled brass hangs on the outer gate of the castle (pl. 4). This publicly proclaims the castle to be a fortification of value to the country at large. The idea, incidentally, is commonly voiced in the context of royal licences for town fortification.

That licences were of symbolic importance is further demonstrated in statistical terms. For example, there are far fewer licences than fortifications – a curious disjunction if all fortifications had to be licensed for the security of the realm. Moreover, the vast majority of licences issued to private individuals were granted to those of knightly or clerical status (around two hundred) rather than to the titled or high nobility. Throughout the entire Middle Ages only three dukes

and fifteen earls ever received a licence from the king to fortify residences as castles. This clearly does not accord with the number that must have been demanded by this group had the monarchy acted to curb their power through such licensing.

It is significant, too, that the internal evidence of the licences illustrates a concern with more than mere fortification. Many additionally confer permission to enclose land and create parks or – as in the case of Oxburgh in Norfolk – to found markets. Such licences are, in effect, comprehensive passports to the trappings of medieval lordship. Quite as significant are the wide variations apparent in what they say. Considering the tendency of the chancery to develop textual formulae in commonly issued documents, such variations strongly imply that the licences are rehearsing terms suggested by the petitioner. In other words, rather than the king issuing these documents on his own terms, the chancery was obligingly providing licences à la carte to those who were prepared to pay for them. The texts of licences should, therefore, be understood as expressing the demands and opinions of those to whom they were issued. As a matter of fact, this is entirely in keeping with the practice of issuing royal licences for other undertakings, such as the establishment of religious foundations.

Viewed in these terms, licences offer a valuable insight into the interests and concerns of builders. They can also offer valuable evidence for dating buildings, though there are complications in using them for this purpose. The Oxburgh licence, for example, includes a pardon for work already undertaken, evidence that the licence was acquired as an afterthought.

In other cases, it would appear that licences were issued as a blank cheque sanctioning the present and future construction of buildings. On 7 April 1474, for example, Lord Hastings, the chamberlain of England, received a licence from Edward IV simultaneously to fortify with walls and battlements four sites (or possibly five) within his estates and create hunting parks of 2,000 or 3,000 acres beside each of them. It is very hard to see what work actually followed upon this extraordinarily ambitious grant. Confusingly, there were already castles on two of the sites – Bagworth (Leicestershire) and Slingsby (Yorkshire) – and there is no record of major alteration to either in this period. Meanwhile, his work to the other pair of manors mentioned – Ashby de la Zouch from 1472–3 and Kirby Muxloe in 1480, both in Leicestershire – respectively anticipated and followed the licence.[24]

No less problematic than the use of these documents to date architectural projects is the categorisation of the buildings associated with them. It might be supposed that residences actually licensed as fortifications in the Middle Ages might be judged as castles by a scholarly tradition primarily concerned with defence as a yardstick of architectural title. This is not in fact the case. A building such as Oxburgh, for example, despite its licence and an impressive array of battlements (see pl. 302), has not been deemed truly defensible by modern scholars. As a result it has not conventionally been entitled a castle.

It is the deliberate intention of the definition of a castle proposed in this book that such a judgement should be laid open to challenge. There is no record of what Oxburgh was actually called in the 1480s, but it makes no sense to divide this off from the tradition of castle building. The licence suggests that Sir Edward Bedingfeld saw fortifications as central to the character of his residence and his social identity. In a sense it is this understanding of the architectural trappings of fortification, not the quality of the defence they provided, that identify the castle.

THE SETTING OF CASTLES

Castles have never existed in isolation and to a limited degree this book must necessarily treat the features that were typical of their immediate landscape. Amongst the most architecturally prominent of these were the religious foundations – monasteries and colleges of secular priests – that grew up in the shadow of every great residence in the Middle Ages, whether a castle or not. These served two principal functions. In an age that acknowledged the direct intervention of God in human affairs, such foundations were spiritual resources, their prayers of direct benefit to the living and the dead. They were also instruments of political advertisement, indicating by their architecture and decoration the wealth and power of the family that patronised them.

These two functions were complementary in many ways, but especially with regard to the dead. Both before and after the Reformation, the churches associated with great residences served as dynastic mausolea. The gathering of dead generations of a family within a church was not only desirable in social and religious terms, it also served an important didactic function. By their memorials, effigies and coats of arms, these collections of tombs illustrated in physical form the illustrious descent and alliances of the family they celebrated. Such collections survive today in considerable numbers, often when the house or castle that they attended upon has long since wasted away. But where the alliance of residence and church is still apparent – as at Warwick – the modern visitor can still be impressed by the human face of the past. Indeed, there are few more immediate ways of appreciating the historic population of a great residence and their dynastic claims than by encountering them, face to face, in imperious and silent effigy amongst their ancestors.

Castles also had an associated economic and physical landscape. Though the precise form of this varied over time it typically comprised three elements. First, there was the estate that sustained the castle; second, as a section of this, a park (or parks) over which the owning magnate had rights of hunting; and third, there might be a settlement or borough, which developed under the fortifications or within their embrace. It is one reflection of the integration of the castle within the landscape that the massive destruction of castles in the aftermath of the Civil War was not simply an assault on potential military strongholds. In many cases their demolition or slighting was more thoroughly malicious, encompassing not merely fortifications but all the attendant symbols of lordship, including parkland and fishponds. Such actions were part of the disgrace and overthrow of a whole social order, a secular counterpart to the Dissolution of the Monasteries. There was nothing inevitable about the ruin of castles such as Corfe, Kenilworth and Raglan in the 1640s, and their destruction must have seemed quite as surprising to contemporaries as the demolition of Buckingham Palace or the sack of Westminster and the Houses of Parliament would be to us.

1

THE ENGLISH CASTLE

Westminster Abbey (pl. 5) and Clifford's Tower in York (pl. 6) were both royal buildings probably begun within a few months of one another in 1245–6 at the direct instruction of Henry III. They present what appear to be two completely distinct and contrasting faces of medieval architecture. In the former, long acknowledged as one of the outstanding artistic masterpieces of the thirteenth century in England, we have a great church, rich, complex and lofty. In the latter we see the forbidding exterior of a castle, a ruggedly conceived tower, solid and windowless. Even the term tower might be thought generous by some – before a fire destroyed its interior in 1684 it was derisively known as the 'Mince Pie', a name that nicely captures its squat outline. But it is set on a high artificial mound or motte to give it scale, a feature that makes it as much a work of landscaping as of architecture.

These two buildings illustrate a deep-seated difference in idiom between the architecture of churches and castles. The former are the province of virtuoso display and, at their best, highly sophisticated and rich in ornament. By comparison, castles can often (though not always) look very austere, their structures making play with massive volumes and forms rather than delighting in fine architectural detail. They are also

usually much more carefully grafted into the landscape. Such manifest points of difference help explain why these different types of building have until recently often been the subject of study by two distinct scholarly constituencies: the former by architectural historians and the latter by antiquarians and archaeologists. Yet for all these contrasts, Westminster Abbey and Clifford's Tower are occasionally mentioned in connection with one another for a very good reason: both may have been designed by the same man, a certain Henry of Reyns (probably a corruption of Reims).[1]

In the case of Clifford's Tower, the basis for the attribution is a royal writ of 13 March 1245. This directs that a certain Master Henry 'the mason' view the site of York Castle along with other craftsmen to determine how it should be reconstructed, and also that the sheriff of York should see to the fortification of the castle as they direct.[2] That this Henry 'the mason' may be one and the same as the master mason named in the building accounts of Westminster Abbey is plausible, partly because the world of fine architecture has always been a very small one, in terms both of its patrons and its practitioners. There is, consequently, a strong possibility that two independent mentions of a

Facing page: Dover, Kent.

5   The choir of Westminster Abbey, London. The reconstruction of the abbey began in 1246 and the east end of the church was complete by Henry III's death in 1272. Work to the nave progressed very slowly and the construction of the western towers was interrupted by the Reformation in the sixteenth century. The setting for coronations, the shrine of Edward the Confessor and latterly the burial place of England's monarchs, Westminster Abbey is one of the most lavish works of church architecture ever erected in England.
The prestige, scale and longevity of the project, as well as the location of the abbey beside Westminster Palace, the political nerve centre of the realm, contrived to make it vastly influential in architectural terms.

6 (*facing page*)   Clifford's Tower, York, begun *circa* 1245, stands on the top of an artificial mound or motte. Within this earthwork have been discovered traces of a smaller mound that was probably raised by William the Conqueror in 1069. The lobed plan of the building compares to that of the great tower of Pontefract Castle, Yorkshire, perhaps also begun in the 1240s. Entrance to the building was through a rectangular forebuilding tower, which was rebuilt in the mid-seventeenth century with sculpted panels of heraldry. There were formerly small turrets rising between the principal lobes of the building that would have given it a busy outline of the kind beloved in Gothic design.

senior mason in royal service called Henry in the same year refer to one and the same man. But it is also likely because there is every reason to suppose that a master mason of the stature of Henry of Reyns would be involved in at least a consultative role in any significant royal architectural endeavour, whatever its nature.

In this last respect it is important to emphasise that castle construction was not necessarily a distinct expertise practised by a particular group of craftsmen. That is not to say that individual masons or carpenters might not make their career in such work, but that they were usually trained or were concurrently active in the architectural mainstream of church design and construction. There has been some confusion over this point because in the twelfth and thirteenth centuries there is occasional documentary reference to so-called engineers or *ingeniatores.* The title seems to have been adopted as an honorific by senior masons (and occasionally carpenters) and was not in fact a distinct profession.[3] So Maurice the 'engineer' who is documented as overseeing the construction of Dover Castle for Henry II in the 1180s is almost certainly the same man as Maurice 'the mason' or *cementarius* who worked on the great tower at Newcastle in the previous decade.[4] Only in the sixteenth century do there begin to appear specialist engineers of fortification whose principal skill lay in designing cannon bastions on a scientific basis and moving the huge quantities of earth necessary to build them. Even then, the more generalist medieval approach to architectural practice often prevailed: in 1539 several of the men responsible for the design and construction of Henry VIII's artillery castles in the South Downs were drafted from the royal works at Hampton Court Palace.[5]

So the visual difference between Westminster Abbey and Clifford's Tower is in a sense deceptive. These buildings – and this is true regardless of their particular attribution to Henry of Reyns – represent two faces of a common architectural coin. To explore what that means in practical terms is one of the central purposes and justifications of this study. All the buildings presented here are essentially the product of an astonishingly inventive and vigorous English architectural tradition that was born in the Middle Ages but far outlived their end. This tradition was not practised by anonymous geniuses, as is sometimes supposed, but by individuals distinguished for their outstanding ability as designers, technicians and builders. These men – and there is as yet no convincing evidence for the significant involvement of women in architectural practice except as patronesses – were not generally adulated in the manner of architects from the Renaissance onwards. But nor were they in any sense rustic equivalents of such figures. Their particular expertise was a thorough grounding in the craft of masonry learnt as apprentices in a building yard, quarry or lodge. What distinguished the master from his mason peers, however, was a knowledge of practical geometry expressed through drawing.

The medieval tradition of architecture attempted to recreate within buildings what were understood as the spaces, forms, proportions and harmonies of God's universe. It was through drawing that this was achieved and the tools involved were few and simple: a pair of dividers, a measuring rod and a set square.[6] With these it was possible not only to create drawings of a proposed building to impress and enthuse a patron, but also full-scale designs of architectural features for masons to cut stones from. Working in this manner involves some remarkable abstractions, of which one of the most important is the manipulation of plans. So strange might this idea seem that it is worth giving one simple example of what it could mean in practical terms from a late fifteenth-century technical treatise by the German master mason Mathes Roriczer.[7]

In his treatise Roriczer explains how to design a pinnacle by the simple geometrical manipulation of the square plan of its shaft (pl. 7). Within an outline of this plan he draws a series of rotated squares of diminishing size. These are created one within the other by joining the midpoints along the sides of the immediately enclosing square. By this method a strict proportional relationship (which would be expressed mathematically as $\sqrt{2}:1$) exists between each square in the series. The squares can then notionally be stacked up at proportional intervals to create the point of the pinnacle. This process of geometrical design was inherited by the medieval mason from classical antiquity, though its roots are more ancient still. It could also be practised and applied at vastly different levels of sophistication within different buildings and with more or less rigour.

Whatever the functional distinctions between Westminster and Clifford's Tower, both are founded on a common tradition of applied geometry in architecture. Of the two buildings, moreover, Westminster in every way represents the senior practice of architecture. Throughout the Middle Ages church design received proportionately greater ornament as a mark of its sacred purpose. In consequence, it was usually in the

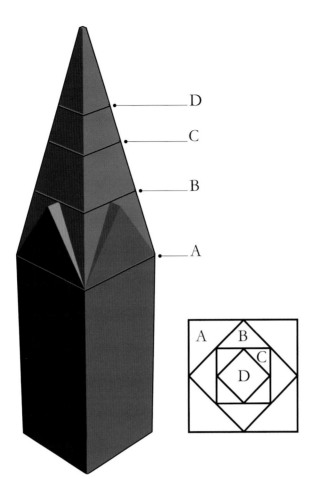

7 A greatly simplified diagram showing the means by which a pinnacle might be designed from its plan. The outer square A represents the plan of the pinnacle shaft and its inner revolutions – B, C and D – the stages by which it is to be diminished to a point. The intervals between the squares are again determined by the dimensions of the plan. The abstraction of relating plans to elevations through practical geometry was fundamental to the practice of medieval architecture. Roriczer's instructions are extremely detailed and incorporate no fewer than 234 separate steps. Another treatise on the same subject, *Fialenbüchlein* by Roriczer's contemporary Hans Schmuttermayer, uses the smaller squares in the series to determine the size of such decorative details as the pinnacle crockets. What Roriczer and Schmuttermayer have done is create an architectural feature by the manipulation of geometric figures, rather than any calculation.

field of church design that architectural experimentation took place. Also, it was in this sphere that masons generally trained. For these reasons, in the ensuing narrative church architecture necessarily figures large. Indeed, it is only by understanding the innovations in this sphere that English secular architecture is properly comprehensible prior to the 1570s. After that date, the situation changed markedly.

The suppression of the monasteries and the ensuing Reformation in the mid-sixteenth century fundamentally transformed the practice of English architecture. The dialogue between domestic and ecclesiastical design that had lent English late Gothic design such vitality broke down, and masons turned instead to a new source of inspiration. With the help of architectural publications imported from France, Italy and the Low Countries, as well as the borrowed expertise of immigrant craftsmen, the medieval building tradition assumed a new mantle and was redeveloped over the sixteenth century in a classical idiom: rich, spectacular and vigorous. One curious consequence is that, even into the 1630s, when the architectural bones underlying the conception and detailing of English buildings

are revealed, they continue to reflect Gothic fashions fresh more than a century before.

While discussing the connections between church and castle design, it is also worth making a brief observation about cost. These two traditions of buildings were intimately connected, but the former was generally much more expensive to realise than the latter. Changes in the value of money and the difficulties of calculating the costs of architecture from the available documentation make it hard to assess the differentials clearly. Nevertheless, Henry III's expenditure in the thirteenth century gives a useful insight into the relative expense of these two types of building that probably remained roughly consistent until the Reformation.

Henry III spent about £41,000 on building Westminster Abbey between 1246 and 1272.[8] This was perhaps the single most extravagant royal architectural commission of the Middle Ages (by comparison, Salisbury Cathedral, erected between *circa* 1219 and 1266 – less the spire – is said to have cost 42,000 marks or £28,000), and the sum not only represents twice the annual revenue of the crown but it was also extracted from an economy a fraction of the scale of our own. Henry's expenditure on castles from 1217 to 1272, meanwhile, has been estimated at approximately £85,000. This money, however, was spent across numerous buildings and even the three biggest absorbed a fraction of the money needed for the abbey: Windsor Castle £15,000, and both Winchester Castle and the Tower of London just under £10,000 apiece.[9] Clifford's Tower at York is unlikely to have cost over £1,000, though works to the castle as a whole absorbed more than twice that sum.[10]

These comparisons should not belittle the expense of castle building. Architecture is, and has always been, breathtakingly expensive and far beyond the ordinary costs of life. Simply, it makes the point that while castle building was vastly costly to undertake, fine church architecture was yet dearer.

THE ENGLISHNESS OF ENGLISH ARCHITECTURE

The comparison of Westminster Abbey and Clifford's Tower can also be used to illustrate the second central theme enshrined in the title of this book: the English character of the architecture discussed. Very little is known about Henry of Reyns, but from his work at

Westminster it is clear that he was familiar with contemporary developments in French architecture and – as his name further suggests – in particular with the rebuilding of Reims Cathedral from 1211. This was the coronation church of the French kings and the metropolitan cathedral of France (pl. 8). One of many detailed indications of his knowledge of this building is the use at Westminster of delicate bars of stone to create patterns within the windows. Such bar tracery is directly copied from Reims, where the earliest substantial examples of the form survive. In consequence of this connection, Clifford's Tower has also been discussed in the context of northern French castle designs, notably Tour de Guinette, the great tower of Etampes (Essonne), south of Paris. This building, constructed around 1140, has in common with Clifford's Tower a four-lobed plan, a very unusual and distinctive design (pl. 9).

But, allowing for their influence, what effect did these French buildings actually have upon their English followers? Though clearly comparable, the points of difference are quite as striking as the similarities. By contrast with the soaring and austere gigantism of Reims, for example, Westminster is diminutive and presents a spectacular display of colour, moulding and carved decoration. Similarly, the two castle designs are startlingly different despite their shared ground plan. Etampes is a high tower set on living rock with massively thick walls. It is entered through a raised door and has a vaulted interior. In each respect it is a marked contrast to Clifford's Tower, which has relatively thin walls, is set on a mound or motte to give it height and is without internal vaults.

In other words, the designs of Clifford's Tower and Westminster are explained only to a very limited degree by the French buildings that have been cited as their models. There is a good explanation in both cases for this divergence: viewed in the light of other English buildings, Westminster and Clifford's Tower make sense. The scale and ornament of Westminster grew out of an English tradition of church architecture, and Clifford's Tower – as will appear later – derived from long-standing conventions of castle design in England. There is, in short, something distinctively regional about both buildings that is fundamental to our understanding of them. Before turning to discuss this idea further it is worth digressing for a moment to make a point about the study of churches and castles as reflected in this group of buildings.

It would be in the interests of the argument presented here if all the comparisons drawn so far were

8 Reims Cathedral (Marne), begun in 1211, was the coronation church of the French kings. It employs delicate bar tracery to ornament the enormous windows that distinguish its interior. The great height of the vault, which is suspended 125 feet (38 m) above the ground, is accentuated by the clusters of thin shafts that rise in stages up the elevation and appear to support it. Reims was quickly outmatched in size by the cathedrals of Amiens, 141 feet (43 m), and Beauvais, 156 feet (47.5 m). Westminster Abbey is 104 feet (31.7 m) high and outstandingly tall by English standards, but an architectural dwarf compared with these French skyscrapers.

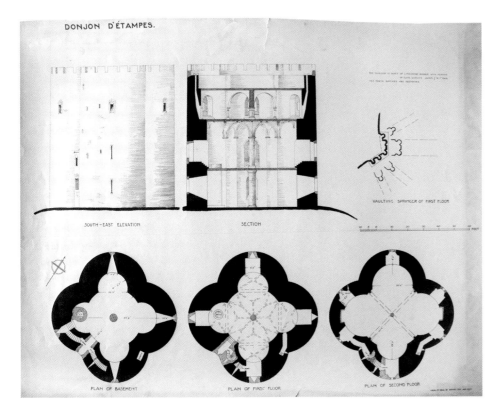

DONJON D'ÉTAMPES.

SOUTH-EAST ELEVATION   SECTION   VAULTING SPRINGER OF FIRST FLOOR

PLAN OF BASEMENT   PLAN OF FIRST FLOOR   PLAN OF SECOND FLOOR

9   The great tower of Etampes (Essonne), built *circa* 1140, elevations and plan by S. Toy, dated 1925. The tower is one of a widespread group of contemporary lobed towers in northern France that includes Ambleny (Aisne), Vic-sur-Aisne (Aisne) and Houdan (Yvelines). All that survives of the building today is its masonry shell. An illustration of Etampes around 1400 in the *Très Riches Heures* of the duc de Berry shows the tower capped by a steep, conical roof. French masons particularly delighted in creating castles with fantastical roofscapes, a taste eschewed to a striking degree by their English counterparts.

correct: that Henry of Reyns did design both Westminster and Clifford's Tower; and that his design of both was respectively inspired by Reims and Etampes. If these things are true – as they may be – then the tower at York is a rare and fascinating example of a thirteenth-century castle building designed by a named architect of outstanding invention. Also, that this man was inspired by foreign example but worked in an English idiom. Yet it is difficult to assert these things with confidence because the comparisons being drawn between these two great churches and castle towers are alarmingly uneven.

For the designer of Westminster, the English coronation church, Reims Cathedral was in every sense an appropriate architectural model. Not only was it one of the most ambitious churches under construction in Europe in the 1240s, but it also shared a common function with Westminster as a liturgical setting for the solemn anointing of kings. Moreover, the connection between the churches is substantiated by numerous detailed and technical comparisons, of which the common use of bar tracery is but one. By contrast, Etampes was built in the early twelfth century and was therefore already a century old when it came to be copied – if indeed it was copied – at York. Added to which there is no circumstantial or further detailed case for associating Clifford's Tower with Etampes

beyond the fact that both have a four-lobed plan. Admittedly, this is a distinctive form but foiled plans were to be used again subsequently and quite unconnectedly in English architecture, for example, at Henry VIII's castle at Deal begun in 1539 (see pl. 318) and Bess of Hardwick's Hunting Tower or Stand at Chatsworth dating from the 1570s (see pl. 350). So do we really need Etampes to explain Clifford's Tower at all?

This question is intended to highlight the very different critical standards that have been applied to the respective study of church architecture and that of its poor cousin, the castle, as well as the assumption in much scholarly analysis that English castle design necessarily followed that of the European mainstream. Continental buildings were occasionally of decisive importance in the development of English castle design. Such, for example, we shall see to be the case with the genesis of the English great tower in the eleventh century, and with the development and detailing of brick architecture in the fifteenth. But, generally speaking, the influence of Continental architecture in England has been invoked too freely by scholars to resolve awkward transitions or anomalies. In large part, this free invocation of foreign models is a consequence of the presentation of castles as purely military buildings: because fortifications are functional, not aesthetic objects, so – it is argued – their design is largely free from aesthetic consideration and naturally transcends political boundaries. In a period where the castle-building classes were international travellers, therefore, fortifications were necessarily designed in the most up-to-date fashion, whether the model was to be found in France or on crusade in the Levant.

The reality is that medieval buildings in England and other parts of Europe are strikingly, even startlingly, different: the discussion of Reims and Westminster has already highlighted that it does not take a trained eye to distinguish between the soaring aesthetic of a French High Gothic cathedral and the dazzling but relatively stunted complexity of its English counterpart. Nor, despite these manifest differences, is there any difficulty in simultaneously recognising them both as great churches produced within a shared culture. In just the same manner as great churches, castles show a remarkable diversity of form across Europe while remaining clearly identifiable as castles.

These differences are not merely apparent as between kingdoms or principalities, but between the regions within them as well. In England, for example, there are several distinctive regional styles of architecture that preserve their identity in recognisable ways right through into the seventeenth century. In broad terms, such English regional traditions can be identified in the south-east, the south-west, the Midlands, East Anglia and the north. Within these regions, and particularly the last, there is considerable diversity.[11] Quite how these traditions emerged or were maintained over time is difficult to say. Often they appear to have been focused either on the different lodges of masons associated with quarries or, before the Reformation, on certain great churches.

To stress such differences is not to imply that these architectural traditions were exclusive or that they developed in hermetic isolation. Regionally, nationally and internationally architectural ideas can be shown to have flowed to and fro readily across Europe (and occasionally even beyond) with bewildering speed and ease. But whereas this exchange has conventionally been explained in terms of a trickle-down of ideas and forms from architecturally dynamic regions to backwaters, and from greater buildings to less, the reality was much more complicated. The various different regions of England were a motive force behind architectural change, sufficiently vigorous to re-digest admired ideas rather than simply to ape them. Added to which, they contributed in different degrees to what might be termed a national idiom of architecture. In this, royal building projects, backed by the unrivalled resources of the king, played a pre-eminent role. They not only set the pace and character of architectural development, they also gave it a loose, national coherence.

Perhaps the best way to summarise these ideas of regional and national idiom is to draw an analogy between architecture and language. Modern English and French, for example, are closely related and have long influenced one another; but they are still different with distinct vocabularies and syntax. In spoken form they also have different registers: they may be spoken with great discipline or slovenliness, in different accents and in dialect. So the traditions of castle architecture in England and France are related but distinct: the French, for example, had a predilection for vaulting important internal spaces and, from the fourteenth century onwards, for spectacular entrance stairs;[12] the English for timber ceilings and great gatehouses. French late medieval domestic arrangements required an upper and a lower hall, English ones a great hall and great chamber. Added to these broad contrasts that help characterise the two national idioms there are also many dialects of architectural expression, which can be further understood through this linguistic analogy.

Different languages can, of course, be used to express the same idea, though differences of vocabulary and syntax can give contrasting and surprising twists of emphasis. And when formally structured they respond in curious and distinctive ways – in verse, for example, the formal Alexandrine is a natural French metre, but English responds better to stately iambic pentameter or the tripping octosyllabic line. So in architecture, as in translation, an admired object from a foreign source is never normally copied but reworked, usually to the point of reinvention. Finally, and most importantly, in architecture, as in conversation, you always do best to speak a language that your present company understands, though the introduction of foreign phrases may add a certain *je ne sais quoi*.

To some extent, this book also treats castles outside the borders of England but within the British Isles. Scotland, Wales and Ireland all have distinctive architectural traditions of their own and it would be absurd to try and do justice to these in an account of this kind. Nevertheless, in some cases, the buildings erected in these regions have a direct bearing on the story of English architecture. Most commonly, this is because attempts at conquest or colonisation have encouraged the erection of what might be described as imperial buildings: architecture created in an English idiom beyond the borders of the kingdom. Such, for example, is the case with the castles erected by Edward I during his late thirteenth-century campaigns in Wales and by Planters in Ulster in the seventeenth century. In as far as these buildings inform our understanding of English castle architecture, it is appropriate to discuss them here.

THE GREAT HOUSEHOLD

To understand English castles it is not sufficient merely to appreciate the purely architectural process behind their creation. Whatever their other qualities, castles were residences, and in order to engage with them we need to have some appreciation both of the communities they housed and of the tradition of grand English domestic architecture that they enshrined.

The fundamental institution of English noble life in both the medieval and early modern age was the household, the personal following attendant on any figure of status, whether male or female, secular or ecclesiastic, young or old. This institution, by its size and magnificence, directly reflected the status of the figure at its head. The greatest English household usually attended upon the king, though certain figures – such as Cardinal Wolsey (d. 1530) – famously vied with this pre-eminence. Most households, however, were very much smaller while broadly following the same overarching structure.[13]

Evidence for the early constitution and organisation of these bodies is largely anecdotal, though an exceptional portrait of the royal household in the 1130s exists in the short text called *Constitutio Domus Regis* or 'The Constitution of the King's House'. From around 1300, a great deal more documentary material survives to inform our picture of the subject. Particularly important is the evidence of surviving statutes governing the life of both royal and noble households.[14] As a whole, this evidence suggests that the household grew steadily in complexity and formality from the eleventh century to the mid-seventeenth. It also shows that, contrary to what is often argued, its essential constitution over this long period of time changed relatively little.

A great household throughout this period can broadly be understood as falling into two sections. The first of these was under the control of the steward. He oversaw the offices or departments responsible for the practical management of the household, notably the preparation and distribution of food. His counterpart in control of the second division of the household was the chamberlain, who worked to imbue the public operations of the household with ceremony and magnificence. Without exception, from the greatest to the least, all branches of the household from the eleventh century to the seventeenth were exclusively or predominantly male; and most of its members were celibate or served in their posts apart from their wives. The only important exception was in instances where the head of the household was a woman, where intimate attendants were female. In addition to these two principal sections, prior to the Reformation all great households also had a clerical component. This group was responsible for the celebration of divine service and the Mass; it also commonly provided the household with a group of literate men who maintained records and accounts. In the royal household it was initially under the control of the chancellor, who additionally kept possession of the great seal for authenticating documents.

These core divisions of the household were all concerned with life indoors, but there further existed a substantial body of individuals whose responsibilities related to life outdoors.[15] Of practical importance were those charged with responsibility for horses. To state the obvious, until the invention of the internal combustion engine, horses were a mainstay of life and were bred to serve every need, from transport to war. Stables, therefore, were enormously important buildings. That is not to say that they were necessarily either prominently sited or architecturally pretentious. To judge from historic inventories and surveys, stables were usually grouped with other service buildings in the outer courts of castles and great residences. And in the manner of such buildings, they were often workaday structures. A survey of Holt, Denbighshire, of 1620 probably reveals what many late medieval castle stables looked like: to the left of the outer gate of this impressive late thirteenth-century castle is a roughly planked timber range. It is succinctly labelled 'stables and other buildings. Ruined' (see pl. 166).

Nevertheless, medieval stables could occasionally be very grand indeed. When one of the flowers of fifteenth-century English chivalry, Richard Beauchamp, earl of Warwick, created new stables for himself at Warwick Castle, they reputedly cost the vast sum of 500 marks (£333 6s. 8d.) and were decorated in some unspecified way with plaster of Paris.[16] These lost stables were almost certainly the model for the great stables begun a century later by John Dudley, duke of Northumberland, at nearby Kenilworth Castle.[17] Both men were appointed to the prestigious post of master of horse for the king, an added incentive for them to house their horses magnificently. The stable at Kenilworth still survives, the pattern of its timber frame cut in the form of the duke's emblem of the ragged staff.

It was probably from display stables of this kind that another type of building associated with horses evolved in the seventeenth century. The riding house was a space created for a type of formal exercise or classical dressage for horses. It was made fashionable in England through the activities of a French riding master who was sent to England to teach horsemanship to James I's son, Prince Henry. One of those who attended the royal lessons was William Cavendish, the future duke of Newcastle. He became an enthusiast for this type of dressage and even published a book on the subject in 1654. At his seat of Bolsover he created an entire range in the outer bailey of the castle dedicated to horses. It included a riding house, a stable and a shoeing house and was detailed in the height of architectural fashion.

Horses were also crucial for the chase and hunting, pastimes that engaged another substantial slice of any great household. In the 1130s, for example, the king's hunting establishment included four horn-blowers, twenty sergeants, several fewterers (keepers of greyhounds), a group of archers – some responsible for keeping the king's bow – knight huntsmen, huntsmen and a wide variety of dogs. The sheer scale of provision for hunting is a reminder of the consistent importance of this sport throughout the period covered by this book. Not only was it a mark of lordly identity but also a chief object of delight, enthusiasm and enjoyment amongst the rich and powerful. As one seventeenth-century historian reported of Thomas, third Lord Berkeley (d. 1361), one of the wealthiest barons of the period:

It seemeth this lord was so much delighted with this sort of recreation, that he and his brothers have kept out four nights together, with their nets and dogs, in hunting of the fox; and surely nature round about his manors of Simonfall and Wotton had fitted the soil and country as invitements thereunto . . .[18]

As the same passage explains, Lord Berkeley kept so many hounds that his packs in six separate manors each consumed more than 44 quarters of oats – about 7 tonnes in weight – in one financial year, 1349–50.

In return for their attendance, the head of the household gave liveries to all his or her followers. The liveries described in the *Constitutio Domus Regis* of the 1130s comprised money, food and goods and were distributed with strict regard to degree. So, for example, the chancellor – who ran the royal administration – received a livery each day of 5 shillings, one fine and two salted simnels (wheat bread), a sextary (probably 4 gallons) of sweet wine and another sextary of ordinary wine, a large wax candle and forty candle ends. Contrary to what a modern reader might assume, these basic benefits of office constituted a valuable income. By contrast, the bearer of the king's bed ate at royal expense and received in addition 3 halfpence a day for his servant and a sumpterhorse with its own livery; the king's tailor was to eat in his own house but had an allowance of 3 pence for his servant; the king's ewer had a 'double diet' with a penny for drying the king's clothes when travelling and 4 pence when the king bathed, except on the three great feasts of Christmas, Easter and Whitsun. It is probably a comment on the marginal importance of women in this environment that the wages of the only one mentioned in the house-

hold – the laundress – were 'in doubt'.[19] Astonishingly, the royal household continued the obligation of feeding its members until 1663.[20]

From around 1200, however, it became increasingly common for liveries additionally to include clothing. This practice perhaps deliberately evoked the Roman precedent of distributing items of dress as evidence of appointment within the state. It was a habit perpetuated by the church with – for example – archbishops collecting a stole termed a *pallium* from the pope as a mark of their office. Clothing was generally dispensed in the form of cloth, the colour and quantity of which reflected the status of the recipient.[21] By the fourteenth century such distributions had become complex and symbolic. Junior figures in a household might receive short lengths of wool inexpensively dyed, senior ones longer lengths of more richly woven and coloured material. The liveries made up from such distributions clearly indicated to whose household a man belonged and, broadly, in what capacity he served. Universities still perpetuate this hierarchical system of dress in gowns and hoods, the inherited medieval livery of an academic. Not only do the colours and forms vary from university to university, but also bachelor undergraduates universally wear slight gowns, masters robes of more generous cut, and doctors or university officials capacious and colourful costume. The English legal system has similar hierarchies of dress for the same reason.

A university college (or an inn of court) provides another useful insight into the medieval household from which it derives. The pyramid of its hierarchy, while steeply shelved, has several intermediary ranks between its apex and base. Within a household each rank operated broadly in relation to those immediately above and below it. So a king was not served at table by a menial servant but by a nobleman, whose attendance redounded to his might and status; and a nobleman would be served by a gentleman of his household. For the head of a household there were obvious advantages in attracting independently important figures into service, not least the power and influence their personal support might lend. In return, noblemen and gentlemen were spurred to service by the benefits that might arise from it. Great offices within a household, and particularly that of the king, could come with attractive perquisites, as well as the opportunity for petitioning provided by personal access to a powerful figure.

Crucially, the medieval and early modern household was a peripatetic institution in attendance on the figure at its head, travelling continuously from residence to residence with all the necessary furniture and utensils. This lifestyle enabled a nobleman to see his far-flung estates at first hand and use up their resources. Long stays, however, particularly by the court, could exhaust local food supplies and place a serious strain on sanitary arrangements. In this situation residences were not so much homes as stopping-off points. Each one provided a series of interiors that could be populated and decorated as necessary to suit the occasion of the visit. This potential flexibility in use can make it difficult to pronounce on the function of spaces within surviving buildings. Particular use is often implicit in the scale and position of chambers within a domestic plan, but in practice every interior could be dressed up to suit the needs of the moment, just as a modern theatre stage can be dressed for different plays. Across the period surveyed in this book, great households gradually travelled less but their peripatetic quality was never entirely lost.

Another complication inherent in relating these human institutions to the architecture of a particular building is that a residence could contain more than one household. This might be the case if both husband and wife were of sufficient stature to possess their own following, as in the case of a king and queen. Alternatively, it might be occupied only by a reduced or core group of staff, a body commonly described from the fifteenth century onwards as the 'riding' household. This was a travelling band, much smaller than its unwieldy 'great' counterpart, that attended the head of a household if he or she visited a residence in haste or for pleasure. In 1512, for example, the earl of Northumberland maintained a great household 166 strong, but his riding household comprised 36 men.[22]

Despite these complications, the architecture of great residences can be properly understood only in the context of the households that served them. The gigantic scale of domestic complexes and their fragmented form reflect the huge numbers of people that might constitute a household and the diversity of their responsibilities, from the huntsman to the cook and the chamberlain to the scullion. Within the building, all the principal chambers had a dedicated staff. That staff, particularly in the more junior branches of the household, would have lived within their designated chamber, working within it during the day and converting it into a dormitory at night with bedding or portable pallets. In such a situation none of the principal chambers in a great house would have been in

any sense private, as we define the word, although some would have approached this, being the preserve of a few senior household figures. Only from the late thirteenth century onwards, and with increasing regularity thereafter, did properly secluded domestic interiors develop for the head of the household alone. The earliest of these were the so-called closets or parcloses overlooking chapel altars that allowed their occupants to perform devotions in seclusion.

By 1400 there were also studies, for example that created for Henry IV at Eltham in Kent between 1399 and 1407 with a ceiling studded with the figures of angels, a desk for the king's books and windows glazed with the images of saints.[23] Something of the exquisite quality of such spaces and their ingenious furnishing is beautifully captured in an uncharacteristically enthusiastic description of one such room in Wressle Castle in Yorkshire by the bibliophile and antiquarian John Leland around 1540:

> One thing I likid exceedingly yn one of the towers, that was a study caullid Paradise, where was a closet in the middle of 8. squares latisid aboute: and on the toppe of every square was a desk ledgid to set books on cofers withyn them, and these semid as yoined hard to the toppe of the closet: and yet by pulling one or al wold cum downe, briste higthe in rabettes [come down to breast height in grooves], and serve for desks to lay bokes on.[24]

The date at which this remarkable study was created is unfortunately not clear, nor does any trace of it survive.

THE ARCHITECTURE OF GRAND DOMESTIC LIVING

In general terms a nobleman's house across the entire period of the 600 years treated in this book can be understood as comprising four essential elements: the services or kitchens, a communal space, the withdrawing rooms and the chapel. The details of their development will be threshed out in the argument of the book as a whole, but it is useful to have an introductory overview of them, particularly since what follows materially differs in some points from the received view of the subject. In the eleventh century the limited physical and documentary evidence suggests that each of these elements was typically represented in a domestic complex by a single structure or

interior, respectively the kitchen, the hall, the chamber and the chapel.[25] The hall aside, which was a shared space, each of these elements corresponded to a branch of the household, the kitchen being the province of the steward, the chamber of the chamberlain and the chapel of the clerical household. Importantly, in early residences it would appear that the respective structures were often physically discrete buildings spread over a considerable area of land.

From the mid-twelfth century onwards these elements of the house began physically to coalesce, though this process did not usually lead to their integration within a regular or coherent architectural composition. Indeed, it remained fashionable even into the late sixteenth century – and occasionally beyond – for the different elements of a house, though physically integrated, to be identifiable from the exterior. This might be achieved, for example, through the use of distinct window forms for different interiors. A good example of this is provided by the late fourteenth-century great tower at Warkworth, which has distinct window types to identify service, public, corridor and withdrawn apartments (see pl. 243). Concurrent with this process of coalescence was the multiplication of rooms within the domestic plan. The only real continuity within it was the great hall. This developed a distinctive architectural language of its own and remained – contrary to what is often asserted – the anchor of English domestic design far beyond the end of the Middle Ages (pl. 10).

The Great Hall

To find the great hall in any house constructed within the period covered by this book is to unlock the key to its overall residential plan. This is true in two senses. First, because the hall was always the first interior that a visitor to a house entered, hence the modern use of the word 'hall' to denote the lobby of a home. Second, because it stood at the crossroads of the domestic plan: accessible from one end of the building were the services and from the other the withdrawing apartments. The great hall was properly the space from which these apartments were considered to be withdrawn.

In 1066 the great hall was already an ancient architectural form in England. Beowulf and the monster Grendel had confronted one another in such a building in Anglo-Saxon legend. And in 627, when St Paulinus had convinced King Edwin to accept Christianity,

10 The Great Hall of Winchester, Hampshire, built in the years 1222–36, is a magnificent surviving example of a type of interior universally familiar in residences across England for more than 1,000 years. The internal arcades dividing the interior into three unequal aisles are a throwback to the design of Anglo-Saxon timber halls. Here they are treated in the manner of church arcades and are carved from polished Purbeck marble. They support a high, open, timber roof. In its present form this is a fifteenth-century structure and probably of lighter build than the original. Henry III instructed that the interior be painted with a map of the world and a Wheel of Fortune, but no trace of this decoration now survives. Suspended on the far wall, however, there does remain the celebrated Round Table of King Arthur, made between 1250 and 1280 (according to tree-ring dating of its constituent timbers) and probably repainted in the Tudor livery colours of green and white in 1522.

a nobleman present had likened the life of man to the flight of a sparrow as it passed from darkness to darkness through the doors of a splendid royal hall.[26] Such early halls were constructed entirely of timber and were distinctive by virtue of their outstanding size within a residential complex.

Though Paulinus might not have recognised the great halls built in England a thousand years later – say at Raglan (Monmouthshire), Cowdray (Sussex), Longleat (Wiltshire) and Wollaton (Nottinghamshire) – these structures nevertheless consciously reflected their ancient ancestry: they were still the largest interiors within their respective houses and each was covered by a gigantic open timber roof. Through the intervening millennium great halls on this model were constructed within every domestic setting, both secular and ecclesiastic, and on a multitude of different scales.

Great halls survive to this day as functioning buildings in surprising quantity, most famously perhaps in Oxbridge colleges. Their survival in this particular context is not coincidental: great halls have always been an architectural symbol of a household, and university colleges are amongst the handful of institutions within which communal living and corporate identity – in the traditional sense – have any reality in twenty-first-century Britain.

Nevertheless, it is important to realise that even in the high Middle Ages the values of community celebrated architecturally by the great hall were at odds with the way in which it functioned. As great houses expanded in size and complexity so was the great hall depopulated, the household being, so to speak, sucked out into the services and withdrawing chambers at either end of it. But this very movement perhaps contrived to make the great hall symbolically even more important as an architectural gesture towards the ancient, but lost, ideal of the household. Its symbolic importance may further explain why it remained so deeply conservative in architectural form.

Of the arrangement of the hall something should be said, because these interiors came to follow a classic layout (pl. 11). Entrance to the hall in the late Middle Ages was usually though a porch set against the extreme of one of its long sides. The porch door led into the so-called screens passage, an area of the hall concealed from the body of the interior by a timber partition or screen. Also opening into the screens passage from the adjacent end wall of the hall were three service doors leading respectively to the kitchen, buttery and pantry. Two doors in the screen gave access to the 'low' end of the hall interior. At the opposite end of the room, and demarcated by a step running across the width of the interior, was the dais at the 'high' end of the hall. This was often lit from the late fourteenth century onwards by a projecting bay or oriel window. Opening from the dais was a doorway to the withdrawing chambers beyond.

In the centre of the hall, usually set slightly towards the dais, was an open fireplace, the smoke from which escaped through a louvre in the roof. Central hearths must have looked archaic even by the fourteenth century, when fireplaces had become commonplace in other domestic interiors. The persistence of such an arrangement within this single space is a reflection of how conventionalised the design of the hall became. That said, hall fireplaces do exist in English buildings from the late thirteenth century onwards, as at Conwy in Caernarfonshire, but they remained unusual.

During meals trestle tables could be laid out within this interior in a fashion still familiar in college halls. The junior members of the household sat at dismountable trestle tables set lengthways along the walls of the hall in the body of the room. Usually their seating would reflect in some way the hierarchy of the household, the more junior sitting towards the screen. In contrast, the head of the household or his deputy sat at a single 'high' table that ran across the width of the dais (pl. 12). Where an oriel window existed, this might be used as a discrete space for senior household servants to dine. This practice continued in some houses into the seventeenth century, as is recorded by one visitor to Lulworth Castle in the 1630s: 'At the upper end of the Hall, is a neat round roome, in one of the Towers, which receives his Lordships private Gentlemen, as that above doth himselfe at Meales.'[27]

In large households – to accommodate the numbers involved and in order for servants to eat – there could be numerous sittings for meals. Such practices are sometimes spelt out in detail, as in the case of the statutes of Eton College probably drawn up in 1452–3 regarding dining in the hall.[28] By the fourteenth century the heads of the households were commonly eating in their withdrawing apartments, rather than in the hall itself. One way of maintaining a link with the ceremony of the hall was to carry food for the head of the household through it in formal procession. The earl of Huntingdon's household statutes in 1609, for example, instruct that when his meat came from the kitchen, an usher was to stand by the hall screen and say in a loud voice: '"By your leave";

11   A reconstruction of the great hall and services at Bodiam, Sussex, begun around 1385, by Stephen Conlin. The arrangement of this range follows the classic late medieval plan. To the far left is the high table on its dais (1), lit by a large window (2). The body of the hall is heated by a central hearth (3) and divided from the entrance or screens passage by a wooden screen (4) with two openings. This passage has external doors to either end, the outer one (5) enclosed within a tower porch. Opening onto the screens passage are three doors, to the buttery (6), pantry (7) and – down a corridor – the kitchen, on the far right (8).

and cause all men in the hall to . . . be bare-headed whilst the meate passeth through.'[29]

Quite when the classic arrangement for the great hall with a screens passage and dais end became widespread is not clear. There are eleventh-century halls, such as Scolland's Hall in Richmond Castle, Yorkshire, that are conformable to its essential details. But if such buildings do indeed anticipate the classic high medieval layout there are plenty of halls even into the late twelfth century that look quite different. The hall of the bishop's palace at Hereford (probably built during the episcopacy of William de Vere, 1186–98), for example, has its entrance porch set in the centre of one of the long walls rather than towards an extreme.[30] Moreover, the first possible references to hall screens (which probably derived from screens in smaller domestic rooms, which are documented from the 1230s)[31] occur as late as the mid-fourteenth century;[32] and the earliest surviving fragment of one probably dates from the 1370s and has survived reincorporated within the sixteenth-century hall screen of the abbot's hall at Westminster.[33]

The hall bay window or oriel too is a relatively late development, the earliest fully fledged surviving example of it being found in the hall at Kenilworth Castle, Warwickshire, of the 1370s. Nevertheless, by whatever stages the classic hall plan developed, one concept it enshrined clearly had a reality throughout our period. This was the division of a single interior between a public and a privileged area, the low and high end of the hall.

Services

While the form of the hall remained relatively constant, the elements of the house around it were transformed beyond recognition over the course of the Middle Ages. The services appear to have fragmented steadily from the twelfth century onwards, a phenomenon that has a very practical explanation. Food was by far the most expensive commodity handled on a day-to-day basis in a medieval household and the process of storing, preparing and serving it was necessarily highly organised. A discrete buttery and pantry, where drink and bread were respectively served to the hall, can be identified at sites such as Oakham Castle in Rutland from the late twelfth century (see pl. 95).

Kitchens too steadily increased in size and complexity, and by the fourteenth century the cooking arrangements of a great residence must have resembled those of a large modern hotel or restaurant with departments independently responsible for preparing different types of food and drink, such as the staples of meat, beer, bread and pastry. The sheer scale of surviving kitchens from the late Middle Ages – as for

13 An anonymous late sixteenth-century depiction of Henry VIII dining. The king is shown in his withdrawing apartments, sitting on a dais beneath a canopy of estate. He is surrounded by courtiers, some of whom wait upon him at table. Canopies of estate were derived from bed hangings and were used in both royal and noble households by the fifteenth century. They became the object of complex protocol akin to that familiar in the context of church liturgy. Visitors, for example, performed obeisance to a canopy and throne even when they were unoccupied. To the right of the interior is a board laid with gold and silver plate, a means of advertising the wealth of the household. Some details – such as the form of the windows and the use of panelling (rather than tapestry) on the walls – may be anachronistic.

example at Durham Castle, which still preserve all their offices – makes vividly apparent the importance of cooking to the household. There might additionally be a separate kitchen for the head of the household, which prepared the types of elaborate dishes the wealthy have always expected for themselves and their favoured guests.[34]

Withdrawing Apartments

The chamber meanwhile grew by degrees into an entire suite of withdrawing apartments, the number, scale and arrangement of which varied from place to place and from period to period. Of particular importance within them, and a consistent feature of ambitious domestic design from at least the thirteenth century onwards, was the great chamber. This was usually directly accessible from the great hall and was typically the grandest room in the withdrawing apartments, suitable for ceremonial and formal receptions.

One feature of the great chamber that survived into the sixteenth century and advertised its origins as a retiring room was the visual focus of the interior: a bed

with a high fabric canopy. Beds were very expensive items of furniture and remained consistently important features of formal English interiors. Throughout the Middle Ages the more public withdrawing chambers contained state beds that might be used as an alternative to a seat by the owner of the house. In imitation of beds, thrones also came to be provided with rich fabric overmantels called canopies of estate (pl. 13). Even so, the use of state beds in England – whose fascinating history remains to be properly traced – probably never died out entirely.

There are in currency misleading terms still regularly applied by scholars to describe withdrawing chambers in medieval buildings, two of which deserve individual mention. The 'Ladies' Bower' is a remarkably resilient but largely fanciful creation of late nineteenth-century sensibility. More confusingly, the word 'solar' is commonly used as a technical term in modern literature to describe a chamber for the personal use of the head of a household. This word, however, was not applied in the Middle Ages to describe the function of a room but its position: a solar was a first-floor chamber. Many solars were withdrawing chambers, but a room so described in the thirteenth century need not necessarily have been so.

One feature of the withdrawing apartments that merits attention is the manner in which domestic rooms were connected. It is typical in modern houses for the principal interiors – such as the kitchen, dining room and drawing room – to open directly off an entrance hall and also to intercommunicate independently. In consequence, there may be more than one route between some of the rooms. But the withdrawing chambers of the buildings described in this book were typically planned in a completely different way, the rooms opening off one another in strict sequence. This physical progression from one room to the next created a hierarchy of interiors, the most important of which was also the most remote or withdrawn from the hall.

The great chamber was always the outermost of these and the bedchamber of the head of the household usually the innermost. Again, it is very difficult to pinpoint the origins of sequentially planned interiors. Some eleventh-century plans are conformable to it but the idea became commonplace only from around 1300. By 1400 such arrangements were sometimes combined with systems of corridor access that potentially short-circuited the sequence. One early and important English example of corridor planning is to be found in the royal lodgings at Windsor Castle begun in 1359. And much earlier Continental examples existed, as in the 1240s work at Castel del Monte in Apulia, Italy.[35]

The Chapel

Before the Reformation, and in Catholic residences thereafter, the clerical order in the household was a distinct body with particular duties. To its priests belonged the exclusive rights of administering the sacraments, of which the most important was the Mass (the ceremonial re-enactment by a priest of the Last Supper eaten by Christ and the sacrifice of Calvary). This conventionally had to be celebrated on a fixed and consecrated altar of stone, a requirement that, in combination with the prescribed ceremonial, necessitated some formal architectural provision for its setting.

Such was their particular importance that chapels and their altar spaces were nearly always signposted architecturally on the exterior of a building. This could be done by projecting the chapel from an otherwise regular plan – as at William the Conqueror's White Tower in London. Alternatively, or in combination with such treatment, the chapel windows could be elaborated in some way. At Maxstoke Castle in Warwickshire, begun around 1342, the chapel window is by far the largest in the building and set with rich tracery (see pl. 210).

Throughout the Middle Ages great residences typically had at least two interiors with altars. One of these was usually attached to, or directly communicated with, the withdrawn apartments. From at least 1300 until around 1350 chapels attached to the withdrawing apartments were commonly located between the hall and the great chamber, and in many cases – as at Little Wenham, Suffolk, of *circa* 1270 – opened directly off the latter. Thereafter it became more common for chapels of this kind to be located outside the sequence of withdrawing chambers but overlooked from them by means of galleries or narrow openings termed squints. Such an arrangement permitted the priests and clerks of the chapel to go about their tasks without interfering with those of the chamberlain's staff. In some exceptional cases, such as royal palaces, however, even after this shift a chapel was sometimes additionally maintained beside the bedchamber. Where they existed, such intimately placed chapels were always very small and for the exclusive use of the head of the household.

The second space for the celebration of the Mass was generally more publicly accessible and might take a variety of forms. At one extreme it might be a small and privately owned church set within the precincts of a house or castle, as at Haddon Hall, Derbyshire, and Farleigh Hungerford, Somerset (the latter in fact a parish church swallowed up by the expanding castle between 1441 and 1443 and henceforth used as a private chapel).[36] But equally it could be an adjacent parish church, a college or even a monastery patronised by the owning family.

Depending on the precise form it took, such foundations might be staffed either by a single priest or a great community and they might additionally make provision for education and almsgiving. These churches would usually have been used on great feast-days by the patronal family and were often additionally developed as family mausolea. The procession to and from churches on Sundays and feast-days gave opportunity for staged public appearances by the nobility, which allowed for the distribution of alms and the reception of petitions.[37]

Despite their different status and potential variety of scale, both chapels and churches usually contained a pew for the head of the household. How this was arranged in the eleventh and twelfth centuries is a matter for conjecture, but the broad arch on the western nave wall of St John's Chapel in the Tower of London may have been intended to frame a royal throne set on a dais. If so, the king would have sat in a slightly elevated position within this royal chapel, facing the high altar at the opposite end of the building. It may be significant in this respect that the slightly later Cappella dei Normanni in Palermo, Sicily, has a similar – if restored – arrangement of this kind, dating from the mid-twelfth century.[38] Another arch of this type survives in the 1130s forebuilding chapel of the great tower at Portchester in Hampshire (see pl. 16).

In England by the thirteenth century, and in some cases possibly before, pews were being enclosed in some way to form a so-called closet. From within the closet it was possible to view the Elevation during Mass – at which the consecrated bread and wine, just transformed into the Body and Blood of Christ, were displayed to the congregation – and practise devotions in private. Indeed, closets were probably the first truly private spaces in English domestic life. At their simplest, they took the form of fabric tents that could be set up and dismantled as was convenient (pl. 14). Such

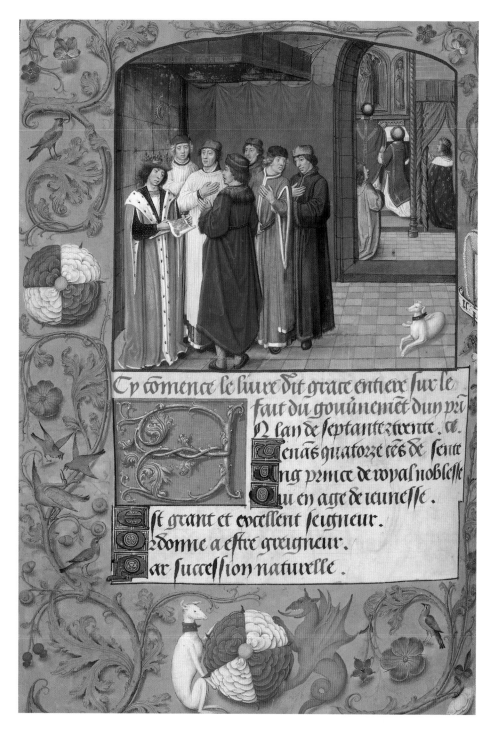

14 The frontispiece of a Flemish manuscript, *Grace entiere sur le fait du gouvernement d'un Prince*, about the upbringing of a prince. It is dated 1500 and decorated with the devices of Arthur, prince of Wales (d. 1502). In the foreground is a prince amongst his advisers. The room is hung with fabrics and he stands beneath a canopy of estate. In the background he is shown at chapel, kneeling in a closet like a tent watching the celebration of the Mass. Both the fabric closet and the canopy of estate are furnishings that appear to have derived from beds, usually the most valuable single items of furniture in any great house.

structures were evidently derived from bed canopies, and one of the first documented spaces of this kind is known to have doubled as such: the Painted Chamber of Westminster Palace, a great chamber built by Henry III (d. 1272), incorporated a huge day-bed, the canopy of which enclosed a squint into a neighbouring chapel.[39] The earliest permanent closets survive from the late thirteenth century in such buildings as Edward I's castles of Conwy and Beaumaris. These are small chambers overlooking the altar, an arrangement that effectively separated the head of a household from his following (pl. 15).

After the Reformation the necessity for the ecclesiastical wing of a household on the medieval scale simply disappeared: without the Mass the communities maintained for its celebration and attendant ceremonial were redundant. And with their departure went some of the special architectural status of the chapel. This is not to say that chapels ceased to be important. New ones continued to be built and, depending on the piety and convictions of the family, could feature prominently in the daily running of the household.[40] Furthermore, there was great pressure on individuals of all ranks publicly to demonstrate religious conformity, a circumstance that may have changed the nature of devotional practice fundamentally. After the Reformation, however, the chapels of conforming Protestants rarely communicated directly with the withdrawn apartments, although some outstanding courtiers of Protestant persuasion did create chapels that in form and even iconography hearkened back to the pre-Reformation. Such is the case, for example, with the chapel of Hatfield built by Robert Cecil, first earl of Salisbury, between 1607 and 1611.[41]

While the collegiate and monastic foundations associated with great residences also lost their religious communities in the mid-sixteenth century, the churches of those that escaped suppression often survived in parish use. In such cases, the relationship with the adjacent residence usually remained close and was expressed physically by their continued use as family burial places. It is worth observing too that the medieval tradition of establishing religious foundations beside great houses and castles did not die in Protestant England. Elizabeth I's favourite, Robert Dudley, earl of Leicester, for example, founded two institutions in association with his principal castles, a proposed cathedral at Denbigh and Lord Leicester's Hospital at Warwick. He was also involved with his brother, Ambrose, earl of Warwick, in trying to estab-

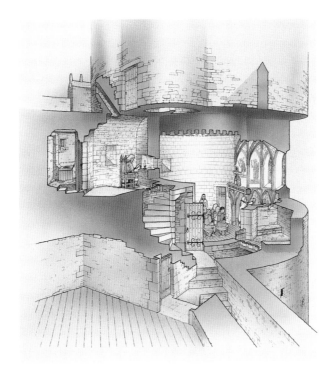

lish a preaching college at Warwick (see below, pp. 441–6). These were intended, just as their medieval predecessors had been, as institutional advertisements of status, charity and Christian nobility.

Latrines

Despite the difficulties that surround the identification of nearly all rooms in surviving medieval and early modern domestic buildings, there is one commonly encountered interior whose purpose is immediately apparent: the latrine. These are today usually termed garderobes, as if that word were in exclusive use as a technical term in the historic past. In fact, the historic vocabulary for describing latrines in account-books and literature is both colourful and diverse.

A selection might include gang or gong (from the Anglo-Saxon meaning 'a place to go'), or the Latin *cloacum*, *necessarium* and *reredorter*. To these might be added jake (a French form of john or jonny). Another widespread euphemism was 'the small or private place', which is still in use today in the Welsh *tŷ bach*.[42] The most popularly applied word, however, was privy. So, for example, when one of Chaucer's characters in *The Canterbury Tales* – an unfaithful bride – wished to dispose of her lover's letter in complete secret: 'She rent it all to clouts at last / And in the privy softly it cast' ('The Merchant's Tale', lines 1953–4).

The physical form of latrines to which these names might have applied varied enormously from holes in the ground to purpose-built structures. In castles the close proximity of large numbers of people in community demanded some formal provision for the disposal of human waste. Throughout the period covered by this book, a properly constructed latrine usually took the reassuringly obvious form of a bench with a hole in it. Seats might be of stone, but were more commonly wooden. A few examples survive, for example that in the fourteenth-century barbican at Thornton Abbey, Lincolnshire.

There survive from the sixteenth century (and there surely existed long before this) lids with handles that could be dropped across the holes in the seats of latrines to prevent smells coming back into the building. In addition, earth or sand might be provided to throw down into the latrine to dampen the smells. In 1532, for example, dry sand was provided for Henry VIII's 'jake' in his lodgings in the great tower at Dover.[43]

What physically distinguished different types of latrine was the means by which they discharged. Most commonly, the bench either projected from the castle walls in its own cubicle, throwing excrement and urine outside the building, or it opened into a chute or shaft that dropped within the thickness of the wall to a cesspit or drained outside. For convenience, latrines arranged in the latter fashion could be clustered together at one point within the building. The most typical arrangement was to have tiers of latrines at different levels set back to back around a single shaft. By stepping the latrine seats outwards at each consecutive floor in a range or tower, the fall from the uppermost to the ground could be uninterrupted.

The latrine towers or blocks created in this fashion are a feature of grand residential planning from the eleventh century to the sixteenth, and the provision within them could be impressive. William Rufus's great tower at Norwich begun in the 1090s, for example, accommodated what were probably eight two-seater latrines along one wall of its principal floor. At Beaumaris, begun in 1295 and initially garrisoned by about 130 men, the inner ward of the building alone was supplied with forty-five latrines stacked in groups within the depth of the wall. These arrangements should be viewed in the context of monastic planning, where the reredorters or latrine blocks adjacent to the dormitory were invariably capable of accommodating scores of people at once. One suggested explanation for this remarkable scale of provision in monasteries is that –

to prevent improprieties of behaviour – monks usually used latrines in community at set moments of the day.[44] It is not beyond the bounds of possibility that at least in the eleventh and twelfth centuries similar regulations were observed in secular households.

Generally, latrine blocks appear to have been intended for communal household use; at Hampton Court in the sixteenth century, for example, there was a 'common house of easement', two storeys high with ranks of latrines on each level.[45] Some great residences additionally possessed what are graphically described as 'pissing places'. One such possibly stood beneath the principal stairs of Edward III's upper ward palace at Windsor, built in the 1360s, where the hordes of courtiers and visitors could conveniently relieve themselves.[46] A pissing place modelled on that at Windsor may survive in the same position in the great tower of Warkworth, Northumberland. Some earlier buildings possess fittings that may also have served as urinals, for example, a dish and external spout in a small wall chamber within the great tower at Orford in Suffolk, begun in 1165.

Households could require encouragement to use such facilities. At the Tudor palace of Greenwich an account describes 'Plasterers whiting the walls of the inner court as also of making diverse red crosses upon the said walls that none should piss against them.'[47] Presumably, the intention was that no Christian would urinate on a cross.

The sanitary provision for members of the household at large is much easier to unpick than that for their masters and mistresses. It is quite possible that the important and powerful in certain periods used public latrines like everyone else; but they may equally have always expected greater privacy or comfort. In addition, women and their small circle of attendants may have demanded or been required to use separate facilities. In the eleventh and twelfth centuries there are occasional instances of isolated latrines that appear to be reserved for the use of particular people. At Portchester, for example, the first floor of the great tower begun around 1130 possesses one grouped set of latrines (now largely infilled with concrete to stabilise the building), which were presumably for the use of the household. Meanwhile, there is a single latrine in one corner of the principal withdrawing chamber. It incorporates a candle niche in one wall, indication that those who used it at night were to have the luxury of light. This may have been a royal privy. Later documentation is explicit about such arrangements and

further suggests that there were expectations of comfort. At Kenilworth in 1313–14, for example, 32 shillings were paid for enlarging and rebuilding the 'earl's latrine' (the earl of Lancaster). This presumably projected like a hut from one of the castle buildings because the account shows that it was covered in 1,500 shingles.[48]

Of course, even from an early date, the rich may not necessarily have used fixed latrines at all. One alternative would be a chair or stool that contained a removable pot that could be cleaned out. Not only might such an arrangement be much more comfortable than a fixed bench but, if properly managed, it would have avoided the whole problem of bad smells. The word 'close stool' to describe such items of furniture came into English use in the early fifteenth century.[49] But did Edward III have such furniture, or even the pleasure-loving William Rufus? Or English queens? If they did, we are missing important evidence for the appointment of the most luxurious chambers in medieval England.

That use of an isolated latrine was a mark of status is implied by the increasing provision of such facilities for senior members of the household by the late Middle Ages. So, for instance, the mid-fifteenth-century two-storey lodging range at Gainsborough in Lincolnshire possessed four chambers on each floor; every one was served by its own latrine and fire, the flues combined within a series of boldly battlemented brick stacks. This type of arrangement became common in the sixteenth century.

The maintenance of latrines was necessarily intensive to avoid smells. Where possible, rainwater might be washed through latrine chutes to clean them, as in the late fourteenth-century great tower at Warkworth and the great tower of Dover Castle, built by Henry II in the 1180s. In the latter case, water from the roofs was channelled down the main latrine stack on the north side of the building.

The alternative to an open drain was the cesspit, which in a large building needed to be dug out regularly. Examples of these survive from the early twelfth century within the great towers of Rochester (Kent) and Castle Hedingham (Essex), both of which are otherwise architecturally connected. At each place, the latrine pits opened *into* the basement of the building and their mouths must have been boarded closed between scourings. It is conceivable that this extraordinary arrangement was dictated by a reluctance – for defensive reasons – to create outward openings in the walls of the tower. Whatever the case, it must have required extremely efficient management if the whole building was not to stink. By the sixteenth century digging out cesspits or clearing the mouths of latrine chutes was a well-documented and specialist task undertaken by so-called gongscourers.

Latrine chutes might create weakness in the fortifications of a castle and in some cases they were protected to prevent a determined attacker from climbing up inside. In the walls of Conwy Castle, begun in 1282, for example, there is a surviving example of a masonry bell constructed over the base of a latrine chute to obstruct access to it.

Water Supply

A great medieval household required huge quantities of water for tasks such as cleaning, brewing and cooking.[50] Where possible, the bulk of that water was provided directly from a natural source such as a spring, a river or even a pool. Contrary to what might be supposed, this need not have lain within the embrace of the defences. At Chepstow, Monmouthshire, for example, water was winched up from a spring-fed cistern at the base of the castle cliff.[51]

If no water supply of this kind was available, the most common solution was to dig a well. Across the period covered by this book, large residences commonly possess several wells to supply water as directly as possible to the places where it was needed, such as the brewery and the kitchens. The breadth and depth of such wells varied greatly. Probably the biggest in England survives in the inner bailey at Beeston, Cheshire. It drops 330 feet (100 m) and is lined with cut masonry for the first 200 feet (61 m) of its depth. So great was the labour of digging this vertical tunnel that the well remained incomplete in 1304, more than seventy years after the castle was begun: according to a surviving account of that year, water had to be carried to the castle from a furlong away by two women.[52]

A shallow well could easily be worked by hand using a rope and a bucket. In a deep well, however, the sheer weight of the rope or chain and the drawing vessel meant that it had to be operated by some kind of mechanism. This could include a counterbalance or a system of pulleys to ease the labour of lifting the water. Usually this was housed in a functional shed that protected the well-head from contamination and dirt. On occasion, however, a well mechanism might be housed more impressively. At Alnwick in Northumberland, for example, the double pulley wheels for the four-teenth-century well in the inner bailey are handsomely framed in an arch beside the gateway.

Medieval designers were also fully alive to the possibilities of using rainwater to supply their needs. In the late twelfth-century great tower at Conisbrough, Yorkshire, for example, rainwater could be stored for use in two cisterns in the turrets at roof level. And when the pools near the royal castle of Queenborough, Kent, were polluted by salt in 1375, a cooper called Robert Man was paid to mend the water casks that collected 'rain water coming down through lead pipes within the circle [court] of the castle'.[53]

The distribution of water within castles is a subject in its own right. As the work of the two women at Beeston illustrates, this might be done over long distances by hand. Water from the earliest castle wells was probably distributed in exactly this way, as from the well in the basement of the eleventh-century White Tower in London. By the early twelfth century, however, it was quite common – in great towers at least – for water to be accessible at one or more levels of the building. Such is the case in the colossal great tower at Rochester of the 1120s. Here the well shaft was carried up through the full height of the building and was made accessible at each level through a cupboard-like opening closed with wooden doors.

In the same period, monastic buildings began to incorporate much more sophisticated arrangements for the supply of water. The most celebrated example is that documented in an exquisite plan of *circa* 1165 at Christ Church Priory, Canterbury.[54] This made use of wells and rainwater, but its principal source of water was a spring 1,000 yards (just over 900 m) away with a 40-foot (12 m) drop to the buildings. It was distributed via pools and cisterns and pipes throughout the entire monastery with a minute attention to detail. There was even an outlet beside the window where refectory plates 'were tossed out for washing'.

That such sophisticated water systems were adopted in contemporary castle buildings is made clear from the great tower at Dover, Kent, begun in 1181. Its water supply was fed by an immense well nearly 250 feet (76 m) deep and lined in cut stone for nearly two-thirds of its depth. There still survive in the fabric of the tower sockets for a long-lost mechanism to operate this. The water raised was poured into a water tank at the head of the well and distributed throughout the building through a network of pipes that must have been laid in the fabric as it was being constructed. At their outlets these pipes – which vary in gauge from 3.5 inches to an inch (9 to 2.5 cm) – must have been closed by taps to prevent the system draining.

There can be no doubt that the Dover water system was as carefully planned as that at Canterbury, but without documentary evidence it is impossible to understand fully its function. In a damaged condition, the extent of the piping is also frustratingly difficult to reconstruct.[55] To date, only two outlets from it have been properly identified and there is no clear evidence as to how the water was being used, whether for washing or cooking. The location of the well room on the third floor of the building – rather than at roof level – is also slightly mysterious because it means that the principal apartments could not have benefitted from this water supply. Perhaps to make up for this deficiency, the water system in the great tower also made use of rainwater. That from one side of the roof was channelled off to fill a lead-lined tank. It is not clear what purpose the water in this tank served or whether it was connected to the piped water system. The remaining rainwater appears to have gushed down the latrine turret on one side of the building, presumably to cleanse it.

Even if we cannot fully understand their purpose, the arrangements at Dover (which are incidentally paralleled in the great tower at Newcastle begun in 1168), underline the potential sophistication of water supply in luxuriously appointed residential buildings by the late twelfth century. Nor – if we trust the documentary and physical evidence (much of which remains poorly studied) – did expectations diminish. If anything they grew. From the thirteenth century onwards there are numerous references to bathrooms in both palaces and castles, though no example of one has survived. The fabric of buildings also occasionally incorporates basins for washing hands. A particularly fine series from the late thirteenth century can be seen in the lobbies to all the main lodging chambers and the side entrance at Goodrich, Herefordshire (see pl. 152).

In kitchens, meanwhile, great ingenuity was displayed in storing and managing water. This might be raised from wells and channelled into tanks for use, as in the thirteenth-century kitchen at Caernarfon,[56] or supplied from a distance by timber pipes in a continuous stream, as in the 1440s kitchen of Herstmonceux, Sussex.[57] In the public parts of a house – including gardens – water also became an object of display, so much so that by the sixteenth century it was common to be confronted in the inner court of a great house with a conduit or fountain fed by spring water.[58] These structures were commonly display pieces, ornamented with architectural detail and sculpture. A fine example survives at Little Leighs Priory in Essex, probably created around 1550 by Richard, Baron Rich. To underline his baronial status it is decked like a castle with battlements. Rather more remarkable is the depiction of the fountain in the forecourt of Henry VIII's palace at the Field of Cloth of Gold (see pl. 322). In symbol of Christian majesty this flowed with wine on which – to judge from the painting – the public drank itself to fisticuffs, vomiting and oblivion.

Heat and Light

Probably the most ancient fireplace arrangement in grand domestic English architecture – and one certainly long pre-dating the Norman Conquest in 1066 – is the open hearth. To accommodate a fireplace in the centre of a room requires only a suitable platform on which the fuel may burn and some means of ventilation. Domestic fuel throughout the Middle Ages – it should be explained – was almost always wood. Coal with its toxic fumes appears to have been used only for industrial processes and then only where it was readily available either through mining or naturally cast ashore by the erosion of exposed seams beneath the seabed. It was, however, widely adopted for domestic use in the seventeenth century, and this brought about a metamorphosis in the form of fireplaces and fire grates that is beyond the scope of this study.

It was the system of ventilation for open fires that appears first to have enjoyed architectural embellishment, though the process by which this developed must effectively be extrapolated backwards from much later surviving evidence. There survive from relatively modest houses of the thirteenth century, for example, glazed tiles made for the ridge of a roof with vents to allow smoke to escape.[59] This rudimentary system of ventilation is likely to have been used in grand buildings of the eleventh century, though no explicit evidence survives to prove the point. In large rooms such systems of ventilation could be enlarged to create a so-called louvre (from the French *l'ouvert* meaning 'the opening'), a roofed structure set on the apex of the roof with slats to allow the passage of air and smoke.

A great house or castle from the thirteenth century onwards typically possessed two externally prominent louvres. One stood over the kitchen, where the heat from numerous fires and the smells of cooking needed to be dissipated. Because great kitchens were quite commonly centrally designed structures – the kitchen of Durham Priory, for example, was erected between 1367 and 1374 on an octagonal plan, and that built a century later at Gainsborough, Lincolnshire, was set out on a square – the louvre lent them a very distinctive outline. Consequently these buildings can be easily recognised in historic views of great houses (see pls 296 and 299).

The second louvre of a house always stood above the great hall, where the open fire persisted as a matter of convention far beyond the close of the Middle Ages. Here it gave further visual prominence to the tallest and largest building within any residence. The earliest great hall louvre to survive in Britain – albeit in adapted form – is probably that in the Abbot's Hall at Westminster, built in the 1370s. This is a simple structure: a rectangular section of the roof raised up by a foot or so to allow the escape of smoke. Louvres were not necessarily workaday structures, however. Almost contemporary with this early survival was a spectacular pair of louvres in the form of pinnacles over Westminster Hall. These are known from a sixteenth-century view of the palace by the artist Wyngaerde and one survives today in nineteenth-century reproduction. Such elaborate louvres remained very popular over halls in the fifteenth and sixteenth centuries.

Open fires were practicable only in large spaces. It is possible, therefore, that in more intimate rooms braziers might have provided a more manageable alternative to them. If these were fuelled by charcoal, they could have been both efficient and relatively free from smoke. Because braziers are portable objects that required no architectural fixture there can be no proof of this fact. There do exist, however, luxuriously appointed rooms from the twelfth century without fireplaces. One such, for example, is the great tower at Dover, which possesses no trace of an original fireplace. In the circumstance, it seems reasonable to suggest that this building was warmed by braziers or some portable source of heat.

The alternative to the open fire, which existed throughout the period covered by this book, was the fireplace. Some of the earliest English fireplaces are found in the White Tower at London, under construction by 1081. In their original form (they have been mutilated over time) these would have appeared strange to modern eyes, being projected almost entirely into the volume of the room that they served. That is to say the hoods of the fireplaces swelled out from the wall surface and their backs sloped steeply inwards towards the ground, so that the fire itself would have stood at the angle of the floor space. To extract the smoke there is a small, domed space in the thickness of the wall above the fire. This vented to the exterior laterally through several small holes.

By the early twelfth century a new kind of fireplace arrangement was coming into fashion. This employed a flue rising vertically through the wall to carry off smoke through a chimney set on the parapet. The earliest evidence for chimneys is provided by such survivals as the chimney fragments excavated from Old Sarum Castle, Wiltshire, built before 1139. Strange as it may seem to say, the history of the chimney in the English architectural tradition is very remarkable and will be traced in some detail through the pages of this book. Chimneys not only served to enliven the outlines of castles, but also advertised to the world at large the warmth and domestic comfort of the building they served.

As a result, chimneys were sometimes treated as miniature works of architecture in their own right. They might also be decorated in abstract ornament or carry devices that underlined the function of the building they stood on. The thirteenth-century royal apartments at Conwy, for example, had chimneys surmounted by crowns. And there survives at St Briavels, Gloucestershire, a chimney with a hunting horn, presumably a reference to the role of the castle as the estate centre of a large surrounding royal chase.

Over the later medieval period the form of the fireplace in grand English houses gradually changed. Projecting hoods became much less common during the fourteenth century and disappeared almost entirely by the fifteenth. In their stead, fireplaces commonly became recessed internally within the depth of the wall – essentially the familiar modern arrangement. What remained consistent, however, was the position of fireplaces in grand English domestic interiors. There are many exceptions to the rule, but from the eleventh century onwards it was normal for fireplaces to be positioned to the side of a chamber on one of its long walls. Moreover, they were often placed off-centre so as to privilege the high end of the interior with their heat. This contrasts, for example, with the mainstream French practice of placing the fireplace at the end of a room, behind the dais.

Fireplaces were obvious objects for ornament. The first decorated examples are cut with abstract patterns and date from the early twelfth century, as in the great tower of Castle Hedingham of the 1140s (see pl. 72). By the mid-thirteenth century there is record of over-mantels being decorated with figurative schemes. For example, in January 1240 the keeper of the king's works at Westminster was ordered to build a chimney in the queen's chamber and decorate it with 'a figure of Winter, which as well by its sad countenance as by other miserable distortions of the body may be deservedly likened to winter itself'.[60]

The taste for making the fireplace and its over-mantel a prominent and richly decorated furnishing within any well-appointed English domestic interior persisted into the seventeenth century. More often than not in the late Middle Ages, overmantels dis-played heraldry. Their subject matter, however, was evidently very varied. So too were the materials used in their creation. Some overmantels probably incor-porated wall paintings or specially made tapestries. In the great hall of Kenilworth, Warwickshire, of the 1370s, for example, there are large blank panels over the surviving fireplaces that could have framed hang-ings. From the mid-sixteenth century moulded plaster also became a popular material for fireplace overman-tels. A particularly fine and early example of around 1555 survives at Broughton in Oxfordshire, its figural decoration probably modelled by a craftsman trained in the French royal works at Fontainebleau. The vast majority of English overmantels, however, were of stone or timber.

It is a noteworthy curiosity that the types of deco-rative overmantel created for fireplaces in English buildings were almost never applied to the frames of internal doorways. This is again in contrast to French taste, where by the fifteenth century this idea was a commonplace. It is hard to explain the English disin-terest in this type of decoration. One possibility is that tapestries and other wall hangings were usually hung in grand interiors so as to obscure doorways.

One last means of heating rooms deserves very brief mention. From the evidence of excavated fragments it is clear that by the sixteenth century the Continental taste for large ceramic stoves had spread to England. Stoves, however, never appear to have enjoyed very wide popularity in great residences. Only one notable example is known in the context of a castle. This was an imported sixteenth-century German stove at Henry VIII's coastal fortification at Camber, Sussex.[61]

It is relatively rare for grand domestic interiors in the period covered by this book to possess architectural fittings for lamps, candles or lights. Most sources of artificial light would have been portable or suspended in a chandelier of wood, iron or brass. Such objects have generally been swept away over time and need not concern us here. By far the most common architectural light fittings are small wall niches. These are usually found in dark and confined spaces such as corridors or latrines. Within smaller domestic chambers lamps were sometimes mounted on projecting brackets to either side of the fireplace. This arrangement is quite common in projecting fireplaces of the late thirteenth century and can be found, for example, in the tower chambers of several of Edward I's Welsh castles includ-ing Beaumaris and Harlech.

Larger fixings for lamps are little more sophisticated and most stand in public rooms. The fourteenth-century great hall at Bolton, Yorkshire, for example, has broad ledges set high in the side walls. These are presumably supports for multiple lights. There are also occasional instances of external light stands, such as the pair incorporated to either side of the arch hood of the 1390s porch door at Portchester. Presumably they were intended to light guests to the threshold of this royal castle hall.

ARCHITECTURAL PLANNING

Grand medieval residences of all kinds were most typ-ically arranged with their principal elements disposed around one or more courtyards. This was a very flex-ible method of planning and one that developed nat-urally from the Anglo-Saxon tradition of building residences with numerous physically discrete build-ings. From 1350 onwards (and occasionally before) there was a tendency to regularise such courtyards for grand effect, and in the mid-sixteenth century an active interest in imposing symmetry upon them. One constant feature of such designs throughout all these changes, however, was that the principal withdrawing chambers of the residence were at first-floor level. In practical terms, this meant that there needed to be at least one substantial flight of stairs within any residence; and there developed two conventional ways of incorporating such a stair within a courtyard plan.

One possibility was to place the stair externally at the entrance to the hall, which was itself raised up onto first-floor level (pl. 16). The origin of this arrangement is very hard to pinpoint for lack of evidence. A first-

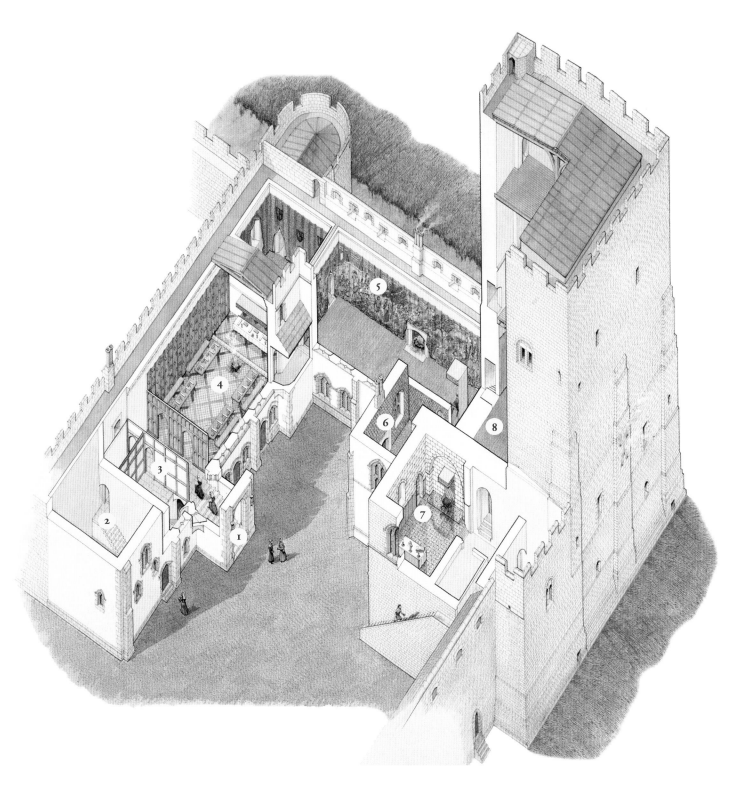

16 A cut-away reconstruction drawing by Stephen Conlin of the inner bailey of Portchester, Hampshire, as rebuilt by Richard II between 1396 and 1399. All the principal apartments of the residence, including the hall, were here arranged at first-floor level around a courtyard. The main stair was incorporated within the hall porch and lit by small external light brackets (1). Running clockwise around the courtyard are visible the kitchen (2), the buttery and pantry (3), the hall with its central hearth (4), the great chamber (5), the so-called Checker Chamber (6) and the chapel (7) with an arch in one wall perhaps intended to frame the king's seat. To complement these apartments the twelfth-century great tower (8) was reordered internally. It probably contained the king's bedchamber.

floor hall is shown as the setting for a feast in the eleventh-century Bayeux Tapestry, and the earliest surviving secular example of the form is to be found at Scolland's Hall in Richmond Castle, Yorkshire, probably completed by 1089. One possible source for the idea was refectory design in monastic planning, though the early evidence for this is scant in England. Certainly, on the basis of later rebuildings, the monasteries at Canterbury and Gloucester can both be presumed to have possessed first-floor refectories in the eleventh century and fragments of such arrangements survive at both Durham (pre-1080) and Norwich (planned in the 1090s).[62] Whatever its origins, the form of the first-floor hall with an external stair continued to be popular throughout the Middle Ages and was particularly favoured in major residences and palaces, such as the mid-sixteenth-century Hampton Court in Middlesex.

Alternatively and more commonly, if the hall was at ground level, the stair to the withdrawing apartments was usually placed beyond the dais door at the entrance to the great chamber, the outermost withdrawing room (pl. 17). Until the thirteenth century, such stairs could be external and were usually termed oriels (confusingly, the same word later came to be applied to windows). Subsequently, they became internalised and from the mid-fifteenth century began to develop into elaborate display pieces. The possibilities such stairs presented for ornament ensured the ultimate triumph of this arrangement. From around 1500, following such prestigious models as Henry VII's Richmond Palace, the great stair, so-called, became a fixture in grand domestic design (pl. 18).

Placing the hall at a different level from the withdrawing apartments created the potential space for two additional withdrawing rooms immediately accessible from it: one at the foot of the great stair beneath the great chamber and another at the low end of the hall on the first floor above the buttery and pantry. The latter might be accessed up a stair directly from the hall or by a stair within the porch. Set in close proximity to the kitchen fires, chambers over the services – or adjacent to them[63] – may sometimes have been specifically intended for winter use. From around 1400 chambers in both positions often came to be called parlours. The name comes from the chamber in a monastery reserved for conversation with visitors and hints at the relative informality of these spaces in comparison with the great chamber. It is interesting to note that over the same period monasteries were themselves creating more private chambers in similar fashion. At Durham Priory in the sixteenth century, for example, except on feast-days the monks ate their meals in a room called The Loft, which was accessible up a stair at the services end of their refectory.[64] Grand living in the secular and religious spheres was never far removed.

This arrangement of a massive ground-floor hall with first-floor chambers to either end remained sufficiently familiar even in the late sixteenth century to be described by Sir Philip Sidney as the setting for one episode in his verse romance *The Countess of Pembroke's Arcadia* (London, 1593). One of the numerous castles described in the narrative possessed a great hall:

> . . . so stately made that the bottome of it being euen with the grounde, the roofe reached as hie as any part of the castle, at either ende it had conuenient lodgeings. In the one end was (one storie from the ground) *Philocleas* abode, in the other of euen height, *Pamelas*, and *Zelmanes* in a chamber aboue her . . .
>
> [Book 3, Chapter 21]

Any Englishman or woman from at least the twelfth century to the seventeenth would have recognised this conventional disposition of chambers in a grand domestic building.

In the context of castles there developed an alternative to – or at least a distinctive variation upon – courtyard planning: rather than scatter the elements of a residence it was possible to stack them up within a tower. The appeal of this arrangement is obvious: a tower is an intrinsically impressive structure, advertising by its height and ornament the power of the owner. At their most ambitious, tower residences could incorporate complete domestic plans with storage spaces, kitchens, services, a chapel, a great hall and withdrawing apartments (pl. 19). Towers with complete domestic plans are relatively rare, but they may be found across the entire period covered by this book from Norwich Castle (begun around 1095) to the Little Castle at Bolsover (begun in 1612). Importantly – and surprisingly – such structures nearly always coexisted with a courtyard residence that duplicated all their interiors. Such double provision can be explained with confidence only from the fifteenth century, where the courtyard and tower residences respectively answered the different domestic needs of visits by the great and riding households.

17 A reconstruction drawing by Chris Jones-Jenkins of the great hall range at Warkworth, Northumberland, as remodelled around 1480 by Henry Percy, fourth earl of Northumberland (d. 1489). The main entrance to the hall was through a tower porch (1), which was decorated with an impressive display of family heraldry. The hall was internally divided by an arcade (2), and there was a building with service and lodging chambers at its low end (3). There were two stairs at the opposite end of the hall giving access to the great chamber. The principal of these (4) was enclosed within a second tower porch (5). This porch also had an upper chamber at the level of the hall roof, possibly a banqueting chamber (6). The household chapel (7) was overlooked by a large balcony closet that opened off the great chamber (8).

Much more commonly, however, towers were used in castles to complement the arrangements of a courtyard plan. So, for example, it was popular for the dominating tower of a castle complex to house the principal withdrawing chambers of the residence. In this way, the most important interiors in the building were reared up vertically and given visual prominence. This could be done by building one single tower of outstanding size. Such, for example, is the case with the great tower at Tattershall, Lincolnshire, built in the 1440s, which rose up like a skyscraper above the other castle buildings. By contrast, the innermost withdrawing chambers in the regularly planned fourteenth-century castle at Maxstoke, Warwickshire, were housed in a tower just slightly larger and more richly detailed than its neighbours. As we shall see, ideas of courtyard and tower planning were open to endless and inventive variation in the tradition of English castle architecture.

WEAPONS AND THE TRAPPINGS OF FORTIFICATION

Within the narrative of this book are accounts of individual campaigns and sieges that illustrate the changing role of castles in English conflicts from the eleventh century to the seventeenth. Siege warfare, of course, is a large subject in its own right, and it may seem presumptuous here to condense into a few pages something that has been the dedicated theme of whole books.[65] Nevertheless, to contextualise the discussion of the individual episodes treated below, it seems appropriate to offer a very brief introductory overview of the principal weapons used in castle warfare and the way they developed over time. Also, to explain to the reader in general terms the ways in which castle fortifications operated.

Fortifications of all kinds fundamentally serve to separate with advantage those who man them from those who attack them. In castle architecture, that separation was achieved by a combination of three forms: the wall, the tower and the ditch. In whatever material they were realised, the height and breadth of these structures determined the strength of a fortification. Scarcely less fundamental to the repertoire of castle architecture was the battlement or crenellation, a tooth of stone projecting from the parapet of a wall or tower that offered protection from missiles to those who

18 The Great Stair at Knole, Kent, built by Thomas, first earl of Dorset, between 1605 and 1608. It connects the dais of the great hall at ground level with the great chamber and other withdrawing apartments on the first floor of the building. As the main ceremonial thoroughfare of the house, the stair was intended to amaze visitors with its splendid decoration and *trompe l'œil* effects. It is constructed entirely of timber but is painted to look like marble. Apart from the heraldry, nearly all the decoration – which includes depictions of the *Ages of Man* and the *Five Senses* – is copied from Dutch prints.

19   A cut-away reconstruction by Chris Jones-Jenkins of the great tower of Warkworth, Northumberland, begun around 1380. All the chambers necessary for grand domestic living are incorporated within this remarkable design. On the principal floor are shown: (1) the porch, (2) the hall, (3) screen and screens passage, (4) buttery, (5) pantry, (6) kitchen and (7) pastry kitchen. There were also withdrawing chambers on the far side of the tower, and service and storage chambers in the basement. A central light well (8) brought light to the inner walls of the principal chambers and rainwater collected in it was used to flush through the latrine chutes in the tower. The domestic arrangements in this tower duplicated those provided in the bailey below (see pl. 17), and were probably for use by the earl's inner or riding household. The central turret (9) is a watchtower and commands wide views over land and sea.

defended it. To all intents and purposes, English medieval masons inherited the essential forms of fortification from Roman example, though they are all in fact much more ancient still.

The separation effected by such fortifications dictated that weapons used in castle warfare had to be thrown or fired. Over the six centuries covered by this study, the technology of such weapons changed immensely as the mechanical weapons of the Middle Ages – the sling, bow, crossbow and catapult – gave way to muskets and cannon charged with gunpowder. In the same period, these changes were to transform the theory of fortification. That said, two important points need to be made. The first is that the gunpowder revolution was very protracted, extending in England over two centuries from roughly 1300 to the 1540s. Only from this latter date did the use of artillery in warfare begin to reform the fundamental planning principles of fortification in England.

Second, that the huge cost of the relevant military expertise and hardware has always prevented the full exploitation of the technology available. This means that even outdated fortifications that might technically have been obsolete in practical terms rarely were so. During the 1630s and 1640s, for example, medieval castles that might have been hopelessly vulnerable to a proper seventeenth-century siege train could in fact offer prolonged resistance to forces without the artillery or resources to press home an attack. As we shall see, too, on occasion in the Civil War the sheer scale of some medieval fortifications, such as the great tower of Raglan, Monmouthshire, proved impervious to weapons of a power unimaginable when the building was first constructed nearly 200 years previously.

This latter point leads on to another important general observation. Hard-pressed and set-piece sieges in English history have been very unusual events. Apart from anything else, they required enormous resources to wage and a degree of determination that is only naturally the product of a complete political breakdown between the sides involved. Indeed, they have consistently been almost the exclusive preserve of what might reasonably be described as civil wars and conflicts with England's neighbours, Scotland and Wales. Even in these cases, castles much more often surrendered in response to wider circumstances than fell through force of arms. One consistently common tactic for besiegers who could afford the time was to blockade a castle. Then they could wait at relatively little personal risk for the food to run out, for an opportunity provided by treachery, or – more usually – for wider political events to isolate the castle garrison and encourage their surrender. Nevertheless, precisely because great sieges were inherently unlikely, when they did occur the results were always remarkable.

The lightest of the weapons that could be used in siege warfare was the bow (and from the late thirteenth century its refined counterpart, the longbow). This could fire rapidly and – depending on its size and the skill of the archer – was a powerful weapon. The longbow, for example, was highly effective at about 200 yards (180 m), though the arrows could fly much further.[66] As a result, it remained an important weapon in English warfare on sea and land well into the sixteenth century. In castle warfare from the mid-twelfth century onwards, however, the bow had an important rival: the crossbow. This was a hand-held weapon that was drawn taut for loading, sometimes with a mechanism, and operated with a trigger. It fired a short missile termed a bolt with great accuracy. The range of these weapons must have varied, but it probably equalled or exceeded that of a longbow.

It remains uncertain at what date the crossbow was introduced to England, but the weapon may have been used at the battle of Hastings in 1066. Certainly, the technology to make it was available then, though the celebrated ban on the use of the weapon issued by the Second Lateran Council in 1139, except against infidels, may briefly have discouraged its use. Nevertheless, by the late twelfth century the crossbow had clearly emerged as the weapon of choice for mercenaries and the garrisons of castle. It was lethal, claiming huge numbers of prominent casualties. Richard I, for example, was fatally wounded in the shoulder by a crossbow bolt while inspecting the fortifications of the small castle of Châlus-Chabrol (Haute-Vienne) prior to an intended assault on 26 March 1199. Even in 1469, at the siege of Caister, Norfolk, it was still claiming English victims in the context of siege warfare.[67]

Given the range of crossbows, such casualties make strikingly apparent how close the opposing sides in a siege had to be in order to engage with each other. The assailants would have needed to stand well within 200 yards of the walls to have much hope of picking off a defender. And in the course of an attack, they must have been much closer. A hard-pressed siege presumably had something of the quality of trench war: a conflict of attrition fought at close quarters with cold brutality.

For the purposes of a castle garrison, the crossbow was valuable both because it could be fired in a relatively constrained space and because its trigger mechanism allowed it to be used spontaneously to pick off a target that was only momentarily visible. Its use from within the defences of a castle also softened the chief disadvantage of the crossbow, which was that it took longer to load than its hand-drawn rivals. By the thirteenth century crossbows were also being scaled up in size and mounted on the battlements to create a very powerful medium-range weapon termed a springald. Four such weapons, for example, were mounted on the angle turrets of the great tower of Chepstow in 1298–9 (see pl. 31).[68]

The heavy artillery of the high Middle Ages were stone-throwing machines, for which medieval chroniclers had many generic names including *petraria* and *ballista*. With their dismountable timber frames, these were portable machines of war and by the thirteenth century they were being managed and maintained by a highly paid group of senior carpenters (and sometimes masons) entitled *ingeniatores* or engineers.[69] The simplest form of catapult, almost certainly known and used in England by the late eleventh century, is today generally termed a perrier or *perrière*. This comprised a pivoted throwing arm with a sling and a stone at one end and a team of men pulling on ropes at the other to fire it. Perriers must have been able to fire large numbers of missiles in quick succession, but the human brawn that powered them must also have made them erratic and inaccurate to use.

Much more formidable was the trebuchet, which was possibly first introduced to England during the invasion of Prince Louis of France in 1216.[70] It probably became thereafter the most common stone-throwing machine by simple virtue of its accuracy: the throwing arm of the trebuchet was counterbalanced with a heavy weight that exerted an even force when the machine was fired. If the missiles placed within it were of the same weight, therefore, they would fall in exactly the same spot time and again. It is likely that many of the greatest catapults of the thirteenth and fourteenth centuries were trebuchets (see pl. 185), but chroniclers and medieval accountants rarely give information about the technical form of these machines. Rather, as in the case of Edward I's siege train at Stirling in 1304 with the king's coveted 'war-wolf', they list their names and enthuse about their size.[71]

Medieval sources also use the word 'mangonel' to describe catapults. In modern writing this word is often applied as a technical term to describe a third type of catapult in which the one end of the firing arm was fixed in a bundle of twisted ropes. The tension of pulling the arm into a loading position created sufficient energy in the ropes to fire a stone. Mechanisms of this kind were undoubtedly used by the Romans. Whether they were ever used in English medieval warfare or, indeed, whether chroniclers were so obliging as to use terms with technical exactitude is debatable. I know of no English manuscript illustration of a mangonel (as the term is presently applied). Whatever the case, it is from the central part of this word that the modern word 'gun' comes.

Just how destructive were these machines? The question is in fact very hard to answer. No fragment of a stone-throwing machine has ever been convincingly identified in England and none survives abroad. The best evidence we have for their form are numerous stylised illustrations in manuscripts, some technical descriptions in medieval treatises and a tantalising plan of a trebuchet in the enigmatic early thirteenth-century sketchbook by the Frenchman Villard de Honnecourt.[72] This last drawing was not only intended to be viewed in conjunction with a counterpart elevation drawing (which is now lost), but is also very hard to interpret in most points of detail. This has not prevented this material from being used collectively to serve as the basis for several modern reconstructions of siege machines in the last twenty years, notably at Caerphilly (in 1991–2), Dover (1997–8) and Chinon.

The most crucial piece of missing information for such reconstructions is information about the changing size of such catapults. We do know that medieval carpenters had access to trees of a much greater scale than exist today, but it is only educated guesswork as to exactly how big such engines could be at their largest and – therefore – how powerful they were. What do survive, however, are catapult stones: a good collection, probably dating from the fourteenth century, remains, for example, at Pevensey in Sussex. These are substantial objects, some more than 20 inches (50 cms) in diameter. Cumulatively, the fall of such missiles could presumably have damaged even heavy masonry.

Catapults, it must be emphasised, were used as much by the garrisons of castles as by those that attacked them. At Kenilworth in 1266, for example, those operated by the garrison proved particularly effective. Amongst other things they destroyed a timber tower for 200 crossbowmen erected to threaten the walls.[73] This raises quite interesting questions about the manner in which engines were mounted in castles. In some cases special platforms were evidently erected for them. A good example is the rectangular 'engine tower' or *gynnetour* mentioned in the outer bailey at Criccieth, Caernarfonshire, in 1343.[74] Another such platform of around 1325 has been tentatively identified at Pevensey to the south of the great tower (see pl. 94). Elsewhere, they perhaps operated blind from behind the shelter of the curtain wall.

For a besieging force the practical problems of operating stone-throwing machines must have been acute: the machines can have had little greater range than the crossbows used by the defenders. As a result, it must have been necessary to bring them very close to the castle walls and create platforms with screening fortifications to protect the catapult teams. Earthwork platforms for supporting catapults have been identified at only one English site, at Berkhamsted, Hertfordshire, from the siege of 1216.[75] The case for the identification seems tendentious in the extreme if for no other reason than it presumes that the siege works were left essentially undisturbed beside an occupied castle for several centuries.

While both sides in a medieval siege generally employed the same weapons and technology (in as far as their resources allowed), the attackers also needed to close the distance created by the fortifications. One means of doing this was by collapsing the defences, either by demolishing them with missiles or undermining their foundations. The latter was usually achieved under the cover of a strong awning, often termed a 'sow' or a 'cat', as in the hard-fought siege at Bedford in 1224.[76] Alternatively, or in combination with such an approach, it was possible to try and overtop the fortifications with a tower and dominate the castle defences, as was attempted at Dover in 1216.[77] There are also occasional references to battering rams, as again at Stirling in 1304.

For the besieged, it was important to maximise the strength of the fortifications and increase the firepower that could be focused on any approach to the defences. To this end, the battlements of walls and towers could be protected by wooden shutters or enclosed by galleries, which are variously termed hourdes or brattices (see pl. 100).[78] From the late thirteenth century it also became the practice to project the battlements out beyond the face of the wall on stone brackets. By opening out the floor space between the brackets as chutes it was possible to drop missiles to the foot of the wall from behind the protection of the battlements. The arrangement was termed a machicolis (see

pl. 162). A similarly conceived feature that begins to appear from slightly earlier in the century is the murder hole, an opening in the vault of a gate passage through which defenders could drop missiles on assailants (see pl. 213).

Another important defensive feature that duplicated the tiers of defence from a wall was the arrow slit or loop. These were openings through which an archer or crossbowman could fire his weapon. Arrow loops become common in English castle architecture only from the late twelfth century. In defensive terms the form of a loop was conditioned by three considerations. Externally, it had to be as narrow as possible to afford the maximum of protection from missiles being fired at the walls. At the same time, loops had to offer a sufficiently good outward view for a defender to be able to mark a target properly. Finally, to be truly effective, the inner splay or embrasure of the loop needed to be formed so as to allow an archer or crossbowman to take a firing position with his weapon. It is this later detail – invisible to the onlooker – that distinguishes in technical terms between a narrow window and a proper loop.

At their simplest and prior to *circa* 1200 arrow loops commonly take the form of a vertical slit with an inner splay cut at a continuous angle through the whole depth of the wall. That splay could either be arched, as in the towers added to the motte at Lewes, Sussex, after 1202, or covered in a lintel of horizontally laid stones, as in King John's North Gate at Dover, complete by 1216.[79] Occasionally, early loops were grouped under a single arch, such as those paired together in the walls of around the 1190s at Framlingham, Suffolk. Alternatively, there is a unique twelfth-century instance of a series of individual loops served by multiple splays in the Avranches Tower at Dover of *circa* 1190. The Avranches Tower is particularly interesting because the loops and splays are so short that they can have been used only by crossbowmen. Archers would have required much taller splays and more space to draw and fire their bows.[80]

Over the course of the thirteenth century loops became the object of variation and experiment. Where a vertical slit offered too narrow an outlook, it could be intersected by a second horizontal slit to create a so-called cross-loop. Some early examples appear in Lunn's Tower at Kenilworth of around 1210 (see pl. 105). This arrangement greatly improved lateral vision. On very rare occasions, as in the fortifications of the 1250s at White, Monmouthshire, the two arms of the horizontal slit are not aligned. The purpose of this odd asymmetry is not clear, although it has been suggested that it made the loop more difficult for an attacker to shoot through. Certainly, a practical test of the arrow loops at the castle in 1980 suggested that firing into them from outside the walls was much less difficult than might be expected; roughly one in three arrows might pass through the loop at 25 yards (23 m) range.[81] Another common modification to a loop or a cross-loop was to splay one or more of its terminations to increase the view of it. These splays might be externally expressed as roundels or half-diamonds.

Arrow loops were often positioned with evident care. They might be clustered at vulnerable points (see pls 115–16) or staggered on different levels to maximise the field of fire (see pl. 133). In other cases they are ingeniously integrated into the architecture of the building as a whole, as in the gatehouse of Warkworth, Northumberland (see pl. 108). At the same time, there was a clear appreciation of the theatrical possibilities of these loops. At Caernarfon, for example, the walls of the 1280s incorporate a tier of dummy arrow loops at basement level to add to the threatening appearance of the defences (see pl. 163).

In considering the development of castle fortifications it is worthwhile making reference to one idea that haunts the historiography of the castle. Great claims have been made for the importance of The Crusades in advancing the science of fortification in Europe; also, by extension, for the influence of late antique and Byzantine architecture on Crusader castles.[82] The case for the influence of late antique and Byzantine fortifications is greatly complicated by the loss of so many buildings and the invocation in their place of north African exemplars, which, in the words of one modern authority, were 'constructed half a millennium before and a thousand miles away and could not possibly have been known to any of the Crusader castle builders'.[83] Also, by the fact that by the twelfth century the Byzantine Empire was itself no longer in command of the resources to build works on the scale of the walls of Constantinople.

There are similarly knotty problems to confront in connecting Crusader and English castle architecture. Again, the loss of buildings has made it hard to establish exactly what different generations of crusaders saw. Added to this, while it seems easy to recognise architectural ideas from the West in Crusader buildings, the scale of those buildings is infinitely greater and their detailing is in almost complete contrast to that of their contemporary English counterparts. The best evidence for the influence of Crusader architecture remains linguistic: the derivation of the word 'barbican', an outer fortification to a gate, from Arabic. Nevertheless, it seems to me that a detailed case for the technical exchange of ideas remains to be convincingly proved.

The gradual process by which all the mechanical weapons of the Middle Ages – the bow, crossbow and catapult – were superseded by gunpowder successors remains poorly understood for lack of detailed information. Guns begin to be noted in campaigns fought by English armies from the early fourteenth century, as at the siege of Berwick in 1333. By the late fourteenth century they were also being used sufficiently widely for castle fortifications to accommodate them. Gun loops seem to have taken one of three forms. For small hand-held guns there appear from the 1360s onwards loops with outward openings in the form of an inverted keyhole.[84] The circular opening was a space for the muzzle of the weapon and the slit above enabled the gun to be aimed. One building of the 1380s that preserves an impressive collection of such loops, all carefully positioned to afford a maximum field of fire, is the Westgate of Canterbury, Kent (see pl. 230).

Heavier guns could be mounted in larger openings of a similar type. In these loops the circular opening is often slightly separated from the sighting slit. Until the sixteenth century heavy guns were generally loaded at their inner or breech end rather than from the muzzle. This meant that they could be permanently fixed into place rather than recoiling after firing. The typical arrangement, therefore, was to lash the barrel of the gun to a wooden carriage that was in turn fixed into the fabric of the castle. Even when the gun has long disappeared, a telltale sign of this arrangement is the existence of sockets in the masonry to either side of the inner splay of the loop. These were the fixings for a beam to support the gun barrel. Good examples of such loops survive in the late fifteenth-century fabric of Richard III's gun tower at Warwick.[85]

The third type of opening for artillery is simply a large square window within a wall or parapet. Arrangements of this kind appear to have enjoyed relatively short popularity in England in the late fourteenth century, though for longer on the Continent. A series of such openings exist along the tops of the walls of the inner bailey at Portchester, a firing gallery for hand-held guns completed in the 1380s. Rather larger guns may have been accommodated in the roughly contemporary upper storey of Caesar's Tower at Warwick

The Ancient and Loyall Citty of YORK

or the Cow Tower constructed along the line of the city walls at Norwich in 1398–9 (see pl. 317).[86] On occasion, the arrangement of these different types of gun loops is minutely documented. In 1381, for example, the mason Thomas Crump was commissioned to make ten 'arketholes' 3 feet in length without cross slits and seven 'little doors' 2.5 feet square for the works at Cooling Castle.[87]

While castles adapted themselves to guns, these weapons were also being adopted by besieging forces. When the duke of Norfolk descended on Caister in 1469, for example, his 'army' enclosed three parts of the castle and came with 'weapons termed in English *gonnys*, *culveryns* and other ordnance of artillery, with archers etc.'.[88] Because great guns were sufficiently prized to receive names, chroniclers more commonly just give these, as at the siege of Bamburgh in 1461.[89] To modern eyes early guns look so gawky that it is easy to write them off as absurdities. The evidence, however, suggests that great guns were powerful if erratic weapons. For those who could afford them, the chief difficulty was assembling a siege train of sufficient size to do real damage.

For the gun properly to transform fortifications, however, two further changes were required. The first was the mass production of relatively reliable weapons. The second was a more technical appreciation of the way in which guns could be used to greatest effect both to defend and reduce fortifications. Both things happened in England during the early sixteenth century, an unexpected outcome of the Reformation. From 1539

Henry VIII disposed of most of the wealth he had appropriated from the church in hostilities with the Catholic powers of Europe. As part of this process he created a series of coastal artillery fortifications that employ multiple bastions (see pl. 318).

The bastion was an earthwork – in these cases faced in stone – that projected from the line of a fortification. Its structure had to be thick enough to absorb the impact of heavy shot and broad enough to provide a platform for the operation of artillery to answer any attack. The bastions of Henry's castles at sites such as Deal and Walmer in Kent also incorporated broad parapets with curved forward angles to deflect shot. In the lower levels of the building individual gun openings were provided with small flues to draw off the smoke. These fortifications were further countersunk in deep moats so as to present a small target to hostile artillery. They were also planned so that no part of the approach or any corner of the moat was concealed from the defenders' guns.

The eccentricity of Henry VIII's bastions is that they are semicircular. In Italy, the principle that bastions should be triangular in plan to improve the sighting of guns from the fortifications was already well established. That idea was only properly realised in English castles at sites such as Carisbrooke on the Isle of Wight and Berwick-upon-Tweed in the later sixteenth century during the reigns of Henry's children, Edward VI, Mary and Elizabeth. And this technology broadly still applied in the mid-seventeenth century, when the kingdom was riven by the Civil War.

FORTIFICATIONS IN THE LANDSCAPE

Before confronting the narrative history of the castle, it is important to make one final point about fortifications in the English landscape up until the seventeenth century. Having looked in the opening of this chapter at Clifford's Tower in York as an isolated work of architecture, it is instructive to stand back and view it from a distance as part of the wider city on the eve of the Civil War (pl. 20). At this date York preserved in all essentials its late medieval appearance: it was enclosed by walls and entered through a series of gate-houses. Within the embrace of these fortifications only the most ambitious buildings were visible. Clifford's Tower was the single element of York Castle visible from afar, but for all its prominence it was (and is) entirely dwarfed by the outline of the Minster. Prior to the Reformation, St Mary's Abbey, which is here seen as ruins to the far left of the scene, would also have overshadowed the city. This view is a powerful reminder of how the English landscape was articulated by fortifications and the manner in which every institution – here the city, the castle and St Mary's Abbey – symbolically and physically defined itself through the use of walls and towers.

2

THE CASTLES OF THE CONQUEST

WILLIAM I

The death of the childless king, Edward the Confessor, at Westminster Palace on 5 January 1066 precipitated perhaps the most important, and certainly the most celebrated, disputes of succession in English history. On the following day Harold Godwinson, earl of Wessex, was acclaimed king of England and crowned in Westminster Abbey. Not long afterwards, two distant rivals for this rich prize heard the news and prepared for war. At the battle of Stamford Bridge in Yorkshire on 25 September, Harold successfully defended the throne against the first of these, Harold Hardrada, king of Norway and sometime captain of the imperial guard at Constantinople. But this great victory was followed just a week later by a catastrophic reverse that famously gave Harold's crown to the third contender.

On the very same wind that carried the fleet and humbled remnants of Hardrada's army home, another invading force set sail for the shores of England. At its head was William the Bastard, duke of Normandy, a figure familiar to posterity simply as 'The Conqueror'. On 14 October, at the field of Hastings, he killed King Harold and routed the Anglo-Saxon army. After further fierce campaigning, William's coronation was celebrated at Westminster Abbey on Christmas Day,

1066. According to the contemporary account by William of Poitiers, a chaplain to the duke, it was an ominous affair. The nervous guards outside the church mistook the shouts of acclamation offered in an unfamiliar tongue for treachery and fired the neighbouring houses. Another authoritative account adds that in the pandemonium that ensued, the Conqueror, perhaps for the only time in his life, completely lost his nerve and sat trembling uncontrollably on the throne.[1]

The early years of William's reign (1066–87) amply matched the events of his coronation. Rebellions, invasions and punitive campaigns racked the kingdom, and, when affairs at last began to settle in the 1070s, a new political order had been created in England. Amongst the most far-reaching changes was the emergence of a new ruling class: most of the spiritual and temporal governors of England were foreigners within the kingdom, bearing strange names, wearing different clothes, their hair cut in different fashions and speaking a different language. But quite as important and outlandish as their personal habits were the institutional and architectural novelties they introduced. Amongst these are usually listed the castle and the system of land ownership that sustained it, the so-called feudal system.

Facing page: Chepstow, Monmouthshire.

THE GENESIS OF THE CASTLE

As conventionally understood, the castle and the feudal system that were introduced to England at the Conquest found their origins in parts of what are now France and Belgium during the breakdown of civil order that accompanied the collapse of the Carolingian Empire in the tenth century. For reasons of self-protection, the powerful magnates that took control of the former counties and duchies of the empire began to fortify their own houses. These buildings, it is argued, were materially different from any previous form of fortification in Europe. Whereas, for example, the forts of the Roman Empire were built for garrisons and publicly supported by the state, castles were privately financed and built to protect the interests of the individual that owned them. Equally important, they were associated with a new form of property tenure. The owners of castles managed their land for specifically military purposes, parcelling it out by 'fee' or *feodum* to support a following of soldiers. This system of securing a following through grants of land has been termed feudal after the *feodum* – or landholding – that characterised it. As a result, castles became a physical embodiment of lordship, landholding and military might.[2]

That some kind of new building came into existence around AD 900 in France is most powerfully suggested by architectural evidence; but it should be emphasised that our knowledge of this is extremely limited. Two methods of fortification appear to have been used to defend residences in this period. The first was the construction of a ditched enclosure with a stone wall or timber palisade. This form of defence has come to be termed a bailey after later medieval usage of the Latin word *ballium* and is difficult to distinguish on physical grounds alone from the types of fortification that might be erected around any medieval settlement in Europe. Much more remarkable, however, and often built in combination with such fortified enclosures, was a high tower, a feature without obvious precedent in domestic architecture.

Such towers might take a variety of forms and be built in varying combinations of earth, stone and timber. Of these combinations, free-standing structures of stone were undoubtedly the most costly to erect and prestigious to own. These were usually rectilinear in plan, comprised several floors and were to be entered through a raised doorway. Their internal arrangements could be very varied (see pp. 109–19).

21 A view of the great tower of Loches (Indre-et-Loire), *circa* 1012–35, from the east. An entrance stair is enclosed in the subsidiary section – or forebuilding – of the tower to the right (1). The tower is an imposing architectural expression of the wealth and power of its builder, Fulk Nerra, count of Anjou (987–1040). It is constructed throughout of cut blocks of stone and its faces are divided into regular, vertical sections or bays by tall buttresses. The particular form of the buttresses is paralleled in such contemporary church architecture as the nave of Saint-Remi at Reims (Marne). The uppermost floor was ringed by a timber gallery, the sockets for which remain clearly visible (2). The relatively tall and narrow proportions of Loches were probably to inform a group of early great towers in England, including those at Corfe and Rochester.

Quite how ambitious such great towers might be, even from a very early date, has recently been demonstrated in startling terms. At Loches, Indre-et-Loire (pl. 21), there survives one of the highest great towers in Europe. On account of its size, the complexity of its internal plan and the quality of its cut masonry, this tower has previously been dated to the mid-twelfth century. But tree-ring dating of timbers taken from the building suggests that it was in fact erected nearly a thousand years ago, between 1012 and *circa* 1035.[3] The re-dating of Loches illustrates the degree to which new scientific methods can enhance our understanding of undocumented buildings. Such findings must not be treated uncritically, but it is exciting to think of the insights that can be expected from this quarter in future years.

Incidentally, the conventional case for dating Loches illustrates a common problem in the received analysis of early castle buildings in the absence of documentary or scientific evidence: the assumption remains that architectural design necessarily develops from the simple to the complex and from the small to the large scale. But what Loches makes clear – and what is actually consistently apparent – is that when vast power and wealth were combined with the degree of ambition that seems to have so distinguished the eleventh-century magnate, almost nothing was impossible. And the builder of Loches, Fulk Nerra, count of Anjou (987–1040), possessed all three in abundance.

An alternative system of creating a tower was to raise a motte. In classic form, this was an artificial mound of earth encircled by a ditch, its summit crowned either by a tower or by a fortified enclosure (pl. 22). Whatever their precise form, the buildings on the summit of the motte were usually approached up a long bridge or flight of steps. The structures associated with mottes in the tenth and eleventh centuries were generally of timber and have been lost. As a result, our most vivid impression of their appearance is provided by artistic representations of castles. In fact, Normandy prior to the Conquest appears to have possessed very few mottes, though this fortification was well known both to the Conqueror and his followers.[4]

The genesis of the motte as a building type has long tantalised scholars and it will probably never be known quite why, where and how this kind of fortification first developed.[5] In large part, this is because gathering basic data about mottes – such as their date of construction and their original shape – is so complicated. Quite as problematic is the enormous diversity of mottes in terms of shape and form, a subject that will be discussed in detail below (pl. 23). Moreover, categorising them in relation to, or distinguishing them from, natural features can be difficult. Is there a material difference, for example, between a tower set respectively on an artificially created mound, a scarped hill or a high crag? Should these all in fact be deemed mottes or are they different? Does it matter?

The motte and stone tower, which were often constructed in combination with a *ballium* or bailey, identify a new type of building in the Western tradition of architecture: the castle. Moreover, in their developed forms they share numerous formal similarities. Perhaps the most obvious of these is that both were elevated structures entered up a flight of steps. They were also both vastly expensive and labour-intensive to raise. Indeed, their physical ambition directly and deliberately reflected on the power of the builder. In expression of this, both could also be known by the same word in the eleventh century – *donjon*.[6] The name derives from the Latin *dominatio* or lordship. Curiously, in the case of some mottes, a *donjon* could also come to represent lordship in legal terms and confer upon its owner rights of labour service.[7] Remarkably, in some cases this association continued until the French Revolution in 1789.[8] Incidentally, it is the powers that such lordship gave that also explain the more familiar English usage of the word dungeon to mean a prison. Meanwhile, the popular modern term for these buildings – keep – gained currency only in the sixteenth century.[9]

It is these architectural forms distinctive of castles, well developed on the Continent by the mid-eleventh century, as well as the feudal system that sustained them, that the Normans are understood to have introduced to England. Also, it is through them that they are understood to have consolidated their conquest. In the much-quoted words of the monk historian Orderic Vitalis, writing *circa* 1080:

> For the fortifications called castles by the Normans were scarcely known in the English provinces, so the English – in spite of their courage and love of fighting – could only put up a weak resistance to their enemies.[10]

That the castle was introduced to England by the Normans is an assertion that – in general terms – is impossible to refute. Moreover, it will become apparent that the early architectural history of the English castle is intimately bound up with the Continental

ancestry of these buildings. Nevertheless, it would be mistaken to regard 1066 as an absolute starting point for the story of the castle in England.

The conquest of England was just one episode in a massive Norman expansion that culminated thirty-three years later with the fall of Jerusalem to the crusaders. In this expansion the Norman sword was given fearsome edge by its association with the Papacy and a vigorous new reforming movement that was transforming the institutions of the church across western Europe. It is often forgotten that England was the trophy of a campaign specifically sanctioned by the pope, as The Crusades were later to be. Yet this Norman expansion was much more than a product of Christian and opportunist militarism. Underpinning its success was something far subtler and infinitely more powerful. For whatever reason, there was developing in eleventh-century Europe a new sense of cultural initiative and conviction that the Normans succeeded in articulating. Even before the Conquest the winds of this cultural change were being felt in England and this circumstance must materially complicate our appreciation of the impact of Norman rule. Edward the Confessor, for example, was himself familiar with Normandy, having been brought up at the ducal court in Rouen. He was clearly impressed by what he saw because on his return to England he reconstructed his palace at Westminster and began to rebuild the adjacent abbey church (the predecessor of the present structure), in a fashion copied from contemporary buildings in Normandy.[11] Completed in time for his burial in 1066, it also stood waiting substantially complete for the coronation of William the Conqueror, a statement of Norman cultural imperialism foreshadowing the political takeover.

In the world of castle building, too, England had had a foretaste of the future. Edward the Confessor showed favour to several followers whom he brought back with him from his exile in Normandy, and some of these men appear to have built castles on land granted to them. Only three have been plausibly identified and these all lie along the unstable Welsh border at Richard's Castle, Ewyas Harold and Hereford. This small clutch of sites built by pre-Conquest Norman settlers has always been admitted within the canon of early castles in England.[12] Restored at the Conquest and, in the case of Hereford at least, much altered latterly, nothing is known for certain of their original form.

Our appreciation of the Norman Conquest must also be coloured by the Anglo-Saxon world. For all the massive changes it brought about, the Norman settlement was profoundly flavoured by the political and cultural order that it supplanted. This was in part because William regarded himself as the rightful heir to the English throne and consciously strove to uphold its traditions, even though he ended up transforming so many. It was also because – contrary to what was believed even forty years ago – part of his English inheritance was an impressive architectural tradition. The excavated remains of such great Anglo-Saxon churches as the Old and New Minsters at Winchester demonstrate that England possessed buildings on a scale to rival anything in contemporary northern Europe.[13] It is for these reasons that Anglo-Saxon England remains directly relevant to the story of the English castle.

THE ANGLO-SAXON
CONTRIBUTION

In 1912 the historian Ella Armitage published a defining work in the modern study of the English castle. Entitled *The Early Norman Castles of the British Isles*, it presented a compelling case for supposing that the castle had been introduced to Britain by the Normans. Prior to this time, the early history of the castle in England had been very differently understood in some circles. In popular terms, many castle buildings were believed to have Roman origins and still more to have been created from the fifth century onwards during Britain's so-called Dark Ages. Even an early nineteenth-century author like Walter Scott, who aspired

to historical accuracy, happily described the late twelfth-century great tower of Conisbrough Castle in Yorkshire as a Saxon structure in his novel *Ivanhoe* (first published in 1819). Armitage showed that, in the vast majority of cases, castle sites were first documented and developed during the immediate aftermath of the Conquest.

In the context of castle studies, therefore, Armitage's contribution was a very important one. But her conclusions have become curiously distorted in the context of a wider historical debate about the impact of the Norman Conquest on England. At one extreme of opinion within this debate are those who have chosen to emphasise the transforming qualities of the Conquest; at the other are individuals who consider that its effects are grossly overrated and have attracted far too much attention. Often underpinning the more outspoken statements of opinion on either side have been thinly veiled sympathies, both political and racial – an irritation with grand narrative histories of the great and the good; support for the underdog Anglo-Saxons; or admiration for the irresistible might and achievement of the Normans.[14]

That such different perspectives have developed is in part a reflection of the difficulties in rescuing a convincing picture of Anglo-Saxon England from behind the events of the Conquest. This is strikingly illustrated in the case of buildings. No great church or major residence in England today is known to preserve any substantial standing fabric from before the Conquest.[15] Our understanding of grand Anglo-Saxon buildings must be gleaned, therefore, from a combination of documentary references, fragmentary sur-

24 (*facing page*) Dover, Kent. Throughout its history, the development of this great castle has been conditioned by the massive earthworks that form a huge U-shaped enclosure dropping to the sea cliffs. These are thought to have formed part of an Iron Age hill fort, though evidence for this is equivocal. At the centre of the enclosure – behind the inner bailey and the great tower built by Henry II in the 1180s – are the Roman Pharos and Anglo-Saxon church, St Mary in Castro. It is these latter that are thought to have been enclosed with a new ditch by William the Conqueror during his eight-day stay in 1066.

vivals of modest buildings and the slowly mounting evidence of excavated remains. We are not overwhelmed by the quantity of early Norman architectural survivals either, but by contrast they are numerous. Presented with such a blank, it is not surprising that some received scholarship on this subject has simply ignored the problem of Anglo-Saxon architecture altogether and chosen to present the Conquest as a new beginning. According to this analysis, the Anglo-Saxons built fortified settlements called *burhs*, which were communally maintained and manned. These were completely different from Norman castles, the private strongholds of an individual lord garrisoned by feudal followers.[16] As is increasingly being acknowledged, however, to treat *burhs* and castles in such sharp contrast is to sacrifice truth for clarity.

The word *burh* simply means a fortified place and was applied in Anglo-Saxon England to a wide variety of sites, not just fortified settlements. Amongst these, for example, is the *burhgeat*, the residence of a thegn or man of knightly status. Even from the title, which literally means 'the gate to the *burh*', it is to be presumed that such buildings had two architecturally prominent features: an enclosing fortification and an entrance. These surely must qualify in conventional terms as castles.[17] For all its limitations, the physical evidence would further corroborate this conclusion. At sites such as Portchester in Hampshire and Goltho in Lincolnshire, archaeological excavation has revealed the remains of what appear to be such private fortified dwellings of thegns.[18] These are relatively modest sites, the former set inside the walls of a Roman fort and the latter with its own enclosure, but their very existence demands a subtler formulation of what distinguished a Norman castle from its Anglo-Saxon predecessor.

Just to complicate matters further, the fortifications built on either side of the Conquest manifestly have much in common. If some *burhs* had a private function, then so did many castles have a public one. For example, it is becoming clear that the vast majority of major castles were planned in direct conjunction with a settlement. Moreover, all castles – despite their much-vaunted private ownership and construction – seem to have been understood as belonging to the king. As a result, they had to be rendered up by loyal magnates on demand at moments of crisis.[19] Finally, both types of fortification were sustained in very similar ways: although the legal terms used were usually different, castles and *burhs* were erected, maintained and garrisoned by a system of levied labour. In

fact, many castles were probably erected by the Normans enforcing on a local population the very legal obligations that they owed to a *burh*.[20]

The interpretative difficulties that these ambiguities create can perhaps best be understood in the context of one of the four sites that are to receive particular attention throughout the narrative of this book. Dover Castle commands the mouth of the River Dour, the only natural harbour along this cliff-lined stretch of the English coast, and controls the shortest sea crossing between England and the Continent. As a result, Dover has been of importance since prehistory as the gateway to England, and its white cliffs have grown to be a symbol of national identity. The earliest remains on the site are believed to be a huge Iron Age hill fort, the U-shaped perimeter defences of which form the outer enclosure of the present castle (pl. 24).[21] Roughly in the centre of this, and towards the natural summit of the castle hill, are the remains of a first-century AD lighthouse or Pharos (pl. 25).[22] This structure was reworked around the year 1000 as the tower of a church. At this time the interior of the fort is believed to have been occupied by a settlement, though the precise nature of this is unknown.

In 1051 two versions of the Anglo-Saxon Chronicle record an affray in this rather dimly understood site. The so-called E Version records that a certain Eustace, count of Boulogne, went 'up towards the *burge*' at Dover with his followers and there fought with the *burh* men, killing twenty 'within and without'.[23] In the D Version, however, Dover is referred to in rather different terms: at a later stage in the narrative it describes a demand that Eustace be handed over, along with what are described as 'the Frenchmen who were in the *castelle*'.[24] This is the earliest use of this French-derived word 'castle' in the Chronicle and would be of independent interest as such. But this particular description of Dover is the more remarkable because the site was subsequently to figure prominently in the events of the Conquest, and numerous reliable authorities refer to it repeatedly as a *castrum* or *castellum* prior to its passing into Norman hands. So, for example, William of Poitiers describes Harold in 1064 promising to deliver the *castrum Doveram* that he had built with his own money to William the Conqueror.[25] He then also records the arrival of William at Dover immediately after Hastings:

This castle (*castellum*) stands near to the sea on a rock which is naturally steep on all sides, and has

furthermore been patiently chipped away with iron tools, so that it is like a wall of towering height equal to the flight of an arrow on the side washed by the sea . . . After the surrender of the castle (*castro*), he spent eight days in fortifying it where it was weakest.[26]

If contemporaries could so variously describe the same building – as a *burghe*, *castelle*, *castro* and *castellum* – it is hard to see why modern scholars with the most exiguous of physical evidence should claim clearer vision.[27] This is the more particularly true, since the sites that can be invoked to illustrate the Anglo-Saxon character of Dover – such as the *burhgeats* of Goltho and Portchester – are so modest by comparison as to be virtually irrelevant as parallels. The case of Dover is important to set out, not because it proves or disproves the existence of Anglo-Saxon castles, but because it shows how unhelpful and dogmatic it is to assert a sharp contrast between pre- and post-Conquest fortifications. To do so additionally ignores two specific points of continuity between *burhs* and castles that suggest themselves from the limited evidence available.

The first is the great hall, which passed with undiminished prestige through the Conquest as an essential element of any substantial residence. Halls were a feature common to secular buildings across Europe, but the scale and attention with which they came to be treated in England after the Conquest are probably best explained in terms of Anglo-Saxon tradition. One reason for this is that on Anglo-Saxon estates duties were sometimes owed not to an individual but to a particular hall.[28] This is an interesting contrast to the system described above by which duties were owed in France to a *donjon*. Second is the gatehouse. Again, in European terms, the gatehouse or gate tower is a common feature of grand architectural design, both secular and ecclesiastical. But in no kingdom is that tradition as consistently strong or ambitious as in England. One explanation for this is that the later English tradition of gatehouse architecture traces its origins back ultimately to the Anglo-Saxon *burhgeat*.

Yet for all the problems implicit in distinguishing between fortified buildings before and after the Conquest, there is undoubtedly something new about the Norman castle in England. The principal reason for making this assertion is that there is still no convincing case for supposing that either great towers or mottes were ever erected by the Anglo-Saxons. This fact alone constitutes a good reason for suppos-

ing that fortified Norman buildings were in some respects speaking a different architectural language from that of their predecessors. Quite as important is the evident scale of castle building in England in the aftermath of the Conquest. This is shown by the relatively higher visibility of castles in the historical record than that of the Anglo-Saxon buildings they replaced. Whereas references to the residences of Anglo-Saxon thegns need to be hunted down, castles flood the narratives and administrative documentation of post-Conquest England. Indeed, the particular circumstances of the Conquest were to create a quantity and scale of fortification that clearly beggared that even of contemporary Normandy and its adjacent duchies.

THE YEARS OF CONQUEST

William the Conqueror's coronation on Christmas Day, 1066 brought the principal events of the Norman Conquest of England to a close within the tidy span of a single year. But while Norman rule was henceforth a reality, its permanence and significance – which seem so clear in retrospect – were far from established. Castle building reflects the three broad stages by which the Norman political settlement may be understood to have set down its roots. First were the events of 1066, which prompted the construction of a small group of castles in the context of William's successful military campaign. Then, between approximately 1067 and 1071, a second generation of buildings was created with the intention of securing territory and towns under the new regime. Though many of these castles were also established in the course of further campaigning, work to them was generally not undertaken in such hurried or uncertain circumstances as those of 1066. Lastly, and in some cases absorbing sites from these first two categories, were the castles associated with the steady consolidation of Norman rule during the 1070s. It is these last castles that will be the focus of the next chapter, but the former categories of building – which might be dubbed castles of campaign and of conquest respectively – also repay brief consideration.

In broad outline the events of the Norman campaign of 1066 are well known. After months of waiting, a favourable wind at last carried William's invasion fleet from Saint-Valéry on the Picardy coast to Pevensey Bay in Sussex, where the army disembarked on the morning of 28 September. This landfall is unlikely to have been fortuitous. Commanding the natural har-

26 Pevensey, Sussex. The oval outline of the Roman fortifications of the late third century AD that occupy the end of a peninsula formerly enclosed by sea and marsh. The massive masonry walls with projecting D-shaped towers remain substantially intact. They incorporate bonding courses of brick and were faced with very neatly cut blocks of stone bonded with pink mortar. This colour was achieved by grinding brick into the mortar mixture. Commanding good beaches for disembarking his army and with space to set up camp, the fort was an ideal landfall for William. The remains of a ditch cut across the original causeway in front of the Roman gate in the foreground have been tentatively associated with the fortification of the site in September 1066. In its present form the inner bailey in the distance is essentially a creation of the 1250s (see pl. 131).

bour of the bay, which has since been largely drained, there still survive the remains of one of the most complete Roman forts in Europe (pl. 26). It was almost certainly within the walls of this building that the Norman army spent its first night on English soil, perhaps fortifying the site with a ditch cut across the landward end of the castle peninsula. One account of the landing written a century later describes the army as bringing with it a complete castle for erection at Pevensey.[29] Prefabricated timber fortifications were widely used in this period and this story could record some genuine use of them in 1066.

The next day the army moved along the coast to Hastings and there built a castle. It is entirely a matter for conjecture whether the later medieval castle at Hastings stands on the site occupied during the campaign or whether any feature erected in 1066 survives here. The original campaign castle is, however, depicted on perhaps the most celebrated work of art associated with the Norman Conquest, the Bayeux Tapestry (pl. 27). Almost everything about this extraordinary piece of medieval embroidery remains a matter of current debate: who commissioned it; who made it; when precisely it was made; and how it was intended to be displayed. All these questions lie outside the scope of this discussion, but the fact remains that the

tapestry includes some of the most sophisticated representations of northern European architecture to survive from the eleventh century. To look at it is to see the events and buildings of the Conquest through the eyes of contemporaries.

The image of Hastings shows a group of workmen labouring with picks and shovels to cast up an artificial mound or motte. This earthwork is depicted with bands of colour, a detail conceivably intended to represent its method of construction in layers.[30] On top of the motte depicted in the tapestry is a low structure, almost certainly a timber enclosure. In comparison with all the other architectural images on the tapestry this is very plain and it is possible that the artist was trying to convey in this way its qualities as a hastily erected structure.

Whatever the case, judged from its depiction on the tapestry, the castle at Hastings would be the only campaign castle known to be constructed with a motte. This observation highlights both a common assumption and a practical issue. The assumption is that every Norman castle needs a motte. That this is untrue is illustrated by the most superficial overview of the early castle sites treated in this and the next chapter. The practical issue is that the castles erected in the course of the 1066 campaign were presumably built first and

UT EO DE RETUR: CASTELLUM: AT·HESTENGA CEASTRA HIC: WIL

27 The Bayeux Tapestry, late eleventh century, probably produced at Canterbury. This scene shows the construction of Hastings Castle. The diggers have iron-shod shovels and two of them are fighting. The significance of this combat is unfortunately not known but it is likely to record a particular event not otherwise recounted in the written sources. The castle motte is shown as a striped mound of earth surmounted by a fortification. There are no steps shown leading up to it, a curious point of contrast with the other mottes depicted on the tapestry. Possibly, this detail and the omission of any architectural ornament on the structures that surmount it reflect the character of the castle as a hastily erected structure.

foremost to protect the Norman army; moreover, that this function would best be served by a fortified enclosure like the Roman fort at Pevensey. In this sense, the depiction of Hastings Castle on the tapestry as a motte is of interest. If a motte really was built – which seems attractive given the accompanying detail of fighting labourers – it might reflect an intention to establish Hastings as a fortified landing point held by a small garrison when the army moved on.

From Hastings the army marched north to meet and defeat King Harold's army on 14 October. But this victory at Hastings elicited no response or capitulation from the English nobility, and after four days of waiting William continued his campaign. He marched first to Dover, where he captured and further fortified the cliff-top fortress. Again, we have little idea as to what work he undertook here. It is generally supposed that he ditched around the natural hill in the centre of the present castle enclosure, on which stand the Anglo-Saxon church and the Roman Pharos. Excavations have revealed traces of a ditch in this area cut through a Saxon cemetery, which might plausibly be associated with this operation.[31] His communications by sea with Normandy secured, William then took Canterbury, the principal seat of England's church, before proceeding northwards to London. When his entry to the

city was contested, he marched around it, wasting the countryside as he passed. Remarkably, at no point on this circuit, which was undertaken in early December, is particular mention made of castle construction. Eventually, William received the invitation he had been awaiting to accede to the English throne, probably at Little Berkhamsted in Hertfordshire.[32]

CAMPAIGN TO CONQUEST

It was in London, already the principal city of the kingdom, that what might be termed the first castles of conquest as opposed to campaign were erected. The *burh* was defended by its circuit of Roman walls and William the Conqueror, aware of the 'inconstancy of the numerous and hostile inhabitants', ordered the construction of 'fortifications' to control it, 'for he saw that it was of the very first importance to constrain the Londoners strictly'.[33] Two castles can be associated with this direction. The first of these occupied an enormous site that straddled the full length of the western city defences. After 1087 this castle was fragmented and a substantial area of it was absorbed into the city. At the same time, however, two new castles were created within its former bounds (and possibly within its inner

59

Map labels:
York (2)

Lincoln

Chester
Stafford Nottingham
Shrewsbury Tutbury

Wisbech

Alrehede
Warwick Huntingdon
Wigmore Worcester
Clifford Hereford Cambridge
Ewyas Harold
Monmouth Oxford
Chepstow Berkeley
Wallingford
Old Sarum London (2)

Dover
Winchester
Montacute Arundel Hastings
Exeter Pevensey

N

50ml   50ml
100km   0   100km

28 A map of the castles known to have been founded between 1066 and 1070. With such limited evidence available, the process of castle foundation in the years immediately after the Conquest is very difficult to elucidate. There can be little doubt, however, that it was shaped by a very fast-moving political situation. The vast majority of documented castles in this period were established in towns and cities.

bailey): Baynard's Castle, on the site of modern Blackfriars, and, as a subdivision of this, Montfichet's Castle near present-day Ludgate Circus.[34] The second castle founded by the Conqueror stood at the opposite side of the city on the site of the Tower of London. Excavations at the Tower suggest that this castle at first comprised only a fortified enclosure at the angle of the Roman wall. At some stage in the 1070s work began in this last castle to the celebrated White Tower, an operation that clearly identified it as the principal one in the city.[35]

For the next three years, between 1067 and 1070, nearly every castle known to be founded by William the Conqueror was similarly to be set within *burh* defences. These castles were erected during the course

of the long campaigns that he so energetically fought to suppress rebellions and control his kingdom. In sequence, the securely identified sites are Exeter in 1067; Warwick, Nottingham, York, Lincoln, Huntingdon and Cambridge in 1068–9; Worcester by 1069; Old Sarum by 1069–70; and York (a second castle), Chester and Stafford in 1069–70 (pl. 28). In virtually every case, the Domesday survey of 1087 records the financial impact caused by the construction of these castles. In Huntingdon, for example, the revenue of twenty houses in the city was lost as a result of the new castle.

It used to be thought that this figure of lost revenue recorded the physical destruction of property caused by the erection of defences. No doubt houses were razed to the ground, but the implied scale of some destruction suggests that Domesday may additionally be accounting for other changes in income that are not now properly understood. In Lincoln revenue from 166 houses was similarly lost, a surprisingly high figure,[36] and in York the new castles absorbed the entirety of one of the seven shires into which the city was divided.[37]

Of the castles in this list, perhaps the best preserved is that at Exeter (pl. 29), the remains of which offer valuable insights into the types of fortification being raised in this period. Exeter Castle comprises an earthwork enclosure set just inside the existing city defences and is without a motte or great tower. The high inner banks to the encircling ditch are a common feature of early castle design and must have supported timber defences, more of which will be said in the next chapter. Deeply set within the high inner bank to the enclosure is the main entrance to the castle, an impressive eleventh-century gate tower in stone. The details of this building with triangular arch heads and heavy mouldings are strongly Anglo-Saxon in flavour, and would suggest that it was begun soon after the fall of the city in 1067. Viewed as a whole, the enclosure and its gatehouse might consciously evoke the architecture of a *burhgeat*.

At the same time that such royal foundations were being established, many other castles were evidently being erected, though their distribution remains poorly understood. Following the submission of London in 1067, for example, William of Poitiers describes the Conqueror as travelling 'to diverse parts of the kingdom', where:

As custodians of castles he assigned stalwart men whom he had brought across from Gaul, on whose loyalty and valour he relied equally; and with

them he placed a multitude of foot soldiers and knights. To these he distributed rich fiefs, for the sake of which they would willingly bear toil and danger.[38]

These castles presumably included some new foundations, but the site of only one – at Guenta – is subsequently named in this passage by William of Poitiers. It is illustrative of our ignorance that this site has been variously identified as Norwich and – as is now generally accepted – as Winchester.[39] Similarly, following William the Conqueror's departure for Normandy that same year, the Anglo-Saxon Chronicle lamented that the Norman regents of England 'stayed behind here and built castles widely throughout the nation, and oppressed the wretched people, and always after that it grew very much worse'.[40]

William fitz Osbern

In only one case is it possible to rescue some information about this process of castle foundation by William's followers in the immediate aftermath of the Conquest. William fitz Osbern was linked by ties of blood to the ducal family of Normandy and had grown up in the company of the Conqueror, with whom he shared a long and close friendship.[41] He proved a crucial figure in the invasion of England, furnishing the Norman fleet with what was evaluated in one list as a force of sixty ships and men. Besides such practical support, he was also useful in encouraging the army in the face of ill omens. According to the Chronicle of Battle Abbey, for example, William fell and cut himself while landing at Pevensey. His men were much dismayed, but fitz Osbern, 'a man of admirable probity and very clever', at once turned the event to advantage, explaining that he had grasped England with both hands and consecrated it as his inheritance with his own blood.[42]

In the aftermath of the battle of Hastings fitz Osbern's rewards were very rich indeed. In 1067 he was raised to the greatest English dignity, that of an earl. He also appears to have received most of the landed property formerly held by Harold as earl of Wessex. This extended in a huge swathe across England from the Isle of Wight on the south coast – where he probably established Carisbrooke Castle[43] – up to Herefordshire on the Welsh border. It also incorporated the city of Winchester, the former capital of the Wessex kings. In one area of this enormous belt of land fitz Osbern's activi-

29   Gatehouse of Exeter, Devon, begun *circa* 1067. This large tower (its entrance archway now blocked) may have been intended to look like the gatehouse of a *burhgeat*. Certainly, the upper windows have triangular heads, a peculiar detail often encountered in Anglo-Saxon architecture. Many eleventh-century buildings were informed by Roman models, and the tall, outer arch framing the gatehouse façade is probably drawn from the design of triumphal arches. A much grander reworking of this idea is encountered in the west front of Lincoln Cathedral, begun in the mid-1070s. To the left of the gateway is visible the steep slope of the castle earthworks dropping to the ditch.

ties as a castle builder are particularly well documented. To secure his territories along the Welsh border, and to extend his interests, he is credited in various documentary sources with having established a series of castles.[44] These buildings must all have been begun within five years of the Conquest because in February 1071 the earl was killed while on campaign in Flanders.

Five new castles can be associated with fitz Osbern in this immediate region: Monmouth and Chepstow in Monmouthshire, Berkeley in Gloucestershire, and Clifford and Wigmore in Herefordshire. He was also responsible for the refoundation of pre-Conquest castles at Hereford and Ewyas Harold in Herefordshire. Most of these buildings are connected with staking out territory along the Welsh border, taking advantage of the principal rivers and their crossings. Despite their frontier role, they all avoided the kinds of destruction of property described in royal, city foundations. Two of the castles – Clifford and Wigmore – are specifically described in the Domesday survey as standing on land that lay 'waste' or unexploited prior to the Conquest. Chepstow was also probably built on wasteland, and Berkeley, which is described as 'a little castle' (*castellulum*), was on the site of what had previously been the centre of a royal estate, now in fitz Osbern's hands. As such, it possibly stood on the site of an existing residence. It is not known whether the two refounded castles stood on the sites of their predecessors, but it seems likely. Certainly, at Hereford, Domesday recorded no loss of revenue resulting from the construction of a castle.

The designation of Berkeley as a *castellulum* is one of several details that implies some hierarchy amongst the castles in the earl's possession. In this case, the diminutive almost certainly referred to the relatively small size of the landholding attached to it. This influenced the numbers of knights who might receive fees on the territory of the castle and, by extension, presumably the scale of its buildings. The relative importance of the castles is also reflected in the scale of the religious foundations associated with them. One mark of the particular importance of Chepstow in the group, for example, was the foundation here by the earl of a Benedictine priory, a daughter house of the abbey of Cormeilles in Normandy. With the exception of Hereford, a cathedral city, none of fitz Osbern's other castles in the region had a religious foundation of such stature attached to it.

Of the physical form of these foundations it is impossible to speak with much certainty. Berkeley,

Wigmore, Clifford, Hereford and Ewyas Harold possess, or are known to have possessed, mottes. It is probable that some or all of these mottes were in part the creation of William fitz Osbern. Similarly, there remain at Clifford and Ewyas Harold earthwork remains of fortified enclosures or baileys (pl. 30). These are probably eleventh century and give an accurate impression of the original size of the baileys created by their Norman builders before the Conquest. It seems likely that the earthworks of all these castles were originally fortified entirely with wooden structures. Monmouth and Chepstow occupied naturally powerful sites that were likewise probably strengthened with earthworks and timber defences. Both these latter castles also preserve today the remains of great towers constructed in stone. In the case of Monmouth, the building probably dates to the twelfth century, but that at Chepstow is certainly earlier.

Whether the great tower of Chepstow was actually constructed by fitz Osbern remains a matter of contention. All authorities agree that it is an eleventh-century building and a case has recently been put forward for attributing it to William the Conqueror. He took control of the castle soon after the death of his friend and clearly had both the means and the time to build on this scale.[45] But an attribution to fitz Osbern cannot be ruled out entirely. By virtue of his friendship – and kinship – with William the Conqueror, fitz Osbern enjoyed quite exceptional resources. He also had a particular interest in Chepstow, as is shown by the monastic foundation he established there. Chepstow was, moreover, a foundation of special importance in his landholdings: the castle had river access to the Bristol Channel, which made it a convenient centre for the earl's territories on either side of this body of water. It was also conveniently placed to act as a springboard for incursions along the south coast of Wales. If fitz Osbern were responsible, the tower would be the earliest work of Norman secular architecture substantially to survive in England.

The great tower at Chepstow is a long, thin structure, a proportion unique amongst surviving English buildings of this kind. Later alterations, including the addition of an upper floor, have obscured some features of its original design, but in most points these are still clearly legible. As first built, the tower comprised two floors: an entrance level and an imposing upper floor. In the manner of all grand architecture of this period, the building speaks the language of Roman imperial architecture (see below, Chapter

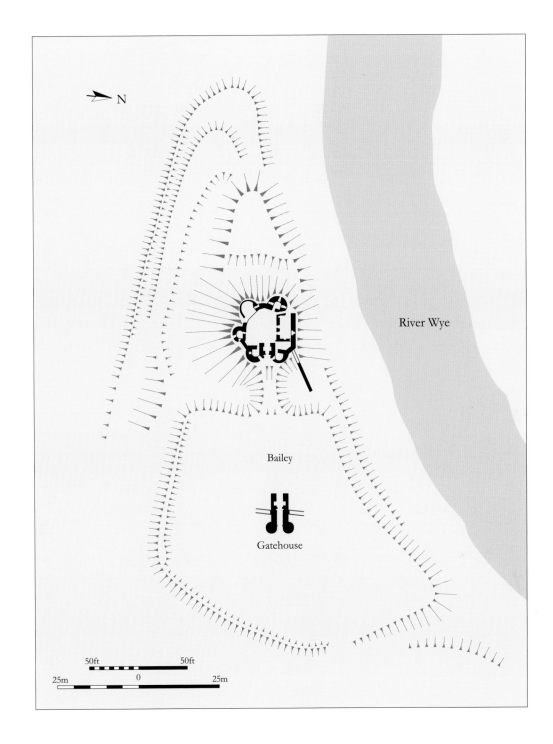

N

River Wye

Bailey

Gatehouse

50ft · 50ft
25m · 0 · 25m

Three): its walls are constructed of regular blocks of masonry and articulated at intervals by narrow buttresses. Running as a thin cord around the outer faces of the building is a course of Roman brick, probably looted from the nearby ruins of the legionary fortress of *Venta Silurum*, modern-day Caerwent (pl. 31). Around the massive entrance door, the mortar between the stones has been made pink with a mixture of ground brick, again a technique faithfully copied from Roman buildings.

The interiors of the great tower must have been cavernous and dark. Most of the windows are arranged to overlook the cliff, and the walls on the landward sides of the building are very thickly built, presumably for defensive reasons (pl. 32). Each floor appears to have stood open as a massive rectangular space, a plan that might suggest that the interior was intended primarily for ceremonial rather than domestic use. Whether or not this was the case it is clear that the most important room was on the upper floor. At this level the

31 (*facing page*)   The great tower of Chepstow, Monmouthshire. Only the lower two storeys of the building were erected in the eleventh century. A timber stair presumably gave access to the raised archway that formed the main entrance to the interior. Pink mortar has been used to fill the masonry joints around the door, a colour created by adding crushed brick to the lime mix. This technique is faithfully copied from Roman fort architecture, and is found, for example, at Pevensey (see pl. 26). Roman too is the detail of a brick bonding course that runs over the top of the door and through the tower walls. The bricks used are Roman and must have been taken from nearby ruins.

32   Chepstow, Monmouthshire, plan of the great tower. This shows the thicker wall towards the landward side (south) and the arrangement of north-facing windows overlooking the cliff. The straight-sided opening at first-floor level (1) was a doorway and must have opened onto a lost balcony or staircase. The former is more probable since there is no means of securing a door within the opening, which would be necessary if it was a point of access. The series of blind wall niches at first-floor level (2) may have been designed as recesses for seats.

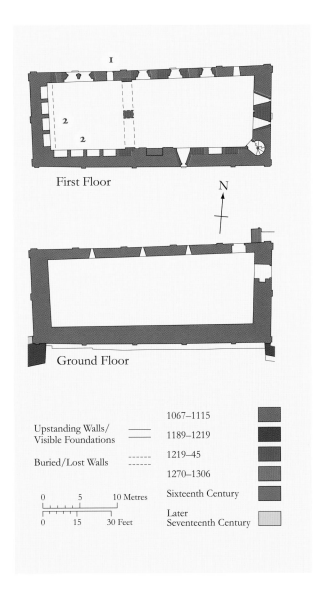

First Floor

N

Ground Floor

Upstanding Walls/
Visible Foundations ——

Buried/Lost Walls - - - - -

1067–1115

1189–1219

1219–45

1270–1306

Sixteenth Century

Later
Seventeenth Century

0   5   10 Metres

0   15   30 Feet

thicker walls are filled with continuous blind arcades, possibly a series of architectural seats for rather comfortless formal gatherings. Framed within these niches are the remains of a zany decorative scheme that is believed to be eleventh century: an irregular band of brick plaster set across a white ground. The interior contains no fireplace or built-in latrine and the only humanising touch is to be inferred from a door that opens out over the cliff face. This must have led to an external gallery or balcony that commanded fine views across the River Wye (see p. 48).

Viewed in its totality, what William fitz Osbern created along the border with Wales was a small network of castles on different scales. What is remarkable about these buildings – though it cannot be assumed elsewhere in the wider kingdom – is that none of them appears to have been destructively obtruded into the territory they consolidated. In this respect they contrast with the first generation of royal castles built in former *burhs*. But castle foundation by the Normans was about to take on a much more predatory character. During the 1070s William the Conqueror appears finally to have lost his patience with the old order of Anglo-Saxon England. From this point forward his policy of settling the kingdom became more intrusive. In the process castles underwent an extraordinary transformation, both in institutional and physical terms: they developed into the administrative hubs of a new Anglo-Norman kingdom, the instruments of its government in peace as well as war and the principal beneficiaries of its resources.

3

THE CASTLES OF SETTLEMENT

WILLIAM I

William the Conqueror (1066–87) and his followers effectively locked castles for the long term into England and its landscape through a system of territorial endowment. At its simplest, such endowment took the form of an estate, variously termed an honour (or honor), a rape or a castlery, of which the produce, revenue and labour were directed to sustain a castle at its focus. One of the most important labour contributions of the estate towards the castle (and certainly the most studied) was a system of knight's service, by which individuals received parcels of land in return for military duty including garrison service. But it could take other forms as well, many of them far less well understood or documented. For example, smaller parcels of land termed serjeanties could be granted out to maintain a castle cook, carpenter or porter.[1] On a wider scale, meanwhile, tenants might be obliged to maintain earthworks and fortifications.[2] In some points this system built on inherited systems of Anglo-Saxon obligation, but it took them much further. By this means, castles became inextricably bound up with land, the primary source of wealth and power in pre-industrial England.

The sheer scale of land redistribution after the Conquest deserves emphasis if the full significance of this moment as a watershed is to be comprehended. In the immediate circle of the Conqueror a very small group of men, many of them royal kinsmen, enjoyed winnings that might guarantee them places in a list of the richest men in history (though to appreciate this it is necessary to suppress entirely modern monetary values and think of one pound as a very considerable sum). It has been calculated, for example, that eight men came to enjoy what were then astonishing annual incomes of over £750. Exceptional amongst these were William fitz Osbern and the Conqueror's half-brother, Odo, bishop of Bayeux, the latter of whom received about 1,700 hides of land. The hide was an administrative rather than a fixed measure, but the extent of this holding necessarily constituted hundreds of thousands of acres and extended over twenty-two English counties. It yielded more than £3,000 per annum.[3]

A more representative figure of this exceptional group was Richard fitz Gilbert, probably a childhood friend of the Conqueror, who enjoyed an income of more than £850 per annum. His estates and those of his wife extended over nine counties, though there were concentrations in two areas, one in Suffolk and Essex and the other in Kent and Surrey. Each came to support a major castle: Clare and Tonbridge respec-

Facing page: Ludlow, Shropshire.

tively.[4] A further ten individuals, scarcely less outstanding, enjoyed revenues of between £400 and £650 per annum, and another twenty-four between £200 and £400. Still important and very wealthy were a further thirty-six with incomes of between £100 and £200.[5] One way of comprehending these statistics is to think of the lion's share of the resources of England falling into the hands of around seventy individuals, lay and clerical.

PATTERNS OF CASTLE FOUNDATION

In the vast majority of cases the creation of castleries was informed by inherited patterns of Anglo-Saxon landholding, a Norman taking over the estates of one or more dispossessed Anglo-Saxons. As a result, the properties they received usually comprised complex and interlocking patchworks of estates or manors, often spread over a wide geographic area. A new castle was commonly founded at the geographic core of such a collection of possessions in the densest area of holdings. Alternatively, irrespective of its position within its associated lands, the site of an Anglo-Saxon *burhgeat* might simply be taken over to serve as a castle. Such, for example, seems to have been the case at Castle Acre in Norfolk. In this instance, the East Anglian estates of an important thegn called Toki appear to have passed in the 1070s to a close associate of the king and another outstanding beneficiary of the Conquest, William de Warenne. Excavations at Castle Acre revealed the existence of pre-Conquest buildings, presumably the remains of Toki's *burhgeat*. This site, in other words, was in continuous use right through the tumultuous events of the Conquest as the focus of a group of estates.[6]

A variant on such patterns of continuity was the creation of a castle on a new site but in clear relation to an Anglo-Saxon predecessor. One of the most curious and important examples of this is to be found at Windsor. Prior to the Conquest, Windsor was an important royal manor and residence; King Harold's father had died of apoplexy at a feast in the great hall there in 1053.[7] This Anglo-Saxon residence was kept in operation by the Conqueror. Such was its importance that it regularly served as the setting for the crown-wearing ceremonies that took place on such high religious feast-days as Easter and Christmas. Frustratingly little is known about

these solemn occasions, but they culminated in the king's appearance before his assembled nobility wearing full royal regalia.[8] The manor at Windsor was never apparently fortified, but nearby, above a cliff dropping to the River Thames in the neighbouring manor of Clewer, William began what the Domesday survey describes as 'Windsor Castle'. The name clearly associated the new castle with the earlier Anglo-Saxon residence. Little is known for certain about the early physical form of this castle and a discussion of its architectural development will begin in the next chapter. It occupied half a hide of land, a detail meticulously noted in Domesday. Curiously, 12 shillings continued to be paid by the crown to the lords of Clewer for the occupation of the site every year until 1572.[9]

This treatment of Windsor was by no means isolated. During the Conqueror's reign castles coexisted with major Anglo-Saxon palaces in at least two other crucially important places: at Winchester, a city invested with particular status as the ancient capital of the Wessex kings of England, and at London. In the case of Winchester, as with Windsor, the Anglo-Saxon palace was greatly enlarged by William the Conqueror.[10] The palace was, however, superseded by the castle only after it was destroyed by fire during fighting in 1140.[11] But at London, in an astonishing instance of political continuity, it still survives as the seat of parliament: the Palace of Westminster. These apparently isolated examples of continuity may simply reflect the importance of the particular sites concerned. But it is equally possible that they illustrate much wider practices that in the main pass completely undocumented. Castles were certainly springing up all over England from the 1070s, but it could have taken time for them to fasten their hold and for the institutions that they supplanted to wither away.

Not all castle foundations reflect continuity with the Anglo-Saxon past, however. In some cases, castleries were created for strategic purposes and cut cleanly through established lines of property tenure. Such was the case, for example, along the Sussex coast, where the Conqueror's own army had arrived. By 1073 this had been divided into five rapes (later six), each one owned by a trusted follower or blood relative of the Conqueror. Two of the rapes were attached to campaign castles that had been first established by William after his landing in 1066: Hastings and Pevensey. The other three – Arundel, Bramber and Lewes – were fresh foundations at the mouths of rivers that gave access inland. It is also likely that the Isle of Wight had

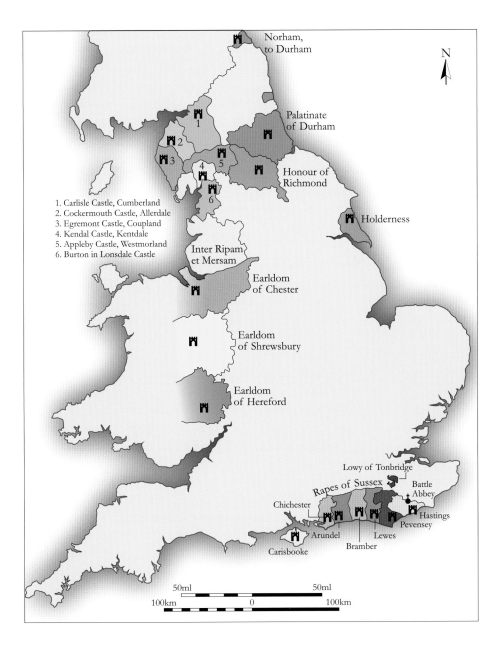

Norham,
to Durham

N

Palatinate
of Durham

1
2
3
4 5
6

Honour of
Richmond

Holderness

1. Carlisle Castle, Cumberland
2. Cockermouth Castle, Allerdale
3. Egremont Castle, Coupland
4. Kendal Castle, Kentdale
5. Appleby Castle, Westmorland
6. Burton in Lonsdale Castle

Inter Ripam
et Mersam

Earldom
of Chester

Earldom
of Shrewsbury

Earldom
of Hereford

Lowy of Tonbridge

Rapes of Sussex

Battle
Abbey

Chichester

Hastings
Pevensey

Arundel

Lewes

Bramber

Carisbooke

50ml   50ml

100km   0   100km

33 A map showing the
principal geographically
coherent castleries
established along the coast
and borders of England by
circa 1100. With the exception
of those in the north-west, all
were created by William the
Conqueror. His foundations
cut through inherited
landholdings and were
intended to support a network

of major castles in the hands
of trusted followers along the
frontiers of the kingdom.
Some monasteries, such as
Battle – the Benedictine abbey
built on the site of the field of
Hastings – were provided with
similar holdings. The practice
of creating discrete blocks of
land to support castles (or
monasteries), however,
remained unusual in England.

Most large castles of the
period, including some
strategically vital ones such
as Dover, were endowed
with complex and far-flung
estates. Redrawn and
elaborated from
N. J. G. Pounds, *The
Medieval Castle in England
and Wales, A Social and
Political History*,
Cambridge, 1990.

become a discrete castlery under the ownership of
William fitz Osbern and that its resources were directed to maintain Carisbrooke Castle.[12] In the early
1070s William began consolidating the border with
Wales in a similar fashion, creating two earldoms at
Chester and Shrewsbury to complement William fitz
Osbern's possession of Hereford. From these bases,
new castles were founded with castleries carved out of
disputed territory beyond the bounds of England. As
we shall see in detail, the north of England witnessed
similar changes in the 1070s, as did the eastern
seaboard down through East Anglia, which was vulnerable to Danish raids (pl. 33).

There was, however, no absolute consistency in the
creation of geographically coherent estates to serve
strategically important castles. Dover, for example,
seems to have had no formally constituted honour
before the twelfth century and responsibility for its
defence appears to have fallen up to then jointly on
the resources of the crown, the earl of Kent and the
constable of England.[13] Moreover, there are examples
of coherent estates being constituted in the aftermath
of the Conquest that evidently had little to do with
military concerns. The abbey founded at Battle on the
site of William's victory over King Harold, for
example, was granted a rape or *luega* within a circumference of a mile that evidently cut awkwardly through
inherited land divisions.[14] This creation, over which
the abbey enjoyed important legal privileges, was evidently meant to underline the special status of the
institution and the fateful battle it commemorated.

At least one early castle estate is likely to have been
constituted in this way: more for honorific than military purpose. There was attached to Tonbridge Castle
in Kent a relatively coherent *luega*, later known as the
'lowy'. This was reputedly granted to Richard fitz Gilbert in compensation for his claim to the castle
of Brionne (Eure), of which he was disappointed.
According to the story, the two landholdings were measured out equally with a rope to ensure the equality of
the exchange.[15] As it stands, the details of the story are
hard to credit, but the odd nature of the Tonbridge lowy
and the legal privileges it subsequently enjoyed do
imply some unusual circumstance of creation.[16]

In all its variety and complexity, the process of
Norman territorial reorganisation was bound up with
important changes to a cornerstone of the Anglo-Saxon
political order. The highest dignity in the English
kingdom was that of an earl. In the 1050s and 60s the
circle of earls usually numbered five or six, and its

34 (*facing page*) Oxford, St George's Tower. Built of rubble masonry on a rectangular plan, this magnificent eleventh-century tower stands beside the Anglo-Saxon western entrance to the city and may be a surviving gate tower from the pre-Conquest defences. If this is the case, the tower was subsequently absorbed within the new castle when it was laid out across the principal thoroughfare of the town in 1071. There is a sealed doorway on the top level of the tower to the left, possibly the entrance onto a lost timber balcony. Many early stone castle buildings seem to have incorporated timber galleries.

members exercised vice-regal powers over the areas they governed, which usually comprised several shires. There is some evidence that in the immediate aftermath of the Conquest the title of earl was equated with that of the Latin *dux* or duke, the greatest Continental dignity. Also, that the Conqueror may have initially intended to perpetuate a system of government operated through a powerful and small group of earls. William fitz Osbern, for example, assumed the title along with vast landholdings in 1067, as did Bishop Odo of Bayeux, earl of Kent, the half-brother of the Conqueror.[17]

Over the 1070s, however, the rank of earl was effectively demoted a grade to that of *comes*, or count: where they fell vacant through death or rebellion, the great Anglo-Saxon earldoms were fragmented into several smaller Norman ones. Meanwhile, the early Norman earls were cut down in size and power. For Bishop Odo and the son of fitz Osbern, this reduction of power was hard to bear and encouraged both into unsuccessful rebellion. In conjunction with its demotion, the title of earl also came to be applied in a slightly different way. As witnessed in the cases of the earls of Chester and Shrewsbury, earls were henceforth generally associated with a particular place. This was a practice borrowed from Normandy, where individual *comes* held one castle as the effective capital of their feudal estate or *conte* (hence the English 'county'). From 1075 all new Norman earldoms, with the complex exception of Northumbria, corresponded to a shire or county and were associated with its principal town. The idea of linking a place with a title was to prove vastly important through the Middle Ages and beyond: it consistently encouraged earls to aggrandise architecturally the places they took their dignity from.

Despite its relative demotion, the body of earls in the eleventh century remained small and very exclusive. There was, meanwhile, a group of powerful men who never assumed this rank but dominated counties (or very large parts of them) in a virtually identical fashion. With so little documentary evidence available, it can be difficult to reconstruct the careers of these figures in much detail. Nevertheless, all had in common a close connection with William the Conqueror and many were of relatively modest origins. One such was Robert d'Oilly, who took his name from Ouilly-le-Vicomte near Lisieux in Normandy. He served in the ducal household of William, whose confidence he evidently enjoyed, and came to England at the Conquest with two brothers. The rewards he enjoyed were substantial, and according to Domesday in 1086, his

estates yielded a respectable revenue of about £260 a year, four-fifths of which was derived from land in Oxfordshire, Berkshire and Buckinghamshire. Much of this land was derived from his marriage to Ealdgyth, the daughter and heiress of a certain Wigot of Wallingford, an Englishman. This match probably took place by 1068.[18] When William the Conqueror's policy towards the English changed, d'Oilly became a useful tool in enforcing the Norman settlement more aggressively in his area of influence.

In 1071 Robert established for the king a new castle within the *burh* defences of Oxford, and three years later, along with a sworn associate and friend, Roger d'Ivry, founded a collegiate church dedicated to St George within it.[19] The new castle was laid across and blocked the main street of the former settlement, a physical statement of hostile and imposed authority.[20] Its motte, which is assumed to have been raised in 1071, still survives; so too does the reconstructed eleventh-century crypt of the collegiate church and, to its west, a tall stone tower (pl. 34). St George's Tower, so-called, has also long been associated with the foundation of the castle. Recent archaeological excavation, however, has raised the remarkable possibility that this was the gate tower that commanded the entrance to the main street of the Anglo-Saxon *burh* of Oxford and that it was incorporated within the castle defences in 1071.[21] If so, it is a reminder of the potential ambition of pre-Conquest architecture. In conjunction with his works to the castle, d'Oilly also built a huge causeway that still serves as the approach to the south side of the city. Seven hundred metres long and supported on seventeen flood arches, this is possibly the first major stone bridge constructed since the Roman period in western Europe and it guaranteed the future prosperity of Oxford.[22]

It was probably while this new castle was being developed at Oxford that the principal settlement in the neighbouring county of Berkshire was being similarly transformed by Norman rule. Until the twelfth century Wallingford was a more important centre in Berkshire than either Reading or Windsor, and by 1071 a new motte and bailey castle had been established there within the circuit of the Anglo-Saxon defences. The castle at Wallingford and the honour that served it were probably established either by d'Oilly's father-in-law or his son-in-law.[23] Whichever the case, they brought about effective Norman control of the economic centres of power in the region and bolstered d'Oilly's hegemony over it. It is significant that towards

35 Edburton Hill, Sussex, an aerial view looking east to Devil's Dyke. In the foreground is the outline of a motte and bailey, one of hundreds of similar castle earthworks in Britain for which no documentary record survives. The silence of the records implies that these castles were the creations of relatively modest figures and were both founded and abandoned before the late twelfth century, when administrative documentation begins to survive in quantity. This particular motte and bailey may be the predecessor of the later Edburton Castle, at nearby Perching, whose fortifications were licensed by the king in 1268 and again in 1329.

the end of his life d'Oilly also became a patron of Abingdon Abbey, the principal monastic foundation in his sphere of power. His generosity to this foundation was apparently encouraged in part by guilt for earlier exploitation of the church. According to the anonymous chronicler of the abbey, his change of heart was brought about by a vivid nightmare in which he was condemned by the Virgin for his rapacious greed and tortured by youths.[24]

D'Oilly's work at Oxford (and indirectly at Walling-ford) is likely to have been underwritten in political terms by his appointment as sheriff of the counties of both Oxfordshire and Berkshire. To the sheriff fell the administration of royal lands in a particular shire, as well as deputed royal authority in certain judicial matters. For an individual with a concentration of land-holdings in a shire or region, therefore, this office materially complemented his position.[25] As a result of the immense power they wielded, sheriffs commonly attracted remarkable quantities of vitriolic and colourful condemnation in the pages of chronicles. Almost without exception, the seat of the sheriff was the royal castle in the county town of the shire. This, for example, was to be the case with the castle founded by d'Oilly at Oxford, which henceforth served as the seat of the sheriff of Oxfordshire. Over the Middle Ages the role of the sheriff was to change considerably, but the office remained a crowning mark of regional power.

The overall rate of castle construction in England during William the Conqueror's reign is very difficult to gauge. In documentary terms, the celebrated Domesday survey of 1086 is a treacherous source, generally mentioning castles only if their foundation affected the income from land in some way. As a reflection of this, just forty-eight castles are referred to in this voluminous and detailed work, most of them incidentally.[26] To this list, modern scholars have added a further forty sites mentioned in documentary sources prior to about 1100, and ten more in Wales. Yet there are good reasons for supposing that these figures represent only a fraction of the total number constructed. Spread across England are hundreds of earthworks that have been identified as castles but for which absolutely no documentary or dating evidence exists at all. It is a reasonable presumption that most of these were created prior to 1200: not only do they compare in physical form to documented earthworks of this date but a functioning castle was unlikely to escape documentary mention past this time. If this pre-1200 dating is allowed, it is further likely that numbers of these buildings belong to the immediate post-Conquest period. The statistics are little more than educated guesswork, but they are startling.

Prior to 1200 it has been estimated that there were established between 950 and 1,150 castles across the country, though not all of them were necessarily occupied at the same time. Of these upwards of 500 were perhaps founded in the decade after 1066.[27] The hundred or so for which we have documentary evidence are generally the largest of these. As regards the more modest and undocumented majority, most were presumably fortified in timber. Very few have been excavated, however, and in most cases we know nothing more of their physical appearance than what their surviving earthworks tell us (pl. 35). These make it clear that despite a huge variety in scale and plan, all incorporate two essential forms either in isolation or combination, the bailey and the motte. Quite who

was founding these remains a mystery, but clearly the castle-building class was much larger than the tiny group of magnates in the immediate circle of the Conqueror. It was perfectly possible, in other words, even for relatively modest landholders to erect and maintain a castle. An example of how such a system operated is vividly illustrated in the case of Richmond, which will be discussed at the end of this chapter.

Precisely mirroring and complementing this process of castle foundation was a huge reorganisation of the church. Two aspects of this deserve particular attention. First, new castleries nearly always spawned some kind of religious foundation. This was often endowed out of the castlery lands, rendering to the castle spiritual dues, just as the other fees within it rendered temporal ones. Second, in the decades following the Conquest there was a systematic movement of cathedral churches to centres of population. For example, the cathedral within what is now the village at Dorchester on Thames, Oxfordshire, was moved to Lincoln between 1072 and 1075.[28] Over time, these changes were to create a coherent system of royal and church government rooted in centres of population and trade; in short, it was to lay the foundations for the administration of the Anglo-Norman kingdom of England. One notable exception to this rule was the construction of a cathedral and royal castle within the Iron Age fort at Old Sarum in Wiltshire. Without sufficient strengths as a civic centre, this foundation failed later in the Middle Ages, and modern Salisbury was established nearby as its successor city in the thirteenth century.

CASTLE ARCHITECTURE AND THE ROMANESQUE STYLE

Trying to piece together an impression of the development of early castle architecture is severely hampered by lack of physical evidence. The vast majority of castle buildings and fortifications in this period were constructed of timber, and practically nothing of these remains to the present day. Moreover, even among stone buildings, surviving eleventh-century structures are far and few between. To compound the difficulties, very few castle sites of this period are documented or have undergone systematic archaeological excavation. Yet the disappearance of so much should not be taken as evidence that these buildings were insubstantial or rudimentary. If the fragmentary remains make anything clear at all, it is that major English castles were conceived of from the first on a truly remarkable scale. Moreover, that by the death of William the Conqueror in 1087 there already existed virtually the complete repertoire of forms that were to serve as the basis for the development of English castle architecture over the next six centuries.

It is common in surveys of castle architecture in the immediate post-Conquest period to distinguish between buildings constructed entirely of wood and those substantially of stone. This distinction was first drawn in the late nineteenth century because it was presumed that timber structures were necessarily less important than their masonry counterparts; and, ironically, it remains as firmly established today even though this view has been so conclusively refuted.[29] As will become apparent, the wide availability of good timber in most areas of the kingdom ensured its widespread use in every sphere of architectural design into the seventeenth century. This resource also sustained a remarkable late medieval exploration in England of the structural and decorative possibilities of timber framing. Nevertheless, to treat buildings in these materials as discrete subjects distracts attention from more important points of similarity.

In the eleventh century wood and masonry were employed both singly and in combination in the creation of castles. They were used to fabricate domestic buildings as well as to articulate and dress earth, which in the form of hills, ditches and mounds properly constituted the fundamental material of most early fortification. Indeed, perhaps more than any other kind of architecture, castles of this period are substantially furnished works of landscaping. As a result, an understanding of both materials is complementary: some impression of lost timber fortifications can be built up from surviving stone structures; and the understanding of stone architecture can in some points be enriched with reference to the probable form of lost timber buildings. Yet for all the comparisons between them, it is important not to lose sight of the special status of stone.

In the eleventh century stone was a highly prestigious material, imbued with particular appeal and associations. In part this was because of its permanence and the difficulties involved in fashioning buildings from such an unyielding substance. For these reasons it was the most appropriate medium for church architecture, buildings designed in the service of God and proportioned in evocation of His creation. In the context of fortifications stone also had the advantageous qualities of strength and resistance to fire. But regardless of their particular function, all stone buildings of this period carried with them something quite as important as any of these qualities: the prestige of Rome. The physical vestiges of Roman imperial power were commoner and more self-evidently impressive in the eleventh-century world than they are today. In structural terms alone, the greatest were far beyond the technical capacity of eleventh-century masons; for example, it was not until the construction of Amiens Cathedral in the 1220s that western Europe had an interior that could compete in height with the Pantheon in Rome, rebuilt in its present form by the Emperor Hadrian (reigned AD 117–38). And there were many potential patrons of architecture in post-Conquest England, notably churchmen, who had seen Rome.

Such considerations aside, the Roman past also obtruded itself in countless ways within the English landscape and, a handful of great churches aside, probably provided its most prominent architectural features. It is in reflection of this that the Norman army landed beside the fort at Pevensey, still doubtless a major landmark on the coast, and that such great cities as London, Winchester and York were still embraced by their late antique fortifications. Inextricably associated with these remains was the imperial political order that had created them, one that rulers across Europe in this period actively sought to emulate. Linked to this was the power and authority of St Peter and his successors, the popes.

As the Conquest gradually became more secure, therefore, it is no surprise that patrons began increasingly to build in stone. Also, that the style of this architecture was sub-classical, just as that of the Anglo-Saxons had been. But the so-called Romanesque style of the Normans was much more structurally ambitious than its predecessor. It also looked different to contemporaries: according to one witness of the post-Conquest construction boom, the churches everywhere were 'going up in a new manner of building'.[30] This visual novelty was almost certainly a reflection of its scale, its initial austerity (relative to Anglo-Saxon building, which often appears to have been encrusted with sculpture) and an interest in the regular articulation of walls with buttresses and windows. The creation of vaults in stone was probably also a complete novelty in England.

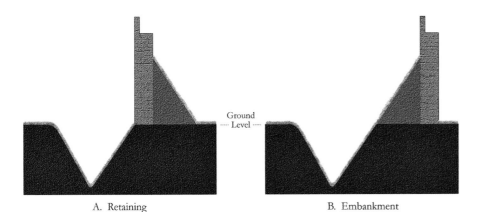

Ground
---- Level ----

A. Retaining   B. Embankment

36 Earthworks could be retained or embanked to create formidable fortifications. In the former system (A), spoil was thrown behind a retaining structure such as a wall on the inside edge of a ditch. This created a ditch with a sheer face rising behind it. By the latter system (B), earth was banked up along the edge of the ditch to make the inner slope much longer than the outer. Both baileys and mottes were created using one or other system of construction by respectively digging in a line or in the round.

Lastly, and as a factor of their monumentality, many Romanesque buildings in stone incorporated passages in the depths of the walls. This type of architectural treatment appears simultaneously in church and castle architecture around the year 1000, as may be seen in the abbey church of Notre-Dame at Bernay, Normandy (begun around 1017), and the great tower at Loches (under construction between 1012 and *circa* 1035). Particularly in castle buildings, such passages can lace the fabric in unexpected ways, as if they were quarried through the walls by some monstrous beetle grub.

Norman architecture also differed from its Anglo-Saxon predecessor in one important technical sense. Masons in the late eleventh century developed the ability to cut stone from its beds in vast quantities and finish it with beautiful exactitude. At Durham Cathedral priory, for example, which was begun in 1093, the different courses of stone run at a constant depth round the walls of the entire building, each one comprising thousands of blocks of masonry cut to a constant height. By any standards, this represents a labour-intensive operation of almost unimaginable magnitude and rigour.[31] It was also hugely expensive and the fact that there was money to pay for it speaks of a remarkable enthusiasm for architecture amongst the new rulers of England.

In all artistic endeavours including architecture, resources were focused on ecclesiastical commissions. As a result, viewed beside many great churches of the period, surviving stone castle buildings can seem rather disappointing in technical terms: for the most part they are composed of rubble masonry and are heavily proportioned. Nevertheless, these were much admired by contemporaries and must have been quite as costly to erect.

Ditches, Banks and Mottes

All castle earthworks in this period are basically variant forms of ditching; that is to say, digging a hole and piling up the spoil. In these terms, bailey enclosures can be understood as examples of linear ditching and mottes as ditching in the round. Statistics of height, breadth and depth do no justice to the reality of big castle earthworks from this period. Even today, after long periods of neglect and slumping, they can still be treacherous to climb. The man hours involved in raising such structures must have been enormous. At a site such as Pleshey in Essex, it has been roughly calculated that the motte alone would have taken one man 24,000 days to raise. And this figure takes no account of the massive bailey earthworks and the fortifications of a large borough or town established beside the castle.[32]

Broadly speaking, earthworks of this period were either retained or embanked (pl. 36). The earth surfaces of the ditch in either kind of construction could be strengthened in a huge variety of ways. Amongst those were the practices of consolidating the surface with turves, rubble or planks of wood. Where a particular site favoured the creation of a moat, clay might also be imported and the ditch lined to hold water.

It is as complements to such earthworks that timber and stone fortifications were constructed. In the case of stone building, the weight of the material made it a practical necessity to build up the wall from natural ground level. As a result, walls were commonly constructed along the firm inside edge of the ditch and used as retaining structures, holding back a weight of earth. This is the case at Richmond (Yorkshire), Rochester (Kent) and Hastings (Sussex), where the huge curtain walls retain a bailey with an artificially high ground level. All these examples, which were probably begun in the 1080s, are massively conceived with walls between 10 and 15 feet (3–4.5 m) thick. This depth was no doubt partly intended for strength, but it also served the practical purpose of making the top of the wall broad enough to serve as a walk. This could then be protected along its outer face by a battlemented parapet and function as a fighting top. In every particular, such retaining designs can be paralleled in Roman fort architecture, for example at Pevensey.

But stone walls are occasionally found in embanked structures as well. Such is the case, for example, at

Tickhill in Yorkshire, probably founded in the 1070s. Here, the high enclosure wall of the bailey is so heavily embanked on the exterior that only a few feet stand clear of the earthwork. Again, the wall is massively thick. The embankment of this wall almost certainly illustrates the form of a standard type of timber fortification. By treating the inner bank as the foundation for a crowning structure lightly constructed in wood, it would have been possible to fashion a high wall-walk along the crown of an earthwork without the need for substantial pieces of timber. Several early castles have huge banks that suggest treatment of the kind, for example, parts of the bailey at Castle Acre (Norfolk) and Exeter (Devon). In such cases timber piles could also have been driven down into the embankment to support the earthwork. By the thirteenth century such fortifications of timber were apparently being variously referred to as *bretasches* or *garrols*, though there is no clear consistency of terminology.[33]

Mottes all appear today to be embanked structures, but some might originally have been retained. Such treatment would have transformed their familiar profile: rather than appearing as mounds with sloping sides, they would have taken the form of huge, straight-sided barrels stepping up from the ground. The only substantial excavated site of this kind is the mid-twelfth-century castle at South Mimms in Hertfordshire, which had a motte retained with timber.[34] Whether retained or embanked, it is assumed that every motte was also crowned by some kind of defensive structure. Besides the depictions found on the Bayeux Tapestry we have little evidence for what these might have looked like in eleventh-century England. In all the tapestry depictions, mottes appear to be crowned either singly or in combination with a perimeter wall and a central tower. As we shall see, this combination also occurs in later buildings. For the present, it suffices to say that the perimeter defence could well have closely imitated the timber structures that fortified embanked ditches. Of the form of central towers on mottes, something may perhaps be deduced from other surviving stone structures of the period.

Wall and Gate Towers

Setting aside *donjons* – that is to say mottes and their stone counterparts, great towers – there is little evidence to suppose that first-generation castles in England possessed numerous towers. Such as were

built stood along the line of a fortification, either to command a wall or a gateway. Moreover, in every case these towers were rectilinear in plan. In the context of wall towers this is curious because Roman precedents for this form, as at Reculver in Kent, are relatively unusual. Roman forts in England generally made use of circular and polygonal designs: the fort at Pevensey (Sussex), for example, preserves solid D-shaped towers; Burgh (Norfolk) solid circular towers; Portchester (Hampshire) hollow D-shaped towers; Cardiff (Glamorgan) solid polygonal towers; and Caerwent (Monmouthshire) hollow polygonal towers. Since eleventh-century masons were quite capable of building in all these shapes, this divergence of form cannot be explained as a reflection of technical incapacity. An alternative possibility is that surviving stone towers were actually following the example of their lost timber counterparts. These would most obviously be built using four upright timbers on a rectilinear plan.

Setting aside the case of Oxford discussed above, only three castle sites preserve remains of wall towers that might convincingly – though not with absolute security – be attributed to the Conqueror's reign. At Hastings there survives a single tower that possibly served as a belfry to an adjacent chapel (pl. 37). Richmond and Ludlow, meanwhile, each preserve several towers within the circuit of a substantial stone-built bailey wall. The two designs form an interesting architectural contrast. At Ludlow the towers appear in plan as crinkles in the line of the wall with only three stone faces and no internal vaults. In these cases, the fourth face of each tower must have been constructed of timber or have opened into buildings within the bailey (pl. 38). At Richmond, meanwhile, each tower is a coherent structure with four, enclosing stone walls. In at least one case, the interior was also barrel-vaulted on two levels (pl. 39).

Curiously, it is the form of the Ludlow towers – the crinkle design – that was to become popular in English architecture, and Richmond, in the light of hindsight, looks eccentric. Nevertheless, all these towers (and also the tower at Hastings) share one interesting point of comparison: in every case, one or more passages pierce the depth of the walls around them. This distinctive feature of Romanesque architecture, which we shall return to, is also paralleled in church and great tower design.

It is amongst surviving gate towers that some of the richest architectural ornament in the castle architecture of the Conqueror's reign is to be found. Given

that such structures appear to have been a defining feature of the Anglo-Saxon thegn's house, or *burhgeat*, it is likely that this reflects a conscious attempt to appropriate the prestige of English architectural forms within the Norman tradition of castle design. The handful of surviving gatehouses from the period is remarkably varied. Richmond has a gate passage flanked by a tower and contrived within the lower storey of a hall block (see pl. 46). At Tickhill there is a much-altered gate tower of low and broad proportions set deeply within the earthwork enclosure of the castle. With its triple gable, it is just possible that this building is meant to imitate the forms of Roman triumphal arches. Between the gables are the mouths of drains, each ornamented with a figure. These are positioned in such a way that, when water pours through, each is unmistakeably intended to represent a man urinating. Most impressive, however, are the tall and massively conceived gate towers at Exeter, Bramber and Ludlow. These have no clear Roman precedent or contemporary French parallel, and their scale suggests a conscious evocation of the grandest architectural form of the period: the great tower.

The Great Tower

Undoubtedly the most prestigious type of castle structure in eleventh-century England was the great tower built of stone. In Normandy prior to the Conquest, such buildings had been the preserve of the ducal family, and their exclusivity persisted during William's reign in England: of the three that can securely be identified as having been begun before his death in 1089 only one – that already discussed at Chepstow – may not have been built by the king. Yet regardless of its precise attribution, Chepstow is really a building of secondary importance in the grand narrative of great tower architecture in England. Quite different from it in physical terms are its two great counterparts: the great tower at Colchester (pl. 40) and the celebrated White Tower at London (pl. 41). In this magnificent pair of buildings are to be found in fundamental terms explanation for the whole future tradition of great tower architecture in England.

Only the White Tower at London is documented to any useful degree in the eleventh century.[35] Sometime after 1077 William the Conqueror placed a certain Gundulf – a cleric trained in Rouen with an expertise in building and the bishop of Rochester – in charge of

37 The eleventh-century tower at Hastings, Sussex, viewed from the interior of the castle. It may have served as the belfry for the castle chapel, the thirteenth-century chancel arch of which is visible in the distance. The tower is built up against the outer wall, which is pierced by a wall passage at this point. Towers of this period are commonly rectangular in plan. This may be a borrowing from timber buildings, which might naturally be erected with four angle posts.

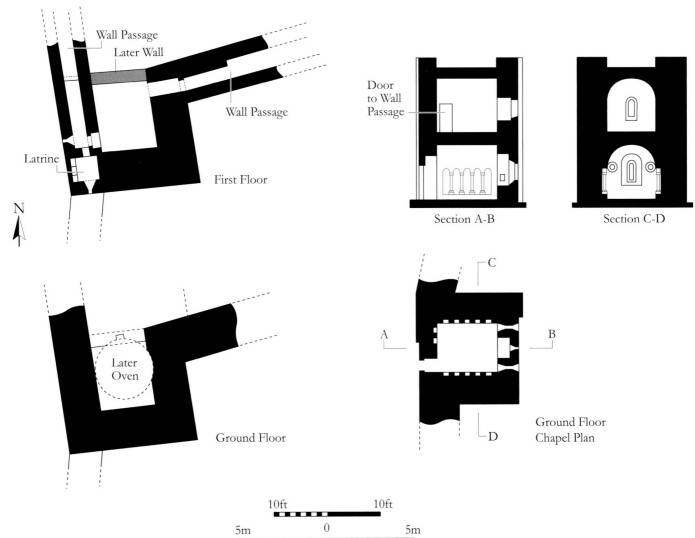

Wall Passage
Later Wall
Wall Passage
Latrine
First Floor

N

Door to Wall Passage

Section A-B

Section C-D

C

A

B

D

Later Oven

Ground Floor

Ground Floor Chapel Plan

10ft   10ft
5m   0   5m

38 (*facing page, top*)   Ludlow, Shropshire. The inner bailey of the castle may have been fortified in stone as early as the 1080s. This early dating is partly suggested by the architectural detailing of the great tower (originally the gatehouse – the ghosted outline of its blocked entrance arch is still faintly visible). To the left is one of the eleventh-century towers that punctuate the line of the early wall (see pl. 39). Stone for all the buildings was probably quarried from the ditches of the castle, which were straight-sided and in places about 80 feet (25 m) wide.

39 (*facing page, bottom*) The eleventh-century wall towers at Ludlow, Shropshire (left), and Richmond, Yorkshire (right), illustrate two traditions of tower design in English architecture. At Ludlow the tower is created – in effect – by crinkling the line of the wall outwards on a rectilinear plan to create a three-sided structure. The fourth, inner side was later infilled with masonry but, when first built, was presumably closed in with timber. There are wall passages in the structure. At Richmond the towers are coherent structures with four walls and incorporate barrel vaults. The lower floor of the tower shown here contains the chapel and preserves decorative wall arcades. Notice that the first floor was accessed through a side door entered down a passage in the thickness of the wall. A grant of the chapel in the castle made in 1088 or 1089 can reasonably be assumed to date the Richmond tower.

constructing a great tower in London.[36] Of the two castles already established within the Roman walls of London, that chosen for this architectural dignity stood on the Thames foreshore at the eastern fringe of the city and commanded its river approach. Recent dendrochronological dating of structural timbers from the Tower suggests that it was under way by 1081 and completed by the Conqueror's son, Henry I, around 1100. It quickly became a symbol of royal power in London and was famously described in the 1170s as 'a fortress, palatine, massive and strong, its walls and its floors rising from the deepest foundations and its mortar tempered with the blood of animals'.[37] That the tower at Colchester was begun by William the Conqueror is inferred from a charter issued by Henry I in 1101 by which Eudo the Steward was granted 'the city of Colchester and the tower and castle and all the fortifications of the city, as my father had them and my brother and myself'. No further details of the purpose or date of the tower are provided.[38]

In their present form the two buildings in some ways look quite different. The White Tower is constructed from a mixture of cut stone and rubble masonry, much of the former being imported from the stone quarries at Caen in Normandy. By contrast, Colchester is a low, broad tower in a curious piebald mix of stone and reused Roman brick. Its odd and stunted proportions are the result of demolition work undertaken in the seventeenth century, when the upper floors were blown up with gunpowder. This loss has made some details of the original design a matter of controversy. As will become apparent, however, there is good reason for supposing that Colchester broadly followed the White Tower in its conception. Amongst other things, this probably means that it was intended to rise likewise to a height of four storeys. The ground plan of Colchester is the largest of any great tower in Europe, an astonishing 110 feet by 151 feet 6 inches (33.5 by 46.2 m), while the London Tower, though still remarkably big, covers only 97 by 118 feet (29.6 by 36 m).

Despite such differences, the evidence for the close architectural relationship of the two buildings is clear. Both are rectangular in plan and outline, with massive walls and projecting turrets in every corner. It should be emphasised that in post-Conquest England nothing of this form or scale had ever been seen before in the realm of secular architecture. Within the upper storeys of both buildings were incorporated complex systems of passages and small rooms. This distinctive interest

in lacing thick walls with chambers is paralleled in great church design. The interiors of both buildings were also originally divided internally by cross or spine walls that rose through the full height of the tower. Spine walls are a common feature of English great towers into the seventeenth century. The White Tower possesses one such spine wall, but Colchester originally contained two in reflection of its outstanding size. What most clearly connects these buildings, however, and distinguishes them from every other subsequent English building of this type, is the large semicircular projection or apse in the same relative position within the plan. In both cases this accommodated a tall, stone-vaulted chapel set over a crypt.

Before discussing the two towers further it is important to acknowledge a problem inherent in the analysis of all great architectural projects in the absence of basic documentary information. Precisely because of their scale, such buildings are more likely than any others to be erected over a long period of time and undergo changes of plan during the course of construction. In the absence of drawn designs or other evidence, the only means of pinpointing changes of plan is to identify inconsistencies within the fabric. Yet the harder you look, the more inconsistencies you are likely to find. These can range from the relatively obvious, such as abrupt changes in carved detail and stone type, to the subtleties of the mortar composition that binds the masonry together. In either case, it can never be more than a matter of informed judgement which inconsistencies are incidental and which important: whether, for example, the appearance of a new stone type in a building marks a break in construction and design or simply the opening of a new quarry in a continuous and planned operation.

As a result, both these towers could reasonably be presented as muddled architectural projects. The protracted construction of the White Tower between around 1070 and 1100, for example, does raise the possibility that the completed building may have differed materially from the original design of 1070. That this possibility should be taken seriously is suggested by the tower at Colchester, which appears to be the product of at least two undated periods of building. At second-storey level, for example, there are clearly preserved within the walls the fossilised remains of battlements. This raises the question whether the building was actually begun as a tower at all or as a low, walled enclosure. To my mind, there is a powerful reason in their close similarity for supposing that both towers were

Ground Floor

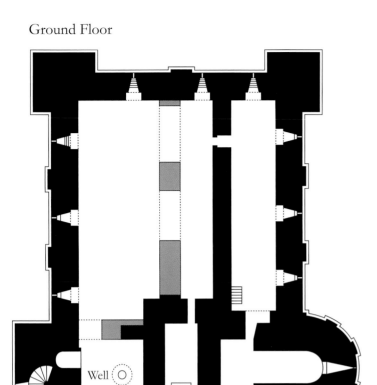

Well ○

First Floor

20ft   20ft

10m   0   10m

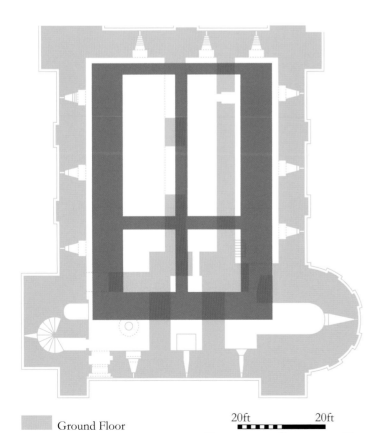

Ground Floor
Roman Foundations

20ft   20ft

10m   0   10m

probably completed much as designed. Not everyone would agree, however, and this in turn is a reflection of the varied opinions that have been expressed about the architectural sources for these great towers.

Broadly speaking, three suggestions have been put forward to explain the unusual size of these two buildings and their curious plans with projecting apses. The first is that they were an architectural response to the particular circumstances of the Conquest. In order to protect himself more effectively from his subjects, it is argued, William the Conqueror played with compressing all the chambers for grand domestic living into single, massively conceived stone towers. It was the need to incorporate an appropriately grand royal chapel within a constricted plan that determined the distinctive design with a projecting apse. Explained in these terms, Colchester can be treated as a gawky experiment and the White Tower as a polished and perfected architectural follower of it. The idea on which this analysis is predicated – that these great towers can be understood as complete residences – has proved hugely influential in the modern discussion and presentation of related buildings.

A more beguiling explanation for the two towers was put forward after excavations at Colchester in 1977. In 1920 it had been shown that the great tower actually enclosed the foundation platform of the Roman Temple of Claudius, a feature that explained the extraordinary size of the ground plan. It was now further revealed that the chapel apse might also stand on the foundation of a Roman predecessor, a circumstance that provided a convincing genesis for the whole design. Added to which, it made the architecture of the building almost iconographic: the tower could be seen as an attempt by the Conqueror to appropriate the Roman past and to present himself as a modern emperor. On this analysis, Colchester again was likely to be the architectural leader and London the follower.[39]

The third explanation for these towers until the 1990s sounded rather thin for lack of evidence. According to this, both buildings were modelled on lost Continental prototypes, the most likely source being the great tower in the ducal city of Rouen in Normandy. One circumstantial point in favour of this association was that the Rouen tower stood in the same relative position – beside the River Seine against the city defences – as the White Tower in London. The tower at Rouen was demolished in the thirteenth century and its plan is probably irrevocably lost, but the fact that Continental buildings unquestionably did influ-

ence these designs has now been demonstrated in the most compelling terms.

An excavation of a castle at Ivry-la-Bataille in Normandy from 1967 to 1982 revealed the remains of a building not only with a plan of the same general form as Colchester and the White Tower, but also with very similar internal dimensions to the latter (pl. 42). Even more importantly, while the plan of Ivry was actually the creation of two building campaigns, the full design appears to have been complete by 1040 at the latest.[40] In other words, it stood complete as a possible source for the English buildings at the time of the Conquest.

Assuming that such close similarities with Ivry cannot be a matter of chance, it seems reasonable to assume that these English buildings are copied from Norman models. What is not clear, however, is whether Ivry is the specific structure that the London and Colchester towers imitate or whether all three structures follow the example of the lost tower at Rouen. On the face of it, it would make sense if they did. Certainly, it would be very appropriate if all these buildings followed the architectural example of the building that symbolised the power of the dukes of Normandy. Whatever the case, viewing the three surviving towers together clears up at least one point about their relationship: Colchester is clearly revealed as the odd building out in the series, not the source for the distinctive design they share. This in turn helps identify the Tower of London as the crucial building in the future development of great tower architecture in England.

Some idea of the prestige of Ivry – and indeed the whole genre of great tower architecture – is shown by a colourful tale in circulation around 1100 regarding its construction by a woman called Albereda, wife of the count of Bayeux. Orderic Vitalis speaks of this 'famous tower, huge and immensely strong' as follows:

The story goes that a noble lady had as an architect (*architectus*) Lanfred, who was then famous above all other artisans in France for his skill, and after his construction of the tower of Pithiviers had been appointed as master of works; and that after she had completed the castle (*arcem*) of Ivry with great toil and expense she had had him executed so that he could never design a work like it anywhere else. Afterwards she herself was slain by her own husband on account of that very same castle (*munitione*), because she had attempted to expel him from it. So the fickle wheel of fortune turns each day and the state of the world is subject to many changes.[41]

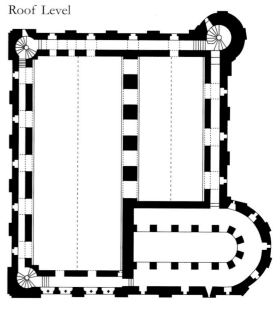

Roof Level

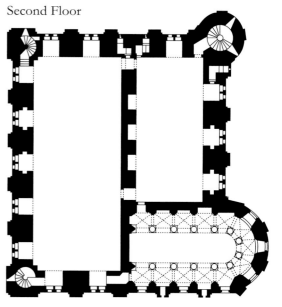

Second Floor

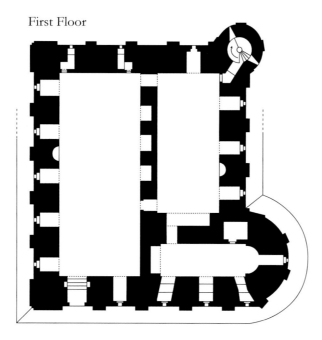

First Floor

20ft   20ft

10m   0   10m

N

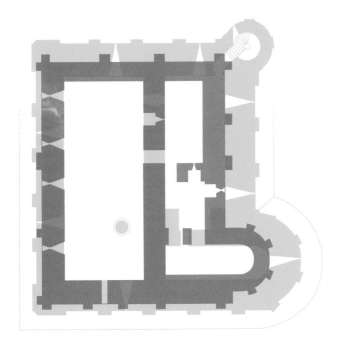

41 (*facing page*) The White Tower, London, a photograph of 2020 and a plan. The tower was under construction by 1081 and completed after 1102. When it was begun, no building on this scale had ever been seen before in the secular sphere in England. It was designed on a rectangular plan and rose four storeys high, its exterior divided by regular buttresses. A chapel block projected from one corner, its position expressed on the exterior by the curving apse. All the levels of the building were connected by a spiral stair in the circular north-east corner turret. The tower comprised three floors, with the roof of the upper floor countersunk within the parapet level. Its interior was divided by a spine wall, which was pierced or decorated with arches on the upper levels. The present roofs on the corner turrets are Tudor, but they replace earlier structures and may represent an intended feature of the original design.

42 The great tower of Ivry-la-Bataille, Normandy, was reputedly built by the 'architect' Lanfred around 990–1011 for Albereda, wife of the count of Bayeux, who murdered him for his trouble. The full plan of this great tower developed in two stages, but was probably complete by 1040. In its final form, the reversed plan (blue) closely resembles that of the Tower of London (red) both in outline and dimensions. It was demolished in 1449 during the Hundred Years War. The evidence of Ivry makes it certain that the English tradition of great tower architecture derives from Norman example. It also raises the possibility that both Ivry and the Tower of London were modelled on the principal building of this kind in Normandy, the lost great tower of the dukes of Normandy at Rouen.

N

Basement, The White Tower, London

The Great Tower of Ivry la Bataille, Normandy

N

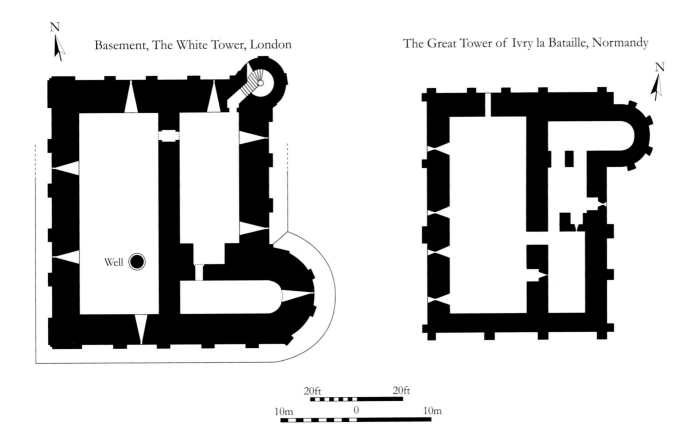

Well

Whatever its truth, one detail of the narrative merits particular attention. In his entire history, Orderic Vitalis uses the word *architectus* only twice: once to describe the unfortunate Lanfred and once to describe God as the creator of the universe. There could be no more eloquent testimony to the admiration in which these buildings were held by contemporaries.

DURHAM AND THE NORTH
OF ENGLAND

Having tried to set the development of castles in this period in context, it is now worthwhile to tell the story of a particular experience of Norman rule. Until 1068 William the Conqueror had been happy to leave the earldom of Northumbria, with its complex internal politics, to its own devices. In that time, two earls had been murdered and a third, Cospatric, had revolted. William responded by appointing a Norman, a certain Robert Cumin, to the earldom. It was not a happy experiment. According to the monk chronicler Symeon of Durham, writing shortly after 1104, Cumin arrived in Durham on 30 January 1069 at the head of 700 men. The Norman earl and his followers had pillaged the countryside on the way north and the Northumbrians gathered outside the town to have their revenge. At first light they rushed through the gates and slaughtered the earl's men, leaving the streets piled with bodies and running in blood. The earl himself was lodging beside the cathedral in the bishop's residence and tried to defend himself. But the house he occupied was set alight. 'Some of those who were inside were burned to death, others rushed out through the doors and were at once cut down. Thus was the earl killed on 31st January with all his men, apart from one who escaped wounded.'[42]

The rival earl of Northumbria, Cospatric, who was somehow implicated in this gruesome episode, now joined forces with a wider rebellion, the most serious of William's reign. The rebel forces, swelled by a Scandinavian army, met at York in September 1069 and the Norman castle garrison there, which had been planted in the city less than a year earlier, sallied out to attack it. They were killed virtually to a man and the castle torn down. These events set the scene for widespread disturbances right across the kingdom, which took some months to suppress. But when the campaigning was over there was a notorious reprisal. Over the winter of 1069–70 William laid waste to the north of England in a calculated act of destruction (familiar today as the Harrying of the North) that shocked even eleventh-century observers. In January 1070 Earl Cospatric submitted to William, though he was cautious not to appear in person. His submission received, Cospatric began his own tour of destruction, amongst other things sacking the cathedral church at Durham after having advised the bishop and community to flee. The unfortunate bishop then tried to leave the kingdom. By 1071, however, he had mysteriously arrived at the Isle of Ely instead, where he was captured in the company of the celebrated resistance fighter Hereward the Wake.[43]

In the aftermath of these events, William was left with an opportunity to rethink his whole policy as regards the north of England. There were three political regions that needed his attention and these corresponded in very rough terms to modern-day Yorkshire, Co. Durham and Northumberland combined with the lowlands of Scotland. Only the first of these was clearly part of the kingdom of England. Since it lay prone from William's ferocious policy of destruction, Yorkshire was a relatively easy prey to political reorganisation. York, one of the wealthiest cities in the kingdom, was provided with a second castle to create a remarkable fortified complex on the south side of the city. When completed, the two mottes of these castles stood to either side of the River Ouse. Connecting them and partially enclosing what later developed as the principal of the castles was an artificial lake or mere.

At the same time, the wider countryside was broken down into a series of huge castleries, though the speed at which this occurred is difficult to establish. To protect against Scandinavian incursions, William granted a certain Drogo de Breuvrière lordship of the Holderness peninsula. Drogo is reputed to have founded Skipsea Castle, which today survives as a huge motte set within the remains of an extensive mere. He later fled from this rich possession after murdering his wife, a relative of the Conqueror.[44] At about the same period geographically compact honours were constituted to support the Yorkshire castles of Richmond (more of which below), Tickhill and Pontefract. According to some authorities, the last of these received its name from a 'broken bridge' that delayed William's forces for several days during the winter campaign of 1069 (pl. 43).[45] On the western seaboard, new castleries were also developing as a result of a grant in 1070 to Roger, the new earl of Shrewsbury, of all the land between the rivers Ribble and Mersey. By the time of Domesday an

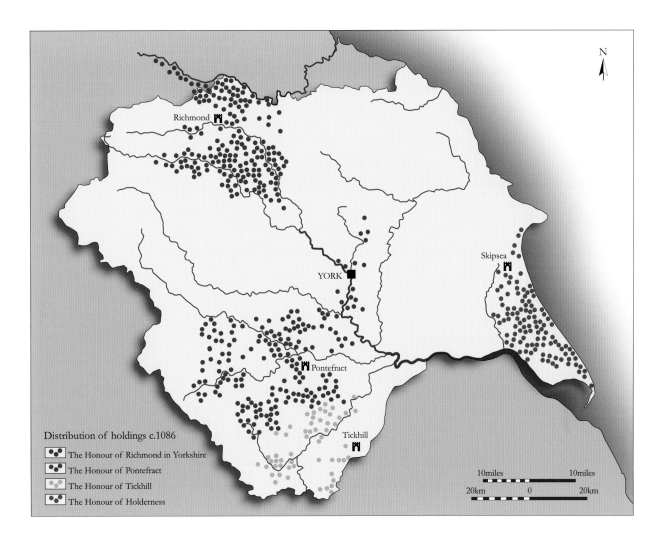

43 The four great compact honours created across Yorkshire in the 1070s: Pontefract, Richmond, Holderness and Tickhill. Every dot represents a landholding. In each case, the castle supported by these honours was placed in a convenient and central position for the administration of the associated estate. The honour of Richmond also possessed land much further afield than Yorkshire and remained one of the richest prizes of English dynastic politics into the sixteenth century. After P. Dalton, *Conquest, Anarchy and Lordship: Yorkshire, 1066–1154* (Cambridge, 1994).

honour had been established as far north as Cockermouth. All these new castles were associated with a borough and some kind of religious foundation.

But the association of the areas north of Yorkshire with William's realm was far from established. Indeed, it may be because they were believed to be beyond the bounds of the kingdom that they were excluded from the Domesday survey. Yet peripheral or not to England, the region had powerful claims on William's attention. This was true in a practical sense because the boundary with Scotland needed to be resolved. But there was another point of interest that was quite as important. Northumbria had been one of the cradles of European Christian culture in the seventh and eighth centuries, and its affairs in this period had been celebrated by the saint and father of English history, the Venerable Bede. Completed in 731, Bede's single greatest work was *The Ecclesiastical History of the English People*, which offered a compelling account of the conversion of England by a heroic cast of saints and kings. As the title suggests, his writings articulated

a sense of common English identity. They also gave Northumbria and its Anglo-Saxon monasteries a place in the European consciousness. As events were to prove, Bede's history was familiar reading for many men in post-Conquest England, both secular and clerical, who saw in his work the portrait of a golden age of English piety, culture and achievement.

The greatest of the Northumbrian saints described by Bede was Cuthbert, bishop of Lindisfarne (d. 687). Cuthbert was an important figure in his own lifetime, but circumstances extended the force of his personality beyond his death. The writings of Bede and other admirers lent his personal history a remarkable depth and authority. Even more important, his corpse remained fresh and incorrupt, imbuing his cult with startling immediacy. From the ninth century onwards the declining kingdom of Northumbria found in Cuthbert and his body a political anchor and there developed within it two related geographical spheres of influence. North of the River Tees, as far as fighting could secure it, stretched the power of the earl of Northumbria. His principal seat was at Bamburgh, a short sail from St Cuthbert's island bishopric at Lindisfarne. This dramatic outcrop of granite had been first fortified in 547 and on purely textual evidence it might be deemed another interesting contender for the title of an Anglo-Saxon castle.[46] South of the Tees to Yorkshire there extended St Cuthbert's own domain focused on Durham, the site where his body had lain since 995. This large area was under the earl's authority, but it was complemented by that of the bishop and his monastic community. By the twelfth century it was named, and its population termed, 'The Saint's People' or *Haliwerfolc.*

William the Conqueror's first direct intervention in Northumbria was the appointment of a new bishop of Durham. In 1071 he invited a cleric from Liège called Walcher to fill the office. Walcher was a Lotharingian by origin and, at the time of his consecration, a venerable figure with rosy features and a full crop of white hair.[47] He was installed at Durham by Earl Cospatric during Lent 1071. A full year later William himself marched north to deal with the problem of the Scottish border. He advanced up the coast, his army supported by a fleet of ships, and Malcolm, king of Scotland, paid homage to the English king without a fight. Apparently the only castle built on the campaign was erected on the return route for the protection of his bishop when William passed through Durham.[48] This dearth of campaign castles and the failure of Walcher to begin a castle at Durham the previous year are both interesting reminders that the construction of these buildings was not an automatic reflex for the Normans. As a symbol of its close relationship with Cuthbert, the key of the castle was hung in the later Middle Ages above his shrine.[49]

Durham stands on a naturally defensible peninsula of land created by a tight loop in the River Wear (pl. 44). This peninsula was probably fortified from its first occupation around 995. Certainly, an unsuccessful siege by the Scots in 1006 culminated in the heads of St Cuthbert's vanquished enemies being washed by women and set on poles along the walls.[50] William's new castle appears to have been built just within the line of these early defences, closing the natural circuit of protection offered by the deep cut of the encircling river. There seems no reason to doubt that the position and basic form of the present building, which comprises a bailey and high motte, were established in 1072. Moreover, it seems likely that the first fortifications were of timber, since they were erected with suf-

ficient speed to withstand a siege in 1075. But almost from the first there must have been the determination to build in stone because – as will be discussed in the next chapter – less than twenty years later the castle seems to have boasted a complete circuit of masonry walls and several substantial buildings in the same material. Remarkably, remains of two of the latter still survive.

To the west of the bailey was erected a gigantic stone hall block, one of the largest ever constructed in England. The hall within this building was set on first-floor level and was completely rebuilt in later centuries. Parts of the undercroft on which it stood, however, survive and give a sense of its former proportions. The second eleventh-century building in the castle is a chapel, which occupies the north-east corner of the bailey beneath the motte. That the chapel stands remote from the hall is typical of early domestic plans, which often have their principal elements widely separated from one another. This astonishing survival, one of the most complete eleventh-century interiors in England, is rectangular in plan. Dividing it into twelve vaulted bays are six tall columns, their capitals ornamented with carved foliage and animals (pl. 45). It is possible that the building formerly possessed an upper floor, in the manner of some royal and episcopal palace chapels on the Continent.

Both the hall and the chapel could have been begun by Bishop Walcher, but the latter at least is more probably connected with his successor. In 1080 Walcher was brutally murdered, another victim of Northumbrian internecine politics, and a cleric from Normandy called William St Calais was appointed in his place. Walcher appears to have patronised architecture in the idiom of his native Lotharingia, but the castle chapel looks Norman in detail and form and therefore seems likely to belong to St Calais' episcopacy.[51] It can probably also be dated prior to 1093 on the basis of a specific architectural contrast. In that year St Calais laid the foundation stone for one of the masterpieces of the Romanesque style in England, the priory and cathedral church of Durham. That the castle chapel shows no stylistic connection with this magnificent new church suggests that it pre-existed it. As it appears today, set beside the towering form of the cathedral, the castle of the bishops of Durham perfectly expresses in architecture the formidable alliance of church and state that the Norman possession of St Cuthbert's body created. Its rich ensuing history will be traced in some detail through the pages of this book.

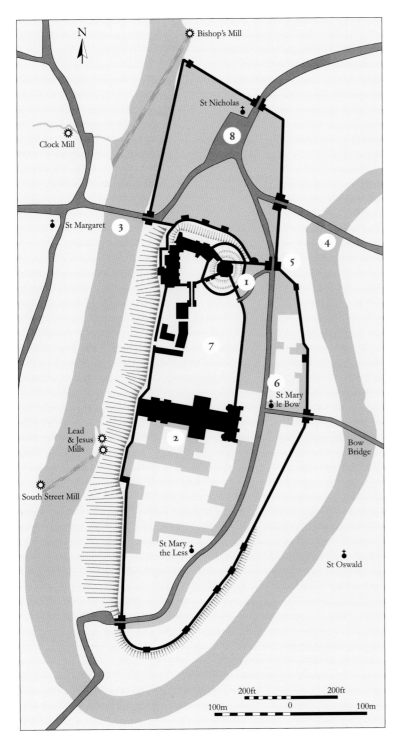

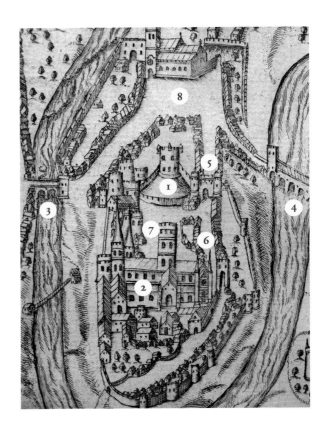

RICHMOND, YORKSHIRE

There is no single building that more effectively illustrates the historical and architectural themes of the first generation of castles in England than Richmond in Yorkshire. Dominating the cliff-lined valley of the River Swale, this is perhaps the best-preserved eleventh-century castle in England. While it is clear that Richmond was amongst the numerous new castles erected across the kingdom in the immediate aftermath of the Norman Conquest of 1066, the exact circumstances of its foundation remain obscure. One twelfth-century poem credits William the Conqueror with building the castle in 1068–9, but there is no substantive evidence for this at all.[52] Much more probable is the late medieval tradition that it was founded by Alan Rufus, count of Penthièvre in Brittany, to protect his northern estates from the dispossessed Anglo-Saxon nobility of the region. These estates were given to him by William the Conqueror after 1071, and the castle was probably established shortly after this event.[53]

That the foundation of the castle was directly connected to the Conqueror's gift appears to be corroborated by the Domesday survey. At this time Richmond, then called *Hindrelag*, was listed amongst Alan Rufus's possessions, one of an enormous body of estates that he owned across England. The survey entry makes no reference to a castle, but one almost certainly existed

44 A plan of Durham showing the line of the late medieval fortifications and Speed's view of the city, published in 1611. The town sits on a peninsula created by a tight loop of the River Wear. The motte (1) was built in 1072 across the neck of this naturally defensible site, protecting the town and the cathedral priory complex (2). It also overlooks the two bridges that cross the river: Framwellgate (3) and Elvet (4). The whole peninsula was understood to form part of the castle in the Middle Ages and was entered through North Gate (5). In reflection of this understanding, the street that runs down the peninsula to the right of the drawing is still divided into so-called North Bailey and South Bailey (6). Until the early twelfth century the market of the town lay between the cathedral and the castle (7). It was then moved to a new site on the far side of the peninsula beside St Nicholas's Church at the top of the picture (8).

because Alan's lands are incidentally described as forming a 'castlery', or an estate organised to sustain a castle.[54] That this unnamed castle stood at Richmond is implied by the fact that a core of Alan Rufus's lands was later constituted as an honour that was focused on Richmond. It seems reasonable, therefore, to interpret this Domesday allusion as proof of the castle's existence by 1086, and an early reference to what became known much later as the honour of Richmond. This was one of the largest and richest endowments of its kind, the lands of the honour spreading over eight counties and supporting a body of 180 knights. Forming the core of this honour of Richmond was a huge estate confiscated from the Anglo-Saxon earl Edwin for his part in the rebellion of 1069. Considering the unsettled state of Northumbria at this date, therefore, it is likely that this honour and its castle were intended by the Conqueror as the northern defence to England.

When the earliest stone fortifications were raised on 'the strong hill' or 'Riche Mount' established by Alan Rufus is not clear, but they probably stood complete – or were well advanced – by his death in 1089. The early date of these structures is partly implied by the close physical relationship of the castle and town: in plan, the two form unequal segments of a large circular enclosure (pl. 46). Presumably, therefore, the two must have been set out together and this in turn suggests that Richmond was planned from the outset as a joint castle and town foundation. Indeed, there is unusually early documentary proof of the existence of a borough at Richmond in a charter of 1136–45. This makes reference to liberties enjoyed by the burgesses of Richmond under Alan Rufus's brother, Alan Niger, who died in 1093.[55] In reflection of their integral plan, the town was actually called the 'bailey' in the sixteenth century.[56]

From the surviving remains at Richmond it is still possible to build up a good impression of the form of the castle planned by Alan Rufus. Apart from the construction of a great tower over the main entrance to the castle in the 1160s, the buildings remain little altered. The principal triangular enclosure was encompassed on two sides by ditches and a massively thick curtain wall constructed of rubble masonry. Built along the eastern curtain were three square-planned mural towers, some laced with wall passages. One of these contains a chapel, almost certainly that granted by Alan Rufus to the monks of St Mary's Abbey in York. This gift can be dated by the comparison of charter texts to 1088 or 1089.[57] Preserved within it are faint traces of painted decoration.[58] To the south the

45   The Norman Chapel, Durham, was probably built by Bishop William St Calais between 1080 and 1093. It is a rugged but elegant interior with vaults supported on tall columns. The rectangular space is lit by several high-set windows and preserves parts of an eleventh-century floor comprising slabs of stone laid in a herringbone pattern. The carved capitals with swirls of decoration at each corner are ultimately derived from classical models. Here, however, figures and animals have been introduced to enliven their design. It is possible that there was formerly an upper chapel on the floor above: some royal and episcopal palace chapels were arranged on two levels. This was certainly the case with another castle chapel of the bishops of Durham at nearby Auckland.

46 A plan of Richmond, Yorkshire. Viewed as a whole, medieval Richmond takes the form of a large circular enclosure, out of which the castle has been cut like a slice of cake. Such integral planning of castles and settlements is not at all unusual. In the mid-sixteenth century the town was still known as the bailey, an indication that the whole of this eleventh-century foundation was considered to be part of the castle. Shown on the plan are the eleventh-century entrance, later overbuilt by the great tower (1); the chapel tower of St Nicholas (2); and the gate to the garden (3). The dotted lines on two sides of Scolland's Hill indicate the position of timber galleries.

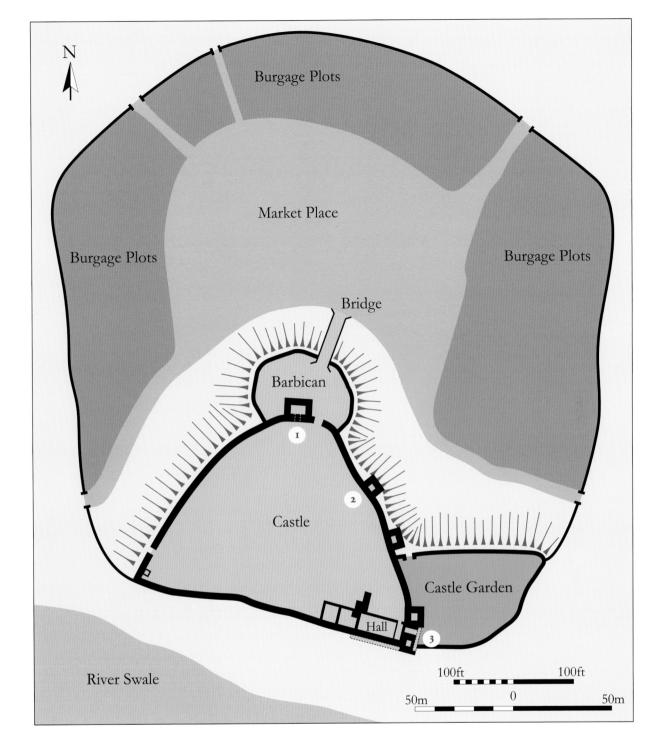

third face of the triangular castle perimeter is protected by cliffs dropping down sheer to the River Swale. Perched on the side of the cliff at the south-eastern corner of the enclosure is Scolland's Hall. The name of this hall has been in currency since at least 1400 and refers to a steward of the castle who died between 1146 and 1150. Scolland is recorded as a witness of charters for upwards of fifty years, a circumstance that perhaps explains the celebration of his name.[59]

The great hall of Richmond Castle, as with the much larger eleventh-century structure at Durham, was at first-floor level. Access to the hall was provided up an external stair, an arrangement possibly inspired by the arrangement of refectories in monastic plans of the period. Its interior was covered by a high-pitched roof and lit along both sides by large windows. At the far end of the hall was a small chamber, possibly for Alan Rufus to withdraw from company in the hall, and

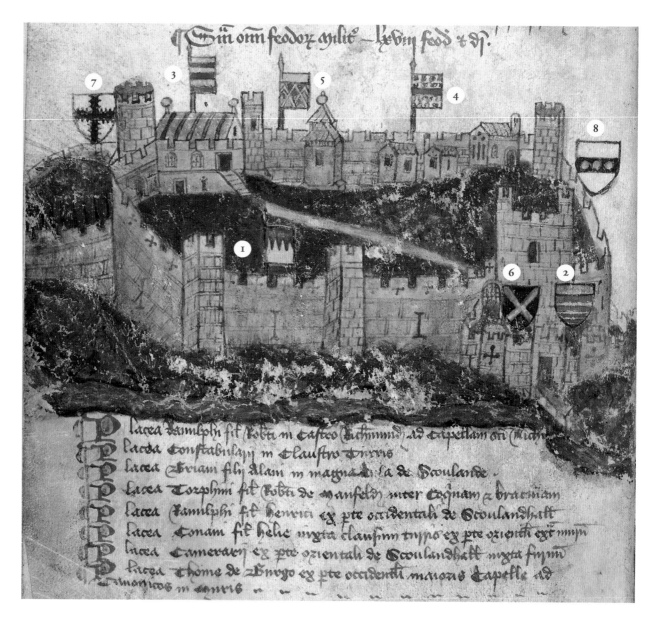

47 A view of Richmond, Yorkshire, from the north, of *circa* 1400, with the arms and banners of those responsible for castle-guard displayed on the walls. The text beneath reads:

1 Place of Ranulph, son of Robert, in the castle of Richmond by the Chapel of St Nicholas
2 Place of the Constable in the enclosure of the tower
3 Place of Brian, son of Alan, in the great hall of Scolland
4 Place of Torphini, son of Robert Manfeld, between the kitchen and brewhouse
5 Place of Ranulph, son of Henry, to the western side of Scolland's Hall
6 Place of Conan, son of Helie, beside the enclosure of the tower to the eastern part outside the walls [i.e. the barbican]
7 Place of the Chamberlain to the east of Scolland's Hall beside the oven
8 Place of Thomas de Burgo to the west of the greater chapel of the cannons within the walls.

The picture illustrates a book recording the landholdings of the honour of Richmond. The particular combination of names listed in the caption indicates that the artist reconstructed the castle-guard at Richmond in the 1190s. Why he should have chosen this particular moment in the history of the castle is not clear. It may be that this is the earliest date for which there was relevant documentary evidence available.

beside this a latrine tower. On two sides of the hall block there remain sockets for what appear to have been external wooden galleries. What function these served is not known, but they may have been for recreation rather than defence: one overlooked the River Swale and the other a lobe of land projecting from the main castle enclosure. This was probably the site of the garden described in the 1280s as 'pertaining to the castle', a function it may have served since the eleventh century.[60]

As far as it is possible to judge from the remains, the original masonry structures of the castle seem to have been constructed as part of a single building operation. They display, moreover, many of the characteristic features of Romanesque. Several of the towers include heavy stone vaults; there are large quantities of cut masonry; and the surviving sculpture is sub-classical:

the hall and main entrance are ornamented with simplified imitations of Corinthian capitals. Such decoration finds close parallel in other late eleventh-century church buildings in the north of England, such as the new York Minster, begun around 1070. It also compares to such Continental detailing as the crypt capitals of Bayeux Cathedral, begun before 1077, interesting evidence of the passage of architectural ideas from Normandy to England.

From surviving documentary evidence it is possible to reconstruct broadly how this castle operated at its first foundation. The lands of the honour were distributed to Alan's followers in return for knight service. Many of these men were fellow Bretons, and the most important also served as Alan's senior household officers. His steward, Wimar, received land from the honour sufficient to support fifteen knights; the castle constable, Enisant Musard, land for thirteen knights; his chamberlain, Odo, land for eleven knights; and his butler, another Alan, land for two knights. Beside these officers, other men also became substantial landowners within the honour, including Scolland the steward, who held land for five knights' fees. There are the earthwork remains of undocumented castles on the properties known to have been owned by many of these men. From this evidence it has been deduced that the lands attached to two or more knights' fees gave an individual the financial resources to build their own castle. Richmond Castle, in other words, was spawning offspring through its household officers.[61] Over time some of these officers additionally endowed religious foundations from their fees, including the abbeys at Easby and Egglestone.

The manner in which castle-guard operated in practice is difficult to reconstruct. To judge from the evidence of other sites, service was usually organised in two-month blocks, with the largest number of knights serving over the summer. But a fourteenth-century drawing of Richmond suggests that sections of the defences were the responsibility of particular individuals (pl. 47). Whether this system applied in the eleventh century is not clear. Nevertheless, it is apparent that by the thirteenth century knights were expected to maintain houses in the castle where they performed service.[62] The practice could be very long standing and in some cases rented plots of town land, termed burgage, may have been used for accommodation by knights performing their castle-guards.

Richmond illustrates the full complexity of a major, first-generation castle. Its physical remains are the expression of an entire social and political order imposed onto England by the events of the Conquest. In the years to come, that order was to intensify its hold yet further and the buildings it produced were to grow even more confident. But the character of architecture in England was to change too. The events of the Conquest created a complex cultural hybrid: the wealthy and sophisticated stock of Anglo-Saxon England grafted with a vigorous Norman stem. In the extraordinary flowering and fruiting of the maturing tree the qualities of both partners in the union became apparent.

4

THE AGE OF MAGNIFICENCE

WILLIAM RUFUS, HENRY I, AND STEPHEN

AND THE ANARCHY

William the Conqueror died early in the morning of 9 September 1087 at the priory of Saint-Gervais, on the outskirts of Rouen. He had been briefly stirred from sleep by the great bell of the nearby cathedral toll-ing for Prime and, after committing his soul to the Virgin, silently expired. The event provoked chaos amongst his assembled followers. According to Orderic Vitalis:

> . . . the wealthiest of them mounted their horses and departed in haste to secure their property. Whilst the inferior attendants, observing their masters had disappeared, laid hands on the arms, the plate, the linen, and the royal furniture, and hastened away, leaving the corpse almost naked on the floor of the cell.[1]

This episode and its circumstances almost perfectly symbolise the character of the Conqueror's achieve-ment. They also reflect the troubled nature of the political settlement that his successors were to inherit. For more than a century, the death of every Anglo-Norman king was to bear comparison with this sordid scene.

The response of those around the bed underlines the degree to which William's authority was personal; his death threw everything into uncertainty and threat-ened to strip his legacy as naked as his corpse. Perhaps the only clear thread of continuity that extended beyond it was an acknowledgement that his three sons were the heirs to his possessions, lands and titles. Having said that, there was no consensus as to what constituted an equitable division of this inheritance. According to Norman precedent, two sons might rea-sonably have been disinherited in favour of the eldest. Curiously, however, the Conqueror tried formally on his deathbed to divide his possessions between the sons, Robert and William Rufus receiving Normandy and England respectively, and the future Henry I a huge sum of money.

This settlement can never have seemed very con-vincing; nor did it prove to be so. The dynastic strife it promised was already a reality: the frustrated ambi-tion of William's sons had been causing difficulty for some years, and Robert, the eldest, was in open rebel-lion at the time of his father's death. Trying to control sons was to prove one of the curses of old age amongst all those Anglo-Norman kings who successfully begot them. Writing of the first Angevin king of England, Henry II (d. 1189), in the late twelfth century, Gerald of Wales recorded that the king had a picture of an

Facing page: Corfe, Dorset.

eagle being attacked by smaller birds painted in his chamber at Winchester Castle. Henry understood himself to be represented by the eagle and the smaller birds as 'my four sons, who will not hesitate to harry me even unto death'.[2]

The instability that such competition for power created within the ruling family was further amplified by the nature of the Anglo-Norman realm. Normandy and the heartlands of England were integrated through powerful ties of aristocratic interest. Nevertheless, they were physically divided by the sea and preserved their own distinct political character, with most powerful families having a predominant interest on one or other side of the Channel. The relationship between the kingdom and the duchy, moreover, had a curious imbalance that further rendered it sensitive. William's death, and his later burial, in Normandy reflect the political dominance of the Norman element in the realm: Normandy was the cultural homeland of the Anglo-Norman settlement, providing the rulers of England with their language and identity. But it offered only a fraction of the wealth of England. This might naturally have orientated the affairs of the realm towards England, but Normandy was locked into the affairs of France and the gateway to rich acquisitions there. Promise of these and the entanglements of French politics redressed the balance of interest. One important practical upshot of this situation was that every Anglo-Norman king spent considerable periods of time in France. Such absences could last for years at a time and might account for the greater part of the reign.[3]

The tensions inherent in the Anglo-Norman realm underlay two civil wars in 1088 and 1101, each of which was attended by important political casualties. This high turnover of figures in the inner circle of power in England was further increased by the unsuccessful outcome of a number of rebellions, such as that of Robert de Mowbray, earl of Northumbria, in 1095. The two sons of the Conqueror, therefore, who inherited the throne after him – William Rufus (1087–1100) and Henry I (1100–35) – had at their disposal large quantities of confiscated property and therefore the means to elevate trusted supporters to positions of great power. One consequence of this was that the patterns of castle construction continued essentially unbroken from the 1080s through both their reigns. That is to say, the crown continued to monopolise absolutely the resources for major castle construction. These were manifested in royal building projects of quite remarkable ambition and often connected to the construction

of great towers in stone. At the same time, however, both kings also extended the resources to build to their immediate family and a small circle of favoured individuals. There were important changes, however, in prospect.

Despite the purges caused by rebellion and civil war, by the early decades of the twelfth century a new English aristocracy was clearly in embryo. It is one mark of this phenomenon that some great families began to adopt names derived from English estates – such as Clare in Essex – rather than Norman ones. Circumstances now conspired to help shape the identity of this group more clearly. On 25 November 1120 the succession to the throne was brought into question by a completely unexpected dynastic catastrophe. On a journey between Normandy and England a royal pleasure boat, *The White Ship*, filled with men and women born to greatness, foundered and sank. Amongst those lost were Henry I's seventeen-year-old son and illegitimate daughter, the former reputedly drowned while trying to save his half-sister. The tragedy served to heighten the dynastic importance of all the survivors. Outstanding amongst these was Stephen of Blois, a grandson of the Conqueror. He had diarrhoea when *The White Ship* set sail and this indisposition, combined with his perspicacious observation that the crew were drunk, dissuaded him from travelling on that fateful voyage.[4]

Henry I attempted to create a succession through his only other legitimate offspring, a daughter called Maud or Matilda. In 1125, following the death of her husband, the Emperor Henry V, Matilda was recalled to England. Then, on 25 December 1126, the barons were required to acknowledge her as heir to the throne. It was an arrangement that broke with all precedent and opened up the worrying possibility of the kingdom passing through marriage to the control of another person or dynasty. With reluctance and the proviso that the barons should have a say in Matilda's marriage, however, the oath was taken. And the first to take it was Stephen of Blois. But the barons were right to be worried. On 17 June 1128 Matilda was secretly married to one of the great enemies of Normandy, Geoffrey, count of Anjou. It was a fiery match between two figures of passionate temperament and from it was born the future Henry II in 1135. This marriage immediately put pressure on Henry I's proposed dynastic settlement. The barons had been cheated, and some were discontented by the abhorrent dynastic alliance that Henry I had effected. As a result, the planned succession backfired and within a month of the king's death on 1 December 1135 Stephen of Blois (d. 1154) had been crowned king of England.

The speed at which his takeover occurred implies that the operation had been minutely planned in alliance with Stephen's brother, Henry of Blois, bishop of Winchester. Empress Matilda appeared to have lost any hope of her inheritance. As events were to prove, however, she was still very much in the game. Over the next five years a combination of private grievances amongst the barons, pressure from Scotland and Angevin incursion in Normandy meant that Stephen began to lose control of the realm. In the same period he also alienated his brother, Henry of Blois, and by extension compromised the support he had enjoyed from the church. These difficulties all advanced the cause of Matilda and her party, headed by Henry I's illegitimate son, Robert, earl of Gloucester. Her supporters, moreover, won a decisive advantage in the struggle when Stephen was captured in the battle of Lincoln on 2 February 1141. The king was imprisoned, first honourably and later in chains, and with the support of Henry of Blois, Stephen's estranged brother, Matilda prepared for her own coronation.

Then in an amazing reversal of fortunes Matilda succeeded in snatching defeat from the jaws of victory. Confident of her position, she behaved with such imperious, unbending and alienating arrogance that even her friends and allies had second thoughts about making her their ruler. Stephen's wife, also called Matilda, was able to summon sufficient resources to topple the empress from her prospective throne and in the ensuing campaign to capture the earl of Gloucester. Soon afterwards, Stephen and the earl were exchanged, and the kingdom now entered a long and protracted struggle for power known familiarly as the Anarchy. Modern assessments of the nature of this conflict have varied, but contemporary sources are of one mind in regarding this as a calamitous civil war. Their accounts cannot be read uncritically, but as one monk of Peterborough famously lamented:

> . . . every powerful man made his castles and held them against the king; and they filled the land with castles. They greatly oppressed the wretched men of the land with castle-work; then when the castles were made, they filled them with devils and evil men. Then both by night and by day they seized those men whom they imagined had any wealth, common men and women, and put them in prison

to get their gold and silver, and tortured them with unspeakable tortures . . . These things we suffered for nineteen long years for our sins and they said openly that Christ and his angels slept.[5]

In the events of the conflict between Stephen and Matilda were laid the foundations for an architectural revolution. The royal monopoly on the resources to build that had characterised the reigns of William the Conqueror and his two sons cracked and collapsed. From the 1140s, not only was royal power compromised by the conflict for the throne, but also Stephen and Matilda began to woo and back supporters in an open competition for political power across the realm. In reflection of this phenomenon, the exclusive estate of earl was assumed or handed out with a freedom inconceivable at any earlier date: over the course of the reign the number of earldoms more than quintupled from around seven to thirty-seven, most coming into existence between 1138 and 1152.[6] At the same time, entire regions came under the sway of individuals freed from the constraints of effective royal control. These men usurped or were granted many of the powers that had formerly been the preserve of the king, from the administration of justice to the minting of currency.

Amongst the plethora of castles built in the course of the fighting – the vast majority of which were temporary creations – was a small group of major new creations, often founded with attendant burial churches, boroughs and parks. These were the first castles of their kind created in post-Conquest England without direct royal subvention or support. They made manifest, moreover, the power of a nobility whose interests and identity were explicitly vested in England. It is a mark of the resources available to this group that their castles made extensive use of stone. And it expresses their ambition – particularly amongst the ranks of earls – that so many were dignified with stone great towers. These buildings, so long the preserve of the king and his immediate circle of family and favourites, now – in a very limited sense – became democratised. From this period onwards, in fact, there developed an association between noble title and this most prestigious type of castle building that was to outlast the Middle Ages.

CASTLE BUILDING AND THE KING

To whatever degree castles were originally erected to overawe a newly conquered people and defend the borders of the kingdom, within a generation of the

Conquest they appear to have been primarily significant in the violent internecine disputes of the Anglo-Norman elite. The first of these conflicts erupted in 1088, when William Rufus found himself confronted by a powerful alliance of barons who supported the claim of his elder brother, Robert Curthose, to the English throne. Amongst his leading opponents were the two half-brothers of William the Conqueror, Odo of Bayeux and Robert of Mortain. They were besieged and starved out of Pevensey Castle after a six-week siege directed personally by William Rufus. Odo was then escorted to his former headquarters at Rochester by a small group of his captors. Upon arrival, his escort tethered their horses and

> ... called on the men in the town (*oppidanis*) to open their gates, such being the wish of the bishop, who was present, and the order of the king [William Rufus], who was not. The defenders could see from the walls that the bishop's face contradicted those who spoke on his behalf, opened their gates and sallied out at top speed, seized the horses, tied up the bishop's escort and led them all off as prisoners.[7]

William Rufus soon arrived at the walls of Rochester and summoned an army of Englishmen to help besiege it. He also raised two temporary or siege castles outside Rochester to prevent anyone from getting in or out of it. Throughout this encounter, there is some ambiguity as to what exactly was being defended by Odo and his men, the town or the castle or both. Different accounts call Odo's stronghold different things. Whatever the case, the defenders were eventually forced to sue for terms and marched out with the honours of war, with their horses and arms. Nevertheless, they forfeited all their English property, which reverted to the king.[8] Odo himself returned in disgrace to Normandy and later died on his way to Jerusalem in the First Crusade.[9]

A few years later, in 1095, record of a rebellion by another outstandingly powerful baron tells a similarly colourful tale of castles warfare in another corner of the realm. Robert de Mowbray, earl of Northumbria, became involved in a dispute with the bishop of Durham that eventually pushed him into revolt. The king marched north and besieged Newcastle, which was held by Mowbray's brother. After the castle fell he went on to assault a smaller castle at Morpeth, where he allegedly captured Mowbray's best knights. From Morpeth, the king pursued the earl to the historic stronghold of the Northumbrian earls, Bamburgh, and laid siege to it, but: 'when the king saw he could not conquer it [Bamburgh], he ordered a castle to be made in front of it, and called it in his language *Malveisin,* that is in English "Bad Neighbour", and set it strongly with his men and afterwards went south'.[10] Following the departure of the king, Mowbray made a daring attempt to turn the tables on his opponents. With the intention of seizing back his lost stronghold at Newcastle and cutting off the royalist forces that besieged him, he secretly set sail from Bamburgh with a small force and landed on the headland of Tynemouth. This was both the site of a monastery patronised by the earl and a natural stronghold, which was possibly fortified as a castle. Unfortunately for him, the royal forces at Newcastle got wind of his plan and marched out to attack the headland. After a few days, Tynemouth was taken and in the bitter fighting Mowbray was himself wounded in the leg and captured. He spent the next twenty or thirty years as a royal prisoner and appears to have died as a monk of St Albans abbey, of which he was a notable patron.[11]

In the light of such narratives, it is small surprise that castles have come to be presented in many historical works as a destabilising influence on the kingdom: strongholds for barons to exploit the weaknesses of the Anglo-Norman realm and its cycles of dynastic violence. Also, that a king had to wrest control of castles from the hands of his over-mighty subjects if he were to control his realm. He did this on the one hand, it has been argued, by building castles as part of an arms race with them; and on the other, by regulating their construction and attempting to demolish such as were illegally erected, so-called adulterine castles.[12] In the light of recent scholarship it would seem that this analysis is fundamentally flawed on a number of levels. This is a point that deserves attention if the true influences at work on castle building and ownership in this period are to be properly appreciated.

Although castles might be built and held by individual barons, it is quite clear that the king reserved the right to occupy them at times of need. The refusal to render up a castle to royal authority was an act of rebellion, hence the scenes described above in 1088 and 1095. This was an assessment explicitly endorsed by a visiting papal legate in a case in 1135, who judged that 'all the chief men, in accordance with the customs of other peoples, ought to hand over the keys of their fortifications to the disposal of the king, whose duty it is to fight for the peace of all'.[13] In other words, there was no reason for an arms race because the king technically held all castles, whoever actually constructed them. Added to this, such an assessment lumps all castles together in one category, whereas in fact there were clearly two.

By the end of the Conqueror's reign, there had become firmly established in England a landholding pattern – the castlery or honour – of which the castle was both symbol and guarantor. This system was fundamental to the Anglo-Norman political order and was actively expanded and consolidated during the reigns of both William Rufus and Henry I. Not only did it accompany Norman power as it extended into the north-west of England and deeper into Wales, tying new land into the kingdom, but it was also continuously being reconfigured and intensified as new families gathered together the necessary lands to sustain a castle. This often occurred at the expense of an existing castlery that was split up or destroyed by marriage alliance, death without heirs or political wreck. The limitation of landed resources, however, necessarily ensured that the number of castles with estates remained relatively constant. Moreover, from about 1100 the threshold of wealth necessary for castle construction seems to have begun to rise and the overall number of castles in the country to begin a very long and gradual decline.

The alternative to these foundations with honours were castles of warfare, which were little more than fortifications of convenience. In the vast majority of cases, castles of warfare were positioned to prey upon the estates of a greater castle, either as siege works or to assert control over disputed land. Such, for example, was the 'Bad Neighbour' erected by William Rufus outside Bamburgh in 1095. This is the category in which there was a particular explosion during the crisis of the Anarchy. Such castles might take a variety of forms. There survive the remains of motte and bailey siege castles raised in the Anarchy, for example, just beyond the walls of Corfe (Dorset), Arundel (Sussex) and Farnham (Hampshire).[14]

Alternatively, a siege castle could be created out of a church: William of Aumale, earl of York, briefly converted the Augustinian priory at Bridlington into a castle in 1143 in his struggle for power with the Gant family.[15] And at Hereford in 1140 Geoffrey Talbot:

> Entering the church of the Mother of God, the Cathedral Church of the episcopal see, and impiously driving out the ministrants at God's table, he recklessly brought in a throng of armed men. The townspeople were disturbed, both because the graves of the newly dead were dug up to provide

earth for ramparts and because at one time it was visible that catapults were being put up on the tower from which they had heard the sweet and pacific admonition of the bells, at another that missiles were being shot from it to harm the King's garrison [in the castle].[16]

Information about the physical form of such a conversion has been supplied by the excavations at Coventry Cathedral, which uncovered evidence for the fortification of the half-completed nave with a ditch during the Anarchy.[17] Hastily created and short-lived, very few castles in this category were significant in architectural terms.

In order to understand the patterns of investment in the great honourial castles of the kingdom it is necessary to understand the role of the king as a patron. Far from struggling for survival in the face of baronial competition, William Rufus and Henry I remained unrivalled leaders in castle construction. This situation was a natural product of political circumstances. Once secure on the throne, both men held all the trump cards in their hands: land was held at the king's pleasure and his resources and power defied all competition. Both, moreover, busily prosecuted their own building projects, and it deserves particular note that royal castle works were without peer in terms of ambition and scale in this period. This is particularly reflected in the construction of great towers of stone, a subject that is discussed independently below. It is also apparent, however, in the grand conception of many royal projects in this period. One instance that must serve to represent the potential scale and scope of royal castles in this period is the redevelopment of Windsor Castle by Henry I.

According to the chronicler Henry of Huntingdon, Henry I held his Easter crown wearing in 1110 at New Windsor, 'which he himself had built'.[18] This statement conceals the fact that Henry I was in fact recasting the castle created by William the Conquer. It hints, however, at the scale of the reworking that Windsor now underwent and a qualitative change in its status: from this moment it decisively superseded the long-serving Anglo-Saxon palace nearby, which now became known as Old Windsor. Frustratingly, nothing is securely known about Henry I's work to the castle beyond the fact that it included the creation of a new palace complex. Also, that these new buildings – which probably stood in the upper ward – were of sufficient pretension to serve as the setting for Henry's marriage in January 1121 to Adeliza of Louvain. Coinciding with his

48 (*facing page*)   A plan of Kenilworth, Warwickshire, showing the castle ruins in their present form. The main castle enclosure is approached over a long causeway from an outer fortification of uncertain date called The Brays. Within the main area of the castle, as defined by the mere and other artificial pools (all now drained), there has probably always existed an inner bailey in the shadow of the great tower. Around this unchanging visual focus, the buildings at Kenilworth were constantly adapted during the five centuries of its occupation to create a complex architectural palimpsest.

works to the castle, three other important changes occurred that also signal Windsor's new importance.

In 1121 Henry I founded a new abbey at nearby Reading. The foundation was conceived on a gigantic scale, the proportions of its church rivalling the largest not only in England but also in Christendom.[19] In the same year, reference is made for the first time to the town of Windsor, a settlement possibly moved from Old Windsor in 1110.[20] That this site was being deliberately developed by the king is indicated twenty years later, when land was acquired for the purpose of enlarging the 'borough' at Windsor. The focus for this settlement was a market set at the gates of the castle.[21] This developed under the control of the constable of the castle, a royal officer with sweeping local powers. Finally, by Henry I's reign, Windsor Forest had been attached administratively to the castle and provided a chase for the king to pursue the pleasures of hunting.

Such royal building operations set a standard of magnificence that the leading members of the court actively sought to emulate: they likewise built great castles with attendant boroughs to stimulate trade and commerce; religious institutions for their spiritual welfare; and parks for hunting and entertainment. Yet until the monopoly of royal power was broken in the Anarchy, the means to undertake such operations came only from the king. Indeed, it could be argued that prior to the death of Henry I no major castle building went on without tacit or direct royal approval. To act without this was a dangerous game, even for a great magnate. As the earl of Hereford commented to Reginald, abbot of Evesham (1122–49), fortifying a castle invited the king to occupy it.[22] The wisdom of the earl's words and the realities of castle foundation in this period are well illustrated by Kenilworth, the fourth and final castle central to the narrative of this book.

THE KING AND THE FOUNDATION OF KENILWORTH CASTLE

Both William Rufus and Henry I had found in Henry, earl of Warwick, a particularly loyal follower. Reward had come in the form of almost unparalleled power in Warwickshire with authority even above the king's sheriff. But when the earl died in 1119 he was replaced by Roger, a son of doubtful commitment. To neutralise the power of the heir, Henry I appointed a royal favourite, Geoffrey de Clinton, as sheriff of the county at some time before 1121. Clinton was a man who owed

everything to Henry I and had risen to power in his service to the office of chamberlain to the treasury. To this royal appointee, the young earl of Warwick was then compelled by Henry I to grant from his own honour a very substantial estate of about seventeen knights' fees. The process of making over this land was completed by 1124, and immediately afterwards Clinton began work on the establishment of a new castle and priory at Kenilworth, a mere 5 miles as the crow flies from Warwick.[23]

Although the start of work to the castle is not documented, it was presumably under way by the spring of 1125. At this time a community of Augustinian canons was established at the priory, a religious order much favoured by Henry I and the inner circle of his court. Both castle and priory were established on royal land and there can be no doubt, therefore, that the king had directed exactly where Clinton was to build. Meanwhile, Clinton continued to bolster his position by establishing in Warwickshire a following of compatriots from the Contentin. This process culminated in 1139 when his nephew became bishop of Coventry; according to rumour, the post had been purchased from the king.

Kenilworth Castle was probably laid out as a fortified enclosure on an island within a mere, the latter detail being apparent from a grant to the canons of the priory to take fish from the water (pl. 48). If further evidence were needed of direct royal involvement in this project, one building provides it. The architectural centrepiece of the present castle is a great tower of immense proportions. This stands today as a broken wreck, one of its massive walls having been blown out with gunpowder during demolition work in the 1640s (pl. 49). A building of this scale was far beyond the resources of Geoffrey de Clinton or his heirs, and for this reason it has generally been dated to the late twelfth century, when the castle was in royal ownership. This attribution, however, does not square comfortably with the documentary evidence: from the surrender of the castle to Henry II by the Clintons about 1173 there survives a continuous run of royal financial records that make no mention of substantial works to the buildings before the close of the century. Yet the tower was evidently in existence by 1190, when money was set aside for its repair. A much more satisfactory explanation, therefore, is that Geoffrey de Clinton began this building with the financial support of the king. This would agree with several other pieces of evidence.

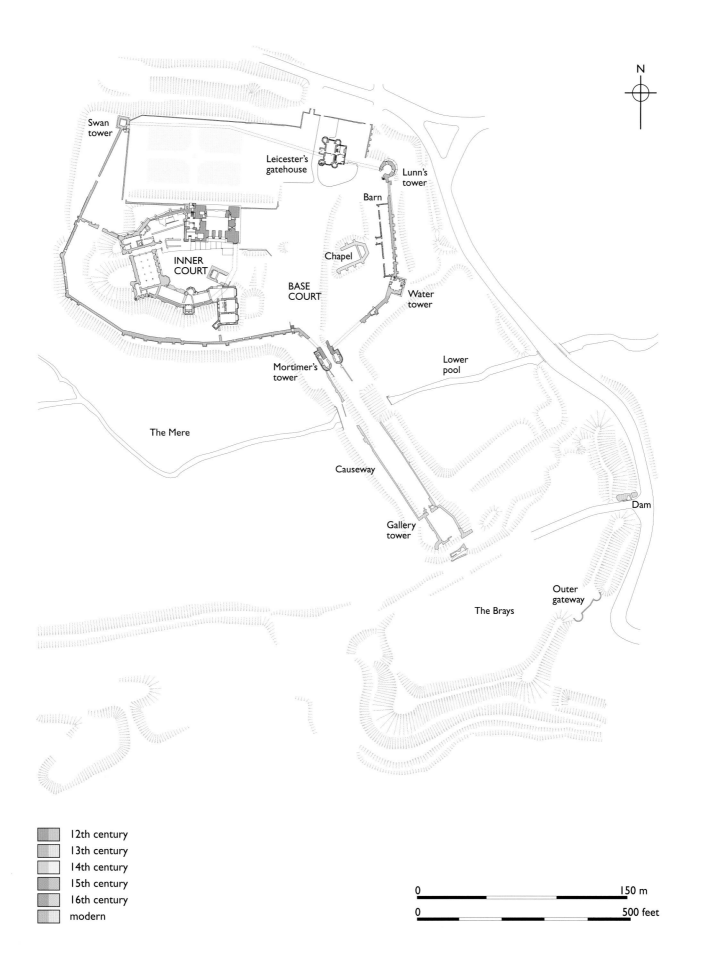

Swan
tower

Leicester's
gatehouse

Lunn's
tower

Barn

Chapel

INNER
COURT

BASE
COURT

Water
tower

Mortimer's
tower

Lower
pool

The Mere

Causeway

Gallery
tower

Dam

Outer
gateway

The Brays

N

12th century
13th century
14th century
15th century
16th century
modern

0   150 m

0   500 feet

49   The great tower of
Kenilworth, Warwickshire, in
a photograph of 1872 taken
prior to heavy nineteenth-
century restoration work.
Known by the sixteenth
century as Caesar's Tower, this
building was repeatedly
remodelled during the life of
the castle. It was probably
begun as the centrepiece of
Clinton's castle in the 1120s,
but a subtle change in the
masonry between the second-
floor windows and the arrow
loops on the third (1) may
suggest that construction was
interrupted by his fall from
power in 1130. The tower
stands on an unusually
massive plinth (2). It is known
from documentary evidence
to have contained a chapel,
which was probably located in
the ruined forebuilding to the
left (3). The window openings
were enlarged in the sixteenth
century and a clock was
installed in one angle tower.
Evidence for square-faced
clock dials on two sides of
one angle turret are visible
here (4). During Elizabeth I's
visit to the castle in 1575 the
hands were symbolically
stopped at 2 p.m., the perfect
moment to receive a guest.
The archway into the inner
bailey was immediately
adjacent to the great tower
and one side of it remains as a
projecting stub of walling (5).

A change in masonry and detailing within the great tower at Kenilworth suggests that the upper floor was a late twelfth-century addition to the building. This implies that work to the tower was interrupted before the structure had been completed, a circumstance that might be explained by the dramatic disgrace of Clinton in 1130, more of which below. Also an intriguing architectural parallel for the tower exists. Kenilworth was one of two castles that came into existence on the estate that was created for Geoffrey de Clinton. The other stood at Brandon between Rugby and Coventry (pl. 50). Excavations at Brandon have revealed the footings of a much smaller tower that bears unmistakeable similarities to the great tower at Kenilworth.[24] Particularly distinctive are the massive corner towers and deep, stepped plinths of both buildings. The most logical explanation for their similarity is that Brandon was begun as a modest copy of Kenilworth when the Clintons owned both properties and wished to emphasise the association between them. Conveniently for the purposes of dating, Brandon passed out of their control in the mid-twelfth century, which suggests that both buildings pre-date this.

On this analysis, Kenilworth is not a baronial castle foundation in the conventional sense, but a royal creation. And similar patterns of royal patronage can be inferred in numerous contemporary situations, most particularly in the context of castles built by bishops, which will be discussed below. One other secular foundation of this kind that deserves individual mention on account of its exceptional state of preservation is the castle at Portchester in Hampshire. Established within a Roman fort (pl. 51), Portchester controlled the natural harbour of Portsmouth, and a castle was probably founded here after the Conquest. Some time after 1120, however, it came into the possession of William Pont de l'Arche, chamberlain of the treasury.[25]

Pont de l'Arche appears to have rebuilt the castle completely, possibly at the behest of Henry I, who is known to have stayed here on several occasions on his way to Normandy. A start to the work is almost certainly signalled by the foundation of a priory at Portchester in 1128. The church (which still survives) and its conventual buildings were erected in one angle of the fort enclosure. In the other William created an inner castle bailey with a great tower, a wall and a ditch

50 Plans of the great towers at Brandon (above) and Kenilworth (below), both in Warwickshire. These two buildings share many formal similarities including the use of massive corner turrets, heavy buttresses and stepped plinths. Brandon Castle was also founded by Geoffrey de Clinton and stood, like Kenilworth, environed with a series of flooded pools. These were substantially enlarged in the early thirteenth century, and the resultant flooding caused the monks of nearby Combe Abbey to sue the owners for damage in 1225.

(pl. 52). Outside the fort walls there existed a settlement, though it seems unlikely that it was ever formally constituted a borough, and the castle stood conveniently close to hunting ground in the forest of Bere.

That castle building at sites such as Kenilworth and Portchester was not being undertaken as part of an arms race is also apparent from their physical form. The kind of workaday fortifications that were constructed during the Anarchy bear no relation in scale, form or design to the leviathan projects undertaken during the periods of peace. These peacetime creations were much more than fortifications. They were architectural trophies of wealth and status, symbolic of outstanding political success and undertaken by figures basking in the warmth of royal favour.

In the late 1130s this situation started to change as leading members of the nobility began to take the political initiative from the king. This is particularly apparent across Norfolk, Suffolk and Essex, where a group of earls began independently to build several castles on a scale to rival Clinton's subsidised Kenilworth. Outstanding amongst them was William d'Albini. In 1138 he was married to the widow of Henry I, Adeliza of Louvain. It was a match that catapulted him into the first ranks of the nobility and, in the view of one hostile commentator, turned his head: 'As a result he became arrogant and inordinately conceited so that he could not bear anyone to be his equal, and anything that our world possessed that was special, apart from the king, was worthless in his eyes.'[26] At the time of his marriage he was made earl of Lincoln, but this title was traded in for that of earl of Sussex in 1141. With this latter dignity came control of Arundel Castle and its rape or honour. Albini responded with a series of architectural projects on a scale that is hard to parallel for a member of the nobility before 1135.

It was probably soon after his wedding that the principal family castle at Buckenham was abandoned. In its place, 'New' Buckenham was laid out nearby at the territorial expense of the Bigod family.[27] This was conceived on a very grand scale: a castle with its own borough and park. As a mark of its outstanding ambition, New Buckenham included a stone great tower on a circular plan (pl. 53). Work to this was probably nearing completion in 1146, when the site of 'Old Buckenham' castle was granted away to support a new Augustinian priory. It is expressive of the spirit in which Albini worked that the grant was conditional on the old castle being destroyed. Meanwhile, a second

Brandon Ground Floor

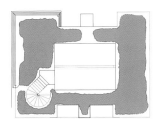

Kenilworth Ground Floor

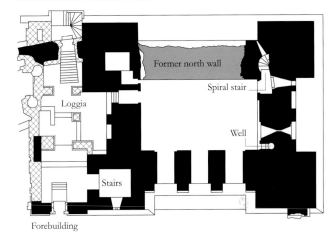

Kenilworth First Floor

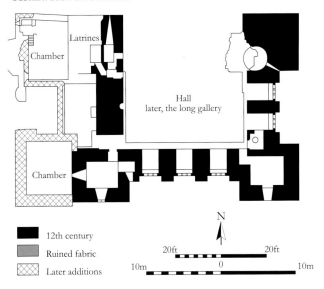

■ 12th century

▨ Ruined fabric (grey)

⧄ Later additions

51 (*above*) A Roman fort was built at Portchester, Hampshire, to command the natural harbour of Portsmouth between AD 285 and 290. It was laid out on a rectangular plan with D-shaped towers at regular intervals. A *burh* was established here during the tenth century and the remains of a later Anglo-Saxon *burhgeat* have been excavated on the site. In 1128 a monastic foundation was established in one corner of the Roman enclosure by William Pont de l'Arche, Henry I's chamberlain of the treasury. Probably at the same time he built the inner bailey and the great

tower of a castle in the opposite corner. Much of the stone for these operations was acquired by stripping away the masonry from the inside of the Roman wall, reducing it in width for most of its length from roughly 10 to 5 feet (3 to 1.5 m).

52 (*right*) Reconstruction by Terry Ball of the inner bailey of Portchester, Hampshire, in the mid-twelfth century. The great tower was erected on the angle of the Roman defences, probably around 1130. Prior to it being heightened in the later Middle Ages, it was low and box-like, a proportion

inherited from the White Tower at London. Some details of the building – such as the form of its buttresses – find regional parallel in the great tower at Guildford in Surrey, which is probably contemporary. The two external faces of the tower were plainly detailed, but those overlooking the bailey were ornamented with large, decorated windows. Internally, the building was divided through its full height by a spine wall and comprised a basement and first-floor level. Access to the upper floor was up a stair housed in a forebuilding with a chapel.

castle on a similar scale was also in the process of creation at Castle Rising. This was again established with a new park and borough.[28] As we shall see, its great tower was modelled on that of the royal castle at Norwich. Finally, at Arundel, and in celebration of his coveted title, Albini probably erected the tower on the motte of the castle (see pl. 58). One later member of the family so admired these buildings that he adopted the great tower as a symbol on his seal for authenticating documents (pl. 54).[29] Perhaps he perceived them as underlining his royal connections.

BISHOP BUILDERS

One group of patrons in this period deserves individual attention for their exceptional importance as castle builders. The small group of men who occupied the seventeen medieval bishoprics of England had a formative influence on the world around them. This was in large part by virtue of their role in the government of the church, a compelling force in the medieval world both politically and spiritually. But it also reflected their remarkable status and connections. Most of those appointed in this period came from a small circle of clerks involved in royal administration and were personally close to the king. Both for this reason, and because their office could not pass to offspring – even if they had them – they were attractive agents for the crown. Without a future generation to save for, bis-

hops also naturally tended to throw their resources wholeheartedly into the world. As a group, they deserve to be viewed after the crown as the greatest builders of the entire Middle Ages. In personal terms, they were also amongst the most remarkable.

Three great bishop builders of this period have received considerable scholarly attention and such is the scope of their work that it is impossible not to break briefly into lists. The first is Roger, bishop of Sarum or Salisbury (1103–39), who, as chancellor of Henry I and justiciar of England, became a second ruler of the kingdom.[30] He built or substantially reworked five major castles, all in the context of wider estates, religious foundations and boroughs. Prior to the events of the Anarchy, he ranks as the greatest builder of the early twelfth century. In order of importance, the projects were the cathedral church and castle at Old Sarum (Wiltshire);[31] Sherborne Castle (Dorset) – the abbey was the seat of his bishopric up until 1075; Devizes and Malmesbury (both Wiltshire); and Kidwelly (Carmarthen).[32] Roger's son or nephew Alexander, dubbed 'the Magnificent', became bishop of Lincoln (1129–48), and began work around 1135 to a massive new castle at Newark and to another at Banbury (Oxfordshire) in 1136.[33] And lastly, Henry of Blois, a grandson of the Conqueror and brother of King Stephen, who was bishop of Winchester, one of the richest sees in Europe, for an extraordinary forty-two years (1129–71). In 1138 it was noted that he had built 'a palace with a strong tower' at Wolvesey in

55 (*facing page*) An aerial view of the massive earthworks at Old Sarum, Wiltshire, in origin an Iron Age hill fort. The cross-shaped foundations of the cathedral church, begun in the late eleventh century and much aggrandised by Bishop Roger, stand in the outer circuit of the defences (1). In the centre of the site is the castle enclosure (2), entered through an imposing twin-towered gatehouse with D-shaped towers. The castle was dominated by a great tower (3), which was probably erected around 1100, incorporating an annexe and forebuilding in imitation of Corfe (see pl. 64). Beside this stood a large courtyard of stone domestic buildings (4). Relations between the cathedral and the castle were strained. In the early thirteenth century the cathedral, later surmounted by its celebrated spire (5), was transferred to the newly established city of Salisbury. The move followed complaints by the canons that the garrison made them fearful of attending services and the constable refused the congregation access to the church.

Winchester,[34] as well as castles at Taunton (Somerset), Downton (Wiltshire), Merdon and Bishop's Waltham (both Hampshire) and Farnham (Surrey).[35] These were castles he continued to alter throughout his long life.

Not just the castles, but also the whole spectrum of building projects undertaken by these men astonished contemporaries. One twelfth-century commentator, William of Malmesbury, wrote of Bishop Roger of Sarum:

He was a prelate of great mind and spared no expense towards completing his designs, especially in buildings, which may be seen in other places, but most particularly at Sarum [and at Malmesbury]. For there he erected extensive edifices at vast cost and with surpassing beauty; the courses of stone being so correctly laid that the joint deceives the eye and leads it to imagine that the whole wall is composed of a single block.[36]

This quality of masonry finish, formerly the exclusive preserve of ecclesiastical architecture, was used by this group of patrons in their castle building to an unprecedented extent. It was, however, just one extravagance upon which others were laid. Their buildings were also enriched with large quantities of carving, much of it in the form of geometric patterns. These were remarkably varied and wittily applied to underline the relative importance or relationship of the spaces that they decorated. At Old Sarum such ornament even extended to the chimneys of the castle, which were carved with complex geometric patterns. Lastly, the castle buildings erected by this group illustrate an interest in formal and regular planning: at Wolvesey, Old Sarum (pl. 55) and Sherborne there were created residential complexes arranged around stone-built courtyards.[37] This idea may have been indebted to the form of monastic cloisters or the house erected by Henry I in the upper ward at Windsor by 1110. Whatever the explanation, they exceed any other surviving residential complex in scale and grandeur.

There is one other bishop of this period whose architectural patronage was quite as spectacular but remains much less widely appreciated. In 1099 a royal clerk, Ralph 'Flambard', a favourite of William Rufus, was appointed bishop of Durham, perhaps after purchasing the bishopric. The nickname came from the colour of Ralph's hair and it celebrated his personality as a flaming brand or incendiary. In 1101, following the death of William Rufus, he was sent in chains by Henry I to the White Tower at London as

a popular scapegoat.[38] Here, he more than justified the reputation of his name:

. . . One day a rope was smuggled to him in a gallon of wine. The generous bishop then proceeded to lay on a great banquet at which his guards ate with him and became intoxicated with all the wine they had consumed. When they were completely drunk and snoring soundly, the bishop produced the rope and tied it to the column which stood in the middle of a window of the tower: holding his pastoral staff with him, he climbed down the rope . . .

The rope proved too short, but he jumped down safely and escaped.[39] Flambard later came to terms with Henry I and began a redevelopment of Durham and its castle.

What is chiefly remarkable about Flambard's work is the scale on which he conceived it. Under his direction, the heart of the late medieval and modern city was effectively brought into existence. Writing from the perspective of the cathedral monastery, one of the monks at Durham wrote of his achievements:

Although the city was naturally fortified, he made it stronger and more majestic with a wall. From the chancel of the church to the stronghold of the castle he constructed a wall of great length. The space between the church and the castle, which had been occupied by many dwellings, he made as flat and open as a field, so that the church should be infected neither by the contamination of their filth, nor the danger of fires. He joined the two banks of the river Wear with a stone bridge, a major construction supported on arches.[40]

The clearance of present-day Palace Green between the cathedral and castle is a particularly remarkable piece of town planning, creating a huge open space by medieval urban standards (see pl. 44).

To this list of buildings must be added Flambard's work to the castle, which the monk does not mention. Within the walls he constructed a massive new hall block at right angles to that created by his predecessors in the eleventh century. The building was damaged by fire in 1154, and its present form owes much to the work of his twelfth-century successor, Hugh du Puiset, and will be discussed below. He also rebuilt the gatehouse to the castle itself. This building was much reworked in the nineteenth century but may originally have taken the form of a gate passage flanked on either side by a rectangular tower (pl. 56). All the

56 An engraving of Durham Castle by S. and N. Buck, dated 1728. To the left it shows the two tall hall ranges set at right angles to each other in the bailey. On the right is the motte with its great tower of stone erected in the late fourteenth century on the site of the earlier timber tower described by Prior Laurence. By the time this engraving was made, the great tower had also been incompletely reordered in the early sixteenth century and repaired as a ruin by several later bishops. The great gate described by Prior Laurence in the twelfth century as strong enough to be defended by a woman is in the centre. It preserves an early twelfth-century entrance arch and vault, which share decorative details with the nave of the cathedral priory completed by Bishop Flambard. The building was heavily reworked in the late eighteenth century, but the plan, with two projecting towers to either side of the gate, is medieval. By the late Middle Ages the approach to the gate was enclosed by a fortified court or barbican.

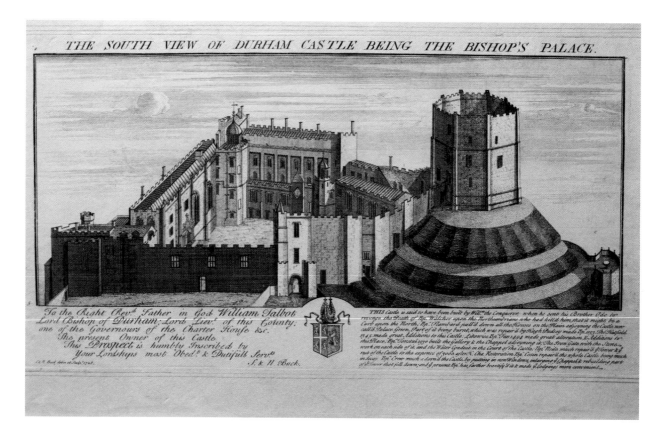

THE SOUTH VIEW OF DURHAM CASTLE BEING THE BISHOP'S PALACE.

surviving work Flambard undertook in the castle bears close comparison in architectural detail to the nave of the adjacent cathedral, which he also completed.[41]

An eyewitness account of Flambard's castle is provided by Laurence, prior of Durham, in a poem of the 1140s that describes the city of Durham. The poem is so high flown that translated quotation is rather confusing, but the text deserves summary. Laurence begins by dilating on the natural strength of the town, its walls and its gates. Only then does he move to the castle, which stands in an open space like a queen, commanding all that it overlooks. The first object to attract his attention is the fortress (*arx*) on the motte. From the summit of this, a tower of warlike aspect springs up into the sky, supported on four great posts and ringed by a beautiful gallery. Evidently this was a timber structure, possibly similar to the tower depicted on a stone capital at Westminster of around 1100 (pl. 59). Around the tower is a circular wall and access to it is gained up a bridge. This is of such majesty and scale that the slope is gentle and easy to walk. Descending this bridge metaphorically, Laurence leads us to the bailey. This is no barren space but packed with buildings. Here stand two great palaces, each with its own porch, and beside them the chapel, supported on six columns. Laurence conjures up a picture of the bailey

busy with activity and colour. At its centre is a well providing an abundance of water. The imaginary tour concludes at the mighty gate to the castle, so strong as to be defensible by a woman. From this extends the bridge onto Palace Green, which the castle shelters from north winds.[42]

In the context of the longer description, Laurence's treatment of the castle serves to make one particularly important point: that the tower where he begins his description is the physical centrepiece to the whole of Durham. In other words, what the poem actually calls 'the castle', and what modern audiences now think of as the same, is actually the bishop's bailey in a much bigger physical entity also known in the Middle Ages as Durham Castle. The peninsula of the medieval town was formerly divided into a further two baileys and their extent is reflected today in the two names – North Bailey and South Bailey – that are applied to the single long street that runs along its length. Many of the houses along this street are known to have belonged to individuals performing knight service at Durham and they formed, therefore, an integral part of the castle. The tower of Durham symbolised the bishop's control over everything within the embrace of the wider castle walls: his palace, the town and the cathedral priory.

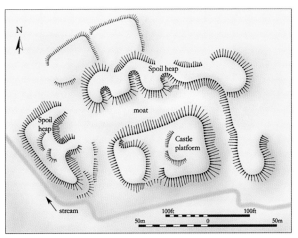

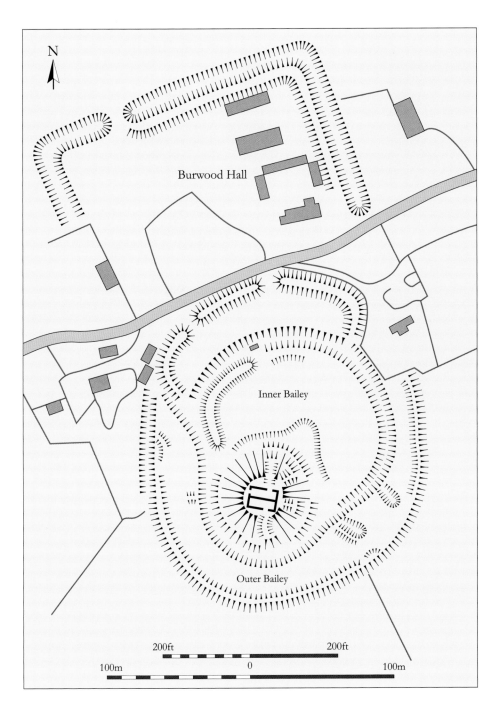

Burwood Hall

Inner Bailey

Outer Bailey

200ft   200ft

100m   0   100m

Spoil heap

moat

Spoil heap

Castle platform

stream

100ft   100ft

50m   0   50m

57 (*above and top right*) Two examples of regularly planned earthwork defences: Mileham, Norfolk (above), was a castle and borough foundation, but Burwell, Cambridgeshire (top right), was a creation of the Anarchy. It was here that an arrow fatally injured Geoffrey de Mandeville, earl of Essex, during a confrontation in 1144, probably in August. He was killed while inspecting the defences of this newly built castle, which had been erected to threaten his lines of communication. It is likely that the work of constructing the ditches was incomplete when he arrived there, hence the curious spoil heaps around the main rectangular enclosure. In the later Middle Ages other buildings were erected on the site and may have further confused the plan.

ARCHITECTURAL CONTINUITIES

The Motte and Gatehouse

In certain points, the continuities in castle architecture between the late eleventh century and the early twelfth need not detain us. Earthworks continued to be the mainstay of castle design in the form of mottes and baileys. These remained as variable in scale as before, though certain regions – notably East Anglia – seem to have developed several unusually massive designs. The tradition of earthworks in the area – at sites such as Castle Acre, Norfolk, and Pleshey, Essex – probably resulted from poor local stone supplies. A small minority of earthworks created in this period across the kingdom are set out in regular forms, including circles and rectangles. At Mileham, Norfolk, for example, a round castle plan intersects with a rectangular borough enclosure to create a plan in the shape of a keyhole, and at Burwell, Cambridgeshire, which was under construction in 1144, a rectangular bailey was planned (pl. 57).

The vast majority of fortifications that surmounted such earthworks probably continued to be constructed in wood, and our knowledge of their form is as circumscribed as before. But a growing number of surviving stone buildings inform our appreciation of these lost structures. From around 1100 there occur the earliest examples of masonry fortifications added to mottes. Virtually without exception these take the form of stone walls that encircle the summit of the mound, a structure termed a 'shell keep' in much modern literature. Perhaps the finest surviving example of such a stone enclosure of this kind from the 1140s is to be found at Arundel in Sussex, which is a regular circle in plan (pl. 58). Entrance to it was through a splendidly ornamented door, the restored

remains of which still survive. Another early and particularly well-preserved example of this form survives at Lincoln. Such defences were presumably widely paralleled in timber.

Of the interior arrangements of such fortified motte enclosures we know virtually nothing. If the summit was large enough it might accommodate numerous buildings, though no substantial examples of such structures survive from the twelfth century. It is a noteworthy curiosity that mottes surmounted only by low buildings enclosed within a wall are a peculiarity in twelfth-century Europe as a whole. The closest parallels for such English buildings are to be found in the Netherlands, for example, the twelfth-century motte fortifications at Leiden.[43] More commonly in France and in other English sites, the motte wall enclosed a free-standing tower, as was evidently the case at Durham. Several stone examples of such structures have been excavated, of which Farnham is perhaps the most celebrated. The central tower in this case was built up on foundations stretching right through the depth of the motte to natural ground level.[44]

Numerous castle gatehouses from this period survive from across the country, often in a very fragmentary or reworked state. Almost without exception, these take the form of a rectangular tower with a centrally placed gate passage running through it. Intriguingly, many of the largest stand in castles with mottes rather than great towers, as if they are making up for an architectural deficiency. This is the case, for example, with the gate towers at Arundel, Lewes and Lincoln. Two gatehouses of episcopal build also deserve individual mention. The first was erected by Bishop Alexander at Newark, Nottinghamshire, around 1135 as the architectural focus of a towered castle. This was an unusually grand building and contained a suite of domestic chambers, a design broadly following in the tradition of Ludlow. At Old Sarum there was a gatehouse designed with a pair of D-shaped towers flanking the gate passage.[45] The precise date of this building is uncertain, but it could well have been built by Roger before 1139. If so, this twin-tower design is – along with Flambard's entrance to Durham Castle with rectangular towers described above – the earliest of its type in England and a later staple of English castle architecture. The design was possibly inspired by Roman precedent.

Finally, it is worth observing that, with the exception of gatehouses, it seems to have remained rare in this period to construct towers along the length of a

58   Arundel, Sussex. A view of the motte surmounted by its so-called shell keep. This stone enclosure was probably built by William d'Albini to celebrate his title from 1141 as earl of Sussex. He received the castle and its rape through his wife, Adeliza, widow of Henry I. As first constructed, the masonry enclosure on the motte was laid out on a circular plan and entered through a richly ornamented door. This blocked entrance is partially visible to the right of the towers added to the structure about 1380. To the left of the photograph is visible the rear of a large gate tower probably built around 1100 and also remodelled in the fourteenth century. It was typical for castles with mottes rather than great towers of stone to possess prominent gatehouses.

great towers commonly developed an elaborate entrance system with a stair and porch housed within a subsidiary tower, termed a forebuilding. Some of the grandest also incorporated unusually complex internal plans. Evidence for processes of variation and addition is apparent by 1100 in two outstanding great towers erected under royal patronage at Norwich (Norfolk) and Corfe (Dorset).

A castle had existed at Norwich since at least 1075, when it featured in the events of a rebellion. But this building was completely refashioned by William Rufus, a king notorious for the extravagance of his lifestyle. He began work on a great tower, an operation that almost certainly coincided with the translation of the cathedral to Norwich from Thetford in 1094. Excavation has shown that the heart of the early castle took the form of an earthwork enclosure. In preparation for the new building this was filled and then heaped over to create a huge motte with a flat top. On this was begun a squared-planned tower, its foundations secured against the settlement of earth in the newly raised motte with baulks of timber. The building appears squat, a proportion emphasised by the absence of corner turrets. Its detailing bears direct technical comparison to that of the cathedral rising beside it (pl. 62).[46]

The façades at Norwich were divided into grids by a combination of regularly placed buttresses and tiers of arcading. In classic medieval fashion, the treatment of the outside of the building advertises the internal design: the tall basement level is without external ornament, a reflection of its mundane purpose as a storage area (it also originally incorporated the only rubble walling in the building, though this was replaced by a disapproving architect in the nineteenth century). By contrast, the upper floors have always been faced in cut stone with levels of arcading corresponding to the levels of interior chambers and, on the top storey, to the setting of the roof. The varied tiers of arches reflect the complex split levels of the interior and impose an ingenious geometric order and system of proportion on what would otherwise appear to be an irregular arrangement of windows.

Attached to one side of the tower is a raised porch or forebuilding, which received a broad entrance stair rising from the top of the motte (pl. 63). Apart from the example at Corfe, there is no exact precedent in English architecture for this feature. Earlier great towers, such as the White Tower and its Norman predecessors, had probably been provided with timber

59 Westminster Palace, London, a capital of *circa* 1100. The sculpture shows a soldier with an axe and shield collapsing on his knees at the foot of a staircase that leads up to a tower on four posts. He has just been struck down by a spear thrust by a defender from the tower. With its four supporting posts, this structure accords well with Prior Laurence's description of the great tower on the motte at Durham. The form of the tower depicted here as a raised platform with an open space beneath is very intriguing. It may explain such stone structures as the forebuilding of Norwich, which has an upper chamber supported on a vault (see pl. 63). The patterning on the platform walls may represent painting on the timber to make it resemble masonry. The weapons of other defenders are visible above the parapet.

wall. Such as exist or are known are rectangular in plan and either open-backed – as at Portchester – or four square, as in Roger of Sarum's work at Sherborne. In this case, the towers stand on the outer corners of the castle enclosure and are laid out in clear symmetrical plan (pl. 60). To judge from the surviving entrance tower of the castle, these must have been impressive structures, built throughout of finely cut masonry (pl. 61).

The Great Tower

This period witnessed an extraordinary flowering in the tradition of great tower architecture. Such buildings remained a distinguishing feature of the most ambitious castle foundations, and prior to the death of Henry I appear always to be associated with royal patronage, either directly or through figures of royal blood or notable favourites. From the late 1130s onwards, however, and during the Anarchy, several earls additionally built them as symbols of their wealth and power.

In broad terms there occurred from the late eleventh century the aggrandisement – in terms of ornament, quality of masonry and complexity of planning – of the early great tower tradition in England as represented by the Tower of London. In particular, English

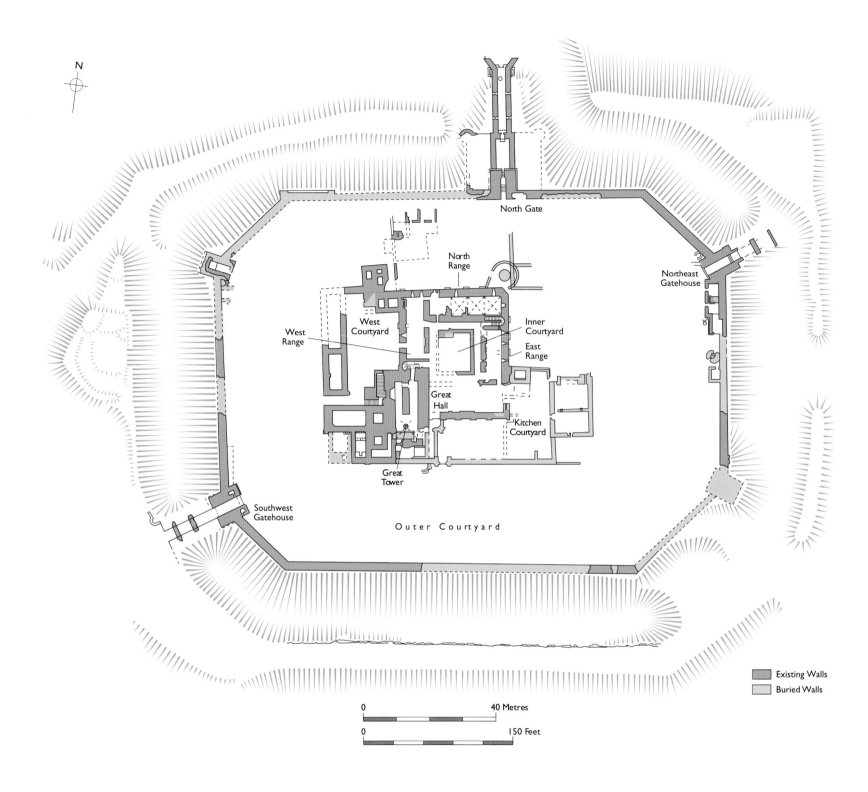

N

North Gate

North
Range

Northeast
Gatehouse

West
Range

West
Courtyard

Inner
Courtyard

East
Range

Great
Hall

Kitchen
Courtyard

Great
Tower

Southwest
Gatehouse

Outer Courtyard

Existing Walls

Buried Walls

0   40 Metres

0   150 Feet

60 (*facing page*) A plan of Sherborne, Dorset, built by Roger, Bishop of Salisbury (1103–39). The castle is regular in design: it comprises an inner court dominated by a great tower and enclosed by a curtain wall with symmetrically placed towers and gates. Sherborne was a particularly important possession for Roger. He was abbot of the great monastery here until 1122, and the church had been the cathedral of his see of Salisbury before 1075. The castle was seized from him in 1135 and remained in royal hands until the mid-fourteenth century, when it was granted to the earl of Salisbury. Bishop Wyville of Salisbury used the opportunity to win it back for his see, in whose hands it remained until the Reformation.

61 The south-west gate of Sherborne, Dorset, was probably built around 1120. It gives a good impression of the scale and architectural quality of the largely ruined outer wall and towers of the castle. Extensive use is made of exquisitely cut blocks of stone with very fine mortar joints. The interior of the gate was remodelled and new windows were inserted within it by Sir Walter Raleigh. He was granted the castle by Elizabeth I in 1592 and reordered the buildings, including the great tower. He also built Sherborne Lodge nearby.

entrance porches and stairs. Indeed, such is the lightness of the forebuilding at Norwich that it might be a realisation in stone of a timber structure erected on four posts.

The head of the stair and the forebuilding door were divided by a drawbridge, the only obvious concession in the design to defence. Sadly, the interior of the great tower at Norwich has been entirely gutted. As a result, there has been considerable scholarly debate about the original form of the building. What all accounts agree on, however, is that it comprised a complete and complex domestic plan, including a hall (which stood two storeys high), chambers, a kitchen, a chapel and a battery of sixteen latrines, evidence of eleventh-century courtly standards of hygiene.[47]

Set on a natural outcrop of rock, the great tower of Corfe Castle remains one of the great landmarks of the south-west (pl. 64); and it was deliberately constructed to be so. Demolition work with gunpowder in the 1640s has added to, rather than detracted from, its dramatic outline. In the absence of documentary evidence, the tower has been variously dated, but its architectural details and the form of its beautifully regular stonework would most plausibly suggest a date in the late eleventh century, possibly even in the 1080s.[48] Despite having been reordered on many occasions in its long history as a residence, the original form of the tower is relatively easy to reconstruct. It was designed on a square plan and rose four storeys high, a building tall in proportion to its breadth (unlike Norwich). Rising up the full height of the tower was a spine wall, which divided the basement and each of the two upper floors into two unequal rooms. The top storey of the building enclosed the roof and is ornamented externally with a blind arcade of arches.

Access to the interior was provided via a forebuilding, approached up an external stair. This is a much more complex structure than the example at Norwich, comprising three storeys and an internal stair with doors into the tower on first- and second-floor levels. The only obvious precedent for this multiple-storey forebuilding design is at Loches (Indre-et-Loire), built between 1012 and *circa* 1035 (see pl. 21). This possesses the sole stone forebuilding in France that can be reliably dated prior to 1100 and is by far the most complex ever constructed on the Continent. That these far-distant buildings were directly related in architectural terms is further suggested by the tall proportions that they share.[49] Projecting from the tower beside the fore-

62 Norwich, Norfolk. A view of the south face of the great tower, begun in the 1090s. In startling contrast there stands beside it the lift shaft associated with the development of a new shopping mall opened in 2000. The tower was erected on a huge and freshly raised motte that incorporated earlier earthworks and, consequently, the building settled unevenly. It was refaced in the nineteenth century, when all the original external ornament was faithfully replaced. As originally built, the basement was of rubble construction and the upper levels were of cut stone, a finish that externally reflected the relative importance in functional terms of the two. The decorative arcades on the tower exterior are arranged in horizontal bands that observe strict proportions. The rich architectural detailing of the great tower is directly derived from that on the cathedral, which was established in the city in 1094. Presumably the projects were connected.

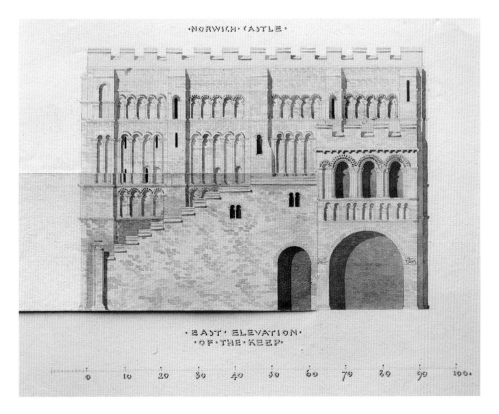

·NORWICH·CASTLE·

·EAST·ELEVATION·
·OF·THE·KEEP·

0 10 20 30 40 50 60 70 80 90 100

63 Norwich, Norfolk. Wilkin's watercolour survey of the east façade of the great tower was engraved for *Archaeologia*, 12 (1796). The stepped wall to the left conceals a flight of steps that rose to the forebuilding on the right. Between the head of the steps and the forebuilding turret was a drawbridge that spanned the pit created by the narrower of the two arches in the drawing. The broader arch within the turret is very richly treated in architectural terms: within it is a richly detailed rib vault (not visible here) and there are sculpted figures of lions at capital level on the exterior. Earlier great towers in England appear to have been entered up timber staircases. The light construction of the forebuilding, really an elevated porch, suggests an origin for the design in timber architecture.

building at Corfe is a second subsidiary structure, an annexe. Such is the organisation of doors in the main tower that although the masonry of the two structures is not interlaid they must have been planned together. On its upper floor the annexe contains a chapel and below a series of latrines.

Between the Tower of London, Norwich and Corfe are to be found the architectural ideas that informed to different degrees every major great tower of the twelfth century in England. Each building, moreover, fathered direct copies. Norwich inspired the great tower of Castle Rising, Norfolk, begun by William d'Albini after his brilliant marriage to the widow of Henry I, Queen Adeliza, in 1138 (pl. 65). Like its model, Castle Rising incorporates all the interiors necessary for domestic living on a grand scale, including a hall, kitchen, chamber and chapel (pl. 66).

The design of Corfe, meanwhile, is likely to have been the model for the series of castles constructed or expanded by Roger, bishop of Sarum, including perhaps the lost great tower of Devizes.[50] Finally, the Tower of London is the most likely inspiration behind Henry I's great tower at Bamburgh (pl. 67), a building of unique and complex internal design. The unmistakeable point of comparison in this case is that Bamburgh incorporates a first-floor chapel vaulted throughout in the body of the tower, a feature other-

wise unparalleled in English design outside London and Colchester (pl. 68).[51]

But particular ideas from these three buildings were also independently reworked as part of a wider and ever richer tradition of great tower design. This developed along regional lines and followed a discernible pattern. Typically, the first great tower in a particular area was of royal construction. Such a building might reflect very disparate architectural sources, a natural consequence of the geographical breadth of royal patronage in this period and the relatively small number of highly trained masons capable of overseeing a project of this complexity and scale. Then the royal building fathered local copies that emulated its distinctive features.

The development of a local tradition of great tower design is best illustrated across the northern border of England, which both William Rufus and Henry I wished to claim at the expense of Scotland. William Rufus first subdued the area and divided the western seaboard into castleries. It was probably in his reign that work began to a great tower at Lancaster, then the most northerly centre of royal power. This important building is unfortunately inaccessible today as a prison and it is not clear what internal features are original or inserted. But Henry I then drove the border north, consolidating his power with the construction of two further great towers. The first of these was probably begun in the 1120s at Bamburgh, the ancient seat of Northumbrian royal power and now the castle of the king's sheriff in the county.

Bamburgh appropriately borrows its proportions and internal design from the Tower of London, but the mason constructing it obviously felt the need for a stone forebuilding, a feature that its model lacked. This he created by contriving a stair and entrance lobby within one very thick wall of the tower. The idea was then directly copied at Henry I's second great tower in the region, at Carlisle. This was probably begun in symbolic conjunction with Henry's plantation of a bishopric in the city in 1133, part of an attempt to give the western seaboard a proper political focus. It is notable that the idea of a swallowed forebuilding enjoyed considerable subsequent popularity in the north, being copied at Richmond Castle, Yorkshire, in the 1160s (see pl. 84).

Although strictly outside the scope of this book, it deserves mention that such patterns can also be discerned in Normandy. They illustrate the degree to which the architectural epicentre of the Anglo-

64 Corfe, Dorset, view of the great tower from the east. This building was the first great tower erected in the south-west of England. It could have been built at any stage from the 1080s onwards. As such, it also has a claim to being the first castle building in England constructed entirely of cut stone, a quality of finish usually reserved for church architecture. Unlike the Tower of London, it is tall in relation to its plan, a proportion that may suggest a connection with the great tower of Loches (see pl. 21 above). Buttresses articulate the exterior of the tower at regular intervals and the roof of the original building was countersunk to the level of the external blind arcade. The tower possessed a forebuilding and a second subsidiary tower or annexe (visible to the left). It is probably in imitation of this building that several later south-western great towers, such as Old Sarum and Sherborne, incorporate annexes. The interior of the main tower comprised two upper floors over a basement. It was divided internally at each level by a spine wall. Curiously, there appears to have been no means of access in the body of the tower between the first and second floors. This implies the existence of a stair within the forebuilding tower in the manner of Loches. The building had no corner turrets, an absence imitated in many later great towers of the south-west.

65 (*top*) The great tower, Castle Rising, Norfolk. It was probably begun around 1138 by William d'Albini, the husband of Henry I's widow, Queen Adeliza. In several details, including its low, squat outline, Castle Rising is evidently a copy of the royal tower at Norwich begun by William Rufus forty years before. The forebuilding is very richly treated with sculpture, as befits its role as a grand entrance to a hugely expensive and prestigious building. The pitched roof is a thirteenth-century addition.

66 (*bottom right*) Plans of the great tower at Castle Rising, Norfolk. Its internal arrangements seem to follow those of the gutted interior of the great tower of Norwich, in as far as the latter can now be reconstructed. On the principal floor it is possible to identify with reasonable security: the hall (1), perhaps with a throne niche (2), a kitchen (3), a great chamber (4) and a chapel (5). The chapel altar stood beneath a vault in the thickness of the wall. Access to the apartments was through a grand door from the forebuilding (6), now blocked. There may also have been a balcony accessible from the principal chambers (7). On the ground floor were service and storage chambers.

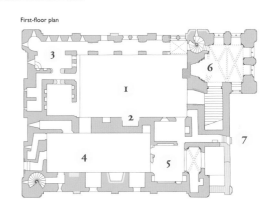

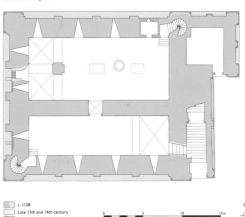

CASTLE RISING CASTLE FLOOR PLANS

First-floor plan

Ground-floor plan

c. 1138
Late 13th and 14th century
16th and 17th century
19th century

Norman realm had shifted its focus decisively by the mid-twelfth century from Normandy to England. For example, Henry I's great tower of Falaise is clearly modelled on Norwich, as may be the forebuilding arrangement at Arques.[52] Henry I, indeed, was as active in creating a network of great towers in his Norman dominions as in England.

While great towers of this period can be fitted within architectural family trees, it is nevertheless important to emphasise that this approach does not do them full justice. This is true partly because there are many missing buildings, which makes it difficult to piece together a complete picture of how this tradition evolved. In the south-west, in particular, there are some crucially important buildings about which little is securely known, notably at Taunton,[53] Bristol[54] and Gloucester.[55] All three great towers were probably built in the reign of Henry I, but little more can be said about them with confidence. Another difficulty with studying this genre of architecture too formally is that great towers were prodigy buildings that were devised to stagger expectation and outshine rivals. To make this point, it is worth turning briefly to two quite different, but related buildings, in the first division of the genre.

In January 1127 Henry I granted custody of Rochester Castle to William de Corbeil, archbishop of Can-

First Floor

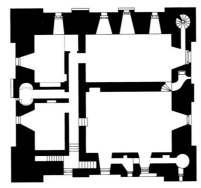

Second Floor

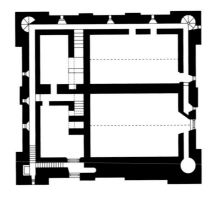

Ground Floor

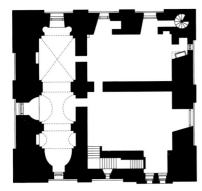

Roof Level

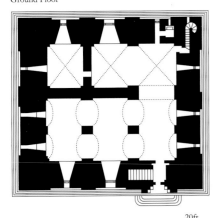

20ft   20ft

10m   0   10m

67 (*facing page*)   The great tower of Bamburgh, Northumberland, was built by Henry I, possibly under the direction of a mason called Osbert who was at work in the castle in 1131. From 1095 Bamburgh was the northern-most royal castle in England and the seat of the sheriff of the county. This building, in the tradition of the White Tower of London, was presumably meant to advertise in stone and mortar the presence of royal authority in

this remote and independent corner of the realm. The base of the tower is richly moulded, a highly unusual and lavish treatment found in only a handful of early twelfth-century buildings (see pl. 70).

68 (*above*)   Plan of the great tower of Bamburgh, Northumberland, showing the probable form of the twelfth-century structure. Instead of a forebuilding, the entrance stair has been swallowed into

one wall. This idea was subsequently copied in several great towers in the north of England, including Carlisle and Richmond. The arrangement of the interior with two cross walls set at right angles is extremely unusual and difficult precisely to parallel. It allowed for the creation of a fully vaulted chapel at first-floor level, a detail doubtless drawn from the example of the White Tower at London.

terbury, and to his successors in perpetuity. As part of the grant, the king also gave permission for the construction of a fortification (*municionem*) or tower in the castle.[56] William de Corbeil was otherwise a remarkable architectural patron – amongst other projects he completed the new cathedral church at Canterbury and oversaw the re-foundation of Dover Priory – and he responded (possibly with royal subvention) by creating what one contemporary commentator described as 'a noble tower of outstanding size' at Rochester (pl. 69).[57] To the tops of its corner turrets, the great tower at Rochester is in fact the tallest great tower in Europe. Its tall proportion and complex forebuilding arrangements may ultimately be derived from Corfe, but this parentage does not explain its exceptionally spacious and richly detailed interior.[58]

In this respect, the tower at Rochester was probably informed by a building that reverses its proportions. At the time it was begun, work to a great tower at Canterbury is likely to have been well advanced. After Colchester, this has the largest plan of any great tower in Europe: a suitable mark of royal power in the governing city of the English church. In reflection of its size, the tower was internally divided by two spine walls and possessed an internal complexity of chambers to match Norwich or Bamburgh. From what can be reconstructed of its badly mauled details, it was also richly decorated with architectural sculpture (pl. 70). As a particular mark of extravagance, the tower rose from a delicately moulded plinth. The connection between these outwardly contrasting buildings at Rochester and Canterbury is suggested by a later building that shows an awareness of both. Aubrey de Vere (d. 1194) acceded to his patrimony in 1141 after his father's murder in a London riot. In the same year he received the title of earl of Oxford from the Empress Matilda. It was probably shortly after this event that he began a great tower built entirely of cut stone at Castle Hedingham, Essex (pl. 71). The tall proportions and complex internal arrangements relate it directly to Rochester. Its distinctively moulded plinth, however, shows that its designer also knew Canterbury.[59]

Following in the footsteps of great towers constructed by the king and his immediate circle was an ever increasing field of lesser buildings that clearly emulated their architectural example. Generally speaking, these are very simple structures, comprising a set of small chambers stacked one above the other. The tower at West Malling in Kent, a building long assumed to be part of a castle and attributed to Gundulf,

bishop of Rochester (though perhaps neither supposition is correct), stands at one extreme of this tradition.[60] In the manner of the Tower of London and Corfe it is ornamented on the exterior with arcades and comfortably appointed within. Rather more modest is the great tower at Goodrich in Herefordshire.[61] Goodrich (see pl. 150 below) may appear to belong to a different architectural world from the massive structure of Kenilworth. Nevertheless, it was designed on a rectangular plan and possessed a raised entrance, two of the classic characteristics of great tower architecture in this period.

With the architectural variety of these buildings in mind, the thorny issue of function should be addressed. The received understanding is that great towers are to be interpreted as residential buildings. To follow the logic of their plan, therefore, their architecture needs to be discussed in relation to a list of interior features necessary for grand domestic living in the period – the hall, the chapel, the chamber, etc. On this basis, great towers have been divided into two categories. The first of these are large buildings that – it is supposed – could comfortably incorporate a hall. Buildings of this kind, it is argued, comprised complete domestic plans. By contrast, those deemed too small to accommodate a hall have been treated as sets of withdrawing apartments or so-called solar towers. In these cases the assumption has been that the hall and other missing chambers stood around the building in the castle bailey.

Such analysis is not wholly misconceived, but it overlooks an important complication: the tradition of great tower architecture is demonstrably one of form and not function. What patrons wanted was a rectangular tower of great size that formed the visual centrepiece to a castle. That such structures were not of consistent function is powerfully suggested by the variety of their internal arrangement and placement within castle complexes. Instead, it is useful to think of three overarching types of great tower design. The first is exemplified by Norwich and its followers. These buildings can usually be understood as coherently planned residential buildings and are distinguished by the number and variety of their internal chambers. Such designs are very rare and stand in contrast to the mainstream. Most other great towers can be categorised according to whether they were erected with or without a spine wall. The former usually incorporate two large chambers on each floor, one slightly larger than the other; the latter a single chamber on each level.

69   A photograph of *circa* 1920 of the great tower of Rochester, Kent. The tower was built by William de Corbeil, archbishop of Canterbury, between 1127 – when the king gave permission for the construction of 'a fortification *municionem*) or tower' in the castle – and his death in 1136. To the tops of its corner turrets, this is the tallest Romanesque great tower to survive in Europe. Its principal front to the right is regularly planned with a symmetrical arrangement of windows. These advertise on the exterior by their number, size and ornament the gathering grandeur of the interior spaces they light. To the left is the forebuilding, which is approached up a stair that wraps around one angle of the tower. There was a chapel in the upper floor of the forebuilding. The tower incorporates cut stone imported from Caen in Normandy. At the heads of the walls are sockets for a projecting timber gallery or *bretasche* (see pl. 102).

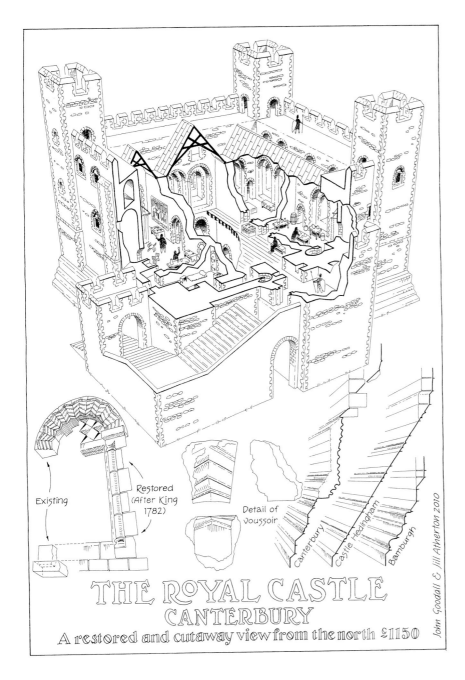

THE ROYAL CASTLE CANTERBURY

A restored and cutaway view from the north c.1150

Existing

Restored (After King 1782)

Detail of Voussoir

Canterbury

Castle Hedingham

Bamburgh

John Goodall & Jill Atherton 2010

70 A cut-away reconstruction by Jill Atherton of the great tower of Canterbury, Kent, probably built in the first quarter of the twelfth century. After Colchester, in terms of its plan this is the largest great tower ever constructed in Europe. It has suffered the demolition of its upper floor and all internal partitions since the late eighteenth century. The original form of the tower, however, can be reconstructed with reasonable confidence from a combination of documentary, visual and archaeological evidence. All the principal apartments appear to have been at first-floor level and included a hall, chamber and kitchen. Early descriptions of the building imply the existence of a continuous corridor in the depth of the wall at roof level, a feature paralleled in the Tower of London. The building rises from an ornamented plinth, a very unusual detail paralleled in England only at Hedingham and Bamburgh (see inset detail). The windows of the principal floors were ornamented with chevron, potentially a very early instance of this architectural ornament. Several features of the forebuilding are conjectural, including the gateway at the foot of the stair after the fashion of Rochester. A raised doorway, however, does exist that might have given access to its parapets.

The vast majority of great towers in the second and third categories, regardless of their size, were probably built as part of a larger residential plan. The most obvious illustration of this is to be found in designs where the great tower is integrated within a wider complex of stone buildings. Such, for example, was the case at Sherborne in Dorset, where the great tower forms part of a courtyard residence (see pl. 60). In this case, the building probably housed a chamber for its builder, Roger, bishop of Sarum. But at the bishop of Winchester's palace at Wolvesey, a similarly integrated tower appears to have served as a kitchen.[62]

Even great towers that demonstrably stood in physical isolation often appear to have been built in conjunction with other substantial stone buildings. Considering that it was still typical in this period to disperse the elements of a house, this arrangement must have seemed quite natural. A particularly grand illustration of this is the great tower at Castle Hedingham, built by the earl of Oxford after 1138 (pls 71–2). In its original form, this contained only one upper chamber of any scale and the likelihood is that it served a ceremonial rather than a domestic function.[63] Added to such physical survivals is a body of documentary evidence for royal castles. This clearly illustrates that many castles with great towers also possessed what are called 'king's houses', evidently separate royal residences. The Tower of London, for example, had one such by 1166.[64]

Great towers have long been represented as fortified houses, discrete and powerfully designed buildings in which the new rulers of a war-torn realm could live in safety. The strength of a great tower was part of its beauty to a twelfth-century onlooker, but its appeal was much more complex. These were prodigy buildings, standing as the visual focus to a castle, much as a church did in a monastic plan.[65] Their rectangular outline would have been increasingly familiar across England as the twelfth century progressed, a symbol of Anglo-Norman rule (pl. 73).

CASTLES OF THE ANARCHY: KENILWORTH AND DURHAM

Rather than try to present an overview of castle building through the dramatic and complex events of the Anarchy, it seems appropriate here to try and appreciate its impact through the particular experiences of two

castles central to the narrative of this book: Kenilworth and Durham. At the death of Henry I in 1135, Kenilworth was in the hands of a minor also called Geoffrey de Clinton, the son of the castle founder. The earl of Warwick saw in this situation a welcome opportunity to be rid of the neighbours planted on his land by the king. A hard-fought battle then ensued in 1136–7 between Clinton, who was a ward of his uncle, and the earl. Of the course of the fighting, nothing is known beyond the incidental details provided by two charters. One issued by the young Geoffrey *circa* 1138 records his recovery of the castle and honour of Brandon. Since Brandon was one of the original elements of the barony of Kenilworth, this suggests that the earl had briefly captured it.

The second charter was issued sometime before 1144 by the earl of Warwick's steward. In it, he agreed to make recompense for the damage he had inflicted on the estates of the priory of Kenilworth. Such destruction of property is typical of the warfare of the period and suggests that the area around Kenilworth had been systematically ravaged in order to put pressure on Clinton. But Clinton evidently proved impossible to oust and, probably in the summer of 1138, a treaty was drawn up between the two parties by which Clinton was guaranteed the barony but as a feudatory of the earl. To seal this, a marriage was organised between the earl's daughter and Geoffrey. Clinton was now safe in his barony and the earl back in control of the county. At Kenilworth, in other words, the breakdown of royal order permitted the earl of Warwick to reassert his position following a humiliating curtailment of power enforced by Henry I.[66] Similar episodes were enacted across the country.

Events in Durham were of much greater moment.[67] Early in 1141 the chancellor of the king of Scotland, William Cumin, visited Durham to find Bishop Geoffrey Rufus on his deathbed. He saw in the ailing body a magnificent opportunity for his own preferment to the see. Secretly persuading some of the bishop's officers to join his cause, he raced north to speak to his master. King David of Scotland was eager to extend his power southwards and readily backed the plan. Unfortunately, the bishop died on 6 May while Cumin was still away. But Cumin's friends kept the news secret by closing the gates of the castle to all comers and eviscerating the bishop's corpse. So there was a fresh cadaver to be exhibited when Cumin returned to the city. Confident of wider support for his prize he immediately seized the castle.

71 Castle Hedingham, Essex. The great tower was probably begun by Aubrey de Vere after he chose his title as earl of Oxford in 1141. This astonishing building is constructed throughout in beautifully cut stone. It shares numerous points of similarity with the great tower at Rochester, from the generic – it comprises five storeys (rather than the more usual four) – to the curious and technical: the latrine chutes of both buildings originally emptied into the basement rather than outside. The plinth of the tower is moulded, a highly unusual detail. In this case, the form of the moulding is similar to that found at Canterbury. It seems reasonable to assume, therefore, that the mason responsible was familiar with the grandest twelfth-century great towers in the south-east.

72 A photograph of 1920 of the ruined interior of the great tower of Castle Hedingham, Essex, probably begun around 1141. Raised above the basement and first-floor entrance level was a two-storey chamber divided by the broadest surviving Romanesque arch in Britain. The wall gallery that runs round the upper part of this room is ornamented so as to imply a prescribed direction of movement around it (some decorative sculpture is faced one way rather than being cut in the round). This is one of several details suggesting that the building was conceived with specific ceremonial uses in mind. As originally built, a pyramidal roof sat within the upper tier of windows (not visible here). The underside of the roof was probably ceiled in to conceal the timbers from beneath. New floors have since been installed within the tower.

Cumin was now in control of the see but he required formal appointment to it. Political events guaranteed him the support of King David and the local barons, who acknowledged him as overlord. His appointment was also endorsed by the Empress Matilda, currently triumphant in the ongoing civil war. But Cumin could not get the archdeacon of Durham and the chapter of the cathedral priory to elect him to the office. To his annoyance, they appealed over his head to Rome for a free election. In revenge, Cumin hounded the archdeacon from the diocese and settled down to rule the bishopric by *force majeure*. Besides the chapter, his only important opponent was a baron called Roger de Conyers. It may be significant that Roger probably had hereditary rights as constable of Durham Castle, rights that Cumin had presumably overlooked in his bid for power.

As part of his wider attempts to secure the see, Cumin built a motte and bailey castle at Northallerton in 1142. This was intended to protect the Yorkshire estates attached to the see of Durham and was put under the control of Cumin's nephew. To cement this intrusion into the political fabric of Yorkshire, he arranged a marriage between his nephew and the daughter of the virtual ruler of Yorkshire in the civil war, William le Gros, count of Aumale and earl of York.

Despite such prudent measures, by 1143 the tide of Cumin's affairs had begun to change. He not only lost the support of King David but also failed to prevent a canonical election for the bishopric. By this election, an extremely reluctant dean called William de Sainte-Barbe was consecrated bishop of Durham at York on 14 March 1143. Roger de Conyers openly identified with the new bishop and was forced to encastellate his home at Bishopton as protection against the predations of Cumin, who was incensed at the appointment. It was to this motte and bailey castle at Bishopton that Sainte-Barbe came in August of that year to receive the homage of many barons of his see. Supported by an armed retinue, he marched to Durham.

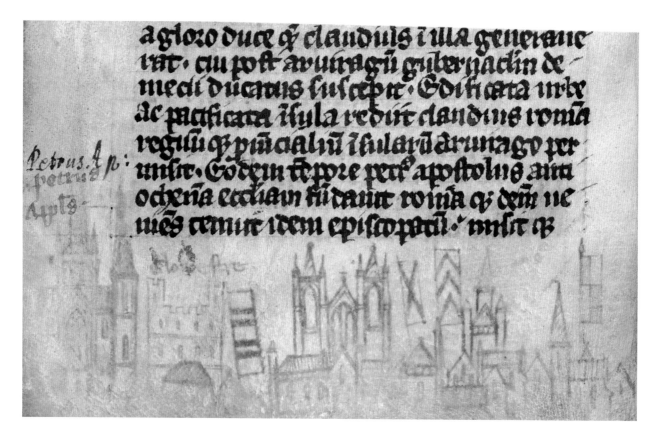

73 This early fourteenth-century view of the city of Gloucester provides a rare glimpse of an English medieval cityscape. Beside the spire of the abbey to the extreme left (now the cathedral) rises the rectangular outline of the castle great tower, architectural symbols of the forces of the church and state that brought the city into being. The great tower of Gloucester Castle was probably built in the early twelfth century. It is one of several important south-western examples of this genre of building – including Bristol and Taunton – to have been demolished.

Cumin refused the bishop entry to the city and determined to prevent anyone within it from supporting his opponent's cause. Early the next morning Cumin's men burst into the cathedral, smashing through the windows of the church and climbing in with ladders. Having roughed up the monks they then began fortifying the building like a castle. According to one account, this attack was undertaken in the fear that the monks would let in soldiers from the bishop's party to fortify the cathedral themselves as a second castle in the city.[68] Whatever the case, this action seems to have precipitated a reign of terror, and Cumin's men began ranging the city and the surrounding country-side looking for spoil. Accounts are vivid in their descriptions of the cruelties they inflicted: 'Some were to be seen being stretched out on racks, others being dragged upwards by their genitals, others shut up in tiny chests placed under stones and almost battered to pieces, others indeed in the depth of winter bound naked outside their homes.'[69]

Meanwhile, the frustrated Sainte-Barbe moved away to nearby Thornley, where he built a castle. But he did not have the power to check the activities of Cumin and he allegedly remained there in great hardship through the winter. In the spring of 1144 Cumin repeatedly attempted to trap the bishop. He also suc-cessfully took Thornley, which was betrayed to him. The terrified bishop fled to Lindisfarne and invoked the aid of King David. The Scottish king was now inclined to support the canonically elected bishop, but was temporarily restrained from intervening by the terms of a truce he was observing. Cumin's hopes now hung by a thread. The day before the truce expired – on 14 August 1144 – in a last bid to secure Durham his men began to convert the parish church at Merring-ton into a castle. Learning of the work, the bishop's barons attacked the building site, which had been almost surrounded by ditches. Cumin's men defended themselves from the church tower, but the castle was taken and its garrison killed or captured.[70]

Cumin's cause now rapidly collapsed. In the face of armed Scottish involvement, Thornley was retaken and control of Durham Castle conceded to Roger de Conyers. On 18 October 1144 Sainte-Barbe was at last received at Durham along with the archbishop of York and the bishop of Carlisle. Within the conventual buildings he was met by Cumin, who prostrated himself and promised to make amends for his mis-deeds. Cumin must then have witnessed the galling spectacle of seeing his rival enthroned as bishop. Six castles had played a role in Cumin's struggle – Durham Castle, the cathedral, Northallerton, Bishopton, Thornley and Merrington. Of these, the cathedral and the last three castles disappeared immediately; Bishopton has an uncertain history; and Northallerton survived as the centre of the bishop's Yorkshire estates into the late Middle Ages. Its survival was guaranteed by the next bishop of Durham, Hugh du Puiset (d. 1195), who extensively restored it. But Durham Castle, the key to the struggle, serenely outlived the conflict.

The experience of Durham during the Anarchy illustrates the rivalries that the strong government of Henry I had held in check. In the absence of an effective ruler this plum bishopric had become the object of open competition in which the contending parties had fought bitterly for supremacy. Castles had been of great importance in waging the conflict, so much so that the numbers in the region had multiplied alarmingly. Once a winner had emerged, they vanished. The struggle over Durham was resolved relatively quickly, but there were conflicts of a comparable scale elsewhere in the kingdom that would be resolved only with the accession of a dynamic, young king who would once more centralise power in his own hands.

5

THE EARLY ANGEVIN CASTLE

HENRY II AND RICHARD I

The protracted civil war in England between Stephen and Matilda was concluded in what might be termed a victorious defeat for the latter. By the treaty of Wallingford in 1153, King Stephen agreed that the kingdom of England should be inherited by Matilda's son, Henry of Anjou. In surety for the succession, a small group of major castles – including London, Windsor, Winchester and Lincoln – were placed in the hands of castellans who swore to deliver them up to Henry upon Stephen's death. This followed a year later, and Henry, an energetic twenty one year old, acceded to the throne without contest. To Henry, the kingdom of England was the crowning possession – in both senses of the word – of his so-called Angevin Empire. Besides England and Normandy, he held Anjou and Touraine by right of his father, Brittany by inheritance from his brother and Aquitaine through his wife. As a whole, these vast territories stretched from the Pyrenees to the borders of England. By the time of his death they included parts of Ireland as well.

Castles were the bones of this great empire, the centres from which it was governed and the means by which it was protected. As a direct result, Henry II (1154–89) necessarily ranks amongst the greatest indi-vidual castle builders of the Middle Ages. His work is very unevenly documented across his possessions, but in England some sense of its astonishing extent is pro-vided by the Pipe Rolls, a series of exchequer accounts that survive in unbroken sequence from 1155. These show that Henry II spent approximately half of his esti-mated annual revenue of £10,000 on his castles in England.[1] By contrast, very little documentation exists referring to his extensive works on castles in France. The partial loss of documentation serves to illustrate that castle building within the Angevin Empire was not centrally organised. Rather, it was episodic, with resources being directed through the relevant channels as need arose.

The results of Henry II's work were almost unfail-ingly spectacular. So too were the endeavours of two of his sons, the Angevin kings Richard I (1189–99) and John (1199–1216). Of these two, however, only the castle building of Richard's reign is treated in this chapter. His attention and resources were for the most part focused outside England. Much of the English building he undertook, moreover, followed on from that initiated by his father and developed architectural ideas that were prefigured from the 1170s. By contrast, John's reign witnessed a profound change in both the

Facing page: Peveril, Derbyshire.

pattern and idiom of castle building in England. His achievement was to lay the foundations for English castle building into the fourteenth century.

One of the most important trends in English castle architecture during the reigns of Henry II and Richard I was a widening gulf between the scale of royal and baronial building. In blunt terms, most baronial castles of the later twelfth century were considerably more modest than their royal counterparts. Surviving traces of them are also correspondingly fewer, being restricted largely to gate towers and stretches of wall. What does survive, however, suggests a steady increase in the use of stone, even in relatively modest projects.

For the barons of the realm, the principal constraining factor on their architectural patronage was the overbearing and intrusive character of Angevin rule. This circumscribed their independence and greatly reduced their resources in relation to those of the crown. A product of their great energy, the power of the Angevins was meanwhile given edge by the celebrated temper shown by all the leading figures in the dynasty. One of Henry II's outbursts, for example, was described like this: 'The king, enflamed with his customary fury, threw the cap from his head, untied his belt, hurled his mantle and other garments from him, removed the silk coverlet from the bed with his own hand and began to chew the straw of the bedding.'[2] This was not a mood in which to meet a king.

As a whole, this period witnessed the emergence of a new emphasis in castle design. Instead of a walled enclosure dominated by a great tower, it became increasingly common to develop castles as compositions of towers. In conjunction with this change, systems of concentric fortification were systematically explored for the first time to create layers of defences. Adding dynamism to these novelties was the emergence of a new building aesthetic. From the 1140s there began to develop in the Île-de-France and its environs an interest in creating delicate stone architecture on a monumental scale. In its native France the so-called Gothic style over the thirteenth century came to achieve its effect by reducing great churches to a fine cage of stone and hanging them with glass. This was arranged in such a way as to conceal the depth of the supporting walls and buttresses and to create thereby interiors of apparent structural impossibility. Its early development, however, was bound up in a fascination with spatial complexity, the creation of large windows, the application of inventive geometry, the visual integration of high stone vaults within buildings through careful articulation, and a fascination with the architecture of classical antiquity.[3]

When the architectural ideas generated by this style began to permeate England in the 1170s, masons showed themselves less interested in the structural possibilities offered by the Gothic style than its decorative and geometric aspects. In the field of castle architecture it was this latter quality that was particularly relished.

THE RESTORATION OF ROYAL ORDER

In England, Henry II's activities as a castle builder were initially conditioned by the events of the previous reign. The collapse of royal authority under Stephen had destroyed the political equilibrium of the realm, and Henry II determinedly sought to restore it. Where the interests involved were not too powerful, it was insisted that contested and royal property be restored to its owner at the time of the death of Henry I. As part of this process of putting the clock back, all castles built since 1135 were declared illegal and Henry II set about demolishing them. Where individuals stood against him he acted directly to break them, often building or appropriating castles in the process. By such activity he brought more castles into direct royal control in England than any previous Anglo-Norman king. In some cases he also consolidated the political settlement he imposed by the plantation of baronial castles, but on a much smaller scale than his predecessors.

The methods by which he worked are well illustrated with reference to East Anglia and the affairs of the Bigod family, one of the most powerful in the region. Hugh Bigod had done well out of the civil war and been raised to the dignity of an earldom in 1140, one of the large number created during the reign of Stephen. In Suffolk he held three castles: Walton, Framlingham and Bungay. At the last of these he almost certainly began work in the 1140s on the obligatory status symbol of a great tower, the remains of which still survive.[4] The earl was instrumental in securing the succession of Henry II, and in 1155 a grateful king confirmed him both in his earldom and the possessions granted to him by Stephen. But it seems that Henry II grew uncomfortable with this state of affairs and in 1157 he confiscated the earl's castles. At the same time he also destroyed the neighbouring castles of

74 The great tower of Orford, Suffolk, constructed between 1165 and 1173. It is laid out on a polygonal plan with three turrets at regular intervals around it and a triangular forebuilding. The walls are laced with passages and chambers to create a complex internal arrangement with several mezzanine levels set between the principal floors. A complete series of domestic and service chambers appropriate for grand living appears to have been incorporated within it, including a chapel in the upper storey of the forebuilding. This view shows the concentration of expensive cut stone around the forebuilding entrance and the use of rubble masonry in less visually important areas. In the foreground are the earthworks that cover the ruins of the walls and towers that formerly enclosed the tower.

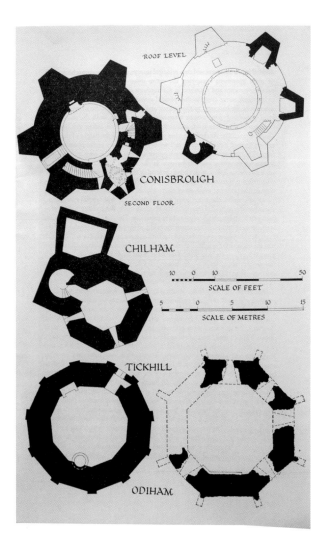

Geoffrey de Mandeville (d. 1166), earl of Essex, at Pleshey and Saffron Walden. In the latter case he flattened a very large great tower probably begun by de Mandeville's father (d. 1144) following his elevation to an earldom in 1140.[5]

Hugh Bigod was later restored to two of his castles – Framlingham and Bungay – probably in return for the sensational fine of £1,000 that was imposed by the king at Nottingham in 1165. The king, however, kept Walton in his own hands, a Roman coastal fort converted like Portchester into a castle with a great tower raised along the line of its outer wall.[6] In exactly the same year, he began work on a castle foundation at Orford that commanded its own harbour, quite possibly channelling the money from Bigod's fine into the new work.[7] This castle was presumably intended as a counterbalance to Framlingham and was established in classic form with a priory and borough. Work to Orford Castle is precisely documented in the Pipe Rolls, which record that between 1165 and 1173 more

than £1,400 was spent on it. Of this amount, £968 was spent in the first two years' work.[8] These huge sums well illustrate the disparity of royal and baronial resources: Orford was a medium-sized greenfield castle development for Henry II. It cost, however, substantially more than the fine, which was intended to push one of the greatest barons in the kingdom to his financial limits.

Orford Castle took the form of a turreted bailey with a great tower at its centre. The bailey is now ruined, but early depictions of the castle show that its stone walls were punctuated at regular points by towers on a rectangular plan. Within this bailey there almost certainly stood numerous buildings, but of their form we know nothing. The great tower, by contrast, is one of the best preserved from the twelfth century in England (pl. 74). It is designed on a polygonal plan, a feature that has received considerable attention. To explain why, it is necessary briefly to digress into the realm of modern castle scholarship.

Towers on circular and polygonal plans, it has been argued, were militarily more effective than the rectangular ones. This is because they presented glancing surfaces to missiles and lacked pronounced angles, which were vulnerable to attack. In consequence, Orford has been hailed as illustrating a new, scientific approach to fortification.[9] Moreover, a number of great towers have commonly been listed as carrying forward its ideas, amongst them three royal buildings, two of which can be dated from the Pipe Rolls: the great towers at Tickhill, Yorkshire, built 1179–82; Odiham, Hampshire, built 1207–12; and Conisbrough, Yorkshire, of the early 1180s. A fourth polygonal tower at Chilham, Kent, is usually associated with a period of royal ownership in the 1170s.[10]

The plans of these great towers can be found together in several standard works on castles, and their similarities are indeed notable (pl. 75).[11] But the most casual comparison also shows that they actually represent two families of buildings. Tickhill and Odiham are thin-walled towers without wall chambers (comparable, incidentally, to such French designs as Henry II's tower at Gisors, Eure, probably a work of the 1160s). Only Conisbrough and perhaps Chilham are true comparisons to Orford, their walls laced by passages and chambers.

Setting aside these niceties, the reality is more complicated than the conventional analysis of these buildings allows. In the first place, there is no tidy chronological change from square to round or polygo-

76 The great tower of Berkeley, Gloucestershire, probably begun in the 1150s, in a photograph of 1916. A 'castelulum' was founded at Berkeley by fitz Osbern immediately after the Conquest, but nothing securely is known of its form. It must have been following the redevelopment of the castle at the direction of Henry II between 1153 and 1156 that the motte was retained within a ring wall to create a bulging tower set with three projecting turrets. The turrets are articulated with narrow buttresses. One turret contains a fine vaulted chapel to serve the motte buildings. Entrance to the motte is via a stair housed in a forebuilding. The motte summit is divided by an arcaded spine wall, which was presumably integral to a cluster of domestic chambers. The hall, kitchen and other bailey buildings were laid out in their present form during the mid-fourteenth century.

nal forms in the great tower tradition, as one would expect if medieval builders actually recognised the former as militarily obsolescent. So, for example, as we have seen, the first round great tower was constructed in England in the 1140s at New Buckenham by William d'Albini, also the builder of the rectangular great tower at Castle Rising. And Henry II was probably erecting round towers from the 1180s onwards at Chinon (Indre-et-Loire).[12] Yet, as we shall see, great towers on a square plan continued to be erected into the thirteenth century. Moreover, circular and polygonal plans were already a feature of many shell keeps, such as Arundel and Cardiff, and the great tower of Berkeley Castle in Gloucestershire. This last building may have been erected under the indirect patronage of Henry II between 1153 and 1156, and is a curious cross between a great tower and a motte revetted in stone (pl. 76).

But if the design of Orford and its late twelfth-century peers does not reflect a response to military needs, what is to explain the clear fashion for such structures? Two answers present themselves. The first is a growing fascination across the architectural spec-trum of church and castle design with complex geometric forms. In this respect, it has been demonstrated that the plan and elevation of the great tower at Orford are generated by a rigorous system of geometry, the former based on a circle with a diameter of 49 feet (14.93 m) (pl. 77).[13] The second is the issue of money. In financial terms, the largest great towers of this period are all rectangular and some of these cost individually as much or more than the whole castle at Orford. That at Dover, for example, probably absorbed a substantial share of the £6,000 spent on the castle by Henry II in the 1180s (see below). From this perspective, the great tower at Orford looks like a miniaturised and geometrically complex version of its grander, rectangular relations: the forebuilding is crushed up as a curious triangular adjunct, and in place of four great corner towers there exist three pronounced turrets around the exterior.

Internally, the Orford great tower comprises a basement and two principal upper chambers, the roof being countersunk within the structure. Contrived within the walls on every level are a series of small

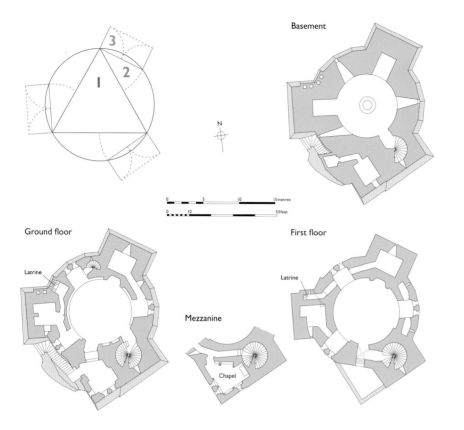

Basement

Ground floor

Latrine

N

First floor

Latrine

Mezzanine

Chapel

0   5   10   15 metres

0   10   50 feet

77 (above) Orford, Suffolk. Floor plans of the great tower with a reconstruction after T. A. Heslop of the basic geometric process involved in generating the design from an equilateral triangle and circle. The position and dimensions of the turrets are determined by the half-length of each side of the triangle. A slightly more complex third stage of geometric planning that more precisely generates the plan has also been proposed, but is not reproduced here. The distinctive and complex geometry of Orford is echoed in several important castle buildings into the fourteenth century, such as the Eagle Tower of Caernarfon (see pl. 165) and the great tower of Knaresborough (see pl. 192). Geometry of this kind could not only be drawn up easily by a mason on a sheet of parchment, but also on the building site itself using ropes and pegs.

78 (facing page, top) An engraving of Farnham, Surrey, published in 1737 by S. and N. Buck. The castle is first mentioned in 1138 as the possession of Henry of Blois, bishop of Winchester, but was demolished in the 1140s. In the later twelfth century Bishop Henry probably rebuilt the walls and towers shown here. The identical architectural treatment of the motte and bailey walls to create a double crown of fortifications with regularly placed towers is typical of the period. By the time this view was taken the towers of the outer bailey had been truncated.

79 (facing page, bottom) A plan of the great tower at Scarborough, Yorkshire, built in the years 1159–69 and shot in two by cannon fire during a siege in 1644. Its designer was clearly familiar with southern English architecture and

perhaps specifically the great East Anglian castles of the 1140s. For example, rather than having a swallowed entrance stair in the manner of Henry I's Bamburgh and Carlisle, there was created after southern English example the earliest externalised forebuilding in the north. A familiarity with East Anglian great towers is particularly suggested by the internal arrangements of the building. The basement and two upper floors were connected by a single, centrally placed stair, a detail otherwise known only at Hugh Bigod's great tower at Bungay, probably a work of the 1140s. And at first-floor level the room was divided by a central arch, a feature paralleled at Castle Hedingham. A curiosity of the plan is that one chamber on the upper floor appears to possess a window throne niche (1).

rooms including a kitchen, latrines, a water cistern and, in a turret at roof level, an oven. The upper floor of the forebuilding is occupied by a chapel, the most richly treated interior in the tower. Reused within some of the great tower fireplaces and an oven are fragments of twelfth-century encaustic tiles, the earliest to survive in England and testimony to the luxurious domestic interiors of the period.[14]

In one important detail, the design of the great tower illuminates the architectural interest in fragmenting castle architecture. The three turrets that rise up the great tower open out at basement level as small, barrel-vaulted interiors. This particular treatment is otherwise common in wall towers of this period; indeed, the particular details of Orford can be compared point by point with those later built by Roger Bigod at Framlingham. It is almost certain, therefore, that the turrets precisely reflect the architectural form of the lost bailey towers. In effect, the great tower is a condensed version of the outer bailey, a turreted wall reared up and drawn tight into a coherent architectural entity. This idea lies at the heart of castle design in this period: that a turreted wall can be adapted to create every element of a castle, from its outer defences to its great tower. The idea could also be applied to motte fortifications, as is illustrated by the late twelfth-century defences of the bishop of Winchester's castle at Farnham (pl. 78).

The construction of Orford shows how Henry II could use a new castle to announce his extended authority; but he also seized and redeveloped castles across the realm as a means of tightening his control of an area. William Aumale, for example, had been appointed earl of York in 1138 and, probably in celebration of the event, established a new castle with a great tower on the impregnable headland above Scarborough, Yorkshire (pl. 79). The land on which the new castle stood belonged to a royal manor and in 1155 Henry demanded it back. When Aumale refused, the king marched north at the head of an army and forced his surrender. Shortly afterwards, in 1159, Henry II began work on a new great tower within the castle, which cost upwards of £650 to construct.[15] A local monastic chronicler, William of Newburgh, claimed that the new building was erected because the earl's tower was decayed with age.[16] But since that building could have been only twenty years old, it seems more likely that Henry II's tower was built as architectural confirmation that the castle had changed hands.

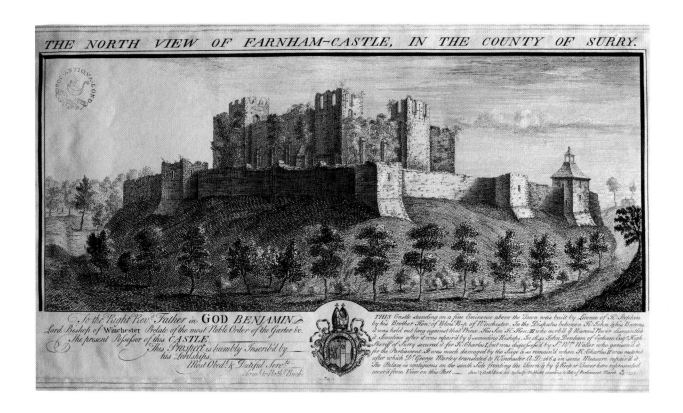

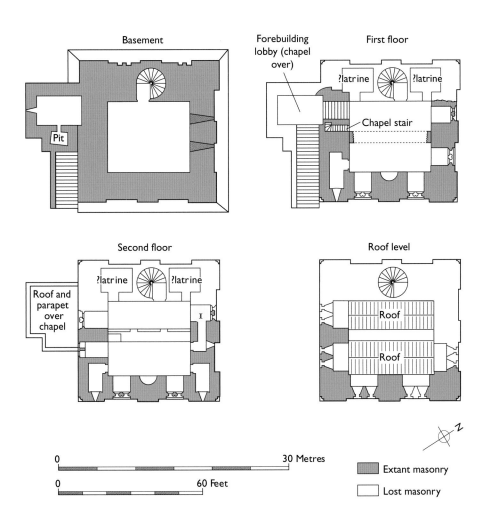

Basement

Pit

Forebuilding lobby (chapel over)

First floor

?latrine

?latrine

Chapel stair

Second floor

Roof and parapet over chapel

?latrine

?latrine

Roof level

Roof

Roof

N

0   30 Metres

0   60 Feet

Extant masonry

Lost masonry

DURHAM AND NORTHUMBERLAND

The accession of Henry II almost precisely coincided with the appointment of a new bishop to the see of Durham, Hugh du Puiset or Pudsey (1153–95). A nephew of both King Stephen and the cardinal and bishop Henry of Blois, Hugh was to prove one of the most extravagant patrons of architecture in the north of England in the late twelfth century. His castle-building career began in characteristically magnificent fashion soon after his appointment. In 1155 a fire swept through Durham Castle and destroyed at least one of its two halls.[17] Hugh created a new domestic range within the gutted shell of this building to the north of the site. This contained as its centrepiece a rich two-storey hall entered through a raised archway of baroque extravagance (pl. 80). The insertion of a floor within this building in the seventeenth century has obscured some details of the original arrangements, but the quality of its architectural decoration can still be admired.

Possibly at the same time as he undertook this work, Bishop Hugh also constructed two new perimeter walls to the castle, each one punctuated at regular intervals with open-backed towers. The first of these walls rose from the gatehouse to the summit of the motte, and the second extended across the back of the castle towards the lower town. Neither survives in its

80 Durham Castle, the splendid entrance to Bishop du Puiset's hall begun after a fire in 1155. It is a mark of the admiration in which this doorway has consistently been held that it has never been substantially altered since its first creation in the mid-twelfth century. The arch did not frame a door but must always have been enclosed within a porch. Its rich carved detailing compares to that found on the monks' door at the north-east angle of the cloister in the neighbouring cathedral priory. The photograph was taken in 1908.

original form, but their details are known from antiquarian description.[18] The bishop also built a gate at the entrance to the Durham peninsula, the architectural core of the so-called North Gate. These changes were seen by contemporaries as part of a wider architectural renewal of the city and indeed the whole diocese. Particularly important in this was an aggrandisement of the cathedral priory, to which he added the present Galilee and donated a sumptuous new shrine of gold, silver and jewels for the body of St Cuthbert's and early England's principal historian, the Venerable Bede.[19]

Outside the town itself Bishop Hugh restored the suburb of Elvet, destroyed during Cumin's struggle for the bishopric, and built the bridge that still connects it to the peninsula.[20] He also ornamented his favoured retreat at Bishop Auckland with new buildings, including a great hall in stone. No expense was spared in this operation, which was probably begun towards the very end of his life and completed by one of his successors.[21] The hall, with its magnificent arcades of polished limestone, was incorporated in the thirteenth century within a grand new castle laid out by Puiset's succes-

sor, Anthony Bek. Although the castle buildings were badly damaged in the Civil War, the hall was afterwards restored as a chapel and survives as the centrepiece of the present bishop of Durham's residence. In many of his operations, Bishop Hugh may have used a mason called Richard, a substantial figure, who owned property and possessed his own seal.[22]

Bishop Hugh was to prove a prominent, but independent-minded figure in the battle for political control of Cumberland and Northumberland. It was this struggle that was to condition castle construction in the region as a whole. Following the death of Henry I in 1135, King David of Scotland had immediately occupied Carlisle, where he was probably responsible for completing the great tower in the castle. Four years later, in 1139, his possession of the city was confirmed by the treaty of Durham, as was the title of his son, Henry, to the earldom of Northumberland. Although certain royal castles in the region, including Bamburgh, were explicitly excluded from the earl's possession, it is clear that he almost immediately took control of them anyway.[23] This settlement was decisively reversed when King David was succeeded on the throne by his young son, Malcolm. Henry II used the opportunity to assert his control over the whole area in 1157.

There followed a spate of castle building across the wider region in the following decade, a process that represented a thorough consolidation of the Anglo-Norman settlement first introduced by William Rufus and Henry I. This was orchestrated by Henry II, who led the way with alterations to the two principal royal castles in the region. It was probably in the 1160s that Carlisle, having been returned into Henry II's hands, was strengthened with a new rectangular gate tower (pl. 81).[24] At about the same time Bamburgh also received a new gatehouse and an inner bailey wall punctuated with two rectangular towers (pl. 82). The latter operations are likely to be associated with fines levied on two individuals in 1169–70 for failing to assist in works to the castle.[25]

While the towers at Bamburgh were being completed, Henry II must have taken the momentous decision to move the seat of the sheriff of Northumberland from this castle to Newcastle upon Tyne. The reason for the move is not now apparent, but it was clearly announced architecturally in 1168, when the Pipe Rolls record the commencement of work to the castle there. Over the next eight years, the operation is known to have absorbed £1,144. The lion's share of this money

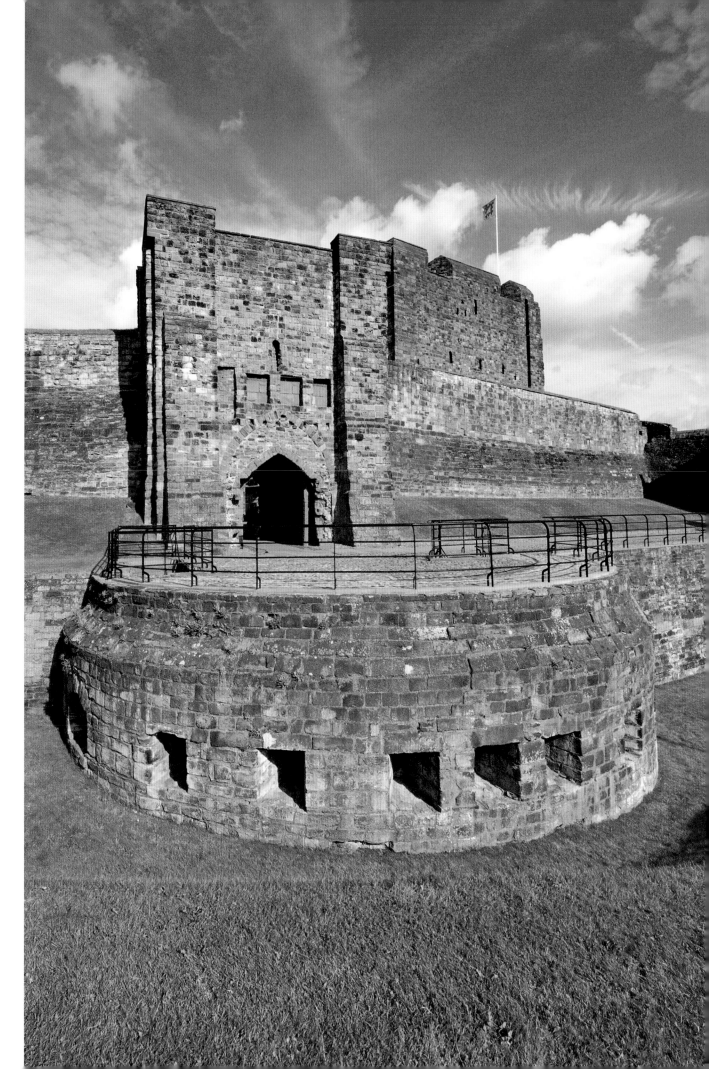

81 Carlisle, Cumberland, the gate tower to the inner bailey. Probably built by Henry II in the 1160s, it takes the form of a rectangular tower with a central gate passage. The date of the building is implied by historical circumstances and the dressing of the original masonry, which is twelfth-century in character. All the details of the gate tower have been heavily reworked over time and the reverse face shows evidence of having been elaborately rebuilt with a display of heraldic carving in the late fourteenth century. The half-moon barbican in the foreground was added around 1542 by Henry VIII's engineer Stephan von Haschenperg. It was formerly a much higher structure, but the upper level was demolished to create a parade ground in the nineteenth century. In the background to the right is the great tower of the castle, cut down by a floor probably in the sixteenth century.

82 The towers and walls of the inner bailey at Bamburgh, Northumberland, were probably erected about 1170. Though much restored, the original form of these wall towers can be accurately reconstructed. Each one preserves a barrel-vaulted chamber at first-floor level (or ground-floor level within the higher inner bailey), which was provided with multiple arrow slits or loops to create firing positions within the depth of the wall. This is a very early English example of arrow loops being created within the depth of the wall to create a second tier of defence beneath the parapet.

went into the construction of a great tower erected under the direction of Maurice *cementarius*, the mason.[26] This was planned with a ground-floor chapel beneath its forebuilding stair and a vaulted basement, both very unusual details. Its principal interior on the uppermost floor is spacious and preserves rare evidence for the structure of its original roof. The great tower is today clearly visible from the platforms of the main city station and stands in exciting conjunction with modern Newcastle. It has survived as a town gaol and, latterly, as the home of the Newcastle Society of Antiquaries.[27]

Only three patrons in the immediate locality had the resources to follow royal example and construct a substantial great tower by the 1160s. The first was Hugh du Puiset, who restored at royal command a castle founded around 1121 by his predecessor, Bishop Flambard, at Norham, Northumberland.[28] Set above the River Tweed, the castle is today dominated by a rectangular great tower of many builds (pl. 83). The core of the building was probably constructed by Flambard as part of his work to the first castle on the site. This was destroyed in 1138, but sufficient of the

83 The great tower of Norham, Northumberland. This building underwent several major reorganisations and enlargements into the sixteenth century at the hands of the bishops of Durham. Hugh du Puiset's late twelfth-century tower comprises the right-hand part of the present structure. Its outline is distinguishable in the changing texture of the masonry. This itself absorbed a yet earlier stone tower built by Ranulf Flambard in the 1120s. By the sixteenth century Norham probably possessed the biggest great tower in northern England by a considerable margin.

fabric evidently survived for Bishop Hugh to enlarge and extend it.[29] He created from a single-cell building a great tower with a central spine wall.

Much further to the south, in Yorkshire, Conan, duke of Brittany, also began a new great tower at Richmond Castle (pl. 84). This was erected on the foundation of the earlier eleventh-century curtain wall to create a dramatic visual centrepiece to the great circular fortifications of the town and castle site.[30] The new building was directly modelled on royal example, with a swallowed forebuilding copied from the royal castles at Bamburgh and Carlisle, a detail discussed in the last chapter.

The third great tower stands at Appleby in Westmorland above the precipitous slopes of the River Eden (pl. 85). It was constructed without a forebuilding and originally comprised two floors set over a basement. In terms of patronage, Appleby is something of an oddity. The tower is first mentioned in 1173,[31] and the most probable candidate for constructing it prior to this date is a certain Hugh de Morville (d. 1173/4),

one of Thomas Becket's assassins.[32] He held the castle and its honour as a royal appointee between 1157 and 1171. But Hugh – who enjoyed the particular favour of Henry II – lacked the resources for a work of this scale, and it is quite possible that the great tower was constructed with royal subventions shortly after 1157. The king certainly did intervene directly in castle building during this period, driving it forward with strategic purpose. For example, when the owner of the border castle at Wark died, Henry II took its repair into his own hands and spent £380 in strengthening the defences between 1158 and 1161.[33]

Some impression of the character and circumstances of lesser baronial building is provided by the example of the Umfravilles. Like many local families in the area, they had probably settled in Redesdale around 1100, but they were formally invested with the barony of Prudhoe in Northumberland during the reign of Henry I. With the ascendancy of King David of Scotland in the region, the Umfravilles paid court to him.

135

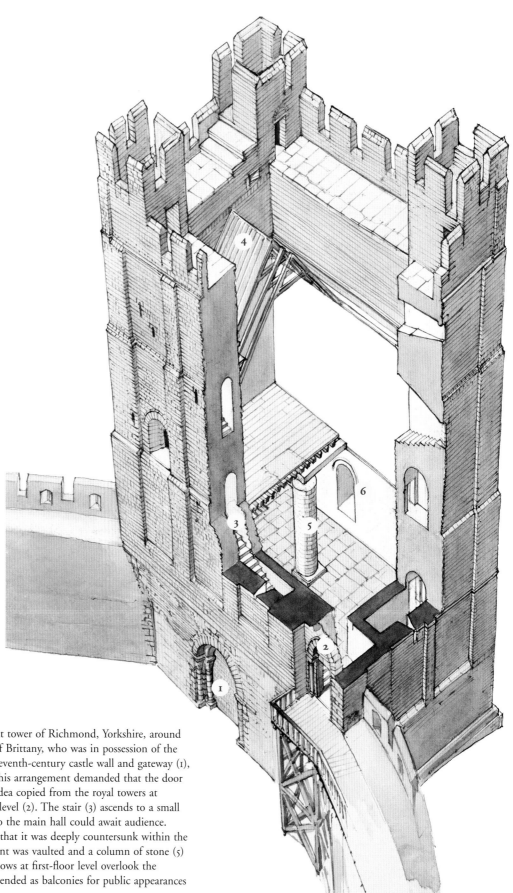

84 Cut-away reconstruction by Terry Ball of the great tower of Richmond, Yorkshire, around
1300. The tower was probably built by Conan, duke of Brittany, who was in possession of the
castle between 1156 and 1171. It was erected over the eleventh-century castle wall and gateway (1),
which were incorporated within the basement level. This arrangement demanded that the door
to the swallowed entrance stair of the new tower (an idea copied from the royal towers at
Bamburgh and Carlisle) had to be raised to first-floor level (2). The stair (3) ascends to a small
vestibule with a window and a bench, where visitors to the main hall could await audience.
Timber sockets for the original roof survive and show that it was deeply countersunk within the
building (4). In the late thirteenth century the basement was vaulted and a column of stone (5)
erected to support the upper floor. The principal windows at first-floor level overlook the
market square (6), evidence perhaps that they were intended as balconies for public appearances
by Conan to the people of the town.

And following Henry II's resumption of power, the head of the family, Odinel, switched his allegiance southwards again.

Three castles are associated with the Umfravilles. The first of these is a motte and bailey castle at Elsdon. Possibly built as a successor to this is the nearby castle of Harbottle. This is also of motte and bailey construction, and a legal wrangle in the early thirteenth century reveals that it was built at the instruction of Henry II, probably immediately after 1157.[34] The largest of the three, however, stood at Prudhoe and may have been the only one in the series with stone fortifications in the mid-twelfth century. In 1170 these probably comprised a wall and a rectangular gate tower, parts of which survive.[35]

A fascinating glimpse of these new northern castles in a military context is provided by the events of the Scottish invasions of 1173 and 1174. Their details are engagingly recorded in the chronicle of Jordan Fantosme, possibly an eyewitness of some episodes he relates. The invasions took advantage of a revolt across the empire on the part of Henry II's sons and were led by William the Lion, brother and successor of King Malcolm. William came first to Wark, where he agreed a truce with the ill-prepared constable, and then to Carlisle. An English counter-attack frustrated his hopes of capturing both castles and he passed with the leave of the bishop of Durham into Yorkshire. Having carved a passage of destruction through the county, his army was confronted by a royal force and withdrew on favourable terms.

The following year he returned and again invested Wark, which had now been prepared to receive him: there is independent record from the Pipe Rolls of payments for corn, oatmeal and a garrison of ten knights and forty squires for the castle.[36] Here he was again frustrated after a bloody encounter. He also suffered a humiliating mishap with his catapult. When it was erected to batter the defences of the castle, the first stone 'barely tumbled out of the sling and knocked down one of his own knights to the ground. Had it not been for the knight's armour and the shield he was carrying, he would never have returned home to any of his relatives.'[37]

The king raised the siege and moved on with his army to Carlisle. After fruitless negotiations there for the surrender of the castle, he led his main force to Appleby. This was apparently without a garrison or provisions, and its constable – 'an old, white-headed Englishman' called Gospatric fitz Horm – immedi-

85 The great tower of Appleby, Westmorland, in a photograph of 1940. The tower signalled the importance of this castle and town as the seat of the county sheriff. It was built in the late twelfth century, but the precise circumstances of its construction are not known. The roof was originally countersunk deeply within the parapets of the building, just above the upper tier of windows. The tower was renovated by the celebrated dowager countess Lady Anne Clifford between 1651 and 1653. She inserted a spine wall and created four floors of guest lodgings within the building. To her belief the building was Roman and she consequently called it Caesar's Tower. Such identification of Romanesque great towers as classical works of architecture was widespread even until the eighteenth century and partly accounts for the enormous prestige they enjoyed.

86 The gatehouse and walls of Egremont, Cumberland, part of the twelfth-century redevelopment of the castle in stone. The contrast between the cut masonry of the gatehouse and the rubble construction of the walls illustrates the conceived importance of the former in architectural terms. There was also formerly a stone vault over the gatehouse entrance passage, but it has collapsed. The foot of the wall to the left of the gate is laid in a hatched masonry pattern termed 'herringbone', a curiously late example of this construction technique. In the background is the castle motte and, built against it, the remains of an impressive late thirteenth-century hall.

ately surrendered it.[38] Continuing his march, William next came to Brough and quickly overwhelmed the outer castle defences. Its garrison, including at least six knights, then retired into a timber tower, which the Scots set on fire. Nevertheless, one of the knights, newly dubbed and determined, still refused to surrender, and having exhausted his supply of spears, tore pointed stakes from the defences and flung them at his attackers.[39] His resistance overcome, the Scots levelled the fortifications and marched on to Harbottle and Warkworth castles, both of which were overrun.

William next turned his attention to Prudhoe, with the intention of repaying the disloyalty of the forsworn follower of King David, Odinel de Umfraville. There the Scots met stiff resistance and, warned of an approaching English army, William retreated northwards to invest another baronial castle at Alnwick. This was also fortified in stone at this date, though only fragments of walls and a gatehouse today remain from the twelfth-century defences. Here, a catastrophe occurred.

An English party of knights from Newcastle found the king taking the air on a hot morning with a small escort. William mistook the party for his own troops and only when they unfurled their standard did he realise his mistake. Heroic to the last, he charged his enemies, but his horse was killed and he was taken prisoner. Amongst his captors was Odinel de Umfraville. William was brought to Henry II as a common miscreant, with his feet bound beneath the horse he rode on. But William the Lion, captured after two years of troublemaking, was not the only object of the king's displeasure. Hugh du Puiset's inaction during these troubles was also brought to account. Henry II seized all the bishop's castles, including Durham itself, which was to remain in royal hands for the next fifteen years.

With one exception, the Scottish invasions of 1173 and 1174 actually made little difference to the steady progress of castle building in the region. In the main, this was relatively modest and focused on the construction of stone walls and gate towers. A grand but typical example of such work is to be found in the late twelfth-century remodelling of Egremont, Cumberland (pl. 86).[40] The exception to this rule was a new great tower at Prudhoe, almost certainly begun in the 1170s. This may well have been an architectural product of Odinel de Umfraville's triumphant and lucrative part in the capture of William the Lion and the ransom of knights in his entourage. Certainly, he emerged from these events as 'the most powerful potentate' in Northumberland, or so the monks of

Tynemouth viewed him. And his exactions on the region included compelling the priory serfs to labour for him on his castles.[41]

This overview of the north should finish with reference to two buildings that are something of an architectural anomaly in both stylistic and circumstantial terms. The most important of these is the castle of Middleham in Yorkshire, part of the honour of Richmond. In the late twelfth century the motte and bailey castle here was abandoned and a completely new castle was erected nearby. This was dominated by a great tower, which is completely out of proportion to the apparent means of the owners, kinsmen of the dukes of Brittany. There is no documentation to identify the builder of the tower at Middleham and its date is uncertain. In stylistic terms, it could be placed at any time between around 1170 and the early 1200s. Rather more modest is the tower and castle at Pendragon, Westmorland, which was heavily reworked in the mid-seventeenth century. The great towers that dominate both Middleham and Pendragon are of relatively thin-walled construction and on a large plan. These details may connect them to each other and the great tower of Bowes, Yorkshire, which was probably constructed by Henry II between 1171 and 1187.

THE ROYAL WORKS AND WINDSOR

Amongst the castle-building projects undertaken across the realm by Henry II, a small group deserves individual notice. One of the most expensive was the renovation of Nottingham, with a stone inner bailey and a great tower perched upon a high rock. This building, which served as the principal royal castle in the Midlands throughout the Middle Ages, has been almost entirely destroyed and is known today only through a seventeenth-century plan (see pl. 292). The relatively small size of the Nottingham great tower may ally it architecturally with nearby Peveril. Erected by Henry II in the years 1175–7 for a cost of just £175, the diminutive tower at Peveril was almost certainly intended as a demonstrative work of architecture: it stands above a cave listed by the twelfth-century writer William of Malmesbury alongside Stonehenge as one of the natural wonders of Britain. According to him, it expelled gusts of air and connected the world to hell. Indeed, since the Domesday survey in the late eleventh century this extraordinary natural feature has gloried under the name of *Pechesers* or the Devil's Arse. The

castle also commanded the very lucrative tin-mining industry in the region.[42]

A consistent object of royal expenditure throughout the reign was Windsor Castle. This had now clearly emerged as the premier English royal castle, and the post of its custodian or *custos* usually went hand in hand with that of the king's deputy and regent, the justiciar of England. Henry's work at Windsor appears to have fallen into two principal phases. In the years 1165–71 the Pipe Rolls record the expenditure of £605 on the 'king's houses' in the upper bailey of the castle. This work presumably involved alterations to the residential complex erected by Henry I. Some of the new buildings were constructed of stone and, when completed, incorporated a cloister and a chapel. They were probably further altered in the next eight years, when another £600 was spent on unspecified works in the castle.

There followed in the years 1171–4 works to 'the wall around the king's houses'. Heightened, restored and otherwise extensively altered, this wall to the upper bailey still survives. Its most distinctive feature is a regular series of rectangular towers, very similar in conception to those at Bamburgh and Durham, but erected on a much more substantial scale (pl. 87). The work of walling the building in stone may also have extended into the lower bailey. Re-walling the castle probably absorbed more money than the £175 explicitly recorded in the Pipe Rolls, but it nevertheless appears remarkably cheap when set against the costs of the king's houses or – in general terms – great tower building. As part of the refortification of the site, the motte was also buttressed and its summit enclosed in a stone wall. One operation at Windsor that is not individually dated is the construction of a second hall against the wall in the lower bailey. Second halls are a mark of the greatest residences in the period, including, for example, Durham and Westminster. Nothing survives of this building, which is first documented in 1196–7, but, remarkably, there does remain a chamber block formerly attached to it.[43]

THE REBUILDING OF
DOVER CASTLE

The rebuilding of Windsor was an architectural undertaking of the first order, but it was to become overshadowed by another far greater. On the evening of 29

87 An engraving by Wenceslaus Hollar of Windsor, Berkshire, published in 1672. It clearly shows the circuit of upper bailey towers created by Henry II in the years 1171–4. By the date of the engraving, the towers had been heightened as part of Edward III's works of the 1350s and 60s. Similarly, the stone enclosure built on the motte by Henry II had been completely rebuilt in the 1220s by Henry III. The late twelfth-century defences of Windsor well illustrate the fascination with fragmenting castles into compositions of towers.

December 1170, in dramatic culmination to his celebrated and bitter dispute with Henry II, Archbishop Thomas Becket was brutally murdered during vespers in Canterbury Cathedral. Henry II bore responsibility for this act and four years later made atonement in startling fashion. At the tomb of the now-canonised martyr he submitted in penance to a public scourging at the hands of the monks: eighty men laying on three strokes each.

Two months after this, in September 1174, a fire cleared the way for a remodelling of Canterbury Cathedral in the new Gothic style. As the cathedral grew, so did Thomas's stature as a saint, and in August 1179 his tomb was even visited by Louis VII of France and the count of Flanders, both of whom were conducted to the tomb from Dover by Henry II in person.[44] To accommodate the burgeoning crowds of pilgrims, a decision was taken, probably in 1180, to reorganise the east end of the new church and construct a public setting for St Thomas's shrine.[45]

Immediately after this, in 1181, Henry II began work on a project that rivalled Becket's new cathedral in scale: a vast remodelling of the castle at Dover. The timing of this project cannot be coincidental. Dover dominated the Straits of Dover, one of the principal crossroads of communication in Europe and an increasingly important sea crossing for Henry II in his relations with the French kings. Moreover, straddling the road to Canterbury, the castle was a visible assertion of Henry's power in the face of Thomas's develop-

oping cult, with its strongly anti-monarchical overtones. The sheer financial scale of this project deserves special notice: over the following eight years the Pipe Rolls record a total expenditure of nearly £6,000 on the castle.[46] On the basis of this astonishing sum, Dover may fairly be considered the single most expensive secular architectural commission of the reign.

Work focused on recasting the interior of the castle with a great tower of gigantic proportions and a surrounding inner bailey. It seems likely on architectural evidence that Henry also fortified at least one section of the perimeter of the outer ramparts in stone and undertook extensive work to the ancient church of St Mary in Castro within the walls. The Pipe Rolls give a good impression of the progress of the operations. The great tower was begun in 1181 and was raised to sufficient height four years later to be briefly victualled and garrisoned. The building was clearly not completed, however, because work to it continued to be mentioned until 1187–8. In the Pipe Roll for the period 1185–6 reference is also made to the construction of the inner bailey wall, what is described as 'the girdle around the Tower'.[47] This late mention of the bailey walls may suggest a staggered construction of the two – a sensible arrangement that allowed the piecemeal demolition of the old castle buildings and a continuity of effective defence.

The Pipe Rolls also identify the architect of the project, Maurice *Ingeniator*, or the engineer, almost certainly the same man as Maurice the mason who

worked on the king's great tower at Newcastle. He received a salary and livery at Dover in 1181 and is documented on the site until 1186.[48] For all the disparity in size between the two towers at Dover and Newcastle, there are many similarities of planning apparent between them – notably in their elaborate forebuilding arrangements and internal systems of water supply – that would argue for their common authorship. But in terms of architectural detail the two buildings are worlds apart. This is an interesting comment either on Maurice's artistic flexibility as a designer or – more probably – his remit in the building work. It may be, for example, that he drew up plans for the design, hence the common planning arrangements, but that in both places other masons took responsibility for creating carved detail.

Maurice's new works at Dover well reflect the contemporary fascination with fragmenting castles into compositions of towers. Each gateway façade to the inner bailey was originally enclosed by a barbican or defensive enclosure. The barbican to the south is now totally destroyed but may have formed an architectural ligature between the new bailey and lost defences around St Mary in Castro. That to the north, however, still survives and it is the more important of the two because it faced the lost twelfth-century entrance to the outer castle enclosure (pl. 88). Passing through this lost entrance the twelfth-century visitor would have approached the north barbican up a steep wooden ramp. Entering within it he was confronted by the high triple-towered gateway façade of the inner bailey. No twelfth-century buildings survive in the bailey, but all the towers within it – bar the gate towers – are open-backed, and some of them evidently had buildings constructed against them, some of them equipped with latrines. What precise function these bailey buildings served is not known, but they may have included the 'houses' of the castle, which were roofed with lead in 1208,[49] and the king's hall documented in 1214.[50]

The great tower stands in the centre of the bailey, a gargantuan structure about 100 feet (30.48 m) square, 90 feet (27.4 m) tall and with walls between 17 and 22 feet (5–6.7 m) thick (pl. 89). Externally, it appears to have been strikingly finished with blocks of Caen stone. These were laid in regular bands to create broad stripes around three sides of the building and were used across the entire central section of the entrance façade. The foundations were laid on the bedrock of the hill and buried beneath an artificial raised mound to give the impression – now lost through infilling – that it stood on a motte within the crown of the bailey. Its design precisely echoes the architectural forms of the north bailey entrance: each face is conceived with three towers, and the forebuilding – a structure of unprecedented and unparalleled size – gives access to the interior through what are effectively two twin-towered gateways, one of them with a drawbridge pit (pl. 90).

The other remarkable feature of the entrance arrangements is the architectural detailing of the fore-

88 (*top*) Dover, Kent, a view of the north barbican and inner bailey, which were probably under construction in 1185–6. The barbican (1) is amongst the earliest built in stone to survive in England. It was approached up a wooden bridge. One foundation pier for the bridge remains embedded in the present stone ramp (2). The entrance to the inner bailey is set to the right-hand side between two towers, which are sandwiched together to create a twin-towered gateway (3). Although the inner bailey appears to form a regular turreted crown to the top of the hill, it actually comprises two high façades set with gateways that are connected to one another by lower stretches of wall. The triple-towered composition of the bailey façade is echoed in the design of the great tower behind (4).

89 (*bottom*) The great tower of Dover, Kent, was begun in 1181, first garrisoned in 1185 but not completed until at least 1187–8. The surrounds of the entrance were entirely faced in cut stone from Caen in Normandy, though the exterior has been so patched and repaired over time that this finish is not easily legible today. On its other three faces the walls were striped with bands of cut stone. Most of the original windows in the building have been replaced over time. In place of the second-floor window to the right above the forebuilding stair there formerly existed a balcony, possibly for royal appearances (1). The great tower continued to serve as the royal lodging in the castle until the seventeenth century, and its interior was repeatedly remodelled, notably by Edward IV in the 1470s and George Villiers, duke of Buckingham, in the 1620s.

90   Cut-away reconstruction of the great tower of Dover, Kent, around 1200 by Terry Ball.
The building is arranged on three floors, which are connected by two spiral stairs set in opposite
corners of the plan (1 and 2). Each floor comprises a pair of large rooms divided by a spine
wall (3) and a number of wall chambers. To reflect the relative importance of the different
floors, the architectural detailing becomes richer on each level. Visitors were taken up the
forebuilding stair directly to the topmost and grandest floor. This stair rose around two sides of
the tower through a pair of twin-towered gateways (4 and 5). Within the lower of these was an
upper (6) and lower (7) chapel. The roof was formerly countersunk within the uppermost
storey of the building (8). Rainwater drained from it was used to flush out the latrines. This
was one element in a sophisticated inbuilt water system that included a rainwater storage tank
and a piped water supply fed from a well chamber on the third floor.

building chapels. There can be little doubt that the upper chapel was for Henry II's private use: it is accessible only down a narrow corridor opening off the high end of the main hall and its interior is vaulted in stone. In contrast, the lower chapel, which faces the visitor on the bottom level of the forebuilding, shows no sign of having possessed any doors and was presumably open to anyone who entered the great tower up the stairway. It was also ceiled in timber. Both chapels use an identical repertoire of architectural mouldings and decoration. In every particular, these resemble the contemporary work at Canterbury Cathedral, although, interestingly, they are applied here to rounded Romanesque, rather than pointed Gothic, arches. More remarkable still, later medieval documentation suggests that the upper chapel was dedicated to Thomas Becket.[51]

If Henry II's reconstruction of Dover Castle was an attempt to appropriate through architecture the cult of Thomas Becket, there is a final sense in which it performed the task to perfection. The form of the tower is associated with royal castles across the whole geographic extent of the Angevin Empire. What could be more appropriate, therefore, than to build one of unparalleled size at this physical crossroad within it? The architectural brilliance of this particular design lies in reformulating this symbol as an ingenious composition of turrets and towers. In this sense, Dover explores the late twelfth century fascination with the simple idea of a turreted wall.

THE REIGN OF RICHARD I

In terms of royal castle building in England, the reign of Richard I is a severe disappointment. Absent from the kingdom for all but six months of his ten-year reign, Richard left his English affairs in the hands of a deputed government, and its architectural endeavours seem largely to have been continuations of Henry II's major projects. Moreover, given the inadequate documentation that has been preserved, it can be very difficult to distinguish between the work of the father and the son. As a result, there is no English equivalent of Château Gaillard, the spectacular castle raised by Richard I in just three years to protect Normandy from the predations of the French king, Philip Augustus. Nor – contrary to what is sometimes supposed – is there any straightforward architectural connection between this operation and contemporary English design.

But the accession of Richard I was productive in another way. Eager to devolve power in preparation for his long absence on crusade and also to raise money for the venture, Richard actively sold up his father's interests for ready cash. The disgraced bishop of Durham, Hugh du Puiset, for example, was one of many beneficiaries of this. Restored by Henry II's death to his full possessions, the bishop at once began preparing to join in the Crusade, furnishing his entourage in magnificent style. Hearing of this, Richard offered him the post of justiciar of England, the governor of the realm in the king's absence. Richard asked in return for the loan of the money that Puiset had amassed for his journey. Negotiations followed, and for a further loan – rumour stated the impossible sum of £11,000 – he granted the bishop the earldom of Northumberland. With such alacrity and evident excitement did Bishop Hugh receive this title, that when Richard girded him with a sword of estate he wryly remarked: 'See, I have made a young earl of an old bishop.'[52]

Richard I's distribution of power, titles and money was to have important repercussions over the next forty years in encouraging baronial families to build. Of the figures that appear immediately to have taken advantage of the king's generosity, two are preeminent. Roger Bigod, having again lost his estates to Henry II after the rebellion of 1173, was able to buy them back with their castles in 1189. He chose to reconstruct Framlingham, which had been partially destroyed by Henry II (pl. 91).[53] As he finished it, the inner bailey of Framlingham is striking testimony to the architectural continuities between the reigns of Henry II and his son. The ring of open-backed towers parallels precisely the treatment of such earlier buildings as Orford, Dover and Windsor (pl. 92).

Another figure elevated to great power by Richard I in 1189 was William Marshal, one of the towering personalities of the period. Born into the troubles of the Anarchy, he almost became one of its victims: as a boy hostage he had been brought to the walls of his father's castle at Newbury, Wiltshire, by King Stephen and his life offered in return for its surrender. His father was completely unmoved and jeeringly commented that he had hammer and anvil to make more and better sons. The king, with the characteristic kindness that made him the contempt of the twelfth-century nobility, could not bring himself to execute the boy.[54] In later life, William Marshal built up for himself a substantial fortune from small beginnings. In 1189 Richard I, in recognition of his loyalty to the

91 The walls and towers of the inner bailey of Framlingham, Suffolk, were probably erected in the 1190s following the demolition of the castle by Henry II. They are unusually tall structures for the period, which perhaps explains why the castle possessed no additional great tower. Their detailing – notably the treatment of latrine chutes and the use of cut stones at the angles of the towers – precisely mirrors that found in the great tower at Orford, begun in 1165. In the fifteenth and sixteenth centuries the internal castle buildings were remodelled, but the exterior was largely left untouched, a fascinating indication of the prestige enjoyed by the gaunt aesthetic of the castle. The only external evidence of the transformed interiors are the fine brick chimneys, probably added in the 1470s or 1510s.

92 A plan of
Framlingham, Suffolk. The
castle comprised a cluster of
baileys set on an eminence
above a flooded mere. These
baileys interrupt the regular
street plan of the adjacent
town, evidence that the castle
was disruptively planted after
the Norman Conquest in an
existing settlement. Enclosing
the central bailey was a high
stone wall, probably built in
the 1190s. This was crinkled
out at regular intervals to
create open-backed towers on a
square – or in one case
polygonal – plan. The layout
follows that of the inner bailey
at Dover. Unfortunately,
nothing substantial now
survives of the twelfth-century
buildings within the stone
enclosure at Framlingham. In
the sixteenth century the bailey
was subdivided into an outer
and a service court, an
arrangement reflected in the
clustering of chimneys to the
south.

93 (*facing page*) The
gatehouse of Chepstow,
Monmouthshire, has been
dated on the basis of timber
taken from its surviving doors
to about 1189. Previously, it
had been described as an early
thirteenth-century building.
The approach to the gate was
formerly enclosed by a fortified
court or barbican. This
probably forced visitors to
approach the gateway obliquely
rather than head-on, as they do
today. The stub of one wall of
the barbican still projects from
the tower to the left. The
sockets and corbels around the
head of the wall may have
supported a crowning timber
gallery or hourd (see pls
99–102). The larger windows
are all later insertions into the
building.

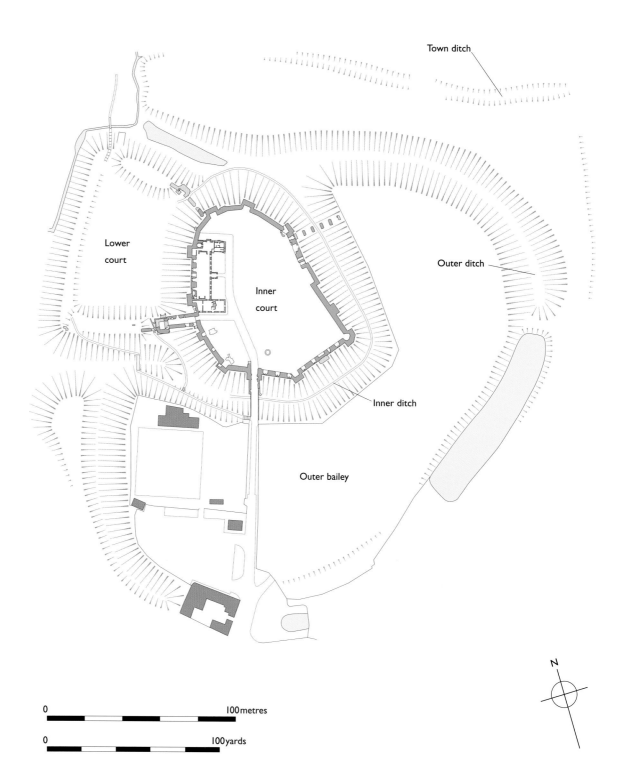

Angevin throne, granted him the hand of the heiress of Richard de Clare, called Strongbow, second earl of Pembroke (d. 1176).

This match raised William to immense fortune, but to his frustration it did not come with his wife's title or Pembroke itself. Instead, he dubbed himself earl of Striguil (Chepstow), one of the principal castles that came with his wife's estates and turned his hand to

reworking this building. His first addition to it was probably the massive gatehouse with its double drum towers: a timber taken from one of the gates to this entrance has now been shown to have been felled before 1189 (pl. 93).[55] The gatehouse may initially have been raised in isolation, but soon afterwards work continued to a series of enclosing walls studded with towers. Some details of the work may hint at

French architectural influence. In particular, four of the five towers and the gatehouse are designed in plan with a complete or almost complete circular core. This is an unusual detail in English design, where open-backed or D-shaped forms were generally more popular.

About royal castle-building operations undertaken in England during Richard's reign little can be said with certainty. The Pipe Rolls record heavy expenditure at Dover (£725) and the Tower of London (£3,339), though the precise nature of the works is now difficult to discern. In both cases, however, Richard was probably responsible for the construction of a substantial tower at an angle of the defences: the Avranches Tower and the Bell Tower respectively. These buildings belong to a small and distinctive group of

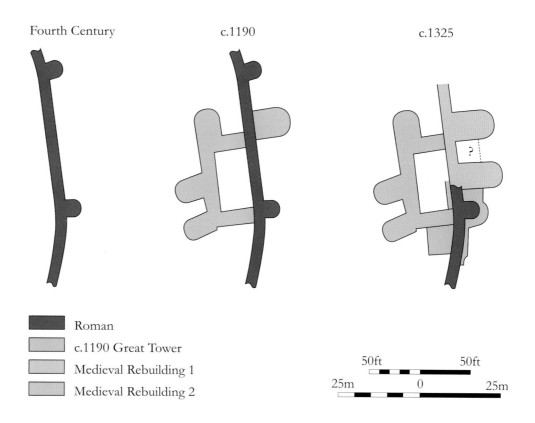

Fourth Century c.1190 c.1325

Roman
c.1190 Great Tower
Medieval Rebuilding 1
Medieval Rebuilding 2

50ft 50ft
25m 0 25m

94 The evolution of the great tower of Pevensey, Sussex. A major structural failure appears to have caused a substantial reconstruction of the tower. There are no convincing parallels for the extraordinary plan of this building, which is almost certainly inspired by the form of the Roman towers along the wall that it straddles. The tower is known from documentary sources to have possessed at least two upper floors approached up a timber stair and to have comprised a complete suite of domestic chambers. Its design explores the late twelfth-century fashion for fragmenting architectural designs into compositions of towers. It also looks forward to the clustering of towers around inner baileys from the thirteenth century onwards at castles such as Clun, Skipton and Alnwick. The phases of development shown here are dated on a combination of documentary and archaeological evidence. It is possible that the rectangular tower added *circa* 1325 was designed as a catapult platform.

large towers on a polygonal or circular plan that were designed to secure an exposed angle in the defences of a major castle.

One other important building project in this period that was probably undertaken at royal expense was the redevelopment of the castle at Pevensey within the Roman fort. This involved the construction of an impressive twin-towered gateway to the inner bailey. Probably in conjunction with this work, a great tower with five projecting D-shaped turrets was also begun (pl. 94). In this case, the design was almost certainly inspired by the drum towers of the Roman walls. Heavily remodelled in the Middle Ages and now a ruin with Second World War pillboxes cemented into it, this bizarre building is problematic to reconstruct.[56]

TIMBER CASTLES

Despite the increasing use of stone in castle architecture, timber clearly remained an important building material in this period. Many castles preserved complete circuits of timber fortification, such as Hen Domen in Montgomeryshire, which was excavated between 1960 and 1988.[57] Even some royal castles, such

as Northampton, remained largely of timber and earth construction into the early thirteenth century. It is known from a poem about the castle of Ardres (Pas-de-Calais) written in the 1180s that there did exist in this period great towers of timber too.[58] Some English examples of such structures are also documented. For example, in 1190 the Jews of York were famously massacred in the castle. The description of the event in manuscript sources is ambiguous, but they possibly took refuge in a timber tower on the motte, which was burnt down.[59] There is also mention that between 1269 and 1271 'a great tower of timber' at Shrewsbury Castle collapsed. This was probably the tower on the motte, but the date at which it was built is unknown.[60]

Some impression of the quality of this kind of lost work and also its high status is provided by the survival of two important castle great halls at Leicester and Farnham.[61] In each case these buildings have been heavily reworked, but both were originally arcaded structures with their timbers cut in the manner of stone to suggest columns and capitals. Such treatment remains typical of timber-frame building right through the Middle Ages. Some idea of their original appearance is provided by the late twelfth-century stone great hall at Oakham Castle in Rutland, a remarkable survival (pl. 95).

95 A view of the great hall of Oakham, Rutland, taken in 1919. This is the finest surviving example of a late twelfth-century great hall in England. It appears to have been organised originally with a low and a high end, the relative importance of each space picked out in the interior sculpture. The hall continued in use as a magistrates' court until 2001, and its roof and floor are modern. From at least the fifteenth century all figures of status who passed through Oakham were obliged to make a gift of a horseshoe that was then hung in the hall or on the castle gate. The origins of this practice are obscure. One of the large horseshoes visible here was formerly inscribed as being a gift of Edward IV.

In war, timber remained the queen of materials; light, flexible and strong. The Pipe Rolls, for example, contain many references to the fortification of castles during crises with what are described as timber *bretasche*. This term might be variously translated as a gallery along a wall head or a stretch of framed palisading.[62] Technical changes in framing techniques in the late twelfth century also made possible the creation of portable timber buildings of great sophistication. Richard I set out on crusade and created one such on his journey to Palestine outside Messina in Sicily. In mockery of the Greek inhabitants of the city, who were known as *Grifones* by the Latin crusaders, this timber castle was entitled 'Mategrifon', meaning 'Kill the Greeks'. Richard I spent the Christmas festivities of 1190–91 in this timber castle and even entertained the French king, Philip Augustus, there. But afterwards Mategrifon was dismantled and shipped to Acre, where it was re-erected as a siege castle outside the city walls.[63]

CONISBROUGH

As the name suggests, Conisbrough Castle in Yorkshire was founded within an Anglo-Saxon *burh* and was already the centre of a substantial honour at Domesday in 1086.[64] Little is known of the early form of the castle, but in 1163 it passed by marriage to Henry II's half-brother, Hamelin Plantagenet, a figure with vast estates across western France and England. Until his death in 1202, Hamelin seems to have treated Conisbrough as a favoured residence. To him can probably be attributed most of the stone buildings that now stand on the site, though not all were necessarily planned together. They exemplify the architectural trends of castle architecture in England over the period covered by this chapter.

Huge earthworks surround the central bailey of the castle, which is enclosed by a high stone wall. Set at regular intervals around this are solid D-shaped turrets (pl. 96). Two of these flank the entrance of the bailey

96 A view of Conisbrough, Yorkshire. Its present remains were largely the creation of Henry II's half-brother, Hamelin Plantagenet, who held the castle between 1163 and 1202. The circuit of the inner bailey wall is regularly punctuated by solid towers on a D-shaped plan. These were probably constructed around 1200 and compare to those built by King John at Knaresborough and Scarborough, Yorkshire. Projecting from the cylindrical great tower at regular intervals are wedge-shaped buttresses, each of which rises above the parapet to form a turret.

From a distance the whole would have created the impression of a forest of towers in the manner of Dover, Orford and Farnham. The great tower is constructed throughout of finely cut masonry and set on a massive plinth like a miniature motte.

to create a twin-towered gateway. The gateway was reworked around 1300 and has since collapsed. Dominating the castle is a great tower on a circular plan. Projecting from it at regular intervals is a series of wedge-shaped buttresses, each of which rises above the parapet to form a turret. As visitors walk up the short stair to the raised door of the great tower they pass between two buttresses that effectively form a second twin-towered gatehouse around the entrance. That these two towers were intended to create a formal composition in this way is suggested by the symmetrical placement of the door and window between them.

The interior of the tower comprises three principal chambers set over a vaulted basement. In this lowest level is a well. On the two top floors the rooms are comfortably appointed with fireplaces and wall basins for washing hands. The upper floor also possesses a vaulted chapel projecting into one of the buttress turrets. It is likely that the second-floor chamber served as a reception chamber and the floor above as a withdrawing room for Hamelin. The hall of the castle and the main kitchens almost certainly stood in the bailey. Even so, the turrets at roof level contained a cistern for water, an oven and a dovecote. In the manner of most great towers, the roof was countersunk within the crown of the building.

One of the curiosities of the great tower at Conisbrough is that there exists a very clear parallel for its unusual design at Mortemer in Normandy (Seine-Maritime), another of Hamelin's castles. The assumption has always been that Conisbrough copies its French parallel, but the reverse is quite as likely.[65] Moreover, Conisbrough is thoroughly rooted in local patterns of design: the absence of a forebuilding, the vaulted basement level and the straight wall staircases are probably all borrowings from the northern tradi-

tion of great tower architecture founded by Henry I at Bamburgh. The detailing of the great tower further emphasises the point and serves to date the building. The ornament and mouldings of the interior compare closely both with those of the great new choir of York Minster, built between 1154 and *circa* 1175, and work at Byland Abbey undertaken in the 1180s.[66] In conjunction with these parallels, a surviving fireplace at nearby Tickhill Castle, probably associated with the royal works of 1179–82, arguably anchors the design in the early 1180s.

Conisbrough Castle reflects in its architecture the wealth and connections of the Angevin ruling dynasty. But the empire created by Henry II, and maintained with difficulty by Richard I, was about to collapse. In the context of its downfall there became established a new architectural style that was to change the face of English castle design.

6

THE GOTHIC CASTLE

KING JOHN AND HENRY III

When King John (1199–1216) acceded to the Angevin throne, the political ligatures of his realm were already strained to breaking point. The French monarchy in its dramatic political recovery under the wily and formidable Philip Augustus had been steadily pushing back the barriers of Angevin power in France. A combination of misfortune and misjudgement early in the reign was enough to add the duchy of Normandy to its trophies of conquest. The process was briefly stayed by two great sieges at Château Gaillard and Chinon, but the inexorable annexation of the duchy was effectively completed in 1204.

French expansion was staked out in clear architectural fashion. Philip Augustus adopted a design of castle tower – the round *Tour Phillipienne*, so-called – that stood in striking contrast to the rectangular great towers of the Angevins. Time and again these were raised within newly captured castles to create powerful statements of a new order replacing the old (pl. 97). On 24 June 1204 Philip Augustus entered Rouen in triumph. He proceeded to demolish the castle and its great tower – redolent of Angevin power – and build his own replacement.[1] By this calculated act of destruction he emasculated the duchy of Normandy and set the seal on the breakup of the Anglo-Norman realm.[2]

The fall of Normandy was to colour the events of John's entire reign. It also lent weight to a circumstance that had in one sense made the loss possible in the first place: a growing rift between Normandy and England. Some of the first hints of this estrangement are signalled not in political events but in light-hearted banter; it was joked among Normans, for example, that English knights had tails. Beneath such pretended differences lay profound divisions and when the break came few hesitated in managing the change or deciding which way to jump.[3]

Nevertheless, at the very moment when the division of the Anglo-Norman realm became a reality, England was in cultural thrall to its political enemy. The French court was clearly emerging as the most admired and powerful in Europe, its protocol and fashions aped everywhere. In this sense the *Tours Phillipiennes* rising in France represented something more than mere political dominance; they also embodied the triumph of the architectural tradition that they sprung from: Gothic.

By 1200, under the wing of the reviving Capetian monarchy, French masons were refining the Gothic style to dramatic effect. In a surge of fresh building – particularly by bishops and their cathedral chapters –

97 Falaise, Lower Normandy, the birthplace of William the Conqueror. The great tower of this castle was begun by Henry I around 1123 and compares in form to that of Norwich, begun by William Rufus around 1095. This passage of ideas across the Channel is a reminder of how sophisticated and admired English Romanesque architecture was in the early twelfth century. When the French king Philip Augustus captured Falaise in 1204, he built a new great tower on a circular plan immediately adjacent to its predecessor. One of the earliest so-called *Tours Phillipiennes*, this staked out his conquest of the castle in dramatic visual terms.

old churches across northern France were levelled to create huge and coherently planned replacements on a scale that dwarfed their predecessors. The new buildings – at sites such as Reims (see pl. 8) and Amiens – were designed in competition with each other, masons and patrons vying to create ever-taller interiors in which stone vaults seemed to float above the ground on walls of insubstantial glass. To make this effect possible, the structure of the church – with its buttresses and thick walls – was externalised and thereby concealed from the onlooker. Meanwhile, the interior was articulated in the manner of a stone cage with columns and fine shafts. These offered an impossibly delicate explanation for the support of the vault. It is this dramatic contrast of delicacy and scale that lies at the heart of what is termed the 'High Gothic' style.

Such virtuouso architectural experiments may seem far removed from the relatively rugged world of castle architecture. Nevertheless, it is tempting to see in the appeal of High Gothic, as well as the cultural attraction of Capetian France, some explanation for a fundamental shift that took place in English castle design

at the start of John's reign. By the 1190s the tradition of castle architecture in England was remarkably catholic, using rectangular, circular and polygonal forms. In this variety is apparent the vitality of Anglo-Norman Romanesque as suffused by the spatial and geometric complexity of early Gothic. But almost overnight, around 1200 the rectangular tower favoured in the Romanesque period passed out of fashion from new English castle building for a century. In its place circular or semicircular, and more occasionally polygonal, designs reigned supreme. So complete is this change that the circular and semicircular tower should properly be understood in the abstracted sphere of castle design as no less characteristic of English Gothic architecture than the pointed arch.

What is so surprising about this change, beyond the speed with which it happened, is that so much else in the English architectural tradition remained constant: the interest in compositions of towers, the predilection for towers without vaults on upper floors, and even the idea of the great tower. French masons would have recognised their ideas in England from 1200, but recoiled in astonishment at some aspects of their reali-

154

sation. Along with French architectural forms, an allied package of ideas and values was also being received that was to have a direct impact on castle building.

CASTLES, HERALDRY AND
THE TRAPPINGS OF WAR

In the popular imagination, heraldry is as inseparable from the image of a medieval knight as his armour or his horse. Yet this formalised system of devices used to identify individuals on the battlefield started to develop properly only from the mid-twelfth century. The earliest important collection of English heraldry occurs in the *Great Chronicle* produced by the monk, artist and historian Matthew Paris at St Albans in the mid-thirteenth century. To accompany the entrance of important characters into his narrative, Matthew inserts a shield with the appropriate coat of arms in the margin of his text. And when that individual dies, the same arms are drawn upside down to symbolise his decease. At the time that Matthew was writing, coats of arms were appearing for the first time on the seals used to authenticate documents. Moreover, heraldry, like the other aristocratic pastimes of hunting and warfare, was beginning to develop its own technical language.[4]

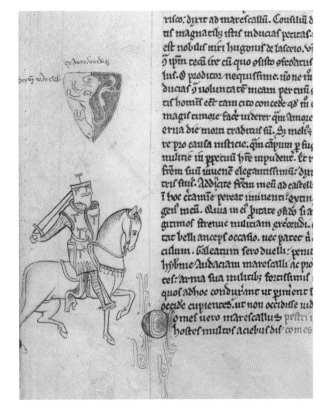

98 Matthew Paris's illustration of Richard Marshal (d. 1234) on horseback beneath his shield. The drawing juxtaposes the Marshal coat of arms with Richard on horseback wearing a surcoat and holding a shield decorated with hammers. This device was almost certainly used during tournaments rather than in battle, when the coat of arms was the appropriate means of identification. In the adjacent text is a description of Richard's capture and death in Ireland. Very similar equestrian portraits of mounted knights with a drawn sword appear on seals of the period.

Such was their perceived importance that disputes over armorial blazons could engender long and acrimonious legal disputes. Amongst the most famous of these in England was fought in the late fourteenth century between the Grosvenor and Scrope families over the right to display *azure a bend or*.[5] A host of nobles, prelates and knights were called on by the court to describe the places in which they had seen these arms displayed and the person identified by them. Their descriptions evoke a world littered with heraldry, and the impression is amply corroborated by surviving physical and documentary evidence. From around 1250 coats of arms may be found applied to badges, to clothing and vestments, to horse trappings, to tombs, in stained glass, on metalwork, in wall paintings, to buildings, to furniture, to doors and shutters, to signposts, above gates and – in their original context – on armour. Even long-dead kings and heroes, such as Edward the Confessor, were provided retrospectively with arms to allow them a place in this new world of display.

In its early stages heraldry observed very few hard and fast rules. Arms were assumed or changed by individuals as needs or liking dictated, and there was no systematic way of distinguishing between the arms of relatives, such as a father, son and brother. Nor, prior to about 1300, were arms combined on shields to indicate marriage alliances between families. But almost from their inception there were some curious sophistications in their usage, one of which is relevant to this discussion. As well as a coat of arms many individuals also wore identifying symbols. One of the best early illustrations of this habit is found in Matthew Paris's *Great Chronicle*, where Richard Marshal is depicted beneath his coat of arms on horseback and wielding a sword (pl. 98).[6] Curiously, his arms in this marginal illustration bear no relation to the decoration on the surcoat and helmet of the figure below, which are covered in hammers, Richard's household badge. What Matthew Paris has almost certainly done here is to depict Richard dressed, not for battle, but for the tournament field.

Tournaments in the twelfth century did not take the popularly imagined form of two knights charging at each other with lowered lances down tidily cleared lists. Such scenes were an innovation of the later Middle Ages. Rather, tournaments were mock battles fought in the open field between contending parties of knights and they graduated almost seamlessly into warfare.[7] Winners took everything from the vanquished, ransoming their armour and horses. Tournaments

99 The south-west gatehouse of Corfe, Dorset, erected by Henry III around 1250. It preserves unusually clear evidence of a projecting timber gallery or hourd: the radiating troughs running through the tops of the tower walls held horizontal beams that supported the floor of this crowning structure. Each beam was further braced from below by an angled timber rising from a small stone bracket or corbel.

combined, in fact, the excitement of war with the thrills of the gambling table, and there were many who were made or broken by them. The tournament field was also extremely dangerous. Besides the crossbow it accounted for more casualties among the great than any other military activity. For this reason the church attempted to forbid tournaments. In England, both Henry I and Henry II enforced this ban for the additional reason that tournament musters might serve as cover for armed rebellions. As a result, for much of the twelfth century this sport could be enjoyed only in France. Stephen's reign, however, had seen some relaxation in this policy, and Richard I began licensing tournaments in England and pocketing the profits for his crusading venture.[8]

Participation in tournaments was necessarily limited to those who could afford or acquire the equipment and this helped establish a sense of common identity amongst them. Indeed, the rise of the tournament co-incided with the emergence of the mutable concept of chivalry, a word that literally refers to the behaviour of *chevaliers* or those who rode horses.[9] Quite as important, it also served to establish two closely related registers of knightly display. Tournaments drew justification from their role as practice for warfare and needed to preserve some flavour of that reality. But the disapproval of the church and the instinct for self-preservation among those who took part in them encouraged a clearer distinction between tournaments and warfare. This led to the adoption of different systems of identification in a tournament from those used on the battlefield. Upon this distinction there gradually came to be established others: the use of sharp weapons for war and blunted ones for tourneying, and – eventually – the evolution of different types of armour for the field and the lists. By the mid-fourteenth century these were often termed respectively the arms of 'war' and 'peace'.[10]

In about the same period, and probably as a prop for such an occasion, the board of the round table that now hangs in the great hall of Winchester Castle was created (see pl. 10).[14]

These wider developments in the culture of knighthood have intriguing parallels in castle architecture of the period. Just as knights began to dress differently for the tournament and the battlefield, so did castles come to develop differing architectural personae for peace and war. The origins of this distinction were practical: a great castle needed to be prepared for action much like an eighteenth-century battleship, and the process could transform its appearance. Amongst the changes commonly effected was the erection of timber galleries variously called hourdes, brattices or alures along the parapets of the castle. These both protected the defenders and allowed them to overlook the foot of the wall on which they stood. Such, for example, were the allures raised around the White Tower of London by Henry III in 1240 after part of the defences had collapsed and rendered the castle vulnerable. His writ dated from Windsor on 10 December directs:

> On the south side at the top of the same tower, you are to make large galleries (*aluras*) in good and strong timber and well-leaded over all facing southwards onto which if need arises men can climb and see down to the foot of the tower to defend it better (*per quas gentes videre possint usque ad pedem eiusdem turris et ascendere et melius defendere si necesse fuit*).[15]

Surviving physical evidence for such structures in England is relatively rare, and while no complete examples survive, some idea of their form can be pieced together (pls 99 and 100). Weaponry might also be raised onto the walls, including heavy crossbows called springalds and other siege machines. In 1313 Edward II's order to raise springalds in the Tower of London during a stand-off with the earl of Lancaster is recorded to have ended all 'hope of peace'.[16]

Finally, heavy, swinging shutters might be inserted between battlements to protect the defenders as they walked along the wall. There are many buildings that preserve evidence for such shutter fixings in England from the late twelfth century to the fourteenth. This usually takes the form of drilled holes for the iron shutter hinge in the sides of battlements (pl. 101). There are also documentary references to the erection of shutters. In the same crisis of 1313 referred to above, for example, Edward II made 'Payment to Thomas of

100 The north tower of Stokesay, Shropshire, has a projecting timber gallery that has been dated using dendrochronological analysis to the 1290s. This is practically the only extant English medieval example of a brattice-like structure in a castle. As at Corfe, the whole structure is supported from below by timbers set on stone corbels (see pl. 99). To the right are the gabled lateral walls of the hall.

Fuelling this interest in distinguishing between warfare and the tournament field was the medieval delight in flamboyant display: in a tournament you could pretend to be someone else, and there was no group of individuals more consistently impersonated than the legendary court of King Arthur.[11] The tale of the Once and Future King was first brought to the attention of the Anglo-Norman aristocracy by *The History of the Kings of England*, written by Geoffrey of Monmouth in the 1130s. Arthur's story subsequently enjoyed enormous popularity across the whole of Europe and was enriched at every retelling. So egregious did it become that, even by the late twelfth century, to describe something as 'a tale of Arthur' was to discount it as nonsense.[12] Nevertheless, in 1191 Arthur's body was revealed after a fire at Glastonbury Abbey, and a fine monument was raised over it. The discovery has every mark of a fraud and was possibly directed by Henry II, who had an interest in discrediting the uncomfortable notion that this heroic king was waiting to resume the English throne. By the late thirteenth century extravagant Arthurian tournaments or 'round tables' were being held in England, such as that organised at Kenilworth for 100 knights in 1279.[13]

 The architectural pace of castle building in England during John's reign was once again established by the crown in a series of six major building projects, each of which is documented in the Pipe Rolls as absorbing more than £1,000.[18] In crude terms this level of expenditure might be regarded as the financial threshold of an outstandingly ambitious building operation. The progress of work reflected the wider fortunes of John's government. In the first decade of the reign, the Pipe Rolls record a gradual increase year-on-year in the quantities of money spent on castles in England with a peak between 1209 and 1212. Thereafter, the breakdown of John's rule brought about a massive drop in expenditure.

Only one of the castle-building operations undertaken by John – at Odiham, Hampshire – concerned a completely fresh foundation. Work to Odiham was under way between 1207 and 1212, and cost £1,154, only £200 less than Henry II's castle on a virgin site at Orford.[19] Modern scholarship has not generally been kind to this building, despite its evident importance and scale. It was reported by one chronicler to have been built by John to enjoy the hunting in the locality.[20] Nevertheless, the castle was to figure largely in national affairs for the next century, and its constableship, with the powers it offered, remained an attractive appointment.

In terms of financial outlay, the most expensive of John's projects was the redevelopment of Scarborough between 1201 and 1212. Costing £2,289, John's work involved the construction of a wall punctuated with D-shaped towers along the landward side of the dramatic castle headland. At the same time, the king further developed the domestic accommodation in the castle, building a chamber block and an aisled hall in the outer bailey. The former is integrated with the line of the wall, and the tower that adjoins it is polygonal rather than D-shaped in plan (pl. 103). This curious modulation of form was presumably intended to draw attention to the position of the royal apartments along the wall.[21]

The chamber block and hall at Scarborough raise an interesting question about domestic living in castles at this period. Both John and Henry III are known to have possessed in most of their principal castles a 'king's house' that stood distinct from the great tower, if one existed. The Scarborough buildings presumably constituted one such house and their existence might

101 The parapets of Maxstoke, Warwickshire, built in the 1340s in a photograph of 1920. A wooden shutter could be hung between every battlement along the wall. Each was suspended from an iron hinge that sat in the diagonal groove cut in the sides of the battlement (1). In this case, it would appear from the form of the grooves that the shutters could be slotted in and out of place. Wood was a valuable commodity and there was no purpose in leaving it out to rot. In other castles, as at Framlingham, Suffolk, of the 1190s, the hinge sockets are just drilled holes, so the shutters were presumably fixed permanently in place. At Maxstoke each chimney takes the form of a miniature tower with a double ring of battlements, a design probably inspired by the fourteenth-century Caesar's Tower at Warwick.

Baldock and William the Shipwright, 2 carpenters working for 6 days to fit swinging hatches between the battlements of the great tower facing St Katherine and on the outer tower towards London.'[17] In this case, the location of the shutters shows that they were being used in vulnerable locations.

The practice of dressing castles for war can probably be traced back into the early twelfth century at buildings such as the great tower at Rochester (pl. 102) and the walls of Framlingham. That it had begun to take on more than a purely practical significance by 1200 is strongly suggested by the architectural evidence: numerous castle buildings (such as the great tower of Conisbrough described in the last chapter) were provided with sockets for hourdes but were evidently designed to appear without them. Indeed, hourding sockets and rich crowns of battlements simply cannot have functioned simultaneously. The intention of such designs was to create a castle that looked magnificent but which could then be converted into a powerful fortification if need arose. This distinction between function and display established a creative tension in castle architecture and, informed by the spirit of chivalry, opened its forms to fantastical decoration.

102 An impression of the mid-thirteenth-century seal of the city of Rochester, Kent. With artistic licence, it shows the east wall of the castle above the waters of the Medway (1). To the right is the castle gatehouse (2), approached across a bridge, and the great tower of the castle (3). Clearly visible at the uppermost level of the corner turrets are projecting horizontal beams (4). In time of war, these beams would have formed the platform on which a hourd could be erected. The sockets in which they sat are still visible in the fabric of the tower and appear to be integral with the original structure, begun in 1127. From the battlements there flies the royal standard emblazoned with lions. The arches spanning the angles between the towers and parapets of the outer wall are a curiosity (5). In a later example of this unusual arrangement at Portchester, Hampshire, there is a latrine contrived in the overhang.

be interpreted as evidence for a move away from great tower living. But it is much more probable that John was actually creating at Scarborough what was otherwise a normal and long-standing arrangement appropriate for a great castle. That is to say, a castle served by both a great tower and a discrete 'king's house'. Certainly, Henry II is known to have possessed a king's house at the Tower of London from at least 1166 and this suggests that the move from great tower to house was not a straightforward change in domestic fashion.[22] The apparent widespread emergence of these buildings in the early thirteenth century is likely to be the result of improving documentation. It may additionally reflect the acceleration or consolidation of an established phenomenon.

When John completed Scarborough he turned his attention in Yorkshire to Knaresborough, where he spent a further £1,294 on the castle between 1204 and 1214. The nature of his work to this site is difficult to reconstruct today, but it included the enlargement of the castle ditches and the creation of four gateway tunnels running into them.[23] Subterranean passages of this kind enjoyed a brief vogue in English castle design in the decades around 1200. They were probably intended as a means by which defenders could make surprise attacks on those besieging a castle. The earliest example survives in the upper ward at Windsor,

which was possibly created by Henry II.[24] At Knaresborough the passages were about 9 feet (2.7 m) high and 4 feet (1.2 m) broad. They were cut through the rock from the castle bailey and were closed at the point they issued into the ditch by a portcullis.[25] These defences may give a clue as to the form of the tunnel defences constructed by John beneath the North Gate at Dover, more of which below.

Much better preserved than Knaresborough, and following closely in the pattern of John's treatment of Scarborough, was the remodelling of Corfe Castle. Again, this work fell into stages, of which the first involved the reordering of the inner and western baileys of the castle between 1201 and 1204. Within the upper ward, under the shadow of the great tower, there was constructed in addition a new chamber block that in later documentation was called – as a mark of its splendour – the Gloriette. To judge from the details of this building, the masons employed were probably drawn from the lodge at Salisbury Cathedral, which was then rising from the ground.[26] The second stage in the work began around 1212 and involved extending the line of walls and towers down into the lower bailey (pl. 104). Presumably, all these new walls and towers were erected to replace earlier timber defences.

The last major rebuilding project initiated by John was the reorganisation of the castle at Kenilworth. His most important alteration to the site involved raising the water level of the mere to create the present concentrically arranged inner and outer bailey in the 1210s. He probably also built the causeway approach to the castle from a third, remote bailey called The Brays. The buildings likely to have been raised by him include the top storey of the great tower (see pl. 49) and Lunn's Tower (pl. 105). John may also have erected some of the outer defences to the castle, though these could equally date from the mid-thirteenth century. They include the twin-towered Mortimer Gate at the end of the entrance causeway and the stone defences to The Brays.

As a steady background to all these operations, John continued the refortification of Dover initiated by his father. His work absorbed a further £1,400 and appears to have involved refortifying the northern tip of the castle site, erecting a stone wall with D-shaped towers and a gatehouse, the remains of which still survive embedded in the castle fabric.[27] Partly excavated from the natural chalk, there existed beneath the new stone defences a series of subterranean passages. The purpose of these is not clear today, but they may have been

103 (*facing page*) Scarborough, Yorkshire, an aerial view of the headland dominated by Henry II's great tower, begun in 1159. The castle is defined on its landward side by a huge ditch (1). John's rebuilding of the wall and towers along the crest of this seems to have fallen into two phases, between 1201–6 and 1207–12; and it is probably after the break that the towers changed from being solid to hollow structures along the length of the wall. One tower from the second phase of work is polygonal in plan (it is today cased in red brick) (2), a modulation of form probably intended externally to highlight the position of the king's chamber block that abutted it to the rear (3). Nearby, in the lawn of the castle bailey, are the foundations of a hall (4) and kitchen (5) probably also built by John. These buildings presumably duplicated those already in existence within the inner bailey (6) and great tower. Such duplication of domestic apartments seems to have been common in castles at this date, though the logic behind it is hard to explain.

104   Corfe, Dorset, a view of the great tower and its southern annexe. It is visible between the gate to the middle ward of around 1250 (left) and one of the towers built by John in the second phase of his works after 1212 (right). The thirteenth-century buildings at Corfe are constructed using cut masonry of very high quality, and their detailing is remarkably consistent over the course of the century.

105 A photograph of Lunn's Tower at Kenilworth, Warwickshire, in 1878. The tower was probably built by King John as part of his remodelling of the castle around 1210. Its broad plinth gives the illusion that the tower stands on a masonry motte, an idea found in other twelfth-century buildings such as the great tower of Conisbrough, Yorkshire. The narrow buttresses that taper into the base are not structural but serve to divide the tower visually into regular bays, a Romanesque rather than a Gothic conceit. The arrow loops are very similar to those on the added storey of the great tower, which is presumably contemporary (see pl. 49).

intended as a means of moving men around the fortifications under cover, and possibly also as protection against miners cutting through the foundations of the wall during a siege. From the threshold of John's gate there descended a bridge, at least 150 feet (45.72 m) long and approximately 60 feet (18 m) high from the base of the outer ditch. This dropped to an outer fortified enclosure or barbican surrounded by a timber palisade. Derived from the Arabic words *bab* (gate) and *khan* (courtyard or enclosure), such defensive outworks to gates called barbicans first begin to be mentioned in England towards the close of the twelfth century.[28] The name remains the only convincing connection so far drawn between the world of The Crusades and English castle architecture.

BARONIAL CASTLES IN
JOHN'S REIGN

There was no baron or bishop in the realm who could compete with John's extensive patronage of castle architecture. Nevertheless, the creation of powerful new landed interests in the previous reign did stimulate some remarkable building projects. The most indi-

vidually important of these was undertaken by the now familiar figure of William Marshal. Though otherwise so generous to William, Richard 1 had deliberately withheld Pembroke and its earldom from him in 1189. Ten years later, however, John passed on both prizes. In time-honoured fashion, William responded to his new dignity by redeveloping the seat of his earldom, the castle of Pembroke. The work was almost certainly initiated during the earl's first visit to his castle in 1200 and included as its centrepiece a great tower within the inner bailey (pl. 106).[29]

It is just possible that architectural inspiration for this monumental building lay in the towers being erected by Philip Augustus in France around 1200, the so-called *Tours Phillipiennes*. These would be an obvious source for the circular plan of Pembroke and provide a parallel for the distinctive recessions in external wall plane at each storey. Nevertheless, connecting Pembroke with these designs is awkward in other ways. The earliest *Tour Phillipienne* was probably built in the king's seat at the Louvre in Paris, begun around 1190 and completed by 1202;[30] the remainder were all begun after 1200.[31] Moreover, no *Tour Phillipienne* can compete either in height or breadth with the Pembroke tower. Nor is there any parallel in this group of French buildings for a tower floored in timber and vaulted only at its upper level. The possibility must remain, therefore, that the design emerged independently and that it simply reflects in more generic fashion an awareness of the Gothic fascination for towers on a circular plan. Alternatively, it may refer back loosely to an earlier generation of French great towers on a circular plan, such as that erected between 1170 and 1190 by the count of Blois at Châteaudun (Eure-et-Loir).[32]

Whatever its inspiration, the great tower of Pembroke spawned a host of architectural copies into the late fourteenth century, and at sites across south Wales there stand towers that copy distinctive details from it. The castles of Llawhaden, Laugharne and Kidwelly, for example, all of which sat in the orbit of the earl of Pembroke's power, each possess one tower on a circular plan with an upper vault. It is possible that some of these vaults supported an inner crown of battlements in the manner of Pembroke, though no evidence for such an arrangement now survives. Alternatively, at Manorbier and Cilgerran there are towers with pairs of windows, an arrangement evoking the sculpted openings at Pembroke (pl. 107). Such architectural connections highlight the admiration in which the great tower of Pembroke was held. They possibly

106 The great tower at Pembroke is a huge drum-shaped building four storeys high and with a splayed base. Entrance to it is provided by a raised door at first-floor level (1). This was covered by a timber porch, the sockets for which still remain (2). Directly above the porch is one of two windows in the building ornamented with sculpture (3), an arrangement evocative of the entrance to the great tower of Conisbrough. The floors of the building were of timber and access between them was provided by a single spiral stair rising in the thickness of the wall (4). The uppermost room, however, was covered by a flattened, stone dome. This dome supported three concentric rings of battlements like a papal tiara, a feature otherwise unparalleled in castle architecture of the period. A series of large sockets beneath the parapet indicates that it was possible to erect a timber hourd around the top of the building (5). Given the arrangement of battlements and arrow loops at the top of the tower, however, the whole was clearly intended to be seen without hourding except perhaps in time of war.

Cilgerran, Pembrokeshire. The east tower begun by William Marshal the younger in 1223 is visible to the left. Its paired windows, coarsely rendered in rubble rather than cut masonry, are an architectural reference to the great tower at Pembroke built by William's father. This is one of several thirteenth-century castle buildings in south Wales that make architectural allusion to the great tower of Pembroke. Similar paired windows, for example, are also found at Manorbier and the impressive Barnard's Tower along the line of the town fortifications at Pembroke.

also made a political point: in imitating this building, these castles were paying architectural homage to what consistently remained the principal castle of south Wales and the physical symbol of its earldom.

Meanwhile, John's style of government, and in particular his political use of the office of sheriff, was also encouraging castle building across the kingdom. Many of those he appointed to this office were political outsiders in the counties where they were installed and were actively encouraged to set down roots by the king. So, for example, the barony of Westmorland had been forfeit to Henry II in 1157 by Hugh de Morville and had been held by a series of trusted royal servants ever since. In 1202, however, John appointed a staunch supporter and a nephew of de Morville, Robert de Vieuxpont, sheriff of the county. The following year Robert was granted the barony in full hereditary right and

subsequently worked to secure control of his new possession in the face of claims by other relatives of de Morville. Crucial to his consolidation of power was the enlargement of Brough Castle and the foundation of a completely new castle in 1214 at Brougham (see pls 182 and 183). On both sites he constructed a great tower of stone on a square plan in the Romanesque tradition, an interesting reflection of the prestige still commanded by such buildings.[33]

Similar circumstances probably explain the development of Warkworth Castle in Northumberland over the same period. In the late twelfth century the castle is known to have been very modestly fortified, but in 1199 a man called Robert fitz Roger paid the king 300 marks to have his inherited title to it confirmed. Robert's landholdings at this time were focused in East Anglia and it can be no coincidence, therefore, that his

concern for Warkworth heralded a remarkable expansion of his interests in the north. In 1203 he was appointed sheriff of Northumberland and began to acquire further grants of land in the county.[34] To judge from the architectural evidence of the buildings at Warkworth, it was at about this time that the castle underwent a complete redevelopment. The obvious inference is that Roger determined to express his new position and interests in architecture.

The degree to which the new castle at Warkworth was conditioned by the old is not now clear, but the whole design looks sufficiently coherent for it to have been freshly laid out in the early thirteenth century.[35] The bailey was entered through an imposing twin-tower gatehouse (pl. 108) and possessed substantial residential buildings in stone. To judge from local parallels, the motte was probably crowned by a walled enclosure or shell keep, though this was replaced around 1380 by a great tower that will concern us later. How long the work took to complete is not known, but in the 1250s, presumably in reflection of the alterations undertaken, Matthew Paris described Warkworth as 'a noble castle'.[36]

IRELAND

The Anglo-Norman conquest of Ireland strictly lies outside the scope of this narrative, but the invitation that brought Richard de Clare, second earl of Pembroke, alias Strongbow, to the aid of the king of Leinster in 1170 was to have far-reaching architectural consequences on both sides of the Irish Sea.[37] In many ways, the experience of Ireland in the late twelfth century closely mirrored that of England a hundred years earlier. A series of Anglo-Norman landholdings was quickly staked out along the eastern side of Ireland, each one with a castle as its focus. These often reflected the constitution of earlier native Irish estates and were colonised with religious foundations and boroughs. Many of the larger castles were almost immediately developed in stone and possessed great towers that reflect close ties with architectural developments in England and Wales.[38]

Amongst the most important castle foundations of this first generation was at Trim, Co. Meath, the centre of the lordship of Meath. It was granted by Henry II to Hugh de Lacy (d. 1186), one of the principal figures of the conquest of Ireland. Today, in 2010, Trim bears the scars of astonishingly insensitive development, but

108 The great gate of Warkworth, Northumberland, built around 1200. At each angle of the towers there are polygonal buttresses. Carefully integrated within the overall design are a series of crossbow loops, their bases splayed to afford the maximum field of fire. Above the gate passage there survive stone brackets for a fighting platform, probably added around 1400. There are sockets for timber brattices in each of the side towers. The upper chamber of the gatehouse was well appointed, with large windows facing into the bailey behind. A sixteenth-century survey of the gatehouse describes it as containing a porter's lodge and prison at ground level and the bedchamber of the earl of Northumberland on the upper floor. In the nineteenth century the gatehouse was adapted as a house. It was returned to its present form when the property was taken into state care in the 1920s.

it remains one of the best-preserved medieval settlements in Ireland. The great tower of the castle was built within an earlier earthwork fortification and is of very unusual design (pl. 109). It has recently been shown to be the product of a complex architectural evolution. As first completed, the building stood only two storeys high and was planned in the form of a Greek cross, with a turret projecting from each face of its rectangular core.[39] This design could well have been inspired by motte fortifications in England, such as Berkeley (see pl. 76) and even Lewes, Sussex. Running around its exterior were a series of wooden galleries or hourds, fragments of which have survived embedded in the building. Dendrochronological analysis of these timbers suggests that they were felled in 1175±9, a date that corroborates the statement in the annals known as *Mac Carthaigh's Book* that the castle was built here in 1176.[40]

Meath passed into royal control in 1210 and Trim was then reorganised. Accounts presented to the exchequer for 1210–12 show that money was being spent on the construction of a granary and what is described as 'the strengthening of the tower'. It may be a reflection of the upheaval caused by these changes that when John visited Trim for two days in July 1210 he stayed not in the castle but in a field outside the town.[41] The works to the tower in the 1210s probably involved heightening the central block of the building. Further alterations in the fourteenth century brought the great tower to its present condition. One building directly informed by the example of Trim was the great tower on a rectangular plan at nearby Maynooth, Co. Kildare, probably begun around 1200.[42] This reduces the turrets at Trim to little buttress-like projections in the centre of each wall. Trim may also have inspired the much-altered great tower on a similar Greek-cross plan at Castle Rushen on the Isle of Man, which was perhaps built by Godred (d. 1187), the Danish king of Dublin.[43]

The other outstanding great tower of the period to survive was built to dominate the borough and castle foundation of Carrickfergus, Co. Antrim, by John de Courcy, who invaded Ulster in 1177 (pl. 110).[44] This follows the classic Romanesque form and is set out on rectangular plan. An intriguing insight into the size of the castle garrison in this period is provided by an Irish Pipe Roll entry of 1211–12 relating to Carrickfergus: during the year it fluctuated between six to ten knights (*militibus*), fifteen to sixteen men-at-arms (*armatis*) and three to five crossbowmen (*balistariis*). It also con-

109 The great tower of Trim, Co. Meath, has a distinctive cross-shaped plan with four turrets set around a central block. As first constructed around 1176, it rose only two storeys high. Clearly visible in the masonry are sockets for timber galleries that were erected around the outside of the building and the doors that gave access to them. The upper floor was added in the fourteenth century. The distinctive plan of Trim may have informed the designs of the great towers at Maynooth (Co. Kildare) and Castle Rushen (Isle of Man). This latter was possibly begun by the Danish king of Dublin and a rival of the Lacys.

110 Carrickfergus, Co. Antrim, is still dominated by the great tower built by John de Courcy, who invaded Ulster in 1177. The great tower was probably begun in the 1190s. It has been substantially altered internally since its first completion, though the external outline of the building remains little changed. The principal door of the great tower was at first-floor level and was presumably approached up a stair housed in a forebuilding, now lost. Like many of the major early castles in Ireland, it was built to command a natural harbour, which allowed Courcy easy access to Chester, Dublin and his wife's father on the Isle of Man.

sistently included a chaplain, four watchmen (*vigilibus*) and four doorkeepers (*janitoribus*).[45] Another rectangular great tower was also possibly erected at Dunamase, Co. Laois, though the fragmentary remains of this building are poorly understood. Several early stone castles in Ireland further possessed stone walls and towers, again following closely on English Romanesque precedent. Carrickfergus has a particularly fine wall tower with numerous loops dating to the first quarter of the thirteenth century. More modest examples of similar structures constructed at about the same time exist at Carlingford, Co. Louth.

The Gothic revolution, however, followed hard on the heels of such buildings. Polygonal and drum-shaped great towers began to be erected on an impressive scale from about 1200 onwards. Amongst the first securely dated buildings of this kind is the round tower at Dundrum, Co. Down, complete by 1210–11, and a decagonal great tower constructed by King John at Athlone, Co. Westmeath. This latter cost £129 2s. to

erect and collapsed in 1211, killing the justiciar's assistant and eleven other Englishmen.[46] Work to other such impressive sites as Castleknock, Co. Dublin, and Nenagh, Co. Tipperary, is less well documented but roughly contemporary. The early interest in great towers on a round plan in Ireland may convincingly be associated with architectural developments in the south of Wales through William Marshal's strong interests in both areas. Wall defences too took on circular forms, as is most dramatically illustrated at Trim in the outer curtain or the gatehouse at Carrickfergus, both probably works of the first half of the thirteenth century.

Besides the emergence of Gothic forms, there also appear at the same time three examples of what was to become a classic castle plan of the period: a rectangular bailey fortified at each corner with a drum tower and entered through a twin-towered gateway. The construction of Dublin Castle, the seat of Ireland's government, was ordered by King John in a

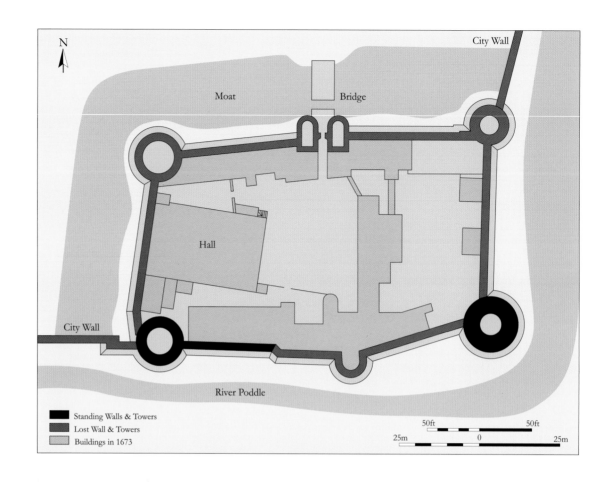

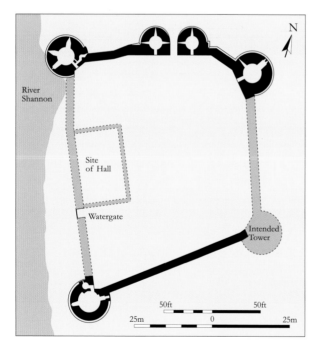

111 Plans of Dublin and Limerick, which are respectively documented as being under construction by King John after 1204 and in 1211–12. The internal buildings shown in Dublin are taken from a map of 1673. It is likely that the hall is the same as that constructed at the direction of Henry III in 1243 'in the manner of the hall at Canterbury'. The buildings shown at Limerick have been exposed by excavation. The only documentary evidence for the construction of Limerick is a Pipe Roll entry for 1211–12, for political reasons a year of intense investment by John in castle building. It is a sum that matches the greatest royal castle-building operations of the period in England, a reminder of the relative expense and importance of this project to the crown. The designs of both castles reflect the early thirteenth-century Gothic interest in quadrangular planning and the consistent use of towers on a circular plan. It appears that Limerick was never completed with a fourth tower, though one was presumably intended.

mandate of 1204 (pl. 111). A strong castle was to be built 'with good ditches and walls' for 'the custody of treasure and other purposes'.[47] Building operations seem properly to have got under way only some ten years later, between 1213 and *circa* 1230. By this time work was also in progress on another major royal castle at Limerick, which was the object of the massive expenditure of £733 16s. 11d. in 1211–12.[48] No less important was the third major building in this group at Kilkenny, the principal castle of William Marshal. It was probably begun either when he first visited Ireland in 1200 or after 1208.

All these designs were executed on what were, to all intents and purposes, virgin sites and offer a fascinating insight into the ideals of castle construction in this period. Their essential design was to continue in fashion throughout the century, as at Roscommon Castle, constructed by the royal governor or justiciar of Ireland in the 1270s. John's activities in Ireland in 1211–12 correspond with the high watermark of his power and compare in financial terms to his most ambitious works elsewhere. From 1213 conflict within his realm dragged England by degrees into a damaging civil war.

Within sight of Windsor Castle, at the meadow of Runnymede on 15 June 1215, King John was forced to set his seal to the articles of what has become the most celebrated document in English legal history. Magna Carta was a charter of liberties for the barons of England, an attempt to protect themselves from the arbitrary exercise of royal power. John had inherited the fiery Angevin temperament and was intermittently capable of decisive action. He earned himself a reputation, however, for lechery, easy living, cruelty and deviousness. There is considerable documentary evidence, too, that he delighted in modest gaming or gambling. John had not the least intention of observing the terms of Magna Carta and sent off a letter the following day to the pope with a doubtful account of events in an attempt to have the agreement quashed. By the end of the same year civil war had broken out. Its events colourfully illustrate the role of castles during a great political crisis in the thirteenth century. They also established the foundations of a new political order in the kingdom.[49]

At first the rebels had the initiative, seizing London in September 1215 and appealing to the French king, Philip Augustus, for help. They then marched south and seized Rochester Castle with a force of ninety-five knights. Their aim was to bottle John up in Kent, where he was awaiting the arrival of an army of mercenaries from the Continent. Heavy storms delayed John's muster and destroyed many of the incoming ships, but having gathered his depleted forces, he marched north to Rochester. There he occupied the town, which was being fortified against him, and broke the bridge across the Medway to isolate the city from London. He then set about reducing the castle, bombarding it night and day with catapults. Famously, the siege closed in on the great tower, begun in 1127 (see pl. 69). The events leading to the fall of the castle, during which part of the tower was undermined and collapsed, are clearly legible in the repaired fabric of the building. A contemporary account of the crisis of the siege evokes the situation vividly:

> When all the other defences were broken down, the great tower (*arx*) alone stood intact, though it too was damaged by the barrage of stones; it was older than the other buildings but constructed more soundly. Then miners were sent in. One side of the building was brought down, but the defenders took

up a strong position in the other half, for the great tower was built in such a way that a very thick wall separated this part from the side which had fallen. Never in our age has a siege been driven so hard, or resisted so bravely. But after days without respite, the men in the tower, besieged there alone and without assistance, were struck by terrible hunger; they had only the flesh of horses to eat and water to drink (which was particularly hard for them, being accustomed to finer food). At last the end came. First they threw out all the men who seemed least able to fight on: the king took some of them and cut off their feet. Then, soon afterwards, all the rest were captured and except those who claimed Benefit of Clergy, they were put in chains. The King kept the knights and most eminent prisoners for himself, and granted the remainder to others. From the enormity of his rage, it seemed that he was going to have the whole army put to the most terrible death, but in fact he only ordered the hanging of one man, a crossbowman; they say that John had fostered him from childhood. All the other rebels were desperate at this news; some fled in fear back to London, others took refuge in monasteries, and now there were few who cared to put their trust in castles.[50]

The loss of faith in the castle was not perhaps quite as complete as the chronicler suggested: Rochester was restored at the start of the next reign and the great tower subsequently became the object of major repairs costing more than £1,000 in the 1250s.[51] Having celebrated Christmas at Nottingham Castle, the royal army set out on campaign to ravage the territories of rebels in the north of England. Few details of the campaign are recorded, but it was evidently a brilliant success. By 14 January 1216 John was in Berwick-upon-Tweed, Northumberland, having relieved sieges at several places and capturing numerous hostile castles, including Belvoir, Pontefract, York, Richmond and Alnwick.[52]

But in the meantime the rebels in London were beginning to receive reinforcements from abroad and they also had a new leader. In the face of papal opposition, Philip Augustus was reluctant to claim the English crown. He chose instead to sanction the efforts of his son, Prince Louis, who was duly elected king by the rebels. Louis arrived in England on 21 May 1216 and John lost control of the kingdom. Canterbury opened its gates to the invading prince; Rochester fell after a short siege; and Louis entered London in triumph on 2 June. He then marched west and took

Winchester, the second capital of England, with a number of surrounding castles. Only Odiham, John's newly built castle, held out for any time, its feisty garrison of three knights and ten sergeants defending themselves with a valour that amazed the French.[53] By the end of the summer Louis had added to his territorial gains an impressive following of English barons. John meanwhile equivocated and issued numerous writs instructing sheriffs to destroy castles he could not garrison across the country. At Portchester, Hampshire, for example, the order was given to level the castle to the ground, or to destroy it with fire should that prove too difficult.[54] It seems very unlikely from the architectural evidence that his orders here, or elsewhere, were followed.

But three castles did hold out for John against Louis' forces: Windsor, Dover and Lincoln, the last captained by its redoubtable chatelaine, Nicola de Hay. Of the course of the Windsor and Lincoln sieges we know little, but that at Dover is described in detail by an anonymous chronicler in the *Histoire des ducs de Normandie et des rois d'Angleterre* who was either present or informed by an eyewitness.[55] The castle was held by the justiciar of England, Hubert de Burgh, with a force of 140 knights and 'a great number' of men-at-arms.[56] Probably no other castle in England could field a garrison of this size, which reflects Dover's importance and the scale of its landed endowment. Hubert was also a seasoned commander in siege warfare, having gallantly led the year-long defence of Chinon in Touraine against Philip Augustus in 1205 following the fall of Rouen.[57]

Louis arrived with his army in early July and encamped for a few days in the town of Dover. On several occasions during this time, the garrison paraded themselves in full armour outside the barbican that protected the main castle gate and Louis' crossbowmen went out to shoot at them. Some idea of the proximity of the forces in this bizarre ritual is suggested by the fact that one crack shot, a crossbowman called Ernaut, was actually chased and captured by men from the castle. His subsequent fate is unfortunately not recorded.[58]

Soon afterwards, on 22 July, the siege proper began.[59] Louis divided his forces between the castle and the town and sent his ships to sea so as to encircle the castle completely. Work then began on the erection of catapults to bombard the gates, walls and 'a very high castle made of hurdles', presumably a siege tower of timber-frame construction. Louis then sent his miners into the ditch with a protective awning to undermine

the barbican wall, which was stormed soon afterwards.[60] Huart de Paon, a horse soldier, was the first to mount the breach, and a popular knight called Pierre de Creon, the captain of the barbican, was fatally wounded in the assault. The miners now set to work in the main castle ditch beneath one of the towers of the great gate, which they collapsed successfully. An intense battle began as Louis' forces attempted to take the breach, but they were successfully resisted by the garrison, who plugged the gap with great timbers torn from the castle buildings.[61]

Following this check, Louis struck a truce with the castle garrison. Four days later, on 18 October, King John died at Newark. Louis, having unsuccessfully tried to persuade the Dover garrison to support his claim in the light of this news, disconsolately returned to London. The death of John was a watershed for both sides, though its effects were slow to be felt. In his place there was crowned at Gloucester his son, the nine-year-old Henry III. Over the winter Louis returned to France, and in his absence, lured by promises of redress for grievances and with the innocent figure of the young king in place of his father, there now began a steady flow of counter defections to the royalist cause. Louis returned in the spring and reversed some of the losses he had sustained. One notable siege he undertook was that of Berkhamsted Castle, Hertfordshire, which he encircled with siege machines. These unleashed such a shower of missiles that the garrison were forced to surrender on account of 'the damnable stones' that ceaselessly rained down upon them.[62]

Soon afterwards Louis determined once more to capture Dover. Leaving one part of his army before the gates of Lincoln, he returned south, bringing a siege machine of prodigious size to pound the defences.[63] William Marshal, the leading supporter of Henry III, saw in the division of the French force a tactical opportunity. In a confused street battle in the city of Lincoln on 20 May he successfully destroyed one part of Louis' army. Then at the battle of Sandwich, on 24 August, Hubert de Burgh inflicted a crushing defeat on the fleet of ships bearing reinforcements from France.[64] Louis was forced to acknowledge defeat.

THE YOUNG KING

Henry III (1216–1272) was perhaps the most obsessive patron of art and architecture ever to have occupied the throne of England. Certainly, it is not until the

112 A photograph taken in 1922 of the North Gate or Norfolk Towers of Dover, Kent. After the damage inflicted by the siege of 1216–17, the principal gate of the castle built by King John with its two towers (1) was repaired and a third tower with a beaked front inserted to block its old entrance passage (2). This created a curious trinity of towers at the northern tip of the castle. Beneath these, an existing system of tunnels in the chalk was substantially enlarged and access created to a new tower at the bottom of the moat. From this tower – called St John's Tower (3) – there extended at first-floor level a drawbridge that gave access to a further series of tunnels in the barbican. The arch of the drawbridge pit survives but was infilled with brick in the eighteenth century and is here obscured by ivy (4). There were also sally ports (gates to allow the defenders to make unexpected attacks) into the moat (5). The scale and complexity of these underground arrangements are best paralleled by Henry III's works at Winchester in the 1240s.

reign of Charles I that he finds a serious rival. It has been estimated that during his fifty-seven-year reign, the longest in medieval English history, he spent the astonishing amount of £85,000 on his castles alone.[65] Moreover, these sums were spent by a punctilious bureaucracy. As a result, Henry's likes and dislikes are registered with beguiling detail in hundreds of surviving documents.[66] From these, for example, it emerges that he ordered the White Tower at London to be whitewashed, almost certainly the reason for its popular name today. The circumstance is known from Henry's characteristic concern that the effect should not be spoilt: on 10 December 1240 he directed that the gutters of the building be extended to the ground 'so that the wall of the tower, which has just been whitened, may be in no danger of perishing or readily falling outwards through the trickling of the rain'.[67] The overall effect clearly pleased him, because he also ordered that the towers of Rochester and Corfe be whitewashed as well.[68]

Although such interests properly lay to be discovered in the future, the reign of the nine-year-old king opened with a burst of castle restoration. The tutor of the king and the bishop of Winchester, Peter des Roches, undertook a certain amount of this work,

including the redevelopment of Winchester and its surviving great hall (see pl. 10). Much more important, however, was the castle building connected with, or overseen by, Hubert de Burgh, the defender of Dover and justiciar of England. He emerged by stages as the dominant political figure of the minority and by extension as its greatest castle builder, both as a baron and on behalf of the crown.[69]

It is difficult to assess the extent to which Hubert de Burgh directly supervised these operations, but in some points they may reflect his own considerable experience as a soldier. As a group these works, which focused on the sites directly involved in the fighting of 1216–17, informed the development of English castle architecture for the remainder of the thirteenth century. They also drew directly on French architectural precedent to a remarkable degree, a reflection of contemporary admiration for this rival monarchy and its art. It is worthwhile, therefore, to consider them individually and with some attention to technical detail.

Between 1217 and 1230 nearly £8,000 was expended on the castle at Dover after the damage inflicted by the siege.[70] The North Gate, which had been partly destroyed by mining, was rebuilt as a trinity of towers (pl. 112). Beneath this extended an underground entrance

passage – an enlargement and extension of one created by King John a few years before – which descended to an isolated tower in the bottom of the moat. This, the St John's Tower, serves effectively as an outer gatehouse to the castle: in its basement are doors to allow surprise sallies into the moat and at first-floor level a drawbridge giving access to the outer barbican through a further series of underground passages. Later alterations have somewhat obscured the character of this arrangement but some sense of the appearance of the lower tower is provided by the great gate erected at Trim in the 1240s, which was possibly modelled on it (pl. 113). The combination of a tower and passage system on this scale is paralleled only in Henry III's work of the 1240s at Winchester, now largely lost.

Two further gatehouses were also constructed on either side of the castle at Dover. That to the east, called the Fitzwilliam Gate (pl. 114), was very similar to the newly adapted North Gate. It was fronted by a cluster of three solid turrets. Each of these is beaked, a feature unprecedented in England but also found in a small group of earlier Angevin buildings in France erected around 1200, such as Loches (Indre-et-Loire), Le Coudray-Salbart and Parthenay (both Deux-Sèvres in Poitou).[71] Below it there extended a long, vaulted passage, which emerged beyond the outer castle ditch. Along the length of the passage were several gates that swung down from the roof of the vault (a unique feature in this period) and at its mouth there stood a small tower with a portcullis.

The third and last of the new entrances to Dover Castle was Constable's Gate. This can probably claim to be the largest gatehouse ever erected in England: it stands about 120 feet (36.5 m) wide and 60 feet (18 m) deep. Where the building overlooks the moat its walls drop downwards from the gateway almost as far as they rise above it, a total frontage nearly 120 feet in height (pls 115 and 116). From the gate there extends a high bridge with a drawbridge that led to a barbican on the ridge between the two outer ditches of the castle. The barbican, now largely destroyed, was a walled enclosure with an outer gate tower. As the name suggests, Constable's Gate was constructed as a self-contained residence for the constable of the castle. The domestic arrangements within it are very unusual: a vaulted hall at first-floor level runs through the building along the top of the gate passage.

As a group, all three new entrances to Dover share several notable points of comparison. Each is properly to be understood as an architectural ensemble built

113   East gate, Trim, Co. Meath, was built at some uncertain date in the early thirteenth century. A circular gate tower with a fortified bridge as an outwork, it is very similar in conception to

St John's Tower at Dover. Although the Trim gate has been plausibly compared to early thirteenth-century buildings in Poitou, such as Coudray-Salbart, it is more likely that this design is

drawn from English sources. If so, it would date to the 1240s, when many of the ideas first articulated at Dover began to be reproduced widely in England.

entirely from stone: a gatehouse, a bridge and an outer tower. This is a dramatic departure from English precedent where such ensembles – where they had existed – were usually of a combination of materials; even at Dover the barbican attacked in 1216 had been a timber and earth enclosure. The form of the new gates, moreover, was probably allied to the architecture of contemporary fortified bridges to towns. One detail that suggests this particular provenance is the stretched plan of the outer tower to Constable's Gate. This shape of tower sits very comfortably across the piers of a bridge, as can still be seen, for example, at Monmouth (pl. 117). Indeed, it is just possible that the first example of this distinctive shape occurred on London Bridge, begun in 1176 and one of the marvels of late twelfth-century engineering. The form of the original outer gate to London Bridge is not known, but it took exactly this form when it was rebuilt during repairs in the fifteenth century.[72]

Whatever the case, these stretched towers appear in several later gatehouses built by Henry III, notably the great gate of Scarborough, built between 1243 and 1245, and the Black Gate at Newcastle (pl. 118). It is a noteworthy curiosity that the thirteenth-century entrance to the cathedral of Lausanne, a church otherwise deeply indebted to English example, also incorporates this form.[73]

Besides the rebuilding of the entrances to the castle at Dover, work also began to complete the walls and towers around the outer bailey. The new towers were all D-shaped in plan, but possess little rectangular side projections, a curiosity we shall encounter again (pl. 119). They also incorporate unusually deep plinths – termed spur bases – in the manner of Constable's Gate. These serve to link the rectangular foundation on which each tower is set with its semicircular superstructure. The detail is copied from some of King John's work at Dover, the designs for which were probably derived in turn from Angevin castles in France. Notable as a comparison are three towers at Chinon, generally dated to between 1180 and 1200 (pl. 120).[74]

That said, the architectural origin of the spur base in castle design is probably much older. Indeed, it is likely that the detail was revived from Roman example: the Gallo-Roman fortifications of Carcassonne (Aude), for example, incorporated towers possessed of these features.[75] And French masons were to experiment further with the architectural decoration of tower plinths, as can be seen most dramatically in the early thirteenth-century towers at Fère-en-Tardenois (Aisne)

114 Fitzwilliam Gate, Dover, Kent, built in 1220. Beneath the gate there extended a passage in the form of a vaulted corridor nearly 200 feet (70 m) long. For much of its extent, the vault over this corridor has now been removed. The passage was carried on a bridge with a drawbridge pit across the ditch of the castle (the partially infilled drawbridge opening is visible to the bottom left). It was also closed by a series of gates that swung down from the roof and at the end by a portcullis. Examples of tunnel entrances to gatehouses are known in England – for example, the mid-twelfth-century Water Gate at Sherborne Castle, Dorset – but the scale of the work at Dover is without parallel in England or France.

First floor

N

Section

0   15 metres

0   15 yards

- c. 1200
- 1221–30
- 1805
- 1883

Ground floor

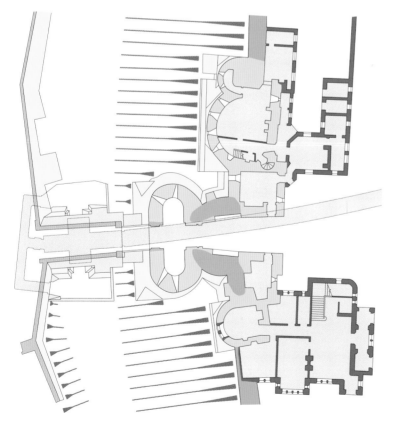

115 (*facing page, top left and right, bottom left*)   Plans and cross-section of Constable's Gate, Dover, Kent, begun after 1217. The gate was created around one of King John's D-shaped wall towers, the crown of which still rises through the centre of the building. A new gate passage was punched through the front of this and a series of new towers built around it. On one side a conjoined large and small tower were constructed with a battery of arrow loops to overlook the approach to the barbican. A single tower of similar form was erected on the other side. This conceit of clustering towers was to enjoy some popularity in the thirteenth century at castles such as Allington, Kent, begun around 1281, and Barnwell, Northamptonshire, erected by 1266 (see pl. 146).

116 (*facing page, bottom right*) Constable's Gate, Dover, Kent, in a photograph of 1922. The gatehouse was begun after 1217 as the new principal entrance to the castle. It was by far the largest gatehouse ever constructed in England. The whole structure is a complex composition of towers. Its main front is formed by a tower planned in the form of a stretched circle. Constable's Gate remains in use to the present day as the official residence of the deputy constable of Dover. It has consequently undergone major alterations in both the eighteenth and nineteenth centuries. The approach to the gatehouse along the ridge between the two outer ditches of the castle was fortified by a barbican, now lost.

117 (*above*)   The Monnow Bridge at Monmouth is a rare surviving example of a type of fortified bridge once common in England. It was probably built in the late thirteenth century and remodelled in the fourteenth. The gate tower straddles one of the bridge piers and takes the distinctive form of two D-shaped towers placed back to back. From the thirteenth century onwards, castle gatehouses in England were nearly always planned in conjunction with bridges over ditches or moats. These could either be fortified in their own right or lead to barbicans beyond.

118 (*right*)   The Black Gate, Newcastle, Northumberland, built by Henry III between 1247 and 1250 at a cost of more than £500. It had a façade on an oval plan with D-shaped towers set back. The upper, polygonal storey is a later addition to the fabric. The gate projected into the castle moat and the bridge extending from it ran to a barbican, now destroyed. This arrangement would have resembled that of the Monnow Bridge. The detailing of the gate, including the pair of trefoil niches for statues that flank the main entrance, compares to that found on the contemporary west front of the priory church at nearby Tynemouth.

in Picardy. The interest in the form, however, seems to have passed out of fashion relatively quickly in France.[76] By contrast, as we shall see in the next chapter, English masons were to develop it vigorously in the later thirteenth century.

When Dover was completed it evidently became an object of particular pride for the young monarch, to such an extent that in November 1247 the constable of the castle was instructed to take one visiting dignitary, Gaucher de Châtillon, on a conducted tour of the site. Henry III directed that Dover be shown to him 'in eloquent style (*faceto modo*), so that the nobility (*nobilitas*) of the castle shall be fully apparent to him, and that he shall see no defects in it'.[77] It is very rare to be provided with such unambiguous evidence for the aesthetic appreciation of castle architecture in the thirteenth century. That the king wished Dover to appear 'noble' to his visitor is significant too. The particular word could equally be used with much the same connotations of warlike grandeur to flatter the military aristocracy who created and occupied these buildings. In the context of a castle, architecture could be understood quite literally to express social identity.

Quite as important as the Dover works were concurrent operations at Windsor. In 1224 Hubert de Burgh was appointed custodian of Windsor Castle and set in train a repair programme that would absorb more than £1,000 in the next six years. Since the siege little had been done to the castle beyond the reconstruction of the great hall. There followed in 1224–5 works to the motte, where a new walled enclosure was erected on the summit. Motte fortifications of this kind are often supposed to have passed out of fashion in the twelfth century and the operation is important in demonstrating that this was not the case. The new building was probably higher than that constructed by Henry II, being termed 'the tower' or 'great tower' in the accounts, and was filled with 'houses'. Its masonry shell and apron or enclosing wall probably survived little altered until the heightening of the building by the architect Sir Jeffry Wyatville in his work to Windsor between 1824 and 1840.[78]

The remainder of the 1220s work concerned the lower bailey, which was bisected along the edge of the motte ditch with a wall to create a lower and middle ward. The new wall was provided with its own ditch and given a small rectangular gate tower. Two large D-shaped towers were built beneath the motte towards the town in the middle ward and connected with a curious bow-shaped wall. Around the lower ward were created a series of defences, which included a gatehouse on the site of the modern entrance. This did not approach the scale of its counterparts at Dover, but documentary record shows that it was fronted by two towers. In the 1240s it was provided with a barbican, the site of which had to be cleared by the demolition of houses. A wall set with three D-shaped towers was also built across the western end of the lower ward (pl. 121). This incorporated decorative bands of masonry and a passage, termed a sally port, for launching surprise attacks, was created beneath it.[79] D-shaped in plan with rear walls of masonry (rather than open-backed), we shall see that the new towers at Windsor are typical of Henry III's later castle architecture.

Closely following in the style of these major works at Dover and Windsor were alterations to three other castles of the first importance. At the Tower of London the royal apartments of the castle were improved and two towers were erected along the waterfront.[80] It was probably at the same time that a twin-towered gateway was constructed at the entrance of the inner bailey to the castle, the so-called Coldharbour Gate. Meanwhile, Hubert de Burgh also commissioned the reor-

121 Henry III's wall across the western end of the lower ward of Windsor, Berkshire, with the Clewer Tower (left) and Almoner's Tower (centre). It is described as being under construction in 1230 A broad tunnel from the basement of the Clewer Tower formerly opened into the moat, an arrangement reminiscent of the much larger underground works at Dover. The Almoner's Tower rises from a sloping base. This detail – found on several of Henry III's towers at Windsor – serves the same structural purpose as the Dover plinths: it tidily connects a square base with a semicircular superstructure. Like the Dover plinths, this particular form was to have extensive architectural progeny in late thirteenth-century English castle design. The walls are laid with stripes of lighter coloured stone, a decoration possibly evocative of Roman building techniques.

ganisation of the outer defences of Bamburgh, Northumberland, with new walls and drum towers (pl. 122). Finally, Lincoln Castle was repaired in the aftermath of the siege it had sustained by the forces of Prince Louis. A tower known as Cobb Hall was constructed in the north-east angle of the castle.[81] At the same time, the gatehouse was reorganised with a trinity of towers and, like those at Dover, with a substantial stone barbican (pl. 123).

This clutch of royal building projects at Dover, Windsor and Lincoln were amongst the most important undertaken during the reign of Henry III. They introduced the developed preferences of Gothic design – with its rigour of planning and consistency of detail – on a grand scale to England and were to prove immensely influential. The architectural ideas they generated – notably the use of spur plinths, the creation of monumental gatehouses with integrally planned stone barbicans and the clustering of towers – are to be encountered repeatedly through the next century in English castle design. Over the next chapters there will be repeated references to the architectural ideas they enshrine.

BARONIAL CASTLES OF THE MINORITY

In the first years of Henry III's reign, it is likely – though very little documentary evidence survives to confirm the fact – that one of the most architecturally active groups in the realm was its sheriffs. These agents of royal authority, many of whom had been appointed by King John, greatly benefited from the breakdown of central authority caused by the civil war. Released from close supervision, they were briefly able to exercise sweeping local powers and to harness the resources

122 (*above*) Bamburgh, Northumberland, viewed from the south-west. The castle underwent extensive repairs over the 1220s at the instruction of Hubert de Burgh. It was probably in this period that the series of towers on the south side of the castle was erected. Particularly substantial is the tower on the far left of the view. Designed on a circular plan, it commands this angle of the defences and fits into the tradition of large-scale towers found in several major late Angevin castles, such as the Avranches Tower at Dover and the Cockhyll Tower at Scarborough. The king's carpenter was regularly employed at Bamburgh between 1220 and 1227. Timber was assembled for his use from various sources, including the castle of Nafferton, which was abandoned and disassembled at this date.

123 (*right*) A reconstruction by Tig Sutton of the east gate at Lincoln as rebuilt after the siege of 1216–17. It incorporates a trio of towers applied to the façade of an earlier gatehouse. As in the case of the Fitzwilliam Gate and North Gate at Dover, the central tower in this triple composition was beaked. Also, the gatehouse was provided with a stone-built barbican with two towers – effectively an outer twin-tower gate. This is the earliest known example of a type of regularly planned barbican that was to remain popular into the fifteenth century in both town and castle gateways. The gatehouse survives but, unfortunately, the barbican has been demolished.

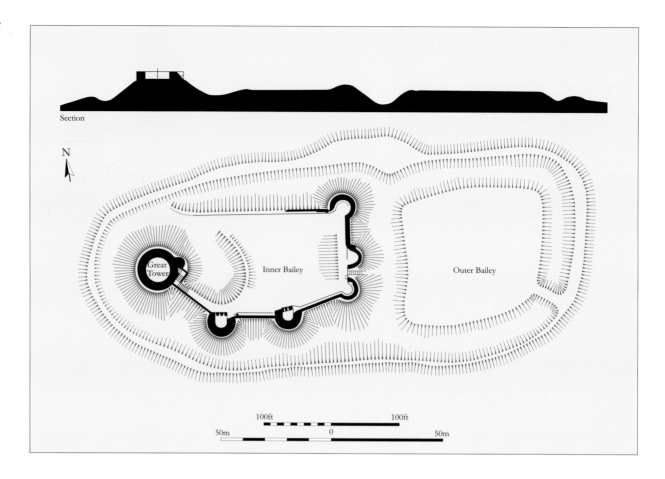

124   Plan and cross-section of Chartley, Staffordshire. The castle comprised two baileys, of which the outer was presumably fortified in timber and is reduced today to an earthwork. Its inner bailey, however, was enclosed by a stone wall set with identical D-shaped towers, two of which were drawn together to form a gatehouse. Dominating the castle was a drum-shaped great tower, now largely destroyed, on a motte. One peculiarity of the great tower is the inclusion of a small projecting turret like a nose, a detail that relates it to a number of other buildings in the west of England and Wales.

of the crown for building. Such freedom was to prove short-lived. In 1223 a general order was issued by the council governing the realm for the surrender of all royal castles and shrievalties. By this order Hubert de Burgh effectively disinherited his political opposition.

At Bedford in 1224 the castle was famously held in resistance to the change. Narratives of the ensuing siege record that the castle had been largely rebuilt by the sheriff of Bedfordshire, Falkes de Bréauté, which probably dates it to the decade or so before 1224. Also, that his additions comprised a towered outer bailey of masonry and a motte surmounted by a great tower. Excavation has also revealed that the castle ditches were faced in stone.[82] The siege of Bedford, attended in person by the young king, was bitterly fought and absorbed very substantial resources. In its final stage, the defenders retired to the great tower, which was split by a mine. When the castle fell the entire garrison, led by Falkes's brother, was executed and the castle razed to the ground.[83]

From 1223 onwards castle building increasingly became the preserve of powerful baronial interests. One outstanding figure in this respect was Ranulf de Blundeville, earl of Chester and of Lincoln. Between

his return from crusade in 1220 and his death in 1232, he was the chief opponent of Hubert de Burgh. He built three castles across his far-flung estates at Chartley (Staffordshire), Beeston (Cheshire) and Bolingbroke (Lincolnshire). All three castles incorporate circuits of walls punctuated by consistently detailed D-shaped towers and twin-towered gatehouses. In every case, however, these common Gothic elements were marshalled in slightly different ways to create what might be understood as three types of castle typical of mid-thirteenth-century design.

Chartley Castle was the principal of the castles begun by Ranulf. It stood in proximity to the Cistercian abbey of Dieulacres, Staffordshire, which he founded in 1214 and where he later chose to be buried. The inner bailey of Chartley was fortified with a regular circuit of walls and towers, two of which were drawn together around the entrance to create a gatehouse. Dominating this circuit of fortifications and set on a motte was a great tower on a circular plan (pl. 124). The great tower at Chartley actually belongs to a small family of great towers that possess an additional projecting turret or turrets. This very distinctive detail is found in a series of buildings along the Welsh march

125 Longtown, Herefordshire, was probably erected in the first quarter of the thirteenth century. The great tower on the motte is circular in plan with three regularly placed turrets projecting from it, one of which is just visible to the right. These turrets relate the tower to a group of contemporary buildings in the west of England, including Chartley. The idea of combining intersecting towers and turrets on a circular plan is encountered in English architecture from the eleventh century, as in the eastern chapels of Norwich Cathedral, Norfolk. The early thirteenth century, however, saw a particular vogue for the idea in castle architecture in buildings such as Constable's Tower, Dover.

at Skenfrith, Caldicot and Longtown (pl. 125). All these towers were associated with mottes and were probably erected in the 1220s and 1230s. They probably relate, moreover, to the fascination with clustering towers and turrets encountered at Dover. A related outlier to this group possibly existed at Helmsley in Yorkshire, in the north-east corner of the inner bailey, though so little of it now survives that it is hard to say much about it (see pl. 128).

There are conflicting accounts of the foundation date by Ranulf of Beeston Castle (pl. 126). Facing into England, the castle was probably a creation of the mid-1220s and intended to protect Ranulf's earldom of Cheshire from Hubert de Burgh's growing power. It occupies a natural outcrop of rock that had been used as a fort in the Iron Age. The castle comprised two baileys, each entered through a wall set with D-shaped towers. In form and detail, the inner bailey defences compare closely to those at Chartley, but there is no dominating tower. A good parallel for a corona of towers on a motte is to be found at Clifford in Herefordshire, almost certainly begun in the 1220s

by Walter Clifford (d. 1268; see pl. 30), or in the north of England at Sandal (pl. 127), probably built in the 1240s.[84]

Bolingbroke, the third of Ranulf's castles, is a variation on the same idea. This stands on low ground and comprises a single, moated bailey enclosed by a circuit of D-shaped towers. Two of these have been brought together to form a gatehouse. The castle is first mentioned here at Ranulf's death in 1232, and its date of foundation is not known. One of the towers incorporates an internal arrow loop looking back into the bailey, a distinctive detail found at both Beeston and Chartley and one that hints at common authorship of all three castles. Excavations have shown that the early domestic buildings within the walls at Bolingbroke were all of timber, as was probably also the case with the other castles (though the domestic buildings at Beeston may never have been built).[85] Within the ruins of the towers are visible today checker-board patterns laid in white stone, presumably the remains of a decorative treatment to the walls as still survives at Windsor. This type of enclosure castle has many parallels across

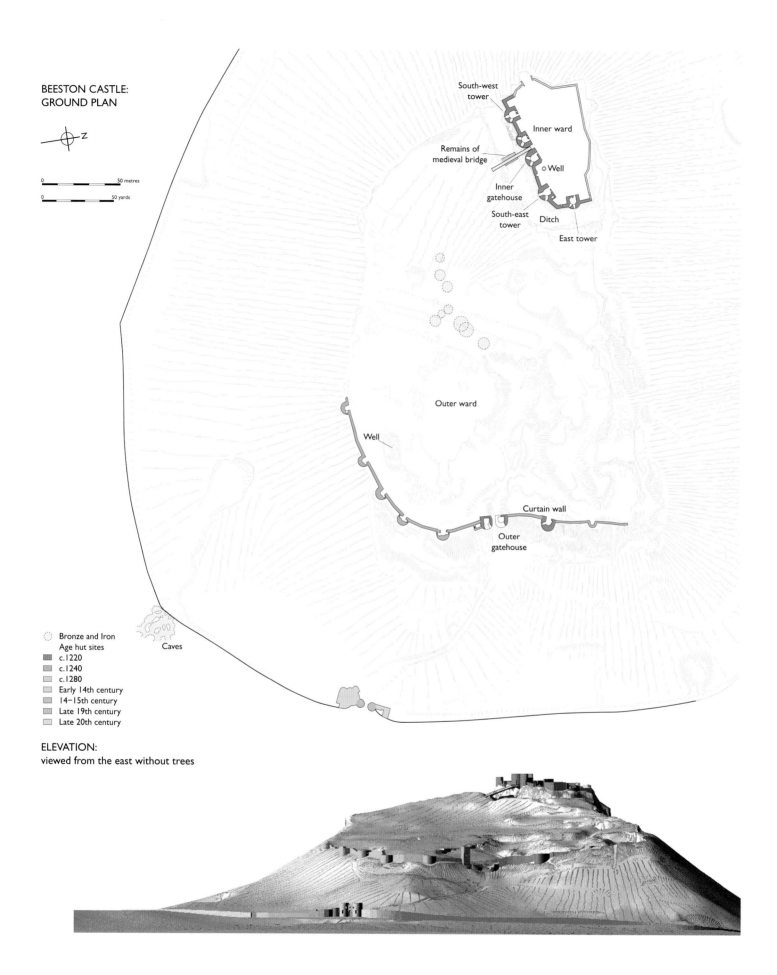

BEESTON CASTLE:
GROUND PLAN

N

0 ____ 50 metres
0 ____ 50 yards

South-west
tower

Inner ward

Remains of
medieval bridge

Well

Inner
gatehouse

South-east
tower

Ditch

East tower

Outer ward

Well

Curtain wall

Outer
gatehouse

Bronze and Iron
Age hut sites
c.1220
c.1240
c.1280
Early 14th century
14–15th century
Late 19th century
Late 20th century

Caves

ELEVATION:
viewed from the east without trees

the country on both elevated and lowland sites, such as Whittington (Shropshire) of around 1221, Tattershall (Lincolnshire), licensed in 1231, and the inner bailey of White (Monmouthshire), built in the 1250s.

Another form of castle not represented by Ranulf's work, but which deserves mention, was one dominated by a gatehouse. Designs of this kind had an architectural pedigree stretching back into the eleventh century at such sites as Bramber, Ludlow and Exeter. While on campaign in Wales in 1224 Henry III began work to one such building at Montgomery, a replacement for the nearby timber castle of Hen Domen. The site was carefully chosen by his advisers (probably Hubert de Burgh) on a site that 'seemed untakeable to everyone'.[86] Its fortifications were dominated by a twin-towered gatehouse with solid, three-quarter, drum-shaped towers.

THE GREAT TOWER

Mottes and great towers continued to be adapted and developed in major castles across the kingdom in this period. At Lewes, for example, two new towers on a polygonal plan were erected along the line of the wall crowning the principal motte of the castle (pl. 129). The operation can plausibly be attributed to William de Warenne, the son and heir to the great estates of Henry II's half-brother, Hamelin Plantagenet (d. 1202). William inherited the castle in 1202, a date that would accord well with the detailing of the towers and their internal arched arrow-loop openings. As in the case of Windsor, the work to the motte fortifications at Lewes was presumably associated with the repair of domestic buildings on the summit of the motte. The eleventh-century great tower at Chepstow was likewise remodelled by the sons of William Marshal in the 1220s and 1230s. There is one documentary record of this work, a gift of ten oaks by the king for alterations to the tower in 1228.[87] Their changes included the insertion of windows with bar window tracery, some of the earliest to survive anywhere in Britain and easily pre-dating those at Westminster Abbey (see Chapter One).[88]

In some cases, completely new great towers in a Gothic idiom were also created. Robert Roos, alias Furstan (d. 1226 or 1227), a prominent figure in northern politics, for example, undertook an ambitious remodelling programme of his principal castle at Helmsley. Here he created a roughly rectangular inner

126 (*facing page*) Plan and elevation of Beeston, Cheshire. The castle occupied the site of a former Iron Age fort on this prominent outcrop overlooking the Cheshire plain. In the huge outer bailey the towers have open backs and are quite lightly built. By contrast, their counterparts in the inner bailey are more massively constructed and backed in stone. This particular architectural graduation is a commonplace of Gothic castle design across Europe. The castle buildings of the 1220s appear to have been left incomplete and in 1303–4 there is record of raising, battlementing and roofing towers in the inner bailey. There is other evidence of the incomplete building works: the ground level of the inner bailey, for example, remains very uneven to this day. As a result, it could never have been laid out with substantial domestic buildings in the Middle Ages.

127 The excavated motte of Sandal, Yorkshire, with the remains of buildings probably erected in the 1240s and demolished in 1646 on the orders of Parliament. The motte was enclosed by a cluster of four towers and had a formidably arranged system of access. Visitors crossed to a walled barbican in the moat (1) across a bridge from the right. They then turned through 90 degrees and crossed over a second bridge to a twin-towered gatehouse at the base of the motte (2). From this there rose a ramp to a second twin-towered gateway at the summit of the motte (3). Built throughout of well-cut masonry, this sophisticated architectural composition loosely resembles in form, quality and scale such late thirteenth-century entrance arrangements as Edward I's gate to the Tower of London. The photograph was taken from the top of the extended ladder of a Wakefield Fire Brigade engine during excavations between 1964 and 1973.

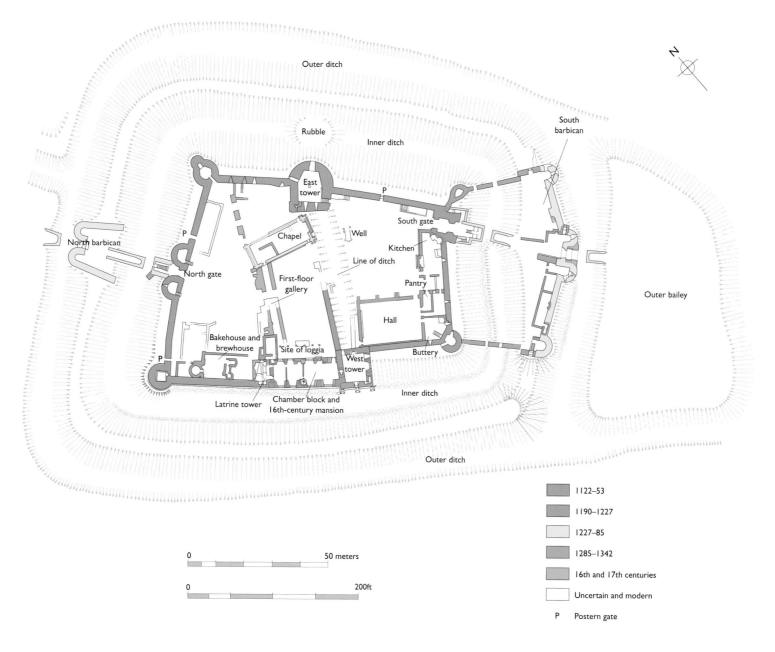

Outer ditch

Inner ditch

Rubble

South barbican

East tower

P

North barbican

P

North gate

Chapel

Well

South gate

Kitchen

First-floor gallery

Line of ditch

Pantry

Outer bailey

Bakehouse and brewhouse

Site of loggia

Hall

West tower

Buttery

P

Latrine tower

Chamber block and 16th-century mansion

Inner ditch

Outer ditch

N

	1122–53
	1190–1227
	1227–85
	1285–1342
	16th and 17th centuries
	Uncertain and modern
P	Postern gate

0   50 meters

0   200ft

bailey fortified with drum towers and enclosed by double ditches. The whole was dominated by a D-shaped great tower along the line of the inner bailey wall (pl. 128). A similarly sited D-shaped tower was also built at Bramber, probably during documented alterations to the castle in the 1260s.[89] This stood on deep spur bases, a detail that links it with the royal works at Dover of the 1220s. In the far north of England, meanwhile, two outstandingly ambitious great towers on circular plans were erected at Barnard Castle, Co. Durham (pl. 130), and at Bothwell, Lanarkshire, both probably works of the 1240s.

Bothwell is perhaps the most ambitious thirteenth-century castle building in Scotland. It was the centre-piece of a castle begun after 1242 by Walter of Moray or his son, William, but never completed. The buildings were constructed entirely of cut stone and its great tower, with three floors and a basement, just scraped the prestigious threshold of 100 feet (30.5 m) in height. It is encircled on its inner face by a stone-lined ditch. The tower was partially demolished in 1337 during the Anglo–Scottish wars, but this inner façade remains well preserved. It may have been built in rivalry with that created by the Balliol family at Barnard Castle. Not exclusive of this, it is also possible that the marriage of the Scottish king, Alexander II, in 1239 to Marie de Coucy connects this tower with the great tower at Coucy (Aisne), begun in the 1220s. The

128 (*facing page*) A plan of Helmsley, Yorkshire. The principal bailey of the castle is enclosed by a double ditch. Its thirteenth-century fortifications include a series of angle towers on a circular plan and a massive D-shaped great tower (see pl. 184). The northern angle tower possesses a curious secondary turret. This distinctive detail may relate the buildings here to the royal works and such tower compositions as the Constable's Gate at Dover of the 1220s. To either end, the approaches to the castle were fortified by barbican gates with open-backed D-shaped towers. Beneath the gate passage of both principal gates are stairs that drop to the moat, an unusual arrangement that allowed for access only when the gate was shut. Unfortunately, nearly all the defences of Helmsley were razed to the ground after a long Civil War siege in the 1640s.

129 Lewes, Sussex, a view of the motte and the stone enclosure on its summit. The two polygonal towers were probably added to the much earlier wall by William de Warenne soon after he inherited the castle in 1202. Typical of this period are the deep plinths of the towers and their numerous recessions of plane. The arrow slits are staggered as they rise up the building and, on the top floor, they sit at the angles of the two towers. This unusual arrangement was presumably intended to improve the field of vision from the tower. In some places the slits were later widened to create windows. An early twentieth-century excavator of the motte described this huge earthwork as being partially constructed of chalk blocks. If true, this method of construction makes it as much a work of architecture as an earthwork.

130 (*facing page*) An aerial view of Barnard Castle, Co. Durham. To the left and dominating the inner bailey is the great tower that was probably built in the early thirteenth century by John de Balliol (d. 1268). He was an outstandingly powerful figure in Anglo–Scottish affairs and controlled substantial estates in Galloway through his wife, Dervorguilla (d. 1290). The tower is built on a circular plan using blocks of regularly cut stone and was integrally constructed with the adjacent chamber block.

French tower, tragically demolished by a mine in 1916, was one of the prodigy buildings of the European Middle Ages.

THE ROYAL WORKS FROM 1227

The event that effectively released Henry III from his minority (which ended officially in 1227) was the political disgrace of Hubert de Burgh in 1232. One of its many consequences was that the king began to indulge to the full his own fascination with building. The greatest operation of his majority was the complete reconstruction of Westminster, both the abbey and the palace. As a whole, the project absorbed something approaching £55,000. Allowing for the changing value of money and the relative scale of the medieval economy, this was probably the single largest act of royal patronage in English history. Castles, however, were also in the forefront of expenditure and in particular Windsor and Winchester. From 1230 these two sites received more than £10,000 each, an astonishing sum.[90] The lion's share of this money was spent on the reorganisation and decoration of domestic buildings, which were the object of endless and bewildering changes.

Virtually nothing now survives of these works, though a tantalising insight into the colour and quality of the domestic interiors familiar to Henry III is provided by the fragmentary remains of two thirteenth-century wall-painting schemes at Windsor. These survive within what are today the buildings of the royal college of St George.[91] At Windsor, Henry III worked on two palace complexes, first on the buildings in the lower ward and then on those in the upper ward. By contrast, his work at Winchester focused on what the documents suggest was a rectangular courtyard residence with towers at each corner. This sounds rather like a small Gothic castle set within the wider defences.[92] The arrangement may have been the inspiration for such celebrated later buildings as the inner bailey of Conwy, more of which in the next chapter.

In the later part of his reign Henry also spent between £1,000 and £3,000 individually on another group of important castles: Nottingham, York, Bristol, Chester, Gloucester, Rochester and Corfe. All these works were again accompanied by changes to domestic buildings, which were increasingly being erected in stone rather than timber. The most impressive survival amongst these is the slightly lonely porch to the great

hall at Bristol, with its elegantly rib-vaulted reception space. The fortifications have not fared well in physical terms. Where they remain they are variations on now-familiar architectural themes: D-shaped towers and twin-towered gatehouses. As such, they need not concern us in detail.

One of the most curious buildings in this Gothic idiom is Clifford's Tower at York, begun around 1245 (see pl. 6). Its clover-leaf plan makes play with the idea of compositions of circular towers, perhaps an evocation of the rings of towers created on mottes such as Sandal. A very similar tower on a lobed plan was also probably begun at royal direction in Yorkshire at Pontefract in the 1240s. It was heightened and elaborately remodelled in the late fourteenth century (see pl. 334).[93] Beside these various royal operations there remains to be discussed another widely influential castle programme undertaken by Henry III at the Tower of London, but for present purposes this can be set aside for independent consideration at the close of this chapter.

BARONIAL CASTLES OF THE LATER REIGN

Trying to rescue some picture of the wider patterns of castle construction from behind this group of well-documented royal projects is beset with difficulty. To judge from a gap in the issue by the crown of licences to build castles from 1231 to 1253, there appears to have been a lull in building during the early years of Henry III's personal rule. Despite the very unsatisfactory nature of such evidence, this would agree with what might be expected from the political circumstances of the period: a series of relatively rapid shifts in power that prevented any particular group of individuals consolidating their position. Hubert de Burgh was briefly superseded by the king's former tutor, Peter des Roches, as the leading figure in the royal administration. His rule proved unpopular and the influence he enjoyed over the king was broken following Henry III's marriage to Eleanor, the daughter of Raymond Berengar, count of Provence, in 1236.

This match was brokered to help bolster Henry III's claims to his Angevin inheritance in France and served to internationalise English domestic politics. Attractive and intelligent, the twelve-year-old queen secured Henry's affections and introduced several of her Savoyard kin to the court. Much to the frustration of other established interests, this small circle was soon reaping rich rewards. Particularly important were three uncles of the queen. On her marriage she brought with her William of Savoy, bishop-elect of Valence, who died in 1239 and whose pivotal role at court devolved on his two brothers. Peter of Savoy was granted extensive property in England, including the great honour of Richmond in 1241. Meanwhile, in the same year, his brother Boniface became archbishop of Canterbury.

Initially, the Savoyards treated such advancement as a means of serving their wider dynastic ambitions in Europe and in relative terms neglected their English possessions. Although elected archbishop of Canterbury in 1241, for example, Boniface's first visit to England occurred in 1244 and lasted only for a few months. It was not until his second trip in 1249 that he was actually enthroned at Canterbury. Only in the 1250s did his residences in England become more regular. Nevertheless, of his twenty-nine years in office, most were spent abroad. It is a final mark of his allegiance and interests that he chose – almost uniquely amongst the medieval archbishops of Canterbury – to be buried away from his metropolitan church and outside England at the Cistercian abbey of Haute-combe, Savoy.

Peter of Savoy behaved in a similar fashion to his brother. In 1242, the year after receiving Richmond, he was granted custody of Pevensey Castle and its honour for a period of ten years. This valuable gift does not appear to have stimulated any architectural response until he managed to secure the castle in hereditary right in 1246. Soon afterwards the inner bailey of the castle was rebuilt with a new wall and a series of D-shaped towers (pl. 131). Curiously, two of these towers remained incomplete until at least 1318, when they were described as never having been battlemented or covered in lead.[94]

The exact timing of Peter of Savoy's work to Pevensey is not definitely known, but it is likely to have coincided with the replacement in 1254 of the feudal obligation to maintain the timber fortifications of the castle – termed *heckage* – with an annual cash payment. Presumably this labour was no longer necessary because the walls were now entirely stone-built.[95] There are several other castles where similar feudal services were commuted to money in the course of building operations, as at Dover during its reconstruction by Hubert de Burgh[96] and at Bramber, Sussex, in 1267–8.[97] The implication is that the refor-

tification of castles with complete circuits of stone walls was becoming steadily more common.

The Savoyard interest in England was further strengthened in 1247 with the marriage of two of the queen's kin to Edmund de Lacy, earl of Lincoln, and Richard de Burgh, lord of Connaught, both of whom were royal wards. At the same time, however, a powerful rival dynastic interest was established at court. In the same month, May 1247, the king invited four of his half-brothers and a half-sister to England as part of a calculated attempt to expand the royal family. Three of these siblings, children of Henry's mother Isabella of Angoulême by her second marriage, were immediately given prospects in England: Aymer de Valence was made bishop-elect of Winchester; William de Valence was given the hand of one of the co-heirs to the earldom of Pembroke; and Alice was married to John de Warenne, earl of Surrey. The architectural activities of this group – known collectively as the Lusignans – will be considered in the next chapter.

The Savoyards and Lusignans not only came into competition for power over the 1250s, but were also jointly distrusted in some quarters as interlopers on the English domestic scene. These rivalries were eventually to precipitate a civil war. Against this background of gathering domestic tension there appears to have been a growth in castle construction, possibly as a reflection of intensifying political competition. Such activity extended quite far down the scale of baronial inheritances and by the 1260s included numerous figures in royal service, as well as several bishops. For example, Warin de Bassingbourne (d. 1269) was a knight of sufficient importance to receive the office of sheriff of Northamptonshire in 1267.[98] The previous year he was licensed to encastellate two manors, one at Bassingbourn, Cambridgeshire, and the other at Astley, Warwickshire. Unfortunately, in neither case is there clear evidence of what was created.

The outstanding castle builder of the 1250s, however, was Henry III's younger brother, Richard, earl of Cornwall. He emerged as the greatest landholder in England after the king and from 1247 enjoyed the lucrative responsibility of reissuing the coinage for a period of ten years. He undertook work to his castles across the south-west in the early 1250s. These included the foundation of a new castle 'on the mountain at Mere' (Wiltshire), for which he received royal licence in 1253. Nothing today survives of this building besides the great hill on which it stood. A building account of 1300, however, records that it was encircled by a ring

of six towers.[99] It was probably in the same period that he established a castle on a remote and inaccessible headland at Tintagel in Cornwall, which he had purchased in 1237. This castle can never have had any strategic or economic value and, aside from its chapel, appears to have been all but abandoned within a century. Rather, it was almost certainly a chivalric folly, constructed on the supposed site of King Arthur's conception. To judge from its remains, it was extremely modest in architectural terms and possessed no substantial towers.[100]

Within the earldom of Cornwall as a whole, Richard was involved in the repair of several existing castles. In the absence of proper documentation, the full extent of his work is unclear, but the most substantial operation was the remodelling of Launceston, Cornwall. It would seem from the architectural evidence of the surviving ruins that he created much of the present castle. This included the construction of a high tower on the summit of the motte, which was formerly encircled by two apron walls. At the same time he fortified the bailey with a circuit of stone walls with two gatehouses and at least one large tower on a circular plan. The buildings at Launceston were detailed with cut masonry but otherwise constructed using local stone laid as rubble masonry.[101]

For all his activities in the south-west, the earl's castles in this region were primarily of importance as administrative centres. His favourite residence was in fact at Berkhamsted, Hertfordshire, within easy striking distance of London. Here he is recorded as having erected a three-storey tower in 1254, evidently a structure of some ambition.[102] A surviving account of 1269 also records that he was involved in wider repairs to the castle including the barbican and buildings on the motte. It is unfortunate that very little now survives of these buildings, which may have been of considerable architectural interest.

On 29 April 1257 Richard, earl of Cornwall, departed from England with a view to securing election as Holy Roman emperor. Using his huge financial resources, he succeeded in winning over the support of three of the seven electors to the throne: Ludwig, count palatine, and the archbishops of Cologne and Mainz. Late in May, on the feast of the Ascension, he was crowned at Aachen and then journeyed deep into the Rhineland attempting to consolidate support. Richard's bid was ultimately to fail, but in this first year he enjoyed enormous success. His absence from England, meanwhile, had a disastrous effect. The removal of his steadying political influence

131 The north side of the inner bailey of Pevensey, Sussex, rebuilt around 1250 by Peter of Savoy. Its walls and towers are built of regularly cut blocks of stone and possess deep plinths. In most details the towers are identical, with three internal floors, the uppermost of which served as a comfortable lodging chamber with a fireplace. Each floor was made independently accessible from the bailey, an unusual planning feature. One of the towers (right) had a vaulted basement, and was probably the principal in the group. In the wall beside every tower was a doorway opening into a latrine (1). The latrines evidently took the form of timber huts projected out over the moat, which originally extended to the buildings. The inner face of the wall was lined with buildings heated by fireplaces. It is known from a survey of 1318 that two of the three towers begun in the 1250s at Pevensey remained incomplete and thatched, a reminder that even ambitious castle buildings could be abandoned unfinished for long periods of time.

served as a catalyst for rebellion, and upon his return in 1258 England was in the grip of civil war.[103]

THE BARONS' WAR, 1258–66

The long-running confrontation between Simon de Montfort, earl of Leicester, and Henry III in the Barons' War, which dominated the politics of Henry III's later reign, had little direct bearing on castle architecture. Its events, however, included notable sieges at two of the castles on which this book focuses. The first of these involved the king's loyal son, Edward, at Dover, where a group of captured royalists were kept for security by the rebel garrison in the great tower of the castle. According to one rather florid contemporary account, these fourteen knights were held in chains, but with the complicity of three guards, one of whom secretly gathered food from the town, they broke free, and:

> . . . at once fortified the door from the inside to exclude those within the castle, who began vigorously to attack in their desire to break in. The defenders constructed a strong wall against the inside of the door to block it against entrance from the hard-fought assaults that they were continuously receiving and only with difficulty repelling. When he heard the news, the Lord Edward flew from London to Dover without even sleeping. Having gathered a not inconsiderable force, he boldly attacked the aforesaid fortress from the front. Those within the tower were well provisioned and began to press from there upon those without, hurling down from above spears and crossbow bolts with great forcefulness, of which they had an abundant supply in the tower. The garrison, who were being indefatigably attacked from both within and without, could not continue to resist this divided assault. They were compelled hastily to give to the eldest son of the king this copiously provisioned castle, only just saving their lives and arms.[104]

So might the very greatest castle of its age, what Matthew Paris described as the 'key of England', fall in almost absurd circumstances.

The hostilities of the Barons' War were concluded at Kenilworth, where the surviving rebels held out after the decisive royalist victory at the battle of Evesham on 3 August 1265. A large royal army gathered outside the walls of the castle under the direct command of the king and a siege began in earnest on 25 June 1266. Every mode of attack was attempted, but the water defences of the mere, combined with the firepower of catapults in the castle, frustrated every assault: a wooden tower that could hold 200 crossbowmen was smashed by missiles, as was a fortified cover for miners termed a 'bear'; and the boats prepared for another major attack.[105]

The king also made use of the spiritual forces at his disposal and brought a legate, an archbishop and two bishops to excommunicate those in the castle. As the red-vested legate performed the ceremony, a clerk and surgeon in the castle called Philip Porpeis dressed in a contrasting white cope and conducted a comic counter-excommunication of the legate, the king and his followers from the walls. Meanwhile, the garrison left the main gate open throughout the siege in mockery of the king's efforts.[106] Starvation, rather than military might, eventually brought about their surrender on 14 December 1266. The terms that were negotiated show that the king was quite as desperate to bring this operation to a close as the beleaguered garrison.

THE TOWER OF LONDON AND TONBRIDGE

In 1238 or 1239 Henry III initiated a building programme at the Tower of London that was to have a formative influence on the future of castle design in England. His intention was greatly to expand the site and to create around it an outer circuit of walls enclosed by a wide flooded moat of enormous proportions. As part of the work he gave the great tower of the castle its modern name, whitewashing the building. The operation greatly alarmed the citizens of London – who were nervous of the king's intentions – and proved ill fated. As the chronicler Matthew Paris smugly records, on the evening of 23 April 1240, the feast of St George, 'the stonework of a certain noble gateway which the king had constructed in the most opulent fashion, collapsed as if struck by an earthquake together with its forebuildings and outworks'.[107] Construction was resumed with redoubled vigour, but exactly a year later to the day in 1241, the new walls of the castle again collapsed. According to the dream of one London priest, Matthew reported, it was struck down by the ghost of the furious St Thomas Becket, a firm ally of all who fought royal tyranny.[108] After these

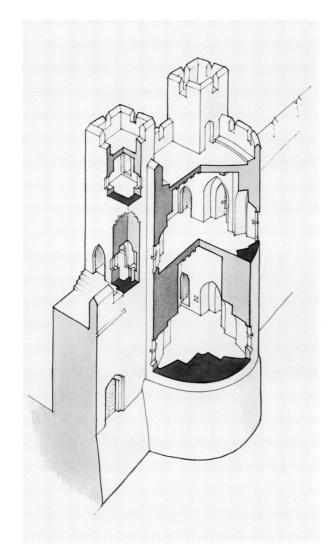

132 A cut-away drawing by Terry Ball of Broad Arrow Tower, Tower of London, one of the perimeter towers built by Henry III along the east side of the castle enclosure. The tower is D-shaped in plan and has a rear wall of stone. Its most distinctive and important feature is the pair of rectangular turrets projecting to either side of the building like ears. A comparable arrangement with only one 'ear' can be found in the towers erected by Henry III in the 1220s on the west side of Dover Castle (see pl. 119). Ear turrets were to become a widespread feature of castle architecture during the late thirteenth century.

setbacks, operations dragged on until Henry's son, Edward I, acceded to the throne. He inherited this botched project and in turn invested heavily to bring the castle to what is effectively its full modern extent.

Despite this chequered history, some fragments of Henry III's work at the Tower do survive along the north and east perimeters of the castle. These serve to illustrate the scale of the project and its salient features. The outer walls of the new castle were regularly planned to create a roughly rectangular enclosure and were set at intervals with towers on a D-shaped plan. Crucially, several of these towers can be shown to have possessed two turrets projecting like ears from the rear of the building (pl. 132). Also, there exists a small gate or postern in the eastern wall. This implies that there was a broad bank of earth and perhaps some outer fortification along the inner edge of the moat, most probably an apron wall. The importance of both these details will become apparent.

Of Henry III's magnificent gatehouse nothing survives, though the foundation of an associated tower set asymmetrically in front of it within the moat – presumably one of the 'forebuildings' described by Matthew Paris – was excavated in the years 1995–7.[109] The existence of such a feature implies a generic connection with the Dover works of the 1220s, the first English gatehouse designs to incorporate substantial stone outer defences. Several more specific features of its design, however, can possibly be inferred from an important group of late thirteenth-century gatehouses in other royal and baronial castles. In all sorts of details, these appear to look for architectural inspiration in the royal works of the 1230s and '40s. One very attractive possibility is that they took as their model the plans for Henry III's lost entrance to the Tower of London.

The most impressive of these buildings is a twin-towered gatehouse at Tonbridge probably built in the 1250s by Richard de Clare (d. 1262), earl of Gloucester and the richest baron in England (pls 133–5). In every respect this is a virtuoso and extravagant work of architecture. Even the arrow loops are externally ornamented with delicate mouldings and there survive fragments of a richly detailed chimney that perhaps comes from it. It was originally approached through a tower in the moat, which, according to an eighteenth-century plan, was set asymmetrically before the entrance in the manner of that excavated at the Tower of London.[110] This and other technical points of comparison aside, there is compelling circumstantial evidence for linking it to the circle of royal masons employed by Henry III and specifically those familiar with building operations around London.

The form of the gatehouse at Tonbridge was to be widely imitated over the next fifty years, a sure sign that it was much admired. As we shall see, in many cases such copies (which henceforward will be described as Tonbridge-style gatehouses) appear in later de Clare castles. Nevertheless, beyond the evident connections of Tonbridge with the king's works in London, three further circumstances point to a royal origin for its design. The next chapter will explore the first of these – that in the next reign the king, Edward I, was to build as many Tonbridge-style gatehouses as the de Clares, and he was unlikely to be copying their buildings. Second, that other patrons with no obvious connection to the de Clares also built Tonbridge-style gatehouses. At Llansteffan, Carmarthenshire, for example, there is a small Tonbridge-style gatehouse that was probably built as part of the redevelopment of the

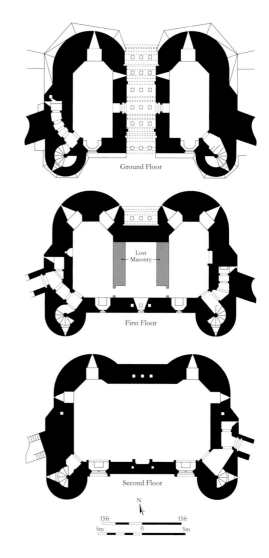

Ground Floor

Lost
Masonry

First Floor

Second Floor

N

15ft   15ft
5m   0   5m

133 (*above*) The façade of the great gate of Tonbridge, Kent, probably built in the 1250s and possibly modelled on the lost gatehouse begun by Henry III at the Tower of London in 1238 or 1239. It formerly stood at the head of a fortified bridge. An eighteenth-century plan by Edmund King shows a barbican tower at the opposite end of the bridge, since demolished. The gate is entirely built of cut stone and its detailing is boldly conceived. The twin towers that flank the entrance are connected by a massive arch. They rise from spur bases, a treatment ultimately rooted in the royal works at Dover and Windsor of the 1220s. This is one of many features that suggest the building was designed by a mason in the king's service.

castle begun around 1265 by William de Camville.[111] Finally, that the acknowledged masterpiece of de Clare castle architecture, Caerphilly, where the Tonbridge-style gatehouse is first known to be copied, is itself almost certainly an architectural descendant of Henry III's ill-fated operations at the Tower. It is to this building at Caerphilly, therefore, a fully fledged expression of the tradition of Gothic castle design that had evolved in England since around 1200, that this chapter should finally turn.

CAERPHILLY

On 11 April 1268 Gilbert de Clare, earl of Gloucester, the son of the builder of the Tonbridge gatehouse, began work to a new castle at Caerphilly, Glamorgan, in the south of Wales.[112] The building was intended to secure the northern border of his lordship of Glamorgan from Llywelyn ap Gruffudd, recently acknowledged by Henry III as prince of Wales. Llywelyn deeply resented the castle, which he regarded as an affront to his authority. After appealing uselessly for Henry III to intervene in its construction, the Welsh prince attacked Caerphilly on 13 August 1270, overrunning the defences and destroying what he could. Earl Gilbert was outraged and set to work once more. Despite difficulties with the king, the castle was prob-

ably almost complete by Henry III's death in 1272. This aggressive assertion of power paid off sufficiently for Caerphilly to be further expanded in the 1280s. It remained an important castle in Glamorgan until it was overshadowed by the development of Cardiff by the Beauchamp earls of Warwick in the 1420s.

Caerphilly was essentially a product of political ambition, built and garrisoned with surplus cash from the greatest baronial inheritance in England. It was also a greenfield development, and its architecture offers a clear insight, therefore, into the architectural fashions of the 1270s. The castle buildings were restored and the water defences re-excavated between 1928 and 1939 by John Crichton-Stuart, fourth marquess of Bute. Within the original castle fabric are several buried features, such as overbuilt battlements, which constitute interesting evidence for changes of design in the course of construction.

134 (*facing page, top right*) Plans of the great gate at Tonbridge, Kent, *circa* 1250. The two most significant features of this building are the scale of its conception, which permitted it to incorporate substantial domestic apartments, and the arrangement of towers: to the front are a pair of large D-shaped towers and to the rear a pair of staircase turrets. In respect of its scale, the design of Tonbridge is almost certainly derived from Constable's Gate at Dover. Pairs of stairs at the rear of gatehouses can be found elsewhere in England from about 1200 onwards, as at Warkworth, Northumberland. But the insertion of the stairs within twin ear turrets is likely to be connected to Henry III's work at the Tower of London (see pl. 132).

135 The inside façade of the great gate at Tonbridge, Kent, *circa* 1250, has a different character from the gaunt exterior front. It is framed by two stair turrets, and comprises at second-floor level a pair of delicately detailed windows that light a large chamber across the full width of the building. This probably served as a hall. There is fine figural sculpture in the building, for example, on the hood moulds of the upper windows. It is comparable in style to that found in the choir of Westminster Abbey. The high quality of the cut stone and such details as the delicate decorative mouldings round the arrow loops hint at the great expense of this building.

In all essentials, its inner bailey bears generic resemblance to the Gothic castles erected by King John in Ireland, with four corner towers and a twin-towered gatehouse (pl. 136). Several details, however, distinguish it from these earlier buildings. Most obviously, the symmetrically planned inner bailey incorporates an extra gatehouse in the Tonbridge style (pl. 137). Moreover, the inner bailey is enclosed with a broad bank of earth retained by an apron wall. This arrangement permitted the garrison to operate two tiers of defence simultaneously in the event of a siege.

The Caerphilly earth bank and apron is a regularised version of a long-standing defensive arrangement favoured particularly – though not exclusively – on low-lying castle sites. King John, for example, created similar concentric defences in stone on the central island at

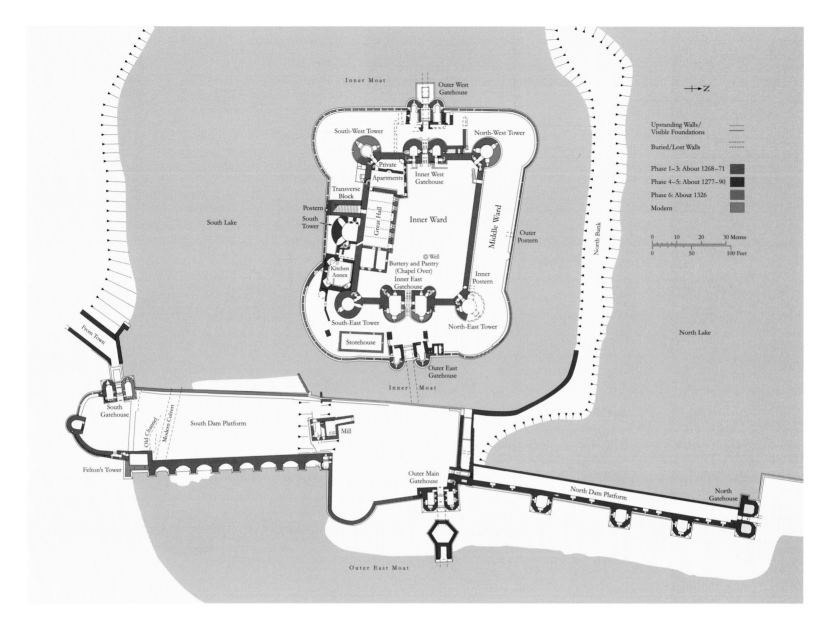

Kenilworth and there may have been timber examples of outer or apron defences in the context of double ditches, such as existed at Helmsley by the 1220s. At Caerphilly, however, the apron additionally possesses bulges at each corner. Finally, in the design of 1268 – and also in the 1280s extensions to the castle – several towers in the castle rise from deep, spur plinths.

In all these particulars, Caerphilly might plausibly be represented as drawing its architectural inspiration from royal building operations of the period. More specifically, it would relate to Henry III's hazily understood grand design for the Tower of London as it has

been represented here: a regularly planned inner bailey enclosed by an earth bank and a moat and perhaps entered through a Tonbridge-style gatehouse.

Whatever the case, the wider architectural activities of the late thirteenth century demonstrate that Henry III's reign had laid the foundations for an integrated and sophisticated tradition of architecture focused within the royal works in London. It was this tradition that was to inform the design of one of the most famous series of castles erected in the Middle Ages. And it is to these buildings, begun by Henry III's son, Edward I, that the narrative must turn next.

136 (*facing page*) Caerphilly, Glamorgan, plan of castle. The enclosing lake is retained by two dams, one of which was probably added to the site in the 1280s. The castle itself sits on an artificial island and comprises two concentric rings of fortification on a regular plan: an outer apron wall and an inner bailey with massive walls and towers. Beyond these is an elaborate system of outer defences, including a great barbican fortified in stone. The plan of this castle is almost certainly based on Henry III's designs for the Tower of London.

137 An internal view of the great inner eastern gate of Caerphilly, Glamorgan, built between 1268 and 1274 and reconstructed in the years 1931–3. This building closely resembles the gatehouse at Tonbridge with two large outer towers and a pair of inner stair turrets. Its principal upper chamber was lit with two large windows, though the tracery has been incorrectly recreated. There are numerous small points of detail that corroborate a connection between Caerphilly and the royal works. For example, above the entrance arch is an unusual chute or loop of a type first found in St John's Tower at Dover built by Henry III after 1217 and the gatehouse at Leybourne, Kent. Another Tonbridge-style gatehouse on the southern barbican at Caerphilly (built between 1268 and 1271) incorporates spur bases, the first ever constructed in south Wales.

7

THE KING'S WORKS
AND WALES

EDWARD I AND EDWARD II

Edward I (1274–1307) was crowned king at Westminster on 19 August 1274, after a leisurely return from crusade. His name was a distinct oddity in the French-speaking court and reflected the devotion of his father, Henry III, to the saintly, Anglo-Saxon ancestor of the English kings, Edward the Confessor. Edward I was to prove a formidable ruler. Armed with a flexible conscience and enormous physical energy, he effectively put the English monarchy back on its feet after the political disasters of Henry III's reign. In large part Edward's achievements in this respect were founded on his activities and prowess as a soldier: his repeated need to place armies of unprecedented size into the field drove forward the development of his administration. And his military successes bolstered his power, prestige and resources. Only late in his reign did the equilibrium of this arrangement begin to break down, notably during his interventions in the Low Countries and his celebrated attempt to claim lordship over Scotland. One important, incidental side effect of his concern to raise money for war was a remarkable evolution in the institution and stature of parliament, the body that made possible the direct taxation of the kingdom.[1]

For many enthusiasts, Edward I is unquestionably the greatest castle-building king ever to have occupied the throne of England. His claim to this accolade is derived principally from the chain of castles that he constructed in north Wales during his conquest of the region from 1277. These are rightly numbered amongst the outstanding works of medieval architecture to survive in Europe. The greatest of them – the castles of Caernarfon, Conwy, Beaumaris and Harlech – are commonly represented as the culmination of the English castle-building tradition. They reflect, according to some authorities, the apogee of the English castle, the moment at which the needs of defence were perfectly balanced in the scales of design with an understanding of architectural effect. From this moment forward it is conventional to claim that architectural effect was increasingly to be preferred at the expense of defence; that the decline of the castle was about to begin.[2]

Outstanding though the royal Welsh castles are, they do not properly mark the beginning or the end of anything in the grand narrative of English architecture. Nor should they be allowed to eclipse the wider castle-building activities of the reign. Rather, they constitute another stage in the flowering of the Gothic castle tradition that was first introduced to England in the reigns of John and Henry III.

This tradition was not only to continue to evolve through Edward I's reign but also into that of his ill-starred son, Edward II (1307–27), whose contribution to the vitality of English architecture in the early fourteenth century is often overlooked. Born in the midst of one of Edward I's castle-building sites, Edward of Caernarfon had a career that could scarcely contrast more markedly with that of his father. Edward II was humiliated on the battlefield, embroiled in bitter conflict with his nobility, deposed by his own wife and finally murdered at Berkeley Castle. Whether true or not, the lurid details of his death – that he was eviscerated with a red-hot poker thrust up his backside – demonstrate what most contemporaries clearly regarded as the catastrophic failure of his rule.[3] Nevertheless, as a boy Edward II is known to have been given a toy castle by his father (how fascinating it would be to know what this medieval toy looked like). In retrospect, the gift is symbolic of the close relationship between the architectural endeavours of the two reigns: the castle building of one was in many important respects inherited from – and developed by – the other.[4]

To do justice to the exceptional richness of English castle architecture during the reigns of Edward I and Edward II it is appropriate to divide this treatment of it into two chapters. Presented in this first chapter is a discussion of the overarching trends of castle building in the period and an architectural history of the royal castles in Wales. In the second there is discussion of castle building in the wider realm, including that associated with the attempted conquest of Scotland.

THE KING'S WORKS AND ST STEPHEN'S CHAPEL, WESTMINSTER

Underpinning the whole development of architecture in this period was the emergence of an architectural practice of undisputed pre-eminence in England: the so-called king's works. During the thirteenth century the building operations of the crown had become more sustained. They had also developed what might be described as a seat of operations at Westminster, where Henry III had lavished such vast resources on the palace and abbey. As a result, the body of craftsmen working for the crown became regularised and their architectural output correspondingly coherent in style. The supremacy of the royal works was assured both by its association with the person of the king, the great-

est patron of architecture in the realm, and through the developing sophistication of architectural drawing. This latter point deserves some enlargement.

There survive today very few English medieval architectural drawings, but both documentary sources and a handful of surviving examples on stone or plaster (as opposed to parchment) make it clear that they existed in some quantity from at least the early thirteenth century.[5] Certainly, it is from this time that the earliest Continental drawings survive, notably the design of a great church façade known as the Reims Palimpsest and the notebook of Villard de Honnecourt.[6] Technical drawings of architecture might serve several important practical purposes in the execution of projects. Using them, for example, it was possible for a master mason to design a building without necessarily being on site, or to press forward in consistent style an inherited architectural operation. It might also allow admired details to be copied easily or to facilitate the use of common forms on completely different scales. That is to say, a drawing of a large window or church elevation could easily be adapted to serve on a miniature scale as the basis for the design of a small statue canopy. Drawings could also be stored away, and in the course of time collections of them naturally built up in the possession of interested institutions and families of masons. No body was better placed to collect a larger and more varied drawings archive than the king's works, and from the thirteenth century onwards there is clear evidence of its masons leafing through this collection and cherry-picking ideas from old designs.

The king's works as an entity grew steadily in importance throughout the thirteenth century, but it properly came of age in the context of a single, extraordinary new commission. In 1292 Edward I began work on a new chapel of St Stephen attached to what was by now becoming firmly established as the seat of royal government in England, the Palace of Westminster. The new building was commissioned in direct emulation of the celebrated Sainte-Chapelle in Paris, the chapel of the French royal palace on the Ile de la Cité. Consecrated in 1248, the Sainte-Chapelle was the purpose-built shrine of no less an object than the Crown of Thorns worn by Christ at the Crucifixion, a relic purchased by Louis IX in 1241 at a fabulous price. The Sainte-Chapelle strove to create the richness of a reliquary of precious metals and jewels on a living scale, and its interior clearly dazzled contemporaries and inspired copies across Europe.[7] One commentator

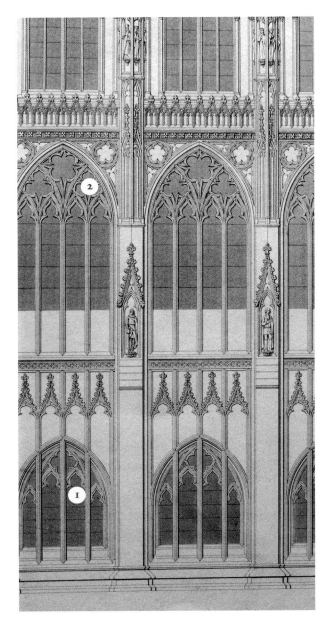

138 The south side of St Stephen's Chapel, Westminster, London, an engraving published by F. Mackenzie in 1844. Begun in 1292, St Stephen's was intended to compete in splendour with the Sainte-Chapelle in Paris. The upper and lower chapels were integrated visually on the exterior by the bars of stone that ran through the two floors. It was this idea of a visual grid that was to inform the Perpendicular style in the fourteenth century. Internally, the mason responsible for the initial design, Michael of Canterbury, created a visual correspondence of large-scale and decorative elements that fascinated future generations of English masons. The tracery patterns depicted here in the upper windows are hypothetical reconstructions, but they accurately show two mannerist details that occur in Michael's other works: some of the arches have slightly pinched tops, a form termed a 'Kentish tip' (1), and the ornamental cusps in the upper trefoils are split to create angular and exaggerated patterns (2). Both these details repeatedly occur in the context of major castle projects into the early fourteenth century. They speak of the widespread influence of Michael of Canterbury and of the king's works.

estimated that the building alone cost £40,000, and when Henry III of England visited Paris in 1254 popular songsters jested that he covetously wanted to take the chapel home.[8] Flamboyantly but faithfully recreated in the nineteenth century by the great French restorer Viollet-le-Duc, it remains one of the outstanding sights of Paris to this day.

In its final form, St Stephen's, Westminster, was probably quite as expensive as its Parisian model, though unfortunately it has not fared as well in physical terms (pl. 138). The main chapel was converted at the Reformation into the debating chamber of the House of Commons – previously a body without a regular chamber of assembly – and was completely recast after a great fire swept through the palace in

1834. Only the crypt today survives. Yet the loss of this building should not distract from its formative importance in the history of English architecture. The chapel was to have a long and involved history of construction, with work continuing intermittently for a period of more than sixty years. The longevity of this building project at the administrative nerve centre of the realm, along with its sheer ambition, were no doubt the crucial factors in ensuring its long-term importance. As a direct result, St Stephen's became one of the principal training grounds for leading artisans in many disciplines, from painters to masons, over several generations.[9]

Although some alterations were made to the chapel in the course of its construction, the building essentially respected the original designs devised by its first master mason, Michael of Canterbury. As his name suggests, Michael's experience lay in the south-east of England, where he had served since 1275 as master mason of the cathedral priory of Canterbury. With brilliant inventiveness he adopted the rich, miniature architectural detailing of contemporary French High Gothic cathedral portals to serve as the basis both for the full-scale architecture of the chapel and its furnishings. By this means he created a design in which there was a correspondence of detail between the whole and its component parts. At the same time, he further developed the Gothic fascination with complex stone tracery patterns. The original window patterns of St Stephen's have been lost, but a medieval copy of its east window survives at Canterbury Cathedral.[10]

St Stephen's Chapel is a fully fledged expression of the so-called Decorated style of Gothic design. Its also contains the seeds of an entirely new style of Gothic architecture, the Perpendicular. These terms beg many questions of definition, but the former might be said to celebrate the spirit of the Sainte-Chapelle. That is to say, buildings in the Decorated style combined architecture, glass, paint and sculpture to spectacular and jewel-like effect. They departed from French example, however, in their sense of architectural propriety. In place of the elegant refinement and intellectual rigour of the Sainte-Chapelle, accomplished Decorated designs verged on the fantastical, delighting in complexity, movement and ornament. This style of design was developed to startling effect in the early decades of fourteenth century and is the subject of the following three chapters.[11] The history of the Perpendicular dominates the subsequent remainder of this book.

PATTERNS OF CASTLE PATRONAGE

During the course of Edward I's reign castle construction became increasingly reserved to the ranks of the greatest families. The reasons for this are not far to seek: Edward I's attitude towards the barons of the realm verged on the predatory. His legal reforms sought actively to curb their power and withheld from them the kinds of grants of income and land that had traditionally provided them with the means for grand architectural commissions. The king's reserved attitude towards this group is reflected in other ways too. He created no new earldoms during the thirty-three years of his reign and repeatedly made difficulties over great inheritances in order to bolster the finances of the crown. In 1274, for example, after the death of the countess of Aumale, he provided backing for a pretender to her inheritance. When the pretender's suit succeeded, he bought him out for a mere £100 and added this valuable earldom to his own possessions.[12]

While the crown was solvent, royal patronage of castles made up for the drop in the pace of baronial building. Then a crisis in royal finances in 1297 brought most of the king's projects to an abrupt halt. For this reason, Edward I's architectural legacy was to prove very mixed. At his death in 1307 several of the castles he had begun in Wales stood substantially incomplete, as did the great new chapel of St Stephen at Westminster. Moreover, two fires at Westminster and Windsor had damaged the royal apartments in both places. Without money to repair them in full they passed to Edward II as partially gutted ruins.[13]

But if Edward I reduced baronial building and failed to bring some of his own castle-building projects to fruition, he can nevertheless be credited with creating a new class of architectural patron. Directing the process of re-forming royal government across the kingdom were a handful of trusted advisers and a circle of royal clerks. These men reaped rich financial rewards and many turned their resources towards the patronage of architecture, both secular and ecclesiastical. Time and again they drew their craftsmen for such projects from the pool engaged by the crown and so disseminated the architectural language of the king's works widely.

The accession of Edward II saw no immediate resurgence in royal or baronial building. Moreover, as the reign progressed, the new king's patronage of avaricious favourites, notably the Elder and Younger Despensers, diverted funds away from the circle of royal clerks who had done so well out of his father. The most important objects of royal resources, meanwhile, were the northern Welsh castles. These had been starved of money in the last years of Edward I's reign, and two of them – Beaumaris and Caernarfon – were brought by his son to the condition in which they are now familiar. In the north of England, a temporary ascendancy over Scotland and the wealth it generated encouraged considerable castle building to the south of the border. The disastrous English defeat at Bannockburn in 1314, however, plunged the area into poverty and chaos for more than a decade. Only when conditions began to settle did castle building begin again across what was now firmly established as a violent border. This was particularly encouraged by the crown's investment of money in the defence of the region, both directly and through the medium of powerful families.

These patterns of patronage bestow upon the architectural activities of the two reigns a sense of geographical progression as the focus of castle building moved in response to political events. In the 1270s there was a busy exchange of ideas between London – the seat of architectural change – and the south of Wales, where the great lords of the Welsh borderlands or march were busy staking out territory. Over the 1280s, however, in direct consequence of Edward I's military campaigns, the north of Wales emerged as the centre of architectural activity. Finally, in response to the king's interventions in Scotland, it travelled to the north of England, where the building efforts of Edward II's reign were particularly concentrated. This progression, starting in London, offers a convenient structure for the following two chapters.

THE TOWER OF LONDON

When Edward I was crowned king in Westminster Abbey on 16 August 1274, the seat of his authority in the capital of the realm must have looked an architectural shambles. The line of outer defences to the Tower of London begun by Henry III was still in the course of construction and it is even possible that the gap created by the collapse of the great gate in 1240 was still blocked by a timber palisade. The sorry condition of the building would have been borne in upon Edward directly during the coronation celebrations if – like other kings – he processed in state from the Tower to Westminster Abbey. It may be no coincidence, therefore, that following his accession the Tower of

139 A reconstruction by Terry Ball of Edward I's riverside entrance to the Tower of London, begun in the 1270s. Viewed in its entirety, this impressive arrangement of two twin-towered gatehouses and a D-shaped barbican looks back to Henry III's architecture of the 1220s, notably the barbican of Constable's Gate and the remodelled North Gate at Dover, as well as the gatehouse of Lincoln Castle. Yet to these designs the Tower adds impressive regularity of form. One important ancestor of this ensemble is the entrance to the motte of Sandal, Yorkshire, of the 1240s (see pl. 127). The outer D-shaped barbican became known as the Lion Tower because it was the home from at least the reign of Edward III of the king's menagerie. As the royal beasts of England and carnivores, the lions were, of course, a patriotic and exciting curiosity.

London became the object of one of the largest building programmes of the reign, works to it absorbing £21,000 over the next ten years. No other castle-building operation by Edward I approached the expense of this costly undertaking.

The master mason directing the operation was a certain Robert of Beverley, who had been placed in charge of works to the Tower by Henry III in 1270. Robert's career perfectly illustrates the centralised and varied operations of the emerging king's works. He is first documented cutting vault bosses for Westminster Abbey in 1253 and rose to be appointed master mason of this great project in 1260. Over the next decade he established himself by degrees as the leading mason in royal employment until his death in 1285. In this position he undertook such diverse tasks as erecting temporary stalls, kitchens and halls for Edward I's coronation festivities and creating in 1276 an effigy of Henry III using 300 pounds of wax.[14] He was otherwise involved in various castle projects. In 1274, for example, he was sent to Dover to survey damage after the collapse of a wall and to estimate the cost of repairs, evidence that he had direct knowledge of this great castle.[15]

Edward I's work to the Tower of London began in May 1275, when tools and labour were assembled to dig a moat. How this operation related to Henry III's earlier ditching around the castle is not clear. All that can be said with certainty is that when Edward I's operations were complete there existed an immense tidal moat at least 160 feet (50 m) wide on the three landward sides of the castle. It is some indication of the scale of this labour that the ditch was cut and flooded

under the direction of an experienced and foreign specialist, Master Walter of Flanders; also that the operation cost more than £4,000, nearly a quarter of the huge sum spent on the whole site in the next ten years. This moat enclosed the existing castle with more than 100 feet (30.5 m) to spare on each side. Along the inner edge of this wide earth berm – and built on piles into the River Thames – was constructed a low apron wall.[16] This ran parallel to the main walls to create a double line of fortification enclosing the site. At each corner the line of the wall bulged outwards to form a broad bastion in exactly the manner of Caerphilly.

Two substantial new entrances were created along the line of the walls, both presumably designed by Robert of Beverley. The most elaborate of these was a new land gate in the south-west corner of the expanded castle. It comprised a complex sequence of buildings: an outer, D-shaped barbican and two gatehouses separated by a long causeway set with drawbridges (pl. 139). The second of the new gates was a river entrance, St Thomas's Tower, known today as Traitors' Gate (pl. 140). As a whole, this rectangular building with small drum towers on each outer corner bears striking relationship to the inside façade of the Tonbridge gatehouse or the more massively conceived hall and chamber block probably erected in the 1240s by Henry III at Shrewsbury Castle.[17] Indeed, the design of Traitors' Gate appears to be a Tonbridge-style gatehouse turned inside out and it was to have an important architectural progeny: as will subsequently become apparent, it is from this essential form that one of the classic English gatehouse forms of the later Middle Ages derives (pl. 141).

140 (*above left*) A reconstruction by Terry Ball of St Thomas's Tower, now known as Traitors' Gate, at the Tower of London built in the 1270s. The first floor of the new building was almost certainly designed to serve as an extension to the royal apartments and is described in 1276–7 as containing 'a hall and a chamber'. Its windows were glazed with coloured glass, and one of the turrets served as an oratory that was occupied by a hermit called Geoffrey. Beneath the apartments was a wet dock, and the gigantic inner arch of the gatehouse (not visible here) was of sufficient span for the royal barge to turn within the shelter of the building. Running within the first-floor walls is a shooting gallery with internal and external arrow loops.

141 (*above right*) The gatehouse of St Augustine's Abbey, Canterbury, Kent, completed around 1308. It corresponds in many technical details to the work of Michael of Canterbury at St Stephen's Chapel, Westminster, and was almost certainly designed by him. In overall conception it compares to the inner façade of the Tonbridge-style gatehouse (see pls 135 and 137). It is from buildings of this type that a whole family of late medieval gatehouses derives, including those in the tradition of Cambridge collegiate architecture. It is noteworthy that each floor of the building, from the relatively austere gateway level to the ornate upper storey, has a distinct architectural character. Masons enjoyed varying the detailing of buildings in this way for aesthetic reasons.

Robert of Beverley also took responsibility in his work for the completion of the circuit of walls and towers begun by Henry III in the 1240s. In certain points of detail the new towers compare closely with the old, some of which Robert must have worked on in the previous reign. The largest, the Beauchamp Tower, was substantially completed in one year between June and December 1281 over the ruins of Henry III's gatehouse to the castle (pl. 142).[18] This tower and its adjacent wall are also noteworthy for their materials of construction. Although externally stone built, the wall cores are of brick that is documented as having been imported from Flanders. Brick was not to emerge as a popular building material in the south of England until the early fifteenth century, and its presence is remarkable. It is just possible that Robert was familiar with the material from his native Beverley, where brick was widely used.

Edward I's works to the Tower transformed the castle in physical terms and it is tempting to present them for this reason as being completely distinct from those planned by Henry III. But the evidence of the buildings themselves argues the reverse: that the Tower

142   Tower of London, the Beauchamp Tower, substantially completed in 1281 on the site of the gateway begun by Henry III and which twice collapsed, in 1240 and again in 1241. The tower is D-shaped in plan and set to either side with turrets that stick out prominently like ears. One of these ear turrets contains a stair and the other a series of chambers serving the main rooms in the tower. Both the tower and its adjacent wall are built in brick faced with stone. The bricks are documented as having been imported from Flanders. The tower follows precisely the form established by Henry III from the 1240s (see pl. 132).

as completed by Edward I was in fact little more than an aggrandised version of his father's intended castle. Just as Robert of Beverley inherited Westminster Abbey and observed with few revisions the design of his predecessor, so at the Tower he appears to have continued an established remodelling programme in a relatively consistent architectural style. Certainly, there is nothing within Edward I's new buildings that suggests any major change of plan or design following the resumption of work in 1275. This is the more significant because the only surviving precedent for the form of Edward I's castle is Caerphilly, which, as discussed in the previous chapter, is itself almost certainly derived from Henry III's incompleted plans for the Tower of London.

Caerphilly was not alone amongst baronial castles built in the Welsh marches to reflect the influence of the royal works. Across the region, the competition between rival baronial families, with the wealth and semi-independent status they enjoyed, continued to encourage architectural commissions on the most remarkable scale. This was particularly true along the southern march and the south coast of Wales, where three families of outstanding wealth set the pace of architectural change: the de Clare earls of Gloucester, the de Valence earls of Pembroke and the Bigod earls of Norfolk. The work of each is worth surveying in turn. In almost every case it reflects the influence of royal building in the south-east of England. Viewed together, however, their castles in south Wales also form a regional group, sharing many common points of detail.

As befitted its great value, the de Clare estate probably sustained the largest and most varied castle-building programme. The foundation of a new castle at Caerphilly by Gilbert de Clare, the Red Earl (d. 1295), in 1268 was accompanied by three satellite foundations in Glamorgan. At Red Castle (now Castell Coch) and Llantrisant these took the form of small walled enclosures set with drum towers. In the 1260s work was also under way to another nearby castle, Llangynwyd, which was dominated by a great gatehouse in the style of Tonbridge. Gilbert the Red next consolidated his interests northwards with the construction of a major new castle in the late 1280s at Morlais, today the bizarre but imposing centrepiece of a golf course. The castle crowns the top of a hill and its diamond-shaped defences are enclosed by ditches hewn from the living rock. There is no gatehouse to the castle at all, simply an archway through one wall, and the irregular perimeter is fortified with a series of D-shaped towers. To either end of the site were much bigger towers on circular plans. The larger of these was almost certainly a great tower, the architectural and symbolic focus of the castle. Its basement, a vaulted octagonal chamber, still survives and hints at the quality of the building itself. Work must have been complete by about 1292, when the castle was seized by the king and forthwith neglected.

Morlais offers one particularly important insight into the design of castles in the late thirteenth century. It is conventional to suggest that fortifications were evolving during this period in direct response to changes in warfare. As part of this evolution the great tower is commonly represented as passing into military obsoles-

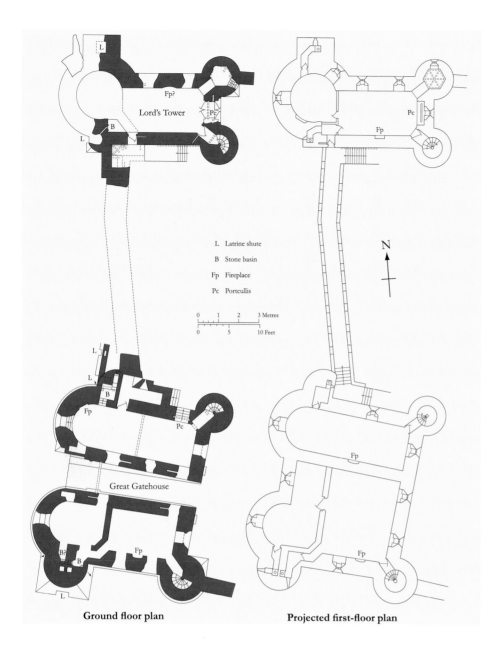

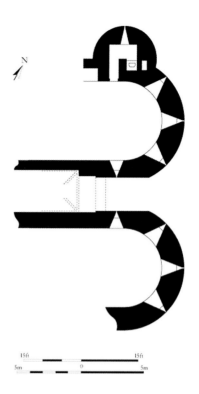

L   Latrine shute
B   Stone basin
Fp Fireplace
Pc Portcullis

0   1   2   3 Metres
0   5   10 Feet

Ground floor plan

Projected first-floor plan

143 (*left*)   A plan of the main front of Llangibby, Monmouthshire, probably built between 1307 and 1314. At either end of this rubble-built façade stood a tower and a gatehouse, each of which is planned in the form of a Tonbridge-style gatehouse. The gatehouse proper is the largest of this type ever constructed and is detailed in cut masonry. Its surviving vaulting compares to that in the tower undercroft at Morlais, another de Clare castle complete by 1292. The pair of turrets projecting at

right angles from the main gatehouse towers is a distinctive addition to the usual plan. Another odd detail is a set of surviving latrines in the main gatehouse with curved backs. The design compares to that of the chapel seats in the Marten's Tower at Chepstow begun in 1286.

144 (*right*)   A plan of the ruined gatehouse at Leybourne, Kent, of around 1266, with its distinctive additional tower projecting to the top. As at Llangibby, this projecting tower incorporated

a latrine. There is another unusual and notable detail at Leybourne: immediately above the entrance arch is a horizontal arrow slit or loop like the opening of a post box. This rare detail is first found in St John's Tower at Dover. It later turns up in the gatehouses at Caerphilly (see pl. 137). Such technical parallels between buildings across a wide geographic area strongly imply that architectural practice was centralised in this period within the orbit of the king's works.

cence, to be replaced in sophisticated castle designs by massive gatehouses. But a comparison of Morlais and Caerphilly, for example, makes the point that there is no such logical progression apparent even within a series of architecturally ambitious castles created by a single patron. The reality is that the existence or non-existence of great towers or gatehouses remained a matter of architectural choice, not of military necessity. Indeed, the chief determining factor of the form of a castle through the Middle Ages was probably the topography of the site it occupied: low-level sites, for example, encouraged the creation of water defences.

Gilbert de Clare's son, also called Gilbert, acceded to the family estates following the death of his widowed mother in 1307 and he enjoyed them for only seven years: in 1314 he was killed at the battle of Bannockburn. It was probably during Gilbert's seven years as earl that work began to another de Clare castle at Llangibby, Monmouthshire. His work to this foundation was continued after 1314 by his widow, Matilda, who held the castle until her death in 1320. Llangibby stands close to two other family castles at Caerleon and Usk, and it is difficult to explain the logic of its location in strategic terms. Enclosed within a large new park, it seems instead to have been primarily intended as a hunting lodge.[19] The castle was set out on a rectangular plan with an imposing façade. This was dominated by a Tonbridge-style gatehouse and a tower in a clearly related architectural form (pl. 143). It should be observed that this gatehouse is the largest of its kind ever constructed, with dimensions twice those of Tonbridge. Unlike any previous Tonbridge-style gatehouse, however, that at Llangibby possesses additional turrets projecting at right angles from the main façade. It is a peculiar arrangement that places the design within the orbit of the king's works and elucidates the operations of this body.

Parallels for the additional turrets at Llangibby are to be found in two buildings of the 1260s in quite different parts of the kingdom, both of which may be related to Henry III's Dover works of the 1220s. The first of these is the gatehouse at Leybourne in Kent, which draws certain details from St John's Tower at Dover (pl. 144). Leybourne gatehouse was almost certainly designed by Robert of Beverley, who supplied 4,000 cut stones to the castle at royal command in 1266.[20] The gift was reputedly made as a reward to its owner, Roger of Leybourne, for saving the king's life at the battle of Evesham. Rather better preserved is the gatehouse of Barnwell, Northamptonshire (pl. 145), which can be dated on documentary evidence to around 1266.[21] Although the name of the designer of Barnwell is not known, his connection with the royal works is suggested both by the high quality of the detailing in the building and by the unusual treatment of its towers (pl. 146). These have smaller towers bulging out of them as if they were growing warts, an idea first developed on a grand scale in Constable's Gate, added to Dover Castle in the 1220s (see pl. 116).

It is the narrowness and technicality of these architectural connections that makes them important. Llangibby, Leybourne, Barnwell and Dover are not directly related buildings in the sense that they inspired one another or were designed by the same mason. Nevertheless, on the basis of very distinctive details – details that no patron would trouble to notice – they can be shown to constitute an architectural family. Given their wide geographic spread and the long period over which they were being created, the most obvious explanation for their relationship is that they were designed by masons who shared a common training and access to an archive of architectural drawings. The demonstrable connections to Dover and the documented involvement of Robert of Beverley indicate that this training was within the king's works rooted in the south-east of England. This reading of the evidence is further corroborated by the analysis of other contemporary architectural projects in the region.

Both the Valence and the Bigod estates in south Wales were derived from the breakup of the great Marshal family inheritance that followed the death of the last male heir in 1245. The castle of Chepstow passed into the hands of Roger Bigod, earl of Norfolk, in 1270, and over the next thirty years he transformed its interior. The mason in charge was a certain Ralph Gogun of London and the exquisite architectural detailing of the buildings he created reflects his cosmopolitan training and connections. His other documented work for the earl included the construction of a castle – possibly Ballymoon, Co. Carlow, in Ireland – and a church at Chipping Sodbury, Gloucestershire. In the 1270s work began to a new residential range in the lower bailey of Chepstow with a new hall and kitchens. Entrance to the range is through a tall porch with what appears to be a small drawbridge pit in front of it. This preserves painted decoration executed in 1292: two shields hung from straps over the door.[22]

Across the bailey from the new range and serving it in the manner of a chamber block was a tower, now known as Marten's Tower (pl. 147). Work to this building is first mentioned in an account of 1287–8 and it was largely complete in 1293. The tower interior preserves substantial traces of decorative paintwork executed in 1292, and there are few buildings that bring closer a sense of thirteenth-century life on the grand scale (pl. 148). With a pair of turrets to the rear, the overall design compares closely to that of the towers created by Robert of Beverley in London. The battlements of the tower are finished with notable richness: besides being elegantly moulded, each battlement is surmounted by a sculptured figure.[23] This is an intriguing and important feature.

The practice of 'inhabiting' battlements with figures is first encountered in England at two places in the 1270s: on the chapter house of York Minster and St Thomas's Gate in the Tower of London. The London figures are recorded only in documentary sources from the period and it is impossible, therefore, to say much about them.[24] At York, however, the inspiration for this form of decoration was almost certainly the collegiate church begun in 1262 at Troyes by Pope Urban IV on the site of his birthplace. The church of Saint-Urbain was one of the most admired architectural commissions of the late thirteenth century in Europe and was otherwise very influential on the design of York.[25] It includes fighting men in the decorative battlements of

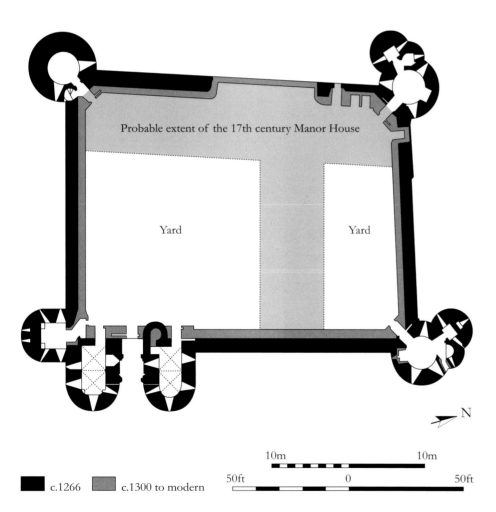

Probable extent of the 17th century Manor House

Yard

Yard

N

10m · 10m

50ft · 0 · 50ft

■ c.1266 · ▨ c.1300 to modern

the seats or sedilia set beside the altar. This detail was probably inspired in turn by a long tradition of illustrating fighting figures in French wall paintings and manuscript illumination.[26] This tortuous passage of ideas through different artistic media and finally from miniature to full-scale architecture is typical of the period and again reflects the influence of drawing. Subsequently, the idea of inhabited battlements was to enjoy widespread popularity, particularly in the north of England.

It is instructive to compare the late thirteenth-century buildings at Chepstow with Bigod's only other major surviving piece of castle architecture. The new twin-towered gatehouse he raised at Bungay in Suffolk can probably be associated with alterations to the castle licensed by Edward I in 1294 (pl. 149). This building appears to have lacked any large domestic chambers to the rear and bears little formal relationship to any of the earl's work at Chepstow. Yet these differences are in some ways deceptive: the masons directing both operations were clearly familiar with architectural developments in the south-east of England. At Bungay the evidence for this is to be seen in the treatment of the towers, both of which rise from sloping plinths. This detail, a variant on the spur bases popular in the southern marches of Wales, is drawn from Henry III's towers at Windsor.

The third of the outstanding castle builders in the southern march was William de Valence, a half-brother of Henry III with extensive interests in France. Along with several other siblings he came to court at the invitation of Henry III. This invitation was intended both

145 (*facing page, top*) Barnwell, Northamptonshire, was begun in or around 1266. Its builder, a certain Berengar le Moyne, was descended from a family who had been granted the manor 'as an inheritance' by the abbot of Ramsey in the early twelfth century. The castle later reverted back to this rich abbey, which may well have contributed towards its cost. To the left is the gatehouse with its third tower set at right angles to the pair flanking the entrance arch.

146 (*facing page, bottom*) Plan of Barnwell, Northamptonshire, *circa* 1266. The asymmetrical clustering of towers is very unusual and is likely to indicate a connection with Constable's Gate at Dover and the king's works. It is not known how the medieval residential buildings were arranged in the castle. In the mid-sixteenth century Sir Edward Montecute (d. 1557) built a new residence within the circuit of the walls. This was pulled down in the late seventeenth century. Plan after B. L. Giggins, 'Barnwell Castle Survey, 1980–5', *South Midlands Archaeology*, 16 (1986).

147 Marten's Tower, Chepstow, Monmouthshire, completed between 1287 and 1293 by the London mason Ralph Gogun. The tower is set to either side with ear turrets, a feature that identifies its architectural parentage in the towers erected by Henry III and Edward I at the Tower of London (see pl. 142). In concession to local fashion, however, the tower rises from a deep, spurred base. There is a chapel at the top of the ear turret to the right, its position identified by a large east window. The battlements are inhabited with sculpture, including the figures of a lawyer, a soldier, a musician and possibly a dancer.

148 (*right*) A reconstruction of the painted decoration of 1292 found in the first- and second-floor chambers of Marten's Tower, Chepstow, Monmouthshire. Each floor is decorated in a similar fashion with an ochre dado edged in red that runs around the windows and doors. Above this is a masonry pattern painted in red onto the wall and a cornice decoration of stylised foliage. Such survivals suggest that fabric hangings remained a rarity even in luxurious chambers in the thirteenth century.

149 (*below*) The gatehouse at Bungay, Suffolk, built by Roger Bigod around 1294. The towers formerly rose from a sloping plinth, the curving line of which is clearly visible to the right (1). This particular form of base first appeared in England at Henry III's buildings around 1230 at Windsor (see pl. 121). Though Bigod's works in Wales and East Anglia reflect regional variations in architectural style, they are all fundamentally indebted to ideas developed in royal buildings in London and the south-east.

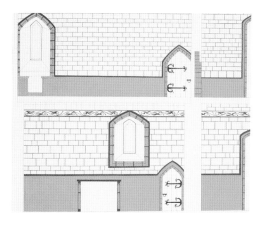

to serve the king's interests in France and to increase for political ends the size of the immediate royal family circle in England. On 13 August 1247, within a week of his arrival, William was married off to Joan, the heiress of the great Marshal lordships of Pembroke, Goodrich and Wexford. William did not formally receive the title of earl of Pembroke – though he did use it – nor initially did he receive sufficient lands to maintain himself in appropriate estate. The difference was made up by lavish grants of other kinds from Henry III, including numerous wardships.

In consequence of such generosity Valence became the object of jealousy and was implicated in the various political crises of Henry III's reign. It is no coincidence that his earliest architectural work in south Wales concerned the remodelling of Pembroke. As the titular castle of the earldom that he claimed, its remodelling was undoubtedly intended to bolster his prestige. Probably in the 1250s or 1260s, to judge from the architectural forms employed, he laid out an impressive new outer bailey wall set with large towers and a new gatehouse.[27] Again, the work may be inspired by the king's works: the gatehouse possesses a pair of rear stair turrets in a fashion comparable to Tonbridge, and the wall towers incorporate clasping turrets in the manner of the Tower of London.

The redevelopment of Pembroke aside, Valence's interest in the south march of Wales and the bulk of his work to castles there probably dates from the late 1270s onwards: in 1273 he raced back from crusade with Edward I, alarmed that his marcher properties were under threat from the earl of Gloucester. In response, he began to extend his own authority in the region and invested substantial sums of money in castle building. It was probably in this period also that Valence undertook work to the castles at Tenby and Haverfordwest. Perhaps the most celebrated operation

Herefordshire. Valence's work
begun around 1275 involved
the complete reordering of the
earlier castle defences, sections
of which survive within the
present walls. The
twelfth-century great tower
was also preserved,
presumably for symbolic
reasons. Stone for the
operation was dug from the
castle ditch. All the
thirteenth-century towers
stand on tall spur bases of
differing form. The variations
in the form of the spurs,
combined with other changes
of detail, hint at the
protracted construction of
the new building, which was
probably completed in the
1290s.

he initiated, however, was the reconstruction of Goodrich Castle in Herefordshire, which sits spectacularly above the River Wye. Work to the present buildings may be related to several royal grants of timber to the site from 1275 onwards.[28]

Goodrich was redeveloped on a compact, rectangular plan, its walls protected by steep slopes and a deep rock-cut ditch (pl. 150). At three corners of the enclosure there rise massive towers and, on the fourth, a great gatehouse (pl. 151). All are set on impressive spur bases. The gatehouse façade comprises a gateway flanked by one large and one small tower. There is slight variation in architectural detail from tower to tower around the castle, a circumstance perhaps suggesting that the process of construction was protracted. Nevertheless, such is the overall coherence of the design that it seems likely that the castle was built to a single plan established around 1275. Integral to this design were the principal thirteenth-century domestic

buildings. These comprised a hall block with its kitchens in one tower and what is probably a chamber block set at right angles to it. The latter is connected to another tower through a monumental double arch reminiscent of that inserted into the great tower at Chepstow by one of the Marshal family in the 1220s or 1230s (pl. 152). All the towers open inwards into rectangular annexes, possibly a feature derived from the side or 'ear' turrets of buildings, such as the Beauchamp Tower at London.

William de Valence also made notable additions to Kidwelly Castle, which he acquired in 1283. The castle had been extensively remodelled in the previous decade by Payn de Chaworth, a prominent marcher landholder, following his return from crusade in 1275. Chaworth's building shows evidence of being influenced by the same architectural currents as the castles of greater families in the region. A substantial loan in 1277 of £360 from the king was probably intended to

151 A plan and east elevation of Goodrich, Herefordshire. The quadrangular castle begun around 1275 was enclosed on two sides by an apron wall. Authorities differ on their dating of the apron wall, but there is a good case for supposing it to be thirteenth century. The gatehouse is in the Tonbridge style but asymmetrically planned in order to fit into position on the corner of this constrained hilltop site. It was integrally designed with a fortified bridge and D-shaped barbican closely resembling that created by Edward I at the Tower of London. One wall of the castle is beaked outwards to preserve the earlier great tower, an accommodation that hints at the prestige enjoyed by these buildings.

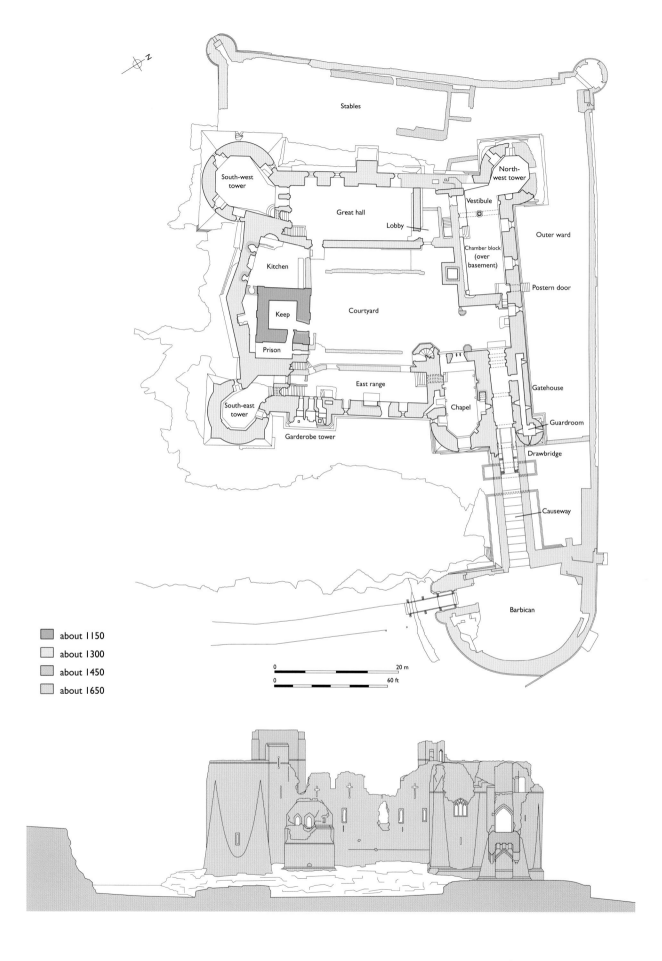

Stables

South-west tower

North-west tower

Great hall

Vestibule

Lobby

Outer ward

Chamber block (over basement)

Kitchen

Postern door

Keep

Courtyard

Prison

Gatehouse

East range

Chapel

South-east tower

Guardroom

Garderobe tower

Drawbridge

Causeway

Barbican

about 1150
about 1300
about 1450
about 1650

0 — 20 m
0 — 60 ft

152   A reconstruction and cut-away drawing by Terry Ball of the late thirteenth-century chamber block at Goodrich, Herefordshire. The principal chamber at first-floor level (1) was connected to the hall (2) by a stair (3) housed in a turret porch (4). The chamber was divided in two by a double arch (5), an arrangement precisely copying that found in the great tower at Chepstow as remodelled around 1230. The area created within the tower beyond the arch may have served as a withdrawing space. Beneath the principal chamber was a large undercroft with a small postern gate into an area enclosed by the apron wall (6). Facing the entrance to it is a washbasin, presumably for the use of visitors (7). Some details of the thirteenth-century buildings at Goodrich, such as its distinctive straight-sided arches (8), are apparently drawn from the north transept of Hereford Cathedral Priory. This building is in turn directly inspired by Westminster Abbey.

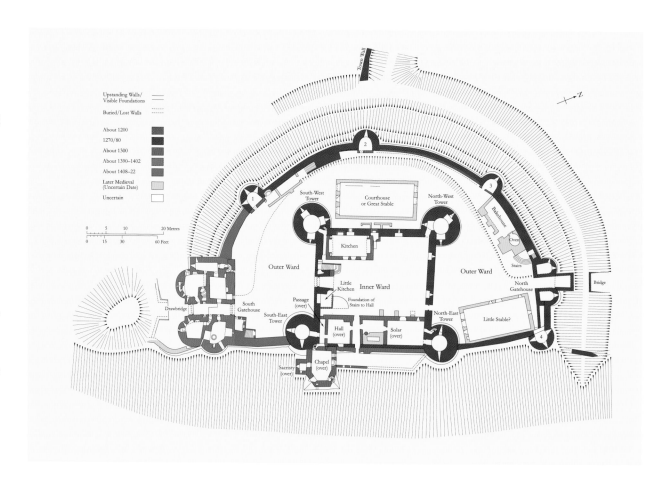

153 A plan of Kidwelly, Carmarthen, founded by Bishop Roger of Sarum (d. 1139), who created the D-shaped enclosure in which the castle developed. The quadrangular inner bailey and apron wall were built in the late 1270s by Payn de Chaworth with subventions of cash from Edward I. With angle turrets and no gatehouse, the bailey compares in conception to Conwy Castle, begun by Edward I in 1282. The most plausible explanation for this similarity is that the designs for both buildings originated in the king's works. That said, Kidwelly is a much more modest creation than its royal counterpart and constructed in a regional style of rubble masonry suited to the local stone. In the 1390s three of the inner bailey towers were raised in height and the great gate begun. As part of this operation one of the towers was vaulted at its uppermost level, a detail almost certainly drawn from the great tower of Pembroke.

support the work and further implies some direct royal involvement in the project. In formal terms Chaworth's castle at Kidwelly bears close comparison to its contemporary, Goodrich: it comprised a rectangular inner bailey with four corner towers in classic Gothic form and was enclosed on three sides by a turreted apron wall (pl. 153). Unlike Goodrich, however, there was no gatehouse to the inner bailey, simply an archway through the wall.

When William de Valence came into the possession of Kidwelly, the work of remodelling the castle undertaken by Payn de Chaworth would appear to have been complete. William nevertheless constructed a series of new domestic apartments within the inner bailey and, connected to them, a polygonal chapel tower set on a spur base. The design of the chapel tower stands in striking contrast to the other castle buildings and reflects the growing popularity of spur bases in the region during the 1280s (pl. 154). The form was probably copied soon afterwards at the nearby castle of Carew, which was remodelled with two towers on spur bases and a new polygonal chapel tower.[29] William de Valence was overlord of Carew at the time and the two building projects are likely to have been connected (see

pl. 338). The examples of Kidwelly and Carew illustrate the way in which architectural ideas promulgated from the king's works might penetrate into the provinces and acquire in their journey there a distinctively regional character. With these buildings in mind it is appropriate to turn now to the north of Wales, where the focus of architectural activity had shifted decisively by the 1280s.

THE WELSH CONQUEST

Edward I's involvement in Welsh affairs was brought about by a disastrous miscalculation on the part of Llywelyn ap Gruffudd, the dominant figure in the complex politics of the region. Llywelyn's brilliantly successful exploitation of political tensions in England during Henry III's reign had won him English acknowledgement as prince of Wales. The title is slightly misleading in terms of modern political divisions: the heartland of his authority was Gwynedd in the north of Wales. Confident in his position, Llywelyn chose not to pay fealty to Edward at his coronation in 1274 and failed to respond to five subsequent summons to

212

154 Kidwelly, Carmarthen, a view of the chapel tower with its deep spurs erected by William de Valence after he came into possession of the castle in 1283. The polygonal form of the tower may have been intended to distinguish the chapel tower from the other towers in the building, an idea repeated at nearby Carew. The distant *circa* 1320 church spire of St Mary's – formerly a Benedictine abbey – with its supporting broaches helpfully illustrates how the spur bases so popular in castles of the region related directly to church architecture. Incidentally, the Westminster-inspired north transept of Hereford Cathedral, which was otherwise very influential on the castle building of south Wales, also possesses buttresses with spur bases.

pay homage. There was no king less likely to overlook such an affront than Edward I. In November 1276 Llywelyn was declared 'a rebel and disturber of the peace', and meticulous preparations were set in train for the invasion of Gwynedd.

Over the summer of 1277 an English army began to muster in Chester. At its height the ensuing campaign was to involve more than 15,000 men, probably the largest military force yet assembled by an English king. With it there gathered huge numbers of craftsmen from across the kingdom, many pressed into royal service and accompanied by armed guards to prevent desertion en route to Chester. Edward was clearly planning a campaign in which new territory was to be staked out with castles. There were precedents for such huge levies of craftsmen in English royal campaigns, for example in John's invasion of Wales two generations earlier, and in Henry II's levy of 500 carpenters to help in his East Anglian activities in 1173–4.[30] What is remarkable in this case, however, is that it is possible to trace through documents for the first time in this and Edward's subsequent Welsh campaigns exactly where the men were drawn from (pl. 155).

As these forces gathered, Edward I created two castles at strategic points within central Wales to press Llywelyn from the south and west. The first of these was begun at Builth, Brecknockshire, in central Wales in May 1277 on the site of an earlier castle recently overthrown by the Welsh. Nothing but the earthworks of Builth now survive, but it is known from extant building accounts that in 1280 it comprised a great tower, apparently in the form of a motte with a stone enclosure on its summit, a circuit of walls with six towers, a twin-towered gatehouse and an outer bailey enclosed in stone.[31] Two months later, early in July 1277, 120 masons and 120 carpenters were drafted for work to a much bigger coastal castle at Aberystwyth in Cardiganshire.[32] Despite the effects of a destructive attack by the Welsh in 1282, it seems likely that the present ruins accurately reflect the form of the original design. It was laid out on a diamond-shaped plan with a concentric inner and outer bailey. Dominating the castle was a great gatehouse, unmistakeably cast in the form of Tonbridge.[33]

Flint and Rhuddlan

Edward joined his forces at Chester on 15 July 1277 and set out a few days later on his expedition, stopping about one day's march away along the ancient Roman road into north Wales at a place known as *Le Flint* or 'the rock'.[34] A new castle was begun here on a low-lying site along the seashore (pl. 156) and under its shadow, in classic form, there was established a borough. All Edward's major castles in Wales were built with direct

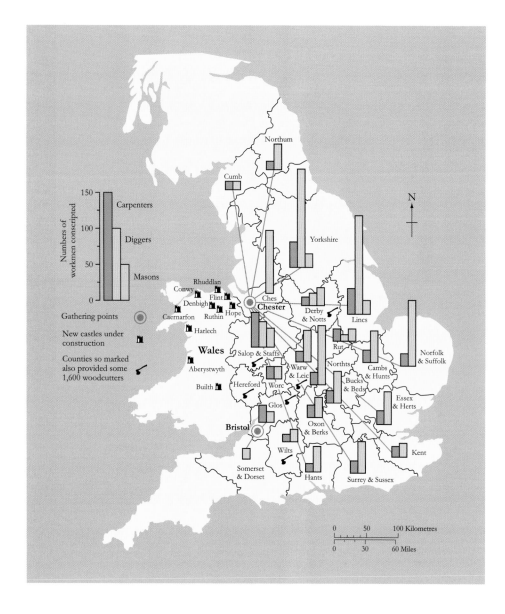

Work finally drew to a close at Flint in 1286, by which time there had been created a castle of two baileys. The inner bailey was set out on a rectangular plan and filled with timber domestic buildings.[36] At each corner stood a tower on a circular plan, one of which was substantially larger than its neighbours. This 'great tower' – as it is called in the surviving building accounts – is set between the baileys with its own encircling ditch, an arrangement that imitates the position and form of a motte in a classic castle layout. But the tower itself is not raised on an artificial mound, and today, without its original upper storey, the ruined building looks curiously squat. It took the form of a broad drum more than 70 feet (21 m) across with walls a staggering 23 feet (7 m) thick. These were opened out on the upper floors to create a ring of chambers running around a central core. There is no clear evidence to determine whether the core of the tower at Flint was floored over to create chambers or stood open as a central light well. If there were floors, this is the broadest tower of its kind ever built in Britain.[37] The great tower of Flint inspired a much smaller (and centrally floored) copy at nearby Hawarden Castle, begun by Roger de Clifford after 1282 and set on a motte (pl. 157).

On 22 August 1277 Edward moved his base of operations another day's march westwards to Rhuddlan, Flintshire. There still survive on the outskirts of the town earthworks from an eleventh-century castle, which Edward may have occupied on his arrival. Almost immediately, however, a new castle was begun a short distance away on the banks of the River Clwyd (pl. 158). The new site was then connected to the sea by canalising the intermediary stretch of the river at vast labour and expense. Edward's intention in building at Rhuddlan was apparently to re-establish a historic border between England and Wales along the line of the River Clwyd. To help consolidate this frontier he founded a new borough beside the castle. As a mark of its intended status, a licence was sought from the pope in 1281 to move the cathedral of St Asaph to Rhuddlan.[38] In the event, however, the proposed move was overtaken by events.

Work to Rhuddlan Castle was to cost the royal exchequer about £9,500 – less than half the expense of the operations at the Tower of London – and was largely completed by 1280.[39] In contrast to Flint it was designed with concentric defences: an outer apron wall with rectangular turrets and a deep ditch enclosing the fortifications of the inner bailey. The apron is known

155   A table illustrating the movement of craftsmen for the construction of Edward I's castles in north Wales for the campaign of 1282–3. It was Edward I's ability to focus resources in this way that made him such a formidable enemy. The map illustrates graphically exactly why the king's works was such an effective centralising influence on architecture: it reached out to every corner of the realm and sucked craftsmen into its projects. Taken from the *History of the King's Works*, vol. 1, 183.

access to the sea, certainly with the intention of making them easily accessible by ship. Timber was floated down the coast to form palisades around the new site and by the middle of the August there were 2,300 men employed there: 1,270 diggers, 320 woodmen, 330 carpenters, 12 smiths, 10 charcoal burners and 200 masons, the last under the direction of a certain Master Thomas of Grantham.[35] Many of these men were soon afterwards moved on to other sites, including a new Cistercian abbey at nearby Vale Royal. Edward I laid a foundation stone for the abbey church, a building of cathedral-like proportions, on 13 August 1277, and the mason Walter of Hereford was placed in charge of the site. The king's interest in this ecclesiastical operation – which he abandoned mysteriously in 1290 – illustrates that he had other than purely military priorities.

156 (*above*) Flint, a view of the inner bailey begun in July 1277 with the great tower in the foreground. It stands free of the angle of the inner bailey and was approached from it over a bridge. The arrangement appears in plan very much like a motte at the angle of a castle bailey. The raised platform of the outer bailey is visible to the left. All the walls and towers are constructed using cut stone, an indication of the huge resources thrown at this castle. Most of the building materials were delivered by sea, visible to the right. In the years 1301–3 a 'gallery of wood, noble and beautiful (*carola lignea nobilis et pulchra*)' was added to the top of the great tower. There is unfortunately no evidence as to what this structure looked like. The defeated Richard II was a prisoner at Flint when he met Henry Bolingbroke, earl of Derby, in 1399.

157 (*right*) The great tower and motte of Hawarden, Flintshire, built by Roger de Clifford after 1282. This building is a copy of the nearby great tower at Flint. It replicates the ring of wall chambers found at Flint, but on a much smaller scale, as a continuous corridor. One additional wall chamber may have served as a chapel. There is clear evidence at Hawarden that the central well of the tower was floored over with timbers to create floors. The masonry of the tower at Hawarden is of quite different character from that of Flint. It compares to that found in earlier buildings of the region, such as Beeston, Cheshire.

158 (*above*) Rhuddlan, Flintshire, a view over the River Clwyd, which was canalised by Edward I at great expense to link the castle to the sea. The apron wall was the first part of the defences to be laid out. It dropped to the side of the river to secure the connection. The castle, which was completed between 1277 and 1280, was intended to secure a historic border between England and Wales. Almost as soon as it was complete, however, Edward I determined to assume control of the whole principality. In plan, the inner bailey is diamond-shaped,

its walls punctuated by arrow loops and set with six drum towers. These are identical in design, but at two opposite corners a pair of towers is drawn together in mirror image to create a gateway. This use of identical architectural units in isolation and combination hearkens back to such late Romanesque works as Henry II's Dover.

159 (*facing page*) A view of Harlech, Merionethshire, begun in April 1283 under the direction of a Savoyard mason called James of St George's and largely complete by 1289.

The castle is set on a high outcrop that formerly dropped to the sea. It comprises an outer apron wall and an inner bailey, the latter set with corner towers and dominated by a Tonbridge-style gatehouse. Amongst the internal buildings was a re-erected Welsh hall, perhaps an architectural trophy of war. The remote and inaccessible location of Harlech made it a perfect place of last defence. In the Wars of the Roses between 1450 and 1470, it was held by both Lancastrians and Yorkists after their causes had otherwise collapsed.

to have been the first part of the castle to be laid out, the intention evidently being that it should protect the site and workforce from attack during the course of construction. The royal apartments within the castle were of timber and probably ranged around the courtyard of the inner bailey. In 1283 the queen had a little fishpond, lawn and garden seats set out within it, elegances hard to imagine today in the rugged ruin that survives.[40]

Llywelyn ap Gruffudd recognised that he had no chance of resisting Edward's forces and came to terms in September 1277. Two months later he paid homage to Edward at Rhuddlan and the whole episode seemed to be over. In 1282, however, Llywelyn was forced to join a revolt against Edward I led by his brother Dafydd. The response was crushing. Three English armies marched simultaneously into Wales and Llywelyn himself was killed in a skirmish near Builth, run through with a spear by a common soldier who did not recognise his victim. Edward I now took control of

Gwynned, which he secured with three new castles. In April 1283 work began to the castle of Harlech in Merionethshire (pl. 159). This was a building closely related to Aberystwyth and dominated by a Tonbridge-style great gatehouse.[41] Much more important and ambitious, however, were the two castles and associated towns that were intended in turn to serve as the administrative heart of this newly conquered principality.

Conwy and Caernarfon

The principle residence of the defeated prince of Wales, Llywelyn ap Gruffudd, was situated on the River Conwy beside the abbey of Aberconwy. This abbey was the senior Cistercian foundation of Wales and the burial place of Llywelyn's ancestors, the house of Gwynedd. Edward I arrived here in March 1283 and set about the transformation of the site. A huge new borough, the largest of the Welsh conquest, was laid out and enclosed in a stone wall with twenty-one towers and three gatehouses. Almost miraculously, this circuit of fortifications survives virtually intact. The new town was built over the earlier monastery and the Cistercian monks were sent to a new site at Meanan, 8 miles away. All that remains of the original abbey today is its church, which was turned to parish use.

Also subsumed within the town plan were the carefully preserved remains of Llywelyn's Hall, probably the main interior of the Welsh prince's former residence.[42] This stood, or was re-erected, against the new town wall a short distance from the king's hall, the office of the royal clerks, the intended future administrators of Wales. This hall and its attendant buildings are likewise lost today, but their position is indicated by the impressive battery of twelve latrines built to serve them along the line of the town wall. The juxtaposition of the hall and the offices may suggest that Edward intended to create a miniature Westminster at Conwy, a palace to serve as the administrative centre

160 A view of Conwy,
Caernarfonshire, largely built
between 1283 and 1287 at a
cost of £15,000. The castle
takes the form of a series of
towers connected by walls. As
originally completed, the
rubble walls of the castle were
rendered and lime-washed. It
possesses no dominant
gatehouse. Presiding over the
town, there is still apparent
here some sense of what an
astonishing creation – and
imposition – Conwy Castle
was. The towers of the inner
bailey, where the royal
apartments were located, are
distinguished by the addition
of tall subsidiary stair turrets.
This detail may have been
drawn from the 1220s
Lanthorn Tower, which
formed part of the queen's
apartments at the Tower of
London. There were wooden
gates on the parapets to
prevent people wandering
from the outer bailey into the
royal apartments.

for Wales and with a Welsh hall – an architectural trophy of war – nearby. As at London, where Westminster and the Tower stand to either side of the city, this palace and castle physically bestrode the new capital of Wales.

Conwy Castle presides over Edward I's new town as a gigantic symbol of royal power (pl. 160). Unlike the castles begun in 1277, it is constructed with rubble masonry. To conceal this fact the exterior was rendered and whitewashed. Its original appearance, shimmering brightly above the water and the town, must have been magnificent. The castle is arranged around two baileys set with eight great towers (pl. 161). These are of much more massive construction than the town walls, a feature that drew attention to their relative importance. Around the castle inner bailey, where the royal apartments stood, the towers are further distinguished by additional turrets that rise high above the parapets. One possible source within the king's works for this detail is the Lanthorn Tower of the 1220s at the Tower of London.[43] At either end of the castle is a small barbican enclosure. That facing the town was approached up a fortified bridge, while the other, which descended to the water, contained a royal garden.

It is particularly noteworthy that there are no gatehouses to the castle: the main entrances are simply archways set in short sections of curtain wall. These are protected from above by a remarkable architectural innovation. Running along the wall head is a continuous projecting balcony of stone, a so-called machicolis (pl. 162). The feature clearly derives from the timber galleries termed hourdes, alures or brattices that had long fortified the towers and walls of castles. Their creation of stone in the case of Conwy, however, is remarkable and there are no clearly dated precedents for such a feature along the heads of curtain walls in either England or France. They presage a hugely important fashion for turning the temporary trappings of war into permanent architectural features. Another distinctive decorative treatment found at Conwy is the placement of upright stones on the tops of the battlements like a jagged row of teeth.

The castle at Conwy was largely completed in an astonishing five building seasons at an estimated cost – along with the new town – of about £15,000. But when work finished it was no longer the chosen seat of royal authority in Wales. That distinction had already passed elsewhere in the most bizarre circumstances. In May 1283 a Roman sarcophagus was discovered at Arfon, a coastal town near the Roman legionary fort of Segontium. Some memory of this Roman connection survived and it seems that the site was associated with Magnus Maximus, reputed to be the first independent ruler of all Britain. He was also celebrated as the husband of the Empress Helena, who found the True Cross on which Christ died, and the father of the Emperor Constantine. As a result, the occupant of the sarcophagus was variously identified as Maximus

161 (*top*) A plan of Conwy, Caernarfonshire. The present domestic ranges in stone probably replace timber predecessors and may have come as an early afterthought to the design. Certainly, they fit clumsily into place and their partition walls at certain points crash into windows within the outer curtain. As complete, they respect the original division of the castle into two baileys. In the outer of these stood the ancillary and public buildings of the castle, including the great hall. The inner bailey was occupied by the royal apartments, all of which appear to have been set at first-floor level. They are the most complete survival of their kind from the period. For a reconstruction of the royal chapel and closet in the north-east tower, see pl. 15.

162 (*bottom right*) The south-west tower and west gate wall walk at Conwy, Caernarfonshire, begun in 1283. The battlements of the latter – now lost – were projected forward on the stone brackets along the wall head. This created a space through which it was possible to drop missiles to the foot of the wall without leaning over the parapet. This arrangement, termed a machicolis, is undoubtedly derived from timber hourding (see pl. 100). Notice the teeth of stone on the tower battlements. This curious detail is derived from castles in Savoy, the homeland of the principal mason involved in the construction of the castle, James of St George's. The teeth do not seem to serve a practical purpose but are decorative, adding to the busy outline of the building. There is one other securely identified English example of this decoration in the walls of St Mary's Abbey, York, probably begun in 1318 by masons who had served in Wales.

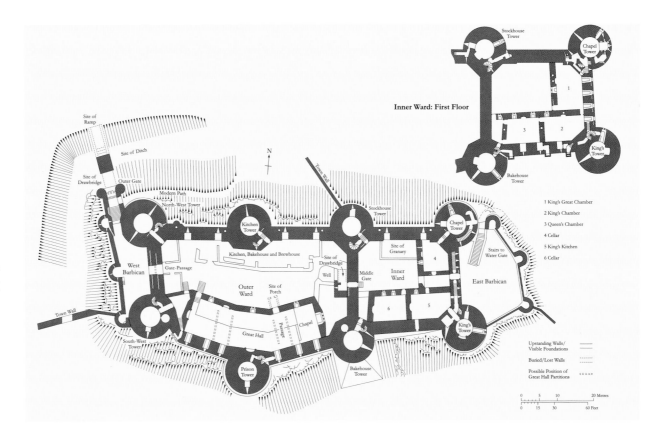

himself or Constantine. What Edward I made of this discovery is unfortunately not recorded, but it can be no coincidence that by June work had begun to a new castle and borough nearby at what became known as Caernarfon, the former enclosing the motte of an eleventh-century predecessor: Edward I wished to appropriate the prestige of this spot to himself.[44]

In pursuit of this aim the new castle, which was begun under the direction of Walter of Hereford (the master mason of Vale Royal Abbey), is unmistakeably Roman in inspiration (pl. 163). It is probably in reference to Roman design, for example, that the towers are of polygonal plan and incorporate softly contrasting bands of stone. This latter feature runs through into the adjacent walls in the manner of Roman brick bonding courses. So clear are the Roman references that the whole composition of the castle has famously been compared to the walls of Constantinople.[45] It is much more likely, however, that the design combines Roman example in Britain with south-eastern English architectural practice.

Polygonal towers are not a widespread feature of Roman fort architecture, though several Welsh buildings – such as Caerwent – preserve structures on this plan. It may have been this circumstance that encouraged Edward's masons to design the towers of Caernar-

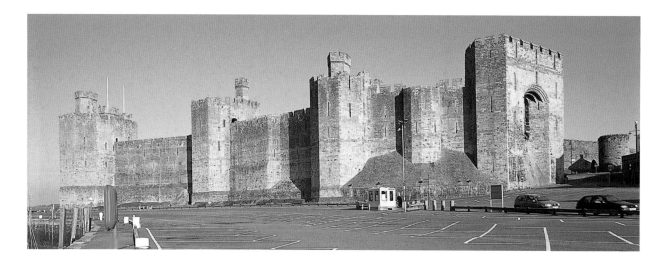

fon in this form. But there may also have been a link with the Pharos at Dover Castle, probably then – as now – the tallest standing Roman structure in Britain. The Pharos was reputed in the Middle Ages to have been Julius Caesar's treasury, and offers an intriguing parallel for the full polygonal plans of several of the Caernarfon towers (see pl. 25).[46] A connection with the south-east would also provide an attractive precedent for the banded masonry in the walls, a feature that also appears in Henry III's additions to the lower ward at Windsor Castle (see pl. 121).

In one technical detail, the architecture of Caernarfon was revolutionary. Great English churches of the thirteenth century – such as Westminster Abbey (see pl. 5) – commonly incorporated much richer mouldings than their European counterparts. That is to say the architectural features they incorporate, such as vault ribs, doorways and arcade arches, were not simply squared off but cut into complex forms composed in cross-section of numerous rolls, hollows and other shapes. These mouldings had the visual effect of making the architecture appear both more delicate and linear, each feature being defined by numerous composite elements. In as far as castles had used mouldings up until the 1280s, the forms employed were drawn from church design (for example, the detailing of the great tower at Dover of the 1180s being drawn from the contemporary works at Canterbury). At Caernarfon, however, a new aesthetic of castle moulding was born. Here, the busy detailing of contemporary church forms was eschewed in favour of bold, broad mouldings termed waves that visually underlined the strength of the building. The idea of using bold mouldings of this kind subsequently enjoyed great popularity in both castle and church design.[47]

Caernarfon Castle was arranged around two baileys (pl. 164). Enclosing the motte of the earlier castle on the site was the outer bailey, entered through an almost symmetrical façade comprising a central gate, two turrets and two towers. The gatehouse must have been approached up a long and high timber bridge and was apparently planned on a wedge-shaped plan. There is a precedent for this unusual form in a very elegantly finished gatehouse probably built in the 1260s at Tamworth in Staffordshire. Dominating the inner bailey at the opposite end of the castle was the Eagle Tower. This was completed by Edward II with its eponymous eyrie of stone birds in the battlements. The form of the building reflects a very mannered use of geometry. It is laid out as a decagon with three tall, projecting turrets, an effect reminiscent of Henry II's Orford. Internally, the wall chambers continue the geometric theme and are laid out on hexagonal and octagonal plans (pl. 165). This ring of wall chambers is comparable to that found in the great tower of Flint.

This consistent use of polygonal forms was echoed in the great gatehouse that was erected after 1296 to dominate the town façade of the castle. The building is fortified to a degree remarkable even for a medieval castle, its entrance sealed by five doors, six portcullises and commanded by scores of arrow loops and murder holes. Above the central archway is a life-size statue of an enthroned king. The gatehouse was possibly not a feature of the castle as first designed, though it copies the idiom of the earlier architecture closely. Much of the interior was never completed, but it is clear from the ruins that the entrance passage extended back to a vaulted chamber on an octagonal plan. From this there must have opened left and right doors into the two baileys. As well as resonating with the form of the

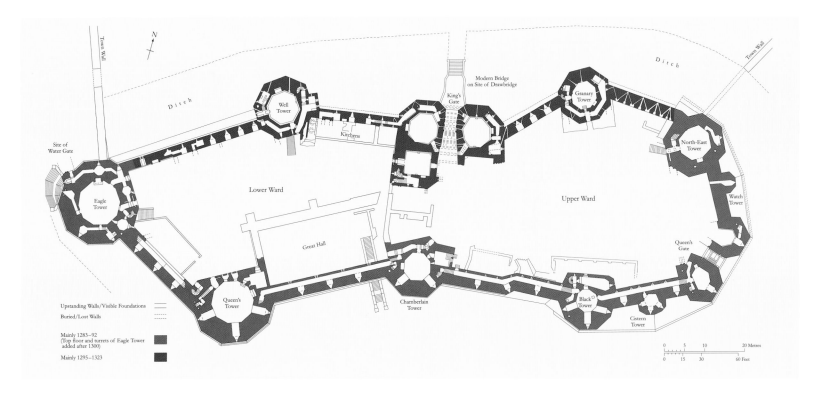

165 (*right*) A cut-away reconstruction of the Eagle Tower at Caernarfon around 1320 by Chris Jones-Jenkins. The tower takes its name from the colony of stone eagles – the birds of imperial Rome – that inhabit the battlements. These are in fact an addition of Edward II's reign. The tower is very complex in geometric terms. In plan, it makes ingenious play with polygons and a triangle, the latter demarcated in plan by the three turrets that rise above the building. This particular combination of forms is common to several virtuoso castle buildings stretching back to Henry II's great tower at Orford, Suffolk (1165–73). Around the principal interiors of the tower, which presumably served as royal withdrawing chambers, is a ring of rooms on both hexagonal and octagonal plans. The arrangement recalls the ring of mural chambers in the earlier great tower at Flint.

castle towers, this curious octagonal chamber within the gatehouse reflects a wider fascination with polygonal forms in the period, of which more will be said in the next chapter. This is particularly apparent in such influential ecclesiastical designs as the octagonal chapter house at Westminster Abbey, begun in 1260.

Besides constructing the royal castles described above, Edward I was active after 1282 in refortifying several former Welsh strongholds, such as Castell y Bere (Merionethshire), Criccieth and Dolbadarn (both Caernarfonshire). The work undertaken at these sites involved little more than repairs and slight extensions to the existing buildings. What connected all the royal castles, great and small, however, were the terms under which they were held by the king's officers. In no case was a castle attached to a specific body of land that served as a castlery in the manner of foundations in the eleventh or twelfth centuries. Nor were any associated with major religious foundations or a substantial park. These castles were built as instruments of government for an absent king and they depended on the royal exchequer for their survival.

Baronial Castles

Edward I did not attempt, however, to govern the whole of the newly conquered territory directly. The estates of the dispossessed Welsh nobility – as distinct

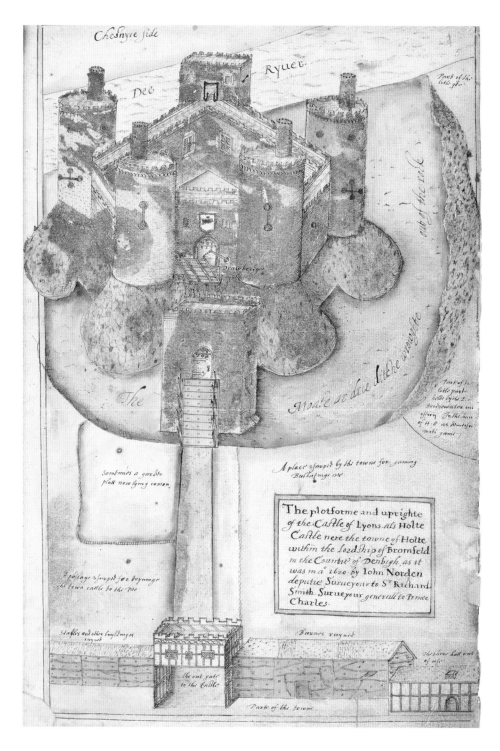

Within the image (as drawn labels):
Cheshyre side
Ryuer.
Dee
The plotforme and uprighte of the Castle of Lyons als Holte Castle nere the towne of Holte within the lordship of Bromfeld in the Countie of Denbigh, as it was in aᵒ 1620 by Iohn Norden deputie Suruey eour to Sʳ Richard Smith Suruey eour generall to Prince Charles.

166   An early seventeenth-century survey of Holt or Castle Lion, Denbighshire, by the surveyor John Norden. Holt was built by John de Warenne, sixth earl of Surrey (d. 1304). The castle was laid out on a pentagonal plan with five principal towers. With one exception these were drum-shaped and possessed tall stair turrets, a design reminiscent of Conwy. One of the towers, possibly containing the principal withdrawing apartments, was rectangular. All the internal domestic buildings seem to have been built of stone. The main gate, which was ornamented with a sculpture of a lion, was approached through a free-standing barbican tower in the moat. The drawing also shows the timber-built gatehouse and ancillary buildings of the base court to the castle, including the stable to the left. Timber courts of this kind were a common feature of medieval castles, but few traces of them survive today.

from the lands of their prince – were passed on to a small circle of English magnates. With one exception the previous year, all these grants were made in 1282 following the suppression of Llywelyn and Dafydd's revolt. They constituted the only major territorial distributions made by Edward I during the reign and they were to prove of great subsequent importance, serving to bind Wales into the dynastic politics of England. In each case the grant of land led to the construction of a castle, and some of these were quite as ambitious as their royal counterparts. But whereas the royal building works are well documented, very little is known about the construction of these magnate castles beyond the fact that they stood complete in the first quarter of the fourteenth century. In each case, the design and form of the new buildings were closely related to those of the king's castles.

One of these castles, Hawarden, has already been remarked upon as including a reduced copy of the great tower at Flint. Hawarden was probably begun by Roger de Clifford shortly after a castle that he had built on the site in breach of a treaty was sacked by the Welsh in the rebellion of 1282 (see pl. 157). Reginald de Grey, justiciar of Chester, worked on two new castles, one passed on from the king during its construction at Ruthin, Denbighshire (which was established with a borough), and another at Hope, Flintshire. In neither case is the castle well preserved today, though there are sixteenth-century depictions of Ruthin that give a good sense of its medieval appearance.[48] In certain points its design evidently echoed that of Conwy, the inner bailey towers for example being distinguished by tall stair turrets. At Castle Lion, Denbighshire, today known as Holt, John de Warenne began a castle with an inner bailey laid out on a regular pentagonal plan. The drum towers that stood at each corner of the plan again looked very similar to those around the inner bailey of Conwy, possessing prominent staircase turrets. Also in the manner of Conwy, there was no gatehouse but an entrance arch punched through a wall. Early drawings show that above this there stood a statue of a lion (pl. 166). Another castle on a regular plan and without a gatehouse was erected by Roger Mortimer at Chirk, Denbighshire. This building was probably begun around 1300 and bears a striking resemblance to the final great royal castle in Wales, Beaumaris, which remains to be discussed below (pl. 167).

Perhaps the most ambitious baronial castle in the group, however, was constructed on the hilltop at

Denbigh by Henry de Lacy, earl of Lincoln. In the manner of Conwy, the new building occupied the site of an important Welsh palace and was intended to signal in stone and mortar the change of regime. The king visited the earl at Denbigh in October 1282, shortly after he had granted away the lordship to de Lacy. In their conversation the two men evidently discussed plans for the development of the site and when he left Edward I made a small contribution of £22 towards the forthcoming operations.[49]

It would appear that the rebuilding of Denbigh fell into two broad stages. In typical fashion, resources were first focused on enclosing the town and castle perimeter to protect the new inhabitants and builders from the Welsh. Following the completion of this outer defensive circuit, attention then turned to the town façade of the castle. From the differences in form between the outer and town walls of the castle, it would seem that the two phases did not follow a common plan (pl. 168). The early outer wall is a relatively modest affair with regular, open-backed towers. By contrast, the town wall of the castle was vastly more ambitious and set with polygonal towers in the manner of Caernarfon. Work to it probably began after 1295, in the aftermath of a revolt that overwhelmed the defences of the town and castle.

Along this town façade was erected the most architecturally sophisticated gatehouse of the thirteenth century. It comprised three polygonal towers drawn together on a triangular plan around the entrance and a central, octagonal porch. Once again, the design is clearly connected to the gatehouse at Caernarfon, with the important difference that the latter is too tightly crushed into the castle plan ever to have incorporated three towers or to have stood in such proud isolation. Another intriguing parallel with Caernarfon is the use of polychrome stone decoration in the gatehouse; rather than striped, the buildings at Denbigh are chequered. This pattern was also extended to the main gate of the town, the impressive Burgess Gate (pl. 169). Work to the Denbigh gatehouse was never completed. As the antiquarian John Leland observed in the 1540s, the building might otherwise 'have beene counted among the most memorable peaces of workys yn England'. He also said that the earl abandoned operations after his eldest son was killed falling down the castle well.[50] The earl's children were unfortunate in their games, another son tumbling to his death from the walls of Pontefract in pursuit of a ball.

Besides these baronial castles in the newly conquered territories of Wales, the northern march also saw considerable related architectural activity in this period. Probably around 1290, the earl of Arundel, Richard Fitzalan, added a great tower to his castle at Clun, and Geoffrey de Geneville began work on a splendid new series of domestic apartments in the castle of Ludlow (both Shropshire). Whether these operations were encouraged by the pressures of war is

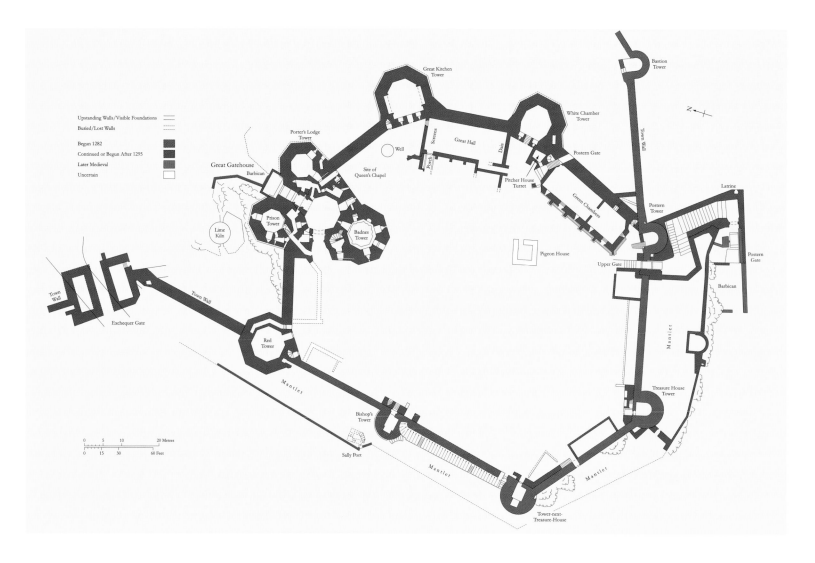

Upstanding Walls/Visible Foundations
Buried/Lost Walls

Begun 1282
Continued or Begun After 1295
Later Medieval
Uncertain

an open question, but it seems unlikely. Rather, they reflect an important economic departure in the region. During the late thirteenth century sheep farming was undertaken on a grand scale for the first time by several great marcher lords. The climate of the region was perfect for the production of soft and highly prized wool, and the new venture proved hugely lucrative. Not only did the magnates grow rich and plough money into architecture, but so too did their agents, including Laurence of Ludlow, the builder from 1291 of Stokesay, Shropshire (see pl. 174).

In the meantime, affairs in Wales had an impact across the Irish Sea. At Greencastle, Co. Donegal, Richard de Burgh, second earl of Ulster and lord of Connaught (d. 1326), began in 1305 a castle that was apparently influenced in its details by Caernarfon.[51] De Burgh had served as a young man in Edward I's Welsh campaigns and was knighted by the king at Rhuddlan in 1283. His work to Greencastle followed a string of generous royal grants in return for his service

in Scotland in 1303, which included right of free chase in certain of his estates and a pardon of all his debts at the Irish exchequer. Although never appointed justiciar of Ireland, he was an outstanding figure in Irish affairs. The earl also constructed a castle at Ballymote, Co. Sligo, in 1300.[52] It seems unlikely that de Burgh was personally influenced by the example of royal building, though that possibility cannot be ruled out. Rather, that he recruited his skilled labour force in Ireland from the group of craftsmen press-ganged into royal service for the Welsh wars.

BEAUMARIS AND THE THIRD WELSH WAR

In March 1284, by the terms of the Statute of Rhuddlan, Edward I divided north Wales into counties after the English style and placed the area under the control of a justiciar. He also tried to establish his own dynasty

168 (*facing page*) A plan of the castle at Denbigh, the seat of one of the richest medieval baronies in the English realm. The building operations fell into two phases. A stone wall with D-shaped towers was erected to protect the whole hilltop site from 1282. Then, probably after 1295, an inner wall was constructed to divide the castle from the town to the east. The polygonal form of the towers of the second phase points to a close connection with the works at Caernarfon. Particularly intriguing is the great gatehouse on a triangular plan with three towers enclosing an octagonal porch. Denbigh possessed an extensive collection of stone-built domestic buildings, still a relatively rarity in this period when timber remained in widespread use.

169 Denbigh, Burgess Gate to the town, probably begun in the 1290s. It stands on deep spur plinths similar to those found in the southern march, as at Goodrich, Chepstow and Carew. The feature is otherwise unparalleled in northern Wales. As in the main gatehouse of Denbigh Castle, there is a decorative band of chequered masonry at parapet level. The gate passage is formidably defended with rows of murder holes.

of Welsh princes. The queen, Eleanor of Castile, was sent, heavily pregnant, to Caernarfon and was delivered there on 25 April 1284 of a son, the future Edward II. At the time the castle and town, begun less than a year earlier, must have been a building site, which shows that the location of the birth was an act of policy. Indeed, as early as the sixteenth century the story was told that when Edward I heard of the delivery of the child he gathered the Welsh leaders together at Rhuddlan. There they demanded of him that he appoint a prince of their own country to rule them and one who spoke neither French nor Saxon as his native tongue. Edward promised them all this, and in delight they requested in addition that the prince be without reproach. Edward I's smile cannot have flickered for a moment. Agreeing to their every demand, he smugly proffered them the baby in fulfilment of his pledge. Since the baby spoke no language at all, the men were informed, his first words could be in Welsh if they so chose. Edward of Caernarfon was not in fact created prince of Wales until 1301, but the story may contain an element of truth.[53]

For the Welsh, the new English government established by the Statute of Rhuddlan proved harsh, and within ten years simmering resentment flared up into revolt. The administration was taken completely by surprise. Virtually every one of the new castles erected by Edward I and his barons was quickly overwhelmed, and the sheriff of Caernarfon was lynched in the capital of the new province. A hard-fought campaign

during the winter of 1294–5 crushed the rebellion. It culminated in an attack on the island of Anglesey, which had to be launched from the mainland across a long bridge of boats. In its aftermath, a castle was begun at Beaumaris to control the island (pl. 170). The operation was directed by a master mason called James of St George and at first was pressed forward at incredible speed. Within the first six months nearly £7,000 was spent on the operation; more money had been expended more quickly on this one castle than any other in the Welsh conquest.

On 27 February 1296 James of St George and a colleague wrote a letter to the king describing the state of affairs at the castle. One thousand craftsmen were employed on the site at the time, and they worked under the protection of 10 mounted soldiers, 20 crossbowmen and 100 soldiers. By this date the walls were already 20 feet (6 m) high at their lowest point. Four of the castle gates were hung and locked each night and the water channel from the sea was deep enough for a 40-ton vessel to come to the gate. To press the work forward, they reported, would require 400 masons, 200 quarry men, 30 smiths, 2,000 workmen and an unspecified number of carpenters. Meanwhile, to move materials 100 carts, 60 wagons and 30 boats would be needed. There was already a shortage of money to pay both labourers and the garrison, and at least £250 would be needed every week for the coming season if work were to be completed. The letter ends with a final plea: 'And, Sirs, for God's sake, please be quick with the money for the works, as much as ever our lord king wills; otherwise, everything done up till now will have been of no avail.' But the royal finances could not sustain this pressure. Over the next two years expenditure gradually declined and then dried up altogether. After the expenditure of approximately £11,500 over three years, Beaumaris was left incomplete.[54]

JAMES OF ST GEORGE AND THE DESIGN OF EDWARD I'S WELSH CASTLES

As a group, the castles begun in north Wales during the reign of Edward I are striking for their evident architectural variety. Almost every genre of castle design discussed in this book so far is represented: castles with mottes, concentric defences, great towers

170 A plan of Beaumaris, Anglesey, begun in 1295. Set out on a flat, shore site, the castle is regular in layout with two concentric rings of fortifications: an inner bailey and an outer apron. Its inner bailey is symmetrically arranged with six drum towers and two Tonbridge-style gatehouses. There is scant surviving evidence of the internal domestic chambers, which were evidently secondary to the conception of the castle. The broad moats connected to the sea, and ships could dock against the walls of the castle. A town was planted beside the castle and one window of the parish church that was created to serve it possesses tracery with split cusping. This technical detail points to the connection of the masons who built it with the architecture of the king's works and south-east England.

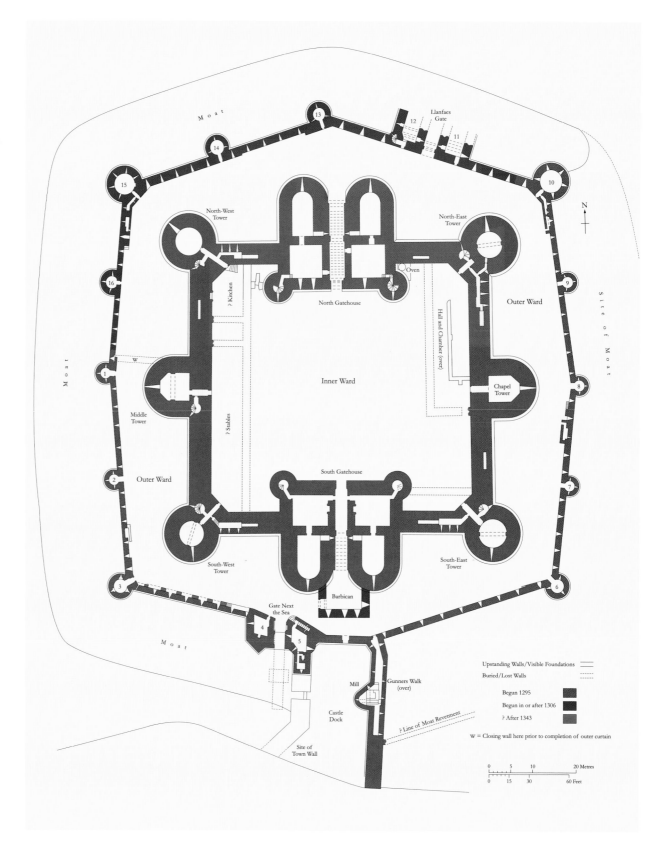

and gatehouses, compositions of towers as well as regular and irregular plans. Such diversity of form is notably absent from most major castle-building programmes of the Middle Ages, for example, the magnificent series of late thirteenth-century castles built by the Teutonic Knights in Pomerania in modern Poland. It unquestionably reflects the inventive and vigorous English architectural tradition from which the designs were drawn, stemming from the early thirteenth-century royal works at Dover, Windsor and London. As has been discussed, the origins of the Tonbridge-style gatehouse, as well as many other details of design, such as the striped walls of Caernarfon and perhaps the polygonal forms of its towers, are to be found in these English buildings.

This point is important to make because the conventional assessment of the Welsh castles has been very different. They have been presented as the work of James of St George, the mason mentioned above for his work to Beaumaris. Although previously known to scholars, James of St George was attributed a central role in the design of the Welsh castles by Arnold Taylor in an article of 1950.[55] Taylor was not only the outstanding scholar to have studied these buildings in recent years but also the saviour of Conwy from a grossly insensitive road development scheme in the 1990s. He showed convincingly that James came from Savoy, where he had practised as a castle builder in the 1260s; that he had fallen in with Edward I on the king's return from crusade and subsequently come to England; and that he had travelled to Wales on 9 April 1278 'to ordain' works to the castles there.

Documentary evidence leaves no room for doubt that James of St George was a leading figure in the king's works from the moment of his arrival in Wales. So too that he was a mason, since he is described as such in the building accounts of Flint. Taylor, however, also wished to see him as mainly responsible for the design of the Welsh castles and cast him as a genius who transferred to Wales the architectural and engineering skills he had learnt in his native Savoy. Only in this way could Taylor explain the sophistication of

these buildings, which he saw as essentially unparalleled in England.

In support of this view Taylor identified several features or details in the Welsh castles that he understood to be of specifically Savoyard origin.[56] Two of these are well observed and convincing. It seems clear, for example, that the best precedents for particular window designs at Conwy and the curious teeth of stone that rise in triplets from the battlements in the same castle are to be found in Savoy (see pl. 162). Other technical comparisons drawn by Taylor, however, are not specific to the Welsh and Savoyard castles as he argued. The use of semicircular arches (as opposed to pointed ones), for example, is widespread in English castle architecture of the thirteenth century: to give just two instances, it appears in the architecture of Leybourne, Kent, and Barnwell, Northamptonshire, of the 1260s. Meanwhile, the technique of laying scaffolds as ramps – rather than in horizontal lifts – is found in earlier Welsh buildings, such as the 1220s great tower at Dolbadarn.

Nevertheless, Taylor was clearly right to see the influence of Savoy in Edward I's buildings. The difficulty comes, however, in seeing the diversity and scale of the Welsh works in what are by comparison the very modest Savoyard castles associated with James of St George. If some of the trimmings of the Welsh castles demand a Savoyard explanation, their architectural bones require an English one.[57] A case in point is the repeated use of gatehouses in the style of Tonbridge. A much more satisfactory explanation for James's role is that he was directing a workforce of English designers – men who had in fact begun several of the castles before James even arrived in Wales. From that moment on, James certainly oversaw building operations, but it was the king's works and its masons that lent the castles attributed to him such outstanding diversity and confidence. But the exceptional castle-building opportunities he enjoyed doubtless made him exceptional too; and by the time of his death James of St George may well have been, as Taylor suggested, one of the greatest military architects in English history.

8

THE KING'S SERVANTS AND THE ARCHITECTURE OF WAR

EDWARD I AND EDWARD II

Beyond Wales and its marches, the most important builders in the reign of Edward I (1274–1307) were, almost without exception, figures reared to power and influence in the king's administration. The bountiful rewards of royal service are well illustrated in the career of a figure such as Anthony Bek. Born into a modest Lincolnshire family, Bek is first documented in royal service in the 1260s as one of Henry III's clerks. He subsequently studied at Oxford University and in 1270 accompanied the Lord Edward on crusade. Here Bek won the confidence of the future king and enjoyed sufficient trust to be appointed an executor when Edward was forced to undergo a medical operation at Acre. Amongst many other marks of favour Bek received upon his return to England was the office of constable of the Tower of London in 1275. In this capacity – between all his other varied and important services to Edward – he was nominally responsible for the remodelling of the outer walls of the castle discussed in the previous chapter (though a certain Giles of Ardenarde actually oversaw the work). Such was his growing wealth and favour that in 1281 he received licence to construct a castle at Somerton in Lincolnshire, his home county. Constructing a castle in this period was generally the crowning achievement of a brilliant

career, but within two years of beginning Somerton Bek became involved in a legal dispute that was to alter the register of his architectural patronage fundamentally.[1]

On 25 June 1281 Archbishop Wickwane of York arrived in Durham during the absence of the bishop, Robert de Insula. His intention was to make a formal visitation of the cathedral priory and thereby assert jurisdiction over it. The action struck at the heart of the special legal status enjoyed by Durham and was vigorously resisted. At North Gate, the entrance to the castle precinct, the archbishop's entourage found its way blocked by the bishop's knights, who refused it passage. The archbishop excommunicated the monks in return and attempted another visitation in September. This time he was forced to retire to the city church of St Nicholas and, having been threatened by a mob, made an ignominious escape.[2] The dispute subsequently escalated, and in 1283 Edward I sent in his trusted servant Anthony Bek to arbitrate. Halfway through the proceedings, however, the bishop of Durham died. It was easy in the circumstances to persuade the monks of Durham that their interests would be best served if the king's agent was made bishop. Bek was duly elected and consecrated bishop of Durham

171 The ruins of the great hall of the bishop's palace at Wells, Somerset, built by Bishop Burnell in the 1280s. To a thirteenth-century visitor familiar with halls designed with multiple gables on their lateral walls (see pl. 174), the extraordinary thing about this building would have been its battlemented parapets. The hall was licensed for demolition by the king in 1552, but was left to decay until the eighteenth century, when one side of it was pulled down to make it look more romantic. A late fifteenth-century description by William Worcester makes it clear that the interior was divided by arcades into a central space with flanking aisles. Archaeological investigation has revealed the remains of an encaustic tile floor that formerly covered the interior.

172 (*facing page*) Acton Burnell, Shropshire, built by Bishop Burnell in the manor of his birth under a licence issued in 1284. It stood within a larger enclosure bounded to one side by a church, which was also splendidly rebuilt by the bishop. Its quadrangular plan is reminiscent of Romanesque great towers, though its walls are of relatively thin construction. The external arrangement of windows reflects the function and importance of the internal chambers. Its interior was partitioned by walls and – possibly – an arcade. All the principal rooms were raised to first-floor level. Formal entrance to the tower was up a stair to a porch in a corner turret. At the opposite end of the building were the bishop's withdrawing chambers. They were served by a latrine tower built centrally in the west wall, shown in this view.

on 9 January 1284 at York. Despite the location of the ceremony, there was no concession to the archbishop over the rights of visitation. Indeed, the issue remained a matter for contention until as late as 1949, which must make it the longest-running dispute in English legal history.

As bishop of Durham, Bek at once began to consolidate the rights of his see with aggressive determination. This process was informed by the administrative and legal reforms that had so strengthened Edward I's royal power in the kingdom as a whole, and it culminated in 1293 with a successful challenge to the power of the king's agent in the region, the sheriff of Northumberland, between the rivers Tyne and Tees. The following year the bishop's sweeping powers were acknowledged by parliament. None of these changes could have happened without the support of Edward I, but they nevertheless concentrated extraordinary power, wealth and independence in Bek's hands. In time-honoured fashion these changes were accompanied by a wholesale reformation of the see of Durham in both architectural and institutional terms. His work in these respects is not very well documented, but circumstances suggest that most of it took place prior to 1299.

New colleges of priests were established to serve the important churches at Lanchester and Chester-le-Street, in 1283 and 1286 respectively.[3] A third such institution

was also established at Bishop Auckland in 1292, almost certainly in tandem with the encastellation of the manor there. This had served since the twelfth century as the country retreat and hunting lodge of the bishops of Durham. As part of Bek's new work to Bishop Auckland, the site was enclosed with new fortifications and the domestic buildings improved with the addition of a two-storey chapel.[4] Only the castle great hall, which was begun by Bek's late twelfth-century predecessor, Hugh du Puiset, substantially survived destruction when the castle was largely demolished in the aftermath of the Civil War in the 1640s. The arcaded interior of the hall was later transformed into a chapel in the years 1661–6.[5]

Probably at much the same time, Bek also greatly enlarged the castle of Northallerton, the administrative seat of the bishops of Durham in Yorkshire. Nor did Bek ignore his needs in and around London, buying and rebuilding the manor of Eltham just outside the city in 1295. It was here that Bek finally died in 1311, and the manor house subsequently developed into one of the great royal palaces of Yorkist and Tudor England.[6]

Yet the most magnificent operation undertaken by Bek was appropriately reserved for the seat of his authority at Durham Castle. Here work began to a new hall on the foundations of that constructed in the eleventh century by Bishop Walcher. Some fragmen-

tary elements of this new structure remain visible in the present building, including its principal doorway and the remains of several windows decorated with stone tracery and flanked by free-standing shafts of stone. Unlike that at Bishop Auckland, the interior of the hall at Durham probably stood open as an undivided space without arcades. To judge from the detailing, the work almost certainly dates from around 1280.

On only a slightly more modest scale, the pattern of Bek's career and patronage was anticipated amongst prominent churchmen at the close of the previous reign. Godfrey Giffard, bishop of Worcester and a former chancellor of Henry III, for example, received licence to encastellate Hartlebury in Worcestershire in 1268. This castle, which appears to have been begun by a predecessor in the 1250s, served as the principal seat of his successors to the see until the Civil War. His brother Walter also rose to high office and as archbishop of York received a similar licence to fortify Cawood in Yorkshire in 1272, already an important residence of the archbishops of York. The list of building bishops more exactly contemporary with Bek would include the unscrupulous Bishop Langton, who rebuilt Eccleshall Castle in Staffordshire and fortified the close of his cathedral at Lichfield, erecting as part of the work

a grand new palace with an encastellated gatehouse and wall towers.[7] Record of a fatal accident at Newark in 1284, when a mason called Walter de Newport fell from a turret of the castle, may suggest that the surviving curtain walls and polygonal towers were under construction by the bishop of Lincoln, Oliver Sutton.[8]

But perhaps the most celebrated in this circle of clerical builders is Robert Burnell, who also accompanied the future king with Bek on crusade. On his return to England in 1274 he was made chancellor, and the following year bishop of Bath and Wells. In the 1280s Burnell greatly extended his principal palace at Wells. As part of this work he constructed a new hall on a scale to rival Durham – it stood 142 feet long and 60 feet (18 m) wide (pl. 171).[9] Around the same time, in 1284, he was also licensed by the king to fortify the manor house of his birthplace, Acton Burnell, Shropshire (pl. 172). The tower Burnell raised there is laid out on a rectangular plan with corner turrets and incorporates all the chambers necessary for grand domestic living. In typical medieval fashion the different window forms advertise the varied functions of the rooms within.[10] Burnell's buildings make apparent an important new departure in castle architecture that deserves detailed consideration.

THE TRAPPINGS OF FORTIFICATION

Both the hall at Wells and the tower at Acton Burnell were probably designed by the same master mason and have many architectural details in common. They also appear very similar in overall form, with boxlike proportions and battlemented outlines. In the case of Acton Burnell, these features unmistakably associate the design with the long tradition of great tower building in England. As such, the tower is an elaborate but entirely conventional piece of castle architecture. Not so the identically treated great hall at Wells. For contemporaries familiar with the gabled walls typical of halls in this period (see pl. 174), this building must have appeared very striking: the hall – itself a building with no defensive pretensions and part of a wider residential complex – has adopted in isolation the architectural features of a castle for grand effect.

The practice of dressing buildings regardless of their function with the trappings of fortification would appear to be a revolution of Edward I's reign. Henceforth it was to become a commonplace of every type of English architecture. The phenomenon has presented students of the subject with what has conventionally been understood as a problem. If castles are essentially functional works of fortification, it has been a reflexive response to try to distinguish amongst the growing body of buildings that adopt the trappings of defence those that do so for specifically military purpose. By this criterion – supposedly – is the Real Castle to be identified. Yet as most scholars admit, the process of identifying functional fortifications is deeply subjective and – in all but the clearest cases – fraught with difficulties. So, for example, while no one has claimed the great hall at Wells as a castle, judgements on the residence at Acton Burnell – with its thin walls and large windows – have been very mixed. To some, its defensive weaknesses are such as to disqualify it from being a castle.

To suppose that you can identify a core group of Real Castles amidst this mass of fortified architecture is not so much incorrect as misguided. In part, this is because contemporaries were actively interested in making the distinction difficult to draw. Since castles remained the defining architectural symbol and benchmark of lordly status, it was a point of positive interest to dress any building of pretension with fortifications to make it – if not a castle – as castle-like as possible. As a result, if there is any distinguishing

litmus test to identify a castle it is to be found in the combined qualities of its owner's status and the scale of the landholding attached to it. This understanding demands a broad judgement of what should be deemed a castle. It also determines that whether or not a particular building is a castle, the fortifications it incorporates are necessarily to be understood as works of castle architecture.

These issues aside, to dismiss Acton Burnell from the ranks of the castle on grounds of indefensibility is to ignore for convenience one crucial piece of evidence. Burnell, and nearly all builders in his position both secular and ecclesiastic, sought a licence from the king to build fortifications around the residence they were constructing (see Chapter One). These documents, which have been categorised and dubbed 'Licences to Crenellate' by nineteenth-century historians, began to be issued in quantity from the early thirteenth century onwards. The terms of these documents suggest that regardless of what the building they sanctioned actually looked like physically, and whether or not they were genuinely defensible, the idea of fortification was central to their identity. In this sense, such licensed buildings should be understood as castles: residences made magnificent through the trappings of fortification.

One result of giving buildings of all kinds the trappings of fortification was to make the prestige of the castle more widely accessible. As well as bishops, prominent royal clerks might aspire to the prestige of castle buildings, creating on a miniature scale the architecture of their social superiors. A particularly fine example of this is Little Wenham in Suffolk, probably built between 1279 and 1294/5 by a royal clerk called Master Roger de Holebrok (pl. 173). As well as reordering the neighbouring parish church, Roger constructed a new residence for himself. In its original form this residence almost certainly comprised a timber hall and services attached to a tower-like chamber block.[11] The latter building alone remains today in almost miraculously good condition. Its internal arrangements are fairly typical of such structures: the spacious principal chamber is raised above a vaulted undercroft and opens into a chapel. What is remarkable, however, is that the whole building is crowned with battlements. So castle-like does it look, that it has often been described as a tower house.

Clerics were not alone in exploiting the opportunities of administrative office. Secular figures, too, raised themselves to favour and great wealth in royal service and turned their winnings to architecture. Sir Stephen

173 The tower at Little Wenham, Suffolk, probably built between 1279 and 1294/5 by a royal clerk called Master Roger de Holebrok. It is L-shaped in plan with the principal apartments raised to first-floor level above a vaulted undercroft. These almost certainly served as withdrawing chambers for a timber hall that stood somewhere to the left of the building. A spiral stair in the central turret connects the chambers at different levels and gives access to the roof. The tower stands in a moated enclosure and is built of brick with stone detailing, an unusually early use of this combination of materials. As in the case of Edward I's works at the Tower of London, the brick may be imported.

Pencester, for example, became an important figure in the administration of Kent during Edward I's reign and served as sheriff of the county, warden of the Cinque Ports and constable of Dover Castle. He sought two licences to crenellate as he grew in power, one at Hever in 1271 and another at Allington in 1281, the latter in conjunction with the right to hold a market and fair.[12] Both buildings have been much altered subsequently, but Allington preserves a series of semicircular towers probably built by him.

Edward I's need for cash also encouraged another category of aspirant castle builder: the merchant. The most celebrated figure of this kind was Laurence of Ludlow, reputedly the richest merchant in England and a supplier of bullion to the royal mints. His money came from the wool trade and he was an important agent in this commodity for various magnates on the march, who were farming it for the first time.[13] In 1291, after having purchased the manor of Stokesay in Shropshire, he received licence from the king to fortify it (pl. 174). This still preserves intact its thirteenth-century great hall and is dominated by a tower of complex plan.

With the accession of Edward II (1307–27), architectural patronage by royal servants diminished appreciably. Resources became concentrated in the hands of favourites and the numbers of individuals able to build contracted sharply. One contributory factor to this situation was the relative instability of the royal administration. Not only did Edward II generally fail to control church appointments, but also his own officers came and went with bewildering rapidity. For example, over the twenty years of his reign there were fifteen changes of treasurer, and ten keepers of the Privy Seal.[14]

That said, there were still some royal servants who became patrons of architecture. John Markenfield, for example, took the opportunity of his appointment as chancellor of the exchequer in 1310 to get a licence to fortify his manor house at Markenfield in Yorkshire. The new post was rather less glorious than its later character would suggest,[15] but it marked him out as one in a circle of Yorkshire clerics favoured by Edward II. Markenfield's new residence was on a sumptuous scale, its principal structures enclosed within a moat. The development and function of the surviving buildings, which are battlemented throughout, have been contested of late (pl. 175).[16] Whatever the reality of its development, the form of the building and the timing of its construction beautifully illustrate the perceived link that continued to exist between political power and castle architecture.

174 (*facing page*) A view of Stokesay, Shropshire. The castle was rebuilt by Laurence of Ludlow following his purchase of the manor in 1291. He was a pioneer in the region's wool business, and the castle was an expression of his financial success and standing. From a distance, the two principal elements of the residence he created are clearly legible – the hall and the great tower. Superbly preserved, they offer a rare glimpse of a contrast that would have been widely familiar to a thirteenth-century audience: the hall with its high roof and gabled walls; the tower with its level and battlemented parapet. The great tower takes the very unusual and complex form of two divergent polygonal towers. This may reflect a particular late thirteenth-century fashion in the southern Welsh marches for using pairs of towers conjoined at right angles, as may be seen at Brecon, Abergavenny and Crickhowell.

175 (*above*) Markenfield, Yorkshire, was built by a royal clerk called John Markenfield under a licence issued in 1310. There survives from this period an L-shaped residential block in one corner of the rectangular moated site. Within this, the principal apartments are raised above a vaulted undercroft. To the left is a large chamber, presumed to be the hall, which was entered up a stair within an external porch. The line of the porch roof is clearly visible as an inverted v-shape. To the right was the great chamber, now heavily remodelled, which was connected to the roof and basement by a spiral stair. Between the hall and chamber is a chapel. The wider landscape of Markenfield is unusually well preserved. There survive the earthworks of an adjacent court, as well as substantial stretches of the medieval park wall.

THE CROWN IN THE WIDER REALM

Throughout Edward I's reign considerable work was undertaken to royal castles that were not in the front line of political events. By comparison with the greatest Welsh castles, expenditure on these buildings can seem modest, but in real terms they were often substantial. At Cambridge, for example, £2,630 was spent on remodelling the castle between 1284 and 1298. Work to this building was never completed, presumably because of the financial difficulties of the crown from 1297, but its essential form as a motte and bailey castle with a large gatehouse entrance can be reconstructed from documentary evidence and early drawings.[17]

A similar reordering of Rockingham Castle, Leicestershire, took place between 1276 and 1291 at a total cost of £1,252, with improvements to the domestic chambers and defences. It was probably as part of this work that the gate to the castle was fortified with two

large drum towers in finely worked masonry.[18] At Richmond, Edward I repaired both the twelfth-century great tower and the domestic apartments during the 1290s. He may further have been responsible for raising each of the eleventh-century wall towers by a storey (see pl. 46).[19] Several other Romanesque great towers – including that at Dover – were also repaired during the reign, clear evidence that these buildings had not been relegated to the dustbin of architectural fashion as is sometimes supposed.[20] Perhaps the most ambitious operation of this kind was the repair in 1287–9 of the hall in William Rufus's great tower at Norwich, which cost more than £600.[21] Finally, at St Briavels in Gloucestershire, between 1292 and 1294, a new gatehouse was built, closely allied in some points of detail to nearby Goodrich, at a cost of £477 (pl. 176). Set in the depths of a huge royal forest, St Briavels was the administrative centre of crossbow bolt production for the royal armies.[22]

Yet the most spectacular royal castle in this category was not built for the king at all but for his wife, Queen Eleanor of Castile. She was granted control of Leeds Castle in Kent in 1278 and greatly expanded it over the next twelve years, though the operation is poorly documented.[23] The centrepiece of her new creation was an island residence within the mere that surrounded the castle (pl. 177). This was termed the 'Gloriette', a title reserved in this period to particularly sumptuous apartments in several major castles. The outer bailey of the castle was connected to the Gloriette by a long barbican bridge and was enclosed by a curtain wall set with D-shaped towers. Running water was supplied to the castle by a conduit and the buildings incorporated a purpose-built bath for the king, which was constructed or repaired in 1291–2. Beside the main castle gate there stood a mill.

A figure of royal blood whose building projects also deserve particular attention is Edmund, earl of Cornwall, who acceded to the title in 1272. The richest man in England after the king, he was particularly lavish in his patronage of religious institutions. Notable amongst these was Hailes Abbey in Gloucestershire, which his father, Richard, earl of Cornwall and king of the Romans, had founded. To this he bequeathed a phial of Christ's blood; and he probably initiated the rebuilding of the church choir with radiating chapels in the form of Henry III's great abbey church of Westminster. His titular county of Cornwall had been administered since the Norman Conquest from Launceston, where the principal castle of the earls was loc-

176   The gatehouse at St Briavels, Gloucestershire, built between 1292 and 1294 at a cost of £477. In overall form it relates to the Tonbridge-style gatehouses popularised by the king's works in the later thirteenth century. Indeed, the series of spurs – rather than the more usual pair – that ornament each tower precisely echo the treatment of the gatehouse at Tonbridge. In other particulars, however, the building reflects the architectural peculiarities of the Welsh marches. The arches, for example, have almost triangular heads, a treatment derived from the thirteenth-century works at Hereford Cathedral. This detail is also found at nearby Goodrich. The entrance passage was closed by three portcullises, each backed by a pair of heavy doors. Some of the smaller doors opening off the entrance passage also possessed portcullises, an unusual detail paralleled at Tonbridge.

177 (facing page)   Leeds, Kent, is encircled by a large lake or mere. The royal apartments in the Gloriette, shown to the left, are connected to the main castle bailey by a bridge. They included a chapel and a closet, now much restored. The building to the right was constructed in 1822. Leeds consistently remained a popular resort for kings and queens throughout the Middle Ages and was repeatedly adapted to suit their needs. It was successfully taken by force in 1321 as part of a carefully planned operation by Edward II to overcome his opponents.

178 (*top*) The great tower of Restormel, Cornwall, was constructed in the 1270s by the earl of Cornwall. Close to the administrative centre of the lucrative tin-mining industry at Lostwithiel, the earl redeveloped this castle as his principal Cornish seat. The building appears to follow deliberately in the tradition of Cornish castles held by the earls, all of which (except Tintagel) possessed mottes with walled enclosures on the summit. In the bailey beside the tower – which was counter-intuitively described in a survey of 1337 as being outside the castle – was a hall and chapel. A park for hunting was also established beside the castle.

179 (*bottom*) The great tower at Restormel was laid out in the 1270s on a circular plan with a ring of chambers arranged around a small central court. Its regular scheme was interrupted only by the entrance gate and the chapel. The principal apartments, including kitchens, a hall and chamber, were on the upper floor of the building. In a survey of 1337 mention is made of a lead water conduit that supplied the kitchen and a valuable alabaster sculpture of the Virgin in the chapel. The distinctive plan of the building anticipates several important castle designs over the next century, including the great tower at Flint and Queenborough, Kent.

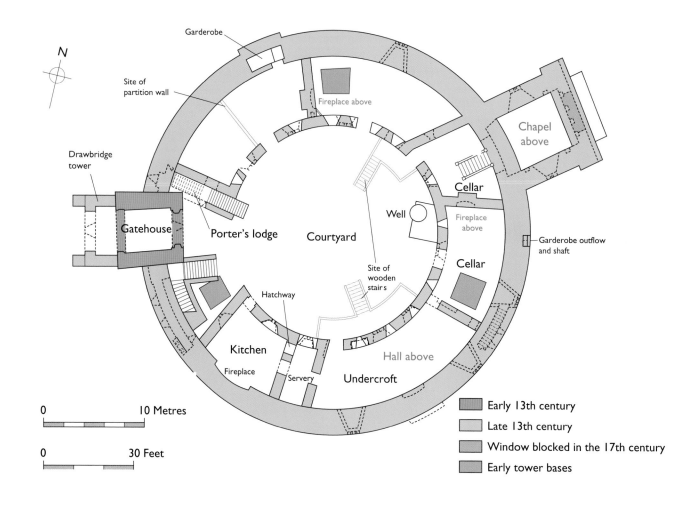

N

Garderobe

Site of partition wall

Fireplace above

Chapel above

Drawbridge tower

Cellar

Well

Gatehouse

Porter's lodge

Courtyard

Fireplace above

Garderobe outflow and shaft

Cellar

Site of wooden stairs

Hatchway

Kitchen

Fireplace

Servery

Hall above

Undercroft

0   10 Metres

0   30 Feet

■ Early 13th century
□ Late 13th century
■ Window blocked in the 17th century
■ Early tower bases

of the motte at Totnes in Devon. If he did so, the work presumably followed a survey of 1273, which described the castle as being in an advanced state of ruin.[25] Edmund died in 1299 without issue and was buried at Hailes Abbey. At his death, the wider possessions of the earldom spanned the entire kingdom and supported a network of castles almost without parallel for their quantity and scale. Edward I received them gratefully, but they were to find another master in the reign of his son: Piers Gaveston, whose career will engage us in a moment.

THE GREAT CAUSE AND THE NORTH OF ENGLAND

On a stormy night in March 1286, while riding to meet his wife at Kinghorn in Fife, Alexander III of Scotland was killed falling from his horse. His death was the opening incident in a celebrated dispute over the succession to the Scottish throne that was to drag England and Scotland into prolonged and damaging conflict. Alexander's only direct heir was his granddaughter, Margaret, the Maid of Norway. When she died on her way back to the kingdom, the inheritance was opened up to a wider field of contestants. Through his own direct intervention and the agency of the bishop of Durham, Anthony Bek, Edward I established himself as arbiter in the inheritance dispute. The two pre-eminent rivals that emerged in the so-called Great Cause were Robert Bruce, earl of Carrick and lord of Annandale, and John Balliol, the lord of Barnard Castle, Co. Durham. In November 1292, following prolonged discussions at Bek's castle of Norham, Edward determined in favour of Balliol, who was subsequently installed as John I of Scotland.

The basis for Edward's intervention in the Great Cause was his claim to feudal overlordship of Scotland, itself an issue of long-standing contention between the English and Scottish kings. Balliol, however, was prepared to perform homage to Edward I for Scotland in return for the throne. Having received this, Edward I immediately began to make aggressive assertion of his feudal position, and relations between the two kingdoms soured. In 1295, inept in his management of affairs and unable to satisfy Edward I, John was deposed by a council of Scottish nobles. This body then made an alliance with the French king, Philip IV, who was at war with England. Edward I was amply furnished with reasons for war and in March 1296 he

180   An engraving of Trematon published in W. Borlase, *Antiquities, Historical and Monumental of the County of Cornwall* (London, 1769). The castle was bought by Richard, earl of Cornwall, in 1270, the year before his death. A survey of 1337 specifically attributes the domestic buildings of the castle – including a hall, kitchen and two-storeyed chamber – to his son, Earl Edmund. These were timber-framed. Edmund may also have built or repaired the stone circuit of walls, including the enclosure on the motte. A house was built in the bailey in 1807.

ated. But Launceston was peripheral in geographic terms to the county and Edmund moved his seat of authority to the more central Lostwithiel. It was almost certainly in conjunction with this move that he substantially remodelled the nearby castle of Restormel during the 1270s.

On the top of the castle motte at Restormel was laid out a ring of buildings on an almost perfect circular plan nearly 130 feet (40 m) in circumference (pl. 178). The only elements that broke the regular outline of this ring were the gatehouse to the motte, which was preserved from the earlier castle on the site, and the chapel. Arranged within this structure were all the apartments of a great secular residence, one of the most complete suites of such chambers to survive from the thirteenth century in England (pl. 179). This remarkable structure is certainly to be understood as a fashionable version of an architectural form – the motte with a low walled enclosure on the summit – common to all the major castles held by the earl in Cornwall. Across such a large geographic area and within the estates of a wealthy earldom, the consistent preference for such enclosures on mottes (over free-standing great towers of stone) is remarkable. It may suggest that the form was thought of as symbolic of the earldom and was being actively used by Edmund as a mark of his lordship in the region.

Edmund was also involved in repairing other castles in Cornwall, including Trematon (pl. 180). Here he created a new group of domestic buildings in timber frame within the masonry fortifications of the castle, which he may additionally have repaired or remodelled.[24] It is also supposed on the basis of stylistic evidence that he repaired the wall encircling the summit mustered an army in Newcastle upon Tyne with the intention of conquering Scotland.

Berwick-upon-Tweed was the first town to fall to Edward I and its male population was massacred. Immediately thereafter work began to a new fortified borough and castle on the site. Edward himself ceremonially moved a wheelbarrow of earth to inaugurate the building operations of what was to become the new seat of Scotland's administration.[26] Aside from being accessible by sea, the choice of Berwick as an administrative centre for Scotland is remarkable. Set in this most southerly corner of the Scottish kingdom, it speaks volumes about the geographically limited nature of English interests.

Berwick Castle has suffered severely, both from later adaptation and from the construction of the railway station and the spectacular Royal Border Bridge completed by Robert Stephenson in 1850. Nevertheless, there survive fragments of two polygonal towers almost certainly begun in the 1290s. One of these formed part of a gatehouse that is otherwise described in medieval documents as forming part of an exceptionally elaborate fortified entrance complex.[27] The form and detailing of both surviving towers – in terms of plan and details such as arrow loops – resemble those found on a grander scale at Caernarfon Castle. This is the first of many indications, also substantiated in the documentary record, that numerous of the king's masons moved from Wales to Scotland.

From Berwick Edward subdued Scotland in an astonishing twenty-one-week campaign, seizing all the major castles on his route and defeating the Scots at Dunbar. Having formally deposed King John in a deliberately humiliating ceremony, he passed on the royal seal of Scotland to his new lieutenant, remarking coarsely: 'He who rids himself of a turd does a good thing.'[28] In symbol of the annexation of Scotland he removed the Stone of Scone, on which the Scottish kings were crowned, to Westminster Abbey. There it remained in its specially constructed thirteenth-century throne until 1996, when, in another calculated act of propaganda (by the Conservative Government of John Major) amidst much pomp and ceremonial, it was packaged back off to Edinburgh. Scotland appeared to suffer in this conquest the fate of Wales, but its situation was in fact very different. Unlike Wales, Scotland was a kingdom and enjoyed close ties with England in both familial and political terms. These circumstances lent its resistance to Edward's direct rule both conviction and resilience.

Within a year of the conquest there was popular rising against the English government led by William Wallace and backed by Robert Bruce, grandson of the former claimant to the throne. In 1298 Edward I responded with another massive invasion and again defeated the Scots in a pitched battle at Falkirk. This victory, however, did not regain him control of the kingdom. Scottish resistance was withdrawn beyond the reach of his forces and effective English government was limited to the south of Scotland. At great expense during a period of financial difficulty, Edward launched three further campaigns into Scotland, in 1300, 1301 and 1303. In each case the Scots refused to meet the English army in the open field. Castles consequently came to play a crucial strategic role for the English: it was only by controlling them that it was possible to hold on to Scottish territory between campaigns.[29]

Despite the increasing importance of castles, Edward I never built in Scotland in the way that he had done in Wales. Existing castles tended to be patched up or slightly expanded rather than redeveloped. Moreover, most of the building that he did undertake in Scotland was of timber. At Linlithgow, for example, Edward created a palisaded enclosure or piel to serve as the winter quarters for his army in November 1301. The following spring he determined to strengthen what was described as 'la fermete de Linliscu'. In discussion with James of St George's, who had come to Scotland from Wales, an indenture describing the proposed work was drawn up: a gatehouse and two towers were to be erected in stone along the perimeter of the palisade and the site enlarged to incorporate the nearby church as part of the outer defences. Had this plan been executed, Linlithgow would have been the most ambitious Edwardian fortification of the conquest after Berwick. But its relative modesty is in marked contrast to Welsh precedent. In the event, however, the whole operation was completed in timber and only its earthworks survive.[30]

Part of the reason for this modesty of construction was certainly financial: by 1296 the English administration was vastly overstretched and money was running short. It may also have become difficult to raise sufficient manpower. In 1297, for example, the king's workmen in Scotland refused to travel to Dunfermline because of the arrears of wages they were owed.[31] Probably more important, however, was the existing pattern of feudal landholding in Scotland. Edward I was not carving out new territory for himself as he had done in Wales. Rather, he was trying to get himself recognised as an overlord by an established group of barons. These men already possessed castles, some of them buildings of considerable architectural pretension. There was – in other words – no need for the same scale of royal building as in Wales.

When the coercion of the Scottish nobility clearly began to fail, Edward tried to drive forward the conquest in 1298 by granting Scottish estates to English nobles. In some cases these estates were offered to new lords prior to their capture, but in no case did such grants encourage castle construction on any scale. This indicates both the politically tenuous nature of these gifts and their limited financial value. Such work as is attributed to new owners – often rather doubtfully – seems to have involved only minor repair or the addition of some new element to the defences of individual castles. At Kildrummy, Aberdeenshire, for example, the similarities of the gatehouse to that at Harlech have won this building an English attribution.[32] Perhaps the most ambitious castle of the campaign was erected in the 1290s (it was described as just begun in August 1298)[33] by a Scotsman, Sir Ralph Siward, at Tibbers, Dumfriesshire. Edward I promised to contribute £100 to its cost, and the project was of sufficient importance that when the treasury failed to pay up the full sum the king wrote an irritated note in June 1302 demanding that money be found.[34] This is a relatively modest stone castle on a rectangular plan with drum towers.

There emerges from the documentary evidence of the reconquest of Scotland after 1296 much fascinating information about the conduct of sieges. These were the only tangible military successes the English enjoyed. The siege of Caerlaverock in 1300 – an impressive triangular castle of the 1270s – was even celebrated in a contemporary poem, which describes the two-day confrontation in detail. The account is strikingly concerned with heraldry and is hard to unpick in many details, though it explains the situation and form of the castle in such detail that the poem must have been written by, or its composition informed by, an eyewitness:

Its shape was like that of a shield, for it had only three sides all round, with a tower on each angle; but one of them [the towers] was a double one (*jumelee*), so high, so long, and so large, that under it was the gate with a drawbridge (*pont tournis*), well made and strong, and a sufficiency of other de-

fences. It had good walls, and good ditches filled to the edge with water; and I believe there never was seen a castle more beautifully situated (*plus belle de lui seoir*), for at once could be seen the Irish sea towards the West, and the north a fine country, surrounded by an arm of the sea.[35]

Interestingly, the poem also stresses the scale, splendour and comfort of the English camp, its tents strewn with leaves, herbs and flowers picked from the surrounds.[36] The castle was invested by sea and land, and the fighting comes across as comprising rather confused episodes of frenetic stone throwing preceded by an unhappy massacre of foot soldiers, who launched the attack.

What emerges from the records of this and other sieges is an impression of the extraordinary diversity and scale of resources that Edward commanded, as well as of the invention, flexibility and mobility of timber-frame military hardware. At Bothwell in 1301, for example, a huge tower or belfry covered in hides was constructed to overtop the defences and was brought to the site on thirty carts from Glasgow.[37] Even more remarkable was the provision of three bridges for the army to cross the Firth of Forth in 1303. These were constructed at King's Lynn in Norfolk and brought north by sea in a fleet of ships. Each bridge incorporated a fortified gate with a drawbridge. Two were also mounted with a type of large crossbow called a springald.[38]

The most elaborate siege of the campaign was also its last. For three months in 1304 William Oliphant held Stirling for King John. The English queen and her ladies, who joined Edward I outside the walls of the castle, were provided with a viewing loft from which to observe the siege in comfort. They cannot have been disappointed. A host of stone-throwing machines were brought to the castle, many of which were sufficiently large to be individually named in the accounts with titles such as 'the Parson', 'the Vicar', 'Gloucester' and 'Weland'. To create the counterweights for some of these catapults it was necessary to strip lead from surrounding church roofs, though it was piously instructed that the altars of the affected buildings should remain protected from the elements. A great battering ram was also constructed to force an entry into the castle. But Edward's pride and joy was the 'war-wolf' or *lupus guerrae*. This leviathan stone-throwing machine took fifty men and five master carpenters more than a week to assemble and the Scots

surrendered before it was complete. Edward, however, insisted that the garrison remain in the castle till the weapon had been tested.[39]

The fall of Stirling brought about the final collapse of King John's cause and in 1305 Edward imposed through parliament a new settlement on Scotland. His new royal lieutenant and warden of Scotland was John, duke of Brittany, who may have taken the opportunity of his appointment to develop his ancestral castle at Richmond. Within a year of the 1305 settlement, however, English rule was once again challenged. Robert Bruce, who had surrendered to Edward I in the winter of 1301–2 and contributed his own catapults to the siege of Stirling, laid claim to the throne of Scotland and was crowned at Scone on 25 March 1306. In its first year the cause of Robert I enjoyed little success, but it survived. Edward I was too ill to fight in person, and having marched north was forced to winter in Lanercost Priory in Cumberland. From a distance, he meted out unusually savage punishment to captives implicated in what he regarded as a rebellion. Amongst other things, he famously displayed Bruce's sister, Mary, and the countess of Buchan in cages from the walls of the castles at Roxburgh and Berwick. In the spring of 1307 there followed the defeat in skirmishes of two of his principal commanders and on 7 July the king himself died on the march to Scotland.

The death of Edward I brought about a profound change in the Anglo–Scottish conflict. Robert I was now able to consolidate his position, winning over Scottish opponents and stabilising his kingdom. The English, meanwhile, prepared for a renewal of the war under Edward II. Their wait was accompanied by a flurry of castle building as the winners from the war spent their money and prepared for the next round of hostilities. Particularly prominent were two of Edward I's principal commanders in the Scottish wars. Henry Percy, in origin a Sussex knight, had been richly rewarded in royal service and amassed properties in Cumberland, Westmorland and Yorkshire, as well as grants of land in the Scottish lowlands. It was probably with the intention of recapturing the latter properties that in 1309 he bought the castle and barony of Alnwick. At the time he was clearly engaged in consolidating his wider patrimony, having received licence in October 1308 to fortify manors in his Yorkshire estates at Leconfield and Spofforth and his Sussex seat of Petworth.[40]

Henry Percy's work at Alnwick amounted virtually to a complete reconstruction of the heart of the castle and probably followed immediately upon its purchase

181 The Middle Gate at Alnwick, Northumberland, was probably built in the 1310s and divides the two outer baileys of the castle. Its fenestration is largely nineteenth-century, inserted by the architect Anthony Salvin during his restoration of the castle from 1852. The D-shaped tower to the left rises from spur bases similar to those found at Caerphilly, Goodrich, Chepstow and Carew. The detail implies that the master mason at Alnwick was connected with the king's works and the castles of the previous generation in south Wales. It is likely that the eighteenth-century battlement figures replace fourteenth-century originals.

182 A view of Brougham, Westmorland. The great tower in the centre was built around 1214 by Robert de Vieuxpont. After 1309 Roger Clifford heightened the tower and ringed it with new buildings: a new gatehouse and barbican to the right and an outer wall lined with domestic buildings including a chapel. The towers along the wall were rectangular in plan. The upper chambers of the great tower and gatehouse were connected to create an extended sequence of withdrawing chambers. These remained the most important domestic chambers in the castle throughout its subsequent history: according to her diary, Lady Anne Clifford used one of the rooms above the gate as a bedchamber in the 1650s. She also describes it as the room in which her father had been born and her mother had died. James I was received at Brougham in 1617.

183 A view of Brough, Westmorland, across the former castle ditch. Robert Clifford constructed the D-shaped tower and hall block in the foreground. Together they housed a complete suite of grand domestic apartments. These perhaps resembled the apartments that he created at nearby Appleby, which have been much reworked subsequently. The castle was restored by the dowager countess of Pembroke, Lady Anne Clifford, between 1659 and 1661. She stayed here regularly and divided her time between what she called the 'Roman Tower' of around 1200 – in the background – and the fourteenth-century apartments. When she resided in the latter her own bedroom was in 'Clifford's Tower' to the right, which she named after its builder.

in 1309. A new inner bailey was constructed in the form of a circle of D-shaped towers enclosing the domestic apartments. Probably in conjunction with this he also built the Middle Gate that connects the two baileys of the castle. This included a single tower rising from a spur base in the style distinctive of such castles as Goodrich and Caerphilly (pl. 181). The detail strongly implies the involvement of a royal mason in the work.

Robert Clifford was also well rewarded for his services in the Scottish wars. His English landholdings lay in Cumberland and Westmorland and he further received grants of Scottish estates. Like Henry Percy, he worked quickly to develop the castles on his properties during the enforced lull in hostilities. In 1309 he received licence to crenellate the castle at Brougham in Westmorland, which he enclosed in a new stone wall set with rectangular towers and a gatehouse (pl. 182). The great tower at the heart of the site was raised by a storey and its upper floor provided with an elegant oratory.[41] This arrangement may have compared closely to that in a lost tower begun in 1308 for the king at nearby Carlisle Castle, later known as the Queen Mary Tower.[42] Immediately beside the great tower at Brougham, Clifford also constructed a connected pair of gatehouses that incorporated spacious domestic apartments. On the front of this there now survives a reset foundation stone with an inscription recording

the mid-fourteenth-century work of Robert's grandson to the castle. It reads simply: 'Thys made Roger'.

In 1310 Clifford further received the lordship of Skipton from Edward II and fortified the inner bailey in stone. The circuit of D-shaped towers that he erected is very similar in both form and scale to that found at Alnwick. In technical detail, the towers also bear some formal points of comparison with the roughly contemporary work at Chirk in Denbighshire. Whether he also constructed the outer gate at Skipton, as has been asserted, is open to question.[43] In the same year Clifford remodelled the baileys at Brough (pl. 183) and Appleby in Westmorland. In each case he erected new domestic apartments that were linked to a tower on a D-shaped plan.

The prizes of the Scottish wars were also turned to architectural use much further from the border. William, Lord Roos played a prominent role in Edward I's Scottish campaigns and was appointed joint lieutenant and warden of Scotland in 1308. He was probably the figure responsible for further improving Helmsley Castle in Yorkshire in the first decade of the fourteenth century. Besides rebuilding the hall, he raised the great tower of the castle dating from the 1220s by a storey and provided it with ear turrets in the unmistakable fashion of the Beauchamp Tower at London (pl. 184). It was probably Scottish plunder

184 The great tower of
Helmsley, Yorkshire, was
begun in the first quarter of
the thirteenth century. It is
D-shaped in plan, though
the outer face was demolished
when the castle was slighted

in the 1640s. In the early
fourteenth century the tower
was raised in height by one
storey. As part of this
operation it was provided
with little ear turrets, a detail
of design popularised by the

royal works. The surprisingly
delicate moulding of the
battlements compares to that
found on the Marten's Tower
at Chepstow, which is securely
attributed to a London mason
(see pl. 147).

from Edward I's campaigns that later gave Sir Edmund Bacon the wherewithal to fortify his manor at Gresham in Norfolk around 1318. Here he raised a quadrangular castle in classic Gothic form with a drum tower at each corner. Nothing but the outline of this moated site now remains.

By 1311 Robert I was sufficiently established in Scotland to go on the offensive and begin regular raids south of the border. He had no intention of capturing English territory, but simply to prey upon it. The results in some areas were crippling. Edward II, meanwhile, remained embroiled in political difficulties and the north of England was forced to look to its own safety. Ongoing castle projects may have been hastened forward in the circumstances, but there is little evidence that the situation elicited any architectural response at all. Indeed, the interest of northern barons was now focused on internal English politics rather than the unwelcome disturbances along the Scottish border.

In the meantime, important English castles in Scotland began to fall into Robert's possession. The Scots pursued a policy of demolishing these buildings to prevent their reoccupation. Perth was captured in 1313, as were Roxburgh and Edinburgh early the following year. Stirling also agreed to surrender if it was not relieved by midsummer 1314. Edward II was finally compelled to meet the crisis and led a large army north in what was clearly viewed by contemporaries as a trial of strength. Within sight of Stirling, at Bannockburn on 24 June, the larger and better-equipped English army was routed and Edward II himself narrowly escaped capture. From this moment forward, until the unconditional acknowledgement of Scottish independence by the treaty of Edinburgh on 17 March 1328, the theatre of the Anglo–Scottish conflict moved decisively south of the border. Carlisle was unsuccessfully invested by the Scots in 1315 (pl. 185), and in 1318 Berwick itself, the base of the English conquest, fell. These disasters coincided with a famine in the years 1315–17. Royal administration in the north of England collapsed and the region became prey to Scottish extortion on a spectacular scale.

The overall effect of these events was to create a series of violent but very localised fluctuations in economic and political fortune. Paying heavy tribute to the Scots and with the revenue from their estates disastrously reduced, the owners of northern estates were not readily moved to undertake architectural projects of any kind. Some individuals chose to escape from the situation altogether. The son and heir of William, Lord

185 (*top*) The opening initial of a royal charter issued by Edward II in 1315–16 granting the city of Carlisle to its citizens. In and around the letter 'E' is portrayed the Scottish siege of 1315, a defining moment in the medieval history of the city. The knight about to hurl his spear at the top centre is identified by the heraldry on his shield as Robert Harcla, who led the defence. Beside him a mounted crossbow or springald is being wound up by a defender. To the left is a Scottish trebuchet or catapult loaded with a stone. Beneath the walls there is a group of attackers, one with a pick, one with a shield and spear, one with a bow and arrow and another climbing the walls. Unlike their Scottish opponents, the English are shown in armour.

186 (*bottom*) The outer wall of Pickering, Yorkshire, erected by Edward II between 1323 and 1326. It is very significant that all Edward II's towers at Pickering are rectangular in plan. They are in fact the first towers on this plan constructed by royal masons since the Gothic revolution of the early thirteenth century. Towers on a rectangular plan were to be one of the staples of castle architecture in the Perpendicular style. The detailing of the towers is boldly conceived with heavy mouldings drawn from the castle works of Edward I's reign. At intervals between the towers there were small turrets projected at parapet level from the wall, fragments of which survive.

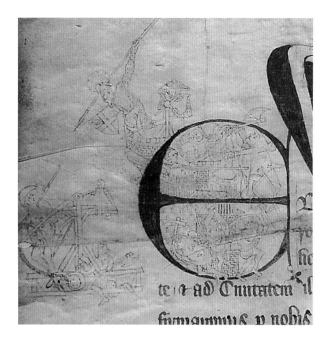

Roos of Helmsley, for example, rendered up the border castle of Wark in return for lands in the more peaceful south of England.[44] In this critical situation, the resources of the crown gradually became central to the defence of the region. These were particularly expended on provisioning castles with men, who could be deployed to frustrate raids and swell the numbers of expeditionary forces.

At Warkworth in 1319, for instance, four men-at-arms and eight *hobelers* or light cavalry were provided

by the king to serve with the existing garrison of twelve men-at-arms. And in 1322 the constable joined the royal army on its march into Scotland with twenty-six *hobelers* from the garrison. Nevertheless, morale was sufficiently low for these forces to neglect their duties and in 1322 Edward II wrote to reprimand the constable of Warkworth for failing to intercept Scottish raids. There were also complaints that some constables had started to charge men for nights of safety within the walls of the castles they commanded.[45] In some cases, however, even the safety provided by castle walls was in question: there were difficulties maintaining garrisons, and walled cities, including Durham, became depopulated.[46]

In 1322 Edward II was nearly captured in Yorkshire while returning from another disastrous campaign into Scotland. The event was a prelude to a truce that at last gave the border some respite from Scottish incursions. Many castles such as Carlisle underwent long-awaited repairs, and others were enlarged. At Prudhoe, for example, a piel or palisaded enclosure was constructed outside the castle in 1325–6 at royal direction. Its purpose is not known and only its earthwork outline survives. The most important architectural project, however, was the remodelling of Pickering Castle in Yorkshire. Between 1323 and 1326, at the king's direct command, a new stone wall with towers on a rectangular plan was constructed along the southern and eastern sides of the castle (pl. 186).[47] Rectan-

187 A reconstruction by David Simon of Piel, Lancashire, around 1350. The castle was built by the abbots of Furness, a wealthy Cistercian abbey with responsibilities for the defence of the western march with Scotland. They received a royal licence for its construction on 26 September 1327. The castle was presumably intended to control trade with the Isle of Man and Ireland. Apparent in the great tower – which is designed on a four-square plan with two spine walls – is the unfaded spirit of Romanesque castle architecture. The tower is entered through a projecting porch, which is integral conceptually with the building (though the masonry of the two structures is not bonded together). Inside the tower were two grandly conceived upper floors set over a basement level. Its parapets were crowned by watch turrets. The tower was enclosed on the landward side by two concentric lines of fortification. There is a local parallel for the form of the outer towers in the fourteenth-century works at Gleaston a few miles away.

gular towers had never entirely fallen out of favour in the north of England during the thirteenth century. Nevertheless, these are the first examples of structures in this form produced in the king's works since the twelfth century. They look forward to the renewed popularity of the form across England in the four-teenth century.

Two other notable buildings from early in Edward III's reign deserve mention in the present context, both of which were undertaken by religious institutions in close proximity to strategically important harbours. At Lindisfarne, a cell of Durham Priory, the vulnerable convent was fortified with an enclosure wall and the church built up with a parapet of battlements. This architectural conversion probably took place around 1330 and was subsequently regretted by the monks, who petitioned that the cell be rendered defenceless in 1385.[48] On the opposite coast, in Lancashire, the wealthy abbot and convent of Furness received a licence from the king in 1327 to build a castle on a tidal island at Piel (pl. 187).[49] The castle occupies a large rectangu-lar site on the shore and possessed at its heart a massive great tower on a rectangular plan. The abbey, which

247

188 A photograph taken in 1872 of the Water Tower, Kenilworth, Warwickshire, probably built around 1310. During the subsequent restoration of the tower the doorway in the lowest storey was patched over. The luxuriously appointed rooms in the upper floor with large windows must have enjoyed fine views. It is significant that the detailing of the original window tracery (visible to the left) is austere and archaic in form, a conceit found in other castle buildings of the fourteenth century, such as Alnwick (Northumberland) and Bodiam (Sussex). Such detailing may have been intended to make the exterior look rugged and old, characteristics appropriate to a castle. With spur bases and large cross-shaped arrow loops, the Water Tower appears to relate to late thirteenth-century architecture in south Wales and the march, as at Goodrich, Herefordshire.

had shouldered considerable military responsibility in the north-west, also constructed more modest towers on several neighbouring manors such as Dalton.[50]

EDWARD II AND THE POLITICS OF FAVOURITISM

By a charter dated 6 August 1307 at Dumfries, just one month after the death of his father, Edward II bestowed the recently extinct earldom of Cornwall and all its estates upon a Gascon knight called Piers Gaveston. By any standards the grant of this great landholding was an extraordinary gift and it was followed in quick succession by other outstanding marks of favour. On 26 December 1307 Gaveston was appointed regent in anticipation of the king's absence in France. He then played a leading role at the coronation in February 1308, bearing the crown in procession and fastening a golden spur to Edward's left foot. The king's generosity was prompted by an affection that had first sprung up between the two men in the closing years of the previous reign. The precise nature of their relationship – whether fraternal or sexual – is not now clear, but to most observers it was made unpalatable

248

both by its strength and by Gaveston's behaviour. At the coronation, for example, his extravagant dress in regal purple furnished with pearls as well as his arrogant deportment so disgusted the king's brothers-in-law, Charles de Valois and Louis d'Evreux, that they left the celebrations early.[51]

Gaveston quickly developed a formidable array of enemies and pressure mounted on the king to have him removed from court. This was briefly achieved in June 1308, but Gaveston returned seven months later and the tension between the king and his opponents intensified. By 1309 there emerged as the leader of the opposition or reforming party the figure of Thomas, earl of Lancaster. A cousin of the king, Thomas was both by birth and inheritance a powerful man with a patrimony comprising the three earldoms of Leicester, Lancaster and Derby. Following the death of his father-in-law, Henry de Lacy, in 1311, he added to these possessions the earldoms of Lincoln and Salisbury and clearly emerged as the first peer of the realm. This impressive body of titles and possessions brought with it an income of about £11,000 a year and a huge belt of contiguous landholdings in the north Midlands, southern Yorkshire and Lancashire, besides numerous outlying estates across England and Wales. It also permitted him to maintain a following of around fifty knights, many of whom were powerful enough to maintain retinues of their own. As events would prove, he could field a small army when the need arose.

Lancaster was a central figure in forcing the king in March 1310 to appoint twenty-one so-called lords ordainer, a group charged with reforming the realm and its government. Inevitably, they pressed for Gaveston's exile and the favourite left England in October 1311. Two months later he was back and was reunited with the king at Knaresborough. As we shall see at the end of the chapter, this castle had been specially remodelled for him at royal expense. Soon afterwards, at York, Gaveston was defiantly restored to all his English honours. Lancaster hurriedly orchestrated a northern campaign to seize the exile. The royal party narrowly escaped capture at Newcastle upon Tyne, where the king's treasure was seized, and Gaveston took refuge at Scarborough Castle. After a ten-day siege he surrendered with promise of safe conduct and began a journey southwards, possibly to Wallingford Castle, as a prisoner. On the way, at Deddington in Oxfordshire, one of Gaveston's inveterate enemies, the earl of Warwick, captured him in an early morning raid. A summary trial followed at Warwick Castle presided

189 Dunstanburgh, Northumberland, was begun in 1313 on the site of an Iron Age fort. Its great gatehouse looks southwards towards the sea and England (1). The towers along the wall probably date to the 1320s and are rectangular in plan, a very early example of this form in a court-connected building. The idea of projecting subsidiary turrets out at the head of the wall (2) is also found in Edward II's contemporary works at Pickering, Yorkshire. The first tower to the right (3) was subsumed within the constable's lodgings and the tower to the extreme right incorporated a small gate (4).

over by Lancaster. Amidst scenes of public rejoicing, he was led a few miles to Blacklow Hill on the earl of Lancaster's estates, and executed.[52]

Gaveston's execution split the reforming party and poisoned the king against those implicated in it. Lancaster was himself forced into political isolation and he responded with a spate of castle building. The full details of this are impossible to reconstruct in detail, but surviving accounts show that during 1313–14 major architectural works were under way in at least five of his principal castles. At his favourite residence of Pontefract in Yorkshire a new tower was in the course of construction, and at Tutbury, the focus of the earl's Staffordshire estates, the gatehouse of the castle was being rebuilt (see pl. 335). In the same year the castle at Melbourne in Derbyshire, now destroyed, was in the course of reconstruction. Finally, at Kenilworth work was in hand on a new collegiate church in the outer bailey, a very early example of a type of religious foundation that was to become an essential element in the greatest late medieval castles. Possibly in conjunction with this work the lower bailey defences at Kenilworth were reorganised with the construction of the Water Tower (pl. 188).

Besides his activity in the heartlands of his power, the earl of Lancaster also built one castle outside his sphere of influence on the very fringes of the realm. At Dunstanburgh in Northumberland a new castle was

begun in 1313 on a dramatic coastal promontory above a small harbour (pl. 189). It made use of the defences of an earlier Iron Age fort and was encircled on its landward side by a series of three specially created meres, which were possibly protected by lost outer defences of timber (pl. 190). The castle controlled no important estates owned by the earl and was erected in an area where he had no substantial following. In the circumstances it seems most likely to have been intended as a bolthole should the political situation in England become untenable. During 1313–14 work was under way on the gatehouse that served as the architectural focus of the castle, under the direction of a certain Elias the Mason. The gatehouse at Dunstanburgh is essentially a very large version of a classic twin-tower gatehouse of the period, incorporating substantial domestic apartments to the rear (pl. 191). Following the completion of the gatehouse, probably around 1320, a wall punctuated by rectangular towers was constructed running down to the sea.

In 1314 the earl of Lancaster's situation in England was transformed by the catastrophe of the battle of Bannockburn. The earl had refused to join the royal expedition and in the ensuing crisis the king was forced to sue for his support and accept the reform of the court. Within two years, however, the earl of Lancaster had fallen out with Edward II and a new group

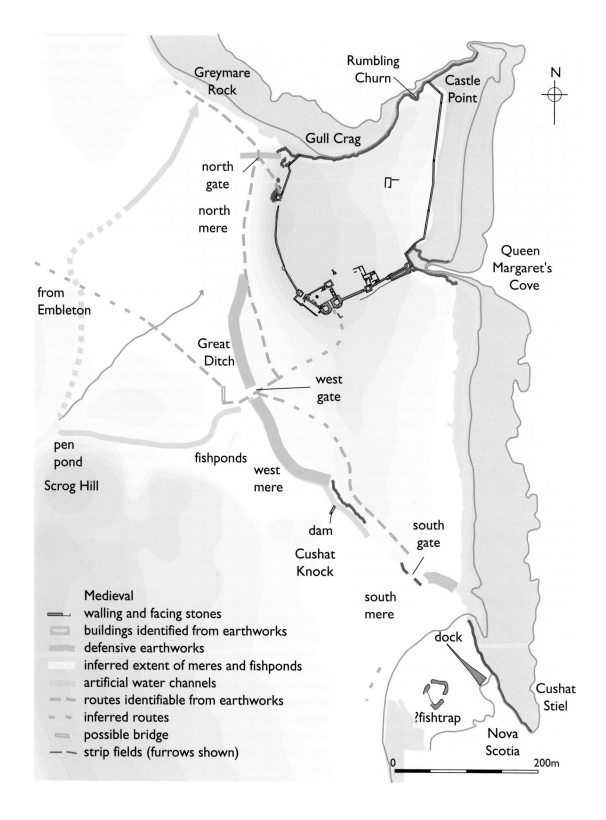

190 An English Heritage survey of 2006 by Alastair Oswald of Dunstanburgh, Northumberland. It has revealed a complex surrounding medieval landscape. The landward approach to the castle was from the west. It crossed a line of artificial meres fed by natural springs and regulated through a system of sluices. The meres defined an outer bailey that was probably fortified with timber palisades and gates. The fresh water from the springs was also used to supply small fish-ponds. On the seashore beneath the castle and facing the main gate was a quay for ships and beside it a fish trap. The scale and elaboration of the Dunstanburgh landscape was by no means unusual in the period. The arrangements were simultaneously of defensive, aesthetic and economic importance.

of royal favourites began to establish themselves. Principal amongst them were a father and son, the Older and Younger Hugh Despenser. The Older Despenser was a long-standing associate of the king and had been driven from the court by Lancaster in 1314. One mark of his political rehabilitation was the grant of an ancestral castle at Elmley in Worcestershire in 1317.[53] Unfor-

tunately, little survives today of the buildings on the site but their restoration may have been connected with the early fourteenth-century remodelling of the choir at Tewkesbury Abbey, which was chosen as the family mausoleum. His son rose to favour only from 1319, by which time an unexpected dynastic disaster had presented the prospect of a rich prize.

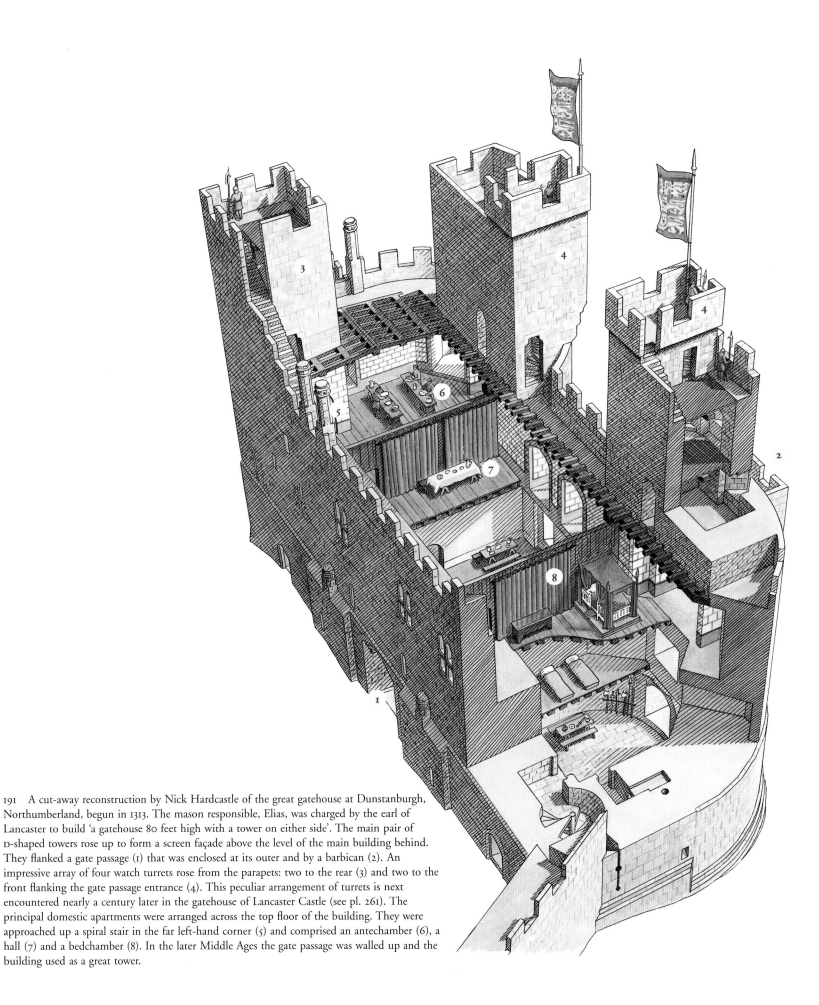

191 A cut-away reconstruction by Nick Hardcastle of the great gatehouse at Dunstanburgh, Northumberland, begun in 1313. The mason responsible, Elias, was charged by the earl of Lancaster to build 'a gatehouse 80 feet high with a tower on either side'. The main pair of D-shaped towers rose up to form a screen façade above the level of the main building behind. They flanked a gate passage (1) that was enclosed at its outer and by a barbican (2). An impressive array of four watch turrets rose from the parapets: two to the rear (3) and two to the front flanking the gate passage entrance (4). This peculiar arrangement of turrets is next encountered nearly a century later in the gatehouse of Lancaster Castle (see pl. 261). The principal domestic apartments were arranged across the top floor of the building. They were approached up a spiral stair in the far left-hand corner (5) and comprised an antechamber (6), a hall (7) and a bedchamber (8). In the later Middle Ages the gate passage was walled up and the building used as a great tower.

The mightiest casualty of the battle of Bannockburn was Gilbert de Clare, the earl of Gloucester, who died without children. His patrimony, therefore, devolved upon his three sisters, one of whom had been married in 1306 to the Younger Despenser. It is a mark of his character that Despenser attempted to choose his own portion in advance of a formal settlement by seizing Tonbridge Castle in 1315. Without royal support at this date, he was forced to relinquish his prize. From 1319, however, and acting in conjunction with his father, he used the king's favour to set about appropriating not only Tonbridge but also the lands of all three de Clare sisters. Such unfettered greed eventually drove the marcher lords to rebellion.[54] By prior agreement with the earl of Lancaster on 4 May 1321, there began a campaign in which every single Despenser castle in south Wales was ransacked, with particular attention being given to their financial records.[55] In this destruction we have probably lost all evidence for the designers of the de Clare castles. On 14 August Edward II was forced by this powerful alliance to exile the Despensers on pain of being deposed.

The king capitulated, but then acted quickly to restore his favourites. Having been joined on the Isle of Thanet by the Younger Despenser – who had used his brief exile to engage in piracy and had attacked Southampton – Edward II moved against his enemies in October 1321. The first undertaking was a carefully orchestrated siege of Leeds Castle in Kent. This was followed by a brilliantly successful campaign into the two heartlands of baronial opposition. By mid-January resistance in the marches of Wales collapsed in the face of the royal army. Then, on 16 March 1322 the veteran soldier Robert Harclay defeated the dispirited forces of the earl of Lancaster at Borough-bridge in Yorkshire as they retreated northwards towards Dunstanburgh.

The next day the earl of Lancaster was himself captured, and brought to trial and condemned to death in his own great hall at Pontefract Castle. His downfall at the hands of an unpopular monarch transformed his posthumous reputation from that of an over-mighty subject to simple 'Thomas', a martyr. Within six weeks of his execution miracles were being reported at his tomb and Edward II was compelled to post guards to keep people away. So did the obdurate earl at last become an object of popular devotion.

In celebration of his victory, meanwhile, Edward II created the Older Despenser earl of Winchester and Robert Harclay earl of Carlisle. He also directed a remarkably bloody purge of his political opposition, with the result that for the next four years the position of the Despensers was unassailable. Their wealth and security now encouraged them to undertake the wholesale restoration of their castles. In architectural terms this appears largely to have been a matter of patching and improvement, but it did include one outstandingly important building, the great hall erected at Caerphilly by the Younger Despenser. The master mason responsible was a certain Thomas de la Bataile, who had previously worked on the remodelling of Leeds Castle for Edward I's queen, Eleanor of Castile (he was possibly from Battel Manor at Leeds). And the interior was roofed in 1326 by William Hurley, master carpenter of St Stephen's Chapel, Westminster.[56]

The prolonged conflict between the king, his favourites and the reformers combined with the disasters of the reign – both natural and politically induced – profoundly coloured architectural patronage at every level. Leaders on both sides actively encouraged their followers to seize control of local government, and areas of England became subject to the arbitrary rule of petty tyrants. In Northumberland, for example, the earl of Lancaster maintained an extremely unsavoury following that included several figures implicated in the internationally notorious assault on a party of churchmen including two cardinals in 1317. The earl, indeed, may have actively backed this outrage. In the main, such figures operated on a small scale but some were of sufficient standing to build.

Complaints were made to the king in 1311, for example, that Sir John de Somery so mastered Staffordshire 'that no one can obtain law or justice therin; that he has made himself more than a king there; that no one can dwell there unless he buys protection from him either by money or assisting him in building his castles'.[57] Amongst the buildings almost certainly erected by this man was the great tower of his principal castle at Dudley. There is no evidence to date this building more specifically than within Sir John's ownership of the castle between 1300 and 1321. It is very likely to have been raised as a mark of status following his elevation to the title of Lord Somery in 1308. This ill-gotten castle was later extorted from his successor by the Younger Despenser in 1325.[58]

When the fall of the Despensers finally came it was as dramatic as unexpected. In 1325 Edward II sent both his queen and his son Edward to France on a diplomatic mission. Once there, Queen Isabella refused to return to England until the Younger Despenser was removed from power, claiming that he had intruded into their marriage. In France she fell into the company of Robert Mortimer, a marcher lord implicated in the rising of 1321. He had been imprisoned in the Tower of London, from which he had escaped, with poetic judgement, on the feast of St Peter in Chains. Isabella and Mortimer became lovers and declared their intention of invading England. They landed on 24 September 1326 at Orwell in Suffolk with a small force and Edward II's government fell to pieces. Both the Despensers were quickly captured and executed, the Younger with particular barbarity. Edward II was then taken to Kenilworth Castle, the old residence of his former rival the earl of Lancaster. There he was persuaded to resign the throne in favour of his fourteen-year-old son, Edward, who was crowned king on 1 February 1327.[59]

For the first three years of his reign, Edward III was nothing more than the puppet of Isabella and Mortimer, whose regime proved deeply unpopular. Mortimer emerged as the model of the favourites he had helped topple from power: greedy, unscrupulous and arrogant. In Wales and the Welsh marches he appropriated the former properties of the Despensers, of the earl of Arundel and even his own kinsman, Roger Mortimer of Chirk. In celebration of this concentration of lands, which augmented his legitimately inherited lordships, he assumed the title of earl of March in 1328. English comital titles had always previously been derived from particular places or counties within the kingdom and this departure scandalised some contemporaries. So too did his appetite for display, such as the three sumptuous 'round table' tournaments – presumably Arthurian – that he organised in 1328 at Hereford, Bedford and his patronal castle at Wigmore.

Two castles bear direct marks of Mortimer's spectacular rise to power. Through his wife he inherited the castle of Ludlow, where the withdrawing chambers of the 1290s domestic apartments were reordered with new fireplaces and windows. He also built a new chapel in the castle dedicated to St Peter in celebration of his escape from the Tower of London. Much more important than these operations, however, was his reconstruction of Wigmore in Herefordshire. This great castle remains one of the most evocative on the Welsh march. Recent consolidation work has attempted to preserve the quality of the ruins at Wigmore as a wilderness. It has also revealed evidence for Mortimer's wholesale reconstruction of the site, including work to a new great hall, accommodation and perhaps

even a great tower. He also proved a generous patron of the nearby priory of Wigmore, where he was eventually buried, following what was to prove – as we shall see in the next chapter – a sensational fall from power.

KNARESBOROUGH

The architectural threads of Edward I's and Edward II's varied and architecturally productive reigns are beautifully drawn together at Knaresborough Castle in Yorkshire. For much of the thirteenth century the castle was owned by the earls of Cornwall, whose patrimony reverted in its entirety to the crown following the extinction of the line in 1300. Doubtless influenced by his increasing involvement in Scotland and the excellent hunting provided by the surrounding royal forest of Knaresborough, Edward I repaired the castle and renovated its domestic apartments. He also constructed a new gatehouse, which was begun in 1304. This took the classic form of a twin-towered structure with residential chambers incorporated behind it. One detail shows that its masons were versed in the architecture of south-east England or south Wales: the solid towers rise from plinths set with minute spur bases.

Edward I's investment in Knaresborough was a modest prelude to that undertaken by his son. On 14 September 1307, shortly after his accession to the throne, Edward II formally directed that a new great tower be raised in the castle. It is noteworthy that this direction followed more than a month after the king had granted Knaresborough to Piers Gaveston as the newly created earl of Cornwall. Edward was in effect beautifying Gaveston's property at royal expense and creating an architectural symbol of their friendship. From the attention he lavished on the project and from the remains of the great tower itself, it is clear that the new building was intended to be a work of unparalleled splendour. Its surviving remains not only bring us remarkably close to the realities of court living in the period, but also – with their complex underlying geometry and sophisticated detailing – constitute one of the unsung masterpieces of the Decorated style.

Two masons appear to have been directly involved in work to the Knaresborough great tower: a Trinitarian friar called Brother William and a London mason, Hugh of Titchmarsh (or Tichemers). Their precise working relationship is unclear, but it was Titchmarsh who oversaw the management of the site until the completion of the tower in 1312. Certainly, the detail-

192 A reconstruction cut-away by Terry Ball of the great tower at Knaresborough, begun in 1307. It was designed integrally with a gatehouse (1) that served as the main entrance to the castle. The upper stories of this four storey tower were approached from a vaulted porch (2) up a curving stair (3) closed by a series of portcullises. A small waiting room opened up off the stair (4). The principal chamber was dominated by a throne niche (5) and lined by stone benches. Its dais end was lit by a large window (6). The room above was probably a bedchamber (7) served by a chapel in the upper storey of the forebuilding (8). At the base of the tower were two vaulted levels. One probably served as a storage space (9), the other perhaps as a treasury or wardrobe (10). One curiosity of the tower is the projecting windows in one of the turrets, possibly the first projecting oriels in English secular architecture (11).

ing of the building suggests a degree of expertise and familiarity with the royal works that would most plausibly be associated with Titchmarsh's experience. During his absences on other duties – or to speak to the king – his place was taken by the master mason of York Minster, Hugh of Boudon.[60]

The great tower at Knaresborough was a polygonal structure comprising three upper storeys of domestic apartments set over a basement (pl. 192). As in many Romanesque great towers (such as Dover and Rochester), formal access to the interior was up a large, free-standing staircase. This rose in a curve from a vaulted porch to the first floor of the tower and was originally fortified by a series of three portcullises and several tiers of murder holes. Halfway up the stair was a little lobby with a stone bench, presumably a waiting room for visitors. The principal first-floor chamber still largely survives. It was magnificently appointed with a huge throne niche across one wall, a unique survival from the period. This stands on a dais that was heated to one side by a fire and lit on the other by a large and richly ornamented window. It may well have been in this room on 13 January 1312 that Gaveston met the king upon his third and final return from exile.[61] Little now survives of the upper parts of the tower, but there is documentary reference to a chapel in the building. A sixteenth-century drawing also shows that the battlements were inhabited by a stone garrison of fighting figures.

Underlying the plan of the tower is a highly distinctive geometry. Three solid turrets rose up the sides of the building to demarcate in plan an equilateral triangle. Embraced within this triangle is an octagonal core articulated at basement and first-floor levels by an umbrella vault. The use in plan of superimposed octagonal and triangular forms looks straight back to the great gatehouses at Denbigh and Caernarfon. Another compelling parallel for the whole design at Knaresborough is the Eagle Tower at Caernarfon with its hexagonal geometry, inhabited battlements and triple turrets. What a casual visitor might not appreciate is that these geometric forms also manifest themselves in the detailing of the building. The vault ribs, for example, make play with the geometry of the plan, and penetrate one another. Such is the attention to detail and the sheer quality of the masonry that with half-closed eyes a visitor might imagine the whole structure to be hewn from a single piece of stone.

The great tower of Knaresborough illustrates the strength and dynamism of the English architectural tradition at the start of the fourteenth century: its confident use of complex geometry, an interest in the organic character of architectural form, a technical mastery of cutting stone, and a delight in using buildings for theatrical effect, as evidenced both by the design of the interiors and also the fighting figures surmounting the battlements. All these qualities were to be further explored in the ensuing decades to dramatic effect in the connected spheres of church and castle design. Then quite suddenly in the 1350s, without rejecting them entirely, the course of English architecture was to change decisively once more.

9

THE LION OF ENGLAND

EDWARD III

At the dead of night on 19 October 1330, Edward III (1327–77) and a small band of followers secretly entered Nottingham Castle through an underground passage. The young king, who was just seventeen at the time, was making a daring bid for independence. Crowned three years before, he had lived ever since as the political puppet of his mother, Queen Isabella, and her lover Roger Mortimer, the earl of March. Arriving undetected at the queen's apartments in the castle, Edward and his accomplices surprised and captured the couple after a fierce struggle. 'Good son, good son', the queen implored, 'have pity on gentle Mortimer.'[1] Edward III had none. Mortimer was led off to imprisonment and execution at Tyburn as a common criminal. Isabella underwent a two-year house arrest at Windsor Castle before being sent into respectable retirement, latterly spending much time at Castle Rising.[2] In this characteristically bold exploit Edward successfully won control of his kingdom and there began in earnest a reign that was to mark a watershed in the history of English architecture.

During the opening years of his rule, the resources of the kingdom were largely directed towards Scotland, at whose hands the English had suffered such humiliation since the death of Edward I. In 1329 the Scottish

king, Robert Bruce, died, leaving his five-year-old son David II to succeed him. Those individuals who had been promised or dispossessed of estates in Scotland now saw opportunity to secure them. At their head was the rival claimant to the Scottish throne, Edward Balliol. The campaigns that followed in Scotland, first with the tacit support and then the involvement of Edward III, were notably successful in the field. Balliol was twice installed as king and not only swore allegiance to Edward III but also ceded the lowlands to direct English rule. Nevertheless, he failed to hold on to his prize and the attendant settlement with its tantalising winnings of land repeatedly crumbled.[3]

Though these events plunged Scotland into internal crisis, they also had the effect of restoring the English side of the border to relative order. Scottish raids now rarely penetrated beyond the Tyne and the chaos they caused became contained. Encouraged by this, and by subventions of cash from the crown, the castles of northern England were busily developed and enlarged.

Within a decade England's ongoing conflict with Scotland became subsumed into a much grander political quarrel. Of defining importance in the course of Edward III's rule was the outbreak of the protracted and intermittent hostilities with France that have

Facing page: Alnwick, Northumberland.

become familiarly known as the Hundred Years War. This conflict formally began on 24 May 1337 with the seizure by the French king, Philip VI, of Edward III's possessions in France: the duchy of Aquitaine and county of Ponthieu. Edward III responded by laying claim to the French throne. In its opening stages the financial demands of the war caused widespread resentment and in 1341 the king was worsted in a political confrontation with his critics.

This domestic crisis appears to have matured him and curbed a dangerous tendency to surround himself with favourites, as his father, Edward II, had done. There followed a series of successful campaigns that raised the prestige of English arms to unprecedented heights. In 1346 English armies not only inflicted a major defeat on the French at Crécy, they also captured the allied Scottish king and routed his army at Neville's Cross just outside Durham. Ten years later, in 1356, the French king, John II, himself was captured after another decisive victory, at Poitiers.

For many involved on the English side, these campaigns yielded immense wealth in booty as well as ransoms. It was only natural for English knights and nobles to invest these winnings in architecture, including church and castle building. Yet in many cases, such investment was not immediate. The opportunities presented by the war in France and its heavy demands effectively diverted the energies of the nobility out of England altogether. This is reflected not only in the relative dearth of castle building in England during the 1340s and '50s, but also in the peaceful character of domestic politics over the same period.

The crucial exception to this lull in building was the remodelling of Windsor Castle, undertaken in stages by Edward III from 1348. Financed out of the profits of war – and latterly the immense ransom of John II of France – this project cost more than £50,000 to complete and constituted one of the major architectural commissions of the European Middle Ages. The new buildings at Windsor were amongst the first mature works in a new architectural style – the Perpendicular. Promulgated by a circle of royal masons, the Perpendicular style was to remain current in English architectural design into the mid-seventeenth century.

In 1369 the Hundred Years War was resumed by France with far-reaching architectural consequences. England was caught off balance by the renewed conflict, and the disastrous reverses that followed revived domestic conflict and magnate rivalry, problems that were to spiral out of control at Edward III's death. As the focus of English politics returned home, there began a surge of building activity that was to continue unabated until the close of the fourteenth century. It was to Edward III's building operations and the new Perpendicular style that the architecture of these projects owed their inspiration. And it was in part from the wealth generated by the Hundred Years War that they owed their grandeur. In recognition of its importance, the genesis of the Perpendicular style and its influence in the 1360s and 1370s is discussed on its own in the next chapter.

One crucially important phenomenon of the reign deserves individual introductory comment. In 1348 there occurred the first outbreak of the Black Death in England. It is impossible to quantify the impact of this pandemic on the population in numerical terms, though perhaps as many as one in three people were carried off during its first outbreaks in 1348, 1361–2 and 1369. Nor can the psychological effects of its visitations on the survivors be easily assessed. But the popular notion – informed by Huizinga's classic work, *The Waning of the Middle Ages* (1924) – that the shock of the Black Death sent Europe into a religious, economic and social torpor is grossly misleading. If anything, the long-term effects of the Black Death were invigorating. It brought about a fundamental reordering of English society and a transformation of the economy.

As regards architecture, the inflation of wages that resulted from the Black Death raised the financial and political threshold of castle construction. The contraction of the labour market, meanwhile, increased the relative importance of the royal works in determining the future development of English architecture. In this sense, the stylistic coherence of most major building projects in the later fourteenth century could partly be presented as a product of this pandemic. But the Black Death did nothing to deter the very richest figures in the realm from embarking on splendid building projects. Nor did its effects obviously colour or influence in a direct or quantifiable way the character of architecture in this period.

THE KING AND HIS NOBILITY

By 1330 the ranks of the English nobility had been devastated by the combined effects of Edward I's neglect and the predations of two generations of royal favourites. Over the course of Edward III's reign, not only was this social order revitalised, but also its character was changed.[4] The English nobility had formerly comprised the barons of the realm, those individuals who in feudal terms held land directly from the king as so-called tenants-in-chief. Amongst their number there further existed a small group who enjoyed the title of earl, an honorific inherited from the Anglo-Saxon past. During the fourteenth century new noble titles were introduced and the qualification for baronial estate became inextricably linked to parliament. This latter development evolved from the practice initiated by Edward II of summoning prominent figures to the House of Lords by writ. By the end of Edward III's reign this distinction was recognised as an act of ennoblement termed a barony by writ. Curiously, such summons were not initially regarded as hereditary – though they soon became so – and in this sense the practice was comparable to life peerages in the present day.[5]

Edward III's clear intention in building up the nobility was to bolster his regime and provide leaders for his wars. It was also closely bound up with his attempts to marry off a large royal family advantageously and with sufficient provision of land to maintain their estate. In so doing he laid the foundations for the dynastic politics of late medieval England and established new patterns of castle construction across the kingdom. That he was able to undertake this reform was in part a consequence of the successful military exploits of the reign. These gave the nobility a defined sphere of action and bound its interests up with those of the king. They also won its members prestige and fostered a degree of fellowship that was further enforced by the developing privileges of the peerage within the House of Lords. By the close of the reign the peerage in parliament numbered nearly seventy, of whom ten were dignified by the titles of earl or duke (as opposed to being simply barons).

In practical terms the restoration of the nobility was made possible by the additional resources at the king's disposal. One side effect of the fall of Mortimer in 1330 was a massive release of land to the crown. Not only did the king get Mortimer's own ruthlessly acquired estates and those of his close supporters, but he also received many of Queen Isabella's properties as well. These possessions had been largely ill-gotten gains, either the appropriated winnings of Edward II's favourites – notably the Older and Younger Despensers – or the fruits of political confrontations during the king's minority, such as the execution of the earl of Kent in 1330.[6] Perpetuated within them, therefore, were

several major inheritances, some of which were selectively restored over time.

A case in point was the earldom of March, which was bestowed on Mortimer's son in 1354 after an impressive military career in Edward III's service.[7] Others, such as the inheritance of the extinguished line of the de Clare earls of Gloucester, were broken up and redistributed. Further incrementing this windfall of property were the estates that passed to the crown during the reign through the natural demise of other great families, notably the de Warennes in 1347. Such changes brought about profound shifts in local politics that could prejudice even the greatest castles: the breakup of the de Clare inheritance, for example, brought about the demise of Caerphilly, and the death of the last of the de Warennes presaged the ruin of the ancient castle of Lewes.

These reserves of land made possible the endowment of several new titles at important moments in the reign. The first of these mass ennoblements took place at the parliament of March 1337, where six new earls were simultaneously created: Henry of Grosmont, earl of Derby; Hugh Audley, earl of Gloucester; William Bohun, earl of Northampton; William Clinton, earl of Huntingdon; Robert Ufford, earl of Suffolk; and William Montagu, earl of Salisbury. All but one of these men were near contemporaries of the king and had served as comrades in arms during the Scottish campaigns. Moreover, the last four had been involved directly in the seizure of Isabella and Mortimer at Nottingham in 1330.[8]

At the same time, Edward III created his eldest son, Edward of Woodstock – familiar to posterity as the Black Prince – duke of Cornwall. This was a radical and important departure: the title of duke was borrowed from French usage and had never been attached to an English name before. It clearly established within the ranks of the new creations a sense of distinction between the king's son and his court circle. This distinction was expressed in the joint ceremony of elevation when the new earls clustered in attendance behind their royal duke and future overlord. Along with their titles, the poorest received endowments yielding at least 1,000 marks (£777) per annum, but most already enjoyed large incomes won since 1330. The basic income of an earl seems to have been reckoned around £1,000 per annum, a sum that helps set in context the cost of architectural commissions.[9]

Much attention has rightly been given to the prominent role that this group of earls and the Black Prince went on to play in the Hundred Years War. Indeed, the creation of new noblemen in 1337 was undoubtedly precipitated by the king's need for military leaders in the looming conflict with France. Quite as intriguing as their military exploits, however, is the manner in which they strove to cloak their new dignities in architecture. In pursuit of this object, the patronage of secular and ecclesiastical projects was inextricably linked. The earl of Salisbury, for example, at once established an Augustinian priory at Bisham in Berkshire and persuaded the king himself to lay the foundation stone of the new buildings.[10] In this act of patronage the earl was providing himself with a dynastic mausoleum and complementing an already extensive portfolio of residences and castles. These included the exceptionally rich prize of Denbigh, which he had received in reward for his involvement in the palace coup of 1330. Similarly, the earl of Suffolk became a patron of Leiston Abbey, Suffolk, a foundation long associated with Orford Castle, which he had received from the king.[11] Others created entirely new seats appropriate to their status: the earl of Huntingdon, perhaps the poorest of the new creations, constructed one of the finest surviving castles of the period for himself at Maxstoke, Warwickshire, along with a priory, more of which at the conclusion of this chapter.

The new creations also prompted programmes of castle repair and maintenance that remain an important but largely ignored architectural achievement of the reign. Edward of Woodstock, for example, received four castles with his dukedom of Cornwall at Restormel, Launceston, Trematon and Tintagel. These were surveyed by his officials and in the next few years their buildings were restored.[12] At Trematon and Launceston the repairs to the walls were to be undertaken by the tenants of those owing knights' fees to the castle, evidence for the continued vitality of such feudal exaction.[13] Subsequently, these castles were maintained as the administrative and defensive bulwark of the duchy over the 1350s and 1360s. Restormel with its deer park and the neighbouring Lostwithiel Palace, the administrative centre of the tin-mining industry, was particularly favoured in this process.[14] It may be no coincidence that as a duke Edward wanted a special seat for his authority, linking a palace and castle in modest emulation of Westminster and the Tower of London in the capital.

In 1343 Edward of Woodstock was additionally invested with the title of prince of Wales.[15] As in Cornwall, this prompted a survey of his Welsh estates and castles. There followed such repairs as the reorganisation of the domestic accommodation at Conwy Castle prior to a visit by him in 1343.[16] Moreover, in 1353 the prince became a patron of the Cistercian monastery of Vale Royal, the abbey founded by his grandfather Edward I at the outset of the Welsh conquest.[17]

Edward III's resources for the bestowing of titles gradually dwindled and so too, therefore, did the frequency of their creation. The last significant dignity he dispensed was in 1351, when Henry of Grosmont, son of the earl of Lancaster, was promoted to the dignity of duke of Lancaster. The title was an acknowledgement of the sheer size of his inherited landholdings: with an estimated income of £8,400 per annum, he was by far the richest peer in England with eight times the revenue expected for an earl.[18] This dukedom was celebrated in architecture with work to Leicester Castle, the favourite seat of the new duke. As part of this, a new burial church was erected for his family, St Mary in the Newark. The architectural patronage of the duke and that of his heir by marriage, Edward III's son John of Gaunt, are to be understood in the context of the Perpendicular style that is the subject of the next chapter.

The architectural example set by the titular peerage in developing or repairing castles and their attendant religious foundations was followed as far down the social ladder as money allowed. Particularly active in this respect were newcomers to the junior ranks of the peerage. For this group, a castle might come as the culminating prize of political success. John de Wilington, for example, received a summons to parliament on 29 November 1336 and about a year later was granted the dramatically situated castle of Carreg Cennen in Carmarthenshire.[19] The architectural development of the site is not well documented, but he may well have been responsible for some of the latter phases of the surviving ruins such as the outer bailey.[20]

More commonly, men who were attempting to cut a figure in politics – either at court or at a local level – were forced by necessity to build new castles. In such cases, these buildings were often located near or on the sites of earlier manor houses. Moreover, they almost invariably took the time-honoured Gothic form of a quadrangular enclosure set with towers. Encastellating a manor house in this way was a means of upgrading it architecturally and signalling the pretensions of the owning family. The quadrangular castle had many advantages: it was not only relatively cheap and imposing in an architectural sense but – where

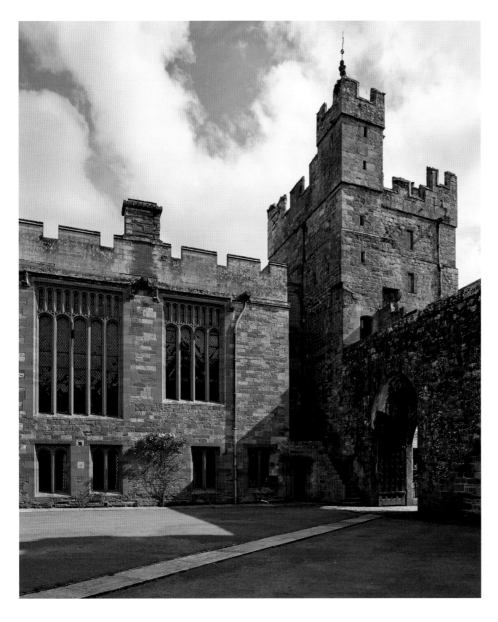

necessary – it was also very flexible. Existing domestic buildings, for example, could easily be incorporated or re-erected within the embrace of new walls. For individuals aspiring to architecture they could scarcely afford, such economies could be very important.

With a few notable exceptions, quadrangular castles of the fourteenth century were not works of much architectural invention or quality. They usually reflect in their design and detailing local architectural preferences and can be grouped regionally. For example, when Ralph, first Lord Dacre, raised his fortunes by marriage he established a new castle at Naworth, Cumberland, to control the border barony of Gilsland. This was licensed in 1335 and remains in occupation to the present day (pl. 193). The existing layout of the castle, though much adapted over time, probably dates back to the first building on the site. It comprises a courtyard enclosure with angle towers on a distorted rectangular plan, a form consistently popular across the north of England in the fourteenth century. In the same decade similar buildings were also begun by figures of local standing in Northumberland at Ford and Chillingham, which were respectively licensed in 1338 and 1344.[21]

Across the south-east, by contrast, quadrangular castles commonly combined towers on both circular and rectangular plans. A case in point is the castle licensed in 1341 at Sterborough in Surrey. This was built by Reginald, first Lord Cobham, an intimate of the king and an active soldier. The castle no longer survives, but drawn and excavated evidence shows that it was laid out on a rectangular plan with drum turrets at each corner and a rectangular gatehouse. As a whole this design compares to such castles as neighbouring Hever, Kent, probably rebuilt around 1380, and Westenhanger, Kent, which received a licence to crenellate in 1343. It also anticipates the design of Bodiam Castle, Sussex, and Shirburn, Oxfordshire, licensed respectively in 1379 and 1383, which will be treated in the next chapter. Several Midlands castles, meanwhile, adopted polygonal towers. This regional preference, found, for example, at Maxstoke (see pl. 210), dates back to such thirteenth-century buildings as Eccleshall, Staffordshire.

In the south-west, finally, round towers were popular, as in the fortifications enclosing the bishop's palace at Wells, which were licensed in 1340, and Farleigh Hungerford in Somerset. The latter building was completed between 1369 and 1383 by Thomas Hungerford, a speaker of the House of Commons raised to promi-

193 The courtyard interior of Naworth, Cumberland. The castle was built by Ralph, first Lord Dacre, to control the border barony of Gilsland, and was licensed in 1335. It was laid out on a quadrangular plan that was distorted to suit the topography of the site. The detailing and form of the building reflects local architectural preferences. At each corner there stood a tower on a rectangular plan, and the entrance was protected by a barbican. Internally, the castle was substantially adapted in the mid-sixteenth century and again between 1602 and 1628 by William, Lord Howard. He refurbished the principal domestic apartments, including the hall and chapel, using material stripped from another family castle at Kirkoswald. The building was gutted by fire in 1844 and nearly all the medieval decoration of the interior destroyed.

194 A plan of Farleigh Hungerford, Somerset. The original castle on a quadrangular plan was completed by November 1383, when a pardon was issued for its construction. A group of existing residential buildings appears to have been incorporated within the present inner bailey. Its four angle towers were capped by conical roofs, a rare treatment in English castle design restricted almost exclusively to the south-west. The castle was extensively remodelled in the 1440s. As part of these changes, between 1441 and 1443 the parish church was enclosed within an outer bailey and assumed into private use. The castle remained in the hands of the Hungerford family throughout the sixteenth century. It miraculously escaped destruction after the Civil War, only to be sold up for demolition in 1705 to clear the debts of the spendthrift Sir Edward Hungerford (d. 1711).

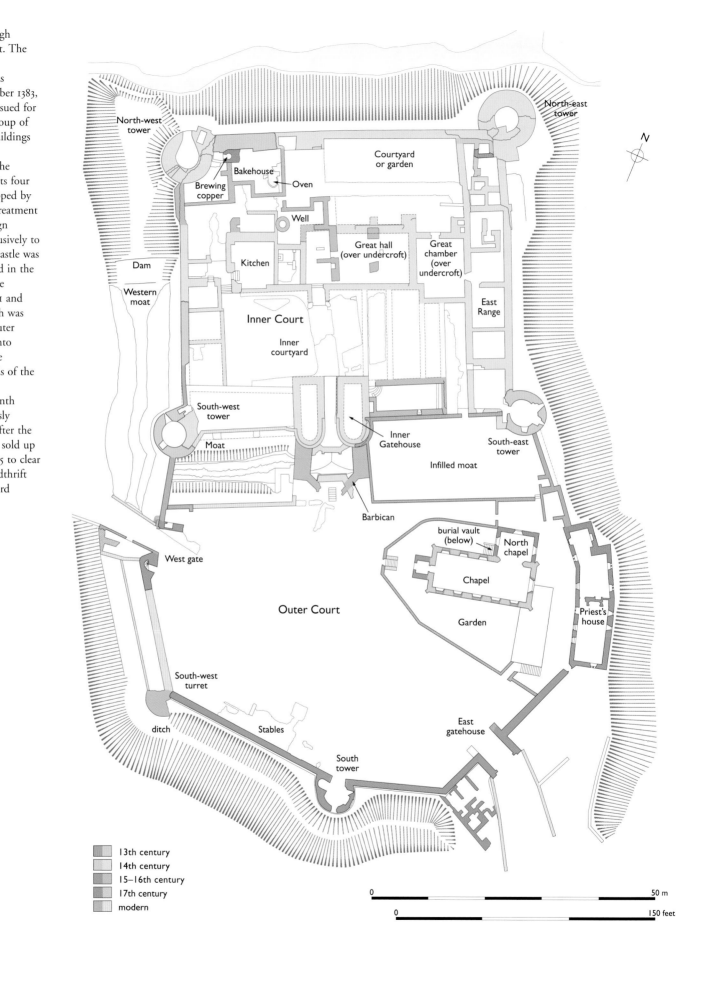

North-west tower

North-east tower

N

Courtyard or garden

Bakehouse

Brewing copper

Oven

Well

Dam

Kitchen

Great hall (over undercroft)

Great chamber (over undercroft)

East Range

Western moat

Inner Court

Inner courtyard

South-west tower

Moat

Inner Gatehouse

South-east tower

Infilled moat

Barbican

burial vault (below)

North chapel

West gate

Chapel

Priest's house

Outer Court

Garden

South-west turret

ditch

Stables

East gatehouse

South tower

13th century
14th century
15–16th century
17th century
modern

0   50 m

0   150 feet

nence through his service to the dukes of Lancaster. Much expanded in the 1440s, the original circuit of towers probably enclosed the buildings of an existing residence on the site (pl. 194).[22]

In most cases it would appear that the intention in quadrangular castles of this kind was roughly to match the proportions of the different towers in order to create a regular design. In deference to long English architectural habit, however, particular architectural emphasis might be given to the gatehouse and one tower in the circuit. This is illustrated, for example, at Etal, Northumberland, which was redeveloped over two generations by the Manners family between 1341 and 1368.[23]

Another important variation in the quadrangular castle form was the compression of the plan into a single, large tower, an idea that harkens back to Romanesque precedent. Perhaps the most impressive example is to be found at Langley in Northumberland (pl. 195).[24] This compact tower on an H-shaped plan was built by Sir Thomas de Lucy (d. 1365), a veteran soldier and a commander at the battle of Neville's Cross, probably around 1350. Such towers found particular favour in the north of England including Yorkshire, where equally ambitious buildings were erected at Harewood (now a ruin) and Gilling (where the basement level survives beneath later rebuilds).[25] They are found throughout the realm, however.

In 1348 a mason called John de Burcestre contracted to build a 'chastel' according to the plans provided by Sir Ralph Stafford on the motte at Stafford (pl. 196). According to the contract, the new castle was to comprise a central block with four angle towers, each of which was to rise 10 feet above the parapets.[26] Sir Ralph had just returned triumphant from campaigning in France. His new castle was an expression of his martial prowess and new-found wealth, but it anticipated the award three years later, in 1351, of an earldom. Another comparable structure is Nunney Castle in Somerset, licensed in 1373 (pl. 197): built by Sir John de la Mare, it comprises a high tower set within a walled enclosure. Sir John was a figure of relatively modest standing, but the previous year he had received the manor of Nunney as a tenant in chief. This technically raised him to the status of a baron, a dignity that the castle celebrates.

While the fortunes of the nobility waxed under the patronage of Edward III, its interests naturally extended into the sphere of church preferment. Familial titles and inheritances were the preserve of an eldest

195 Langley, Northumberland, was built by Sir Thomas de Lucy (d. 1365), probably around 1350. The building is conceived of as a quadrangular castle compressed into a single tower. This idea of compressing a turreted bailey into a tower had been first explored in English castle design in the twelfth century, as at Orford (see pl. 74). The hall is at first-floor level with withdrawing chambers above. The tower to the left houses a massive twelve-seater latrine that serves all the floors. Entrance to the tower was originally through a projecting stair porch that broke the symmetry of the plan (the door visible here is a modern creation). A late nineteenth-century restoration of Langley by the Northumbrian castle antiquarian Cadwallader Bates recreated the array of miniature turrets and battlements that crown the structure today. Confusingly, he also increased the number of windows filled with complex flowing tracery designs. The tower probably stood originally within a larger fortified enclosure.

196 The motte and the remains of the 'chastel' at Stafford, which the mason John de Burcestre contracted to build in 1348. He worked to plans provided by Sir Ralph Stafford, who may have commissioned another, more senior mason to draw them up. According to the contract, the new castle was to comprise a central block with four angle towers, each of which was to rise 10 feet above the parapets. There was a fifth tower in the middle of the south side. The basement level of the building still survives, and the remains show that the towers were polygonal in the fashion of the region. A survey of 1521 was enthusiastic in its description of the building, which was deemed suitable for Henry VIII to use: it enjoyed fabulous views, overlooked a good park, and was built in a uniform fashion with a hall and great chamber at first-floor level, services beneath and numerous chambers. Mention is also made of a 'surveying place' at the low end of the hall. The ruins of the tower were rebuilt in the late nineteenth century and partially demolished in 1961.

son, but ecclesiastical office could provide younger siblings with comparable privileges. In consequence, the nobility eagerly pressed their offspring into the church and the bench of bishops was steadily colonised by men of high birth. Though the episcopacy continued to accommodate individuals of every background, at no point in English history has its membership been so overwhelmingly aristocratic. Bishops had always been great builders, but this lent to their architectural endeavours a spirit almost indivisible from that of their secular relatives. Moreover, during the military successes of the 1340s and '50s there developed a sense of common purpose between the spiritual and secular arms that has few parallels in English history.

THE NORTHERN MARCH

The renewal of the Anglo–Scottish war in the 1330s and the reassertion of English royal authority returned the northern counties of England to relative stability after the disasters of Edward II's reign. It also offered rich rewards for those who prosecuted it on the English side. This naturally encouraged building, and there followed a steady flow of important new castle projects in the region until the close of the century. In both architectural and political terms the border divided into two sections: the so-called western and eastern marches. This division can be understood as broadly corresponding to the bipartite ecclesiastical rule of the area by the bishops of Carlisle and Durham, who remained figures of pre-eminent political importance. The precise means of governing the march varied over time and as the needs of the war dictated. Responsibility for its defence, however, consistently lay with local magnates acting under the direction of royal officers. These officials exercised sweeping powers and enjoyed the promise of financial subsidy from the crown. As a result, such appointments became the object of vigorous competition between the leading ecclesiastics and families of the region.

By governing through the agency of appointed officials the crown effectively diminished its own immediate importance in the march and – by extension – its building. Rather than setting the pace of architectural change, Edward III patronised unusually modest and

197 A cut-away reconstruction of the great tower of Nunney, Somerset, in the 1580s by Stephen Conlin. The tower was built by Sir John de la Mare under a licence issued on 28 November 1373, shortly after he came to enjoy the dignity of a baron. It comprises a cluster of four high drum towers, each five storeys high and surmounted by a conical roof, a form comparable to the towers of the contemporary quadrangular castle at Farleigh Hungerford. Nunney was modernised in the late sixteenth century, probably by Richard Prater, a rich Londoner who bought it sometime after 1560. He slightly raised the floor levels and inserted a spiral stair in the near left-hand tower (1). Internally, the tower comprised a kitchen at ground-floor level (2), a hall on the second floor (3) and withdrawing chambers on the top floor (4). Opening off these into the far right-hand corner tower was a chapel (5). It was recorded in the sixteenth century that the tower with its encircling moat stood within a larger courtyard enclosed on three sides by a wall and on the fourth by the stream beside the site.

piecemeal projects in conjunction with the Scottish campaigns over the 1330s and 1340s. The virtual sum of his operations was the repair of several Lowland castles that had been destroyed by the Scots. In 1334, for example, he re-established Roxburgh as a principal stronghold. A timber piel comprising 2,248 pieces of wood was brought from Newcastle to fortify the site and the buildings were repaired between 1335 and 1337.[27] At the same time the king chose to move his seat of government to York in order to supervise the Scottish campaigns, a striking indication of just how disastrous the events of the 1310s and 1320s had been to the north. To accommodate the influx of royal servants, the castle there was reorganised in the years 1334–6 with new courtrooms and exchequer buildings.[28]

By contrast, the magnates of the march, both secular and ecclesiastic, were busily engaged in castle construction on an impressive scale. Indeed, trying to make sense of buildings along the border is complicated by the sheer quantity and variety of castle remains. Broadly speaking, within the western division of the march, castle design remained highly conservative. For example, there was a continued preference within it for towers on a rectangular plan, a form that had been consistently favoured in the area since the twelfth century. The idea of creating castles with a single dominating tower also remained popular. Across the eastern march, by contrast, there was more varied and sophisticated planning. This situation was a product both of its relative wealth and its importance as the principal corridor of access into the Scottish lowlands. By the 1350s, however, the architectural variety of the eastern march began also to give way to rectangular planning. This shift towards the close of the reign was probably bound up with the growing influence of the Perpendicular style.

Outstanding amongst the beneficiaries of the war and perhaps the dominant secular figure in the march during the early part of Edward III's reign was Henry, second Baron Percy. In 1318 he had inherited from his father an important stake in the affairs of northern England besides claims to substantial estates in Scotland, which he revived in the 1330s through his support of Edward Balliol.[29] His pretensions in the march were strikingly illustrated in a ceremony he enacted at Warkworth in Northumberland, a castle added to the family patrimony in 1328. According to the Percy Cartulary, on 18 July 1343 Henry took and smashed his old seal in the castle.[30] This curious action was almost certainly an evocation of a moment in the funeral service

198 The gatehouse to the inner bailey of Alnwick, Northumberland, can be dated to around 1340 by the heraldry displayed beneath the battlements. It may specifically celebrate the families involved in the English victory at Halidon Hill in 1333 and includes the quartered royal arms of England and France, a heraldic innovation of 1342. The twin towers rise from spur bases, and the battlements are crowned with fighting figures, both borrowings from the architecture of the king's works in the late thirteenth century. This gatehouse is very similar in form to the outer gate, though it is more heavily ornamented and lacks a barbican. Its relative richness is appropriate to its position as the entrance to the domestic heart of the castle.

to the domestic heart of the castle (pl. 198). The new buildings incorporate many of the architectural forms and ideas introduced to the north of England through the royal works in Edward I's reign, including spur bases, a type of shouldered arch termed a Caernarfon arch, and battlement figures. They also illustrate some remarkable departures.

The new defences of Alnwick incorporated towers of semicircular, polygonal and square plan, a variety of forms that had not been seen combined in a single English castle design since the late twelfth century (pl. 199). Moreover, the main front of the castle was laid out on a monumental scale as a regular façade with pairs of towers and turrets flanking a central gatehouse protected by a barbican. Such symmetry of composition is very remarkable at this date. So too is the particular form of the entrance, where the gate and barbican are physically integrated to create a coherent architectural entity (pl. 200).[34] Lastly, the window tracery within the buildings was deliberately austere and evoked in certain cases designs fashionable nearly a century before. In this treatment is expressed in an unusually explicit way the long-standing preference for rugged detailing in castle design. This was in part thought to be aesthetically appropriate to powerful buildings, but it may also have been intended to make the castle look respectably old-fashioned.

In the absence of documentary record the only evidence for dating the work at Alnwick comes from the heraldic decoration of the inner bailey gate. Displayed at parapet level are the arms of the historic lords of Alnwick and several families involved in the Scottish campaigns of the 1330s.[35] The most convincing explanation for the display is that it celebrated the brief fulfilment of Percy's territorial ambitions in Scotland following the English victory at Halidon Hill in 1333. Certainly, this would agree with the particular inclusion of the de Warenne arms: the last earl Warenne was involved in Scottish affairs only in the 1330s and died in 1347. A dating around 1340 is further corroborated by other castle works in the area, three of which deserve individual mention.

The building at Alnwick directly influenced work to two other castles by individuals connected with Henry Percy. At Bothal Castle in Northumberland a new gatehouse modelled on the inner bailey gate at Alnwick was begun by Sir Robert de Ogle, the eldest son of another Robert who was prominent in the affairs of the march. It likewise included a display of shields arranged in hierarchical importance on the

of the bishops of Durham, in which the seal of the deceased prelate was destroyed and its fragments cast into the open tomb.[31] For Percy the smashing of the seal was intended likewise to mark an act of passage. By it he formally abandoned his family's ancient coat of arms and assumed in its place the figure of a blue lion rampant. The new coat of arms – which confusingly was already in currency – was clearly intended to advertise his prowess as a warrior and resonated with Edward III's own fascination with this royal, predatory beast.[32] Percy was in effect representing himself as the lion of the northern march.

The principal seat of Henry Percy's authority, and a convenient forward base from which to manage his Scottish affairs, was Alnwick. Here he continued the architectural development of the castle initiated by his father in 1309, remodelling the outer circuit of defences with new walls, towers and a great gatehouse.[33] In addition, the twelfth-century gate tower that had been preserved by his father as the entrance to the inner bailey was reconstructed with a new façade. The reorganisation of Alnwick was evidently undertaken as a single rolling programme, the detailing of the various towers and gates bearing generic comparison but altering by degrees as the work went forward. For example, the inner bailey gate and the main gatehouse are essentially identical in design, though the former is encrusted with sculpture as befits its role as the entrance

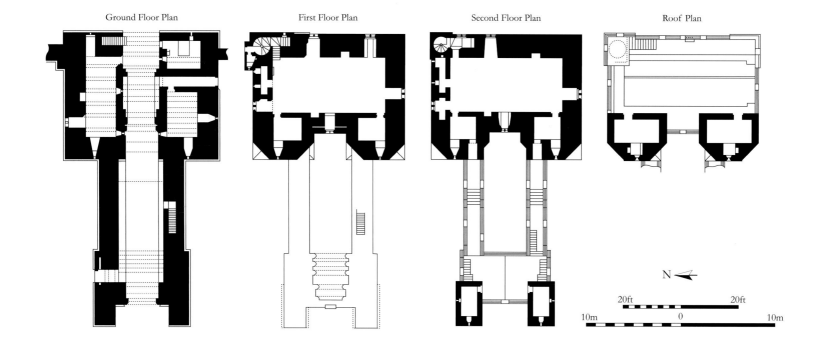

Ground Floor Plan   First Floor Plan   Second Floor Plan   Roof Plan

N

20ft   20ft
10m   0   10m

200   Plans of the outer gate and barbican at Alnwick, Northumberland, built around 1340. The idea of combining a gatehouse and twin-towered barbican had been current in English design since the early thirteenth century in such entrance arrangements as Lincoln (see pl. 123) and the Tower of London. At Alnwick, however, the idea is brilliantly regularised and the two elements integrated. Numerous similar gatehouse barbicans were created across the country in the fourteenth century, as we shall encounter, for example, at Tynemouth, Warwick, Arundel and perhaps Berkeley. These buildings often reflect regional preferences of design in the form of towers and architectural detailing. All incorporated spacious domestic apartments and appear to have served as self-contained lodgings.

building and fighting figures in the battlements. The start of the operation, which may also have included the construction of a great tower demolished in the eighteenth century,[36] probably coincided with the issue of a licence to fortify the castle in 1343.[37] Rather more ambitious was a rebuilding of Prudhoe Castle by Gilbert Umfraville, ninth earl of Angus (d. 1381). He provided the castle with a new circuit of outer towers and remodelled the twelfth-century gatehouse with an extra floor and a new barbican. At the same time new windows were inserted into the great tower, probably evidence for a complete remodelling of its interior in this period.[38] In virtually every particular the forms and details of the new buildings are taken from Alnwick: the types of tracery, arrow loops and the design of the new barbican. The most likely date for the remodelling of Prudhoe is in the 1340s, when Umfraville acted in close alliance with Henry Percy in the affairs of the march.[39]

Another important building erected within the orbit of Percy influence was the great tower of Edlingham, just 6 miles from Alnwick (pl. 201).[40] It was probably built around 1340 by Sir William Felton, a distinguished soldier. He received numerous royal appointments, including the command of Bamburgh and Roxburgh castles between 1334 and 1340 and the sheriffdom of Northumberland in the years 1341–3.[41] The tower is sumptuously detailed and constructed throughout of cut stone. Very unusually for an English build-

ing, the principal first-floor chamber was vaulted in stone. Set to the side of a thirteenth-century hall range, it evidently incorporated the withdrawing chambers of the castle. The refined detailing of the tower suggests that Felton borrowed masons for the work either from the king's works (which he must have been engaged with during the reconstruction of Roxburgh in 1335–7) or, more probably, from Alnwick.

Henry Percy died in 1352 at Warkworth Castle and was buried at Alnwick Priory.[42] The burial illustrates a decisive move northwards in the interests of his family. Throughout the first half of the fourteenth century the heartlands of Percy wealth and power had been in Yorkshire, which had served as a useful base from which to exploit the opportunities of the march. And there is some evidence that Henry Percy continued to regard Yorkshire as a dynastic home. He must, for example, have patronised the superb tomb of the 1340s to an unknown member of the family in Beverley Minster (probably a cleric rather than a woman, as has long been supposed), near his important seats of Wressle and Leconfield.[43] Similarly, he is documented as having repaired the domestic buildings at Scarborough, one of several northern, royal castles that he held in custody.[44]

But Henry Percy's burial in Northumberland indicates the degree to which his family interests, and those of his English co-combatants, were changing fundamentally. The Edwardian Anglo–Scottish war had ini-

tially been waged by those who invested their resources from the wider kingdom to win new lands in the north. Now these conquests were yielding real rewards and transforming the balance of familial interests. By the early fifteenth century the affairs of the march were being conducted by a small and exclusive circle of families whose fortunes were rooted in the area.

There was in the western march no individual figure of comparable stature to Henry Percy, a reflection both of the relative poverty of the area and its comparatively fragmented patterns of lordship. Perhaps the greatest secular lords of the region were the Lucy family. Within the western march the Lucys were owners of the ancient castles of Cockermouth and Egremont and also enjoyed intermittent control of the royal castle of Carlisle. Unfortunately, little is known of their architectural activities on these sites. It is a curiosity that their rebuilding of Langley Castle (see above) in the eastern march reflects western architectural preferences, notably the use of windows ornamented with rich curvilinear tracery; presumably the mason who designed it came from the western march.

The principal political rivals of the Lucys were the two pre-eminent ecclesiastics of the region, both of whom were castle builders. The abbots of Furness fortified numerous manors in this period and erected the castle at Piel, which has already been described. John Kirby, bishop of Carlisle (1332–52), also began a new castle on the site of a manor house at Rose in Cumberland and – remarkably – the remains of this building continue today to serve as the seat of his successors in the see. Rose Castle was probably completed between the issue of two licences to crenellate, the first dated 1336 and the second in 1355 after Kirby's death. It appears from the first to have taken the classic Gothic form of a rectangular enclosure set at regular intervals with towers on a rectangular plan. Enclosing the entire site was an outer apron wall.[45]

While work to it was under way, Kirby became embroiled in an episode that perfectly reflects the perceived importance of castle ownership and the explosive politics of the march. In 1338 the bishop petitioned for the possession of Carlisle Castle on the grounds that he had nowhere appropriate to live in his diocese, his residences all having been destroyed by the Scots. The suit was not rejected outright, but Edward III would only intermittently grant the bishop control of the castle, which was itself in poor repair and manned by a dispirited garrison. To make matters worse, Kirby was increasingly short of money, the treasury having

201 Edlingham, Northumberland, view of the great tower with the footings of the earlier hall block visible in the foreground. The tower was probably built around 1340 by Sir William Felton, and the hall by his father, also called William. At roof level each corner of the tower was capped by a semicircular turret, a very early example of this type of architectural enrichment in England. The tower may give an insight into the design of the lost royal castle buildings at Roxburgh, which Sir William commanded. Its angle buttresses are an unusual feature paralleled in such fourteenth-century buildings as Piel, Lancashire, and Brancepeth, Co. Durham.

failed to pay up for debts incurred in the defence of the march. The bishop solved his immediate needs in 1345 by seizing large quantities of food from the town. This action sparked a brawl in the market place amidst a crowd that had gathered to watch the performance of a mystery play. In retaliation, the garrison ran amok in the town with Kirby allegedly looking on from the castle gate dressed in a full suit of armour.[46]

SOUTHERN ENGLAND

Events in the northern march had a considerable impact on the affairs of the kingdom at large. In particular, the alliance between Philip VI of France and David II of Scotland brought to coastal areas in England and Wales the periodic threat of seaborne French attack. It is important to realise that such raiding has conventionally been treated by historians as the chief explanation for castle building in the south of England in the late fourteenth century. And the threat certainly did have a tangible effect, particularly as regards the repair of existing castles and the hurried provision of garrisons to man them at moments of crisis. In 1335, for example, it was the concern of French attack that prompted the survey and hurried repair of several royal castles along the south coast. The associated documentation provides a fascinating snapshot of these buildings at the time.

At Portchester Castle the surveyors reported that the sea had washed away sections of the Roman wall around the outer bailey and a timber fortification had to be erected to prevent enemy galleys from sailing into it.[47] Meanwhile, on the landward side of the castle extensive new earthworks were created beyond the walls. Both the Landgate and the gateway to the inner bailey were provided with projecting barbicans. At exactly the same time, just across the Solent on the Isle of Wight, money was expended on the repair of Carisbrooke Castle. Between 1335 and 1341 a new façade with a pair of towers was added to the front of the castle gatehouse and the domestic buildings in the bailey were repaired (pl. 202).[48] During the course of the repairs there was a failed French landing on the island.

Over the same period there is some evidence that the nobility and several larger towns took similar precautions. A new barbican was added to the eleventh-century gatehouse of Lewes Castle by John de Warenne in a manner and style comparable to the royal additions to Carisbrooke (pl. 203). The work at Lewes is

202 The main gate of Carisbrooke, Isle of Wight. Its twin-towered façade was added to an existing gatehouse between 1335 and 1341. These alterations were put in hand – according to the surviving works account – 'for fear of the invasion of the Isle this year' by the French. In the 1380s the gatehouse was raised in height and the projecting battlements or machicolis over the entrance added. The gatehouse is approached over a bridge that may have been fortified in the fourteenth century to create a barbican. All evidence for this, however, was swept away during alterations in the years 1597–1602, when the castle was encircled by a new system of bastion fortifications.

not documented, but the detailing of the new building also compares to the demolished Westgate of the town, which was probably built with money raised by a murage grant dated 1334.[49] But castle building in the kingdom at large was neither concentrated along the coast nor did it necessarily coincide with scares of attack. Really grand architectural projects required time and money to carry through and, as a result, they remained closely bound up with domestic politics. Before the influence of the Perpendicular began to be felt, these buildings continued to reflect a fascination with the geometric complexity and idiosyncrasy of the Decorated style.

This process is nowhere better illustrated than in the south-west of England and Wales in the area of the Bristol Channel. In the early fourteenth century Bristol was one of the most prosperous cities in the kingdom and its wealth funded two brilliant and closely related essays in the Decorated style. At some point in the 1290s work began to a new church at the abbey of St Augustine in Bristol, now the cathedral.[50] More than a decade later at St Mary Redcliffe, the principal parish church of the town, a great porch on a polygonal plan was erected to house a relic of the Virgin.[51] Both projects had their architectural roots in the works of Edward I's reign and that crucial royal commission, St Stephen's Chapel, Westminster. The porch was additionally reminiscent of such polygonally planned castle gatehouses as Caernarfon and Denbigh. Both Bristol buildings proved widely influential. (It has even been suggested on the basis of shared details that the designs of St Augustine's were known to Peter Parler, the master mason of Prague Cathedral from 1356.)[52] They also share with each other, and a small circle of buildings that follow them, one highly distinctive form: an arch with a polygonal outline (see arch shown in pl. 204).

Amongst the patrons of St Augustine's Abbey were members of its founding family, the Berkeleys. They created within the rebuilt church both an opulent burial chapel and a series of tomb niches with polygonal over-arches. Thomas, eighth Lord Berkeley (1326–1361), accumulated such wealth that he was dubbed 'Thomas the Ritch' by the seventeenth-century historian of the family, John Smyth. According to Smyth, working from the family muniments that have since been lost, Thomas embarked upon the reconstruction of his seat at Berkeley Castle in the 1340s. This process began in 1342 with the restoration of the 'high tower' of the castle and the addition to it of two connected

203 The main gate of Lewes, Sussex. In the mid-fourteenth century a free-standing twin-turreted gatehouse (1) was erected in front of its eleventh-century predecessor (2). The new gatehouse probably stood on the first pier of a long fortified bridge that spanned the castle ditch. Its builder is likely to have been John de Warenne, seventh earl of Surrey (d. 1347), the last of his family to enjoy the great Warenne inheritance. The gatehouse possesses distinctively detailed cross loops that are delicately outlined with a double moulding (3). These loops are paralleled both in the town Westgate (probably built with money raised by a murage grant dated 1334) and the nearby entrance to Ewhurst. The manner in which the front turrets are projected out is unusual in England in this period (4).

204 The porch to the bishop's hall in the palace at St Davids, Pembrokeshire, constructed in the 1340s. Its door has an arch with a polygonal outline, evidence that the mason who designed the building was connected with Bristol. The walls are crowned by an arcaded parapet. This is ornamented with stone laid in a chequered pattern and also an impressive array of sculpture showing grotesque imagery. The parapet was surmounted by battlements and was evidently intended to evoke a machicolis. Its coloured stone decoration perhaps suggests a connection with the works at Denbigh (see pls 168 and 169).

turrets on a rectangular plan (see pl. 76). The work reputedly cost £108 3s. 1d.[53] There followed between 1344 and 1345 the creation of a new suite of domestic buildings in the bailey, including a hall, a kitchen and a chapel with its own delicately ornamented wall closet.[54] It may also have been in this period that a large barbican – now destroyed – was erected at the entrance to the castle. In broad terms, this probably resembled the barbican at Alnwick: it was entered through a pair of polygonal towers, but little else is known about it.

In the light of Smyth's account it is worth digressing briefly to set the rebuilding of Berkeley in the context of Thomas's extravagant lifestyle and wider patronage. This was funded through his activities as a soldier in Scotland and France and by investment in land. The castle was the principal seat of an enormous network of estates studded with residences and hunting lodges. To these were added the ancient castle of Beverston in Gloucestershire, which Lord Berkeley bought and partially rebuilt in the years 1348–50.[55] In the churches associated with his estates Lord Berkeley made complex provision for the endowment of priests. On a daily basis his kitchens provided food – by Smyth's estimate – for a household of more than three hundred people. These included twelve knights and

twenty-four esquires, each one accompanied by a page. All these men were liveried in a garment of ray and crimson (a type of woollen cloth with stripes), lined with different types of fur depending on their degree.[56] Besides his busy activities as a soldier, Thomas was an enthusiastic huntsman and even stocked one of his parks with white deer. For his agricultural work and pastimes the accounts record his ownership in 1346–7 of 15,381 horses.[57] This was a lifestyle rivalling that of many titled peers.

There are several architectural details that demonstrate that the master mason responsible for the work at Berkeley Castle was trained in Bristol. In particular, the great hall makes consistent use of polygonal arches, clearly a borrowing from St Augustine's Abbey. But Berkeley was not the only major residence to pick up this detail. Exactly the same arch form also appears in another very ambitious residence on the other side of the Bristol Channel. The bishop's palace at St Davids in Pembrokeshire was remodelled during the episcopacy of Henry Gower between 1328 and 1347, and its ruins still substantially survive. Gower was a royal clerk on the model of those raised to power in Edward I's reign through diligent service to the king.[58] At St Davids he created for himself a courtyard residence with two great halls set at right angles to one another

205 The east front of
Warwick, built between the
1340s and 1393/4. Analysis of
technical details including
mouldings suggests that work
began on the gatehouse,
progressed to Caesar's Tower
on the left, and concluded
with Guy's Tower to the right.
Incidentally, the names of
these two flanking towers
celebrate respectively the
fictional connections of the
earls of Warwick with the
world of Rome and the
popular hero of chivalric
romance, Guy of Warwick.
The projected battlements of
the towers and the flying
bridge that connects the two
gatehouse turrets add a sense
of theatre to the design.

(pl. 204). The isolated use of a polygonal arch as the
entrance to one of the halls suggests that there was
again a mason from – or familiar with – Bristol working on the site.

As a whole, however, the palace is less a derivative of
Bristol design than a parallel expression of the same rich
and flamboyant Decorated style. Particularly notable at
St Davids is the treatment of the parapets. These are
crowned with battlements set above a deep arcade laid
with chequered masonry. The overall form of the
parapet at St Davids is clearly intended to evoke the
machicolis running along a castle wall, though in this
case the arcades could not have functioned defensively.
Here they are being applied as an architectural status
symbol and bestow on the palace the character of a
castle. Their rich associated programme of figure sculpture lends further splendour to the display.[59] It may be
the case that the use of chequered parapets was copied
from such castle buildings as the gatehouse at Denbigh.

Probably inspired by St Davids is a hall and inner gatehouse at another of Gower's palaces at Lamphey and a
parapet added to a lodging building at nearby Swansea
Castle. The latter work is attributed to John, Lord
Mowbray, who held the castle between 1331 and 1354.[60]

It was against the background of this Decorated
tradition in the south-west that one outstanding castle-
building operation in the Midlands must be understood. Thomas Beauchamp, eleventh earl of Warwick,
was one of the most celebrated soldiers of his age and
a near contemporary of Edward III. He won honours
at home and great wealth in France during the 1330s
and 1340s. His military career culminated on crusade in
Prussia, where he allegedly captured the prince of the
Lithuanians.[61] It was probably around 1340 that he
began to reorder his seat at Warwick Castle with domestic ranges and a new line of eastern defences (pl. 205).
On the basis of architectural detail it has been convincingly argued that work on this latter project began

with the central gatehouse and its integrated barbican.[62] Soon afterwards, possibly following his rich pickings at the battle of Poitiers, he began a tower to the north of the gatehouse called Caesar's Tower. It comprises five vaulted floors set out on a three-lobed or trefoil plan and is encircled by a crenellated gallery. Work to this was followed by an octagonal tower to the south of the gatehouse, today known as Guy's Tower. This may have been begun after Thomas's death and is known to have been completed in 1393/4 at a cost of £395 5s. 2d.[63]

Caesar's Tower has long been described as a French-inspired work of architecture, apparently because there are no obvious English sources for it.[64] Convincing precedents for the tower, however, are as hard to find in France as in England. An alternative possibility is that it derives from the vigorous and inventive Decorated tradition in the south-west of England. Various features of this exceptional building argue in favour of this, not least the fact that towers with two lobes can be found in the late thirteenth-century architecture of that region, as at Stokesay in Shropshire and Abergavenny in south Wales. In addition, there is a fourth building at Warwick Castle probably also begun by Earl Thomas that certainly is rooted in the court-connected architecture of Edward I's reign. The Watergate comprises four turrets clustered around a central tower (pl. 206). Within it is a polygonal entrance passage, a form so unusual must point to a connection with the porch of St Mary Redcliffe at Bristol and the great gatehouses of Denbigh and Caernarfon.

MONASTIC GATEHOUSES

Over the summer of 1327 Bury St Edmunds in Suffolk was wracked by repeated bouts of rioting. The violence was the result of a long-running struggle by the populace to establish their independence from the great Benedictine monastery at the heart of the town. Fighting was fierce and extensive damage was done to the monastic precinct. In the course of one attack the abbot was abducted from the monastery and several monks were murdered. The battle was also carried out to the surrounding countryside. By the time peace was restored at least thirteen of the abbey manors had been destroyed and livestock worth an astonishing £6,000 was carried off.[65] The breakdown of law and order in Bury in 1327 was specifically bound up with the failure of royal government in the closing year of Edward II's reign. It fed, however, on the growing tensions that

206   The Watergate, Warwick, in 1914. The gatehouse stands immediately beside the motte at the end of the principal domestic range in the castle. It is one in a small group of buildings – such as the porch of St Mary Redcliffe, Bristol, of the 1340s, the great gatehouse of Denbigh and the great tower of Knaresborough – that are designed around an octagonal core. The detailing of the building corresponds closely to that found in the late fourteenth-century east front of the castle and suggests a date of construction around 1360. It is planned with a pair of turrets to the front and a corresponding pair to the rear, the latter each containing a spiral stair. The upper floors were well-appointed domestic chambers. The design of the top window is oddly austere for the period. If the tracery is original, it probably illustrates a desire to use bold and archaic forms in castle architecture.

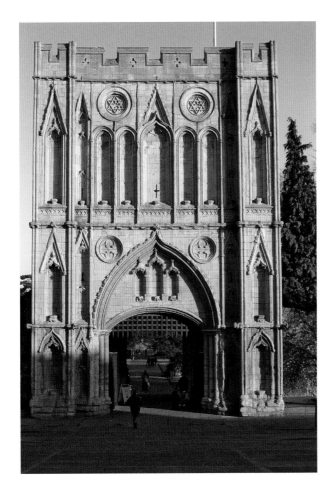

207 The great gate of the abbey of Bury St Edmunds, Suffolk, was built in response to rioting in 1327. A display of heraldry within the gate passage suggests that the lower stages were complete prior to 1346. The rich ornament of the building signals its role as a monastic, rather than a castle, gatehouse. There is something particularly threatening, however, about the way in which tiers of arrow loops peep out from the array of ornament. If the niches that covered the façade were originally filled with sculpture, this building could have shrugged off its imagery at a moment of need and been revealed as a powerful fortification. The gate passage is internally divided by a cross wall. This arrangement created a covered space for the distribution of alms in the mouth of the gateway, as required by monastic convention. A very similar gatehouse was erected in the precinct at Peterborough.

existed between major landowners and the populace at large during the economic changes of the fourteenth century. The local and national confrontations that this precipitated were to come to a dramatic climax in England during the Peasants' Revolt of 1381.

Bury was one of the richest abbeys in England and it responded to the situation in appropriately magnificent architectural fashion. In the aftermath of the rioting the entire perimeter of the convent wall was renewed with fortifications. These were even carried over the river on the so-called Abbot's Bridge, each arch of which could be closed by a portcullis. In conjunction with this operation a new gatehouse was built at the market entrance of the monastic precinct. Covered in architectural ornament and without flanking towers, the gatehouse could not be mistaken for the entrance to a castle (pl. 207). But the rhetoric of castle design is nevertheless clearly apparent in the battlemented outline of this boldly conceived building.[66]

The great gatehouse at Bury is one of several monastic gatehouses in a castellated style that were constructed across England in the fourteenth century. All these buildings play upon the long-standing prestige

of gatehouses in the English architectural tradition and physically express the character of medieval monasteries both as religious and feudal institutions. At William the Conqueror's Benedictine foundation at Battle, for example, where the abbot was responsible for the defence of the adjacent coast, licence was issued to construct a gatehouse as the entrance to its fortified precinct in 1338 (pl. 208).[67] As completed, this building is likely to have incorporated the exchequer and courtroom of the abbey, by this period under the control of lay officers. In reflection of its public role, the principal entrance stair was formidably fortified with a portcullis and murder holes. This gatehouse was possibly encouraged by the threat of French raids along the nearby coast. More certainly, it offered a secure and appropriately grand setting for estate administration.

Concerns for public appearance probably also explain the great gatehouse of Thornton Abbey in Lincolnshire, the largest structure of its kind to survive in England. This was begun in 1377 as a two-storey structure and was then greatly enlarged in 1382 following the Peasants' Revolt.[68] It stands along the line of a wall, fortified with brick towers in the fashion of the neighbouring town defences of Kingston upon Hull.[69] The gatehouse still preserves a spectacular façade set with sculpture, and the building was formerly crowned by battlements and the figures of fighting men. Projecting across the broad moat around the defences is a contemporary brick barbican. The gatehouse interior, which contains no services or kitchens, probably served as a courtroom or exchequer. Estate papers may also have been stored in the warren of tiny chambers within the building.[70] Scarcely less ambitious was the gatehouse erected by the abbey of St Alban, Hertfordshire, following the issue of a licence to crenellate the precinct in 1357.[71]

One architectural feature shared by all these buildings is an internal division of the gate passage with a large and a small archway for cart and pedestrian access respectively. This wall created an internal porch for the distribution of alms to the poor and it immediately distinguishes monastic gatehouses from their counterparts in castles. Indeed, only one great monastic gatehouse of the Middle Ages eschewed this distinctive arrangement and might reasonably be confused, therefore, with the entrance to a castle. This was erected at Tynemouth in Northumberland in the 1390s at the entrance to the naturally fortified headland occupied by the Benedictine priory (pl. 209). Work to the gatehouse was undertaken as a part of a large repair pro-

208 The Great Gate of Battle Abbey, Sussex, photographed around 1880. The gatehouse was probably begun after the issue in 1338 of a licence to fortify the monastery. In this case the large cart and smaller pedestrian entrances run through the full depth of the building and are clearly expressed on the façade. No English castle gatehouse of this period (and very few ever) possessed such a pairing of entrances, which remained architecturally specific to religious foundations. The abbot of Battle had feudal responsibility for the defence of the adjacent coast and the abbey was endowed in the eleventh century with a coherent body of land comparable to that of many early castles.

gramme to the fortifications, which was of sufficient note to receive patronage from an unusually august circle of individuals: on 23 February 1390 the king, Richard II, granted £500 towards it, his uncle John of Gaunt £100 and Henry Percy, earl of Northumberland, 100 marks and 1,000 trees.[72]

Explanation for both the scale of this operation and the castle-like form of the gatehouse is undoubtedly to be found in the very unusual status of Tynemouth itself. The headland served throughout the fourteenth century as an important stronghold against the Scots and was viewed – perhaps somewhat paradoxically – both as a priory and a castle. In the 1340s, for example, one royal agent tried to assert his control over the headland on the grounds that it was a castle and therefore directly subject to the king's authority.[73] The writ of 1390 granting money to the priory works actually describes Tynemouth as 'the priory or castle' (*prioratus sive castrum*). In the light of such ambiguity, the decision to eschew the normal architectural forms of a monastic gatehouse is readily comprehensible. The gatehouse interior formed a self-contained residence with its own services and great hall. It may have been a residence for the steward of the liberty of Tynemouth, who controlled the priory estates, but its intended function is not documented.

MAXSTOKE

In the history and architecture of one exceptionally well-preserved building are exemplified the forces that conditioned castle construction in the period covered by this chapter. Amongst Edward III's young companions at Nottingham in the coup of 1330 was a certain William Clinton. A descendant of the twelfth-century founder of Kenilworth Castle, William inherited modest landed interests in the Midlands during the reign of Edward II. To these he had added important territorial gains over the 1320s: in 1327 he received for his support the castle, manor and hundred of Halton in Cheshire from the grateful Queen Isabella and Mortimer. The following year he made a profitable marriage to the heiress Juliana Leybourne, who brought with her substantial properties in Kent. It is not clear when William first became an intimate of the young Edward III, but following the coup he was quick to enjoy the trust of the newly independent king. In December 1330 he was appointed warden of the Cinque Ports and constable of Dover Castle, and during a tournament early in 1331 the king fought under Clinton's standard – a notable mark of distinction.[74]

William Clinton responded to the king's favour by petitioning in 1330 for a licence to found a college of

209 The gatehouse of Tynemouth Priory, Northumberland, was begun in 1390 with a gift of £500 from Richard II, and cash donations from the two leading peers of the region, John of Gaunt and Henry Percy, first earl of Northumberland. Its principal tower was formerly crowned by angle turrets and battlements, as well as the arms of Prior Robert de Rhodes (ruled *circa* 1440). The gatehouse is indistinguishable from contemporary castle buildings in the region and – uniquely for a monastic building of this kind – makes no architectural provision for the distribution of alms. Nor does it display the wealth of ornament common in monastic gatehouses. Its upper floors comprise a suite of domestic chambers including a hall, great chamber and kitchen. In overall form it compares to the fourteenth-century gatehouses at Carlisle, Alnwick and Prudhoe – though it far exceeds all of these in scale. Its details are paralleled in local castle buildings such as Belsay, Chipchase and Hylton. The gatehouse was converted into a barracks in 1783 and returned to its present, ruinous condition by the Ministry of Works in 1936.

priests at his birthplace of Maxstoke in Warwickshire. This college did not endure long. On 10 March 1337, in reward for his varied services to the king as a diplomat and soldier, William was created earl of Huntingdon. William was poor by the standards of other peers, a difficulty overcome by supplementing his income with grants of lands and rents worth 1,000 marks per annum. The titular seat of his earldom – the castle of Huntingdon – had been demolished by Henry II following a siege in 1173. It is a fascinating comment on the perceived connection between castles and noble titles that in 1341 the king granted him 200 marks in compensation for not receiving this castle.[75]

On the very day of his creation the new earl received licence to establish an Augustinian priory at Maxstoke, a symbolically timed ratification of a reorganisation and enlargement of the college that had been planned some time before. It must have been in conjunction with this new foundation that the new earl also determined to build himself a castle nearby (pl. 210). Licence for this latter operation was issued only in 1345, and – because the earl was childless – the new building was described

as being for Clinton's nephew and heir. Work to it, however, must in fact have been far advanced by this date, because in the previous year the old manor house at Maxstoke was granted away to the priory; the canons converted its buildings into a service court and used the water from its moat to drive a mill.[76] That the old residence could be granted away and adapted in this way suggests that it was already superfluous to the earl's needs. By extension, it also implies that he was already accommodated at the new castle.

Maxstoke Castle formerly comprised two courts enclosed by buildings. The outer or base court stood to the north of the present castle site and is described in two sixteenth-century surveys of the site. It was walled and turreted with a stone and timber gatehouse. Inside stood the ancillary buildings of the castle such as its stables and barns. All trace of the base court has disappeared and there is no clear evidence for its date. The likelihood is, however, that it was laid out in the fourteenth century as part of the original castle plan. Base courts were regularly sited with what seems – to modern eyes – a complete disregard for the architec-

210 Maxstoke, Warwickshire, a view from the north-west in 1920. The castle was begun after 1337 by William Clinton to celebrate his elevation to the peerage as earl of Huntingdon. It was established in conjunction with the foundation of a nearby Augustinian priory. In 1344 the buildings of his earlier manor house at Maxstoke were granted away to the canons of the priory, presumably evidence that the new castle was ready for occupation. This view over the moat shows the chapel window to the right with the roof of the great hall beyond. In the centre is the great tower of the castle, which communicated with the principal withdrawing rooms. The inner bailey was laid out on a rectangular plan with corner towers. There were formerly domestic buildings lining the outer walls. Two sixteenth-century surveys record that beside the four-square inner bailey there stood a base court containing stables and other ancillary buildings. This was walled and turreted in stone and possessed a stone and timber gatehouse. There is also record of a battlemented wall that ran along the inner side of the moat.

tural logic of grand new buildings. In direct consequence, they were often swept away in the eighteenth and nineteenth centuries. Such is the case at Maxstoke.

The inner court at Maxstoke now stands in isolation. It is laid out on a quadrangular plan with a tower at each corner. Around the walls and towers is a broad bank of earth enclosed by a moat. The bank may be a modern creation, but one sixteenth-century survey records a subsidiary wall of stone set with turrets around three sides of the inner court. It is probable that this stood on the inner edge of the moat. Such an arrangement would have created a vastly more complex overall composition of elements than appears today.

The inner court design at Maxstoke can be closely related to other building projects in the wider region. For example, the corner towers are polygonal in plan, a form paralleled in the Midlands at sites such as

Caverswall in Staffordshire. At Maxstoke, however, the most important direct influence on the design is undoubtedly the contemporary work at Warwick Castle. Indeed, the technical points of comparison between them, such as common detailing and the moulding of architectural elements, argue for an exchange of workmen or expertise between the sites.[77]

Entrance to the inner court was through an impressive gatehouse with a pair of polygonal turrets (pl. 211). The gate passage is overlooked by a series of murder holes and its internal vault is ornamented by a multitude of ribs and heavy bosses enriched with foliage. In the battlements and along the wall-walks that extend from it are fixings for wooden shutters that would have shielded the garrison from hostile view, a well-preserved detail of the lost trappings of war (see pl. 101). Rising above the battlements were numerous tall

chimney pots, a long-standing symbol of wealth. These are ornamented with two levels of miniature battlements, a treatment evocative of the tiered machicolations found on the contemporary Caesar's Tower at Warwick (see pl. 205). The passage of ideas from large- to small-scale designs is a commonplace of late medieval architecture.

The interior of the courtyard was formerly enclosed by ranges of timber-frame buildings erected against the outer walls. Many of these were later removed by Richard III, who ordered that they be dismantled and moved to Nottingham in 1485 to supply his works to the castle there. The doors and fireplaces in the exposed walls indicate the position and floor levels of these lost ranges. Some of the original castle buildings do survive, however, encased within later adaptations. Opposite the gatehouse are the curtailed remnants of the high-roofed great hall, the only stone-built structure within the bailey. Beside the hall is the chapel, the position of which is identified on the exterior by a large traceried window. Beyond this lay the principal withdrawing apartments of the castle. They evidently communicated with the adjacent corner tower, which rises a storey higher than its neighbours. Even in a regularised Gothic castle design, there was space for a great tower that drew attention to the power of its owner.

Maxstoke Castle was completed on the eve of an architectural revolution. The example of St Stephen's Chapel, Westminster, had offered masons the opportunity to indulge in rich ornament and complex geometry. But over the 1330s other ideas implicit in its design began to be explored. In the process a new style of architecture was born and it is to this that we must next turn our attention.

211   The main gate of Maxstoke, Warwickshire, in 1906. The building preserves a pair of medieval gates that were decorated after 1438 with ironwork representing the heraldry of the Stafford family, later owners of the castle.

The detailing of the gatehouse – including the form of windows and technical comparison of mouldings – suggests that it was constructed by the same masons who were at work on the gatehouse and barbican of Warwick Castle.

One specific detail further reveals the connection: all the chimneys appear to be miniature models of Caesar's Tower at Warwick, with a ring of battlements projected beneath the lip of each pot (see pl. 205).

10

THE GENESIS OF THE PERPENDICULAR STYLE

EDWARD III

The Perpendicular can perhaps claim to be the most long-lived of any architectural style in English history, its aesthetics and forms current for a period of nearly 300 years. It also remains the least appreciated. The neglect of the Perpendicular style is bound up in part with the wider perception of the period that fostered it – the late Middle Ages – as a cultural autumn in the grand narrative of English History. It also reflects a strong prejudice in this modern age of mass production against the very quality that so recommended it to contemporaries: regularity. As will become apparent, mas-ons working in the Perpendicular idiom sought to impose an architectural logic on the structures they created, subsuming every element of a design into a web of fenestration and carefully modulated moulding. They also favoured the creation of boxlike volumes and were fascinated by the use of rich detailing to lend their rectilinear buildings ornament and busy outlines.

These aesthetic preferences were initially born out of a highly unusual commission in the sphere of eccle-siastical design. Following the murder of Edward II, the king's body was taken to Gloucester Abbey, now the cathedral, and – evidently with the direct help of Edward III (1327–77) himself – work was set in hand around 1331 to enlarge and beautify the great Roman-esque church appropriately as a royal mausoleum. The mason employed to undertake this work was almost certainly Thomas of Canterbury, possibly the son of the designer of St Stephen's Chapel at Westminster.[1] He began his daring transformation of the church in the relatively unimportant south transept, an indica-tion that his monastic patrons wanted convincing that his radical proposal was practicable. What Thomas did was to reface the interior of the twelfth-century build-ing with tall panels of tracery directly derived from the external elevations of St Stephen's Chapel. These mask-ed the Romanesque fabric and cosmetically created an ordered and stylish interior in the Perpendicular idiom (pl. 212). The abbot and convent were clearly delighted and with a few minor alterations this brilliant scheme was subsequently extended across the whole east end of the building.

Within the new church elevations at Gloucester are to be found all the characteristic features of the Per-pendicular. The style was properly brought to matu-rity, however, by another important mason. William Ramsey came to London from Norwich, where for several generations his family had served the cathedral works. He took over responsibility for the completion of St Stephen's Chapel at Westminster and established

himself over the 1330s and 1340s as the foremost mason in royal employment. In various prestigious building operations, notably the new chapter house and cloister of St Paul's Cathedral in London, he further developed the idea of applying rectilinear grids of panelling across elevations.[2] Ramsey died in 1349, very probably from the Black Death, but his ideas and drawings passed into the king's works and were widely exploited for many generations.[3] In the sixteenth century, for example, royal masons were still producing window tracery designs with little decorative quatrefoils of a type that had first been seen in the cloister walks of Norwich Cathedral in the 1330s.[4]

Such reuse of architectural details across long periods of time makes apparent the character of the Perpendicular as an essentially canonic style: it was engaged with the inventive reworking of forms and ideas derived from a canon of mid-fourteenth-century designs. That the Perpendicular never went stale is in part testimony to the sheer calibre of its leading practitioners. It also reflects the vigorous response of regional centres of design to the Perpendicular as promulgated by the king's masons. These centres reformulated the Perpendicular to suit local needs, creating what were in effect regional versions of the style. Their ideas were then reimported back into the architectural mainstream when – as in the case of Ramsey himself – masons were drawn from the provinces to serve in the centralised operations of the king's works.

The popularity of the Perpendicular was in large part due to the circumstances in which it developed. At just the moment when reverses in the war with France were concentrating the energies of the nobility back into England around 1370, the Perpendicular was represented by a newly completed building project of enormous importance: from 1350 work had been under way to transform Windsor into the pre-eminent royal castle in the kingdom. In the process, it also became the seat of the Order of the Garter, a prestigious order of chivalry founded to celebrate the military prowess of England. The new buildings at Windsor were familiar to every member of the court. They were also known to a remarkably wide circle of craftsmen, who had been pressed from every corner of the realm to work here. Indeed, given the reduction of the workforce as a result of the Black Death, there can have been few masons of significance in late fourteenth-century England who escaped working on the site. As a result, Edward III's works at Windsor became perhaps the most influential of the late Middle Ages.

212 The south transept of Gloucester Abbey (now the cathedral) was remodelled around 1331–6. The master mason, probably Thomas of Canterbury, applied grids of tracery copied from the exterior of St Stephen's Chapel, Westminster (see pl. 138), across the interior of the Romanesque structure. He also chose to remove decorative bosses from the intersections of the vault ribs so that the whole interior space dissolves into a complex web of linear patterns. This idea of applying regular grids of panelling to the elevations and vaults of a building was fundamental to the Perpendicular style. It derived from French architectural ideas of the thirteenth century.

WINDSOR CASTLE, PART I:

KING ARTHUR AND ST GEORGE

It is from the records of Edward III's reign that we receive for the first time a detailed impression of the flamboyant lifestyle enjoyed by a young medieval king and his immediate circle. The extravagancies of the court powerfully suggest a group that lived for its own pleasure. Surviving wardrobe accounts, for example, document Edward III's bizarre appearance at a Christmas feast dressed as a pheasant and the decoration of one helmet for the tournament field with a crest comprising 4,000 peacock feathers.[5] One recurrent theme of the king's pastimes was a fascination with the figure of King Arthur and the exploits of the knights of the Round Table. He is even recorded in an armorial roll of 1334 as having fought at a tournament bearing the arms of the Arthurian knight Sir Gawain under the pseudonym of Monsieur Lionel, a name deliberately evocative of the royal beast of England.[6] The circumstance suggests an impressive knowledge of Arthurian romance and a remarkable interest in appropriating its forms to contemporary court spectacle.

Windsor had been somewhat neglected as a royal residence by Edward III in the first years of his reign, but in January 1344 a great tournament was held there. Following three days of combat, the king and his team emerged victorious. In celebration, Edward III declared his intention of founding a chivalric order of 300 men whose members pledged mutual assistance and support for their leader.[7] The model for the new order was to be the Round Table of legend with the king assuming to himself the role of Arthur. Within weeks work began at Windsor on a circular building 200 feet (61 m) in diameter and housing a round table under the direction of the mason William Ramsey and the carpenter William Hurley. This remarkable structure stood in the upper ward of the castle, but it proved short-lived.[8] Work to the building ceased in November and the whole project was abandoned. Various explanations have been offered for this change of heart. These include the distraction of renewed hostilities with France; concern at the suitability of King Arthur (who overlooked the infidelity of his queen) as a role model; and disillusionment following the unfortunate death of Edward III's favourite, William Montagu, earl of Salisbury, from wounds received at the Windsor tournament.

The idea of a chivalric order based at Windsor was, however, revived four years later, on 24 June 1348. During the course of another tournament at the castle Edward III instituted the Order of the Garter. The precise relationship of this order with the earlier Round Table is uncertain, but the very idea of such a chivalric brotherhood was rich with Arthurian association. Unlike its aborted predecessor, the new order was also dignified with an explicit religious affiliation. Less than two weeks later, on 6 August, a foundation charter was drawn up for two new royal colleges of priests to serve existing chapels in the political nerve centres of the realm: St Stephen's Chapel in Westminster and the chapel built by Henry III in the lower bailey at Windsor Castle to honour the Virgin and St Edward the Confessor. Both new colleges were identically constituted with a dean and twelve secular priests or canons – the number of Christ and his apostles – charged with celebrating divine service. To assist in their duties, each of these men was provided with a deputy, a vicar choral, who was responsible for singing services. There was besides a group of four clerks or professional singers, six boy choristers, a verger and two bell ringers. It can be no coincidence that this composition copied that of the French royal chapel, the Sainte-Chapelle in Paris.[9] Of the two colleges, that at Windsor was to function in special relationship to the new Order of the Garter, and its chapel was now additionally dedicated to the martial figure of St George.

As first constituted, the Order of the Garter comprised twenty-five knightly members and the king, in effect two groups of twelve men led respectively by Edward III and his eldest son, the Black Prince. The number was intended to mirror the number of the apostles; but it also conformed conveniently to the usual size of competing teams in court entertainments and tournaments, one reflection of the heady blend of devotion and pleasure that the new order enshrined. As the canons had their deputies, so too did the knights: twenty-six so-called poor knights were to attend divine service as celebrated by the dean and canons on a day-to-day basis. These men were to be worn-out veterans and were to pray for the good estate of the knights, a formidable array of favourites and prominent soldiers. The first meeting of the new order took place on 23 April 1349, the feast of St George, the date from which the college formally recognised its foundation. Famously, Edward III's creation still survives, its membership – now as then – the highest dignity that can be conferred by the sovereign within the English honours system.

213 The entrance passage vault of the Cradle Tower, Tower of London, 1348–55. Its distinctive circular bosses formed murder holes, through which it was possible to drop missiles onto the passage beneath. These are the first known examples of such ring bosses. The detail subsequently became a hallmark of gatehouse designs associated with the king's works in the later fourteenth century. Preserved on the vault are traces of what is probably a fourteenth-century colour scheme: the webbing is of white chalk and the Reigate stone ribs were painted red, a treatment that is still just visible. Similar fourteenth-century colour schemes survive elsewhere, as in the chapel of Our Lady of the Pew in Westminster Abbey.

The Order of the Garter, with its associated college at Windsor, was established while Edward III was still glorying in the military successes of 1346–7 – Crécy, Neville's Cross and the fall of Calais. It is small surprise, therefore, that many features of the order suggest that it was intended to underline the king's ambitions on the French throne. The livery of the order was the blue of France, rather than the more conventional English red. Similarly, its motto was in French, *Honi Soit Qui Mal y Pense* – shame on him who thinks evil of it – and was probably intended to refer to Edward III's claim to France. The curious garter symbol worn by all the brethren may derive from a sword belt and underlined both the military vocation and the obligation of its members. Several other highly prestigious orders of chivalry were established elsewhere in Europe during the Middle Ages, many of them quasi-religious in character, such as the Burgundian order of the Golden Fleece. Nearly all possessed arcane membership symbols, a reminder that they were the exclusive preserve of a tiny, comprehending court circle.[10]

It is almost certain that the royal mason William Ramsey put together the plans for the collegiate buildings to house the new foundation at Windsor in 1348. His death in 1349 meant that the task of constructing them devolved on one of his subordinate masons, and work began under the direction of John Sponlee in 1350.[11] The new college was essentially a reorganisation of the now-ancient palace complex in the lower bailey of the castle, much of which remained gutted after a fire in 1295–6.[12] Henry II's great hall was converted into the college refectory, and the adjacent courtyard of domestic apartments built by Henry III was reconstructed as a new cloister with a chapter house and dean's lodging. Between the cloister and the castle wall were erected timber-frame houses for the canons.

Entrance to the college was through a grand, vaulted porch called the Aerary after the *aerarium* or a treasury on its upper floor. Both in detail and in overall form, the Aerary Porch compares closely with the Cradle Tower, a small watergate constructed by Edward III at the Tower of London as a private entrance to his apartments in the castle between 1348 and 1355 (pl. 213). The similarities underline the close relationship of castle design in the period with all other types of architecture. Since Sponlee was not involved at the Tower at this time, it also illustrates that masons within the king's works were borrowing ideas from a common pool of designs. Almost certainly this took the form of a collection of drawings.[13]

While these operations were under way the existing thirteenth-century collegiate chapel at Windsor was extravagantly reordered. This stood on the footprint of the present Albert Memorial Chapel, but little now remains of it. There is documentary record that new windows and stalls were inserted within the building. From the inception of the order it seems that it was the practice to hang over the stall of each knight a crested helmet and sword. Such a display was probably derived from the practice of hanging arms and armour over tombs, which is documented from at least the mid-thirteenth century.[14] Work to the chapel and college was finally completed in 1367, when a massive altarpiece of alabaster was brought to Windsor from Nottingham. It was carried in ten carts, each drawn by eight horses. To help regulate the life of the college, as well as the court and the teams of craftsmen now at work within the castle, a mechanical clock had been erected at Windsor by 1350. The mechanism and the bell were erected within the great tower on the motte, which soon afterwards became the object of a new building project.[15]

216). Ring bosses are an occasional feature of church vaulting where there was a need to pass ropes into the body of the church for light or bell cords. What has no precedent is the multiplication of such openings within a single space. Almost certainly, these gate-passage bosses were intended as murder holes that could be opened up by removing the lion-head plugs. Similar bosses are found in numerous gatehouse designs of the late fourteenth century, most of which can be directly associated with royal masons. The earliest example of the form, however, is again to be found in the Cradle Tower of the Tower of London, the architectural source for the Aerary Porch of St George's, Windsor (see pl. 213).

THE INFLUENCE OF ST GEORGE'S, WINDSOR

Great castles and residence had always, of course, been associated with religious foundations, but St George's was a new departure in several important particulars. Its form as a college was a relative novelty in England. The convention prior to this date was to establish monastic institutions under an endowment, either Benedictine or – since the twelfth century – usually Augustinian houses. Consequently, the individuals within them were necessarily tied to their communities for life and lived according to the recognised rule of an international order. By contrast, the dean, canons and clerks of St George's, Windsor, were stipendiary officials paid to fulfil obligations set out in a set of statutes that had been drawn up by the king. In this sense, the college was a tailor-made institution, created to serve the needs of its patron.[17]

Another outstanding feature of the royal college was its role as the home of the Order of the Garter. This lent the college an enormous prestige and engaged it with the life of the realm in a variety of important ways. The order constituted in effect a secular equivalent to the bench of bishops – an exclusive group of the movers and shakers in English society with a sense of corporate identity. Its survival to the present day illustrates just how powerful and successful it was. So too does the fact that St George became established henceforth as the patron saint of England, a distinction he appropriated from St Edmund at Bury in Suffolk. It is fascinating in this latter respect to observe that, prior to the Reformation, on their appointment

214 The stair to the summit of the motte at Windsor, Berkshire, in a photograph of *circa* 1913. In its present form the stair is largely the creation of 1439–40, when the mason John Cantelou oversaw its reconstruction. It creates a splendid approach to and from the royal apartments capable, if need be, of accommodating a complete procession in marching order.

In 1353, in conjunction with his work on the college, Edward III began to build a new set of royal lodgings in the castle within the masonry shell on the motte, substantial parts of which still survive. Although structurally modest, these lodgings (and also the canons' houses in the college) nevertheless offer a rare insight into the kinds of timber-framed structures that were once common in the context of castles at this period.[16] The royal lodgings on the motte was approached up a huge stair that was rebuilt in its present form in 1439–40 (pl. 214). Beside this was erected in the years 1358–61 a twin-towered gatehouse, now confusingly known as the Norman Gate (pl. 215). Within the surviving gate passage is a vault with one curious and significant decorative detail.

At the intersections of the ribs there are ring bosses, each one plugged with the head of a royal lion (pl.

215 (*top*) The Norman Gate, Windsor, Berkshire, 1358–61. The mouldings of the gate arch are bold and distinctively bulbous, a mannerism intended to imbue the building with a sense of strength. Such treatment looks back to the moulding forms developed in the context of castle architekture in the late thirteenth century, notably in Edward 1's castles in Wales. The towers of the gatehouse were refaced in the nineteenth century.

216 (*bottom*) The vault of the Norman Gate, Windsor, Berkshire, erected between 1358 and 1361. Each of the ring bosses is plugged by the head of a lion, the royal beast of England. A very similar vault also survives in the Bloody Tower at the Tower of London, where the heads can be lifted out to create murder holes. Edward III was captivated by lions and their symbolism. He also kept lions in the menagerie at the entrance to the Tower of London, which became known as the Lion Gate. The detailing of the vault is in stark contrast to that of the near-contemporary and richly ornamented Aerary Porch to the royal college of St George, a reflection of the different character thought appropriate to the gateway of a castle and a religious foundation within it.

217 *St George and the Dragon*, a wall painting in the castle chapel at Farleigh Hungerford, Somerset. The figure is larger than life and was probably painted in the early 1440s, when Walter, Lord Hungerford, adapted this former parish church as his chapel and included it within the embrace of the castle walls. He had been appointed a knight of the Order of the Garter in 1421 and had himself depicted as a kneeling figure to the right of the saint. Large dedicatory paintings of St George by members of the order are recorded in other castle chapels, as at Goodrich, Herefordshire.

to the order many knights of the Garter suddenly developed a public devotion to their patron, St George (pl. 217). In so doing, they at once advertised their connection to the order and their loyalty to the king.

There are a few isolated examples of colleges being founded in relation to castles prior to 1348, a case in point being proposed at Kenilworth in 1318 by the earl of Lancaster.[18] But from 1348 colleges suddenly became a universal feature of the very greatest residences and castles. Several founder members of the order were directly involved in the patronage of such institutions, often as a means of celebrating important dynastic events. Henry of Grosmont, for example, was created duke of Lancaster in 1351. He was the second man after the Black Prince ever invested with this high dignity in England, and two years later he established a colle-

giate foundation on the most lavish scale at the gates of Leicester Castle.

The college was dedicated to the Virgin and incorporated a hospital established by Henry's father in 1330. It stood in a specially created bailey of the castle called the Newarke or 'new work' just outside the town walls. Besides the hospital with a community of one hundred paupers and ten nurses, the college was served by a dean, twelve canons, thirteen vicars, three other clerks and a verger.[19] This constitution allied it to the new royal foundations of Edward III at Windsor and Westminster as well as their model, the Sainte-Chapelle in Paris. The latter association was made explicit, moreover, by the gift to the Leicester college of a relic from Christ's Crown of Thorns, which had been chosen by the duke as a gift from the French royal collection of relics at the Sainte-Chapelle. St Mary in the Newarke became the burial church of its founder and numerous later duchesses of Lancaster, whose tombs filled the chancel.[20]

Hand in hand with the institutional influence of Windsor went the architectural style it exemplified: the Perpendicular. Indeed, the college church of St Mary in the Newarke in Leicester probably introduced the Perpendicular style to the Midlands, though little is known of its principal buildings because they were destroyed soon after the Reformation. Documentary description reveals that the new college church was unusually sumptuous. Also, that it was cruciform in plan and constructed with a high vault of stone, both features that simultaneously distanced it from the mainstream of parish church design and allied it with the tradition of great church building.[21] Beside it stood a great cloister with a free-standing bell tower, a plan that compares generically to that of the royal college of St Stephen at Westminster and one other important building modelled on Edward III's works at Windsor: New College, Oxford. Some further clues as to its appearance, however, may be provided by another college in the region built in the Perpendicular style.

As discussed previously, Thomas Beauchamp, earl of Warwick and a founder member of the Order of the Garter, was already in the course of reordering Warwick Castle by the time that work to St George's began. He evidently felt the need to keep pace with royal example in his endeavour and began to reform the neighbouring collegiate foundation of St Mary's, Warwick, an institution of distinctive constitution that had been merged with the castle chapel in the early twelfth century. In 1367 the earl integrated all the

218 (*top*)   The chancel of St Mary's, Warwick, in a photograph of *circa* 1903. This splendid interior with its skeletal vaults was probably begun around 1367 and was completed by 1397. Patronised by the earl of Warwick, a founder member of the Order of the Garter, it is the earliest surviving Perpendicular building in the Midlands. The design was probably informed by the lost church of St Mary in the Newarke at Leicester, begun in the 1350s. The side walls are ornamented with miniature battlements and the vaults possess ring bosses filled with angels, both intriguing allusions to castle architecture.

219 (*bottom*)   A view of the east end of the collegiate church of St Mary in Warwick, a view of *circa* 1903. The chancel was reconstructed from about 1367, when the earl of Warwick rationalised the parochial system of the town and placed it under the control of this college. The new chancel was an important architectural source for John of Gaunt's hall at Kenilworth, erected in the 1370s. The polygonal chapter house to the right, for example, seems to have been the model for the projecting oriel window of the Kenilworth hall (see pl. 222). Projecting oriels of this kind – anticipated perhaps in such buildings as the great tower at Knaresborough – were subsequently to become a commonplace of English domestic architecture.

parishes of Warwick under the umbrella of St Mary's and, probably at the same time, began the work of reconstructing the chancel of the church (pl. 218).[22] These collegiate buildings are amongst the most inventive works of the early Perpendicular style to survive and it is unfortunate that the name of their designer is lost.[23] Whoever that mason was, he had undoubtedly served in the royal works and was additionally familiar with the architecture of Bristol and Gloucester.

The internal elevations of the new chancel at Warwick were modelled on those of Gloucester Abbey and comprised two tiers of panelling divided by a miniature parapet of battlements. Over these was set a vault of brilliant design with free-standing ribs crossing the interior beneath a stone ceiling. At the intersection of the ribs are large ring bosses reminiscent of those in the Norman Gate at Windsor, their openings ornamented with angels bearing shields (rather than lions). Like the miniature crenellations, the bosses could be read as a deliberate evocation of castle architecture intended to celebrate the martial prowess of the patron. Within the walls of the chancel were also

created an Easter Sepulchre and an exquisite, vaulted closet for the earl to perform his devotions in private. To the north of the church a small, polygonal chapter house with a flat timber ceiling was constructed (pl. 219). As we shall see, the details of this building, along with those of the chancel, were to be incorporated virtually unchanged into the castle works of nearby Kenilworth in the 1370s.

There are large numbers of lesser figures who followed the king and high nobility in establishing colleges, many on a relatively modest scale. Occasionally, these institutions had very complex histories of foundation that have a direct bearing on castles. Sir John de Norwich, for example, was a distinguished soldier and the son of a chief baron of the exchequer to Edward II.[24] In 1341 he received a licence to crenellate three of his mansions, including Mettingham, Suffolk. Here he built a moated castle, the gatehouse tower, walls and earthworks of which still partially survive.[25] Nine years later, in 1350, he also established a college at nearby Raveningham to serve as the family burial place. But his line was extinguished in 1373 and, after some confusion, the castle became the home of a reconstituted college served by thirteen priests. In this way a dynastic seat became appropriated by the perpetual community that had been created to serve it.[26] There are other examples of exactly this process occurring elsewhere, but other interests usually interfered to prevent it.

Not only St George's Chapel, but also the new royal apartments at Windsor may also have exerted their influence on contemporary castle buildings. At Arundel, for example, the motte was evidently in use by Richard Fitzalan, third earl of Arundel (d. 1376). Nothing of the buildings on the motte within the twelfth-century enclosure wall survives today (see pl. 58), but when the earl died it is recorded that the residue of his fortune – an incredible £60,000 in coin – was found in 'the high tower at Arundel'.[27] This may suggest that the earl had refitted the motte as a suite of withdrawing apartments separate from the residential buildings within the bailey. It may also have been in connection with the royal works at Windsor that the bishop of Winchester reorganised the shell keep of Farnham and gave it a new hall in 1351–3.[28]

Whatever the case, the Windsor works were about to go in a completely new direction and to take castle architecture in the wider realm with them.

WINDSOR CASTLE, PART II: THE UPPER WARD

Following the capture of John II of France at Poitiers in 1356, Edward III appeared to have swept the board of European politics, achieving all his objectives. With a princely ransom in prospect, the king planned a new palace of unparalleled scale in England within the upper ward of the castle at Windsor. The start of the operation is marked by a surge of expenditure on the castle works in 1359, when the existing upper ward buildings were demolished. Over the next ten years a new complex was laid out within the embrace of the twelfth-century walls and towers erected by Henry II (pl. 220). Responsibility for the project fell on the shoulders of three men. John Sponlee, the master mason of St George's, was undoubtedly the designer of the new buildings and directed the opening stages of the operation. In 1361 he was joined on site by a West Country-trained mason, William Wynford, who assumed control of the work three years later. Wynford was subsequently to distinguish himself as one of the most brilliant designers in the Perpendicular idiom. Administering the whole project was the clerk of works, William of Wykeham, later bishop of Winchester and a future architectural patron of outstanding importance.[29]

Despite many alterations to Windsor Castle and the fire in November 1992, Edward III's buildings still constitute the bones of the upper ward. It consequently remains possible to appreciate the sheer scale on which they were conceived. In their regularity and logic the new buildings exemplified the aesthetics of the Perpendicular style. Austere and imposing, Edward III's upper ward also expressed the character of Windsor as a castle. The royal lodging range was erected along one side of the upper ward immediately to the front and left of a visitor entering from the Norman Gate. Set end to end along the internal front of the building were the three great public chambers of the residence raised above a vaulted undercroft: the great hall, the chapel and the great chamber. Together these created a façade nearly 390 feet (85 m) long, which was articulated by a band of tall and identically detailed windows.

This monumental composition was punctuated by a pair of twin-towered gatehouses with polygonal flanking turrets and machicolations. One gave access to the royal apartments and the other to the great kitchens and their associated services. Gatehouses had

220 The upper ward and great tower at Windsor, Berkshire, a detail from an engraving by Wenceslaus Hollar published in 1672. As rebuilt in the 1350s, the interior of the great tower (left) comprised four two-storey ranges in timber frame with low-pitched roofs enclosing a central courtyard. The principal chambers within these ranges, including a hall, were all arranged at first-floor level. Work to the rooms was completed when they were glazed and laid with floor tiles in 1357. The principal apartments in the upper ward (right), begun in 1360, were arranged around three courts that were subsumed behind a regular front comprising the hall (1), chamber (2) and chapel (3). To the extreme left of this façade is the Rose Tower (4), which takes its name from the fourteenth-century painted decoration of its principal chamber. This tower included a small stair that gave the king private access from the inner ward to his innermost apartments. The Rose Tower was to prove very influential, inspiring numerous copies. To a fourteenth-century audience the scale and regularity of the palace front with its identical windows would have been astonishing. So too would the two castle gateways to the state apartments (5) and kitchens (6). They are integrated within the façade, a treatment unprecedented in English design. The other two sides of the ward are enclosed by accommodation ranges for the household (7). Edward III's ranges at Windsor incorporated a system of fenestration with single- and two-tier windows on the lower and upper floors respectively that was to be much imitated.

never been integrated within a building range in this way before and the Windsor frontage set a precedent for the idea, whose subsequent popularity far outlived the Middle Ages in English architectural design. The uppermost chamber of the main gate was a council chamber, which stood proud above the neighbouring ranges. Its position not only removed it from the ears of spies but also allowed councillors to enjoy the views and air from the flat lead roofs during breaks in the discussion. At one extreme the façade terminated in a projecting tower with a tall stair turret and pinnacle. The Rose Tower, so-called, incorporated at ground level a third entrance to the royal lodgings, which was intended for the private use of the king. Its upper rooms were royal withdrawing chambers, one of which preserves beneath panelling the fourteenth-century wall-painting scheme that originally gave the tower its name.

As befitted a work of castle architecture, the whole front was crowned by a parapet of battlements. These were intended to screen the low-pitched roofs of the main chambers and enliven its boxlike outline. In the course of construction, however, the great hall roof was

raised in height, an alteration doubtless made in conformity with ancient English preference for huge open-timber structures in these spaces. Extending backwards from the main façade were three contiguous courtyards. That opening behind the hall incorporated the main kitchens and services. The remaining pair housed withdrawing apartments for the king and queen. This ingenious domestic arrangement, which shoehorned all the principal apartments of a great medieval residence into a regular plan, was subsequently to prove one of the most admired and influential features of the work. Connecting the apartments at both ground- and first-floor level was an extensive system of corridors and galleries,[30] sophistications of planning mistakenly supposed by some authorities to be an innovation of Tudor domestic design in England.

Extending right round the ward, the twelfth-century towers of the curtain wall bestowed upon the exterior an imposing sense of regularity. Their rectilinear outline perfectly complemented the boxy proportions of the new buildings. Enclosing the remaining two sides of the upper ward were accommodation ranges

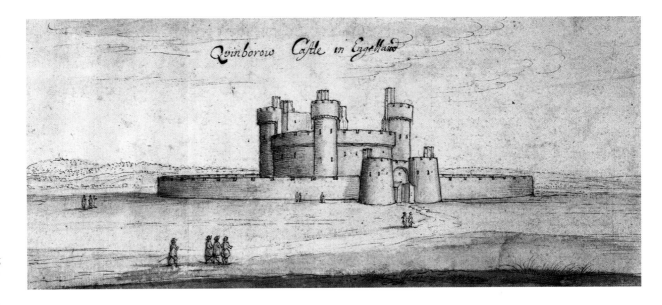

for the king's officers and entourage. These acted as an architectural foil to the main façade, echoing its regularity but executed on a more modest scale. Extending along the main fronts of the accommodation ranges were two tiers of windows, tall arched openings on the first floor and pairs of windows in rectangular frames below. This distinctive pairing of forms was to be widely copied in castle building for the remainder of the century.

THE KING'S WORKS OF THE 1360s

The reconstruction of the upper ward at Windsor was only the greatest of numerous important royal works in the Perpendicular style funded from the war and the ransom of John II of France. Perhaps its grandest contemporary castle project was a completely new foundation on the Isle of Sheppey in Kent (pl. 221). Work to Queenborough – named after Edward III's consort, Philippa of Hainault – began in 1361 and was largely completed by 1372 at the immense estimated cost of £20,000.[31] The project was initially overseen by William of Wykeham, the paymaster of Windsor, and was directed by the master mason John Box. He was another former associate of William Ramsey and active over the 1340s in various commissions at Canterbury Cathedral priory. The castle was unfortunately demolished on the orders of parliament after 1650, an operation conducted with unusual thoroughness. Its remarkable design and its circular plan can be rescued, however, from documentary evidence and limited archaeological excavation.

The design of Queenborough Castle exemplified the aesthetic characteristics of the Perpendicular style. Most obviously, the building was regularly planned and – as befitted a work of castle architecture – austerely detailed. It also reflected the boxlike proportions originally intended at Windsor: all the roofs were of low pitch and lay hidden behind the battlemented parapets. This is in contrast to the fantastical roofscapes popular in contemporary French castle architecture. The castle may have derived its form from walled enclosures on mottes (termed shell keeps), notably that at Restormel, and such related buildings as the great tower of Flint (see pls 156 and 179). Amongst other things, these precedents would explain the circular plan, the internal courtyard and the barbican, which evoke the type of apron fortification seen, for example, on the motte at Windsor. But the monumental quality of the design is remarkable. It may possibly look to designs far away, such as the circular and turreted Castell de Bellver, Majorca, though a convincing connection is difficult to posit. Whatever the case, as will become apparent in the next chapter, it almost certainly contributed to a distinct group of late fourteenth-century great towers in England with central courtyards.

The castle at Queenborough lay within easy striking distance of London by boat and enjoyed growing favour with Edward III as old age increasingly limited his travels to the south-east of England. Another castle favoured for the same reason was Hadleigh in Suffolk, which had first been established more than a century before by Hubert de Burgh and licensed in 1230. As at Queenborough and Windsor, the rebuilding project was under the financial control of William of Wykeham and absorbed the relatively modest sum of about £2,000. It appears to have involved the reconstruction of the royal apartments and the addition of several new towers to the existing walls, though its details are poorly documented. Many of the senior craftsmen involved were drawn from royal building operations, including the master carpenter William Herland.[32]

As might be expected, the surviving buildings at Hadleigh reflect in certain details the centralised operations of the king's works and its associated Per-pendicular style. For example, the two corner towers that today form the most prominent features of the site both incorporate chambers on a hexagonal plan. The idea of combining circular and polygonal plans is implicit in several thirteenth-century tower designs within the royal works, for example, in the gatehouses built by Edward I at the Tower of London. But this specifically hexagonal form is a novelty and is also encountered at Queenborough. It was subsequently to enjoy wide favour across the south-east of England in many Perpendicular buildings of the later fourteenth century, such as Bodiam Castle, licensed in 1385.

Similarly, both towers at Hadleigh have decorative patterns laid into the external masonry made of cut or knapped flint. This type of architectural decoration is common in southern England from about 1400 onwards but its early history is bound up with the work of Michael of Canterbury, the founding mason of St Stephen's, and the Ramsey family at Norwich. As a result, several early Perpendicular buildings make modest play with it, including the Aerary Porch of St George's Chapel, Windsor. It is from these that Hadleigh probably takes its lead.

In the same period, certain strategically important castles in the south-east of England also underwent repair under royal direction. The natural harbour at Portchester served repeatedly as the point of departure for many of the campaigns of the Hundred Years War. It was probably in recognition of its value in this respect that the royal apartments there were reconstructed soon after 1356.[33] Dover Castle, which was persistently described by royal officials throughout the fourteenth century as being in an advanced state of decay, had more than £1,000 expended on it from 1361 to 1377. It is not clear how this money was spent, but judging from official surveys it made little difference to the parlous condition of the buildings.[34] Between 1367 and 1370 the walls of Rochester Castle on the Medway were restored with two new towers. Both the

towers and the detailed accounts recording the expenses of their construction survive.[35]

The last in this group of royal building operations that deserves mention in this context is the remodelling of Westminster Palace, the seat of Edward III's government. Following the foundation of the new college attached to St Stephen's in 1348, the sister foundation of St George's, Windsor, the palace was extensively reordered. As part of the work to the new college, a row of canons' houses was constructed and a great bell tower erected near the present-day site of Big Ben. The royal lodging or so-called Privy Palace was also extended, and a new garden enclosed by a wall and moat was laid out beside it on land appropriated from Westminster Abbey. It was some satisfaction to the irate monks that the keeper of the Privy Palace later choked to death while feasting on a pike caught from the moat. Very little is known of the latter buildings, which were demolished by Henry VIII. Their one surviving element, however, shows a clear affinity to castle design. The Jewel Tower, built in 1365–6, formerly stood at one extreme of the walled and ditched royal garden and was intended as a store for the king's plate and jewels. Set out on a rectangular plan and crowned with battlements, it is comparable in generic terms to the inner bailey towers at Windsor.[36]

Edward III's building projects of the 1360s introduced into English castle architecture a new artistic tension that was to prove enormously fruitful. The Perpendicular style they embodied tended towards cohesion, regularity and consistency of detail. Yet time out of mind, English masons had depended upon irregular composition and varied detailing to emphasise the relative importance of the different elements of a great domestic complex. It was the challenge of uniting these two contradictory demands that was to inspire masons until the close of the century. They were also to inform the architectural patronage of the greatest subject in the realm and a towering figure in English politics: John of Gaunt.

JOHN OF GAUNT AND THE REBUILDING OF KENILWORTH

John, the fourth child of Edward III, was born in Ghent (or Gaunt) in 1340. At the age of two he received the honour and earldom of Richmond, a possession that ensured his future wealth and security. But following his marriage in 1359 to Blanche (d. 1368), daughter of Henry, duke of Lancaster, Gaunt came to enjoy an additional inheritance. In two stages in 1361 and 1362, his wife, by the death of her father and sister, unexpectedly brought him the entire Lancastrian patrimony. At a stroke, aged twenty-two he became the premier nobleman in England and an important force in both domestic and international politics. He also became owner of a huge and varied collection of residences across England and south Wales. Amongst the most important of these were the ancient castles of Lancaster, Pontefract (Yorkshire), Pevensey (Sussex), Leicester, Kenilworth (Warwickshire) and Tutbury (Staffordshire).

In 1372 he surrendered his earldom of Richmond and its castles (including Bolingbroke, where his eldest son, the future Henry IV, was born on Maundy Thursday 1367). By way of return he received other important properties, including Knaresborough and Tickhill, Yorkshire. In London he inherited the Lancastrian palace of the Savoy, which had been sumptuously rebuilt by his father-in-law. Until its violent destruction during the Peasants' Revolt in 1381, this remained his principal base in the capital. His favoured residence near London was Hertford, which had been granted to him by the king in 1360, when – improbably as must have seemed later – he did not have 'castles, houses or other buildings wherin he can lodge or stay as befits his estate'.[37]

The owner of so many castles and with a huge income at his disposal, Gaunt was necessarily an architectural patron of importance. Over the 1360s there is documentary evidence that he maintained the castles on his far-flung estates both as residences and administrative centres.[38] He also garrisoned them when need arose, particularly in Wales. In 1372, however, the register of his architectural interest changed in response to a new departure in his ambitions. In that year he claimed through his second wife, Constanza, the title of king of Castile and León. At the same time, in symbol of his ambition, he quartered his arms with those of Spain. Gaunt persisted in this claim to the Spanish throne for sixteen years but never successfully realised his kingdom. The aspiration, however, required him to transform his public persona: in terms of protocol and ceremonial he became – quite literally – a second king in England. A flurry of building operations followed as all the major residences he owned were extended to accommodate a royal lifestyle.[39] These buildings were realised in the Perpendicular style by craftsmen from the king's works.

The most important of the surviving projects Gaunt undertook in this period was the remodelling of Kenilworth, the seat of his Midland administration. In September 1373, 400 marks were paid to a certain Henry Spenser, 'chief mason at Kenilworth', in anticipation of what was evidently intended to be major building operations at the castle the following year.[40] Both Spenser and his principal colleague in the ensuing works, the master carpenter William Wintringham, had previously been engaged in the reconstruction of Windsor Castle for Edward III.[41] As will become apparent, the buildings they created at Kenilworth clearly reflect the influence of Edward III's operations. Spenser was also evidently familiar with other important local contemporary buildings in Coventry and Warwick, in particular the rebuilding of the castle and the Perpendicular east end of St Mary's, Warwick, probably begun in 1367.

Gaunt's efforts were focused on the reconstruction of the domestic apartments in the castle inner bailey, dominated by the twelfth-century great tower. The centrepiece of the new work was a great hall of unusual form, which was roofed by 1377 (pl. 222). This stood on the footprint of a predecessor remodelled only thirty years earlier in 1347 by Henry, earl of Lancaster.[42] The new hall was raised up on a vaulted undercroft in the manner of Windsor and entered up a long stair though a tower-like porch. Internally, its lateral walls were covered in blind panelling and divided into bays by the timbers of the roof. These timbers appear to have dropped down to floor level at regular intervals to create internal bays. It is likely that the roof followed closely on the design of that erected by Wintringham in the great hall at Windsor. Unusually, there appears to have been no dais step at Kenilworth, so the area of the high table may have been defined by decorated tiles in the French manner.[43] Behind the dais there also existed a set of three fireplaces, a feature almost certainly drawn from contemporary French design. Lighting the dais on the courtyard side was a projecting window or oriel. Windows of this type became a commonplace of English architecture into the seventeenth century, but this example at Kenilworth is the earliest fully fledged example of the form.[44] It may have been inspired by the Rose Tower at Windsor, a polygonal tower projecting from the main façade of Edward III's residential range (which was evidently the inspiration for a 1370s window in the abbot's house at Westminster). Its immediate architectural source, however, is the chapter house of St Mary's, Warwick.

222 Kenilworth, Warwickshire, the interior front of the great hall built in the 1370s. The projecting window or oriel to the left is modelled on the chapter house of St Mary's, Warwick (see pl. 219). To the right are the remains of the porch and entrance stair. The very deep, sloping plinth of the hall range is proportioned in imitation of that on the neighbouring twelfth-century great tower and served visually to integrate the hall within the existing buildings. Along with the unusual austerity of mouldings, it also expressed the character of this building as the hall of a castle.

Set to either end of the hall was a four-storey tower on a rectangular plan (pl. 223). That at the lower end of the hall comprised service chambers, a strong room and the apartments of several senior household officials. Each of its four levels was originally vaulted, a feature paralleled in the pair of towers that flank the main front of the neighbouring castle at Warwick. Beside this tower there extended a court with two kitchens, the larger of which comprised at least four large fireplaces. Such cooking provision was double that of most noble households in this period and speaks of the regal scale of Gaunt's household.[45] Beyond the hall dais and opening out behind the second tower was a series of withdrawing apartments. These could be approached either through the great hall or up a subsidiary stair housed in a second oriel window almost identical to that of the hall. Projecting from this range was a large tower with latrines in its lower two storeys. A pair of retiring chambers on its upper floors offered superb views over the mere and park for the duke. This transformation of the inner bailey was accompanied by the enclosure of a garden on an unknown site and the remodelling of two towers along the outer perimeter of the castle defences.[46]

It is fascinating to observe the ways in which Spenser sought to detail the new buildings at Kenilworth in a way that befitted their location in a castle. The great hall, for example, possesses an exceptionally deep plinth that is proportioned in relation to that on the twelfth-century great tower. Incidentally, this Romanesque tower continued in use over this period: in 1392 it is known to have housed the duke's jewel chamber.[47] In addition, the window tracery of the hall was carefully contrived on a continuous plane with the surrounding wall surface, a detail that lends a curious austerity to this self-evidently sumptuous building. At the same time, Spenser's work at Kenilworth reflects the aesthetic preferences of the Perpendicular style. The external hall façade with its flanking towers, for example, is symmetrically planned and the panelling of the hall interior illustrates an interest in grids of decoration.

Yet Kenilworth was not a straightforward copy of Windsor and its architectural ideas. Whereas Windsor was built to a regular plan with an imposing façade of identical windows, Kenilworth was a much more conventional product of English architectural preferences: an irregular massing of buildings focused on the great tower and hall. Moreover, within the new additions to the castle the medieval love for articulating the various sections of the house by differences in architectural detail was taken to new and highly sophisticated extremes. From the exterior, for example, it is possible to read off the relative importance of every interior by its windows: service chambers are lit by slits or rectangular openings and the residential apartments with traceried openings. The latter are themselves orna-

223 Kenilworth, Warwickshire, the external front of the great hall range built in the 1370s. This is treated as a symmetrical composition with two flanking towers. Such regularity of form allies the building to the works at Windsor. Here, however, there is a much greater variety of window designs employed. The tower to the left with small windows formed part of the services. Now reduced in height, it formerly possessed four vaulted storeys, an arrangement undoubtedly inspired by Caesar's and Guy's Towers in the neighbouring castle at Warwick. The tower with larger windows to the right and incorporated a second oriel to the hall. The pairing of oriels in halls remained a mark of the grandest residences (see pl. 291).

mented in hierarchical order, the most ornate lighting the most prestigious withdrawing spaces. It was Kenilworth's vision of organised difference that ultimately appealed to English patrons above the regimented magnificence of Edward III's Windsor.

Work at Kenilworth was to continue into the 1390s, but in the meantime Gaunt undertook a steady stream of other projects. The residential apartments of the Savoy and Hertford were enlarged and in consecutive years from 1373 instructions were issued for the repair of Knaresborough, Tickhill and Pevensey. Nothing is known in detail of these operations, or of Gaunt's documented expenditure on several other castles in this period, including Melbourne in Derbyshire, Higham Ferrers in Northamptonshire, and Lancaster. Over the same period Gaunt also invested in his estates, for example, rebuilding his favourite hunting lodge in the forest outside Leicester Castle called 'Bird's Nest' in 1377–8.[48]

The one place besides Kenilworth where it is possible to get some sense of Gaunt's architectural labours in the 1370s is at the great Yorkshire castle of Ponte-

fract. A rebuilding programme appears to have been initiated on 18 September 1374, when he wrote to his receiver at the castle exchequer directing that 'the ancient tower called "le Dounjeon" at our castle of Pontefract be enlarged anew with well cut stone so as to be of greater height than the tallest tower of the same castle . . . And the same stone may be taken from the ditch to the south of the same castle or from such other place as our steward or you think suitable.'[49] The 'donjon' that Gaunt altered was a low tower probably constructed by Henry III in the 1240s, a structure very similar in proportion and plan to the contemporary Clifford's Tower at York. From the evidence of early drawings, Gaunt raised this building by at least one storey and crowned it with a spectacular array of small turrets, battlements and chimney pots (see pl. 334). The new great tower was an architectural statement of Gaunt's power. Moreover, it placed Pontefract on equal architectural terms with such major local castles as Conisbrough, Tickhill and Knaresborough, all of which had had monumental great towers added to them over time. As will be discussed in Chapter

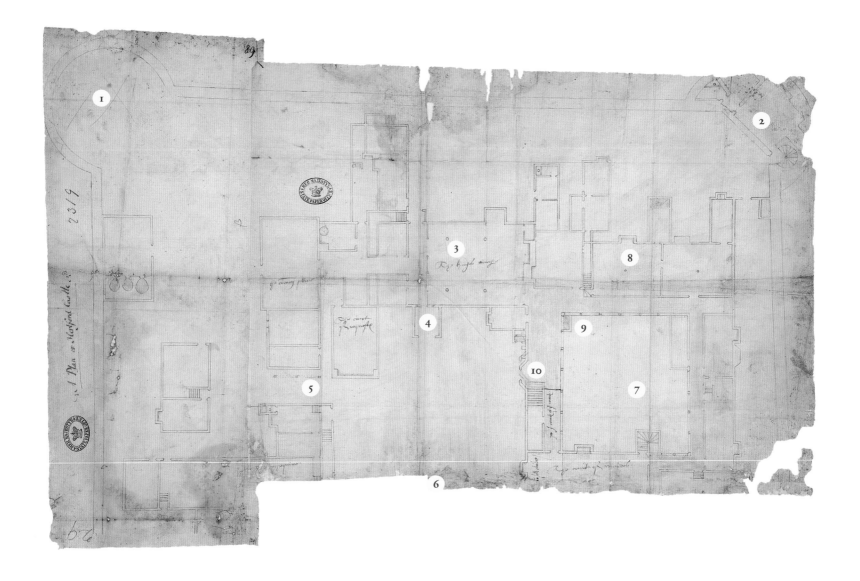

224   An Elizabethan plan of the south-east angle of Hertford Castle, possibly drawn up in 1564. In its totality, Hertford was a motte and bailey castle enclosed by a double moat. Two towers on the line of the bailey wall are marked on the plan (1 and 2). The thin walls of the domestic buildings suggest that they were of timber. It seems almost certain, therefore, that these were the domestic apartments that John of Gaunt contracted William of Wintringham to build in 1380 at a cost of £440. The aisled hall (3) with its porch (4) and screens passage clearly marked is at the centre of the plan. To the left is a substantial services complex accessible via passages (5) from the main castle court (6). The withdrawing chambers are arranged around a cloister with open walks on three-and-a-half sides (7). It is apparent from the depiction of floor posts (8) that the principal apartments were at first-floor level. Also, the position of one latrine drop shows that they oversailed the cloister walks (9). The principal means of access to them was up a large stair with an external porch (10).

Twelve, the reorganisation of Pontefract continued into the reign of Gaunt's son, Henry IV. Few names of the craftsmen involved are recorded, but there was a continued link to the king's works through the carpenter William Wintringham, from 1374 the surveyor of all Gaunt's buildings in England.

Even while Gaunt endeavoured to support his estate as a king in exile over the 1370s, his marriage to Constanza was in difficulties. Gaunt developed a liaison with a lady attached to the household of Queen Philippa, Catherine Swynford. Following Constanza's death, Gaunt married his former mistress. The children of their union were to be of the greatest importance in the dynastic politics of fifteenth-century England. The Beauforts, so-called, were an illegitimate royal dynasty that shadowed and complemented their legitimate counterpart. We will be encountering them and their architecture in the chapters that follow.

Gaunt was to continue maintaining his Lancastrian castles throughout the next reign until his death in 1399, but he was to undertake only one more major rebuilding in that time. For the sake of coherence this deserves mention here. In 1380 Gaunt contracted with William of Wintringham for new houses and a chapel at Hertford Castle. The work was evidently to be executed in timber frame and was to cost the substantial sum of £440. According to the contract, Wintringham was to follow an agreed design and was to receive 100 marks per annum for his labour. It appears to have been completed in 1391–2, with the construction of an almshouse outside the gate and modifications to a chamber called 'Le Parlour' in the castle. In 1392 the mason Roger Skillyngton also received part payment of 750 marks for work he had undertaken at Hertford.[50] Gaunt's buildings in the castle have completely disappeared but they remained in use until Elizabeth I's reign, when they were used as a retreat by the law courts from outbreaks of plague in 1564, 1582 and 1592.[51] Some idea of their design is preserved in a sixteenth-century plan of the castle. This appears to show a rambling residence of classic English form focused upon a great hall but with unusually extensive withdrawing apartments connected by corridors (pl. 224).

ANCESTRY AND LITERARY ROMANCE IN CASTLE ARCHITECTURE

Edward III was not alone in using a legendary figure – King Arthur – to lend authority to his architectural undertakings at Windsor. It was in emulation of royal example that from the fourteenth century onwards a select group of families began to conjure up legendary heroes of their own from the pages of historical romance. These figures made glamorous their distant ancestry and marked them out as exceptional within the ranks of the nobility. Occasionally, such mythical ancestors also came to be celebrated in the architecture, decoration and setting of major castles.

Perhaps the longest running and most architecturally productive relationship between such a hero and a great noble line was that of Guy of Warwick and the earls of Warwick. The legend of Guy, set notionally in the period of the Danish invasions, became popular from the late twelfth century onwards. It exists in several versions, but in broad outline the tale might be summarised as follows. Guy was a young man who

fell in love with the only daughter of the earl of Warwick, a companion in arms to King Arthur. She refused to marry him, however, until he demonstrated his prowess as a knight. Following years of successful adventure across Europe and the Holy Land, Guy returned home to collect his now-willing bride. On the couple's nuptial night Guy climbed to the top of the tallest tower of Warwick Castle. Looking out from this vantage point he was suddenly struck by the worthlessness and vanity of performing great deeds for a woman's hand when the service of God was the true object of life. That night he left his wife and engaged in more years of adventure as a knight of Christ.

While Guy was away on his second tour of duty, the pagan Danes challenged the king of England, Athelstan, to fight for his kingdom against a giant called Colbrond. At divine direction, Guy returned anonymously from his wandering just in time to act as the English champion in the combat. Guy defeated Colbrond and England was saved from the pagans. Nevertheless, after the combat he refused to identify himself and travelled back to Warwick. There he lived in a cave outside the city as a hermit. After more than two years of prayer and isolation he sensed death approaching and sent to his long-abandoned wife to say that if she came to the cave she would be able to bury his corpse. At the same time he also passed on a warning that she would die herself only a few days later. His wife came to the cave, lamented over Guy's body, which she buried, and was soon afterwards laid to rest beside him.

The first of the earls of Warwick known actively to have associated himself with the legend of Guy was Thomas Beauchamp (d. 1369). He possibly began the north-west tower of Warwick Castle and may further have named it Guy's Tower in evocation of the tower on which Guy underwent the conversion of his nuptial night. He certainly possessed a series of tapestries that depicted the legend of Guy, which were hung in the castle, and developed a most remarkable family shrine to the hero. There existed outside Warwick a hermit's cave popularly associated with Guy and known from at least 1334 onwards – probably as a result of the earl's interest in it – as Guy's Cliffe. There, at about the same period, an 8-foot-high (2.4 m) statue of Guy in armour was cut into the living rock (pl. 225).[52]

Guy's Cliffe became sufficiently celebrated to attract tourists such as Henry V, who was no doubt drawn there by his love of chivalric romances. It was also developed by later generations of the family. Follow-

225 The giant figure of Guy of Warwick carved into the living rock at Guy's Cliffe, Warwick, in the 1330s. Guy was probably shown in the act of drawing a sword, and early engravings suggest that his surcoat and shield were painted with the ancient arms of the earls of Warwick, his supposed descendants. An inscription, called Guy's Will, was also formerly carved in the rock nearby. It was indecipherable even by the seventeenth century and has now disappeared entirely. A chapel served by two priests was founded here in 1423 by Richard Beauchamp, earl of Warwick, at the direction of an anchorite hermit of York called Em Rawghtone. The fifteenth-century antiquarian and historian John Rous was one of the priests who served the chapel here.

226 (*facing page*) Hatfield's throne on the south side of the choir still serves as the *cathedra* of the bishops of Durham. In the base of the structure is visible Hatfield's funerary effigy. It was probably built between 1362 and 1371. The form of the throne with tiers of canopied niches framing the seated bishop is similar to that shown on his seal (see pl. 228). Presumably, the lost thrones in the castle hall were of similar design, though set on a lower dais.

For visitors eager to see other tangible evidence of Guy's exploits there was also assembled a collection of armour and relics that was kept in the castle. It is not clear at what date this armour was created, but the sword and coat of mail was an heirloom of the family by 1369.[55] The armour continued to be shown to visitors far beyond the end of the Middle Ages. Celia Fiennes, who visited the castle in the 1690s, recounted:

At the Entrance of the first Court the porter diverts you with a history of Guy Earle of Warwick, there is his walking staff 9 foote long and the staff of a Gyant which he kill'd thats 12 ffoote long; his sword, Helmet and shield and breast and back all of a prodigious size, as is his wives iron slippers and also his horses armour and the pottage pott for his supper – it was a yard over the top; there is also the bones of several Beasts he kill'd, the rib of the Dun Cow as bigg as half a great Cart Wheele: 2 miles from the town is his Cave dugg out by his own hands just the dimention of his body as the Common people say, there is also his will Cut out on stone, but the letters are much defaced: these are the storyes and meer ffiction, for the true history of Guy was that he was but a Little man in stature 'tho great in mind and valour.[56]

Displays of this type were by no means unusual and they are a reminder that pilgrimage and relics were not the exclusive preserve of the church. At Arundel, the two-and-a-half-yard-long sword supposedly used by the hero Bevis to vanquish the giant Ascupart was shown to Captain Hammond during a visit in 1634.[57] This sword still survives at Arundel and is thought to be a fourteenth-century weapon of English make.[58] The same Bevis was depicted on a hanging in the possession of the wealthy noblewoman Juliana of Leyburn in 1367 and valued at £2.[59] Given the focus of her family holdings in the south-east, Bevis was perhaps an assumed ancestor or at least a local hero. The Neville family, meanwhile, celebrated their fictional ancestor called Bulmer (or Berthram Bulmer according to Leland writing in the 1540s)[60] by adding two panels carved with the letter 'B' to one late fourteenth-century tower in their castle at Raby in Co. Durham (see pl. 249).[61] John, Lord Neville (d. 1388), also used Bulmer's initial on his signet seal.[62] And at Dover, King Arthur's association with the castle was celebrated both in the name of the great hall and by a set of bones of one of Mordred's victims.[63] Another important sur-

ing his remarriage in 1423, Richard Beauchamp, fifth earl of Warwick, founded a chantry for two priests on the site. This new foundation was intended to secure a male heir, and the earl was exhorted to its creation by a visionary anchoress in York named Em Rawghtone. One of the priests who served this hermitage was the antiquarian John Rous (d. 1491), and its history is largely known through his writings. In the late fifteenth century the great Beauchamp heiress, Anne, commissioned a new life of the family hero from the monk poet John Lydgate.[53] And her enthusiasm encouraged or drove her husband Richard Neville, familiarly known as Warwick the Kingmaker (d. 1471), to consider further works to Guy's Cliffe.[54]

vival of the genre of object is the Round Table on the walls of Winchester Castle hall (see pl. 10).

The association of Guy of Warwick with a cave chapel was more unusual, though it is worth pointing out that a clutch of such foundations was established near castles around 1400. John of Gaunt had a particular devotion to St Robert, whose cave hermitage stood on the banks of the River Nidd at Knaresborough. Less than a mile away a townsman also created a cave chapel dedicated to Our Lady in 1408 with a life-size sculpture of a knight, probably St George, on the outside.[64] At Warkworth, Henry, first earl of Northumberland (d. 1408), probably built the cave chapel dedicated to the Trinity and the Virgin in the castle park.[65]

Related to this phenomenon of heroic ancestors was the emergence of so-called ancient heraldry during the fifteenth century. This was a type of historic heraldry: blazons attributed to or used by earlier generations of a family. Such ancient arms were enthusiastically displayed by greater noble families on buildings, tombs and domestic interiors during the fifteenth century.

On his effigy at Guy's Cliffe, for example, the hero ancestor of the earls of Warwick was depicted wearing the ancient arms of the family. In 1353 Henry Percy, earl of Northumberland, possessed a tapestry for the hall decorated with the ancient arms of the family.[66] And his successor in the 1480s ornamented the great hall porch of his castle at Warkworth with the two coats of arms in stone. Even the king changed the royal arms in 1405, reducing the number of fleurs-de-lis present in each quartering of his blazon to three. Contrary to what is conventionally supposed, the ancient arms of England did not pass entirely out of use. The whole point was that ancient and modern arms could be displayed together where appropriate to illustrate the longevity of the royal heraldic lineage.

THOMAS HATFIELD AND THE COUNTY PALATINE OF DURHAM

During the 1370s, while Gaunt was enlarging Kenilworth and Pontefract, the palatinate of Durham was enjoying the rule of yet another extraordinary bishop, Thomas Hatfield. A royal clerk appointed to the see in 1345, Hatfield was a decidedly martial cleric and one generally sympathetic to Edward III's wars. Indeed, at Crécy in 1346 he not only came to the aid of the Black Prince on the field during the fighting, but also subsequently conducted the funeral of the most important victim of the battle, John, the blind king of Bohemia. For Hatfield, at least, there was no conflict between his character as a priest and a captain. At his death in 1381 he was described as tenacious of his dignities, tall, venerable, grizzled, tending to portliness, hospitable and generous to the poor.[67]

It was Hatfield's achievement at Durham to articulate in art and architecture the peculiar quality of his office as an ecclesiastic and feudal lord. To understand how he did this, it is necessary to appreciate the relationship between his works to the cathedral church and castle. In the choir of the former he erected a new throne that serves to this day as the *cathedra* of Durham's bishops. Probably built between 1362 and 1371,[68] this tall, canopied monument incorporates at ground level Hatfield's own tomb (pl. 226). The new *cathedra* in the church was undoubtedly conceived of in conjunction with a slightly earlier reordering of the constable's hall in the adjacent castle. This he enlarged to the south so as to create an interior more than 130 feet (39.6 m) long, a hall in medieval England second

227 This oval seal was used by Bishop Hatfield to affirm documents relating to ecclesiastical matters. It shows the patron saint of Durham, St Cuthbert, and the bishop's namesake, St Thomas Becket, with the Virgin and Child above. At the bottom are Hatfield's arms. Oval seals were conventionally used by ecclesiastics and women throughout the Middle Ages.

in length only to Westminster. This operation is probably dated by a contract for the repair of the hall roof with a certain John of Northallerton dated 1351–2.[69] To either end of this vast structure he erected a throne, an arrangement apparently without English parallel. A visitor entering the roughly central door of the hall, therefore, was effectively presented with two halls, each with its own dais throne, extending to their right and left within one space.

This arrangement must have been intended to reflect Hatfield's dual estate as a prince and bishop because it was in the same period that his chancery at Durham created a new seal. Since the late eleventh century the bishops of Durham had always used a single seal of oval shape, a form universally employed by women and ecclesiastics (pl. 227). But during Hatfield's reign a distinction was drawn between this seal for documents regarding church matters and a new seal for those concerned with the palatinate (pl. 228). Significantly, Hatfield's new palatine seal followed the example of the royal seal: it was circular and bore on one side an image of him enthroned wearing vestments. The throne, incidentally, bears generic comparison to that in the cathedral. On the other he was shown on horseback, fully clad in armour as a knight. The medieval vision of priest and lord is here fully realised as an administrative reality.

In addition to the new hall, Hatfield also enlarged the motte of the castle and began work to a new great tower on its summit. Our knowledge of this important building is sadly limited. The tower was altered around

1500, neglected intermittently to the point of collapse in subsequent centuries and then heavily reworked by the architect Anthony Salvin in 1839 at a cost of £5,000 as accommodation for students following the foundation of the University of Durham.[70] The present structure, which still serves this last function, probably incorporates some medieval masonry and witnesses to the polygonal plan of Hatfield's original. From eighteenth-century description it seems that the basement of the building was vaulted and arranged with stairs at each corner; also, that the stone shell was not floored across, but that buildings were ranged around the interior to create a central light well.[71] If this was a fourteenth-century feature it may have derived from such earlier models as Edward I's great tower at Flint. Crowning the structure in the sixteenth century were four little turrets. The detail might be an addition, but it would accord well with earlier fourteenth-century designs in the region, such as the great tower of Edlingham, or even Gaunt's work at Pontefract.

Beyond the fact of its being attributed to Hatfield, there is no firm evidence to date or attribute the great tower at Durham. Nor is it possible accurately to gauge its architectural character. The likelihood is, however, that it was erected in the 1370s. It may also have informed the exceptional and highly sophisticated series of northern castle-construction projects initiated during Richard II's tumultuous reign. It is to these remarkable buildings and the first flowering of the Perpendicular as a national style of architecture that this narrative must turn next.

11

THE TRIUMPH OF THE PERPENDICULAR

RICHARD II

As the darkness grew on the evening of 25 January 1377, a party of more than a hundred mummers passed through the streets of London to the sound of music and revelry. They rode in pairs on horses, their way lit by torches, to meet the heir presumptive to the English throne, Richard of Bordeaux, grandson of Edward III. Some were attired as knights, others as squires; one as an emperor, and another as a pope with a following of cardinals. At the tail end of the procession was a group dressed as papal legates wearing hideous masks, the burlesque villains of the entertainment. The cavalcade proceeded noisily over London Bridge towards the nearby manor of Kennington, where the prince was staying. Richard, a boy of ten, graciously descended from his chamber to receive the mummers in the hall, a splendid interior rebuilt in the 1360s by his late father, Edward, the Black Prince. He was accompanied by his widowed mother and three uncles, the surviving sons of Edward III – John of Gaunt, Edward Langley and Thomas of Woodstock – besides other noblemen. There he was presented with a set of loaded dice and in three throws won a pelisse or cape of cloth of gold, a gold cup and a gold ring. After further gift giving, the delighted prince called for music, and to the sound of trumpets, nakers and pipes the entire company danced, the mummers on one side of the room, the lords on the other.[1]

This carefully stage-managed entertainment took place during the last months of Edward III's reign in a tense political atmosphere. Since the renewal of the Hundred Years War with France in 1369, now a conflict without its former appeal or prizes, the realm had been in growing domestic and economic difficulty. To make matters worse, over the same period Edward III had been increasingly confined by illness and subject to the control of his unpopular mistress, Alice Perrers. The death of his eldest son, the Black Prince, in 1376 made the question of the succession sensitive. Not since the reign of Henry III had England been ruled by a minor, and Gaunt was rumoured, unfairly as it turned out, to have designs on the crown. By their appearance with Richard in this entertainment, the surviving brothers of the Black Prince were demonstrating support for their young nephew.

It was not, however, to prove an enduring alliance of interests. Following Richard II's coronation on 16 July 1377, control of the realm passed to a council dominated by figures from the household of the Black Prince; to all intents and purposes, the royal uncles found themselves politically marginalised. In this arrangement were sown the seeds of a future conflict between a circle of favourites around the king and a disgruntled but powerful group of nobles. The conflict would cost Richard his crown and his life.

For all its political difficulties, however, the reign of Richard II (1377–99) was also a period of outstanding artistic achievement. The king himself was a particularly important figure in bringing this about. He proved to be a man of discerning taste and used art and architecture to underscore his power and regal image. To the same ends he also encouraged the development of complex ritual in his court, with high-flown terms of address and elaborate ceremonial. In later life, for example, Richard II was known to sit enthroned amongst his peers and expect those at whom he looked to bow down in profound obeisance.[2] His innovations in fine dress reputedly included the pocket handkerchief, and he was instrumental in introducing tapestry to English interiors, a fantastically expensive type of woven fabric imported from the Low Countries. Such was the cost of tapestry that it remained highly prized even within the ranks of the nobility into the mid-sixteenth century.[3]

In the uncertain and volatile court, those who enjoyed the fruits of royal service eagerly imitated the example of their lord and master. It is one reflection of this that a steady and growing stream of new castles and residences were erected throughout the reign. Many of these possessed unusually complex systems of withdrawing apartments, apparently a response to the demands of domestic ceremonial introduced by the king at court. The reign also witnessed a large number of outstanding church-building projects, including major works to the cathedral priories of both Canterbury and Winchester. As we shall see, there was a common group of craftsmen involved in these architectural projects, all of them intimately familiar with Edward III's buildings and working within the Perpendicular idiom. At their hands during the reign of Richard II it can be said that the Perpendicular became at last a truly universal style within the kingdom.

THE HOLLOW CROWN

The patterns of castle construction in late fourteenth-century England closely reflected the complex politics of the period, so a brief introduction to the individuals and events that shaped these is essential. Although not a member of the council that governed the king-dom, John of Gaunt was the dominant figure of Richard II's reign both by right and by necessity: he was the eldest of the king's uncles and, as duke of Lancaster, by far the wealthiest peer in England. During the minority he stood behind the throne and acquiesced in the decisions of the ruling council. His role was not an easy one. The outbreak of the Great Schism in 1378 – the establishment of rival popes at Avignon and Rome – polarised European politics and helped intensify the external pressure being exerted on the kingdom by France and her allies, including Scotland. As a result, throughout the 1370s there were continued efforts to garrison and repair royal castles in both the north and the south of the kingdom. This was a process essentially unaffected by the accession of the new king.

Richard's minority ended with the first major crisis of the reign, an agrarian uprising on an unprecedented scale. The Peasants' Revolt of 1381, which was born of the economic difficulties created by the Black Death and the Hundred Years War, caused widespread destruction of property across the kingdom. As the figurehead of the government, John of Gaunt was the personal focus of much discontent and was forced to flee into Scotland. In London, his Savoy Palace was attacked with particular ferocity and its valuable contents wantonly destroyed by the mob. He chose never to rebuild this splendid London residence and the ruin stood until his death as a prominent memorial on the Strand to his insulted dignity.[4] At the height of the crisis the young king personally rode out to parley with the rebels at Smithfield on the edge of London and at considerable personal risk helped to disperse them. One splinter group of the mob stormed the Tower of London, where they discovered Simon Sudbury, the much-hated chancellor and archbishop of Canterbury, hiding in St John's Chapel in the White Tower. He was dragged out, beaten and summarily beheaded.

Having proved his ability and courage in dealing with the revolt, Richard now assumed full control of government. As soon as he did so a circle of favourites quickly emerged. The most notorious of these was Robert de Vere, earl of Oxford, who was evidently regarded by some critics as a second Piers Gaveston. Equally prominent was Michael de la Pole, a man with important mercantile interests, and one of the king's former tutors, Simon Burley. The latter two men were elevated to peerages at the start of Richard's first important military endeavour, an invasion of Scotland in 1385. Michael de la Pole was created earl of Suffolk, a title he immediately expressed in architecture, receiving the same year a licence to crenellate three manors including a seat in Suffolk at Wingfield.[5] The principal façade of the impressive quadrangular castle he began there still survives, as does the nearby church and college founded a few years earlier under his direction. His building activities at Wingfield probably condemned Orford Castle, the county seat of his predecessors, the Ufford earls of Suffolk, to decay.[6] Meanwhile, as a special mark of distinction, de Vere was raised to the entirely novel dignity of marquis of Dublin, in the eyes of chauvinist English opinion a solecism of both title and place. The following year he also became duke of Ireland, the first Englishman not of the royal blood to support such an estate.[7]

In 1385 Richard II balanced his patronage of these favourites by elevating his two uncles, Thomas of Woodstock and Edmund Langley, to the dukedoms of Gloucester and York respectively. Both men lacked the landed resources to sustain these titles and their income had to be made up from the treasury, which was not to prove a reliable paymaster. Nevertheless, over the course of the reign each adopted an ancient castle as his principal seat: the duke of Gloucester chose Pleshey in Essex and the duke of York Fotheringhay in Northamptonshire. Little apart from the earthworks at either of these motte and bailey sites survives and our understanding of their development in this period is limited. At Pleshey, excavations have revealed a rectangular court of buildings on the top of the motte, which were possibly erected by Gloucester.[8] It is also known from an inventory made in 1397 that the castle was richly furnished and contained numerous tapestries, as well as an unusually fine collection of books.[9]

A few more details of the lost buildings at Fotheringhay are known from sixteenth-century description. Some features of the castle recorded at this time may well post-date Langley's period of ownership, though he was attributed in the 1540s as having expended large sums on the castle.[10] One of its baileys was enclosed by buildings and the motte was surmounted by a great tower with several projecting turrets. This building was laid out on a sixteen-sided plan with a continuous two-storey range enclosing a small inner courtyard. Projecting from the parapets was a series of turrets, and it was described in numerous accounts from the sixteenth century onwards as 'the fetterlocks'. The name, clearly referring to the heraldic badge of the house of York, is a fascinating instance of architecture taking on direct dynastic symbolism.[11] To celebrate their importance, the parish churches at both Fotheringhay and Pleshey also came to be served by colleges of priests, though that planned by the duke of York in the former case was properly established only after his death in 1402.[12]

The Scottish campaign of 1385 was not a success, and in its aftermath John of Gaunt determined to go in pursuit of his Spanish throne. His absence from England between 1386 and 1389 removed from court an important stabilising influence. It also attracted the hostility of the king of Castile, whose crown Gaunt claimed, and encouraged the French to reject English overtures for peace. These two Continental powers now came into alliance against England and there followed over the summer of 1386 the most serious invasion scare of the reign. It is one indication of the perceived scale of the crisis that even the monastic community at Westminster Abbey felt bound to play its part. With the permission of the chapter, the seventy-five-year-old abbot and two monks were sent to the coast in armour. Curiously, one of the monks was so tall that when the armour later came to be offered for sale on the open market no one wanted to buy it.[13]

Such a response was not without cause. Serious preparations for an attack were under way on the other side of the Channel and the town garrison of Calais even captured a French ship bearing parts of a timber castle intended to cover the landing of an army on English soil.[14] According to one chronicler, the structure took the form of a wooden wall thickly and densely made, 20 feet high. Every twelve paces (*passus*) along its 3,000-pace length there was a tower capable of holding ten men that rose 10 feet above the level of the wall. The account also states that the structure offered protection for gunners (*gonarius*), perhaps implying some specific physical provision for cannon. It is an additional curiosity that the designer of this wall was captured with his creation. Although his name is not given, he is described as an Englishman and his nationality is probably no coincidence: nowhere else in northern Europe did there exist a comparably sophisticated tradition of timber-frame construction. This captured fortification was erected at Sandwich to serve as a defence against those who had built it.[15]

The threatened invasion never materialised, but the domestic political situation continued to worsen and eventually erupted into violence. On 13 November 1387 Richard's uncle, Thomas of Woodstock, duke of

229   A detail from a view of Westminster by Wenceslaus Hollar, dated 1647. The twin-towered north front of Westminster Hall was remodelled by the king's mason Henry Yevele from 1394. This particular composition – unique in the context of an English hall – was probably derived from the characteristic design of great church west fronts with two towers. Universally familiar to the medieval public, it can be no coincidence that several castle buildings of the 1390s relate to this distinctive composition. The new entrance was also ornamented with a display of sculptures representing English kings, a scheme anticipated in the choir screen of St Paul's Cathedral of *circa* 1327 (and subsequently widely popular). This borrowing of forms and iconography from ecclesiastical design in the seat of royal government was doubtless intended to emphasise the sacral quality of Richard II's rule.

celebrated of these was the remodelling of Westminster Hall, begun in 1394 by the king's mason Henry Yevele and his carpenter Hugh Herland.[17]

At Westminster Hall Richard II recast the main entrance as a twin-towered façade in a fashion evocative of a great church (pl. 229). This conceit emphasised the sacred nature of royal authority in the king's principal hall, an idea further implied by the form of the huge roof that covered it. With thirteen roof trusses supported on the backs of hovering angels, this explicitly referred to the number of Christ and his apostles; here the celestial court hovered in protection and appreciation above its terrestrial counterpart. In artistic terms the reworking of Westminster Hall was to prove very influential, a reflection of its place at the heart of English consciousness and government. It stimulated a fashion for roofs supported on the sculpted figures of angels in both domestic and church interiors into the sixteenth century (see pl. 299, for example). When necessary, the workaday furniture of the royal law courts that usually occupied the public space of the great hall at Westminster could be swept away to create the largest covered interior in the kingdom. The banquets held here were so substantial that they were sometimes policed by mounted officers. On special occasions the deep walls were also ideal for the display of Richard's outstanding tapestry collection.[18]

The early 1390s were a period of political calm and – as we shall see – of intense architectural activity. But in July 1397, entirely without warning, the king moved to revenge his humiliation of 1388–9 and seized the three principal lords appellant. His uncle, Thomas of Woodstock, was murdered, the earl of Arundel executed and the earl of Warwick banished. Using their combined lands as endowments, he undertook in September 1397 the single largest creation of peers in medieval English history. Amongst them for the first time was a batch of dukes. None of these men was of royal blood or possessed the quantity of land conventionally associated with such a title. In consequence they were derisorily described by one critic as the 'duketti'.[19] Richard's ambition in this act of mass ennoblement was nothing less than a fundamental reorganisation of the political map of England with a more numerous nobility of graduated title in possession of smaller estates. This settlement seemed to signal his complete political triumph but, ironically, it set in train the events of his own downfall. Had it lasted longer it would undoubtedly have changed the architectural face of England.

Gloucester, and the earls of Warwick and Arundel presented the king with an indictment of his principal favourites. This group, the so-called lords appellant, then moved to confront the king and force his submission, mustering their forces at Huntingdon, where they were joined by John of Gaunt's son, Henry Bolingbroke, and Thomas Mowbray, earl of Nottingham. On 20 December 1387 the lords appellant intercepted and defeated an army led by Richard's favourite, de Vere, before marching south to London and capturing the king. Following a short imprisonment at the Tower, Richard was forced to throw over his favourites and concede everything that his opponents demanded. He may even have been briefly deposed. As events were to prove, Richard never forgot his treatment or forgave these men.

It was possibly as a direct result of this humiliating episode that over the 1390s Richard increasingly came to emphasise the divine character of his royal estate. As part of this process, he encouraged elaborate forms of address and staged formal crown-wearing ceremonies. He also came to identify closely with his sanctified and remote ancestor, Edward the Confessor. Indeed, in about 1395 he began impaling the royal arms with St Edward's in the manner of a wife with her husband.[16] This affiliation with Edward the Confessor encouraged Richard to numerous works of patronage around Westminster, the site of the saint's shrine. Most

The uncertain atmosphere at court brought about a quarrel between Henry Bolingbroke, the son of John of Gaunt, and Thomas Mowbray, the 'duketto' of Norfolk. It was determined that the quarrel be settled by personal combat at Coventry. The king travelled to attend the combat, staying the night before the encounter at Baginton in Warwickshire, a tower house built by his favourite, Sir William Bagot.[20] The two disputants met the next morning with considerable ceremony before a large crowd. Just before the first blow fell – and doubtless to universal disappointment – Richard intervened and decreed that the two men be banished. His one concession to Henry was that he should enjoy the immense Lancastrian patrimony in the event of his father's death. But when John of Gaunt did die the following year, on 3 February 1399, at his favourite seat of Leicester Castle, it was not a promise Richard found himself able to keep. Within three months he had lost his throne to Gaunt's son.

HENRY YEVELE AND THE KING'S WORKS

Amongst the innovations of the opening months of Richard II's reign was a reorganisation of the king's works, a change that was to have a lasting impact on English royal architecture. It had previously been the case that regional groups of royal buildings or large projects were managed as isolated undertakings, overseen and administered by specifically appointed individuals. Although this practice never entirely disappeared, in 1378 an important departure was made from it. For the first time a small body of men was effectively made responsible for all the king's building operations across the realm. In this arrangement was born what later became known as the office of the king's works, an institution that was to function for the next 400 years. The principal figure in this new organisation was the clerk of the king's works, an administrator and accountant with the power to impress masons and materials. He was supported in his task by a group of purveyors, many of them responsible for individual localities or sites, and his financial dealings were verified by the comptroller of the king's works.[21]

Also appointed in 1378 to undertake the practical work of repairing and creating the king's buildings was a group of five master craftsmen: the king's carpenter, his glazier, his smith and 'surveyor of ironwork', his plumber and his mason. The figure appointed to this last role was a certain Henry Yevele (d. 1400), perhaps the pre-eminent master mason of late fourteenth-century England. Yevele is first documented in London during the 1350s and was named in the accounts for the rebuilding of the hall at Kennington by the Black Prince as the 'prince's mason'. In 1360 he moved into Edward III's service as a 'disposer' of masonry at both the Tower of London and Westminster. It must have been through these operations that he developed his familiarity with the buildings that had shaped the Perpendicular style in the previous reign. His subsequent career involved him in a huge variety of secular and ecclesiastical work both for the king and a multitude of private clients. The loss of documentation has doubtless obscured the full scale of his operations, but it is clear that he undertook a wide variety of architectural duties. These included providing designs (which other masons realised), quality testing new work and acting as consultant. Such was his amassed fortune that he paid for (and doubtless designed) a chapel on London Bridge, a structure central to London's identity and commercial life.[22]

Yevele's wealth, however, was not just derived from building: he is documented as having engaged in other commercial ventures. One of these in particular gives a fascinating insight not only into the extent of his artistic influence but also the probable manner of its operation. Tomb construction in England was always closely allied with architectural practice, and Yevele was part of a consortium that ran the most successful workshop producing monumental brasses in London. The mass-produced output of this workshop, known as 'Series B' brasses, is found literally all over the kingdom. Moreover, brasses of this type were bought by a substantial number of the architectural patrons named in this chapter.[23] In the absence of fuller documentation, this demonstrates that Yevele was connected to the castle-building circle and they to him. Moreover, that it was possible in the late fourteenth century to run a national business requiring a detailed exchange of information between client and artisan from London. As in architecture, the medium for such exchange was drawing, which made possible the creation of 'plats' or designs that patrons could agree to and craftsmen work from.

Yevele was to prove an important centralising influence on architectural practice across the country. His work also illustrates the continued and close relationship that existed throughout the Middle Ages between the spheres of ecclesiastical and castle architecture. But

Hand Cannon·C14th(Hackbutt or Arquebuse-à-croc)
Pitt Rivers Museum, Oxford

35"
1¼"
BORE
a
a

THE WESTGATE
CANTERBURY
A restored and cutaway view from the south c.1400

© Jill Atherton 2010

230 The Westgate, Canterbury, Kent, by Jill Atherton. It was built as part of the wholesale reorganisation of the city defences initiated in 1377 under the direction of Henry Yevele. Work to the gate is documented between 1380 and 1385. The drum towers and boldly projecting machicolis are strongly reminiscent of Edward III's Norman Gate at Windsor (see pl. 215). All the loops in the tower are carefully placed for a maximum field of fire. Shaped like inverted keyholes, they are almost certainly intended for small handguns (see top inset). The gate overlooked the town ditch and was formerly approached over a drawbridge. Many technical details of the building point to the origin of its design in the orbit of the king's works. As with several of Edward III's castle gatehouses of the 1360s, for example, the drum towers stand on two corners of the central gatehouse structure. Another leitmotif of early Perpendicular castle design is the use of ring-boss murder holes in the vault of the gate passage.

he was not an entirely isolated figure and his activities dovetailed with those of other senior masons active in different areas of the country. The names of some of these individuals may be lost to us, but at least two important contemporaries with wide architectural practices can be identified: William Wynford and John Lewyn.

The careers of these three men do not provide a full explanation for the development of English architecture in Richard II's reign but they go a long way in that direction. There was still room for substantial regional variation in architectural practice and for the development of personal styles of design, but there was also a common outlook informed by the king's works. To a remarkable degree, the ideas of the leading royal master mason of Edward III's reign, William Ramsey (d. 1349), were universally adopted and reworked across the kingdom. In that process, the examples of Windsor and Westminster were particularly powerful. Moreover, when these men died, their posts effectually passed to a generation of masons trained in exactly the same context of royal building projects as themselves.

THE SOUTH-EAST

It is conventional to view the south-east of England as the centre of castle-building activity during the late fourteenth century simply by virtue of political circumstance: this was the frontier of England and under repeated threat of hostile attack. Yet while English reverses in the Hundred Years War undoubtedly encouraged attention to the repair and garrisoning of castles along the coast, the direct impact of invasion scares on major new building operations is usually difficult to demonstrate. Architecture has always required sustained investment and the episodic threat of French and Castillian attack did not encourage this. Rather, the patterns of castle construction in Richard II's reign across the country at large – while they occasionally intersect with vulnerable coastal areas – bear no obvious geographic relation to strategic needs. They were commonly accompanied too by undertakings with no connection to fighting: the aggrandisement of neighbouring churches and the creation of parks. Castles were important in war and might serve in its conduct, but they remained first and foremost creations of domestic politics and dynastic good fortune.

There hovers behind the whole process of castle construction across the region the influence of the

231 (*left*) The cemetery gate of St Augustine's Abbey, Canterbury, Kent, built by the monk and sacrist Thomas of Ickham at a cost of £466 13s. 4d. The gatehouse was begun at some date after 1361, but its date of construction is not recorded, nor is the name of the mason responsible. It loosely imitates the form of the principal precinct gate constructed by 1308 (see pl. 141), but incorporates the deep machicolis found on the Westgate of the city.

232 (*right*) The late fourteenth-century gatehouse of Saltwood, Kent, prior to its restoration in 1884. The drum towers and façade were built as part of Archbishop Courtenay's adaptations to the castle undertaken between 1381 and his death in 1396. Built in rubble masonry with slightly tapering towers, this building is nevertheless recognisably similar to the Westgate at Canterbury. Many of its details also point to a connection with the works of Edward III at Windsor and Queenborough of the 1360s. Its turrets, for example, are added to the corners of the main gatehouse and they possess chambers on a hexagonal plan. The gatehouse appears to have served as a lodging, and behind each tower is a battery of latrines.

king's works: everywhere new buildings follow precisely the bold and simplified architectural style – the Perpendicular – first fully articulated in Edward III's redevelopment of Windsor. And where documentation survives, the king's mason Henry Yevele recurrently appears as the leading professional involved. By implication, he enjoyed an effective monopoly on architectural design. His direct involvement is easily traced in the architectural projects of the greatest magnates in the south-east.

The building operations of the archbishops of Canterbury must be viewed against the background of one outstanding commission: the complete reconstruction of the nave of the cathedral priory at Canterbury. This operation was begun by Archbishop Sudbury (d. 1381) and completed under his two successors, William Courtenay (d. 1396) and Thomas Arundel (d. 1414).[24] The design of this magnificent interior, one of the masterpieces of the early Perpendicular style, can confidently be attributed on stylistic grounds to Henry Yevele. His involvement at Canterbury explains Yevele's connection with several other works of secular architecture concurrently patronised by the archbishops.

The first of these was a programme initiated in 1377 to repair the walls of Canterbury, a project jointly financed by the city, the community of the cathedral priory and the archbishop. One of the figures appointed to oversee this project was Henry Yevele, who was also presumably involved, therefore, in creating the most important surviving element of this fortification. Work to the imposing Westgate of the city is first documented in 1380 and was complete by 1385 (pl. 230). Setting aside the question of its specific attribution to Yevele, the designer of this building was evidently aware of the royal castles of Edward III: the gatehouse has murder-hole bosses in the gatepassage vault for example.

It is noteworthy that the Westgate at Canterbury resembles two other contemporary and related gatehouses. Just on the outskirts of the city, the monk and sacrist of St Augustine's Abbey, Thomas of Ickham, built a new gate to the entrance of the monastic cemetery enclosure (pl. 231).[25] Meanwhile, during the 1380s and '90s Archbishop Courtenay was at work remodelling the old archiepiscopal castle on the coast at Saltwood in Kent. As part of this ambitious operation, which included the reconstruction of the castle chapel and residential buildings, a new twin-tower façade was erected in front of the twelfth-century gate tower (pl. 232). The scale of the new façade and many of its details directly ally it with the Canterbury Westgate and by extension with Yevele.

Courtenay was a fierce defender of the rights and privileges of the see, and his building activities – which included the foundation of a college at Maidstone in Kent – could be seen as an attempt to renew the architectural face of his archdiocese. Certainly, he was a man much concerned with questions of public appearance and feudal right – not perhaps surprising given the social tensions of the period and the murder of his predecessor at the hands of a mob. On one celebrated occasion in 1390, for example, the manner in which straw was delivered to his manor of Wingham caused him outrage. The carriers, five tenants who owed the archbishop service, brought the straw 'not openly in carts for his glory, but closely in sacks upon their horses' backs for their own convenience'. Courtenay was furious. The men were summoned to the great hall at Saltwood, roundly told off and forced to perform public penance. This they did on the following Sunday, 10 April 1390, by carrying sacks on their own backs that fully revealed their contents. The attention this episode excited suggests that some contemporaries regarded it as an extreme exercise of feudal rights. Memory of it as an abuse of power lived on until the Reformation and the writings of the Protestant polemicist Foxe in his *Acts and Monuments* (1563).[26]

To some extent, Courtenay's architectural patronage was mirrored by other senior ecclesiastics in the region. The archdeacon of Canterbury, for example, rebuilt his own more modest residence at Lympne in the late fourteenth century, a castle just a few miles from Saltwood. Rather more ambitious than this operation was the work of William Reede, bishop of Chichester (d. 1385), who was licensed to fortify his Sussex manor at Amberley in 1377. Work to the castle, which included the wholesale reconstruction of its domestic buildings, was apparently still under way when Reede's will was drawn up in 1382.[27] Existing buildings on the site conditioned the form of the new castle, which was rambling and irregular. The whole was lent coherence, however, by the construction of a twin-towered gatehouse in the centre of the main façade.

Meanwhile, the foremost secular magnate of the region was no less active as a castle builder than the archbishop. Richard, fourth earl of Arundel and ninth earl of Surrey (d. 1397), was involved in the total overhaul of his seat at Arundel, Sussex. Persistently in conflict with Richard II, he was nevertheless one of the wealthiest peers in England and possessed an astonishing estimated £70,000 worth of moveable goods at his death.[28] In classic form, the remodelling of Arundel castle was connected with the creation in 1380 of a college of priests attached to the parish church of the town.[29] To this day a fourteenth-century iron grille divides the nave of the church from the chancel, which remains the property and burial place of the modern heirs to the adjacent castle, the Fitzalan-Howards, now dukes of Norfolk. The east end of the building is a work of particular architectural ambition and can plausibly be attributed to Yevele on stylistic evidence. One corroborative detail for this attribution is that in 1374 he is documented as the creator of a tomb for the earl's parents.[30]

To complement works to the college, the buildings of the adjacent castle at Arundel were themselves reworked. The eleventh-century gate tower was heightened and extended forward with the construction of a new barbican (pl. 233). Possibly as a continuation of a programme of works inherited from his father, the earl also constructed several new towers around the perimeter of the castle. The precise date of all these operations is impossible to establish without documentary evidence, but they may have continued throughout the 1380s. Certainly, work to the college was still under way in the 1390s, when it was extended by the foundation of a hospital dedicated to the Trinity.[31] While remodelling Arundel, the earl was almost certainly also responsible for works to the castle of Reigate, one of his favourite residences, but little is known about this important lost building.[32] His wealthy and brutal younger brother, John, also aimed to set up a new castle at Betchworth in Surrey as the seat for a cadet branch of the family. He received a licence for this in 1377, but drowned in quicksand on the Irish coast around New Year 1380 during the course of a particularly barbaric military expedition.[33] Work to the building may never have advanced far.[34]

The architectural patronage of John of Gaunt, the last major landholder in the south-east, forms an interesting contrast to that of the archbishop of Canterbury and the earl of Arundel. For all their size and importance, Gaunt's holdings in the south-east were a peripheral element to the Lancastrian estates as a whole. This probably explains why he is not known to have visited Pevensey, from 1372 his principal castle in the region. Indeed, in 1377 he allegedly refused to garrison the castle in the face of French attack, boasting that if it were destroyed he could easily afford to rebuild it.[35] It may have been in consequence of such cavalier treatment that Pevensey was sacked in 1381 during the Peasants' Revolt. That serious damage was done to the

233 The barbican at Arundel, Sussex, was added around 1380 to the front of the earlier castle gate tower. It is built in an expensive combination of knapped flint and bands of cut stone. The design looks back to the kinds of barbicans first created in England in the 1220s. It compares more directly, however, to such fourteenth-century designs as Alnwick (see pl. 200) and the work of John Lewyn at Carlisle (see pl. 246). Visible in the background is the entrance turret added to the motte in the 1380s. All the late fourteenth-century additions to the castle employ a distinctively designed doorway form with a depressed arch, features also found in the contemporary college buildings.

buildings on this occasion is suggested by the fact that no courts could be held in the castle immediately afterwards.[36] Nevertheless, the castle was subsequently repaired and maintained, though no details of the work are recorded.

Gaunt's distance from the affairs of the south-east might have led to the relative neglect of his own castles, but it was architecturally productive at another level. In each county, the gentry were jockeying for local power, and the support of the king or a great landowner could swing the balance in this struggle. One of the desiderata in this competition was a castle, an architectural symbol of status, political power and wealth. The outstanding family in Kent was the Cobhams, whose three principal lines each came to occupy a castle over the fourteenth century. We have already encountered the veteran of Edward III's wars, Reginald, Lord Cobham (d. 1361), who established a seat at Sterborough Castle and a collegiate foundation at Lingfield, Surrey. John Cobham (d. 1399), a distant relative, acquired the manor of Hever by marriage. Probably following the issue of a licence to crenellate in 1383, he created the surviving façade of this castle with its asymmetrically planned gatehouse and flanking towers. But the most important member of the family in Richard II's reign was John, third Lord Cobham (d. 1408), a member of the governing council of the realm during the minority and subsequently a moderate supporter of the lords appellant. The pattern of his patronage and building will now seem familiar.

In 1362, following the death of his relative Reginald, John founded a college that he attached to the parish church of Cobham. The buildings he raised to accommodate the community of priests still survive as an almshouse. So too does the carefully organised series of brasses that commemorate his dynasty within the chancel of the church.[37] Aside from commissioning brasses, much of John's work to the church and college buildings appears from documentary evidence to have been undertaken in the 1380s, long after the initial foundation: in 1383 he not only contracted for work to the college quadrangle and an attached school but also paid for new glass in the church, which he commissioned from the king's glazier, John Brampton.[38] It was probably at exactly this time that he also erected within the chancel a fine new reredos, piscina and sedilia, all of which might plausibly be attributed on stylistic grounds to Brampton's colleague in the King's works, Henry Yevele.

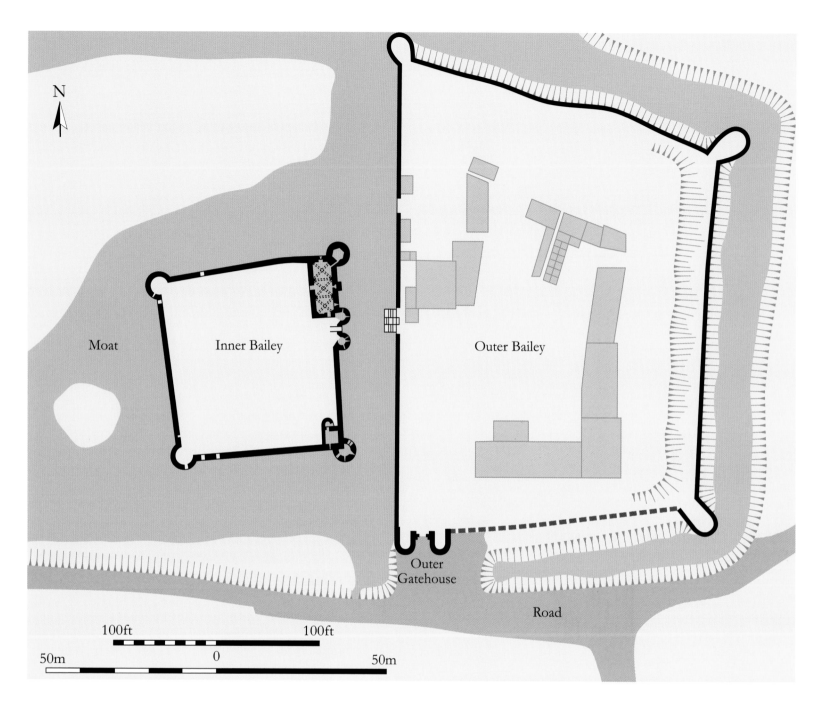

N

Moat

Inner Bailey

Outer Bailey

Outer
Gatehouse

Road

100ft   100ft

50m   0   50m

234 A plan of Cooling, Kent, redrawn from a map of 1877. The castle was licensed in 1381 and built by John, third Lord Cobham. It comprised two rectangular baileys walled in stone and with drum-shaped angle towers. The inner and outer court respectively housed residential and ancillary buildings. Extending along the wall to one side of the inner gate are the remains of a two-storey stone range faced with a decorative chequered pattern of rubble and cut stone. A document of 1382 refers to the upper room of the range as the great chamber. Access to it was via a stair in one of the gate towers. Adjacent to this range was a tower with a hexagonal internal plan, the only tower in the castle treated in this distinctive way. This detail hints at the importance of the tower within the sequence of withdrawing apartments. The castle was previously encircled by water-filled moats. In 1554, during the events of a siege, there is documentary reference to a garden island beside the castle. This may have been created in the fourteenth century.

This attribution is corroborated by Yevele's documented connection with Lord Cobham in a number of other building projects in the same decade. In 1381 he commissioned Yevele to supply designs for a new aisle and porch to St Dunstan's, the parish church of his London home.[39] Significantly, these designs were executed by another mason called Nicolas Typerton, a working arrangement we shall encounter again. Yevele and Cobham were also charged to oversee the construction of the walls of Canterbury in 1385 and repairs to the great bridge of Rochester in 1383 after icebergs damaged its fabric. From 1387 John, Lord Cobham,

contributed substantially to the latter project and founded a chapel on the bridge.[40] Curiously, his generosity almost exactly coincided with Yevele's own undertaking to pay for a chapel on London Bridge, which was constructed between 1384 and 1397.[41] But the relationship between these two men is most strikingly illustrated in another project that appears to have initiated this spate of activity in the 1380s.

On 10 February 1381 John received a licence from the king to fortify his manor house at Cooling, about 7 miles from Cobham. The castle he created lies near the parish church and its defences were formerly enclosed by water-filled moats. It comprises two rectangular baileys walled in stone and with drum-shaped angle towers (pl. 234). Despite its large plan, the outer gate is on a relatively diminutive scale and crowded with fortifications (pl. 235). Suspended from one of its towers is a brass charter with an inscription in English that speaks of the public value of the castle as a defence of the 'country' (see pl. 4). The charter illustrates a point so rarely documented in explicit terms that it is easy to forget: Cooling was not just a functional building but also an architectural advertisement of intent on the part of its builder. To a visitor, the towers and battlements of Cooling could be understood as endorsing the text of the charter and affirming Lord Cobham's stated intention of defending the public weal. By extension, they also celebrated his own vocation as a knight and lord.

Several documents relating to the work survive and they show that there were two principal masons responsible for the work at Cooling: a certain William Sharnale and Thomas Crump, both men previously involved in local royal building projects.[42] Sharnale emerges as the more substantial of the two, receiving a total of £456 for building undertaken between 1381 and 1384. But it is Crump's recorded contribution that is more revealing of architectural processes in the period. According to one document dated September 1381, Crump assessed the total cost of erecting the great gate of the castle as £44. His calculation was based on the measurement of masonry by the perch, a unit commonly invoked in building contracts of the period (see pl. 244). But this document also records that Crump's calculations were independently assessed by Henry Yevele, who evidently surveyed the completed structure. Yevele estimated the cost of the gate at the lower sum of £39 and noticed, moreover, that Crump had failed to create a postern entrance, which had also been contracted for.[43]

235 Cooling, Kent, the outer gate of the castle, which was licensed in 1381. On the right-hand tower is affixed a small brass plaque in the form of a charter with an enamelled seal bearing the arms of Cobham (1). Inscribed on the charter is an English doggerel verse proclaiming the public utility of the castle in defence of the 'country' (see pl. 4). Above the gate is a stone shield, presumably once painted with the Cobham arms. The gatehouse towers are both crowned by a projecting machicolis and cut through with small arrow and cannon loops.

That Yevele assessed Crump's contract strongly suggests that he had some overarching role in the design of the building. Furthermore, that it was possible to judge the completed gatehouse as not having been correctly completed implies the existence of a coherently expressed design for the whole to which he had access. This almost certainly took the form of a drawing.

Incidentally, the surviving documents also provide an interesting insight into the real costs of architecture in this period. It is estimated that Lord Cobham owned lands worth about £300–400 per annum; but the surviving bills for the castle account for nearly £600, and from what they describe, the whole building operation probably cost more than twice this sum. Constructing Cooling must, in other words, have stretched Cobham's finances to the limit. This throws into relief the relative wealth of the earl of Arundel with his tens of thousands of pounds.

Cooling is one of several contemporary castles built in the region by prominent local knights in a spirit of self-promotion. As will become apparent, all these buildings look very similar. Nearby, a certain Roger de Ashburnham created a castle at Scotney in Kent, laid out with two baileys enclosed by moats. Ashburnham was a younger son of a poor knightly family. He inherited Scotney from his mother and set about creating a new seat there for himself. To pay for this he must have enjoyed a large, additional income, either from the profits of war or royal service, though no record of this now survives.[44]

No licence to crenellate Scotney exists and the date of the new castle is unknown. It was presumably complete by the time of Ashburnham's death in the 1390s, and its similarities to the diminutive Cooling suggest that the two buildings were contemporary. The chief difference between the two castles is that Scotney was built throughout in cut stone rather than rubble masonry, an indication of its relative expense. Both buildings also compare to the celebrated castle at Bodiam in Sussex, built by a locally important knight, Sir Edward Dallingridge, under a royal licence issued in 1385.

Dallingridge was a soldier who amassed through marriage and inheritance a considerable estate with a concentration of property in East Sussex including a family seat at Fletching.[45] In the political vacuum created by the demise of the de Warenne family, and with the support of their territorial successors, the Fitzalan earls of Arundel, he came to act as the first knight in the east of the county. This position was put under pressure, however, following the grant of the rape of Pevensey and other manors in the west of the county to John of Gaunt in 1372. The efficient administration of the rape by duchy of Lancaster officials disadvantaged Dallingridge and threatened his local position. He responded violently. In 1381, under the smokescreen created by the Peasants' Revolt, he began a campaign to intimidate the duke's servants and reassert his position. But Dallingridge seriously misjudged his opponent and was worsted in the legal wrangling that ensued.[46] Nevertheless, he was in a powerful position to create trouble in the future and it appears that Gaunt pragmatically came to an accommodation with him.

Bodiam looks suspiciously like the physical product of this reconciliation. The new castle stood as an architectural symbol of Dallingridge's status in the county and was laid out with all the trappings of lordly authority, including a new market, mill and an elaborate surrounding landscape of pools. Its geographic location, however, could be interpreted as a concession to Gaunt. Unlike the family seat of Fletching, Bodiam stood a respectable distance from the heartlands of the duchy estates in Sussex. Regularly planned and enclosed in a broad moat, even as a ruin it remains one of the most popularly celebrated castles in England (pl. 236). Its gatehouses proclaim in heraldry the ownership of the castle and the exterior is deliberately rugged. In the absence of documentation we will probably never know certainly who designed Bodiam. The architectural details of the building, however – including the use of ring bosses in the gatehouse vault and the design of the angle towers with polygonal internal chambers – demonstrate a connection with the king's works. So too does the design of the domestic ranges, the fenestration and regularity of which imitate in very modest form the upper ward at Windsor (pl. 237).

Bodiam is one of several castles in Kent and Sussex that can be connected to the king's works and the Perpendicular remodelling of Windsor by Edward III. But it also compares directly to buildings elsewhere in the south-east. In 1377 Warin, second Lord Lisle, a figure associated with the dukes of Lancaster, received a licence to build a castle at Shirburn in Oxfordshire (pl. 238).[47] Although much altered over time, this building evidently bore a striking resemblance to Bodiam: it was laid out on a rectangular plan with towers on alternately round and rectangular plans in a landscape of pools. The principal entrance possessed a vault with murder-hole ring bosses and the interior ranges appear

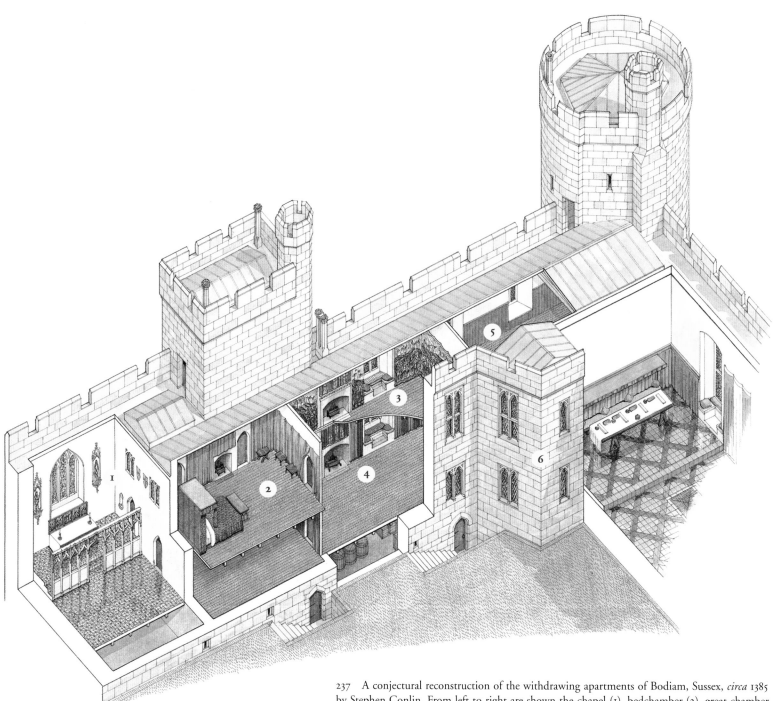

237 A conjectural reconstruction of the withdrawing apartments of Bodiam, Sussex, *circa* 1385 by Stephen Conlin. From left to right are shown the chapel (1), bedchamber (2), great chamber (3) – with a parlour below (4) – and an outer chamber (5). These were connected to the dais of the great hall on the right by a staircase turret (6). The regular proportions of the two-storey ranges enclosing the inner court are ultimately derived from the upper ward at Windsor. So too is the lighting of lower and upper chambers by single- and two-tier windows respectively. A clear effort was made to indicate the function of apartments by the use of different window designs. Moreover, the external windows are plainer than those on the interior, part of a conscious attempt to make the building look austere and castle-like to an approaching visitor.

238 A photograph of Shirburn, Oxfordshire, taken in 1900. The castle was built by Warin, second Lord Lisle, who received a licence in 1377. The original design of a rectangular castle with alternate towers on a round and rectangular plan must be rescued from behind the effects of two substantial rebuildings, one of 1830 and the other by Thomas Parker, earl of Macclesfield, after his purchase of the estate in 1716. Its form as first designed is clearest on the principal façade, which is shown to the right. The entrance vault of the central gatehouse tower still possesses a ring-boss vault like that at Bodiam. Shirburn demonstrates the centralisation of architectural design across the south-east in the late fourteenth century. An estate map made in 1736 by William Burgess shows the castle surrounded by pools. In origin, these bodies of water may be medieval, although they appear here in remodelled form as part of a later, formal landscape.

to have been regularly planned. These similarities between Bodiam and Shirburn highlight the degree to which architectural production had become centralised during Richard II's reign. In the circumstances, it is only a small leap beyond the available evidence to suggest that Henry Yevele was involved in some capacity at both places.

Much ink has been spilt over the question of whether Bodiam would ever have been capable of withstanding an attack. In conventional terms this question is important because Bodiam needs to be defensible if it is to be understood as a 'Real Castle' in the traditional sense.[48] Like many debates of this kind, the terms of discussion – which hinge on such issues as the efficacy of the moat as an obstruction and the operability of arrow loops – are subjective. But, regardless of individual opinions on the matter, it should not be allowed to obscure a point of more fundamental importance. Whatever we may think about the defensive qualities of Bodiam today, there can be little doubt that Dallingridge built something that he regarded as a castle. That allowed, it remains important to comprehend what made it a castle for Dallingridge. In this case the answer is not hard to agree: Bodiam is a residence made architecturally magnificent through the trappings of fortification.

By contrast with the efforts of the nobility and gentry, the crown was not a particularly active patron of architecture in the south-east. There is documentary reference to new fortifications and houses at Wallingford, to a large new tower overlooking the repaired bridge at Rochester Castle and to the repair of Carisbrooke, where the great gate was heightened and a new entrance constructed to the tower on the motte.[49] In 1382 Edward III's great castle of Queenborough was also seriously damaged in an earthquake and two of its towers had to be rebuilt from the foundations.[50] The most significant royal project in the region, however, was the reorganisation of Portchester Castle, an operation that fell into two distinct phases. The first was undertaken by the constable, Sir Robert Ashton, an associate of John of Gaunt, who was appointed keeper of Portchester Castle on 15 February 1376.[51] Henry Yevele is specifically named as the overseer of this project, though another mason took practical responsibility for it.[52] The work involved creating a tower attached to the constable's lodgings on the outer angle of the inner bailey. Incorporated within the tower and extending around the adjacent walls is a covered firing gallery with rectangular openings for handguns, an early example of architectural provision for such weapons.[53]

The second series of alterations to Portchester involved the reconstruction of the residential apartments in the inner bailey of the castle and the reordering of the twelfth-century great tower. This operation began in 1396, immediately following Richard's truce with France and his marriage to the seven-year-old French princess Isabelle. The intention was doubtless to provide a comfortable staging post for the king on future visits to France. In the event, however, he was deposed before work was completed. The new lodgings are the most complete series of royal apartments to survive from the period. Some idea of their internal disposition is provided by the surviving 1370s hall range of the abbot's lodging at Westminster erected by the abbey mason John Palterton and the carpenter William Wintringham, both figures in the orbit of the king's works.[54]

The Portchester residential buildings form a courtyard around three sides of the inner bailey and connect with the first floor of the great tower and the chapel in its forebuilding (see pl. 16). With their two-storey elevations, regular outlines and two-tier upper windows, the Portchester ranges demonstrably derive from Edward III's palace at Windsor. The distinctive murder-hole vault of the royal works is also found in the Landgate to the castle, which was restored at this time.[55]

The king in some cases acted as a vicarious patron of architecture in the region through his court circle. For example, Sir Richard Abberbury, a retainer of the Black Prince who was appointed Richard's 'first master', capitalised on his close connections with the king to consolidate his position in Berkshire and in 1385 received a licence to crenellate his manor of Donnington. All that remains of this castle, which was laid out on a rectangular plan with drum turrets at each corner, is an imposing twin-towered gatehouse (pl. 239). In plan and detail this loosely resembles other known designs from the royal works such as Carisbrooke and Archbishop Courtenay's gatehouse at Saltwood. It also has an entrance vault with inset panels of tracery, a very unusual enrichment in the context of fourteenth-century castle design. Possibly they are a borrowing from the Aerary Porch at Windsor.

Another figure who also rose to prominence in Richard's favour through his service to the Black Prince was Sir John Devereux. He received the residence of Penshurst in Kent and in 1392 was granted a licence to crenellate it. He perhaps responded by enclosing the sumptuous existing manor house on the site with a curtain wall and a series of towers on a rectangular plan

239 The gatehouse of Donnington, Berkshire, virtually the only upstanding fragment of the quadrangular castle erected around 1385 by Sir Richard Abberbury, 'first master' of the boy king Richard II. It has angle turrets flanking the main structure of the gate, a detail common to other Perpendicular gatehouses of the period. Projecting from the front of the gatehouse are the stub walls of a barbican. The gate passage vault is decorated with panels of tracery, a very unusual enrichment in the context of a castle at this date. Indeed, overall the building displays an unusual quantity of sculpture and architectural ornament, evidence of the money lavished upon it. Donnington had several notable later owners, including Henry VI's favourite, William de la Pole, and Henry VIII's brother in law, Charles Brandon. It was demolished after a protracted siege in the 1640s.

scare of 1386. Besides clearing several coastal areas, he outraged the monks of Canterbury by attempting to move St Thomas Becket's precious relics from Canterbury to Dover Castle for safe keeping.[58] Yet for all this activity and the sheer extent of his property, Burley lived on the edge of his means and never patronised architecture. At his execution in 1389 he was in debt.[59] Burley's subsequent burial in London (beneath a tomb commissioned by Richard II) was testimony to his failure to set down roots in any of his extensive possessions.

WILLIAM WYNFORD AND THE SOUTH-WEST

Amongst the first architectural initiatives of Richard II's reign were two royal castle projects of very different character in the south-west of England. In 1377 work was in hand to construct a sumptuously appointed tower attached to the withdrawing apartments of Corfe Castle in Dorset. The new tower was appropriately called 'the Gloriet', probably both because of its sumptuous internal treatment and its juxtaposition to King John's building of the same name. Today, sadly, only its broken foundations remain.[60] Then, in March 1378, the governing council of the realm ordered Henry Yevele and his fellow master mason John Sponlee, Edward III's designer of the upper ward at Windsor, to travel to Southampton and advise on the erection of a new tower in the castle there. This rich town was particularly vulnerable to seaborne attack and its refortification was clearly regarded as an urgent matter in the face of French raids, a rare example of a major architectural project in this period responding to military need. The proposal drawn up by the two men was evidently approved, and in May the same year instruction was given for masons to be impressed in the work.[61]

What both these projects have in common is that they involved a mason named William Wynford. Like his colleague Yevele, he was a master mason who had served since 1361 with John Sponlee as joint 'ordainer of the Works' at Windsor Castle. As well as informing his architectural style, Wynford's service at Windsor introduced him to the clerk of works, William of Wykeham. This connection was to prove enormously important because at every subsequent stage in Wykeham's brilliantly successful church career he employed Wynford: it was probably through his agency as provost of Wells that in 1365 Wynford became master

240   Detail of a view of Penshurst, Kent, by J. Kip and published in John Harris, *The History of Kent* (London, 1719). The engraving shows the house enclosed by a rectangular enclosure wall and a series of towers (now mostly demolished). By the date this engraving was made, these fortifications had been partially subsumed within later extensions. They might have been begun in the 1340s by the merchant and lord mayor of London, John de Pulteney. He had purchased the estate in 1338 and received a licence to crenellate it in 1341. The hall of his 1340s house – identified here by the louvre in its roof – still survives as the centrepiece of the present-day buildings. Alternatively, they could have been erected by Sir John Devereux under a licence issued in 1392.

(pl. 240). If so, this regular composition may have been inspired by the upper ward at Windsor.[56]

Not all Richard II's preferments in the region encouraged new building, however, as the career of one of his most notorious favourites, Sir Simon Burley, illustrates. In the early years of the reign Richard granted Burley various properties along the Welsh border, including the castle and lordship of Newcastle Emlyn, Carmarthenshire, and also that of Lyonshall in Herefordshire. At the same time a plot was hatched to bestow upon him the rich inheritance of the Leybourne family in Kent, to which he had no claim whatsoever. This came to fruition in 1384 and it was supported by Burley's subsequent appointment as constable of Dover Castle and warden of the Cinque Ports. At his installation ceremony, Richard II personally handed him the key of his new castle. The only honour that now escaped Burley was a peerage. As a matter of fact, it seems that Richard II granted him one in 1385 that parliament refused to endorse, an extraordinary mark of disapproval.[57]

Nevertheless, by virtue of his office Burley was now a major figure in Kent and was instrumental in organising the defence of the county during the invasion

241 A detail of the town plan of Southampton, Hampshire, published by John Speed in 1611. This is the only known view of the great tower begun on the castle motte in 1378. The project involved three senior royal masons: John Sponlee, Henry Yevele and William Wynford. It was initially pressed forward with great haste and more than £1,000 was spent in the first year of work alone. Ten years later, the project had absorbed almost double this sum. This view shows the tower as a drum-shaped structure on top of the motte and enclosed by a low wall or mantlet. It is crowned by a projecting parapet – probably a machicolis – and several turrets. Southampton may have been a miniaturised version of Queenborough and a descendant of the thirteenth-century great tower at Flint (see pl. 156).

mason of Wells Cathedral; and that in 1377–8, the same year that Wynford began work at Southampton, he was also described for the first time as master mason to Wykeham as bishop of Winchester.[62] The combination of his two jobs in royal and episcopal service established Wynford beside Yevele as the most influential mason in the south of England during the late fourteenth century.

Of the great tower that was subsequently raised on the motte of Southampton Castle nothing now survives. Even its foundations have presumably been destroyed: a block of flats was erected on the site of the building in the 1950s, a development apparently done without any archaeological investigation. From the surviving building accounts, however, we know that it took ten years to complete and cost just under £2,000, three times the sum estimated here for the construction of Cooling. It would appear to have been a miniaturised version of Edward III's castle at Queenborough, comprising a central tower with turrets at battlement level and enclosed by an outer curtain wall or mantlet (*mantelletum*) with a 'barbican' (pl. 241).[63] It is possible that the central tower itself contained a small courtyard. If so, the design probably hearkens back ultimately to buildings such as Edward I's great tower at Flint. In the sixteenth century it was enthusiastically described by the antiquary John Leland as

'the glorie of the castle, large, fair and very stronge, both by worke and by the siting of it'.[64]

While this remarkable building was under construction, Wynford was very busy elsewhere. He was concurrently engaged on the complete remodelling of Wykeham's episcopal residence at Bishop's Waltham, Hampshire, where he reconstructed a new hall range from 1379 and refurbished the twelfth-century great tower in 1395.[65] As a whole, the operation compares to Richard II's remodelling of Portchester in the 1390s. Then from 1380 he was almost certainly the mason who took responsibility for work to Wykeham's important university foundation at New College, Oxford. And in 1387 he began work to the buildings of its sister school foundation, the college of St Mary at Winchester.

In all these projects the clear inspiration for Wynford's work – perhaps at the behest of his patron – were the royal apartments of Windsor Castle. The relationship is clearest in the case of the two college plans, which unite the hall and chapel in the manner pioneered at Windsor to create a single dominating range enclosed by lodging ranges. At Bishop's Waltham the idea was compromised by the existing buildings on the site, but the hall and service ranges are ordered to similar and imposing effect.

The exchange of ideas between castle and collegiate architecture points to an increasingly sophisticated relationship between different traditions of building in the late fourteenth century. It also reflects the calibre of Wynford as an independent-minded designer, far less slavish in his adaptation of Perpendicular forms than Yevele. In one important detail, however, these buildings all depart from their immediate model at Windsor. Wynford eschewed the regular fenestration of Windsor, preferring instead to light the chapels and halls of his colleges with differently designed windows. In this preference for varied fenestration he was joined by all his English colleagues of the period.

In the 1390s Wynford began work on another group of major projects. At Winchester in 1390 he was joined by Henry Yevele in undertaking a thorough repair of the castle for the king. Only his repairs to the castle great hall, built by Henry III, can today be identified. Four years later as the bishop's mason he undertook the remodelling of the cathedral in the city, an inventive overhaul of the Romanesque fabric.[66] Over the same period he was almost certainly the mason employed in designing one of the masterpieces of late fourteenth-century Perpendicular architecture for a different patron.

In February 1393 John, fifth Baron Lovell, received a royal licence to fortify his manor house at Wardour in Wiltshire.[67] At the time, Lord Lovell was around fifty years old and one of the richest barons in England. He was also an experienced courtier, soldier and diplomat, recorded to have travelled as far afield as the Baltic, Italy, Ireland, the eastern Mediterranean and France.[68] The new castle was built at the end of what is now a remote and peaceful valley, its walls reflected in the water of a wide lake. In its present form this lake is an eighteenth-century creation, but it is almost certainly part of an artificial medieval waterscape. Enclosing the castle site was a walled yard or bailey set out on a polygonal plan, though little is known of how it was arranged internally.[69] It was probably entered through a gatehouse, now lost, and contained service buildings such as stables and storehouses. There stood at its centre the architectural focus of the castle: a huge tower designed on a hexagonal plan around a small courtyard. The main front of the great tower takes the form of a twin-towered gatehouse and rises to an astonishing five storeys in height.

The fourteenth-century form of the great tower must be rescued from behind the effects of a major restoration in the 1570s by the mason or architect Robert Smythson and the destruction caused by a mine detonated beneath it during a Civil War siege in 1644 (pl. 242). As befits a work of castle architecture, the great tower is cleanly and boldly conceived. The walls are constructed throughout of cut stone and rise in stages from an exquisitely moulded plinth to a heavy cornice set with foliage ornament and drainage spouts. Above this cornice would have risen an array of battlements, turrets and chimneys. During the 1570s many of the medieval windows in the tower were replaced to emphasise the symmetry of the design. It is clear, however, that the fourteenth-century windows in the building were of many forms, their relative size and ornament reflecting the importance of the chambers they lit.

Such is the architectural sophistication of the great tower at Wardour that scholars have been encouraged to seek the explanation for its design in Lovell's travels abroad. It has, for example, been mistakenly associated with Concressault (Cher), a building that was not actually begun until 1398, five years after Lovell received his licence.[70] In fact, the great tower was evidently designed by a mason thoroughly conversant with the Perpendicular style and fascinated by the ideas of compact planning pioneered in Edward III's work at Windsor. The heavy and abstracted detailing of the architectural elements, moreover, is taken from Windsor. So too is the form of the hall windows that dominate the tower façade. Its closest architectural parallels are the poorly understood great tower at Southampton and its architectural sources: Queenborough and Flint. In the circumstances, the most likely designer of this building is William Wynford.

From the spectrum of work he undertook, it is clear that Wynford was the leading south-western mason in the late fourteenth century. Whether he monopolised the practice of architecture in the region to the extent that Yevele did across the south-east, however, seems doubtful. In Devon and Cornwall, for example, there are several building projects that have no obvious connection with him. The most important of these was undertaken by Richard II's half-brother, John Holland. He was created earl of Huntingdon in 1388 and received Berkhamsted Castle in Hertfordshire as his seat. In addition, he also received considerable property in the south-west including the manor of Dartington in Devon, which was entirely rebuilt from 1388 onwards.[71] Dartington was planned on a grand scale, and though its details reflect the influence of the king's works, there is no particular reason to associate it with Wynford.

Edward Courtenay (d. 1419), earl of Devon, watched this plantation of John Holland in his geographical sphere of influence with some nervousness. The earl's principal castles were at Tiverton and Okehampton, and both had been extensively reordered in the first half of the fourteenth century. Too little survives in either case to determine whether they were further altered in this period. His brother Sir Philip, however, did establish a cadet branch of the family at Powderham Castle, just outside Exeter.[72] This appears to have comprised a residential complex with a hall incorporated within a lightly fortified court that was entered through a gatehouse. Archbishop Courtenay, the rebuilder of Saltwood, was another of the earl's brothers.

There are also occasional instances of yet more modest castle building in the area. In 1380 William and Margaret Asthorpe, for example, were licensed to fortify their house at Hemyock. The couple were essentially without court interest or great power, though William did serve as an MP and sheriff of Devon. This building took the classic quadrangular form of the *nouveau riche* castle, with drum towers at each corner.

242   A cut-away reconstruction by Stephen Conlin of the great tower at Wardour, Wiltshire, begun around 1393. This tower stood in the centre of a large, walled court on a polygonal plan, parts of which still survive. The twin-towered façade of the building is probably related to Richard II's new entrance to Westminster Hall begun in 1394 by Henry Yevele (see pl. 229). At the heart of the tower was a small courtyard and light well (1). From this a stair (2) ascended to the great hall, which rose from the first floor through the full height of the building (3). Opening off one end of the hall were the services of the castle. Around the remainder of the building extended the withdrawing and lodging chambers. All the principal rooms appear to have been sandwiched between antechambers on a wedge-shaped plan, an arrangement that allowed for the creation of regular interiors within the constraints imposed by the hexagonal design. It also allowed for a complex arrangement of closets, antechambers and latrines. The building incorporates a series of vaulted chambers at ground level for storage (4).

Perhaps in no area of England was the reign of Richard II more obviously transforming in architectural terms than in the north.[73] Here the power and wealth of a handful of great families encouraged a series of castle-building projects of outstanding grandeur and sophistication. Many of the patrons involved were supporters of John of Gaunt in the closing years of Edward III's reign and constituted something of a northern faction at court. Foremost amongst them was Henry Percy (d. 1408), who was created earl of Northumberland at Richard II's coronation in 1377. There had been no northern earldoms since the late twelfth century, and the curiosity of this title would have underlined the singular power of the man whom it dignified. Percy was the richest landowner in the north by a considerable margin and in 1381 further extended his interest with a marriage to Maud Lucy. This brought him property along almost the whole of the northern march from coast to coast, including the Lucy castles and the lordships of Egremont, Cockermouth and Langley.[74]

It was undoubtedly to celebrate his new estate that the earl, in time-honoured fashion, embarked on the construction of a great tower at his castle at Warkworth (pl. 243). This remarkable building, constructed throughout in cut stone, ingeniously combines all the chambers necessary for grand domestic living into a regular and imposing volume (see pl. 19). Doubtless to facilitate the process of design and costing, the structure was laid out using the measurement of a perch (pl. 244). The external detailing of the building is carefully designed to reflect its internal arrangement: the service, public and withdrawing chambers are respectively lit by different forms of window and the earl's bedchamber is marked externally by a sculpture of a rampant lion, the heraldic emblem of the family. As originally completed, the tower possessed a busy crown of battlements, pinnacles, turrets and large chimney pots. Just beneath this there survives a series of sculpted figures of angels bearing shields, doubtless formerly painted with heraldry.

The great tower at Warkworth was almost certainly designed by the mason John Lewyn, a figure central to the architecture of the region in the late fourteenth century. His career is worth unpicking in detail. Aside from possible references to him as a mason working at Westminster in 1351[75] and at Windsor in the 1360s,[76] there is no evidence for Lewyn's involvement in any major royal project of Edward III's reign. He is first securely documented in 1353 in the pay of Durham Cathedral priory and in 1366 was the master mason responsible for the great kitchen in the monastic precinct with its fine star vault. From 1368 there is clear evidence that he was a prosperous and well-established figure. In that year he is referred to as the 'bishop's mason', a role that – depending on when he assumed the post – might have involved him in the construction of the great tower of Durham Castle for Bishop Hatfield. Whatever the case, this lost building with its central light well and turreted outline was almost certainly related architecturally to the great tower at Warkworth. Lewyn also received his first documented commission from the royal works in 1368: the extension of the domestic apartments at Bamburgh Castle. This operation, it later transpired, he failed to complete. Like Yevele, he was also evidently engaged in other business ventures, including the export of wool.[77]

To judge from his documented career, up to about 1370 Lewyn might have been completely disconnected from the inner circle of royal masons and the developing Perpendicular style. By the end of the decade this situation – if it was ever the case – had changed completely. In 1368, as an acknowledgement of his heroic role in the defeat of the Scots at Neville's Cross outside the city, the powerful local baron, Ralph Neville, became the first layman to be buried in the cathedral church at Durham. Soon afterwards, Ralph's son, John, paid to rebuild the shrine of Cuthbert, the cathedral's patron saint, and contributed towards a new reredos for the high altar. This structure, the so-called Neville Screen, with its exquisite architectural frame in the Perpendicular style, was completed in 1380 (pl. 245). It is a testimony to the possibilities of architectural exchange in the period that the screen was designed and built in London (almost certainly by Henry Yevele) using stone from Caen in Normandy and shipped to Durham via Newcastle. The erection of the new screen, witnessed if not overseen by Lewyn, illustrates a delivery of ideas and resources from London that was to transform the castles of the northern march.[78] Indeed, the details of the sculpture plinths and shield-holding angels on the Neville Screen were probably the source for the decorative crown of the great tower at Warkworth.

At exactly the same time that the Neville Screen was under construction, the reorganisation of the king's works in 1378 effectively drew Lewyn in to the nexus of royal masons. Yevele was too far away to involve himself directly in distant, northern projects and he

243 (*above*) The great tower of Warkworth, Northumberland, was probably commissioned by Henry Percy following his elevation to the peerage in 1377 as earl of Northumberland. It incorporates all the interiors necessary for grand domestic living in the Middle Ages and wraps them together into a coherent design. In plan, the tower forms a Greek cross with four polygonal wings radiating from a central, polygonal block. Above the building rises the needle-like outline of a viewing tower with magnificent prospects over both sea and land. The windows signal by their size and ornament the importance of the rooms they light.

244 (*right*) The great tower of Warkworth, Northumberland, begun around 1380, in a plan by Richard Lea. It was laid out using a measurement of 16 feet 6 inches, a unit variously called a rod, pole or perch. Though the building is distorted, a first-floor plan superimposed by a grid of half-rods clearly shows, for example, that the hall measured 2.5 by 1.5 rods and the great chamber 2 by 1 rods, and also that the walls are either a half, a quarter or an eighth of a rod deep. Building contracts of the period often quantify masonry by the rod, so using this unit would have facilitated calculations of cost and material.

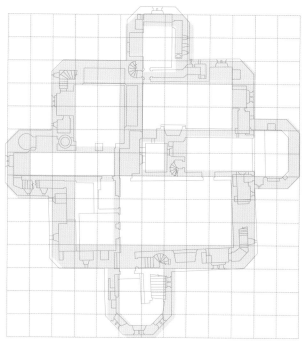

245 The Neville Screen, Durham Cathedral, completed in 1380, was formerly filled with sculpture. It is a striking reminder of the internationalism of the finest architecture: the screen is built of stone from Caen; it was carved and designed in London (almost certainly under the direction of Henry Yevele), and then shipped in pieces to Newcastle for erection in its present location. The band of ornament that completes the lowest storey of the screen may be the source for the decoration found on the great tower of Warkworth. It incorporates angels holding shields and polygonal plinths rising above triangular projections to either side of the high altar.

246 De Ireby's Tower, Carlisle, which was built by John Lewyn under the terms of an indenture dated 13 April 1378 and at a cost of 500 marks (£333). This document gives precise dimensions of the building and pays particular attention to the form of the entrance, which was to be protected by a barbican. It also mentions various interiors within the building, including a hall, a kitchen, a latrine and a prison. The gatehouse was presumably intended as a self-contained residence. In design, it compares to the roughly contemporary Cockermouth gatehouse and looks back to buildings in the region of an earlier generation, such as the barbican gates at Alnwick and Prudhoe.

needed a stand-in. That Lewyn was chosen is shown by the series of royal commissions he received from 1378 onwards. These not only involved him in work across the entire march, a much wider geographical spread than he would perhaps naturally have enjoyed, but also introduced him to all those who exercised royal power and were, by extension, the castle builders in the region. In 1378 Lewyn was instructed to impress masons for work to the royal castles of Carlisle and Roxburgh. Contracts for both operations still survive, though in the latter case the building does not. At Roxburgh – allowing for the belligerent activities of the Scots – he was to build a wall with three towers, one including a gate, a project that continued until 1387.[79] His work at Carlisle involved the construction of a new outer gate with a barbican to serve as a lodging for the warden of the western march at a cost of 500 marks (pl. 246).[80]

Warkworth is of a different order of sophistication from the Carlisle gatehouse and in it Lewyn showed a much more profound familiarity with the early prod-

ucts of the Perpendicular style. The polygonal turrets that project from the core of the great tower at Warkworth, for example, are almost certainly derived from the Rose Tower at Windsor (the privy entrance to the palace and the location of some of the king's withdrawing apartments; see pl. 220). They also show a debt to the polygonal turrets in the residential ranges of Kenilworth. Of the two, this latter connection may be the more important because prior to an acrimonious and public quarrel between the two men in 1381, Gaunt and Percy were close allies. It is not impossible, indeed, that Percy was provided with drawings of Kenilworth or, alternatively, Lewyn received information about the new buildings there when in 1379 he was commissioned by Gaunt to construct a barbican and several houses in his Northumbrian castle at Dunstanburgh.[81] That there was some direct connection between Warkworth and Kenilworth is suggested by the similar forms of window they employ. In particular, the grandest rooms in both castles make use of a

247 Castle Bolton, Yorkshire, probably begun in 1378 and reputedly absorbing £666 every building season for the next eighteen years. The castle comprises four tall ranges laid out on a square plan with rectangular corner towers. On two sides there are also subsidiary turrets placed symmetrically in the plan. In overall form, and in the labyrinthine complexity of its beautifully ordered internal arrangements, the building is indebted to the earlier fourteenth-century tradition of castle building in the region. To these, however, it adds the scale, regularity and boxy outline of the Perpendicular works at Windsor. Bolton remained sufficiently admired for the Scottish kings to copy some features of its design in their great palace at Linlithgow nearly a century later. Beneath the turret at each angle of the main towers, the parapet string course steps up. This detail is to be found in other buildings of the period.

type of arch-head with straight sides, a distinctive form rare in the south and unparalleled in the north.

Yet the Warkworth great tower is not an entirely exotic production. It also incorporates ideas found in other major local buildings, many of which are also explicitly linked with Lewyn. In 1378, probably just before work to Warkworth got under way, Richard, Lord Scrope, then chancellor of England, began a new castle at Bolton in Yorkshire. This impressive building, set on the side of a hill overlooking Wensleydale, still substantially survives (pl. 247). According to the antiquary John Leland writing in the 1540s, it took eighteen years to build with 1,000 marks (£666) being laid out on the works each season.[82] Scrope simultaneously invested in a burial church, massively expanding Easby Abbey outside Richmond and securing a licence in 1392–3 to endow the canons there with lands worth £150 per annum.[83] That he had such huge sums to spend probably reflects the profits of his high office rather than the riches of booty from his campaigning days.

Lewyn's involvement in the project is demonstrated by a surviving contract dated 29 September 1378 by which he agreed to complete the eastern range of the quadrangle, its two eastern towers and the eastern end of the southern range. This contract illustrates the working distinction between the process of design and that of construction: there existed an agreed building design that was being realised in stages. That said, there was flexibility in this system and the description of the buildings in the contract also proves that there were changes of plan in the course of the project.[84] The building incorporates several idiosyncratic features that seem to be hallmarks of Lewyn's work. In the hall, for example, the smoke from the fire was drawn out through flues set in heads of windows. Similarly distinctive is the incorporation of the stair and lobby to the great hall within a turret projecting from the walls. This is identical to the arrangement at Warkworth, where the main stair is contained within one of the projecting polygonal turrets of the great tower.[85]

248   A view of Brancepeth, Co. Durham, built in the last quarter of the fourteenth century and much adapted in later centuries. Although probably begun by Ralph Neville (d. 1367), the castle was most probably completed by his son John (d. 1388).

John Lewyn may well have been involved in the building works and was contracted in 1392 to repair the roads around Brancepeth. The towers that stood around the former outer court of the castle were rectangular in plan and

possessed unusually heavy corner buttresses. Towers of a similar design also exist at the Neville castle of Raby, but they occasionally occur much further afield, as at the so-called Bevis Tower north-west of the motte at Arundel, Sussex.

When it was planned, Bolton was one of the largest castle structures in the north. Yet as it rose from the ground, a newly prominent family was in the process of creating several castles on a comparable scale across the north of England. As already noted, Ralph Neville (d. 1367) had been the hero of the battle of Neville's Cross just outside Durham against the Scots in 1346.[86] His close connections with Durham probably spurred him late in life to rebuild his nearby castle on the outskirts of the city at Brancepeth. In its final form the castle, which was completed after his death, essentially comprised a series of large free-standing towers arranged around two courts.[87] It was much altered in the nineteenth century by the architect Anthony Salvin,[88]

249 (*top*) An engraving of Raby Castle, Co. Durham, by S. and N. Buck dated 1728. The castle was licensed in 1378 but it actually grew organically from the 1340s onwards, with a particular concentration of work falling between 1381 and 1388. Among the additions to the castle in this latter period were the outer apron wall and the central Bulmer Tower, named after a mythical founder of the castle. About 1475 sculpted panels displaying large letters 'B' were inserted around its upper level to celebrate this figure. To the right of this tower is the chapel gate ornamented with fighting figures and a large sculpture of a bull, the Neville family's heraldic beast. The castle kitchen bears a striking similarity to the great kitchen of Durham Priory, begun in 1364 under the direction of John Lewyn.

250 (*bottom*) The Neville Gate at Raby, Co. Durham, can be dated by the display of heraldry beneath the parapet to 1381–8. Many of the windows and details of the gatehouse have been altered over time, though the fringe of decorative cusping on the underside of the entrance arch is original. This latter ornament is found in several northern gateways in the last quarter of the fourteenth century including Thornton Abbey (Lincolnshire), Hylton (Co. Durham), Lumley (Co. Durham) and the inside face of the inner bailey gate at Carlisle. One possible source for this idea is the detailing of the Aerary Porch at Windsor of the 1350s, the entrance to Edward III's college of St George. Covering the entrance passage is a net vault. The projecting towers to either side are set at an angle in a manner reminiscent of the buttresses at Brancepeth.

but several of its late fourteenth-century towers survive. These are all massively conceived on a rectangular plan with buttresses rising to form corner turrets (pl. 248). [89] The scale of the work at Brancepeth set an impressive standard for the future architectural projects of the Neville family. It was a standard they did not hesitate to meet.

In 1378 Ralph's son, John (d. 1388) received a licence to crenellate another important family seat at Raby in Co. Durham. A castle had existed on the site since at least the thirteenth century, but the licence seems to have been an opportunity to expand the building substantially. The old hall and chapel were now hemmed round within a series of free-standing towers, solidly proportioned and several on distorted rectilinear plans (pl. 249). One of these housed a polygonal kitchen comparable in form to that built by Lewyn at Durham Priory, possibly evidence for his involvement here. Work at Raby continued into the 1380s with the construction of an impressive gate tower set with heraldry (dated 1381–8) and to an apron wall enclosing the whole site (pl. 250). [90]

In the meantime John was extending his power south and west into Yorkshire, and established two new centres of influence at Middleham and Sheriff Hutton. At Middleham he inherited a substantial castle, which he reworked with new domestic apartments. By contrast, the existing castle at Sheriff Hutton was abandoned and in 1382 a licence was issued for another building on a greenfield site. The principal court at Sheriff Hutton was laid out on a regular plan with four high ranges set with towers. Descriptions of the castle imply a very similar plan to Bolton, with a spacious stair rising to a hall on one face of the building. In the 1540s the antiquarian John Leland asserted: 'I saw no house in the north so like a princely logginges.' [91] Certain technical details of its design, including the treatment of ornamental string courses in the towers, also strongly imply that Lewyn was its designer (pl. 251). The work of constructing Sheriff Hutton was probably completed by John's son, Ralph, who in Sep-

251 (*top*) Sheriff Hutton, Yorkshire, begun around 1382, relates closely to the design of Bolton. The main court had four principal towers connected by high, stone-built ranges. Sufficient of the towers survives to demonstrate at least one technical point of connection with Bolton: in both buildings the projecting course of stone at the top of each tower steps up at the corners. This detail, unlikely to be noticed by a patron, is almost certainly a mark of Lewyn's common authorship (see pl. 247). On the far side of the castle was an outer or base court, which was described by Leland in the 1540s as having a façade with '3. great and high towers, of which the gatehouse was the middle'. In the sixteenth century the castle served as the official seat of the president of the Council of the North.

252 (*bottom*) Wressle, Yorkshire, a quadrangular castle in the tradition of Bolton and Sheriff Hutton that was begun by the soldier Sir Thomas Percy, probably in 1390s. A brother of Henry, first earl of Northumberland, Thomas enjoyed close connections with John of Gaunt. In the 1390s he became an important courtier and was amongst those elevated to earldoms by Richard II in 1397. The windows of the building are deliberately rugged, a striking illustration of the use of archaic or austere architectural forms in the context of castles. Wressle was substantially modernised in the early sixteenth century by Henry Percy, fifth earl of Northumberland. Only one range of the castle now survives.

253 Lumley, Co. Durham, licensed in 1389. The corner towers are distinctively detailed with buttresses and polygonal machicolations at each angle, a particular treatment found in other buildings in the region into the early fifteenth century, such as Hylton and Bywell. The fabric of this quadrangular castle was substantially remodelled in the 1570s by John, Lord Lumley, who made the castle home to his remarkable collection of art and genealogical memorabilia. In the 1720s the buildings were again reorganised by Sir John Vanbrugh, an astute observer of medieval English castle architecture.

tember 1397 also secured the title of earl of Westmorland. His architectural patronage will be further considered in the next chapter.

Whether Lewyn was yet more widely involved in castle construction it is impossible now to tell. Whatever the case, a consideration of this series of great northern castles would not be complete without notice of two other regularly planned buildings of recognisably similar form and very probably associated with him. At Wressle in Yorkshire, Sir Thomas Percy, younger brother of the earl of Northumberland, created for himself a fine quadrangular castle that followed closely in the tradition of Bolton and Sheriff Hutton (pl. 252). Work to Wressle probably began after 1390, when Sir Thomas emerged as a prominent figure in Richard II's court.[92] The castle includes a series of ruggedly detailed windows that appear incongruously crude in a building of such quality. In fact, they are probably intended to make Wressle look formidable and ancient – in other words, castle-like.

The other building possibly connected with Lewyn is Lumley Castle, Co. Durham, licensed in 1389 (pl. 253). Constructed by Ralph, Lord Lumley (d. 1400), a supporter of the earl of Northumberland and an important courtier, this castle has less massive ranges than Bolton but clearly resembles it in overall conception. Its main gate also incorporates a display of heraldry of a kind that was becoming increasingly common in major castle buildings across the kingdom.[93]

Whoever designed Lumley also worked on perhaps the most splendidly decorated of all northern castle buildings, the great tower at Hylton, Co. Durham. This four-storey building was cast in the form of a twin-towered gatehouse (pl. 254), a design possibly inspired by Richard II's new and distinctive main façade of Westminster Hall. In more local terms it is connected to the nearby gatehouse of Tynemouth Priory, which was being rebuilt at exactly this time (see pl. 209). Across both the principal façades of Hylton is a rich display of sculpture and heraldry. The latter fixes the

254 A cut-away reconstruction by David Simon of the tower at Hylton, Co. Durham, which is cast in the form of a gatehouse. It may be dated on the basis of its heraldic decoration (1) to the 1390s and the treatment of the turrets compares exactly to those at nearby Lumley. The tower possessed battlements inhabited by fighting men, an idea that can be traced back in English castle design to the 1270s and which remained particularly popular in the north of England. It incorporated a complete suite of residential chambers, including a hall (2), services (3), a kitchen, chapel (4) and withdrawing chambers (5). The tower is known to have stood in a fortified enclosure that incorporated various ancillary buildings including a chapel. It was completely gutted after 1950 and is today a roofless ruin. The front of the building displays the arms of all the principal families in the area in hierarchical order beneath the royal standard. Given that Sir William Hylton's rank as a commander or banneret was expressed by the right to fly a broad banner on the field, the emphasis given to this emblem cannot be coincidental. On the reverse side are the arms and helm of its builder beneath the stag that Richard II adopted as his symbol. The closest parallel for this display are the outer faces of the exquisite Wilton Diptych (London, National Gallery), commissioned by Richard II around 1395.

255 Belsay, Northumberland, the pele tower built between 1391 and 1396 as a symbol of John Middleton's restoration to his family estate. Two nearby towers at Chipchase (see pl. 333) and Widdrington were similar in design and were probably erected at about the same time. So, too, the gatehouse at Tynemouth. The Belsay tower preserves remains of fourteenth- and fifteenth-century wall-painting schemes on its principal floor, which presumably served as a great chamber. Contrary to what is sometimes supposed, pele towers rarely stood in isolation. At Belsay the surrounding buildings incorporate some fabric from medieval structures.

construction of the building to the 1390s, during the lifetime of Sir William Hylton (d. 1435), who served Richard II as a commander or banneret.[94] It is possible that the gatehouse formed the entrance to a regular courtyard of buildings that have since been destroyed, but the evidence is equivocal. It could equally have stood as the dominant feature within an older and irregular complex enclosed by walls and ditches.

Hylton is a halfway house between the great northern castles of the nobility and the more modest creations of the gentry, what have popularly become known as pele towers. These are fortified residential towers, usually on a rectangular plan and with corner turrets. Contrary to what is generally supposed, it appears that pele towers were rarely isolated fortifications. Rather they tended to be erected as fortified adjuncts to houses. These buildings are complicated to study: they are poorly documented and rarely incorporate features or detailing that is readily dateable.

Occasionally, however, the history of a family can offer information about a particular tower and by extension about a group of related buildings. A case in point is the impressive late fourteenth-century tower at Belsay in Northumberland, which can be properly dated and understood only in the context of a remarkable tale of dynastic misfortune and recovery (pl. 255).

In 1317 the Middleton family was dispossessed of their manor of Belsay because of the scandalous involvement of the heir to the estate in the abduction of two cardinals travelling on their way to Scotland. By the late fourteenth century the property had passed to a distant relative of the family, John, Lord Stryvelyn. He had no surviving children and arranged a match between his great niece and his disinherited kinsman, John Middleton, whom he adopted as his heir.

Lord Stryvelyn died in 1378, but his widow kept control of much of the estate until her death in 1391, when it finally passed to John's control. By that time

John had inherited other property and he now emerged as a considerable landowner.[95] It was almost certainly to celebrate the restitution of his family estate in 1391 (and before his own death in 1396) that he constructed a tower at Belsay decorated with the impaled arms of Stryvelyn and Middleton. The new building evidently formed one element of a larger house with a hall and ancillary ranges, and was probably contracted locally by a mason who also designed the towers at nearby Widdrington and Chipchase.

THE MIDLANDS AND SOUTH WALES

The Midlands had no well-documented figure who dominated its architectural practice in the same way as Yevele, Wynford or Lewyn. The only individual who might have approached their stature in professional terms was the chief mason of the duchy of Lancaster. In the 1390s this post was occupied by another Windsor-connected mason, Robert Skillyngton.[96] Unfortunately,

so little of his work can be confidently identified today that it is difficult to assess his artistic character with any confidence. Skillington is certainly known to have completed the great lost church of St Mary in the Newark at Leicester Castle, the burial place of the dukes of Lancaster and probably the first Perpendicular building in the Midlands.[97] He also undertook various unidentified operations at Kenilworth in the 1390s and work at Tutbury Castle, which will be discussed in the next chapter. Another major project that Skillington is likely to have been involved with simply by virtue of his post is the completion of Guy's Tower at Warwick in 1393/4, the final element of the great entrance façade to the castle that was begun in the 1340s (see pl. 205).

The work of Skillington aside, there is plenty of evidence for the influence of the Perpendicular style on the architecture of the region. Thomas Woodstock, duke of Gloucester, for example, developed his seat at Caldicot Castle, Monmouthshire, from 1383 onwards with new domestic buildings, a postern tower (pl. 256) and a great gatehouse (pl. 257). Besides the documentary record of his work, there survives in the postern tower door a discretely placed stone with the name 'Thomas' cut upon it within a quatrefoil, almost certainly a ceremonially laid foundation stone. It is an unexpectedly human reminder of the interest and pride that patrons could take in their building projects. The buildings at Caldicot reflect long-standing, local architectural preferences: for example, the postern tower stands on spur bases, a form popular in the south of Wales since the late thirteenth century. Moreover, there appear in the gatehouse mouldings forms that look back to the vigorous tradition of Decorated design in the Bristol Channel.[98] But there are marks of influence from the royal works too at Caldicot: the gatehouse has a vault with ring-boss murder holes and in overall plan (pl. 258) bears a close resemblance to its contemporary at Bodiam in Sussex.

Another building of the 1380s on the south coast of Wales that makes play with Perpendicular forms in combination with locally favoured architectural designs is Llawhaden Castle in Pembrokeshire, which was largely rebuilt by Adam de Houghton, bishop of St Davids (1362–86). Houghton was closely associated with John of Gaunt and jointly established a college with the duke at St Davids in 1366. The new college buildings were erected under the direction of a certain John Fawley, and their details show that he was fully conversant with the Perpendicular style.[99]

256 The postern gate at Caldicot, Monmouthshire, was constructed over two years between 1385 and 1387 at a cost of £54 by a certain Robert the Mason for Thomas Woodstock, duke of Gloucester. According to the agreement drawn up for the work, the tower was to be built on the site of a former dovecote and was to stand 50 feet tall with three chambers, three fireplaces and three latrines. It was also designed to incorporate a vaulted gate passage closed by a portcullis. Additional payments were made for adding the machicolis (50 shillings), an alteration apparently requested by the duke himself. The tower possesses spur bases, an unusual detail in a building of this period in England but consistently popular along the coast of south Wales from the thirteenth century onwards. Carved discreetly into the lowest stone to the right of the doorway is a quatrefoil and the name Thomas. This is probably a foundation stone laid ceremonially by the duke at the start of building work. Another stone from a demolished building in the castle with the name of his wife, 'Alianore', also survives.

While Fawley was involved in the college he was also directing operations at Llawhaden and in 1383 was appointed constable of the new castle, apparently as construction drew to a close.[100] He created a work of hybrid architecture informed by the Perpendicular but conceived in keen awareness of the architectural traditions of the region. The great gate, for example, with its spur bases and banded masonry might easily be mistaken for a late thirteenth-century structure (pl. 259). By contrast, the detailing and interior arrangements of the castle with its massive and coherently planned domestic ranges reflect the influence of Windsor.

THE DEPOSITION OF RICHARD II

The death of John of Gaunt in 1399 and the resumption of his estates by Richard II provoked an unexpectedly fast response from Gaunt's exiled son, Henry Bolingbroke, in Paris. While the unsuspecting Richard was on campaign in Ireland on 1 June, Henry secretly set out for England and conducted a brilliant campaign in which castles played a prominent role. He landed at Ravenspur in the first days of July and moved through the Lancastrian estates in Yorkshire by way of the castles at Pickering, Knaresborough and Pontefract. At Doncaster he was met by more supporters, including the earls of Northumberland and Westmorland. Richard's uncle, the duke of York, who was keeper of the kingdom, soon afterwards threw in his lot with the rebel forces. By the time Richard had returned from Ireland on 24–5 July, his cause was waning rapidly.

After several days' delay, the king rode with a small party to Conwy Castle. When he arrived there on 12 August his principal strongholds in the county palatine of Chester had fallen and his treasury had been seized at Holt Castle. At Conwy he received the earl of Northumberland, who probably assured him of his safety, and escorted him as a virtual prisoner to Flint. There he presumably resided in the great tower still crowned by the 'beautiful and noble ring of timber' erected by his ill-fated predecessor Edward II when prince of Wales. Henry met Richard II at Flint and then escorted him to London.

The focus of these momentous events in Wales and western England should not distract from the wider turmoil caused by Henry's invasion. John Pelham, constable of Pevensey in Sussex, created a diversion for Henry's landing in the north by a spirited defence

257 The great gatehouse, Caldicot, Monmouthshire, begun in 1383. It appears to have contained a suite of domestic rooms that may have functioned as withdrawing chambers from the neighbouring great hall.

The gatehouse is built entirely from cut stone and was richly detailed with sculpture: each upper window was framed with a sculpted architectural canopy. This ornament has largely been defaced. Many technical

details of this building hearken back to the forms of mid-fourteenth-century buildings along the Bristol Channel, including some of the mouldings and the deep arcading beneath the battlements.

335

258 Plans of the gatehouses at Caldicot, Monmouthshire, begun in 1383, and Bodiam, Sussex, of *circa* 1385. Below is an overlay of the two. The internal chambers of the Bodiam gatehouse were not extended backwards as at Caldicot, but otherwise the two designs share many points of comparison, notably the rectangular flanking towers and the projecting side turrets. Such similarities point to the probable common origin of both designs. Most likely, both were drawn up by masons in the employ of the king's works with access to a model technical drawing of a gatehouse plan. It is noteworthy that, viewed in elevation, the completed gatehouses are very different in character. This underlines the point that one plan could be realised by two masons as an elevation in very different ways.

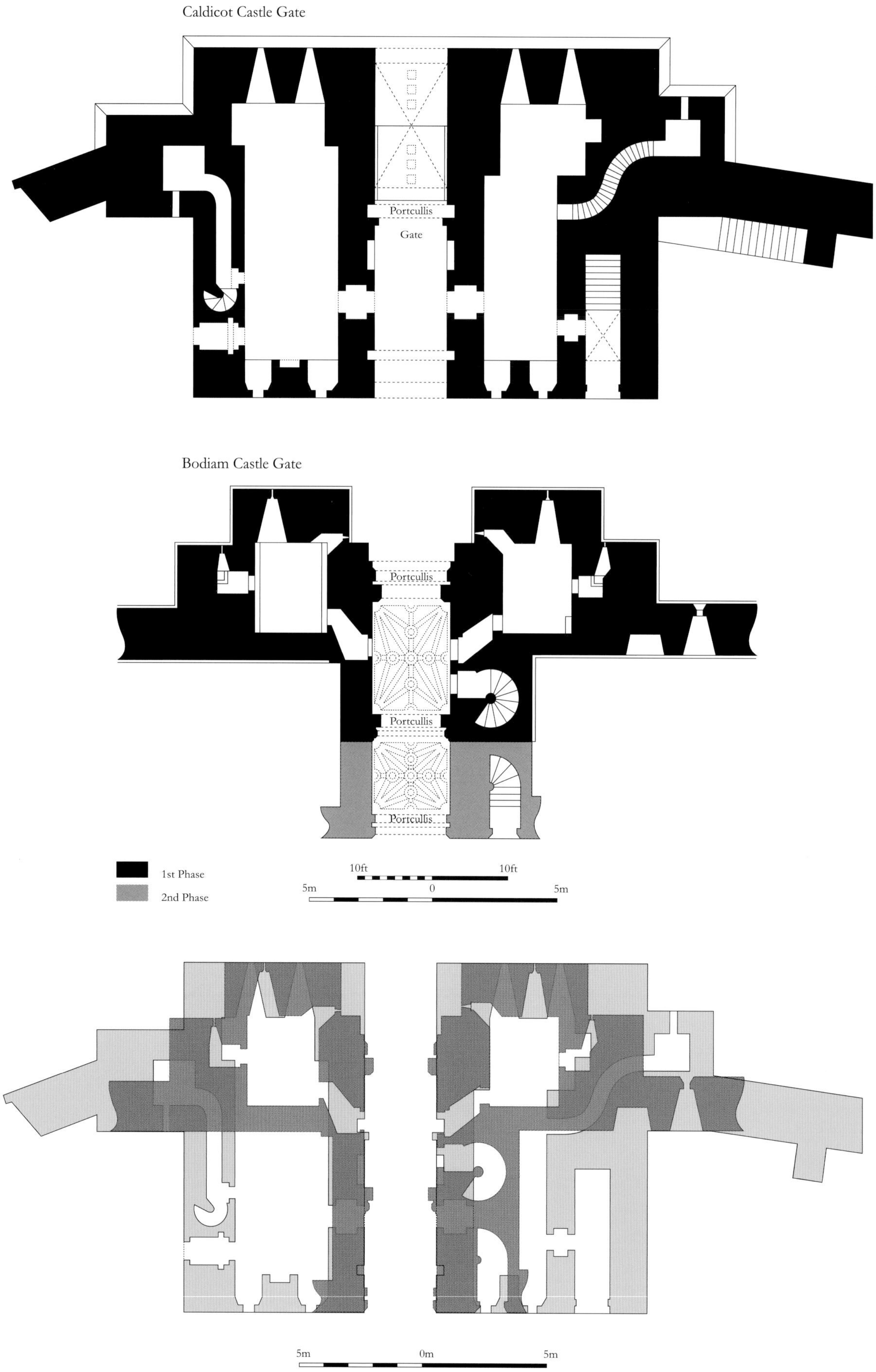

Caldicot Castle Gate

Portcullis

Gate

Bodiam Castle Gate

Portcullis

Portcullis

Portcullis

1st Phase
2nd Phase

10ft   10ft
5m   0   5m

5m   0m   5m

of his castle against the royalists. He wrote plaintively to the duke:

> My dear lord,
> It is right that you know of my position, I am here laid in manner of a siege . . . so that I may not out, nor no vitals get without much difficulty. Wherefore my dear, may it please you, by the advice of your council, to give remedy to the salvation of your castle and the malice of your enemies. The Holy Trinity keep you from your enemies and soon send me good tidings of you.
>
> Written at Pevensey in the castle
by your own poor
J. Pelham[101]

At quite what moment in his campaign Henry determined to seize the throne from Richard is not now clear. Whatever the case, Richard was subsequently deposed and the coronation of Henry was celebrated at Westminster Abbey on 13 October 1399. Every effort was made to lend this doubtful occasion weight. An ampula of sacred oil reputedly given by the Virgin to Thomas Becket (and then unaccountably lost for two centuries) was happily discovered in time for the ceremony.[102] Moreover, in his desire for marks of distinction, Henry may have been the first English king to be enthroned upon the coronation stone of the kings of Scotland, the Stone of Scone.

A few months later, following a rebellion by his former favourites, Richard II was murdered at Pontefract, where he was being held prisoner. The deposition and murder of a king set an ominous precedent for the future and remained firmly lodged in the English historic consciousness. As late as 1597 the lord chamberlain insisted on suppressing the deposition scene of Shakespeare's *Richard II* on the grounds of its sensitivity, and Elizabeth I famously identified herself with the king. Commenting of her own failings after having been innocently presented with a chronicle of the reign by the antiquary and lawyer William Lambarde, she once famously exploded: 'I am Richard II; know ye not that?'

259 The main gate of Llawhaden Castle, Pembrokeshire, completed around 1383 by the mason John Fawley for Adam de Houghton, bishop of St Davids (1362–86). Its two great drum towers rise from deep spurs, a detail consistently popular in southern Wales from the late thirteenth century. The gatehouse is built with roughly shaped blocks of stone and its upper chambers were barrel-vaulted, construction techniques typical of the region. A decorative band of grey stone has been created across the middle of the building. The gatehouse faces down the main street of the town towards the market place.

12

THE LANCASTRIAN AGE

HENRY IV, HENRY V AND HENRY VI

The political difficulties created by the usurpation of the throne by Henry IV (1399–1413) in 1399 brought to a close the forty years of intense architectural activity in England that constituted the first flowering of the Perpendicular style; this chapter concerns its second spring. It took more than a decade for domestic affairs to stabilise and when they did so under Henry IV's heir, the resources of the kingdom were unexpectedly diverted abroad. The madness of the French king, Charles VI, and the rivalry of his principal magnates offered Henry V (1413–22) a perfect opportunity to intervene in Continental politics. In the successful campaigns that followed, many English noblemen won for themselves lands and titles in France. And in 1420 Henry V was acknowledged by the treaty of Troyes as the heir to the French crown. Not since the thirteenth century had English interests extended so far into France or the prestige of the Valois kings sunk so low. One important side effect of these events was that English and French artistic tastes – and particularly that of the breakaway court of the duke of Burgundy, now clearly established as the lodestone of European culture – were brought into close connection. In this contact were laid the foundations for a remarkable period of cultural exchange in all the arts, including architecture.

Famously, Henry V's early death in 1422 frustrated the union of the English and French crowns. The accession of a nine-month-old baby, Henry VI (1422–61), to the English throne was one of three important developments that redressed the balance of power in the ongoing struggle for the control of France. Soon afterwards, the French king, Charles VI, died and opposition to English rule became focused in the hands of his son, Charles VII. Then from 1429 the prestige and power of the new French king were bolstered by the brilliantly successful exploits of Joan of Arc, a shepherdess and visionary who at divine behest donned armour and fought for his cause. Henry VI's minority government now became preoccupied with saving the deteriorating situation in France, a course of action that proved both expensive and unsuccessful. Failure made the government more unpopular and generated political tensions at home. It also helped exacerbate the rivalries between the three royal uncles at the heart of government affairs – John, duke of Bedford (d. 1435), the regent of France; Humphrey, duke of Gloucester (d. 1447); and Henry Beaufort, bishop of Winchester (d. 1446), one of the richest prelates in fifteenth-century Christendom.

Reverses in the war and the approach of Henry VI's majority in the 1430s were additionally important in encouraging Englishmen to abandon their conquests and return from France, thereby intensifying competition for power and court patronage at home. One of these returning noblemen, William de la Pole, earl of Suffolk (later marquis and then duke of Suffolk), emerged as the outstanding favourite of the king when Henry VI attained his majority in 1437. Despite widespread popular resentment, Suffolk and his circle enjoyed a virtual monopoly over royal patronage until the political hegemony he established was dramatically overthrown following his murder in May 1450. Suffolk's death heralded a slow slide into the intermittently fought civil war known as the Wars of the Roses, a conflict precipitated by Henry VI's periods of illness and incapacity from August 1453 onwards. The fortunes of his Lancastrian cause, largely directed by his formidable queen, Margaret of Anjou, and of the rival Yorkists were to fluctuate violently. When the fighting actually began in 1455, until the moment of Edward IV's accession as a Yorkist king in 1461, there was to be relatively little building by the nobility in England.

But prior to the hostilities of the Wars of the Roses, the particular circumstances of Henry VI's reign encouraged an extraordinary spate of grandiose architectural projects. The intense political rivalry between court factions in an atmosphere of relative – if strained – peace spurred leading figures on both sides to build. Money for the work came either directly or indirectly from the royal coffers: those involved usually enjoyed substantial profits from offices of state in the administration either of France or England. Early in Henry VI's reign such posts were usually in the gift of the royal uncles, but as the king grew up they increasingly came to be enjoyed by virtue of royal favour. What distinguished major castles of this generation was the quality and interest of their architecture. This followed in the tradition of the Perpendicular style but was enriched and transformed by Continental ideas. Such a fusion was essentially made possible by the organisation and operation of the royal works. Superficial appearances might not suggest that this was the case, so the point deserves brief explanation.

THE KING'S WORKS

None of the three monarchs that occupied the throne in the first half of the fifteenth century was to prove a great builder. In each case the reasons were different. For Henry IV the acute financial difficulties of his administration precluded the patronage of major architectural projects; for his son Henry V, an overriding interest in the conquest of France focused his resources on military operations abroad; and for Henry VI, the ambitious building schemes he began after his long minority were jeopardised by poor health and his failing government. Nevertheless, such royal works as were begun – notably the construction of a new Lancastrian palace at Sheen by Henry V and Henry VI's foundation of a college dedicated to the Virgin beside Windsor Castle at Eton – were both to prove vastly important in the future evolution of grand English domestic and castle architecture.

So too was the circle of royal masons who undertook these operations. Their experience and training linked them directly to the previous generation of leading architectural practitioners working in the Perpendicular style. Richard II's chief mason, Henry Yevele (d. 1400), was succeeded in his responsibilities at Westminster, Canterbury and the Tower of London by a close associate, Stephen Lote (d. 1417/18). Another London-based mason, Lote had collaborated with Yevele in various architectural projects and the production of funerary monuments.[1] At Lote's death, the post of king's mason passed briefly to William Colchester (d. 1420), who had previously been engaged in such royal building operations as Richard II's great tower of Southampton Castle, Westminster Hall and – by the royal command of Henry IV – in the rebuilding of York Minster. Colchester enjoyed his post only for twelve months before he was replaced in turn by one of Lote's former colleagues, Thomas Mapilton (d. 1438). It is one mark of the friendship between the two masons that Lote bequeathed to Mapilton his collection of architectural drawings (termed 'patrons' in his will).[2] Mapilton also practised from London, though as a young man he had worked in Durham and served the king in France as a craftsman. He was in turn replaced by Robert Westerley, who occupied the post between 1439 and 1461. Westerley's earlier career had involved him in numerous royal building projects, including those at Westminster, Sheen and Rouen Castle.[3]

Besides appreciating the close personal and professional connections between these men and their familiarity with the core buildings of the Perpendicular style in London and Westminster, it is also important to recognise their international experience. To a greater or lesser extent all were directly familiar with buildings in those areas of France occupied by the English. They might also plausibly be supposed to have had access to

260 A photograph of around 1890 showing the internal front of the tower built in the 1440s at Tutbury, Staffordshire. The tower rose three floors in height and was formerly crowned with battlements. At every level it comprised a large and a small rectangular chamber accessed from the rear by a projecting stair turret (visible here). Two drawn surveys of around 1585 taken during Mary, queen of Scots' residence in the castle show that the tower contained three discrete lodgings. The tower was almost certainly designed by the king's mason Robert Westerley. He was sent to the site, along with two masons from the duchy of Lancaster's own works department, to give advice on the project. The day-to-day work was overseen by four masons, and stone for the building came from Winshill quarry near Stoke-on-Trent.

a wide range of other Continental architectural drawings. To what degree English masons became involved in Continental building operations during the early fifteenth century will never now be clear, but their expertise was widely valued. For example, the master mason of Paris and its cathedral, Notre-Dame, between 1431 and 1455 was called John James, a figure of obscure origin but to judge by his name almost certainly an Englishman.[4] And the sixteenth-century Florentine writer Giorgio Vasari implies that there was an English mason amongst the international group of experts assembled in 1420 to advise on the problems of vaulting the presbytery of Florence Cathedral.[5] Although the circle of royal masons in fifteenth-century England might seem small and of restricted experience therefore, in fact it had access to an extraordinary breadth of architectural ideas.

This circle, moreover, maintained a virtual monopoly on grand building design in England at large: the king's master mason remained the first port of call for architectural expertise for those within the orbit of the court. As a result, even when the king was not actively building, his masons were serving the needs of those courtiers and noblemen who were. This process of freelancing by royal masons is very poorly documented, but as in the case of Henry Yevele a generation earlier, it is to be imagined that these men could be involved in various ways – as advisers, remote designers or overseers. Also, that for practical reasons, when undertaking provincial commissions they usually worked in conjunction with a senior and locally based mason. A rare documented example of such working practices relates to the construction of a tower at Tutbury in Staffordshire, a possession of the duchy of Lancaster, in the 1440s. The episode is sufficiently revealing to deserve description.

In 1441–2 masons and workmen at Tutbury cleared the site of an old tower in the castle and laid out the plan for its replacement using ropes and pegs. This was viewed by the steward of the duchy of Lancaster, Humphrey, earl of Stafford. For some reason, he did not approve the proposal and asked for the advice of the royal council, which directed that a tower be built on a different site altogether. Robert Westerley was then sent to give his opinion about the new building and was advised in his decision by two masons from Pontefract, another duchy castle where similar works were under way. The tower was completed over the next eight years by a small core of four relatively junior masons at a cost of about £600 (pl. 260).[6] In the circumstances, it seems reasonable to assume that they worked according to designs drawn up by Westerley. This attribution would agree, moreover, with the sophisticated detailing of the building. It is worth mentioning that in the course of the works, the ownership of the castle passed to Henry VI's queen, Margaret of Anjou, a notable patroness of architecture in her own right. She paid for the completion of the tower and constructed another in the castle.

HENRY IV AND THE DUCHY OF LANCASTER

Despite the shadow cast across his character by the usurpation of the throne, there is no gainsaying the remarkable career of Henry IV. He had been born at Bolingbroke Castle in Lincolnshire, probably in 1366, and as a teenager had been amongst those in the Tower of London when it was stormed during the Peasants' Revolt of 1381. A pardon he issued in 1400 to a certain John Ferrour of Southwark in return for saving his life on that occasion 'in a wonderful and kind manner'

speaks of a dramatic escape from the mob. He spent most of the period between 1390 and 1393 abroad, first travelling on crusade in the Baltic and then going on pilgrimage to Jerusalem. The former journey, which was widely fashionable amongst the English nobility in the period, exposed him to the Teutonic Knights. It is known that he spent Christmas of 1390 at Königsberg and saw many of the order's great castles, including the celebrated Marienburg (or Malbork) in modern-day Poland.[7] What he made of the experience is not now clear, but he later spoke warmly of the military order that had hosted his visit. Following Richard II's judgement of exile he travelled to Paris, where over 1398–9 he attended university debates and engaged in unsuccessful diplomatic attempts to secure a bride of European stature.[8]

As the king of England, Henry united the power and revenues of the crown with the unparalleled resources of the duchy of Lancaster. It was a combination of great incomes that led some of his more optimistic subjects to hope for a reign without public taxation. The hope was never realistic, but in the event his two incomes were never actually united. Rather,

Henry IV decided to run the two concerns separately, maintaining the duchy of Lancaster as an independently functioning and effectively private patrimony. The arrangement was of practical importance because as king of England Henry was too poor to build until the very end of his reign: the usurpation in 1399 plunged England back into an unwanted and costly war with both France and Scotland, neither of which acknowledged him as a rightful ruler. Moreover, in 1400 there broke out a major Welsh rebellion under the leadership of the self-proclaimed prince of Wales, a squire called Owain Glyn Dŵr. It is one indication of the insuperable financial problems faced by the royal administration that six treasurers were appointed in the first five years of the reign.

But as duke of Lancaster and almost irrespective of his difficulties as a king, Henry was the pre-eminent castle builder of the kingdom. In 1402 he initiated a substantial programme of works at Lancaster Castle, which continued into his son's reign. By 1422 a total of more than £2,500 had been laid out on the buildings there.[9] As part of the operation, the existing castle gatehouse was subsumed inside a new building with a twin-towered façade (pl. 261). Ornamented with the king's arms and those of Henry of Monmouth as prince of Wales, the building was probably completed before the latter's accession in 1413.[10]

At Pontefract, meanwhile, the reconstruction of the outer walls of the castle initiated by John of Gaunt in the 1370s continued. Amongst the structures that can be specifically attributed to Henry IV is the Swillington Tower, built between 1399 and 1405 at a cost of £370 14s.[11] This broadly imitates the form and detailing of the earlier towers in the rebuilding sequence, although it stood proud of the walls and was approached over a fortified bridge. The arrangement might relate to the latrine towers termed *danskas* characteristic of the castles held by the Teutonic Knights and personally familiar to Henry IV. Between 1400 and 1409 a large residential tower was erected at Leicester, a major lost structure to judge by its cost of about £500, and new boundary walls were laid out round the castle.[12] Meanwhile, at the nearby castle of Tutbury a new wall and towers were added to the defences under the direction of John of Gaunt's former master mason at Kenilworth, Robert Skillyngton.[13]

Such of these buildings as survive illustrate many points of similarity with earlier works of castle architecture patronised by the duchy (and former earldom) of Lancaster. For example, the Lancaster gatehouse

bears comparison to that begun by the earl of Lancaster in 1313 at Dunstanburgh in Northumberland. Both buildings incorporate four subsidiary turrets within their twin-tower plan in a very unusual combination: there are two turrets at the front flanking the gate passage and two to the rear at the outer corners of the building. In addition, the inner façades incorporate five symmetrically arranged openings: a central gateway with doors and windows on either side. At Pontefract, the great kitchen erected at some period in the fifteenth century bears striking resemblance in its arrangement of hearths to that built at Kenilworth by John of Gaunt in the 1370s.[14] These similarities suggest that like the English kings, the dukes of Lancaster – uniquely amongst the English nobility – undertook a sufficient quantity of building to maintain a works department with a corporate architectural memory informed by a collection of architectural drawings.

The only area where Henry IV was an active patron of castle architecture both as king and duke of Lancaster was in Wales and its marches. The threat of Owain Glyn Dŵr's rebellion encouraged the provisioning of castles and the hurried repair of such royal castles along the border as Chester and Hereford. The latter operation in May 1402, for example, involved plugging gaps in the walls with timber palisades, the construction of watchtowers and the repair of the great tower.[15] At the same time, as duke of Lancaster, Henry raced to prepare his duchy possessions for the conflict. Particularly notable in this respect was his work to Kidwelly, Carmarthenshire, which he inherited from his father. In 1388–9 John of Gaunt had begun a new gatehouse here, but progress to the building was slow until 1403 (pl. 262). Then, under threat of attack, Henry IV ensured that it was rapidly completed as part of a number of essential repairs to make the castle defensible. These included the digging of a new ditch, the repair of hedges (presumably of thorn) and the construction of a timber tower. Kidwelly was besieged several times in the ensuing conflict and although the castle with its small garrison of between nine and twenty-one soldiers never fell, the town was sacked twice.[16]

In its repair of Kidwelly, the duchy was behaving exactly like other landowners in the region. Most major English noble families owned property in the marches, which they needed to protect. Little of the building they undertook in response to the rebellion was architecturally impressive: the violence and the loss of income caused by the fighting precluded any

262 The great gate of Kidwelly, Carmarthenshire, was begun by John of Gaunt in 1388–9 and completed in two further phases of building by Henry IV. The front section of the building was a discrete architectural unit housing the mechanism for the drawbridge and portcullis. To the rear of the gatehouse were the domestic chambers for the constable: immediately over the gate passage at first-floor level was the hall. Above it was a withdrawing chamber. Although very large and impressive, the building is less sophisticated than its contemporary and counterpart gatehouse at Lancaster. Built throughout of local rubble, it is necessarily rugged with few carved architectural details. The bulging towers and the crude treatment of windows are characteristic of local buildings. Evidently, the masons responsible for realising this building were drawn from south Wales.

263 (*facing page top*) Cardiff, Glamorgan, a view of the motte by Paul Sandby, *circa* 1770. As part of the earl of Warwick's alterations to the castle begun after 1423, a tall new gatehouse was built to command the approach to the motte. Little more than a decade after this view was taken, the gatehouse was largely swept away by Capability Brown for the third marquess of Bute. The domestic buildings on the summit of the motte were also probably adapted in the fifteenth century. By remodelling Cardiff, the earl was signalling the future role of the castle as his seat in Glamorgan.

264 (*facing page bottom*) Cardiff, Glamorgan, a view by Paul Sandby of *circa* 1770 of the earl of Warwick's main 1420s residential range to the south-west of the motte. Just peering above the battlements is the top of the principal tower to the rear of the building (1). The inner front of the range was punctuated by four polygonal turrets (2) modelled on Edward III's Rose Tower at Windsor (see pl. 220). This early fifteenth-century range at Cardiff appears to be the direct inspiration for Edward IV's apartments of the 1470s in the lower bailey of Nottingham Castle (see pl. 292). The rectangular tower to the left was erected by Henry Herbert, earl of Pembroke, as part of his alterations to the castle around 1580 (3). The range still survives, but it presently bears the stamp of a magnificent reworking by William Burges for the third marquess of Bute in the 1870s.

but hurried or makeshift repairs until the chief crisis had passed. This came in 1404, when Owain Glyn Dŵr joined in a revolt with the earl of Northumberland, the earl's brother and his son, Harry Hotspur. The earl had been instrumental in placing Henry on the throne and with his kinsmen had secured the northern march against the Scots. Their rewards were rich, but not sufficient to purchase their continued loyalty.[17]

Before the rebel forces could join up, Henry met and defeated the earl's son, Hotspur, at the battle of Shrewsbury on 21 July 1403. He then marched north to confront Northumberland himself. In the event, his journey was wasted. The earl fled to Scotland, and Henry, who was without a siege train, was powerless to take his castles. Indeed, at the Percy castle of Warkworth the king's officer had the humiliation of being denied access by one of the earl's sons on the absurd grounds that the boy lacked the appropriate trappings of estate to receive a royal visitor.[18]

In the circumstances, Henry was more or less forced to pardon Northumberland. But when the earl revolted yet again in 1405 he acted with greater determination. Marching north at the head of a large army he crushed the rebellion and then proceeded to reduce all the Percy strongholds. This time Warkworth fell immediately, and Henry was able to compose a triumphant letter describing the siege from the comfort of its domestic apartments. Because the castle was well provisioned, he wrote, the constable had denied him entry. But upon firing seven shots with his cannon, the garrison had cried mercy, and surrendered.[19]

Owain Glyn Dŵr's alliance with the Percys marked the high tide of Henry IV's misfortunes. From 1405 his affairs began slowly to improve and with them royal castle building began again – though on a modest scale – in the areas troubled by the fighting. The earl of Northumberland had permitted the Scots to sack Berwick-upon-Tweed and in 1405 Henry IV pledged 1,000 marks a year from the revenues of the town to pay for repairs to the fortifications. Then in 1407, as the fighting in Wales finally subsided, building began across the region. At Kidwelly, from 1408 the recently completed gatehouse was reordered and its interiors made more commodious. It would seem that Henry IV's intention was to turn the building into a self-contained residence for the constable of the castle with its own kitchen and accommodation. Meanwhile, in 1409 work began at the royal castle of Carmarthen to repair five towers and construct a gate at the cost of

£100. The next year work was under way to repair 'the great round tower' of Cardigan Castle and to erect a new tower and chambers for the constable. The year after that, in 1411, an instruction was issued to build a new gatehouse at Monmouth. Similar repairs to royal castles were to continue under Henry V. At Carreg Cennen, for example, at least £500 was spent between 1414 and 1421 on the buildings 'recently thrown down by rebels'.[20]

By the 1420s the recovery in Wales began to be reflected in the architectural endeavours of other powerful families, who started to remodel castles as centres of their regional administration along the southern Welsh seaboard. Outstanding in this respect was Richard Beauchamp, earl of Warwick, who acquired substantial estates in south Wales following his marriage to the Despenser heiress Isabella (1400–1439) in 1423. The dowry of his wife did not include the thirteenth-century castle at Caerphilly, and the earl determined instead to reorder the ancient castle at Cardiff. As part of his overhaul of the site he constructed a new gatehouse and erected a tower at the foot of the steps rising to the enclosure on the motte (pl. 263). His principal addition to the castle, however, was a residential range with a turreted inner façade directly inspired by the design of Edward III's upper ward at Windsor (pl. 264). This incorporated to the rear a single, massive tower. It may have been in answer to this new building that the earl of Buckingham also remodelled his nearby castle at Newport, Monmouthshire, in the 1430s and 40s (pl. 265).[21] Only the river façade of this building today survives.

The operations at both Cardiff and Newport make one notable concession to local architectural style: all the towers stand on spur bases. The inclusion of this feature is the more remarkable since – excepting the town gate of Alnwick in Northumberland (see pl. 275) – there is no evidence for its use elsewhere in England at all in this period.

THE NOBILITY AND COURT CIRCLE

One important result of Henry IV's struggle for political survival was the rise to power of several new individuals loyal to his cause. This is particularly true across the north of England where the Percy rebellion raised the political stakes and – after the family's fall from grace – offered opportunities for the redistribution of confiscated property and generous rewards.

265 Newport, Monmouthshire, a view of the roughly symmetrical river front of the castle. Work to it is first recorded in an account roll of 1435. This makes mention of the tower to the left of the photograph (described as the *majoris turris*) and identifies the master mason responsible as a certain Richard More. Stone for the operation was being shipped from Dundry in Somerset, a reflection of the long-standing architectural links between south Wales and the opposite shore of the Bristol Channel. The spur bases are a conscious throwback to thirteenth-century architectural design in the region. The castle was rectangular in plan and the central river gate gave direct access to its principal residential apartments. Work to the buildings was largely complete by 1452.

Ralph Neville, first earl of Westmorland (d. 1425), having backed the usurpation of Henry IV then remained loyal to the crown. He sought to advertise his new-found position as the premier northern earl in architecture. In 1409 he received a licence to found a collegiate church beside his principal castle at Raby, which he had remodelled in the previous reign.

At about this time the earl of Westmorland was also probably engaged in enlarging the domestic apartments at Middleham in Yorkshire. This work, which included the renovation of the bailey and great tower, is likely to have been completed in time for Henry IV's visit to the castle in 1410. Finally, it can be convincingly argued that he renovated the castle at Bywell in Northumberland at some stage after 1415 with a new gatehouse and tower.[22] The surviving gatehouse looks back to the architectural example of such buildings of the 1390s as nearby Hylton, Co. Durham.

Another contemporary castle in the same locality but on a more modest scale that is also informed by the previous generation of castle buildings is Witton, Co. Durham. Built by the head of a prominent marcher family who also helped resist the Percy rebellion, Sir Ralph Eure (d. 1422), Witton was licensed in 1410. Work to it almost certainly coincided with Eure's construction of another tower on a rectangular plan at Ayton in Yorkshire, his wife's patrimonial seat. Evi-

dently, in this case the support of the Lancastrian cause provided Eure with the means for a complete overhaul and upgrading of his principal seats.

Other notable rebuilding projects in Yorkshire undertaken by figures in Henry IV's circle of supporters after the Percy rebellions include Whorlton and Ravensworth. The latter, near Richmond, was owned by Henry, third Lord Fitzhugh (d. 1425). He not only helped suppress these disturbances but was also advanced to high office by Henry V, who appointed him chamberlain and treasurer of England. His income was further supplemented by property forfeited by his relatives, the Scropes at Bolton, who were also implicated in resistance to Henry IV.[23]

To the north-west of England, the vacuum created by the fall of the Percys consolidated the power of Sir John Stanley (d. 1414). A noted soldier, Sir John had served Richard II in Ireland prior to his defection to Henry IV's cause in 1399. At the battle of Shrewsbury he was wounded in the throat while fighting against Harry Hotspur. In its aftermath, when asked how the Cheshire rebels should be punished, he managed to rasp out the curt and bloody advice: 'Burn and slay, burn and slay'.

In 1405 Stanley was granted the lordship of the Isle of Man that had been forfeited by the earl of Northumberland and soon afterwards was appointed a knight of the Garter, steward of the household and constable of Windsor Castle.[24] To control his extensive interests in Cheshire, Lancashire, the Isle of Man and Ireland, Sir John Stanley created a new seat for himself at Liverpool, where he encastellated his residence with a new tower. This building latterly became known simply as The Tower and was demolished by the town corporation in 1826. In the long term, Stanley's acquisitions helped establish his family as an outstanding power in the north-west into the seventeenth century.

No less important as builders than the nobility who profited in the service of Henry IV were the ecclesiastics promoted by the king. Thomas Langley, for example, was a clerk born in Lancashire who entered the service of John of Gaunt and transferred his allegiance from father to son. In 1405 he was appointed chancellor of England and the following year, after failing to secure papal confirmation for his recent election as archbishop of York, he was enthroned bishop of Durham. His estimated income from the see was about £4,000, which made him one of the five wealthiest men in the kingdom. To this he might have added the power and estate of a cardinal in 1411, though Henry IV quashed the appointment. Langley's training in royal service encouraged him to embark on a process of consolidating the palatine powers of the see in much the same spirit as his predecessors, Anthony Bek and Thomas Hatfield. And the renewal of the administration naturally went hand in hand with the wholesale renewal of its buildings and institutions.[25]

Langley's architectural endeavours at Durham seem to have begun in earnest in 1413, when he leased a lime pit and quarry to a certain Thomas Alanson in return for delivering 120 horse loads of lime to the works of the castle of Durham.[26] The work in question was almost certainly the reconstruction of the main north gate to the castle, which commanded the only route up onto the peninsula of the city until its demolition around 1820. This incorporated a gaol and accommodation for a senior palatine official.[27] The gatehouse, which was complete by 1421, was designed to conform to the steeply sloping topography of the site and possessed its own barbican. It is just possible that the designer of the gate was the future royal mason Thomas Mapilton, who was employed at Durham between 1408 and 1416 during the reconstruction of the priory cloister.[28]

The new gate gave added protection to the whole summit of the peninsula, which in turn underwent substantial alteration. In 1416 Langley founded two schools, one for grammar and one for music, on the green beside the cathedral church.[29] It was probably in conjunction with this operation that he financed the reconstruction of the Galilee chapel to the west of the cathedral and the creation within it of his own chantry served by two priests. His successor, Robert Neville (elected bishop of Durham in 1438), later rebuilt the chancery and mint of the bishopric on the green that occupies the heart of the Durham peninsula between the castle and cathedral.

From the 1420s Langley's activities grew in number and pace. It was probably in this decade that he restored the two bridges to the Durham peninsula and remodelled or built at the head of each a gatehouse;[30] also, that he enlarged the great tower of his episcopal castle of Norham with an additional floor and many new windows.[31] Besides the great tower at Durham itself, this was now the largest structure of its kind in the north of England. The work is likely to have been contemporary with another operation in Norham Castle for which documentation survives: the construction in 1422 of a tower, now lost.[32]

In 1429, following a serious fire in Durham Cathedral, the bishop was generous in helping pay for a new central tower to the church. The model for the new structure was the crossing tower then under construction in the metropolitan see of York. It may therefore be no coincidence in view of this point of comparison that Langley was himself very active in Yorkshire. He rebuilt the great gate of his episcopal manor at Howden and the fine surviving hall porch still bears his arms.[33] In 1429 he also presented York Minster with the celebrated St Cuthbert window. Langley's reform of church institutions in his own diocese extended to the reorganisation of the three collegiate churches of Auckland, Lanchester and Chester-le-Street and the reissue of statutes to Sherburn Hospital just outside Durham in 1434.[34] A keen huntsman, it is appropriate that he died in the country residence of the see, Bishop Auckland Castle, in 1437.

THE PERPENDICULAR REFORMULATED

Through the death of Henry IV in 1413 and the undisputed succession of his son, Henry of Monmouth, the Lancastrian dynasty came of age as a royal line. Free from the stigma of his father's regicide and usurpation, the young king was an appealing figurehead and offered the welcome opportunity for a fresh political start. He was already a hardened soldier introduced by his experience of the Welsh revolt to tactics that were to prove devastatingly successful in France. Moreover, he was confronted with a kingdom markedly strengthened by its recent traumas. It was, indeed, a direct reflection of the stability he enjoyed at home that Henry v was able to cast his eyes abroad and fight for the French throne. The results of this political endeavour were to have profound artistic consequences.

That Henry v perceived his reign as a new beginning for the Lancastrian dynasty is strikingly signalled in architectural terms. Over the winter of 1413–14 he began to amass materials for a 'great work' at Sheen in Surrey (now Richmond). Henry v's intention was to establish a new seat of royal power outside London surrounded by three new religious foundations, including a charterhouse and a Bridgettine convent. An important river retreat from the capital had existed at Sheen since the reign of Edward III, but the old buildings had been razed to the ground by Richard II in a histrionic gesture of grief following the death of his first wife there on Whitsun 1394.[35] Work to the new residence was to continue into the minority of Henry VI as the central preoccupation of the royal works. As such, the creation of Sheen and its associated religious foundations was the backdrop against which the architecture of the period developed. It is very unfortunate, therefore, that the buildings of this crucially important foundation have vanished almost without trace.

The work at Sheen was directed by the king's master mason, Stephen Lote. The heart of the new palace was a sumptuous timber-frame residence. Confusingly, this appears to have incorporated an earlier building moved wholesale from Byfleet (near Weybridge in Surrey). In its new location 'The Byflete', as it became known, was transformed with the addition of such ornaments as a 'great figure' in timber of an antelope set over the kitchen, Henry v's heraldic badge.[36] Very few high-quality timber-frame buildings from this period survive, but it is possible that the residence built by Sir John Norreys at Ockwells in Berkshire in the 1440s provides an impression of this important lost palace.[37] The self-contained set of royal apartments in the Byflete was separated from a second court by a moat.

The year after Sheen was begun, Henry v undertook the French campaign that culminated in his victory at Agincourt. For the next decade the king and his nobility became principally occupied with French conquests and affairs. The buildings undertaken in these new pos-

sessions by English patrons are strictly beyond the scope of this book but it is worth commenting briefly on one striking aspect of their architectural character. Whereas in Ireland and Wales the English had built in an exported style, in France they built as Frenchmen: the designs fitted into patterns of local architecture and their domestic apartments were arranged after the fashions of France. At heart this is because the English came to France to commandeer a social and political order rather than to overthrow it. The patronage of William de la Pole, the future favourite of Henry VI, is a case in point. As count of Dreux, he occupied a castle at Bricquebec (Manche) that reflected in its domestic arrangements – with a *salle haute* and *salle basse* (literally 'high' and 'low' halls) – his character as a French nobleman. But when he sold up his French title and returned to England, the house he built at Ewelme from 1446 had a great hall in the English manner.

It might be supposed from this case that the experience of Henry v's conquests had done little to touch English architecture. But the reality was otherwise. French example informed the canon of the Perpendicular style and offered English patrons and masons new ways of realising old ideas. In effect, the ancient forms of English castle architecture were now dressed up in new clothing to dramatic and splendid effect. William de la Pole's new residence at Ewelme was in fact deeply indebted to Continental architecture in its use of a material that over the first half of the fifteenth century transformed English architecture: brick.

BRICKMAKING IN ENGLAND

One of the most important architectural borrowings from the Continent initiated during the reign of Henry v was the use of brick as a fashionable building material.[38] Brick had probably been in continuous use and production in England since the Roman period, its technology – that of firing moulded blocks of clay earth – being directly akin to that used in the creation of floor and roof tiles. But throughout this long period brickmaking in England was largely undertaken as a cottage industry and restricted to localities, particularly along the east coast, where supplies of good building stone and timber were limited. It is one reflection on the small-scale production of this material in England that up to the fourteenth century buildings constructed in the material usually incorporate varied sizes of brick supplied from different sources. A good example of this is the North Bar in Beverley (pl. 266), built in 1409–10: according to the surviving accounts, twenty-one different craftsmen moulded and supplied the 112,300 constituent bricks of this town gate to a variety of different sizes.[39] To all intents and purposes this building is a work of rubble masonry, the different bricks laid higgledy-piggledy to create the fabric of the walls.

By contrast, across a great swathe of northern Europe, from the Low Countries eastwards through the Baltic, brickmaking emerged from the thirteenth century onwards as a large-scale industry. Indeed, there was even a medieval export trade in the material from this region to England, as is documented, for example, in the supply of bricks from Flanders to Edward I's works in the 1280s to the Tower of London. The widespread use of brick in this German diaspora essentially reflected the dearth of alternative building materials in the region. Here large brickyards developed the capacity to produce millions of identically proportioned bricks in a single season. Such bricks could vary greatly in size across this huge geographic area (they were often sized according to local standard measurements, which could vary between towns), but they typically followed a classic proportion: allowing for the necessary depth of binding mortar, the dimensions of an individual brick were half as broad as long. This allowed them to be laid easily in combination both along and across the depth of a wall (as so-called stretchers and headers respectively) in regular patterns or 'bonds' of masonry. Bonded brick masonry of this type was strong and relatively cheap to create when compared with cut stone.

Because of the wide availability in northern Europe of suitable clays, bricks could also usually be made on or nearby the site of a major building project in temporary kilns called clamps, thereby saving costs of transportation. Another advantage was that individual bricks could be moulded into special shapes while the clay was still wet. This facilitated the creation of decorative mouldings for features such as doors and windows. Particularly popular in brick buildings across Europe was the detailing of parapets with ornamented arches, a motif easily expanded in castle architecture to suggest a machicolis. Alternatively, bricks could be cut like stone, a process that might either precede or follow firing. In England, the use of moulded bricks is rare before the later fifteenth century. More commonly, they were cut into shapes after firing, and building accounts regularly make reference to saws and other tools necessary for this.[40]

It was the arrival of this technology of brick mass manufacture, brought by foreign craftsmen, that was to prove so influential in the development of English architecture from the early fifteenth century onwards. As far as it is possible to tell from the limited and relatively modest architectural remains, prior to Henry V's reign brickwork in England seems predominantly informed by eastern Baltic and central European architecture. In the North Bar at Beverley, for example, the use of shield outlines and angled bricks to decorate the façade is paralleled in mid-fifteenth-century buildings across modern Germany and Poland, such as the gates at Tangermunde and Neubrandenburg.[41] Such points of comparison might be explained both by trading connections and the late fourteenth-century popularity of the eastern Crusade amongst the nobility. In the fifteenth century, however, the architectural parallels for the detailing of brick in England shift to northern France and the wealthy cities of modern Belgium and the Netherlands.

The nature and strength of this new architectural connection are apparent on many levels. In linguistic terms it was the French word *brique* – rather than such alternatives as 'wall tile', 'Flanders tile' and the Dutch *beckstein* – that was increasingly adopted in English to describe this material. It would be wrong to think of any standard brick sizes (in the Middle Ages in England, contrary to what is often asserted, there is no overarching typology of brick sizes. Indeed, some buildings are documented to incorporate two or more different standard sizes of brick). Nevertheless, English bricks of the fifteenth century conform broadly in scale to those found in the Low Countries rather than to the larger bricks typical of the eastern Baltic and central Europe. Moreover, when English buildings were erected in bond, the masonry almost invariably comprised alternately laid courses of headers and stretchers. This so-called English bond derives from contemporary buildings typical of the Low Countries rather than the Baltic, where the so-called monk's bond was almost universally employed (courses comprising pairs of stretchers divided by a header). It is significant that there is no surviving fifteenth-century example of monk's bond in England.

It would be mistaken, however, to separate out these two spheres of Continental influence too precisely: there was already a busy exchange of architectural ideas across the full extent of northern Europe. For example, there developed during the fourteenth century in the area of modern-day Poland a distinctive method of

decorating brick termed diaper. In the firing process it was possible to create distinctively coloured bricks, either by over-firing so that they burnt black, or by dusting them in sand that formed a covering glaze. Such coloured bricks could then be knitted into bonded walls to create patterns in the masonry. Diapering found currency across the areas of brick building in Europe during the fourteenth century, and the first surviving example of such work in England is found in a tower at Stonor Park in Oxfordshire.[42] This was almost certainly built by some Flemings (described as 'les Flemyngs'), who were paid in an account of 1416–17 for work to Stonor. The same account records the cost of making 200,000 bricks (£40) and carting them to Stonor from Crockernend (£15).[43]

Nor did England buy in its expertise from a restricted geographic area of Europe. From the anecdotal evidence of surviving documents, there is evidence of craftsmen from northern France and the Low Countries, as well as individuals from the 'Teutonic' region (presumably East Prussia) and numerous 'dochemen'. In this period the denomination could theoretically apply to any speaker of German (or *deutsche*) across the full extent of the Baltic.

Brick was absorbed into the English tradition of fine architecture through two important royal buildings: Henry V's new palace at Sheen and Henry VI's college dedicated to the Virgin at Eton. Although little is known of the form of Sheen, the surviving accounts do reveal that the buildings there made use of two imported materials: much of the stone was imported from the prized limestone belts near Caen in recently conquered Normandy and large quantities of bricks were brought to the site from Calais. How the two were combined is not clear, although there are explicit references to brick chimneys in the outer court. The religious foundations around the palace also made use of this brick. The Carthusian monastery or charterhouse, for example, is known to have included several buildings entirely constructed of the material and the surviving accounts identify two of the senior craftsmen responsible for them as coming from Holland. The remains of brick buildings have also been excavated on the site of the Bridgettine convent, an order with its roots in Sweden. Amongst these was the church, the foundation for which was actually laid in 1426 after Henry V's death. This apparently took the unusual architectural form of the mother house of the order at Vadstena near Stockholm, a fascinating instance of direct architectural borrowing from the Baltic.[44]

266 The North Bar, Beverley, Yorkshire. According to the surviving building accounts, the gate cost approximately £95 to construct and was completed between July and December 1409. Bricks were supplied to the site in small quantities as work progressed by twenty-one different suppliers. The standard cost of bricks was about 3s. 8d. per 1,000, though the cut bricks for the main arch and vault cost 4s. 2d. for the same quantity. The form of the shields and statue niches suggests that the gatehouse designer – who is not clearly identified in the accounts – was familiar with the brick architecture of the Baltic. It was the ability to mass-produce identical bricks that was to transform English architecture in the fifteenth century. The gate was heavily restored in 1867 and the central, stepped battlement is a modern creation.

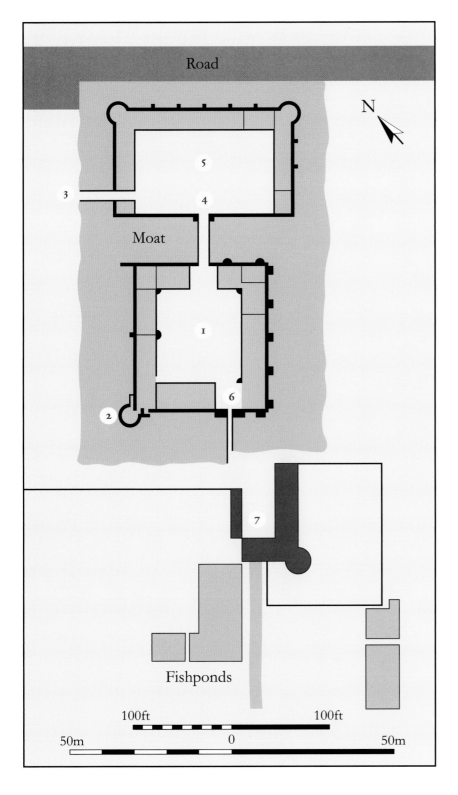

Road

N

Moat

Fishponds

100ft   100ft

50m   0   50m

267 A redrawn version of a ground plan of Caister, Norfolk, by Henry Swinden and dated 1760. It shows the principal, moated court (1) of the 1430s castle enclosed within four domestic ranges and dominated by the great tower (2). This was approached over two bridges (3 and 4) and through the service or base court (5), a classic English arrangement. There was also a smaller postern gate to the inner court (6). Along the top of the plan is the line of the road that runs beside the castle. At the bottom of the plan is another L-shaped range of the fifteenth century, possibly the castle mill (7).

Over the 1430s each of the three royal uncles of Henry VI was to begin a residence that incorporated brick, though none survives or is well documented. John, duke of Bedford, built a small castle at Fulbrooke in Warwickshire that stood within sight of Warwick. According to Leland, writing in the sixteenth century, this was 'of brick and stone' and was demolished in the reign of Henry VIII because its presence was so resented by the earls of Warwick. The materials were allegedly carried to Compton Wynyates, more of which in Chapter Fourteen.[45] Little more is known of the manor of the More in Hertfordshire, which Cardinal Beaufort and a group of associates were licensed to crenellate in 1426.[46] Excavations have shown that the buildings were laid out within a moat-enclosed court and that the walls were of brick laid in one of the only English examples of 'Flemish bond' (alternate headers and stretchers laid in a single course of masonry) prior to the seventeenth century.[47] Finally, Humphrey, duke of Gloucester, created a residence for himself at Greenwich (apparently called Bella Court), now also lost, for which he received a licence to crenellate in 1433. The terms of the licence either imply that the building possessed a dominating tower, or that a free-standing tower could additionally be built in the park.[48] It was to this residence that the duke moved his collection of books, the future core of the Bodleian Library at Oxford.

Two surviving brick buildings of the 1430s probably afford an insight into the architectural influences at play on these three lost buildings. The first of these is a castle built by Sir John Fastolf at Caister in Norfolk. Fastolf was a notable soldier and a trusted associate of the regent of France, John, duke of Bedford, whom he served between 1422 and 1435 as chief steward. As English fortunes waned in France, Fastolf began systematically to sell up his French interests and buy up land in East Anglia.[49] He also undertook several building projects, including the creation of a castle at Caister to serve as his principal seat. Fastolf's secretary, William Worcester, claimed in 1466 that the new buildings had cost £6,000 over thirty years to build and an inventory of their contents shows that they were fabulously furnished.[50] Caister Castle was laid out around three rectangular baileys, each of which was enclosed by a water-filled moat and fortified with towers (pl. 267). It was dominated by a single tower of exceptional height at one corner of the inner bailey (pl. 268). The surviving buildings are constructed of brick produced in clamps 1¼ miles away and detailed in stone (and in some areas with brick plastered over to look like stone).

Work to Caister is documented in a series of surviving building accounts covering the period between 1432 and 1435.[51] These appear to relate to an early stage in the construction process and are of limited help in explaining the form of the building. But to judge from the salaries noted in the accounts, there was a senior mason on site called Henry Wode. This man may be related to the Colchester-based master mason John Wode, who contracted in 1436 to rebuild the great western tower of the abbey of Bury St Edmunds.[52] His presence might explain why some features of the building, such as the hall oriel window and vault, look English in character. Overall, however, Caister is fairly clearly a building inspired from abroad. The rectangular windows of the hall, for example, relate to Continental design and are without English precedent.

Faulkbourne in Essex has a very different but similarly exotic architectural feel (pl. 269). It was built by Sir John Montgomery, again a figure prominent both as a soldier and an officer in the French administration. Work to the building probably began following

the issue in 1439 of a licence to crenellate. In its original form the building – presumably much like the lost residence at Greenwich – comprised a two-storey range adjoining a high tower on a rectangular plan. As at Caister, the windows were all designed with rectangular frames, but the treatment of the whole is much richer. Amongst several other distinctive features the upper sections of the tower buttresses are triangular in cross-section, a distinctive detail found in several English brick buildings prior to 1460. In addition, the battlemented parapets stand on a decorative machicolis of cusped arches. The latter feature, which is carved into the bricks, was later copied in several other local brick buildings.[53] These include Rye, Hertfordshire, a courtyard residence built by a naturalised Dane called Sir Andrew Ogard under a licence to crenellate of 1443 at a cost of more than 2,000 marks (pl. 270).[54]

The architectural exoticism of Caister and Faulkbourne was a short-lived phenomenon. English fine architecture at large – and castle design in particular – was about to be taken in a new direction by the example of a vastly influential new project. In 1440 Henry VI founded a grandiose college dedicated to the Virgin at Eton beside Windsor and incorporating a school. Work began to a sumptuous church and set of college buildings early the following year, which were almost certainly designed by the royal mason Robert Westerley. He intended to create a regular quadrangle around a two-storey cloister, an idea derived from secular architecture on the Continent. Probably in imitation of the upper ward of Windsor Castle, the exterior faces of the quadrangle were punctuated by rectangular turrets (pl. 271). For rich effect, the buildings were executed in a lavish combination of stone and brick. Laid into the latter by a workforce including many foreign craftsmen was an unparalleled diversity of diaper patterns. To add richness to the outline of the building the parapets of the quadrangle were battlemented and set with carved brick chimneys, the latter detail possibly inspired by Sheen.

The future influence of Eton was assured by the circumstances of its construction: not only did it take place under the eyes of the court in Windsor, but also craftsmen from across the country were pressed into service here. Both patrons and masons came away informed by its ideas and there immediately followed a second generation of brick buildings in an English architectural idiom. Outstanding amongst these were three that can confidently be identified as making use of Eton's regular, turreted outline. They may also by

269 (*top*) A photograph of Faulkbourne, Essex, in 1918. Work to this remarkable building evidently began in conjunction with the royal licence issued on 11 October 1439 to Sir John Montgomery (d. 1449) 'to fortify, crenellate and embattle the said manor with walls of stone or brick'. In 1461 the house passed into the hands of the brilliant careerist Sir Thomas Montgomery (d. 1494), who may have substantially enlarged it. This front with its busy architectural ornament is probably all Sir John's work. It has a grid of windows and the tower possesses buttresses with a triangular section, both details typical of brick architecture in the 1440s and 1450s. The brick spire to the right is also medieval. The ornamental blind arcade beneath the battlements that suggests a machicolis is similar to that found at other buildings in the wider region, including Someries, Bedfordshire.

270 (*bottom*) A plan of Rye, Hertfordshire, by J. Oliver published in 1685. The engraving was drawn to explain the details of a plot that was hatched in 1683 to assassinate Charles II and his brother, the future James II. It juxtaposes a plan of the buildings laid out by Sir Andrew Ogard under a royal licence issued in 1443 (centre) with an elevation from the south (above). The main gate gave access to the inner court with a hall, great parlour and great stair, the last presumably leading to the great chamber above. This stood in one corner of a large moated site that was enclosed by a wall with angle turrets and arrow loops. Outside the moat was a base court. All the buildings were of brick. Sir Andrew also rebuilt a residence at Emneth, Cambridgeshire, and died at New Buckenham, Norfolk.

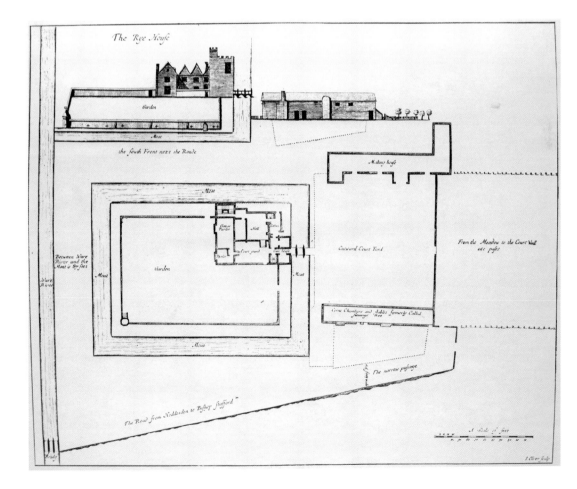

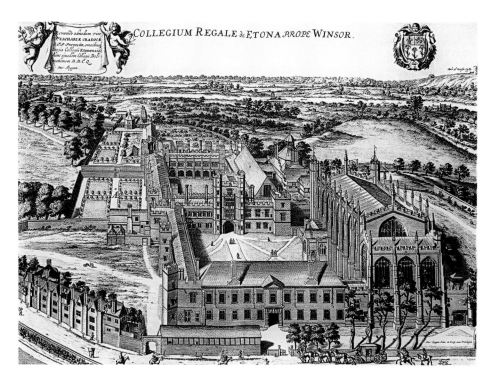

271 A view of the royal college of St Mary at Eton, Berkshire, published by Loggan in 1688. The college was founded in 1440 and has a complicated architectural history. In the distance is the brick court of domestic buildings begun in 1440. This possessed three ranges with rich diaper decoration and a turreted outline probably inspired by the neighbouring upper bailey of Windsor (see pl. 87). The fourth range (right) was the hall, entirely built of stone. The quadrangle was left incomplete at the death of Henry VI and brought to the condition shown here by Provost Lupton in the 1520s. The chapel to the right is the completed choir of a church begun around 1448.

extension be tentatively attributed to Robert Westerley and served further to integrate brick within the wider English building tradition.

One of the most intriguing in this group is the lost residence built by Henry VI's favourite, William de la Pole, at Ewelme, Oxfordshire. Begun in 1446 to celebrate his promotion to the title of marquis of Suffolk, the plan of Ewelme as a regular, turreted residence can be inferred from a demolition valuation of 1612.[55] Two years later, in 1448, Margaret of Anjou began her own educational foundation at Queen's College, Cambridge. Again, this brick building makes clear reference to the forms of Eton with its turreted façade. The third building in the series is the spectacular castle at Herstmonceux, Sussex, created by Sir Roger Fiennes, which is individually discussed at the conclusion of this chapter.

It was not only as a design that the example of Eton was important. The opulent combination of brick, diaper and stone that it pioneered became henceforth a hallmark of the most lavish patronage and was immediately adopted in two outstanding castle projects. In 1439 the lord treasurer of England, Ralph, Lord Cromwell, was preparing to transform his family seat at Tattershall in Lincolnshire. Cromwell had been aggrandising this castle for many years. Not only had he constructed new domestic apartments within the thirteenth-century circuit of walls and towers but also he had considerably expanded the site with a series of

ditched outer baileys. Erected inside these were such additional buildings as the great stable and wool house. These operations had been on a sufficient scale to warrant the establishment of several brick kilns in the locality, which were managed by a certain Baldwin the Docheman.[56]

Why Cromwell now determined on a yet grander project is not clear, though it is probably to be explained in terms of an attempt to bolster his political position. In 1439 he secured a licence to found a college of priests at Tattershall, an essential adjunct to any noble residence, and also massively stepped up brick production in the kilns he controlled. Surviving accounts show that in 1439–40 well over four million bricks were produced, five times the maximum quantity of any previous documented year.[57] The following building accounts are unfortunately lost, but in 1446 work to his new tower, described as 'le dongeon', was well under way.[58] This building was evidently intended to comprise a splendid series of withdrawing chambers. So large was the ground plan that it had to be projected out of the inner bailey into the moat.

This tower is the principal medieval survival at Tattershall today. It stands five storeys high and is constructed in fine, bonded brick with stone dressings (pl. 272). Prominent in the masonry of its walls are complex diaper designs. Both in its combination of materials and use of diaper ornament, Tattershall is probably inspired by the example of Eton. Its corner turrets were formerly capped by lead spires and the whole structure is crowned by a machicolated parapet and a chimney stack ornamented with battlements. At each level from the ground upwards the mouldings and decoration of the building grow richer. This sense of gathering magnificence is particularly apparent in the treatment of fireplaces and vaults. These bear elaborate displays of heraldry and Cromwell's two devices: a purse to celebrate his office as treasurer and the plant Common Gromwell, a pun on his name. Throughout the building there is evidence that the interior masonry surfaces were skimmed over with plaster and painted to look like brick with neat white mortar joints.[59]

In both form and detail the great tower of Tattershall is an essentially English building. The window tracery, for example, employs the rectilinear patterns typical of the Perpendicular style of Lincolnshire. Moreover, the most elaborate vaults are designed with intermediary ribs termed liernes, a detail of English character (pl. 273). Yet these features have been enriched with ideas derived from Continental brick

272 A view of the great tower or *donjon* at Tattershall, Lincolnshire, known to have been under construction in 1446. Ralph, Lord Cromwell had previously improved the domestic accommodation in the bailey and had to create space for this huge new building by projecting it into the moat. The tower set Tattershall on an architectural par with England's greatest castles, and its five-storey outline remains a landmark for miles around. Its combined use of stone and brick laced with diaper designs – undoubtedly inspired by the Eton works – creates an appropriately rich finish for this prodigy building. To underline the gathering importance of the internal chambers, the architectural detailing grows steadily richer at each level. In the years 1912–14 Lord Curzon extensively restored the tower, returning looted fireplaces and installing new tracery (based on surviving fragments). He also rebuilt the upper storey of the tower. The corner towers were originally crowned by four lead spires, the last of which collapsed in the late nineteenth century. Curiously, Lord Curzon baulked at replacing these. Turret spires are in fact a relatively common feature of castle design throughout the Middle Ages. They may have existed, for example, on the White Tower at London from its first completion.

273 The vestibule vault at the head of the main stairs in the great tower of Tattershall, Lincolnshire, 1440s. It combines a system of English rib vaulting with a type of panelled decoration borrowed from Continental brick architecture. The decorative details are made from cut bricks and the geometric shapes were picked out with skims of white plaster, traces of which remain. At the intersections of the ribs are displayed various coats of arms associated with the family, including those of Cromwell himself in the centre. Confronted with this splendid display, visitors can have been in no doubt that they were about to enter the principal apartment of the great tower.

design to create a completely new hybridised form of architecture. The lierne vaults, for example, were ornamented with brick panelling probably derived from the types of decoration found particularly in the gables of Baltic churches and town halls since the thirteenth century. In combination, these forms created a complex vault without obvious European precedent.

In building a great tower at Tattershall, Lord Cromwell was giving an ancient family seat one of the architectural attributes of a great castle. While his work was under way, another outstanding political figure, the duke of York, was at work creating a castle with a tower of similar ambition at Hunsdon in Hertfordshire, on what was effectively a virgin site. The duke acquired the manor in 1445 and probably began the new building the following year: he received on 5 March 1446 an exemption from royal impressment for twelve 'masons, makers and layers of *bryke*' besides twenty carpenters and forty labourers in the area.[60] A year later, in May 1447, a licence to build a tower was procured.[61] Then, probably while the new building was in the course of construction, political circumstances forced the duke to sell the property to his chamberlain, Sir William Oldhall. It must have been under Oldhall's direction that Hunsdon was completed because in 1478 an informed visitor, William Worcester, attributed the whole work specifically to him and enumerated the cost of the tower and its surrounding ancillary buildings of

brick as 7,000 marks (£4,667). In reality, it seems unlikely that Oldhall would have had the money to complete this building alone. Today, only a fragment of the medieval work at Hunsdon survives, but something of its original form can be reconstructed.

The tower stood on a small plot of land enclosed by a moat and low walls with small angle turrets.[62] To the east and west it was approached over a short, brick bridge. From the surviving remains it is clear that the building was cruciform in plan with angle buttresses. Those buttresses that survive are of triangular cross-section and decorated with diaper designs ingeniously laid to run uninterrupted around angles. From the evidence of one surviving window frame and several ornately carved arrow loops it is clear that the structure was detailed throughout in stone. The most reliable witness to the original form of the tower is William Worcester, who implies that it comprised a complete suite of domestic apartments. In the 1480s he wrote of it: 'The height of the said tower with the upper storey called "an oriole" with windows and gilded vanes, is said to be more than a hundred feet from the base of the said tower. Also the length of the great hall of the said tower is 80 feet and its breadth 24 feet.'[63] This description perhaps suggests a tower in which – as at Tattershall – each floor was more richly treated in architectural terms than the last. The oriel was presumably intended to offer splendid views over the surrounding landscape, an arrangement more familiar in such grand sixteenth-century residences as Wollaton in Nottinghamshire (see pl. 351).

The naturalisation of brick within the English tradition of castle architecture that was effected through Eton (as well as Sheen) and developed in buildings such as Tattershall and Hunsdon was to prove vastly important in the long term. From this moment the decorative possibilities of brick were explored in a wide variety of ways by English masons. Particularly important was the use of diaper patterns in walls and the use of rubbed, red brick to create prominent and complex chimneys. But perhaps the most lasting legacy of Eton was the interest in the decorative effects of combining brick and stone. Far beyond the close of the Middle Ages there was a special prestige attached to brick buildings plentifully detailed in stone, as even the early seventeenth-century work of the classical architect Inigo Jones illustrates. And where such a combination was beyond the pocket of a patron, it remained common to skim mortar around the windows and doors of brick buildings to suggest stone.

274 A photograph taken in 1915 of the entrance to the base court of South Wingfield, Derbyshire, built in the 1440s. With a great tower (left), battlemented chimneys and cross loops, this residence speaks the language of castle architecture. Very unusually in an English secular building of this ambition, the gatehouse has two arches for pedestrian and horse traffic. The residence was laid out around two principal courts, which were divided by the hall range. Much of the inner court was demolished without trace in the 1640s. It is not known who designed these buildings, but their detailing hints at the mason's connections with London. Remarkably, Ralph, Lord Cromwell, had sufficient resources to construct this imposing residence in one campaign. It overlooked parkland for hunting and several large pools, the outlines of which can still be traced in the landscape.

ARCHITECTURE AND POLITICS DURING HENRY VI'S MAJORITY, 1437–60

The use of brick throughout the fifteenth century remained an important but relatively circumscribed phenomenon in geographic terms, focused in the east and south-east of England. In this sense, the story of brick architecture in this period tells only one part of a wider architectural tale. For example, while Ralph, Lord Cromwell, was redeveloping Tattershall in brick, he was also at work to another grand residence entirely built of stone at South Wingfield in Derbyshire. Wingfield always appears to have been known as a manor rather than a castle, probably a means of highlighting its juniority as a secondary possession. Imposingly laid out around two courts, however, its ruins are indistinguishable on architectural grounds from those of many castles of the period: the outer court is commanded by a great tower (pl. 274) and the battlemented outer walls are set with turrets and towers. Even the chimney stacks of the buildings are enlivened by miniature bat-tlements. In this sense, South Wingfield is unequivocally a work of castle architecture.

Throughout this period the most lucrative governmental posts – and those most likely to provide the funds necessary for building – remained the financial offices of the crown. Cromwell's successor as lord treasurer, Ralph Boteler, for example, was also a notable builder. Boteler began his career in France during Henry v's reign but refocused his interests in England after his appointment as a chamber knight of the young Henry vi in 1430. Soon afterwards, grants from the king began to follow in quick succession. In 1433 he became constable and steward of Kenilworth Castle and in 1437 he secured the constableship of Conwy Castle, amidst numerous other appointments. His election as a knight of the Garter in 1440, however, was the first mark of outstanding royal favour. It was followed the next year by his appointment as chamberlain of the king's household and his creation as Baron Sudeley. Boteler was granted his title, the first of the reign, by patent.

This was an unusual method of creating a peer and is possibly to be explained by Boteler's curious personal circumstances: his mother – a widow – retained con-

trol of the family seat at Sudeley in Gloucestershire until 1443. He was, therefore, receiving a baronage by royal favour in anticipation of his actual inheritance. His reception in so short a space of a time of both a title and an inheritance was a powerful incentive to build. But the necessary cash was probably provided by his appointment on 7 July 1443 as treasurer of England. Over the next decade, and before his career was dented by the fall of his associate and ally the duke of Suffolk in 1450, he completely rebuilt Sudeley. The castle appears to have taken the form of a rectangular court with corner towers, of which only two survive today.

Only one important architectural patron of the period amassed the wealth to build without serving in the royal administration and his career was very unusual. John Cornewall succeeded in securing a brilliant match to Henry IV's sister, whose eye he reputedly caught at a tournament in York in July 1400. His wife brought a handsome income that he greatly enhanced in the conduct of the war in France. There he not only won some notable prisoners but also pioneered a very lucrative system of brokering ransoms.[64] By 1424 he had bought the manor of Ampthill in Bedfordshire, and proceeded to construct there a substantial castle. According to the sixteenth-century writer John Leland, the castle stood 'stately on a hill, with four or five towers of stone in the inner ward, beside the base court, of such spoils as it is said, he won in France'.[65] Later plans and also a reported model of the castle – now unknown – confirm its arrangement around two courts. They also suggest that there were nine towers in all, each of which was a five-sided polygon in plan.[66] Cornewall died without a legitimate heir and Ampthill was sold to his friend Ralph Cromwell for 5,000 marks, a price allegedly far short of its market value. It was sufficiently desirable, moreover, to become an object of conflict during the Wars of the Roses, when it was seized by the duke of Devon.[67]

Meanwhile, other families had existing castles that they could aggrandise with the financial and political benefits that flowed from royal favour. In the far north, the Percy family undertook dimly understood work to the town and castle of Alnwick, of which the most impressive survival is a town gate decorated with their family emblem of a rampant lion (pl. 275). To the west, the celebrated general in the French wars, John Talbot, first earl of Shrewsbury and Waterford (d. 1453), repaired and adapted Goodrich as a principal seat.[68] And in the south-west, Sir Walter Hungerford elevated his family through service to the Lancastrian dynasty to a position of great authority in Wiltshire and

275   The Bondgate or Hotspur Gate, to the town of Alnwick, Northumberland, was under construction in 1450. Above the gate is a large heraldic panel, now much worn, depicting the Percy family lion. It was carved in 1450 by Matthew, the mason of Alnwick Abbey, for £1 10s. Notice the spurs from which the gate towers rise, an unusual detail that is probably copied from the fourteenth-century works at the castle (see pl. 198).

Somerset.[69] To celebrate his new standing, a series of Hungerford chantry foundations were established across the region. These included one in the parish church at Farleigh Hungerford in Somerset, which was privatised when it was swallowed up within a new outer bailey of the castle between 1441 and 1443.[70]

At a more modest level, those who acted as local agents for powerful courtiers could sometimes amass sufficient wealth to build. John Heydon, for example, was a lawyer who acted on behalf of Henry VI's favourite, William de la Pole, in Norfolk and considerably expanded his family landholding in the county. Probably in the 1440s, at the height of his power (or possibly in the 1470s, the evidence is not clear-cut), he began to rebuild his family seat of Baconsthorpe, which he enclosed within a turreted wall. At the entrance to the residence he built a gatehouse. Castles, then, had still lost none of their appeal for those who possessed – or aspired to possess – political power.

Meanwhile, there were other fortifications being created on a yet smaller scale. The ownership of land – that fundamental guarantor of wealth – was ferociously contended and the law was only one weapon in the armoury of those attempting to secure it. Another was intimidation and armed force, which could be employed with absolute ruthlessness. Ralph, Lord Cromwell, the builder of Tattershall, for example, incarcerated one widow called Elizabeth Swillington during the 1430s, in an attempt to force her to part with her inheritance. This she doggedly refused to do, and in her complaint to Cromwell's executors several years later described being held in both Tattershall and Castle Rising. She also claimed to have lost the sight of one eye due to the conditions of her confinement and the lack of medical attention.[71]

Where the victims were less helpless, fortifications could spring up; in a very modest way this precisely parallels twelfth-century patterns of castle construction during the Anarchy of Stephen and Matilda. One such confrontation took place over the ownership of Gresham in Norfolk in the years 1448–50 between the nobleman Robert Hungerford (supported on the ground by John Heydon of Baconsthorpe) and John Paston, the son of one of Cromwell's henchmen who had brow-beaten Elizabeth Swillington in the chapel of Tattershall Castle. As tension grew, John Paston's efficient wife, Margaret, wrote to her husband in London. The letter, probably composed in 1449, suggests that she was fully possessed of the practicalities of fighting and fortification:

Right worshipful husband,
I recommend myself to you and prey you get some crossbows and windlasses to arm them with and quarrels, for our house here is so low that no man can shoot from it with a longbow, even at greatest need . . . I would that you would get two or three short poleaxes to keep here and as many [armoured] jackets as you can. Partryche and his fellows are sore afraid that you will enter again on them, and they have made great ordnance in the house as I have been told. They have made bars to bar every door crosswise and they have made wickets on every quarter [*side*] of the house to shoot out of, both with bows and handguns; and the holes that have been made for handguns, they be scarcely knee high from the floor, and of such holes have been made five. There can no man shoot out from them with a hand bow.[72]

The letter ends on an incongruously domestic note, asking for sugar, almonds and cloth for a child's gown and a hood, there being – Margaret complains – no good cloth to be had in the town.

CASTLE RETREATS

Parks had been understood since the Conquest as the natural adjuncts to castles, where the nobility could enjoy the jealously guarded privilege of hunting. For this reason, there was a long history of noblemen creating hunting lodges. A case in point is the series of lodges built around Chepstow in the thirteenth century.[73] The ceremony of hunting was never to lose its lordly significance or appeal, but around 1400 there becomes apparent for the first time an interest in parks not only as places of entertainment but also of retreat, and the creation of sumptuous lodgings within them. The inspiration for this probably came from France in the late fourteenth century, where the fashion for such buildings may have been fired by Charles V's commissioned translation in 1373 of the late thirteenth-century garden treatise by the Bolognese Pietro de' Crescenzi.[74]

One of the most celebrated buildings of this kind was the 'Pleasance' erected by Henry V at his favourite Lancastrian castle of Kenilworth. According to a life of the king by Thomas Elmham:

. . . his majesty the king kept Lent [21 February–6 April 1414] at Kenilworth Castle, and in the marsh, where foxes lurked among the brambles and thorns, built for his entertainment a pleasure garden . . . On this site he constructed a delicious place which he caused to be called Plesant Mareys.[75]

The Pleasance on the edge of the mere at Kenilworth was a small house, enclosed by a moat and with at least one tower. To judge from the excavated remains and the description of its timber-frame domestic buildings, it could have loosely resembled a small fourteenth-century castle such as Maxstoke.[76] There is also a roughly contemporary French image of a retreat with a tower and enclosed garden on the edge of a mere at Dourdan (Essonne) within the astonishing series of views of French castles that illustrate the months in the *Très Riches Heures* of Jean, duc de Berry.[77] This image powerfully conveys a sense of the charm and elegance of these creations, essential adjuncts to the luxurious lifestyle of the fabulously wealthy.

It may have been in direct imitation of the arrangements at Kenilworth that Henry VI's queen, Margaret of Anjou, created her own Pleasance at Greenwich. The basis for her new residence was the brick tower and residential range built by Humphrey, duke of Gloucester, which she took possession of and expanded between 1447 and 1453. Set on the banks of the Thames, it could serve as a retreat from the royal London palaces in exactly the same way as the Pleasance at Kenilworth.

Both these royal retreats probably looked back for their inspiration to an earlier generation of buildings. In the 1370s, for example, the earl of Warwick built a house in Wedgnock Park, one of the enclosed parks adjoining Warwick Castle. The building was known as 'Goodrest', presumably as a reflection of its use as a place of retirement. All that survives of it is a double moat crossed by a bridge and part of an outlying fishpond, an arrangement very similar to that at Kenilworth. Documentary evidence demonstrates that the lost buildings were of timber-frame construction.[78]

Probably more important was the example of Henry V's grandfather, John of Gaunt, who liked to indulge in hunting from the lodge called 'Bird's Nest'. This stood on the outskirts of Leicester beside the castle, his favourite seat, and was rebuilt by him in 1377–8.[79] Unfortunately, nothing is known of the architectural form of the Bird's Nest but it is possible that it took the form of a castellated building. Indeed, the residence appears to have been used as a stronghold in a stand-off between rival factions in Leicester in 1524.[80]

From the fifteenth century onwards there are numerous examples of hunting lodges in the form of freestanding castle towers. These often stood within sight of the castles they served. Passing near Tattershall, for example, Leland commented in the 1540s: 'One of the Cromwelles buildid a preaty turret caullid the Tour of the Moore. And thereby he made a faire greatponde or lake brikid about. The lake is communely caullid the Synkker.'[81] One corner of this tower, which is first documented in 1471–2, still survives and there is historic record that it was formerly enclosed by a moat. A similar tower, dated by an inscription to 1488, in a northern architectural idiom survives in Hulne Priory outside Alnwick in Northumberland. It is a reflection of the appeal of the tower and the ruins of the friary in which it stood that it was treated in the 1770s as the focus of the park by the landscape designer Capability Brown (pl. 276). Consequently, the interior of the tower now possesses a charming Georgian Gothic interior and is connected to a summerhouse built by Robert Adam in 1778–9.

HERSTMONCEUX

The first half of the fifteenth century witnessed a transformation of the Perpendicular style at the hands of the leading masons of the king's works. Their principal achievement was to introduce Continental ideas into the English architectural mainstream and – as part of this process – to establish brick within the kingdom as a fashionable building material. Time has not generally been kind to the buildings of this formative period. In at least one case, however, it is possible to appreciate the vigour and invention of castle building at this time.[82]

On 5 February 1441 the treasurer of the household of Henry VI, Sir Roger Fiennes, received a licence to crenellate Herstmonceux in Sussex. The outer walls of the castle he created, which are reflected in the waters of a broad moat, still survive. Its regular and turreted exterior is dominated by a large gatehouse in classic English manner (pl. 277). Nevertheless, this building departs from native convention in a number of ways. Most obviously, it is constructed from brick lavishly detailed with stone. In the gatehouse, moreover, the brickwork is ornamented with diaper designs. This combination of materials and decorative treatment is evidently derived from Eton, with which the building shares a number of further technical points of similarity.

276 Hulne Priory, Northumberland, stands inside the bounds of one of the three medieval parks that formerly served Alnwick Castle. In the midst of this Carmelite friary, which was founded in 1265, the earl of Northumberland built a tower to serve as a hunting lodge. Its interior was attractively Gothicised in the eighteenth century, but there survives a plaque with a dated inscription: 'In this year of Christ 1488 this tower was builded by Sir Henry Percy the fourth earl of Northumberland of great honour and worth that espoused Maud the good lady full of virtue and beauty daughter to Sir William Herbert right noble and hardy earl of Pembroke whose soul god save and with his grace conserve the builder of this tower.'

The interior, for example, was formerly divided into four unequal courtyards. The principal of these incorporated a cloister and gallery in exactly the manner of Eton (pl. 278). At a more detailed level still, the ornamentation of windows and doors compares to that found at the royal college. And, remarkably, there is documentary evidence for a link with the Eton building works. Bricks for Herstmonceux were almost certainly produced locally by a native of Malines in present-day Belgium called John Rowelond. He was present in Herstmonceux in 1436 with two assistants, when he was formally naturalised as an English subject, and his name also appears in the Eton building accounts.

Yet Rowelond was not a master mason, nor was he responsible for the design of this building. His presence is simply representative of a wider interest in

277   A view of Herstmonceux, Sussex, begun by Sir Roger Fiennes under a royal licence issued in 1441. The castle is one of a small group of early brick buildings connected to the quadrangle begun by Henry VI in 1440 as the home of his college dedicated to the Virgin at Eton, Berkshire. Particularly important is the regular façade of the building comprising a central gatehouse with a pair of flanking turrets and corner towers. Read from side to side, this creates a distinctive rhythm of elements – tower, turret, gatehouse, turret, tower – that was to recur in major English buildings into the late sixteenth century. The arrangement is anticipated in some much earlier royal buildings, for example, the east front of Caernarfon Castle (see pls 163 and 164).

imporing specialist craftsmen to England in this period with the technical understanding to make bricks of the quality necessary for fine architecture. The design of the castle is much more likely to have been devised by the king's mason, Robert Westerley. His involvement would explain the technical comparisons with Eton. That Sir Roger had direct dealings with Westerley, moreover, is almost beyond question. Henry VI's direct interest in the Eton works must have involved Sir Roger in financial oversight of the project, and his brother, James Fiennes, was the official recipient on the king's behalf of the first building accounts for the new college.

Aside from all the architectural and personal links that connect Herstmonceux to Eton, there is a final and compelling reason to see its design as emanating from the centralised operations of the king's works. The main

278 A view of the entrance court of Herstmonceux, Sussex, in the 1770s by P. Sandby. The court was enclosed by a cloister at ground level and glazed galleries above, a design lifted directly from Henry VI's quadrangle at Eton. To an English audience, the way in which the cloister walks obstructed direct access across the court between the gate passage and the hall entrance would have been unexpected. The cloister is supported on buttresses with a triangular cross-section, a distinctive detail of several brick buildings in England of the 1440s and 1450s that was derived from the architecture of the Low Countries. More characteristic of English design are the tall and varied chimneys, though their creation of red brick as opposed to stone would also have been a novelty.

façade of the building presents a distinctive rhythm of elements: from side to side there is a tower, a turret, the gatehouse, a turret and a tower. This type of façade may have been inspired by royal castle designs of the thirteenth century, for example, the composition of towers and turrets around the eastern gate of Edward I's castle at Caernarfon (see pl. 164). Whatever its provenance, however, we shall see that this form of regularised façade first found at Herstmonceux was to recur in castle architecture for more than a century to come (and shall be referred to henceforth – rather clumsily – as the Herstmonceux-type façade).

The most convincing explanation for the longevity and popularity of this particular design is that it orig-inated at the nerve centre of architectural production in the Lancastrian realm: the king's works. By the time that Herstmonceux was approaching completion, however, that body was itself on the verge of effective dissolution. With the opening hostilities of the Wars of the Roses all royal building operations ground to a standstill and masons looked elsewhere for employment. They took with them a remarkably consistent experience: nearly all senior masons active in late fif-teenth-century England had demonstrable ties with Eton and by extension the drawing collection of the king's works as it existed around 1450. This experience was materially to shape the future development of castle architecture.

13

THE YORKIST AND EARLY TUDOR SETTLEMENT

EDWARD IV, RICHARD III AND HENRY VII

The battle of Towton, fought on Palm Sunday (25 March) 1461 in blizzard conditions and bitter cold, was one of the largest and bloodiest encounters of the Wars of the Roses. It not only secured the throne for Edward IV (1461–70, 1471–83), but also crippled Henry VI's Lancastrian cause without quite destroying it. Over the next decade, as the new Yorkist regime established itself, there emerged around the king a circle of trusted followers who came to enjoy enormous personal power within defined geographic areas. In architectural terms this method of government was to prove immensely important: it concentrated resources in the hands of a small group with a natural interest in celebrating their power through architecture.

Edward IV's brief overthrow and restoration in 1471 brought about some important changes in the composition of this circle, but the policy of creating royal agents with delegated authority to control regions of the kingdom remained consistent throughout the reign. The result was a series of castle-building projects on the very grandest scale, with a particularly intense burst of construction during the relative peace of his second reign from 1471 to 1483.

The activities of Edward IV's reign were brought to a dramatic close after his death by the usurpation of the throne from the boy king Edward V by Richard, duke of Gloucester, in 1483. Two years later Richard III was himself killed and his army defeated at the battle of Bosworth on 22 August 1485. It seems clear from documentary evidence that Richard III began his own ambitious programme of building shortly before he died, but very little of it was accomplished and its architectural qualities are hard to judge. His fall brought about important changes in the ranks of the nobility, as banished Lancastrian families re-established their fortunes. Moreover, Henry VII (1485–1509), the founder of the royal Tudor dynasty and the victor of Bosworth, chose to rule in a very different way from his Yorkist predecessors. The instability that beset the early years of Tudor government reduced to almost nothing the building works of the crown. It also encouraged the king increasingly to take power into his own hands. Amongst those who suffered from this were the nobility, whose powers and influence Henry VII actively sought to circumscribe. Of those that did have opportunity to build, most were tied to the king by close familial links or were directly dependent on his favour as royal servants.

Then from about 1500 the political status quo changed fundamentally once more. Now secure on his throne, Henry VII embarked on a series of major building projects. The most important of these were the reconstruction after a fire of the royal palace at Sheen – which was renamed Richmond Palace – and the construction of a new Lady Chapel and mausoleum at Westminster Abbey, now known as Henry VII's Chapel. Apparent in such operations is the familiarity of leading English masons with contemporary French architecture. Meanwhile, the furnishings and decoration of these buildings were substantially the responsibility of foreign craftsmen. Both Henry VII's tomb and the high altarpiece in the Westminster Lady Chapel, for example, were the work of Florentine artists. Immigrants had become prominent in such crafts as stained-glass manufacture from the 1440s. By 1500 they had come to dominate the full spectrum of the decorative arts, a trend much resented by their English competitors. As a result, English artistic fashions became closely tied to those of Continental Europe.

In stylistic terms, the buildings treated throughout this chapter are all to be understood as works in the Perpendicular style. They also reflect the same creative dynamics between the secular and ecclesiastical spheres that have become a familiar theme of this narrative. That said, there is apparent over this period a change in the role of the king's works in the wider development of English architecture. Up to the 1440s, it has been argued, this body was at the heart of architectural change across the kingdom, its personnel supplying designs and overseeing building operations widely; also, that the king's mason was individually a crucial figure in this process. Throughout the later fifteenth century, however, it is apparent that this dominant role was being eroded and that major works were increasingly being put in hand by a larger circle of masons. Particularly notable in this respect is a group of masons working in the west Midlands and Oxfordshire, some specifically connected with the patronage of the bishops of Winchester. This change was apparently accelerated by the disruption of royal building projects in the political turmoil of the 1450s and the dispersal of workforces from them.

THE YORKIST SETTLEMENT OF THE 1460S

Edward IV's victory at Towton would have been complete if the Lancastrian royal family had not been absent from the field and able to flee to Scotland. On the international scene there were plenty of figures willing to support their cause and it was not long before the Lancastrian monarch returned to England. On 25 October 1461 Margaret of Anjou landed at Bamburgh in Northumberland with a body of French mercenaries and in open alliance with Scotland. Her hope for a spontaneous general rising in favour of her husband, Henry VI, did not materialise, but Bamburgh and nearby Dunstanburgh castles were rendered up to her by a sympathiser. Soon afterwards Alnwick capitulated to the queen, allegedly for want of supplies. In response, Edward IV marched north in November at the head of a large Yorkist army. The king himself fell ill of the measles at Durham and command passed to one of his principal supporters, the so-called Kingmaker, Richard Neville, earl of Warwick. The earl fixed his headquarters at Warkworth in Northumberland and rode out every day to supervise simultaneous siege operations at all the Lancastrian strongholds. It was from Warkworth, too, that the distribution of munitions from Newcastle was arranged.[1] By Christmas all three castles had capitulated, as had another Lancastrian castle in the north, Naworth in Cumberland. Peace, however, was to prove short-lived.

Within three months of their capture, the newly appointed constable of the three Northumbrian castles, Sir Ralph Percy, yielded them up again to a Lancastrian force. Margaret of Anjou pressed her advantage and marched with a force to besiege the bishop of Durham's castle at Norham. A rapid campaign by the earl of Warwick relieved Norham, but without a siege train his force was powerless to take the established Lancastrian castles. Indeed, Henry VI remained at Bamburgh and ruled what remained of his kingdom from his three Northumbrian bases for nearly a year. He even attempted, unsuccessfully, to capture Prudhoe Castle, Northumberland. For the first time since the Anglo-Saxon period, England had two concurrently regnant kings established within the borders of the kingdom. Unable to deal with the situation himself, Edward IV installed a loyal agent with a vested interest in enforcing the Yorkist settlement in Northumberland. At York on 27 May, three weeks after the Yorkist victory at Hexham, Edward IV created John Neville, Lord Montagu, the brother of his ally 'The Kingmaker', earl of Northumberland. The title had been extinct since the death of Henry Percy, the third earl, in the Lancastrian ranks at the battle of Towton in 1461. According to one fifteenth-century account, the new earl was explicitly charged with reasserting royal control in the north.

The same source describes how the new earl marched with his brother, the earl of Warwick, to Alnwick. Upon their arrival on 23 June the castle submitted, apparently by prior arrangement. The following day Dunstanburgh followed suit. At Bamburgh, however, the garrison resisted and was magnificently warned by the Yorkist heralds:

> . . . if ye deliver not this jewel, the which the king our most dread sovereign Lord hath so greatly in favour, seeing it marcheth so nigh his ancient enemies of Scotland, he speacially desireth to have it, whole, unbroken, with ordinance; if ye suffer any great gun laid unto the wall and be shot, and prejudice the wall, it shall cost you the chieftan's head; and so proceeding for every gun shot, to the last head of any person within the said place.[2]

Then all the royal guns, including Newcastle, the king's great gun, and London, his second gun of iron, were simultaneously fired at the castle and 'the stones of the walls flew into the sea'. After further bombardment, according to this account, men-at-arms and archers stormed the defences. Other sources, with more simplicity and probably more accuracy, state that the garrison simply surrendered after one of their commanders was wounded.

The pivotal part played by Richard Neville, earl of Warwick, in these events reflects his crucially important role in establishing Edward IV on the throne. His rewards were immense, and in the early 1460s his income probably approached £10,000 per annum, by far the largest of any member of the contemporary nobility. Besides the substantial Midland power base he inherited as earl of Warwick, the Kingmaker also received extensive properties in the north-west, as well as the office of warden of the western march. In this sense, his brother's creation as earl of Northumberland was part of a process of dynastic endowment that gave the Nevilles corresponding control over the eastern march. This was further consolidated by the appointment of George Neville, younger brother of Richard and John, to the archbishopric of York in 1464. By the late 1460s the only northern figure who could rival this formidable family triumvirate was Lord Stanley with his landholdings in Cumberland and the Isle of Man. This situation almost proved fatal to Edward IV's rule and was reversed in stages from 1470 onwards.

What architectural use the Neville family made of their power over the 1460s is difficult now to assess accurately. George as archbishop of York assumed control of 'the More', Hertfordshire, which he is credited with having greatly expanded and furnished in the most sumptuous manner.[3] Unfortunately, nothing is known in detail about the form of the building he created or its relationship to the residence on the site for which Cardinal Beaufort and others had received a licence to crenellate in 1426.[4] In the north of England, tradition has also long ascribed the so-called Montagu Tower at the south-east corner of Warkworth Castle to John Neville as earl of Northumberland. There are no known buildings at all attributed to the greatest of the brothers, Richard. This probably reflects the degree to which he focussed his energies and ambitions towards the international stage. It also speaks of the manner in which he treated his far-flung estates: rather than nurture them to create a power base and a loyal following, he exploited them as sources of revenue.

The construction of a new Yorkist order in the north during the 1460s had a direct parallel in Wales, where castles again played a crucial role in the struggle for power. Here the trusted agent of the new regime was a certain William Herbert, who was given responsibility for reducing the Lancastrian strongholds across Wales in 1461. He and his followers captured several castles over the next year. Carreg Cennen, for example, was surrendered to his brother in 1462 and ignominiously demolished over the summer by 500 workmen with picks and crowbars at a cost of £28 5s. 6d. The castle appears never to have been reoccupied. Herbert's chief prize, however, was the castle of Pembroke, which surrendered to him on 30 September 1461.[5] At the same time he also captured Jasper Tudor, earl of Pembroke, whose estate he inherited in February 1462. This was simply one of several important grants made to Herbert that brought him vice-regal powers in Wales and a name for himself in the region as Edward IV's 'master-lock'. By the end of 1462, supplied by the sea and secure in its remoteness, Harlech was the only surviving outpost of Lancastrian resistance in Wales. As the chronicler John Warkworth observed: 'And so Kynge Edward was possessed of alle Englonde, excepte a castelle in Northe Wales called Harlake.'[6]

This continued resistance became a matter of material importance in June 1468, when a small French force led by the attainted Lancastrian earl of Pembroke, Jasper Tudor, landed here. Jasper marched across north Wales, holding courts in the name of Henry VI and seizing Denbigh Castle. Two Yorkist armies set out to destroy this force, one under Herbert and the other

279 The gatehouse façade of Raglan, Monmouthshire, probably begun by William Herbert after 1465. The gatehouse served as the central feature in a range of withdrawing chambers that extended across the whole front of the castle. Few details of the fifteenth-century internal arrangements of this range are now apparent, though it evidently incorporated a gallery space and terminated in a large residential corner tower. At its centre probably stood the great chamber and parlour of the castle, their exterior faces ornamented with richly detailed windows and exquisite heraldic sculpture. These communicated with the great tower (to the left) across a drawbridge.

commanded by his kinsman Sir Roger Vaughan. They met at Harlech and there besieged the castle. It is difficult to distinguish much detail of the ensuing three-week siege from the colourful poetry of the bards, but the castle finally surrendered on 14 August 1468. Reputedly, it was this resistance that inspired the modern Welsh nationalist song 'Men of Harlech'. On 8 September 1468, in recognition of his services and as a culmination to his extraordinary career, Edward IV created Herbert earl of Pembroke. He was the first Welshman to enter the ranks of the English peerage. Herbert was to enjoy the title and distinction for less than a year: in July 1469 he was executed following his capture at the battle of Edgecote.

In the decade of his political pre-eminence in Wales, William Herbert created for himself a castle appropriate to his new-found power and resources (pl. 279). In 1465 the family castle at Raglan in Monmouthshire was declared the seat of an independent lordship by Edward IV.[7] It was almost certainly in conjunction with this change of status that Herbert completely rebuilt the castle. The new work comprised a pair of courts enclosed within a curtain wall and dominated by a colossal great tower (pl. 280). This stands outside the circuit of the castle walls, a position that finds

precedent in such thirteenth-century plans as Flint. It was clearly a highly prized and admired building and had come to be known by the seventeenth century as the Yellow Tower of Gwent. Even the partial demolition of this building after the Civil War has done little to obscure its self-evident ambition (pl. 281). It should be said that Herbert's father has also been suggested as a possible builder of this remarkable structure. The financial outlay necessary for such a huge operation, however, would have been far beyond the means of any other member of the family.

In stylistic terms, Herbert's new castle at Raglan was an architectural importation, its design and detailing bearing no relation to existing buildings in the area. The mason responsible drew on a wide variety of architectural sources from across England in his work. The surviving fragments of machicolis set with cross-shaped arrow loops compare very closely with examples found in the Midlands and specifically Warwick, while the battering of the great tower walls and the distinctive shape of its main entrance door are best paralleled in such court-connected buildings in the south-east as Herstmonceux, Sussex, begun in 1441. But it is within the orbit of the south-western architectural tradition that the building as a whole sits most comfortably. In

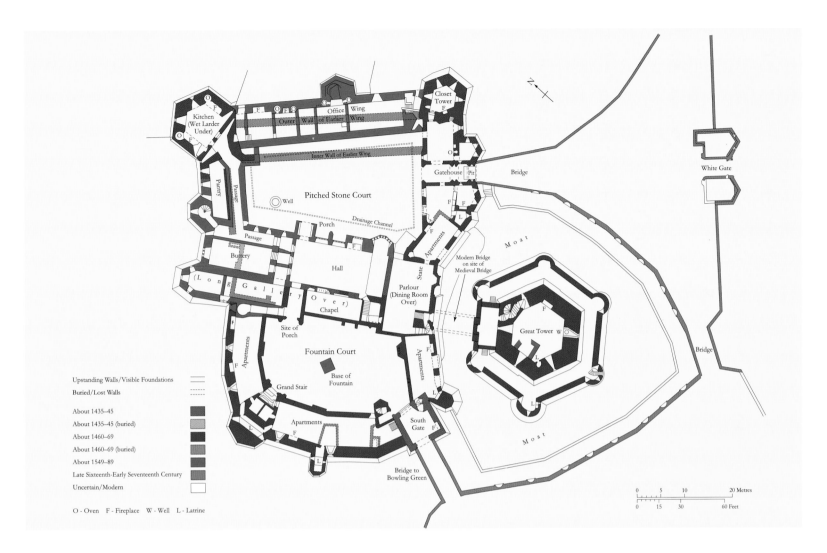

Legend:

Upstanding Walls/Visible Foundations
Buried/Lost Walls

About 1435–45
About 1435–45 (buried)
About 1460–69
About 1460–69 (buried)
About 1549–89
Late Sixteenth-Early Seventeenth Century
Uncertain/Modern

O - Oven   F - Fireplace   W - Well   L - Latrine

280 (*above*) A plan of Raglan, Monmouthshire. The castle has preserved the essential elements of its fifteenth-century layout through numerous later adaptations. Its two internal courts were divided by the great hall, which was rebuilt in its present form during the late sixteenth century. Arranged within the outer court were service ranges and the kitchen tower. The inner court was enclosed by the chapel and a series of apartments, including the principal withdrawing rooms. It is possible that the great tower and the main castle apartments were originally intended to operate separately depending on the scale of the earl's following at any given time. All the towers within the main circuit of the castle

walls are hexagonal in plan and have one point at right angles to the plane of the wall, a design that was to gain popularity in the sixteenth century.

281 (*right*) A reconstruction and cut-away by Chris Jones-Jenkins of the great tower at Raglan, Monmouthshire, probably built between 1465 and 1470. Entrance to it was via a bridge and through a subsidiary tower, an early addition to the original design. The tower is polygonal in plan and formerly stood five storeys high (the top floor and crown of battlements, which were probably projected to form a machicolis, have been demolished). The massive walls are constructed throughout of cut stone and

are impressively battered, an unusual detail probably intended to add an impression of solidity. This solidity was not illusory: during the Civil War the tower withstood a barrage of 18- and 20-pound cannonballs without sustaining any significant damage. At ground level there was a kitchen and on the four floors above a series of withdrawing chambers accessible over a drawbridge from the main apartments in the castle bailey. The direct source for the tower at Raglan was almost certainly Guy's Tower at Warwick, completed in 1393/4. Since the earl of Warwick and Herbert were rivals for power in south Wales from 1461 onwards, the choice of architectural source is unlikely to be coincidental (see pl. 205).

282 A view of Nether Hall, Essex, painted in the 1770s by P. Sandby prior to the ruin of the gatehouse. Nether Hall was built by the richest commoner of Edward IV's Yorkist regime, Thomas Colte, between 1461 and 1471, as the centre of a power base he established for himself in Essex. The moated inner court of the new house was laid out on a rectangular plan with corner turrets and dominated by a large gatehouse, which possesses a remarkable quantity of high-quality moulded and diaper brickwork. Much of the decoration was made to stand out against skims of white mortar, traces of which survive on the existing ruin.

particular, the decoration of the great chamber window compares directly to that of the Deanery in Wells, lavishly rebuilt in castellated form after 1472.[8] The buildings also make use of fan vaults, a form long popular on an intimate scale in the south-west.

As a further favour to William Herbert, Edward IV also constituted the two nearby castles of Tretower and Crickhowell as independent estates in 1463.[9] Whether Herbert built at either site is not now clear, but this distinction reflects their perceived importance as seats of administration. His kinsman and half-brother Roger Vaughan settled at Tretower and built a new residence for himself just beside the castle, an architectural expression of his dependence on Herbert. Vaughan was himself well rewarded for his loyalty to the house of York, but the scale of his work at Tretower reflects the chasm between his income and that of his half-brother.

Several other figures came to enjoy wide powers in particular regions of the kingdom over the 1460s. The Midlands fell under the control of William, Lord Hastings, chamberlain of Edward IV. This area was one of the heartlands of Lancastrian power and for this reason had been chosen in November 1459 by Margaret of Anjou as the setting for the so-called Merciless Parliament, which condemned numerous leading Yorkists. Hastings's new estates included the property of the attainted Lancastrian Lord Roos with Belvoir

Castle and its estates. Writing in the 1540s, John Leland asserted that Hastings had deliberately ruined Belvoir in revenge for having been surprised by a Lancastrian force on his first arrival to survey the site. Also, that he carried the lead from the roofs to undertake his own building work elsewhere.[10] The details of the story seem garbled but they certainly convey the spirit of the period with its massive shifts of power and territorial reorganisation. In the south-east, Henry Bourchier (created earl of Essex in 1461) and his brother Thomas, archbishop of Canterbury from 1454 and a cardinal from 1467, were props to the king's power. Henry eventually supplanted the Lancastrian Fiennes family from Knole, which he substantially enlarged.

There were commoners, too, who benefited from Edward IV's rule in the 1460s. Outstanding in this respect was Thomas Colte, born in Middleham in Yorkshire, a follower of Edward IV's father. In 1461–2 he received a series of very generous grants from the new king besides some important financial offices.[11] It was probably soon afterwards that he began rebuilding a manor house that he owned at 'Netherhalle' near Roydon in Essex. Nether Hall (pl. 282) is one of the most accomplished fifteenth-century works of brick architecture in England, loosely connected with such neighbouring buildings as Rye House, Hunsdon and Someries (see Chapter Twelve).[12] The arrangement of the domestic buildings is not clearly understood, but the principal chambers appear to have been inside the gatehouse. Prior to its ruin in the eighteenth century, record was made of a painted scheme of heroes in one of the gatehouse chambers, probably added in the sixteenth century.[13]

There was also an important group of latecomers to the circle at the heart of the 1460s Yorkist settlement. The king's secret and scandalous marriage in 1464 to Elizabeth Woodville catapulted her considerable family into the forefront of politics, to the frustration of several more established interests. Quite as important were Edward IV's two brothers. The elder of the two, George, was heir to the throne until the birth of the king's first son in 1471. He was created duke of Clarence at the start of the reign and endowed with a complex amalgam of estates concentrated in the east Midlands. His minority was terminated in 1466, after which he appears to have established Tutbury Castle as his principal seat. Not only did he undertake building here (though the details of what he created are unfortunately not known), but also in 1468 approved the maintenance of a huge household incorporating 299 members and costing £4,500 a year to maintain.[14] His younger brother, Richard, aged only nine at Edward IV's accession, did not immediately benefit to the same degree. Although created duke of Gloucester late in 1461, his landed endowment was in the 1460s diffuse and relatively small. This situation would change, however, following the political upheavals that would topple Edward IV briefly from the throne.

THE FALL AND RESTORATION OF EDWARD IV

The king's brother Clarence was determined to secure a bride to suit his estate and his choice fell on Isabel Neville, the daughter and co-heiress of the earl of Warwick's huge estates. Edward IV, however, objected to the match and his stance soured their relations. It also added to the growing tensions between the king and his principal magnate, the earl of Warwick, who saw in the marriage a means of extending his power. In defiance of the king, on 11 July 1469 Clarence and Isabel were married at Calais, then under the control of Warwick. The ceremony itself was celebrated in splendid style by the Kingmaker's brother, George Neville, archbishop of York. Immediately afterwards, Clarence and the earl of Warwick sailed for England,

where they publicised their intention of ending Edward IV's evil government and ridding the country of his councillors. The confrontation that followed at the battle of Edgecote was an overwhelming victory for the rebels. In its aftermath they not only executed William Herbert, the newly created earl of Pembroke, Humphrey Stafford, earl of Devon, and the queen's father, Richard Woodville, Earl Rivers, but also captured and imprisoned Edward IV. The king was sent first to Warwick Castle and then to Middleham Castle in the heartlands of the Neville north. In the meantime Clarence and Warwick tried to rule in the king's name. Their attempt was a disaster.

A wave of violence swept the kingdom as the pent-up tensions of more than a decade of political instability erupted. At Gainsborough in Lincolnshire, for example, a local rival attacked the residence of Thomas Burgh, 'a knyght of the kinges howse, and pullede downe his place, and toke alle his goodes and cataylle'.[15] After the dust had settled, Sir Thomas reasserted his position in the 1470s with a new residence unusually rich in the trappings of fortification and with its own brick great tower (pl. 283). In the far north-west, meanwhile, Sir Thomas Stanley took the opportunity of besieging Hornby Castle, jealous of it having recently passed under the control of Richard, duke of Gloucester.[16] Most famously of all, Caister constructed by Sir John Fastolf became the object of an armed struggle between its occupants, the Paston family, and the duke of Norfolk. Writing less than a decade after the event, William Worcester recorded that the siege lasted for five weeks and three days: 'The duke with his force numbering about 3000 armed men encircled the castle. Three parts of it were placed under the fire of English firearms, guns, culverins, other siege artillery and archers etc.' He lists the twenty-five defenders of the castle and also around forty principal figures in the besieging force. It is open to question how hard pressed the siege really was, particularly since the duke of Norfolk presumably wanted to win the prize undamaged. Indeed, despite the impressive listing of guns in his account, Worcester describes only one casualty: a defender called Dawbeney, who was 'slain by a quarrel', presumably fired from a crossbow.[17]

Powerless to control events, Clarence and Warwick were forced to allow Edward IV his liberty. The king now reasserted his authority by redrawing the political map once more. With the intention of breaking down the Neville dominance of the north, he made overtures to restore the head of the Percy family to his property.

283 (*facing page*) The brick tower of Gainsborough, Lincolnshire, probably erected by Sir Thomas Burgh in the 1470s. It is polygonal in plan with an impressive crown of battlements, turrets and chimneys. The arrow loops and false machicolis add to the martial character of the building. In many technical details the brickwork compares to that elsewhere in Lincolnshire and East Anglia. Sir Thomas additionally rebuilt the hall and kitchen of this residence, both exceptionally fine survivals from the period. He rose to fortune as an intimate of Edward IV and in 1461 was appointed an esquire to the king's body within the royal household. The tower was probably begun following an attack on the house during the brief overthrow of Edward IV's rule in 1469–70. It was complete by Sir Thomas' death in 1496.

To appease John Neville – who had assumed the Percy title of earl of Northumberland – he offered a commensurate south-western estate in recompense. The plan backfired when, after an uneasy truce, the earl of Warwick again rebelled in favour of the Lancastrian dynasty and, with John's support, briefly succeeded in restoring Henry VI to the throne.

Edward IV escaped to Burgundy in the autumn of 1470 with a small circle of followers including Lord Hastings and Richard, duke of Gloucester. He returned to England soon afterwards, however, landing at Ravenspur in Yorkshire on 14 March 1471. In the ensuing campaign, and with Clarence's aid, he won two decisive victories. At Barnet he defeated and killed the earl of Warwick; at Tewkesbury the Lancastrian army was routed and Henry VI's son was counted among the dead. Henry VI died on the night of Edward IV's return to London. According to Yorkist propaganda he was overwhelmed by grief; other commentators assumed that he was murdered. There was some further fighting in Wales and a siege of Pembroke in September, but Edward returned to power substantially strengthened and free of his former supporter who had become his chief rival, Warwick the Kingmaker.

THE MAGNATES OF EDWARD IV'S SECOND REIGN

Clarence was well rewarded for his part in the restoration of Edward IV and entered into the estates of the deceased earl of Warwick, which he held by right of his wife, Isabel Neville. He is credited by the historian Rous, writing at Guy's Cliffe on the outskirts of Warwick around 1484, with having been a great builder. Of his work at Warwick, Rous specifically says:

> He purposed to have done many grete thinges as wallyng the town and have made a out ward to the castell closyng in the barn and the stabull . . . and the low wey callyd the hollow wey in to the town shuld have be usid as was of old tyme. Also this noble duke would have made a set parke of the temple felids a for geyn the castel for a plesans to be in the castel and se the dere and the sporte of hem . . . but froward forteon maligned soor a geyn him and leyd al a parte.[18]

Although Clarence's plans for an outer castle ward, a park and a pleasance to view the hunting may not have come to fruition, it is likely that an extension to the castle withdrawing apartments beyond the hall can be included in his list of completed works. The centrepiece of this was the so-called Spy Tower, which stands against the main range of the castle court (pl. 284). This was almost certainly conceived in conjunction with the duke's proposed landscape changes around the castle, its upper windows and adjacent roof leads offering fine views over the park. The uppermost chamber of the tower is, in effect, what came to be known in the sixteenth century as a prospect or banqueting chamber, a space for retirement and the entertainment of favoured guests.[19]

That Clarence never finished his work at Warwick is largely the fault of his younger brother. Richard, duke of Gloucester, was the principal beneficiary of Edward IV's restoration and received a grant of the Nevilles' great northern estates in reward for his support. Amongst many other major castles, these brought him control in the 1470s of Middleham, Penrith and Sheriff Hutton. There followed a steady flow of offices and land grants throughout the ensuing decade, many of them augmenting his power in the north and even extending his control into the palatine of Durham.[20] Around 1472 he also married the co-heiress of the late earl of Warwick, Anne. This match necessitated partitioning up the Warwick estate with his brother and brother-in-law Clarence. The friction generated by this division was an important factor in bringing about Clarence's alienation from Edward IV and his demise – as tradition has it, drowned in a butt of sweet Malmsey wine in 1476.

Across his growing estate, Richard was evidently a major builder, though without adequate documentary evidence the details of his work are frustratingly hard to reconstruct. His chosen seat was evidently Middleham in Yorkshire: it was here that his son was born in 1476 and where he chose in 1478 to found a college of priests, the essential adjunct to the greatest residences. In the circumstances, therefore, it seems convincing to attribute to Richard several modernisations of the castle and its great tower. In the latter, on the upper floor of the building, he created a tall chamber lit by a tier of raised windows in the manner of a church clerestory. As will become apparent, the refurbishment of ancient great towers is a recurrent theme of castle building in this period. Amongst Richard's other castles, there is also anecdotal evidence for a major reorganisation of Penrith in Cumberland,[21] work at Carlisle[22] and at Sandal in Yorkshire;[23] and repairs to

Barnard Castle, Co. Durham, where he also secured a licence to found a college of priests.[24]

As Richard's counterpart in the north of England, Edward IV created Henry Percy earl of Northumberland in 1471, thereby restoring the family to its former dignity. The earl responded with a complete reorganisation of the family castle at Warkworth, evidence perhaps that he intended the castle to be his seat henceforth. As part of the operation, a collegiate church was begun, its nave quaintly – even absurdly – miniaturised in order to make it fit within the space available. The existing hall and great chamber, meanwhile, were reordered and each provided with a splendid porch tower (see pl. 17). That to the hall was ornamented with a display of heraldic sculpture including the modern and ancient arms of the family. This display dates the operation between 1472 and 1485, and its details associate the masons responsible with the workshop of York Minster. The porch to the great chamber generically resembles the spy tower at Warwick, comprising a stair and an upper prospect chamber. Work to the buildings was interrupted by the murder of the new earl in 1489 and the college was left unfinished. It appears that the earl's politic decision not to commit his following at the battle of Bosworth until a winner had emerged so disgusted his household that they abandoned him to a mob during a tax riot.

Across the Midlands, Edward IV's favoured agent was his chamberlain, William, Lord Hastings. Unlike the great noblemen described up to this point, Lord Hastings was unusual in that he never received an earldom. What he got instead was a very generous body of lands in his native Leicestershire, which was then supplemented by lifetime grants of valuable offices in the area. These included the crucial posts within the Midland estates of the duchy of Lancaster and a host of stewardships from families and religious institutions across the region. Such stewardships were mutually beneficial for both parties: they gave the grantee knowledge of support at court and they gave Lord Hastings nominal control of the land and a cut of the profits from it. To the wealth and power he built up in this quiet fashion were added two generous annuities from the king of France and the duke of Burgundy, material acknowledgement of his influence with Edward IV.[25] A highly sophisticated man, a noted patron of the arts and an intimate of the king, he seems to have enjoyed a respect rarely accorded to favourites.

Lord Hastings had been a beneficiary of the king's generosity since 1461, but his loyalty during the

284 A photograph taken in 1914 of the Spy Tower, Warwick, probably built by the duke of Clarence between 1471 and 1478. It is an architectural descendant of Edward III's Rose Tower at Windsor. In plan, the tower comprises two polygons, one large and one small. The former incorporates in its lower level a grand staircase connected to a gallery in the first floor of the adjacent range and the latter a small and discrete landing space. On the three upper storeys, however, the volumes of the two polygons are integrated to create single chambers. Their external faces, meanwhile, are subsumed within an almost unbroken grid of windows. Access to the upper chamber was up a small spiral stair that projects above the roof, and the battlemented outline of the tower was formerly enlivened with pinnacles. One particular detail that lends visual delicacy to the design is the manner in which each window is enclosed by an additional moulding so as to appear framed within the structure. This curious architectural mannerism is a recurrent feature of many buildings created in the orbit of the king's works during Edward IV's reign.

285 The ruins of the great tower at Ashby de la Zouch, Leicestershire, erected between 1472–3 and 1483. The castle was half destroyed in 1649 following a hard-pressed siege during the Civil War. Built of cut stone throughout, the tower must have been an extraordinarily expensive structure to complete. This view of the internal façade of the building shows the small entrance door at ground level. It is visually connected by a projecting strip of stone to a panel carved with the arms of the owner and builder, Lord Hastings, high above. The windows of the building grow in size and number as they rise up the tower, an arrangement that reflects the gathering grandeur of the interior. All the windows have double mouldings, an odd detail that is paralleled in the Spy Tower at Warwick. The Hastings family arms appear in many places on the building.

Warwick rebellion and the gradual marginalisation of Clarence materially strengthened his grip on the Midlands in the 1470s. It was in reflection of his growing power that at Nottingham on 17 April 1474 he received a royal licence to fortify with walls and battlements no fewer than four manor houses within his great estates: Ashby de la Zouch, Bagworth (and Thornton) and Kirby in Leicestershire, and Slingsby in Yorkshire. By the terms of the same licence he was also permitted to enclose an astonishing 9,000 acres of parkland around these buildings.[26] At one fell swoop he was creating the architectural and landed framework for a lordship in Leicestershire irrespective of its historic castles. He was also making an acknowledgement of family links since the fourteenth century with Slingsby Castle, otherwise a curious geographical outpost in this list. It is one reflection of his radical outlook that he chose as his seat within this creation not his father's principal holding at Kirby but a previously unremarkable if wealthy manor

at Ashby de la Zouch. And it is an expression of his ambition that the religious foundation he associated with his new lordship was no less than the mausoleum of the dukes of Lancaster, St Mary's College in Leicester, which he generously patronised.

Despite the date of the licence it is clear that Lord Hastings's rebuilding of Ashby de la Zouch had actually begun the previous year. In a series of surviving account rolls there is record for the first time in 1472–3 of 'diverse great works within the manor and the wages of carpenters, tillers, masons, plumbers and other artificers and their servants'. Although the sums of money recorded are very small, it seems reasonable to interpret this entry as the start of a new building project here.[27] From this there still remain two towers, both ruined in the aftermath of the Civil War. The larger was a great tower (pl. 285), comprising a first-floor kitchen and a series of withdrawing chambers above (pl. 286). More restrained in detail but scarcely

286   A reconstruction cut-away by Phil Kenning of the great tower at Ashby de la Zouch, Leicestershire, viewed from the exterior as it might have appeared around 1480. The tower was laid out on a rectangular plan and was integrated on all its floors with a seven-storey side turret, shown to the right. It was entered through a small door at ground level (1). From the basement upwards the main chambers served respectively for storage (2), as a kitchen (3) and as withdrawing spaces (4). They were connected by a spiral stair that rose the full height of the building to the roof (5). The subsidiary tower contained small withdrawing rooms (6), latrines and a treasure chamber accessed down a ladder (7). The whole building was crowned by a machicolis and a series of corner turrets. This upper section of the building compares in detail to that of the 1470s gatehouse at Farnham Castle, Surrey (see pl. 297). The principal fireplace in the uppermost chamber is decorated with a row of Edward IV's sunburst badges, an advertisement of Lord Hastings's special relationship with his monarch.

287 A plan of Kirby Muxloe, Leicestershire, begun in October 1480 and left incomplete after 1483. The new buildings were laid out on a rectangular plan around a courtyard within a moat and were enclosed by a double circuit of walls: a tall inner wall against which the residential buildings were to be erected and a low apron wall along the moat edge. Together these would have created a two-tiered array of battlements. The circuit of walls was punctuated at regular intervals by towers on a rectangular plan set with gun loops at ground level. Entrance to the site was through a gatehouse. There may have been a base court planned beyond the moat.

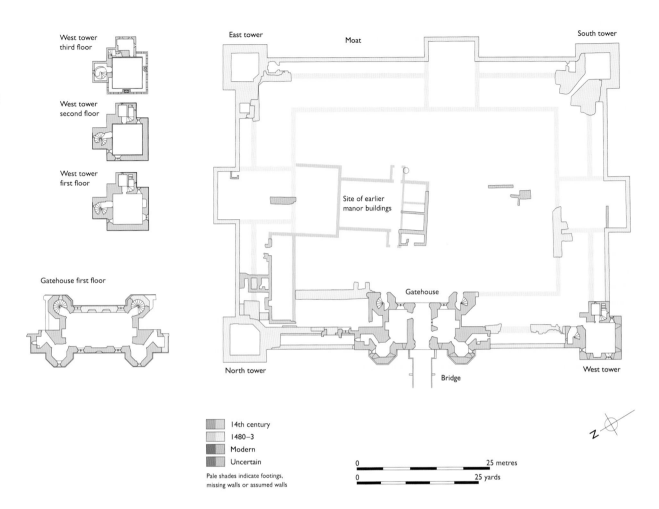

West tower third floor

West tower second floor

West tower first floor

Gatehouse first floor

East tower   Moat   South tower

Site of earlier manor buildings

Gatehouse

North tower   Bridge   West tower

14th century
1480–3
Modern
Uncertain

Pale shades indicate footings, missing walls or assumed walls

0   25 metres
0   25 yards

less ambitious in scale is the kitchen tower, with cooking space sufficient for the royal household.

The two towers stand at right angles to one another along the line of a thick curtain wall with corner turrets. Their arrangement would accord with William Dugdale's description of the towers in 1677: 'as it should seem, and as by tradition it hath been told, built in such a figure, that two more might be placed at convenient distance to equal them'.[28]

That Ashby de la Zouch was planned as a rectangular enclosure with four regularly placed towers makes sense of what is otherwise a rather zany arrangement of surviving elements. It would also speak of the means of William, Lord Hastings. The difference in detailing between the towers could simply express their relative importance and different function: the great tower as the living and architectural centrepiece of the site being by far the most richly treated. Both buildings probably overlooked 'the great gardens' inherited from the previous manor house and described in manorial accounts before the building works began.

While works were still under way at Ashby, Lord Hastings turned his attention to another of the manors listed in the licence of 1474. The rebuilding of Kirby Muxloe is well documented from a surviving series of weekly building accounts, which show that work began in October 1480. Besides preparing the moat and collecting materials, one of the first tasks taken in hand was the clearance of woodland to create a garden.[29] The new buildings were laid out on a quadrangular plan (pl. 287) and erected in locally manufactured brick with details such as windows and doors in stone, a combination of materials first made fashionable at Eton (pl. 288). Indeed, the master mason at Kirby Muxloe, John Cowper, had trained in royal service at Eton in the 1450s. Even more intriguingly, the accounts show that during the early 1480s he was regularly travelling to Tattershall, where he had been responsible since at least 1475 for work to the collegiate church founded beside the castle.[30] This latter project tied him into a complex network of patronage dominated by one of the outstanding builders of the late

288   The entrance front of Kirby Muxloe, Leicestershire, begun in October 1480, is built of brick detailed in stone. The diaper designs in the gatehouse masonry include the initials 'WH' for William Hastings, the sleeve from his coat of arms and other emblems such as a ship and a jug. If the gatehouse was intended to possess three storeys in proportionate enlargement to those found on the surviving corner tower, it would have stood around 100 feet (30.5 m) tall. Excavations in the 1920s revealed the remains of a medieval bridge to the gatehouse and also several blocked cannon loops set below the waterline of the moat, a curious example of a medieval mason's error.

fifteenth century, William Waynflete, bishop of Winchester, more of whom below. It may reflect Cowper's training at Eton that Kirby is extensively decorated with diaper decoration: according to the accounts, four brick masons were specially paid to create 'pictures in the walls' (*pyctura of le walles*) using dark bricks. These were evidently laid into the prepared faces of standing walls, since scaffolding had to be specially erected for the men to work.[31]

The rebuilding work at both Ashby and Kirby was brought to an abrupt close following the summary execution of William, Lord Hastings, in 1483 by Richard, duke of Gloucester. Ashby de la Zouch was patched up with brick buildings by his heirs on a more modest scale than originally proposed and Kirby Muxloe was eventually abandoned. Whether Hastings worked on any of the other sites listed in the licence is not now clear. Minor repairs are recorded in an account of 1468–9 to 'Bagworth Castle',[32] a building referred to in the 1540s by John Leland as 'the ruines of a manor place, like castelle building'.[33] Whatever the case, an

almost unbroken run of Lord Hastings's manorial accounts from 1466 to 1478 makes mention of other architectural operations of which we otherwise would have no knowledge. Folkingham Castle in Lincolnshire, conventionally believed to be a twelfth-century site, for example, was the object of major repairs in the years 1473–6.[34] Unfortunately, there is no upstanding masonry on the site to judge the nature of the works here.

EDWARD IV AND ROYAL CASTLE BUILDING UP TO 1485

Upon his first accession to the throne Edward IV had had neither the opportunity nor the money to embark upon an extravagant building programme. Amongst the only castle works of his first reign were additions to the lodgings of his favourite castle of Fotheringhay (now lost) and the erection of a new gatehouse at Hertford. This latter project was undertaken between 1463

and 1465 at the relatively modest documented cost of over £200. Now the home of the mayor of Hertford, the gatehouse has been heavily altered over time (pl. 289).[35] Hertford is a modest forerunner of the remarkable architectural works of the second reign. These were initiated in splendid style with one of the most ambitious ecclesiastical commissions of the European late Middle Ages.

On 12 June 1475 Edward IV instructed Richard Beauchamp, bishop of Salisbury, 'to build and construct a new chapel in honour of the blessed Mary and St George the martyr within our castle at Windsor'. The direction may have been intended as a votive offering for the success of a large military expedition that was being prepared for an invasion of France and which set off in July that year.[36] If it was, the Virgin and St George were pleased to provide during the campaign the means to pay for their new chapel. On 29 August 1475 Louis XI bought off Edward IV and his army. By the treaty of Picquigny he agreed to pay Edward IV £15,000 immediately and a further annual fee of £10,000. To the disgust of his impetuous ally the duke of Burgundy, who had promised to join the expedition but had failed to turn up, Edward IV returned home to spend his sensational winnings.

Vaulted in stone throughout and laid out on a cathedral-like scale, the new church at Windsor was a chapel only in name and, with small changes to the original plan, took nearly eighty years to complete. In detail, the building shows a familiarity with the whole canon of the Perpendicular style and incorporates specific ideas lifted from such late fourteenth-century buildings as the chancel of St Mary's, Warwick, and the east end of Gloucester Abbey (now cathedral).[37] There could be no more powerful testimony to the capacity of the best masons working in the Perpendicular idiom to reformulate old ideas to brilliant new effect. Surprisingly, the designer of the building was not the king's master mason but a certain Henry Janyns from Oxford. Janyns had worked at Eton in the 1440s and even inherited the drawing collection of the warden mason on the site in 1459.[38] Nevertheless, he was an independent mason and his appointment to this prestigious royal commission is a striking expression of the broken stranglehold of the king's works on architectural practice in the kingdom.

St George's Chapel is a work of castle architecture by virtue of its location, a church consciously intended to complement Windsor as a royal seat in a variety of ways. As a building it expressed the power of the new

289 The gatehouse of Hertford, begun in 1463. It is laid out on a four-square plan with a shallow, polygonal turret at each corner and is built of locally produced brick with stone detailing. The bricks were made by Cornelius Gyles for 21 pence per 1,000 and were laid by nine 'breekmasons'. Running through the centre of the building is a gate passage with what appears to be an eighteenth-century vault. According to the building accounts, there was a machicolis detailed in stone added to the building in 1465. A certain Reginald Langley carved the royal arms over the gate and these were originally painted. It is an open question as to whether any of the crowning decoration on the building today is medieval.

290 An engraving by Wenceslaus Hollar of the return stalls in the choir of St George's Chapel at Windsor published in 1672. To either side of the choir entrance were special stalls for the king (1) and the prince of Wales (2), the former treated as a fantasy castle and ornamented throughout with towers and portcullises. The uppermost tier of the encircling stalls was for the canons of the college and the knights of the Garter. They sat alternately beneath canopies of two types: those of the priests had pinnacles (3), those of the knights battlemented platforms for their heraldic achievements, banners and swords (4). The stalls still survive, though they were adapted in the eighteenth century.

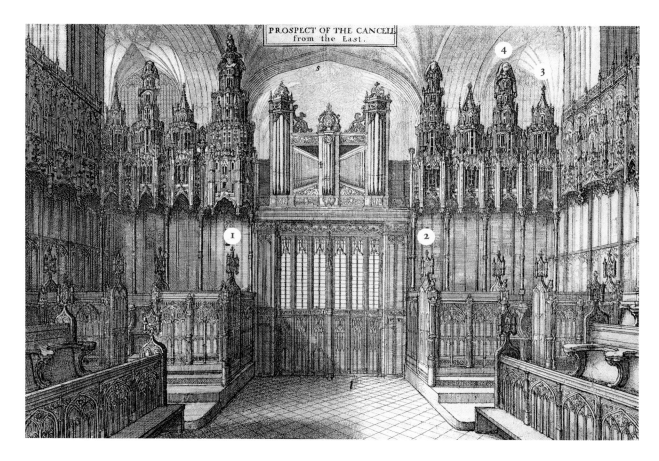

Yorkist dynasty, for whom it was to serve as a royal mausoleum in place of Westminster Abbey. Interestingly, it was explicitly not a burial church of the dukes of York, whose mausoleum at Fotheringhay received the body of the king's long-dead father in 1476 amidst great display.[39] Edward IV chose pride of place within the new building at Windsor for his own sepulchre, creating a curious two-storey chantry chapel embracing the east end of the north aisle. But the new chapel of St George's was also meant to trumpet the prestige of the chivalric order of the Garter. The new stalls in the choir, which were completed in 1483–4, were carefully designed to reflect the curious mixture of the order's martial and religious interests (pl. 290).

The rebuilding of St George's, Windsor, was just one of several important architectural projects funded by the profits of Picquigny. Frustratingly little is known about one of these: a major restoration of Dover Castle. Evidence for the work is principally provided by two sixteenth-century sources. John Skelton (d. 1529), in his elegy on Edward IV, vaguely stated that the king 'amended Dover on the mountain high',[40] and William Darell, writing in the 1580s, claimed that he had spent more than £10,000 in beautifying the castle. Darell's account is so obviously garbled (and also dis-

torted to flatter its dedicatee, Lord Cobham) that it is hard to credit many details within it.[41]

The thrust of both accounts is substantiated, however, by the fabric of the great tower, the upper floor of which was reordered in this period with fireplaces bearing Edward IV's badge of the rose in a sunburst. No other trace of fifteenth-century work now remains in the castle. The reorganisation of the great tower as a set of lodgings perfectly accords with the interest of his principal magnates in creating such structures, as at Middleham, Ashby de la Zouch and Raglan. That the work at Dover took place in his second reign is strongly suggested by Edward IV's patronage – or that of his archbishop, Thomas Bourchier – of nearby Canterbury Cathedral from around 1482.[42] It also ties up with a fragment of documentation that links the supply of bricks for Dover with Edward IV's work to another Kent property.[43]

In November 1475 work began to rebuild Eltham in Kent, the residence aggrandised by Bishop Bek of Durham and subsequently favoured by several kings for its hunting. Nothing now survives of the original domestic ranges created here by Edward IV, though it is known that they were built of brick and incorporated a gallery that enjoyed fine prospects over the city

of London.[44] From the evidence of accounts and limited excavation, it is clear that they were battlemented and turreted, as befitted any great residence of the period. The surviving great hall, however, is testimony to the grandeur of the new work on this constrained, moated and walled site (pl. 291).

Meanwhile, from 1476 there is documentation describing the construction of a tower integral to a lodging range in the outer bailey of Nottingham Castle. The work to the range was unfinished at Edward IV's death and completed by Richard III, as Leland's enthusiastic description of the 1540s makes clear:

> But the most bewtifullest part and gallant building for lodgyng is on the northe side, wher Edward the 4 began a right sumptuus pece of stone work, of the which he clerely finichid one excellent goodly toure of 3 hightes yn building, and brought up the other part likewise from the foundacition with stone and mervelus fair cumpacid windows to lying of the first soyle [i.e. floor] for chambers, and ther left. Richard his brother as I hard ther forced up apon that worke another peace of one lofte of tymber, making rounde wyndowes also of tymbre to the proportion of the aforesaid windows.[45]

A surviving plan of the castle of 1617 suggests that this building was connected closely to the residential range and tower of the 1420s at Cardiff Castle (pl. 292). By extension, it also evidently looked back to Edward III's lodging range at Windsor Castle. Unfortunately, the name of the master mason who initiated the project is not recorded but something of the style of the compass or bay windows may be suggested both by the Spy Tower at Warwick (see pl. 284) and a surviving timber-frame building at Knole, Kent, in Pheasant Court, probably erected around 1470. The Nottingham range and its windows, however, were completed from 1484 under the direction of a mason previously active at Westminster Abbey, William Turnour. The contrasting form of first- and second-floor windows may well have been the inspiration for the types of oriel that survive at sites such as Thornbury, Gloucestershire, begun in 1511 (see pl. 311).

Of the form of the tower Edward IV erected behind this richly detailed range at Nottingham little is securely known. The plan of 1617 shows that it was polygonal, just like its architectural ancestor at Cardiff. An integrally planned turret on one side of the building may also suggest a connection with the contemporary great tower at Ashby de la Zouch built by Lord

291 A view of the hall and dais of Eltham, Kent, in 1937. The hall was begun late in 1475 and probably designed by the king's mason, Thomas Jordan. Its windows are raised high for the display of tapestries and the roof is a fabulous open-timber structure with pendants. The conception and detailing of the hall reflect a thorough familiarity of its designer with the crucial buildings of Henry VI's reign. In particular, the creation at Eltham of a stone hall in a largely brick-built complex looks back to the first design for Eton College begun in 1441. Likewise, the pairing of oriel windows in the hall – a very rare detail – may derive from the plans to rebuild Eton as described in the king's will of 1446. One technical token of the continued influence of Henry Yevele is the enrichment of the oriel windows with intermediary sub-cusping. The overall symmetry of the plan echoes that of St George's Chapel, Windsor.

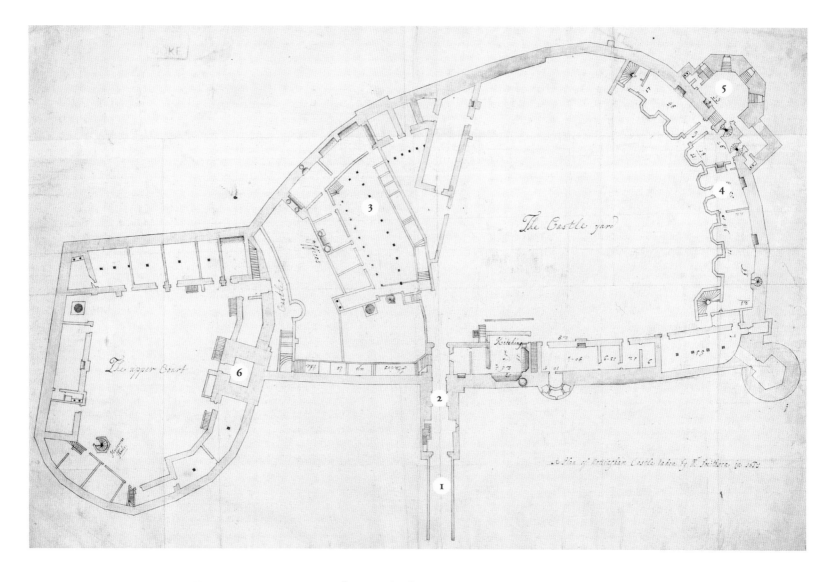

Hastings. He was granted control of Nottingham Castle and Sherwood Forest on 2 March 1475 – just before the building works there began – so a direct relationship between the two projects is an attractive possibility.[46] It should also be said that a facsimile of 'an old sketch' of the castle was published in J. Hicklin's *The Ancient Castle of Nottingham* (Nottingham, 1834). The drawing from which the engraved plate is purportedly taken is not otherwise known, but it looks convincing and shows the tower with a projecting machicolis towards the top.

A much more modest operation undertaken towards the end of Edward IV's reign was the repair of the Tower of London in 1480. Again, details of this operation are not well documented, but it appears that the moat was scoured and that a new barbican was created outside the Lion Gate known as 'The Bulwark'. This fortification, enclosed in brick walls, may have replaced temporary timber defences in the same

area hurriedly erected during the political crisis of 1471 using wine barrels filled with sand. The Bulwark was intended for guns, which were presumably mounted in a pair of drum towers at the entrance.[47] Possibly in conjunction with these alterations a triangular gun turret was also added to the main thirteenth-century gateway of the castle, the Byward Tower. Such angular designs are unusual in England and perhaps derive from the design of bridge piers, the angled faces intended to deflect missiles.

In addition to all these operations, Edward IV was lastly responsible for giving Ludlow Castle in Shropshire an important role in the politics of the kingdom as a whole. The castle had been much used by his father, the duke of York, who had inherited it amongst the possessions of the last Mortimer earl of March. Edward IV assumed the title of earl of March and spent considerable time at Ludlow as a boy. Indeed, some of his letters addressed from there survive. This child-

292 (*facing page*)   A ground-level plan of 1617 of the upper and middle wards of Nottingham Castle by Robert Smythson. According to Leland, writing in the 1540s, the castle bridge (1) was ornamented with the sculptures of beasts and giants. Beyond the gate (2) was a group of domestic apartments including a hall, chapel and services arranged around an open court. This was curiously distorted to suit the topography of the site (3). Edward IV's buildings ran down the opposite side of the courtyard (4). They comprised a range lit by bay windows that backed onto a high angle tower (5). This disposition of elements closely resembles that found in works of the 1420s at Cardiff (see pl. 264). The tower was polygonal in plan with a side turret, the latter detail paralleled in the contemporary tower of Ashby de la Zouch. The Romanesque great tower of the castle stood in the upper ward (6), and its upper levels were approached up an external stair.

hood experience may have encouraged him to establish it as the seat of his own son, Edward. Born in sanctuary at Westminster Abbey in 1471 during Henry VI's brief restoration, the young Edward was created prince of Wales immediately after his father's return to power. In 1473 he was sent with his household to Ludlow, where the administration of the principality known as the Council in the Marches of Wales was settled. There is no documentation relating to the prince's ten-year occupancy of the castle in this prosperous town, but archaeological excavation has demonstrated that the eleventh-century great tower was substantially altered in the late fifteenth century, perhaps following its partial collapse.[48]

The prince of Wales was in Ludlow when his father unexpectedly died on 9 April 1483. On his journey south, Edward IV's younger brother, Richard, duke of Gloucester, intercepted the royal party and took control of the boy. This was the first step in the complex and celebrated struggle for power that culminated in the duke's usurpation of the throne and coronation as Richard III in 1483. Amongst the victims of the usurpation was William, Lord Hastings, who was dragged out of a council chamber in the Tower of London and summarily executed.[49] Famously, too, Edward V and his younger brother also died in the Tower, almost certainly murdered by their uncle.

Richard III's reign was not to prove long-lasting or stable. Yet to judge by the very limited evidence available, it witnessed a surprising quantity of architectural activity. His completion of the lodging ranges at Nottingham has already been mentioned, but he additionally initiated at least two other works.

York Castle had been in a sufficiently parlous state for Edward IV to promise its repair in 1478. No work appears to have followed, however, and restoration waited until his brother ascended the throne. With such a strong following in the north, Richard III had particular reason to be concerned with the county castle of Yorkshire and in 1484 he appointed surveyors to oversee its restoration. From the limited evidence available it would seem that they demolished various structures to clear space for new buildings. Then the battle of Bosworth intervened in 1485 and the castle was left as a gutted ruin.[50]

A second project likewise interrupted by Richard's fall was the erection of a great tower at Warwick Castle. This was possibly undertaken at the instigation of his wife, since Richard had no direct interest in the castle and the local historian John Rous notes Anne Neville's

particular interest in the town. Whatever the case, Rous credits the king 'with great coste of building in the castel',[51] and John Leland, writing in the 1540s, stated that Richard III 'pullyd downe a pece of the waulle, and began and halfe finishid a mighty tower, or strengthe, for to shoute [shoot] out gunns'.[52] The remains of two polygonal corner turrets from this building still project from the north wall of the castle along with internal fixings for cannon. A sixteenth-century plan of the tower shows that it was laid out on a rectangular plan with a kitchen to the rear (see pl. 353). If this arrangement belongs to the fifteenth century, it is probable that the upper chambers were intended to be residential in function. As a whole, this building speaks of the continued prestige of the great tower into the 1480s and also of the growing interest in artillery fortification.

During his short reign, Richard III was well aware of Henry Tudor's plans to supplant him on the English throne. Over the summer of 1484 he travelled to Scarborough and resided in the castle while assembling a fleet to oppose his rival. He apparently had grand plans for the town, which he elevated to the status of a county, and during his visit he began work to an artillery bulwark commanding the harbour from the south-east.[53] The following year he again moved uneasily around the country so as to be prepared quickly to meet any invasion. His preparations were to prove useless. Famously, at the battle of Bosworth on 22 August 1485, Richard III was killed and the Yorkist line of English kings was overthrown. Henry VII, the victor of the field, as he struggled to establish a grip on England and its throne, transformed the architectural scene once more.

THE EARLY TUDOR SETTLEMENT

Contrary to what is popularly assumed, the Wars of the Roses did not end at the battle of Bosworth. During the course of his reign, Henry VII was repeatedly involved in fighting for the crown in an extension of this protracted, dynastic feud. The shadow of the conflict even fell beyond his death: its last victims died at the command of Henry VIII. Busily engaged in securing his rule and consolidating royal finances, it is no surprise that Henry VII initially undertook little building. And as if to affirm the fact institutionally, upon his accession he made no appointments of retained craftsmen to posts within the royal works at all.[54] By contrast with their wary king, the principal political supporters of the Tudor invasion, many of them returned from years of exile, immediately began turning the fruits of their victory to architectural account. All were spurred by a desire to celebrate in tangible form their restoration to power. This activity was encouraged by the early generosity of the king to his followers. It was several more years before Henry VII developed a reputation for miserliness and also for controlling magnates by holding crippling debts over their heads.

One of the most magnificent builders in these early years was John de Vere, thirteenth earl of Oxford. He had fought in the vanguard of the Tudor army at Bosworth and was well rewarded for his long and active fidelity to Henry's cause. It was probably immediately after his restoration that the earl began to rebuild the ancient baronial seat of his family at Castle Hedingham in Essex. The earthwork enclosure of the earlier castle was divided in two to create an inner and outer bailey, the latter serving as a base court with ancillary buildings including a granary, stables and a tennis court. This was entered over a bridge that crossed the broad earthwork ditch. Preserved as the centrepiece to the inner court was the great tower of the castle erected in the 1140s. This was reworked internally and encircled by a new series of domestic buildings built of brick and timber including a hall, chapel and great chamber block. Along the line of the wall were erected at least three new towers in brick, the largest of which was a second great tower. It contained withdrawing apartments and enjoyed wide prospects over the surrounding landscape and little park.[55]

The earl's work at Hedingham is likely to have been completed in time for a royal visit in 1498. All that survives of it today is the fine castle bridge built of brick. At some undocumented time before his death in 1513 the earl also erected another great tower at Castle Camps in Cambridgeshire, an important and valuable manor long in the hands of the de Vere family. There had been a castle on the site from at least the twelfth century and the new buildings occupied the area within the moat. Eighteenth-century views show the tower as a tall thin structure towering over a cluster of later domestic buildings within a walled enclosure. It collapsed in 1738.[56]

Rather more flamboyant in his celebration of prosperity under Tudor rule was the Welshman Sir Rhys ap Thomas. A crucial figure not only at Bosworth but also in other later campaigns of Henry VII's reign, he

gradually emerged as the leading royal servant in Wales. In 1505 he was appointed to the Order of the Garter, an honour that he celebrated with five days of jousting and entertainment at Carew Castle, Pembrokeshire, before the assembled notables of Wales. Deliberately chosen as the climax of this remarkable event was the feast-day of St George (23 April), the patron saint of England and of the Order of the Garter. That morning, to the sound of trumpets and drums, a cavalcade escorted the bishop of St Davids, the primate of Wales, from Lamphey to the castle gates. For the occasion, these were hung with a painting of St George and St David embracing one another, a visual symbol of the amicable integration of Welsh and English interests that the occasion expressed. The bishop and his host proceeded into the castle, and their reception is worth quoting at length from an anonymous early seventeenth-century account. The procession passed into the castle through:

> . . . the first court, which was called the *Platea* or common place wherin people did use to walk; two hundred talemen were arranged all in blewe coates, who made them a lane into another lesse court, called the *pinacotheca*, in which the images, scutcheons, and coat of armours, of certaine of Sir Rice's auncestor's stood, and soe they passed into the greate hall, which hall was a goodlie spacious roome, richelie hanged with cloath of arras and tapestry. At the upper end under a plain cloath of state of crimson velvet was provided a cross-table for the king: on each side, downe the length of the hall, two other tables, the one for Sir Rice alone, the other for the rest of the gentlemen. Here everie man stood bare, as in the king's presence. Within a while, after the trumpets sounded, and the herald called for the king's service; whereupon all the gentlemen went presentlie downe to waite upon the sewer [servant at table] . . . The sewer for the time, Sir Rice appointed his sonn, Sir Griffith Rice, who had binn bred up at court, and therefore hade some advantage of the rest in point of curialitie and courtliness . . . When the king's meate was brought to the table, the bishop stood on the right side of the chaire and Sir Rice on the left, and all the while the meate was a laying downe, the cornets, hautbois, and other wind instruments were not silent. After the table was served and all sett, the bishop made his humble obeysance to the king's chaire, and then descended to say grace, which donn, he returned againe to his

former station. Much pleasant discourse passed betweene them for a time, which ever and anon was seasoned with diversitie of musick. When they saw their time, the table was voided and the meate removed to the side board for the wayters. Then the king's chaire was turned and so everie man at libertie to putt on his hatt. The king's service being finished, Sir Rice went to his owne table, taking only the bishop along with him, whom he placed at the upper end at a messe all alone, and himself at some distance sate him down at another. All the gentlemen there present were pleased; for Sir Rice's more honour, to stand by and give him the looking on, until his first course was served . . .[57]

It is apparent from the surviving fabric of Carew that Sir Rhys transformed the castle in which this entertainment took place.[58]

Another veteran of Bosworth who benefited on a grand scale from the battle was Thomas Stanley. His commitment of forces for the Tudor cause decisively changed the course of the battle and he was rewarded at Henry VII's coronation with the title of earl of Derby. In celebration of this earldom he rebuilt his seat in the north-west at Lathom, Lancashire. Very little is known about this important building, which was ruined following a long siege in the Civil War and then built over in the eighteenth century. Limited archaeological excavation has revealed a stone-faced moat around the site 42 feet (13 m) wide. The best evidence as to its appearance is provided by a sixteenth-century poem, which described it as possessing 'nine towers on high and nine on the outer walls'. Some further gleanings of its size and form are furnished by descriptions of the long Civil War siege, which make it clear that it was powerfully built and substantial.[59] The earl also built a castle at Greenhalgh, Lancashire, according to the seventeenth-century historian William Camden as a defence against those whose lands he had appropriated.[60]

There were other successful agents of royal authority who managed on a smaller scale to take advantage of the change of dynasty: Sir Henry Vernon rebuilt his family castle at Tong in Shropshire around 1500. This important building, splendidly adapted over later centuries, was abandoned and then demolished to make way for the M54 motorway in 1954. You can today appreciate the views it enjoyed from the road. There were also royal officials who amassed wealth sufficient to build. William Cope, cofferer to Henry VII, for example, acquired the manor of Hanwell in Oxfordshire in 1498 and began a castle there. The building was evidently not completed at Cope's death in 1513, and his will specified that the building was 'to be finished and made according as it is begun and according to a platt thereof made', a clear instance of the use of architectural drawings.[61] The work was eventually completed some time after 1518 and there are various copies of an 'old drawing' that show it as a quadrangular building with angle towers, though the details of this are problematic.[62]

In comparison with these figures, one individual who might have been expected to build on a very large scale indeed actually appears to have done relatively little. Jasper Tudor, earl of Pembroke, had been a father figure to Henry VII, and his rewards after Bosworth speak of the trust in which he was held. On the eve of the king's coronation on 28 October 1485 he was created duke of Bedford, and by 7 November he had married Katherine Stafford, widow of the duke of Buckingham. The estates she brought gave Jasper control of a great triangle of land extending across from southern Wales to Essex and up into Derbyshire. If Jasper Tudor built in these properties, no clear evidence survives for his work. The one possible exception is the great chamber block at Sudeley Castle in Gloucestershire, with its delicate clerestory windows, rich detailing and ingeniously contrived chimney flues (pl. 293). There is no stylistic detail that can be used to argue for this attribution contrary to the orthodox one: that it is a work of Richard III.[63] Yet Sudeley was one of Jasper's favourite seats and central to his interest in a geographic sense. After his death, Jasper's widow Katherine Stafford repaired the castle at Kimbolton, Huntingdonshire.[64]

In the early years of the reign castles continued to play a minor role in Henry VII's military campaigns. Harlech, formerly a thorn in Edward IV's flesh, now became an outpost of Yorkist resistance. Meanwhile, during the various Yorkist invasion scares, Henry VII repeatedly moved to Kenilworth and the Midlands in order to respond quickly to attacks. Such, for example, was the case before the battle of Stoke in 1487.[65] Yet his use of Kenilworth was not merely strategic: he built a tennis court here.[66] In 1493 he also established his eldest son, Arthur, and the Council of the Marches at Ludlow Castle. But it was not until the mid-1490s that he began any notable works to his castles and residences.

293 (*top*) Sudeley, Gloucestershire, in 1940. The ruins give a sense of the opulent domestic interiors that were being created towards the close of the fifteenth century. This shell formerly comprised a lower and an upper room, probably a parlour and a great chamber respectively. Both were warmed by fires and had a window projected in the depth of the wall at one end. The grids of windows, a feature of buildings in the Perpendicular idiom, probably displayed heraldic glass and must have let the light flood in. In the upper chamber tapestries would have been hung beneath the cornice on the blank lower register of the wall. The low-pitched roof, accessible up a stair tower from both chambers, was lead-covered and could have been used for walking and recreation on fine days.

294 (*bottom*) An engraving of Henry VII's Tower, Windsor, Berkshire, by Mackenzie and published in Britton's *Architectural Antiquities of Great Britain* (London, 1805–14). The building was attached to the withdrawing chambers in the upper ward and appeared to be a tower only when viewed from the exterior of the castle, where it was defined by two polygonal corner turrets. As they rose up the building, these turrets dissolved into the most spectacular windows set out on complex geometric patterns. There is no obvious precedent for such 'compass windows', though the Spy Tower at Warwick and the lodging range at Nottingham as completed by Richard III show an interest in similar ideas. A more specific precedent might have been the lost 'oriole' chamber on the upper floor of the tower at Hunsdon, Hertfordshire begun around 1446.

HENRY VII AND ROYAL BUILDING

It is no coincidence that the king began to build at the very moment that his nobility ceased to do so: the financial policies that filled the royal coffers bit deeply into the pockets of his subjects. With this money Henry VII was able in just over a decade to leave a very important architectural legacy indeed. In the surge of building activity he undertook, moreover, the Perpendicular tradition was reformulated once more.

Henry VII's first significant architectural projects both concerned castles. Following a royal visit to Corfe in Dorset during an invasion scare in 1496, the substantial sum of £2,000 was provided to repair the castle, an ancestral seat of his mother, Lady Margaret Beaufort. Lead was provided for the roof of the great tower and the fabric of the building shows evidence of changes to doors and windows. Other residential apartments were also repaired, though the demolition of the castle buildings ordered by parliament in 1646 was so complete as to make detailed reconstruction of these impossible. Besides securing the castle as a fortification in a time of crisis, the building operations at Corfe underlined the power of the Tudor dynasty and its political roots in the region.[67]

Much more familiar to historians but actually of comparable cost were Henry VII's alterations to his

royal seat at Windsor. Since their first construction in the 1350s, no English king had seen the need substantially to alter or enlarge Edward III's royal apartments in the upper ward of the castle. The growing taste for seclusion apparent in the 1470s and '80s through the provision of tower residences for inner or 'riding' households, however, was probably the incentive for Henry VII to create a space for domestic living in his premier castle. The king's habit of retirement amongst the intimates of his so-called Privy Chamber is well documented.[68] Consequently, in the late 1490s there began the construction of a new 'tower' to the west of the older royal apartments under the direction of the mason Robert Janyns, a kinsman of Henry Janyns (d. 1483), the designer of St George's Chapel (pl. 294).[69]

Henry VII's work to the tower at Windsor was undertaken in conjunction with further building in St George's Chapel itself, where work had probably lapsed since 1483. Just before the battle of Bosworth, the body of Henry VI was brought to Windsor and laid in unhappy juxtaposition to that of his murderer and rival, Edward IV, in the choir of the chapel. Almost immediately miracles were reported and a pilgrimage cult began to develop around the Lancastrian king, whose reputation for ineptitude was now replaced by sanctity. Consequently, in 1493 Henry VII chose to be buried with his Lancastrian forebear and set in train a campaign to have him canonised by the pope. To create an appropriate setting for his monument, the existing Lady Chapel at St George's was pulled down and a new building begun on its footprint. But just as preparations were set in hand to vault the building in 1498, the community at Westminster successfully convinced the king that Henry VI had intended to be buried in their abbey church. Henry VII now abandoned St George's and switched his allegiance, directing that the body of Henry VI be moved to Westminster.

Confusingly, Henry VI's body never was translated, but in 1503 a new Lady Chapel was in turn begun at Westminster to receive it. Now popularly known as Henry VII's Chapel after its builder, this was deliberately intended as a building of unparalleled architectural splendour. The designer of the new work was almost certainly Robert Janyns, the mason of Henry VII's tower at Windsor. In evidence of the connection, the new chapel makes use of the distinctive projecting or compass windows found in the earlier building, an unusual instance of secular architectural forms being absorbed into the canon of church design (pl. 295).[70] Meanwhile, two close friends of the king ensured that

295   The Lady Chapel, now known as Henry VII's Chapel, at Westminster Abbey was begun in 1503 by the mason Robert Janyns as the burial chapel for Henry VII and his ancestral saint, Henry VI. It was conceived of as a virtuoso work of architecture in the form of a great church, with aisles and high vaults of stone. Its grand conception combined with fabulously rich detailing and complex geometry has consistently earned this building the unstinting praise of visitors from the sixteenth century to the present day. The compass windows around the lower chapels were evidently inspired by Henry VII's Tower at Windsor, also built by Janyns.

296 An anonymous seventeenth-century view of Richmond, Surrey, viewed across the Thames. Henry VII refashioned the Lancastrian palace after a fire in 1497, bestowing on it a fantastical array of turrets, oriel windows and cupolas. The huge concentration of chimneys added to the busy outline of the building. They were of red brick, to make them prominent. Access to the upper storeys of the building was provided by a great stair set within a polygonal angle turret, which was described in the seventeenth century as 'the chief ornament of the house'. The queen's and king's apartments were arranged around a small internal court on the first and second floor respectively. Such planning evokes contemporary French palace architecture, though there is English precedent for it too. There is an oblique view of the hall to the left of the main building and beside it the conical roof of the great kitchen.

building operations at Windsor did not grind to a halt. Dr Christopher Urswick, a canon and later dean of Windsor, supported by the wealth of Sir Reginald Bray, a knight of the Garter from 1501, began to complete the main chapel. Between 1498 and 1509 the entire interior was vaulted in stages with the exception of the crossing. It was intended for a lantern tower, a plan finally abandoned in the 1520s.

Henry VII's change of heart about Windsor was connected to a decisive shift in his interests closer to London. On 22 December 1497 the great Lancastrian residence at Sheen was severely damaged by fire. The event prompted a rebuilding of the palace but one apparently constrained in certain points by the earlier buildings on the site. Most importantly, Henry V's royal lodgings were rebuilt to create a structure like a great tower with a central courtyard.[71] This visual and domestic core of the complex was refashioned with turrets, oriel windows and a fantastical crown of battlements, domes and brick chimneys (pl. 296). Set to either side of the principal court beside the lodgings were the hall and chapel, and beyond were various service courts, a magnificent array of gardens and a convent of Observant Franciscan friars, previously established by the king in 1485. In celebration of his new creation, Henry VII bestowed on the new residence the title of his chief duchy, Richmond.

The name of the mason responsible for the new buildings at Richmond Palace is not certainly known, but his creation was to prove profoundly influential into the 1530s. While the work to Richmond was under way, Henry VII also began three other projects in the immediate environs of London that usefully contextu-

alise it in architectural terms. In 1501 the mason Robert Vertue was instructed to build a tower at the Tower of London. The new building had large windows overlooking the River Thames and formed an extension of the king's lodgings within the castle. The project, incidentally, compares to the exactly contemporary repair of the royal lodgings at Portchester, Hampshire, and the creation of a withdrawing chamber with a fine oriel in the forebuilding to the great tower. The apartments at the Tower of London were further aggrandised in 1506 by the addition of a gallery that gave access to a chamber for the king in the Queen's Tower.

The year after Robert Vertue began work at the Tower he also provided the queen with a plat or design for a new royal residence on the waterfront at Greenwich. Built entirely of brick, this building again incorporated a great tower as its visual centrepiece and was battlemented throughout. Not so the last of Henry VII's buildings in the capital. According to Stow's *Survey of London*, the king began to rebuild Baynard's Castle in 1501 'not imbattoled, or so strongly fortified castle like, but farre more beautiful and commodious for the entertainment of any Prince or great estate'.[72] His comments reflect the degree to which the trappings of fortification constituted a recognised style of architecture in great residential buildings.

So far this chapter has emphasised the degree to which the grand building activities of the crown and nobility were materially shaped by the political vicissitudes of the period. The craftsmen that worked on these buildings and the tradition of architecture that informed their designs, however, were being nurtured within a related but independent sphere: the church.

It is testimony to the remarkable standing enjoyed by the established church in late medieval England – and also its power – that it weathered the dynastic turmoil of the Wars of the Roses completely unscathed. Even the bench of bishops, though deeply implicated in politics, suffered no single casualty by murder or execution during the entire course of this struggle. As a direct result of the relative security they enjoyed, church institutions consistently remained amongst the most important patrons of architecture throughout this period, able to drive forward projects through changes of regime.

In so doing, they carried the English architectural tradition through into the Tudor period in a state of undiminished vigour. The most important patrons in the ranks of the church remained its bishops, and their undoubted focus of interest was on the patronage of learning. Indeed, the contribution of bishops to the development of the universities of Oxford and Cambridge in this period was crucially important to the future of these institutions. This work is relatively well studied, but it is often presented as a discrete endeavour. In reality, the patronage of educational foundations usually took place in the context of a wide spectrum of other building activity, often quite as remarkable and connected with castle and residential architecture.

The outstanding bishop patron of the entire period of this chapter was William Waynflete, who lived into his nineties.[73] Appointed schoolmaster at Winchester, he caught the eye of Henry VI and was appointed first provost of Eton in 1442 and then bishop of Winchester, the richest see in England, in 1447. Despite his strong personal links with the Lancastrian regime, he survived Edward IV's reign and during the prosperity of the 1470s became a prominent builder. Curiously, many of his projects were realised with the resources from dead figures active within the court of Henry VI, to whom he served as executor. The property of Sir John Fastolf of Caister Castle, Norfolk, for example, was materially important to the foundation at Oxford of Waynflete's own Magdalen College, under construction from 1468. To this, and in imitation of the colleges of his predecessor as bishop, William Wykeham, he attached two schools, one in Oxford and the other at his birthplace, Wainfleet in Lincolnshire. And as an executor of Ralph, Lord Cromwell's will he undertook the construction of the collegiate church at Tattershall opposite the castle from *circa* 1475 to 1482.[74]

In the 1470s he also gathered the neglected royal college of Eton under his protective wing, ensuring its future stability and tidying up its zany amalgam of incomplete buildings.

Work to these various sites involved two principal craftsmen: at Magdalen the leading Oxford mason of the period, William Orchard, took responsibility for the project.[75] Here he designed a building in the Oxford collegiate tradition as derived from the fourteenth-century New College but regularised it with a cloister, a feature probably inspired by Henry VI's designs for Eton. Orchard also supplied stone for Waynflete's works to the Eton chapel in the 1470s, but operations here were directed by a mason called John Cowper. We have already encountered Cowper at work for Lord Hastings at Kirby Muxloe in the 1480s and it is worthwhile relating something of his career. Cowper is first documented working as an apprentice at Eton in 1453 and in 1460 was entered in the pay rolls of the college as a mason. He then passed into the service of Winchester College, where he is recorded as repairing a chimney in 1466–7. From 1475 he is recorded as working on the collegiate choir of Tattershall for Waynflete and in 1477, as 'a mason of Winchester', he contracted with Waynflete to build a bridge at Bramber in Sussex. His employment by Lord Hastings at Kirby Muxloe from 1480 to 1483 reflects his status as an established and senior mason with a wide practice.[76]

It is likely that Cowper served Waynflete in much the same way that the mason William Wynford had served the bishop's great predecessor, William Wykeham. If so, a host of important but undocumented projects undertaken by the bishop might plausibly be associated with him, including Waynflete's chantry chapel at Winchester Cathedral. This is one of two monuments that flanked the former shrine of St Swithun, the patron of the church. Certainly, the designer of this remarkable monument had a detailed knowledge of the Perpendicular canon that would be consonant with Cowper's documented experience. So too would two substantial residential projects executed in brick.

The best documented of these is the addition to Farnham Castle, Surrey, of a new gatehouse tower, built between 1470 and 1477 (pl. 297). It must have been at about the same time that Waynflete began the reconstruction of his residence at Esher in Surrey. The only element of this that survives is the much-altered gatehouse with inlaid grids of regular diaper (pl. 298). This was finished some time before 1484 because in that year the timber framing of the gatehouse floor was used as a

297 A photograph taken in 1939 of the great gate of Farnham, Surrey, built between 1470 and 1477 and probably designed by John Cowper. The projection of corner turrets at different levels and the inclusion of a subsidiary tower to the right are both technical details of design that are paralleled in the great tower at Ashby de la Zouch. So too is the heavy machicolis that crowns the structure, though this feature is otherwise widely encountered in the period. Documentary evidence reveals that this building formerly incorporated a complete residence, including a hall and kitchen. It also shows that the red brick façade covered in diaper was further coloured by the application of 200 pounds of red ochre in 1475. As originally finished, the gatehouse must have glowed brilliantly within the castle complex. In a world familiar with buildings finished with shades of whitewash, one appeal of brick was its strong colour. Two seventeenth-century drawings of the castle by John Aubrey show that its original windows were small and regularly set.

point of reference in a contract with a carpenter regarding the construction of the bishop's school at Wainfleet, Lincolnshire. Besides dating the gatehouse, the contract of 1484 is fascinating for the light it sheds on the bishop's working practices as an architectural patron.

Prior to the contract being drawn up, one of the bishop's agents in Lincolnshire, the master of Tatter-shall College, John Gygur, sent a memorandum to the bishop about the school building. In this he observes that the schoolhouse did not need to be very grand and that the craftsman who had engaged to build it, therefore, might be shown 'an example of sum maner [of] house in your nobyl place of Ascher [Esher] that may be example to hym for I remember ye have many dyverse houses of mene byldyng in the same that wold be convenient and acordyng to your entent'.[77] The use of the Esher gatehouse as a point of reference in the ensuing contract of 1484 suggests that the carpenter did visit Esher and looked at the gatehouse with his patron, exactly as Gygur suggested.[78] In view of the visit, it can be no coincidence that the school eventually took the form of a diminutive brick gatehouse, although one without battlements or arrow loops.

Indeed, only in its lack of the architectural trappings of fortification is this building in anyway – to borrow Gygur's word – 'mean'.

Plans and drawings made of Esher by John Aubrey in 1673 show that the residence not only comprised the surviving twin-towered gatehouse but also a turreted curtain wall and a great tower, all apparently of brick (pl. 299).[79] Beside the tower there stood a hall with a great timber roof supported on the backs of angels and a timber-frame gallery that offered prospects over the River Thames. This latter structure was of sufficient grandeur to be coveted by Cardinal Wolsey in the next reign and was carted off to adorn Hampton Court.

Waynflete was by no means alone among bishops in this period in creating residences in the form of castles with massive gatehouses and great towers. In exactly the same period, for example, the manor house of the bishops of Lincoln at Buckden, Huntingdonshire, was transformed by two men also renowned for their patronage of learning (pl. 300). Thomas Rotherham, who occupied the see of Lincoln from 1472 to 1480, has been credited on the authority of John Leland, writing in the 1540s, for building a great tower here.[80]

298 A 1960s photograph of the brick gatehouse at Esher, Surrey, with its bold and varied diaper ornament. The gatehouse is the only substantial surviving element of Waynflete's residence built by 1484. It was refenestrated and internally reworked by William Kent in 1729, who also added the porch shown in this view. The medieval lierne vault over the entrance passage still survives. It is ornamented with classical detailing that was presumably added by Kent. John Aubrey, visiting in the late seventeenth century, recorded that Waynflete's arms were previously carved both on the front of the gatehouse and on the internal vault of its entrance passage. He also noted that the building was crowned by a machicolis and that the gate was protected by a portcullis. There are also shallow, projecting towers to the rear.

Quite possibly the money for this was provided in part by the generous pension he received from the French king after Picquigny in 1475. Whatever the case, one ceiling in the tower is decorated with the arms of his successor to the see, John Russell (d. 1494), who evidently completed the work.[81] Russell additionally enclosed the site within a battlemented wall and added other buildings in brick with superb decoration in diaper and glazed brick. Rotherham also renovated Newark, the ancient castle of the bishops of Lincoln.[82]

It was in this period that the see of Canterbury was occupied by one of its greatest building archbishops. John Morton had spent his early career in the service of the Lancastrian cause and had even accompanied Henry VI and Margaret of Anjou in their two unsuccessful invasions of Northumberland. After the death of Henry VI, however, he came to terms with the Yorkist regime and rose sufficiently high in Edward IV's service to be made bishop of Ely in 1478. During his short period in office he repaired Wisbech Castle in Cambridgeshire (now lost) and extensively rebuilt the bishop's residence at Hatfield, Hertfordshire. The surviving hall range at Hatfield is brick-built, its masonry richly inlaid with diaper decoration. In 1483, upon the accession of Richard III, his fortunes were rapidly reversed. He was arrested with Lord Hastings and after a period of imprisonment escaped to the Continent. There he plotted the return of Henry Tudor and secured papal support for both the Tudor invasion and the king's subsequent marriage to Elizabeth of York.[83] His rewards were in proportion to his achievements.

On 6 October 1486 he was translated at royal behest to the vacant see of Canterbury, which he was to occupy for the next fourteen years. In addition, he became chancellor on 6 March 1487 and in 1493 was made a cardinal. One of the wealthiest men in England, he built in a similar fashion to his peers at Winchester and Lincoln. He chose for his master mason one of the outstanding figures of late medieval English architecture, John Wastell, the future designer of the celebrated fan vaults in the chapel of King's College, Cambridge. The full extent of Wastell's involvement in Morton's building is difficult to assess, though in the 1490s he was explicitly referred to as the archbishop's mason. Allowing for the use of drawings and the example set by figures such as Henry Yevele, he could quite convincingly have had a hand in them all.[84]

Morton's greatest undertaking in the archdiocese was the erection of a great new tower over the crossing of his metropolitan church, the present Bell Harry.

299 A view and plan of Esher, Surrey, by John Aubrey in 1673 (Oxford, Bodleian Library, MS Aubrey 4, fols 45r and 45br). Dominating the view are the great tower (1) and gatehouse (2), the latter with a richly detailed chimney. The kitchen is also visible (9). Aubrey wrote (fol. 48r): 'Eshur-place lies low at the foot of a steepe hill northward: it is a stately pile and strongly built of brick in the Gothig Architecture; a castle-like palace . . . In the hall windows this motto *Est Deo Gratia* and in the . . . the hall [roof] (as in Westminster hall) angels carved in wood susteyning the scutcheons: two are with scrolls scilicet *tibi Xsti.*' The plan shows the great tower – described as 'a kind of keep' – (1) and gatehouse 'with portcullis and hollow battlement' to the bottom right (2). Beside the former is the hall (3). The plan is also annotated with the words court (4), terrace (5), garden (6), little court (7), timber built lodging (8), buttery kitchens (9) and 'lodgings castle like but not so high as a . . . [*sic*]' (10).

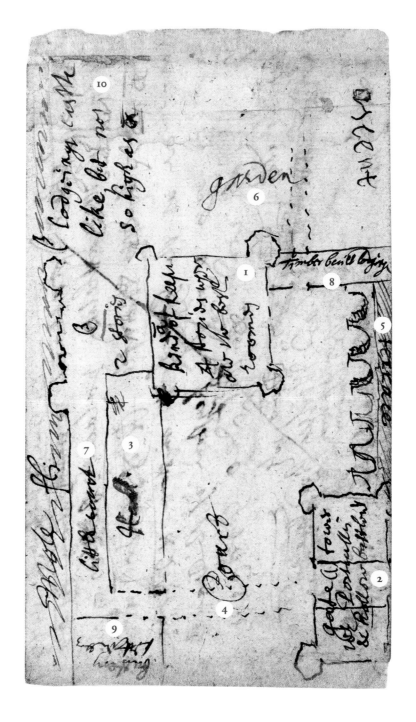

300 A view of Buckden, Huntingdonshire, a residence of the bishops of Lincoln. Thomas Rotherham, also an important benefactor of Cambridge University, began the great tower in the 1470s. The work was completed by his successor to the see, John Russell (d. 1494), who enclosed the site within a battlemented wall and built the present gatehouse. His arms appear on the left-hand gable in a mixture of glazed and orange bricks and stone. The fullest account of the medieval buildings is supplied by a parliamentary survey dated April 1647. It names the tower the 'King's Lodgings' and shows that demolition work during the Commonwealth and in 1839 and 1871 has reduced to nothing the residential buildings at its foot. These included an aisled hall, a cloister, a great chamber and a chapel. The wider setting of the residence, including the layout of gardens and fishponds, is outstandingly well preserved.

At the same time, however, he was involved in improving numerous of the residences owned by the archbishops of Canterbury, including Knole, Croydon, Maidstone and Charing. In addition he completely rebuilt Ford, Kent, now demolished. This building is known from a seventeenth-century survey and drawing to have possessed a great tower of brick with five storeys of well-appointed lodging chambers for his household.[85] Meanwhile, at Lambeth, Surrey, he erected the great gatehouse that still serves as the main entrance to the archbishop's palace (pl. 301). Built in brick with diaper patterns and stone detailing, this battlemented, asymmetrically planned, twin-towered gatehouse is directly comparable to Waynflete's work at Farnham. Viewed from across the Thames, it completes the visual illusion that Lambeth is an impressively fortified residence with an encircling ring of rectangular towers.

The gatehouse of
Lambeth, Surrey, is perhaps
the most important surviving
domestic building begun by
John Morton, archbishop of
Canterbury. It was probably
built in the 1490s under the
direction of the archbishop's
mason, John Wastell. The
gatehouse is constructed of
brick with stone detailing and
the masonry is decorated with
diaper patterns. It gave the
public river frontage of his
London palace the character
of a quadrangular castle.
Contained within its
asymmetric plan were lodging
chambers for senior members
of the household and also the
Prerogative Court of
Canterbury, where until 1858
wills for much of the
kingdom were proved. The
courtroom door employs a
form of bulbous moulding
that enjoyed popularity in a
series of buildings ultimately
descended from Eton.

Morton's funerary monument in Canterbury Cathedral crypt, as well as two of the buildings he worked on – Knole and Lambeth – preserve an extremely unusual bulbous moulding of a kind that looks back to Henry VI's works at Eton of the 1440s (and also such derived buildings as the great hall at Eltham). It is just possible that this detail was born of a direct but complex connection between Wastell and the Eton works. Early in his career, Wastell was in partnership with a senior mason called Simon Clerk. He also later superseded Clerk at the plum post of master mason of Bury St Edmunds Abbey. Clerk is first documented in 1434 helping the master mason of Westminster Abbey carve an image niche on a tower at Lambeth Palace. And from 1453 to 1461 he served as the master mason of Eton.[86] There is no clear proof that Wastell trained under Clerk, but some connection of this kind would help explain the Eton-style mouldings in Morton's work and also the interest at Ford in contrasting stone and brick construction.

Only one other English see could rival the works of Canterbury, Winchester and Lincoln. Richard Fox, one of Henry VII's most able and industrious servants, was enthroned bishop of Durham on 23 July 1495. Over the next six years he undertook a wide variety of

works to the castle buildings there, which included the reorganisation of the hall with a single dais in conventional fashion:

> Out of a great vast Hall in the castle there, [he] did take as much away as made a fair Buttery and a Pantry, even to the Pulpits or Galleries on each side of the Hall, wherein the Trumpeters of Wind-music used to stand to play while the Meat was usher'd in: And on the wall, which parted the said Buttery from the Hall was a great Pelican sett up, to show that it was done by him, because he gave the Pellican to his arms.[87]

The trumpet lofts, which were possibly built by him, still survive above the screens passage but the figure of the pelican is sadly lost.

At the same time a new series of service chambers and lodgings was created at the southern end of the great hall at Durham. This is one of the most complete survivals of its kind from the period, though some parts of it were regrettably lost in alterations during the 1990s. A timber-frame servery court beside the hall gave access to all the principal offices of the kitchen, including an accounting chamber and bakehouse.[88] The great kitchen itself is dominated by two large fireplaces with battlemented overmantels in brick, a very unusual material in the region at the time. Writing to Fox around 1500, Lord Darcy could scarcely contain his enthusiasm for this interior: 'My lord, both I and my lady was in all your new works at Durham, and verily they are of the most goodly and best cast that I have seen after my poor mind, and in especial your kitchen passeth all other.'[89] Over the hatches between the kitchen and servery are inscribed the words of a grace to bless the food that passes over them and also a date, 1499.

The date is significant: it was in 1499 that Bishop Fox successfully concluded a perpetual peace in the north of England sealed by the marriage of Henry VII's daughter, Margaret, and James IV of Scotland. The treaty was the result of several years of diplomacy. In 1494 one of the pretenders to the English throne, Perkin Warbeck, was welcomed into the Scottish court. The ensuing hostilities with England culminated in an invasion during August 1497. James IV's army was checked at Norham, where the ever-efficient Fox had prepared the castle for an assault. He was, in fact, well experienced in such work, having organised an invasion of France in 1492 and supervised the refortification of Calais at the king's command. Encouraged by the personal presence of the bishop, and despite the deployment of guns by the Scots, the castle successfully resisted attack for two weeks. An English army relieved Norham on its way into Scotland and on 30 September 1497 Fox concluded a seven-year truce at Ayton. In 1499, after yet more manoeuvring, he succeeded in extending this Scottish truce. To celebrate the occasion a great feast was held in the castle at Durham.[90] Evidently the building works in the kitchens were also pushed forward to accommodate it.

But not all of Fox's building at Durham was brought to completion. He also began to reorder the great tower on the motte with a kitchen, hall and withdrawing chambers, an undertaking cut short by his translation to Winchester, the richest see in England. Previously disappointed of promotion to Canterbury, Fox allegedly commented smugly: 'whereas the archbishop had a higher seat, Winchester was more succulent'.[91] As bishop of Winchester, he is most celebrated today as a statesman, scholar and the founder of Corpus Christi College, Oxford. Like Waynflete before him, however, he undertook important works at Winchester Cathedral. He also continued at Farnham Castle the works he had left off at Durham, reordering the great tower on the motte with new residential apartments.

The building operations undertaken by bishops at the close of the fifteenth century laid the foundations for the next generation of grand domestic architecture in England. Part of their outstanding achievement was to complete the naturalisation of brick within the English architectural tradition. In the process, the buildings that informed their work in a technical and stylistic sense – namely Eton College and its associated circle of buildings – became established as fundamental points of reference for the next generation of masons. The great brick palaces begun in the two decades following Henry VII's death by Archbishop Warham in 1514–18 at Otford, Kent, and Cardinal Wolsey at Hampton Court, Middlesex, further developed this tradition. Yet the end of the architectural pre-eminence of bishops was at hand. The reign of his son, Henry VIII, was to witness political, social and religious upheavals that were irrevocably to change their place in English society.

OXBURGH AND HADLEIGH DEANERY

In a chapter dominated by great buildings, it is appropriate to turn at the conclusion to see how the forms of castle architecture were perpetuated in more modest residences. Oxburgh in Norfolk is amongst the most celebrated works of late medieval domestic architecture in England. Under construction in 1482 by Sir Edmund Bedingfeld, the young heir to substantial estates in East Anglia, this magnificent brick building presents an intriguing challenge to conventional categories of architecture (pl. 302). Its generally accepted title since the eighteenth century as a 'hall' is an acknowledgement that Oxburgh has long served as a comfortable and well-appointed residence. The fortifications it displays and the moat that encircles the building, however, would seem to belie a merely domestic label. That these were an important element of the design is not merely demonstrated by their prominence in architectural terms but also by the provision in 1482 of a royal licence to crenellate the manor here. On the face of it, a fortified building should be a castle, but in this case the fortifications are just too cosmetic to be functional and scholars have baulked at according it this title.

The conventional way out of this problem is simply to say that Oxburgh is lightly fortified to resist the types of low-level violence that are well documented

302 (*facing page*) Oxburgh, Norfolk, under construction in 1482 by Sir Edmund Bedingfeld. The brick gatehouse is decorated with diaper decoration and tiers of panelling. Internally, the walls are lined out in white to suggest perfectly laid brick masonry, a decorative finish common in brick buildings from the 1440s onwards. Each parapet of the gatehouse was formerly crowned by a centrally placed pair of chimneys, an enrichment now lost. Over the gateway is a broach machicolis and arch. At the rear angles of the gate is a pair of projecting corner turrets.

303 The brick gatehouse of the Deanery at Hadleigh, Suffolk, erected by the successful Yorkist clergyman William Pykenham (d. 1497). There are rich diaper decorations in the brick on each face of the building, clear evidence that – contrary to what is sometimes suggested – the gatehouse was intended to be free-standing. The central windows have been substantially restored but the remainder of the fabric is remarkably well preserved. In contrast to its counterpart at Oxburgh, the gatehouse at Hadleigh possesses no arrow or gun loops. The omission is probably deliberate and reflects the character of its owner as a priest.

304 (*facing page*) The gatehouse of Giffords Hall, Suffolk, probably built before 1520. The habit of aggrandising residences by the addition of new gatehouses was widespread in East Anglia in the fifteenth and sixteenth centuries. These buildings are commonly castle-like in character with turrets, battlements and chimneys. Much of the moulded and cut brickwork on this building was skimmed over with mortar to resemble stone, a finish still clearly visible, for example, around the windows. There is a false central chimney pot, evidence for the enthusiasm for busy parapets.

in this period. It is, in effect, a domestic residence that is conceding to the contemporary need for defence. Implicit in this judgement is the idea that fortification was undesirable, a metaphorical ball and chain on the ankle of domestic architecture that restricted imaginative and luxurious building. Viewed in these terms, Oxburgh is a vestige of a vanishing age, its flamboyant fortifications almost self-conscious of their obsolescence in an increasingly peaceful kingdom. Yet charting the decline of the castle in a building like Oxburgh is completely to miss the point. The wealthy in late fifteenth-century England were not attempting to leave the trappings of fortification behind. These symbols of feudal power remained central to their identity and the social order they served. Arguably, this aspiration underpins the entire history of domestic architecture for the ensuing century.

An insight into just how modulated and self-conscious such play on fortifications might be, moreover, is provided by a contemporary gatehouse closely related in architectural terms to that at Oxburgh. The incumbent of the valuable rectory of Hadleigh, Suffolk, from 1470, and the archdeaconry of Suffolk from 1472, was a certain William Pykenham, a man with impeccable Yorkist connections that would undoubtedly have brought him a bishopric but for the fall of the dynasty in 1485.[92] Following the example of other rich secular and ecclesiastical patrons, he chose to aggrandise his residence at Hadleigh with a new gatehouse in fashionable brick (pl. 303). The building he created, probably soon after 1472, is superbly detailed with cut and moulded brick and its busy outline is

enlivened by a chimney and battlements. There also survive on each elevation traces of diapering patterns, sure evidence that it was intended as a free-standing structure. The addition of a brick gatehouse to earlier buildings in this way is widely paralleled across the region, as at Giffords Hall in Suffolk, built before 1520 (pl. 304). Contrary to what is generally assumed, therefore, there is no reason to think that Pykenham intended to rebuild the whole residence at this date.

Internally, the gatehouse incorporates a porter's lodge and two comfortable upper chambers, one served by a chapel. Within the principal chamber there is a fine fireplace with an overmantel that preserves an extraordinary seventeenth-century interior view of the neighbouring church, perhaps the successor to an earlier wall painting in this space. The vaulting forms and painted decoration of the gatehouse compare in all points to those found at Oxburgh, and in one of the corner turrets there is a dovecote, a symbol of lordly rights in the manor. In every respect, Pykenham was appropriating to himself the forms of lordship. Yet in one detail the building differs from Oxburgh: it possesses neither arrow or gun loops nor a machicolis. Not all of Pykenham's fellow churchmen shared such architectural restraint, but this gatehouse could be read as a symbol of lordship couched in the idiom of a castle but bereft of the essential trappings of war.

Oxburgh and Hadleigh illustrate the sophisticated ways in which castle architecture was developing by the close of the fifteenth century. The gathering storm of a social and religious revolution, however, was to open its forms to yet more inventive exploration.

14

THE RENAISSANCE CASTLE

HENRY VIII

With the accession of Henry VIII to the throne on 22 April 1509, this narrative arrives at what is conventionally regarded as the threshold of the early modern age in England. And this period does feel in so many ways like a new beginning. Over the course of the ensuing reign, the institutions of the medieval church were overthrown and the effects of the Renaissance in learning and art become fully apparent in England. Henry VIII, unlike so many of his royal ancestors, looms out of the past as a real personality. So too do the figures of his court: Wolsey, the proud cardinal of popular imagination; Thomas Cromwell, the Machiavellian architect of the Reformation; Thomas More, the statesman saint; and the king's six wives, from the formidable Katherine of Aragon to the Reforming enthusiast Katherine Parr. Moreover, these figures and the issues they confronted on the public stage continue to resonate in the modern world: does it lie within the power of the state to command not merely the loyalty of its people but also their beliefs? As a final and compelling touch, the brush of Hans Holbein has reared so many characters from this lost world into living beings that we can recognise today, from the imperious figure of the king himself to Lady Guildford, confident and amused in her portrait sketch.

Yet to what extent were such novelties perceived by contemporaries? The question is important because there is a long tradition of English historical writing that has sought to contrast the medieval and Tudor worlds specifically as a means of highlighting the achievements of the latter. According to this analysis, the medieval world and its trappings fell away in the course of Henry VIII's reign (1509–47). In their place there became established in embryo the social, political and religious institutions of modern Britain. One notable victim of this analysis has been the castle. Inextricably bound up with noble identity, castles have been presented as thwarting the process of centralised government. They have, therefore, been categorised as medieval buildings and, by extension, as structures with no place in the brave new world of Tudor England. The fact that castles manifestly continued to be occupied, developed and even built afresh, in as far as it has been acknowledged at all, has been largely treated as a curiosity.

Explanation for the persistent importance of these buildings is to be found in one of the overarching continuities that link what have become firmly established as the discrete middle and early modern 'ages'. Despite the massive political and religious changes witnessed

Facing page: Lullingstone, Kent.

in this period, the English nobility continued to define itself as a body with a military vocation, enriched by the possession of land and distinguished by its ancestry. The pre-eminent architectural symbol of this noble order, the castle, continued in consequence to enjoy enormous prestige. Old and new families competed to control ancient castles and the great landed endowments that went with them. And where monastic buildings were converted to secular use, or new residences were erected on the proceeds of church spoil, they commonly made architectural play with the long-established trappings of fortification: gatehouses, towers, turrets, battlements and arrow or cannon loops. The history of the castle and its architecture in England was very far from over either in 1509 or at Henry's death in 1547.

There also survived through this period the practices of the medieval architectural tradition. Just as medieval and Tudor society have been contrasted so as to set off the latter to advantage, so have their arts. Henry VIII's reign is commonly characterised as Renaissance, a word that literally translates as 'the rebirth'. As a term of art, this is properly a modern usage of the word: it was first applied in the mid-nineteenth century to describe a cultural movement within certain Italian city states from the fifteenth century; a movement that was concerned with the exploration and revival of classical antiquity. This is in contrast to the usage of the celebrated historian of the Renaissance arts, Giorgio Vasari (d. 1574), who in effect used the word *rinascita* to underline the novelty of the work he described and emphasise its quality by connection to antiquity.[1] In the sixteenth century the Renaissance was first and foremost an intellectual movement, its ideas being introduced across northern Europe by scholarly intercourse and fuelling the debates of the Reformation. Its associated artistic forms, however, appear to have been disseminated as a result of the wars fought in Italy by French and Imperial forces from the 1490s onwards.

One manifestation of Renaissance influence was the emergence of what was clearly recognised by contemporaries as a new departure in the arts. Just as the Gothic aesthetic had looked startlingly different to the men and women of Europe around 1200, so did this new fashion inspired by the arts and achievements of ancient Rome seem fresh and exciting to their successors around 1500. The reception of these ideas in England was almost entirely mediated at first through the French court, which had emerged by the early six-teenth century as a much greater, wealthier and more sophisticated institution than its English counterpart. It deserves emphasis that as a borrowed style from this powerful neighbour, the Renaissance in England bears very close comparison to that of every other major artistic movement considered in this book: with the fifteenth-century reception of ideas from the court of Burgundy; or with Gothic forms from the thirteenth-century French court; or the Romanesque of Normandy in the eleventh century.

So, too, with one point of exception, did the manner of its absorption into the architectural tradition resemble those of earlier artistic movements. English patrons and masons were concerned by novelty in art and architecture, not the pursuit of foreign influence as such. What they did, therefore, was to apply Renaissance ornament to what were otherwise wholly conventional buildings in the Perpendicular idiom. The extent to which this process was cosmetic is reflected in the continued dominance of English masons in the oversight of new architectural projects. Where the Renaissance perhaps differed from its forebears, however, was the degree to which foreigners were valued and employed to create fittings of all kinds for the same operations, from painting to panelling. The most fashionable Tudor residences might have been built by Englishmen but they were hung with textiles from Italy and the Low Countries, wainscoted by Germans, glazed by Flemings, and painted or plastered by Frenchmen.

It was possible for the Renaissance to be so cosmetic because – although it might come with a complex package of associated ideas – to all intents and purposes it was quite crudely understood by most English men and women. Indeed, it is scarcely an oversimplification to say that in artistic terms it comprised three admired finishes. The first of these was marbling. Marble began to intrude itself everywhere in grand domestic buildings in the Tudor period. Real and fictional representations of the material were applied to walls, panelling and floors. Often combined with such displays was 'grotesque' or 'antique' work, the second finish. This was a genre of art inspired by the painted decoration discovered within the buried ruins or 'grottos' of classical buildings in Rome. It combined animal and vegetable forms to create playful and fantastical images. One of the great strengths of antique work was that it was without strict rules of application and could therefore be adapted to suit circumstances.

These two finishes alone were incorporated into early Tudor classical ornament. By the late sixteenth century, however, a third finish also became very fashionable. Cartouche work is a style of classical decoration that incorporates figures, architectural detail and a distinctive type of framing termed strapwork (it has the appearance of a broad leather belt twisted and curled around each panel of decoration). This first appeared in England in the 1540s, notably in Henry VIII's palace of Nonsuch in Surrey, but it was further popularised in England through the importation of engravings from the Low Countries. It is a mark of how little troubled contemporaries were by categories and styles of art that this finish was also often described as antique work. Modern scholarship is more exacting.[2]

It is this simplistic grasp of what characterised classical art and architecture for a Tudor audience that helps explain what has conventionally been seen as a problem: why did English patrons and masons, once they had been introduced to the Renaissance, take so long to adopt its forms in a systematic way? The answer lies in their interests. Classicism as learnt, say, from the pages of architectural treatises, such as that produced by the sixteenth-century Vincentian architect Andrea Palladio, is a style of paradigm with correct and incorrect ways of doing things. There had always been proprieties in Romanesque and Gothic architecture, but they were styles of experiment. Until practitioners and patrons were taught to think otherwise, the pursuit of classical forms in England was not bound up with an interest in formal design but novelty and fantasy.

THE COURT AND THE YOUNG KING

Upon his father's death Henry VIII was just seventeen years old, and a council of elder statesmen was hastily convened to determine how he should be treated henceforth. They agreed 'to bring him up in all pleasure for otherwise he might grow up too hard among his subjects as the king his father did'.[3] It was a decision that was entirely to change the face of the court. The young king wanted to enjoy himself with contemporaries and quickly gathered to himself a group of playfellows. These individuals soon invaded the so-called privy apartments, where the king slept and spent his time beyond the public eye. By this change, menial roles previously undertaken by servants around the king were transformed into politically powerful posts. The gentlemen of the privy chamber, as they were known from 1518 onwards, attended the king in his principal withdrawing apartments and became a body of great influence. At their head was the groom of the privy stool, whose responsibilities to attend the king whenever he relieved himself gave unparalleled and regular opportunity to call royal attention to personal concerns or political matters.

The intrigue of the privy chamber lent to the politics of Henry VIII's reign a quality of peculiar and extreme ruthlessness. For those successful within it, it also offered sufficient income to build. Sir William Compton (d. 1528), for example, the first groom of the privy stool, accumulated the wealth to build a new seat for himself at Compton Wynyates, Warwickshire, probably in the 1510s. This building answers the popular ideal of the Tudor residence, what might be termed the domesticated castle: a rambling building, busy with battlements and chimneys and dominated by a tower (pl. 305). Curiously, Compton Wynyates is reported to have cannibalised the materials of an early fifteenth-century castle at Fulbrook.[4]

Henry VIII never showed much enthusiasm for the business of state and his willingness to delegate responsibility for it created over the course of the reign two brilliant royal servants: Cardinal Wolsey (d. 1530) and Thomas Cromwell (d. 1540). It was a mark of Henry's character that both men fell spectacularly from power, essentially victims of the king's involved marital affairs. Their joint achievement was to bring the resources of the whole realm, including those of the church and the nobility, under royal control to an unprecedented degree. In this sense, Henry VIII's rule witnessed under a completely different guise the continued centralisation of government that had been begun by his father. The crucial episode in this process, and one that touched every aspect of life in the realm, was the assault on the wealth of the church from 1534 in the context of the European Reformation. In the process there was established the foundation of a political settlement that would last until the Civil War. As will become apparent, it also brought about a transformation in the practice and patronage of architecture.

Until the 1530s Henry was more concerned with winning prestige for himself as a soldier and statesman in Europe than with building. Not only were all the principal residences he used inherited from his father, but by harnessing the resources of the crown, Wolsey became the foremost patron of architecture in the

305 The rambling outline of Compton Wynyates in Warwickshire in 1915. The buildings cannibalised materials from the brick and stone castle built by John, duke of Bedford (d. 1435), at Fulbrook. This stood within sight of Warwick, just three and a half miles from the town. In 1462 the earl of Warwick got control of Fulbrook, but from 1478, following the death of the duke of Clarence, it passed to the crown and was neglected. Sir William got permission from Henry VIII to demolish it and reused the materials at his own new residence, probably in the 1510s. Whether any architectural features of Fulbrook were recycled as complete entities will never be known, but the possibility is intriguing. The house is dominated by a tower in the manner of a castle.

kingdom. The degree to which Henry VII's palace of Richmond, in particular, remained the measure of grand architecture for the first two decades of the new reign is strikingly illustrated by its use as a model by Wolsey for his greatest proposed work: a new Oxford college called Cardinal College, now Christ Church, begun in January 1525.[5]

The one significant, early work of castle building undertaken by Henry VIII was similarly informed by the previous generation of fine architecture. In 1509–10 Henry began a stone gatehouse for the lower ward of his principal seat, Windsor Castle. This new building was known as the Exchequer because it served as the seat of administration for the honour of Windsor, an illustration of the continued connection between gatehouses and the exercise of feudal rights (pl. 306).[6] It was designed with paired polygonal towers of different sizes on its inner and outer faces. This distinctive form can not only be found in earlier buildings – such as the gatehouse of Oxburgh, erected around 1482 (see pl. 302) – but also in several early sixteenth-century buildings. One such is the gatehouse at Lullingstone, Kent, probably built in the 1510s as part of the wider remodelling of the castle (pl. 307).

None of these gatehouses – Oxburgh, Lullingstone or Windsor – is likely to be copied from either of the others. Nor is there any reason to suppose that they were designed or executed by the same craftsmen: by this stage the monopoly on architectural expertise within the royal works that caused the rash of Ton-bridge-style gatehouses in the thirteenth century had long passed. What their similarity of design suggests instead is that their different masons had access to a common design for a gatehouse which they realised independently. In this case, the probability must be that all three designs were drawn up by masons engaged from, or with contacts in, the long-standing centre of artistic production in the kingdom: London. This point is worth exploring for a moment.

To understand developments in fine architecture across the kingdom in the sixteenth century it is necessary to appreciate the central importance of London craftsmen, as well as the dependence of this London circle of masons on the architecture of the king's works in the fifteenth century. As the gatehouses of Windsor and Lullingstone are prefigured in Oxburgh, so are Tudor buildings more generally informed by an earlier generation of buildings for their inspiration: the king's works of the Lancastrian court. One of the most important stock designs of the period, for example, is the Herstmonceux-type façade with its symmetrical rhythm of elements: tower, turret, gatehouse, turret,

404

306 A view of Henry VIII's Gate, Windsor, Berkshire. The gatehouse was built in 1509–10 and known after its function in the administration of the honour as The Exchequer. It is symmetrically planned and incorporates a large pair of polygonal towers projecting forwards and a small internal pair of turrets with stairs to the rear. Above the gateway, which was formerly approached over a drawbridge, is a panel with the royal arms and above this a machicolated parapet decorated with Tudor badges. Over the course of the nineteenth century the building was much altered: the gate passage was vaulted, the walls refaced and new windows inserted.

tower. As will become apparent, façades of this kind were legion in England until the last quarter of the sixteenth century. Presumably the London masons who copied the type so widely had access directly or at a remove to the drawing archive of the king's works of Henry VI's reign.

Just like his predecessors and nobility, Henry VIII lived a peripatetic lifestyle.[7] Outside the core of royal residences that he most regularly visited in the south-east of England, there was no regular programme of maintenance. Consequently, between stays even the grandest might run to ruin. Some sense of this pattern of neglect followed by urgent repair is illustrated by Kenilworth, which in 1524 was identified by Henry VIII as one of three 'auncyent castels' in royal ownership that should be maintained 'for our resorte and pleasur'.[8] Even so, the repairs at Kenilworth were restricted to rare visits by the king. They were also undertaken with a strict eye to economy. In 1524 itself, Henry v's Pleasance was moved from its place beside the Mere to the outer court of the castle, presumably as a means of providing cheap extra accommodation. There followed more repairs in timber frame, including the reconstruction of the royal lodgings along the east side of the inner court in the years 1530–32. For the glazing of the building 1,040 feet of glass ornamented with the king's badges was brought from London.[9] A survey of around 1545 observed that these buildings could be more appropriately reconstructed in stone taken from the nearby priory at Kenilworth, then recently suppressed.[10] Whether this work was ever undertaken is not known.

THE NORTH AND THE BATTLE OF FLODDEN

It was not until 1513 that Henry VIII was able to arrange his first war. Acting in alliance with the emperor, Maximilian I, who shamelessly manipulated his youthful enthusiasm, the twenty-two-year-old king set out to win himself glory in France. Two years of campaigning brought few rewards, however, and the highpoint of the fighting came with the capture of the town of Thérouanne (Pas-de-Calais) and a cavalry skirmish outside it called the battle of the Spurs (which Henry missed). Henry proudly presented the town to the emperor, who promptly instructed that it be razed to the ground. The site of its cathedral church is still a field.

These events remained forever green in Henry's memory and were recalled with advantages long after the event, as in 1527, for example, when he received a

307 (*facing page*) The interior façade of the main gatehouse of Lullingstone, Kent, probably built in the 1510s by the courtier Sir John Peche (d. 1522) as part of his wider remodelling of the castle. The plan of the gatehouse is very similar to that of Henry VIII's Gate at Windsor but it is notionally reversed. That is to say, if Windsor is the correct way round with its large towers facing outwards and the smaller turrets inwards, then Lullingstone is back to front with its large towers on the interior and the smaller on the exterior.

French delegation at Greenwich. The entrance to the banqueting house where they were to be entertained – a space like the backstage or tiring house of a theatre that was dressed up for special occasions – was decked up in the form of a triumphal arch with a depiction of 'the battle of Thérouanne' on its reverse. This arrangement allowed Henry to welcome the ambassadors, walk them familiarly into the building and then ask them to turn around. The ambassadors were discomfited by the scene they viewed, doubtless magnified as a French disaster, and Henry was vastly amused. The painter of the lost scene was Hans Holbein.[11]

Acting as an ally of France and taking advantage of Henry VIII's absence, James IV of Scotland invaded England in August 1513. His large army advanced immediately to Norham, where the castle was captured after a short siege: the outworks fell quickly but the great tower was held by the garrison for six days.[12] Following its surrender, the Scots went on to capture Wark, Ford and Etal nearby. In these encounters, the Scottish artillery, perhaps including Mons Meg, now preserved at Edinburgh Castle, proved particularly effective. An English response was mobilised under the command of Thomas Howard, earl of Surrey. For the last time in history, the knights of Durham collected the banner of St Cuthbert from the shrine of the cathedral priory and marched to war. The two armies met at Flodden, and in the ensuing battle James IV was killed and the Scots routed. For the English the battle provided glory for everyone. St Cuthbert was particularly represented as the victor of the field and his shrine was additionally decked for the future by the royal banner of Scotland.[13] Meanwhile, several leaders of the English army – rather like their predecessors after Neville's Cross in 1346 – began to build.

For all its completeness as a victory, the Scottish threat was not removed by Flodden. First amongst the buildings to be restored, therefore, were the strategic castles damaged in the fighting. Amongst these was Norham, which was reported to be all but destroyed by the Scots. Work was immediately set in hand to repair it.[14] In the surviving accounts for 1514–15 payment was made to the master mason of 'Durham Abbey' (i.e. the cathedral priory), and it is almost certainly to him that the present form of Norham can be attributed.[15] At this date the office was probably filled by a certain Christopher Scune, who is first documented in 1505 as the mason in charge of the great spire of Louth, Lincolnshire. He was increasingly absent from Louth, however, probably as a result of his northern commitments, and abandoned the construction of the spire there in 1515. By this time he was not only active at Durham but also engaged in rebuilding the nave of Ripon Minster in Yorkshire.[16]

In 1521 Thomas, Lord Dacre, the warden of the march and the leading magnate in the region since Henry VIII's accession, wrote a note on the state of the Norham works. At this time the inner bailey with its great tower was completely restored so that 'with the help of God and the prayer of St Cuthbert it is impregnable'. Little progress had been made, however, on the repair of the outer bailey, though the lower stages of 'four new towers founded for bulwarks' had been erected along the line of the wall. There were sufficient cut stones in the castle, he reported, to complete at least three of these and perhaps all four. As the note makes explicit, these defences were intended for hand-guns and artillery as well as more conventional bows and crossbows.[17] It is a comment on the rapidly developing science of fortification that the defences in which Lord Dacre expressed such confidence were condemned in 1550, just thirty years later, because the towers provided one another with no supporting fire.[18]

Meanwhile, Lord Dacre himself was busy overseeing the repair of Wark for the crown. In 1517 he had requested the help of the master mason of Berwick to help devise fortifications on the site, and in 1519, by way of a plea for more money, he reported on the condition of the works. His principal creation was a 'dongeon' or great tower on the motte of the castle. If the king made up his budget to a full £700, he promised, it would be possible to complete the dungeon besides other towers, buildings and a great gatehouse three storeys high.[19]

Dacre was similarly active elsewhere for the king, notably at Carlisle, the seat of his wardenship. There is heraldic and anecdotal evidence likewise that he rebuilt Askerton and Drumburgh castles, the latter from stones taken from Hadrian's Wall.[20] In as far as the buildings can be reconstructed, their forms appear very conventional for the region with towers on rectangular plans connected by high ranges. To judge from his letters, Lord Dacre also resided regularly at Harbottle Castle, Northumberland. The summit of the motte here was enclosed by a wall set with small gun loops, probably a creation of this period.[21]

Besides repairing strategically important sites along the march with subventions of cash from the crown, both the bishop of Durham and Lord Dacre were concurrently developing other castles privately as major residences. At Naworth in Cumberland, for example, Lord Dacre extensively restored the buildings, an operation recorded by the appearance of his arms and initials in the fabric.[22] The nearby Augustinian monastery at Lanercost, where he eventually chose to be buried, similarly benefited from his attention and there survives an altarpiece almost certainly intended for the high altar of the priory church. This work in a German style bears the Dacre family arms and the date 1514, which may suggest that it was a thank-offering for Flodden. Lord Dacre's most important project, however, was the remodelling of Kirkoswald, Cumberland. Confusingly, the fittings of this castle were taken to repair Naworth between 1604 and 1624, and were then destroyed at their new home by fire in 1844. Within the embrace of the earlier fourteenth-century walls and towers at Kirkoswald were created a new hall, one of the largest in northern England, and a chapel, both with painted ceilings.[23]

Probably the only surviving elements from the lost interiors at Kirkoswald, and a testimony to their former opulence, is a group of wooden sculptures. Most celebrated are the four so-called Naworth Beasts. These giant figures of a bull, a griffin, a ram and a dolphin were designed as supporters for heraldic banners, though it is not known how they would have been arranged or placed. Examination of the figures in 1999 suggested that they were originally painted. It has also revealed that some of the timber used came from an exceptionally ancient oak tree, possibly one of some now-forgotten significance.[24] Rather more enigmatic is a group of small figures also cut in oak showing a group of men of different estate.[25] No precise parallels for this collection of sculpture survive, though they do clearly belong to a long northern tradition of prominent heraldic decoration in castle architecture stretching back to the fourteenth century in such buildings as Alnwick and Warkworth in Northumberland and Hylton in Co. Durham.

The bishop of Durham, meanwhile, was similarly active in his country residence at Auckland, Co. Durham. According to the Durham Chronicle, Bishop Ruthall gave instruction for a banqueting house to be erected here under the direction of a certain Stranwich. This must have been begun around 1520 because the operation was interrupted by Ruthall's death in 1523. It was sufficiently far advanced, however, for a successor, Cuthbert Tunstal, to finish easily after his succession to the see in 1530. Tunstal 'built a certain gate at Auckland, and where there is a chamber at the top for dining, he finished the upper part of a great window

as it had been designed by the sometime bishop Ruthall'.[26] Banqueting houses in this period usually took the form of free-standing towers, for example, those built at Hampton Court in 1538. The particular design of this chamber over a gate and with a large window, presumably of compass form, suggests a structure related to such surviving designs as the entrance of 1538 to Hengrave Hall in Suffolk, more of which below.

Lord Dacre and the bishop of Durham were the greatest patrons of castle architecture across the northern march in the first quarter of the sixteenth century, but they were not alone. Other significant builders in the region included the bishop of Carlisle, who restored Rose Castle in the 1520s, and Sir Edward Stanley, son of the earl of Derby. He was created Lord Mounteagle for his part at Flodden and soon afterwards established his dynastic seat at Hornby in Lancashire, a property long coveted by his powerful family. There he either rebuilt or repaired the great tower of the castle, affixing his arms to the base of the building. This is the only part of his castle that still survives, but the whole of it was described in a survey of the 1580s as 'very fair built, standing stately upon the top of a great hill' and was environed with two parks, a garden and an orchard.[27] To complement his seat, when Lord Mounteagle drew up his will in 1523 he was also planning a new chancel to the parish church in the village. This he exhorted his executors to finish, besides a small chantry foundation supporting two priests, a clerk, five bedesmen and a free school.[28]

One of Mounteagle's regional competitors for power and another veteran of Flodden was Henry Clifford (d. 1523), romantically dubbed the 'shepherd lord' in folklore for his supposed upbringing amongst rustics. The son of a loyal Lancastrian, Clifford succeeded in mending his fortunes in the service of the Tudor dynasty and emerged during Henry VII's reign as a dominant political figure in Yorkshire and Westmorland, where he controlled the honours of Brough, Brougham and Appleby. In reflection of his waxing power he was an active patron of religious houses, notably the charterhouse at Mount Grace and the Augustinian houses of Shap and Bolton. All his principal residences were castles, though there is little positive evidence for his occupation of these: Brough was burnt down after a Christmas feast in 1521 and Skipton housed a number of brass cannon that Clifford had captured on the field of Flodden: three of James IV's culverins known as 'The Seven Sisters', with barrels over 13 feet long and weighing over two tons apiece.

In this list of noblemen builders in the north is one prominent exception. Henry Algernon Percy, fifth earl of Northumberland (d. 1527), enjoyed one of the largest incomes of any peer in the realm, but he was politically marginalised in Northumberland by Lord Dacre. In response, he withdrew southwards to the fourteenth-century heartlands of Percy power in Yorkshire at Wressle and Leconfield. It would appear that both residences were substantially reworked internally by him, and some complete interiors from the former castle can be reconstructed from drawings and surviving fragments of panelling.[29] Leland enthusiastically described Wressle in 1540 as 'the most proper beyond Trent'. He notes that the base or outer court was timber-built, but his description of the inner court, which was laid out on a quadrangular plan, is worth quoting at length:

> The castelle it self is motid [moated] about on 3 partes. The 4 parte is dry where the entre is ynto the castlelle . . . In the castelle be only 5 towers, one at eche corner almost of like biggenes. The gatehouse is the 5., having fyve longginges [lodgings] yn hight, 3 of the other towers have 4 highes in Longginges: the 4 conteineth the botery, pantery, pastery, lardery, and kechyn. The haule and the great chaumbers be fair, and so is the chapelle and closettes . . . so were the gardeins withyn the mote, and the orchardes withoute. And in the orchardes were mountes *opere topiario* [topiary work] writhen about with degrees [steps] like turninges of cokilshilles [cockleshells].[30]

Two surviving books of household statutes from 1511 also show that the earl lived in appropriate and magnificent style. Nevertheless, it may be a mark of his undoubted political frustration that he embarked on no major building projects for which record survives.

When the earl died, his possessions were taken over by the crown, and in 1537 a royal officer admiringly described their extent. After complaining that he had never seen an inheritance more blemished by the folly of its late owner or the untruth of his servants, he wrote that: 'the honours and castles purporten such a majesty in themselves now being the king's as they are in manner as mirrors or glasses for the inhabitants 20 miles compass every way for them to look in and to direct themselves by'.[31] This judgement sums up the continued importance of castles as defining symbols of the realm and its landscape.

THE GROWTH OF THE PEERAGE

Henry VIII celebrated his victories against France and Scotland in time-honoured fashion by the creation of peers. On 1 February 1514 he promoted the marshals of his two armies to rival East Anglian dukedoms. These creations presaged a steady flow of titles that were massively to increase the ranks of the peerage during the reign and served to underpin a great deal of castle building. The victor of Flodden, Thomas Howard, was restored to the title of duke of Norfolk, which had been forfeit by his Yorkist father at Bosworth. At the same time he received a special addition to his coat of arms: the rampant lion of Scotland pierced in the throat by an arrow. Howard subsequently retired to Framlingham, Suffolk, the long-standing seat of the dukedom. There, as was appropriate for so celebrated a soldier and so grand a peer, he occupied a well-appointed residence arranged within the circuit of late twelfth-century castle walls. A surviving inventory taken at the duke's death in 1524 catalogues an impressive collection of furnishings within these lost buildings.[32]

At the same time Charles Brandon, the marshal of Henry VIII's army in France, was elevated to the dukedom of Suffolk, a title recently made available by the Tudor purge of the de la Pole family. Brandon's father had been killed while serving as Henry VII's standard-bearer at Bosworth, a sacrifice that assured him a good start at court. There he had become an intimate of the king as a superb jouster and had appeared in the lists for the coronation challenge in a suit of gilt armour. In France, he had played a significant role in the siege of Tournai and had been given the key of the city upon its surrender and the outlying castle of Mortain.[33] Brandon's dukedom initially came with the majority of the de la Pole estates, including Ewelme in Oxfordshire and the castles of Wingfield in Suffolk and Donnington in Berkshire, all of which he was to occupy and alter.

In 1515, however, Brandon's status changed again in the most remarkable way. In the spring of that year he was sent out to escort home Mary, the recently widowed sister of Henry VIII, who had been briefly married to the French king, Louis XII. While in Paris, at the eager entreaty of Mary herself, he agreed to become her husband. He later justified the act to a furious Henry VIII by explaining that he 'newar sawe woman soo wyepe'.[34]

The match transformed Suffolk's position. He was now not only directly allied to the royal family but also

– during periods of peace with France – enriched by his wife's dower payments amounting to £4,000 per annum. With this income, Suffolk engaged on a long series of new building projects to old and new residences. Amongst the first of these was the reconstruction of Suffolk Place in Southwark.[35] Work to this building was under way in 1518 under the direction of a clerk called Robert Hutton. It is probably a reflection of his French connections that this made use of a new development in brick-making technology introduced from Italy: terracotta. In essentials, terracotta was a means of creating delicately moulded architectural detail. The technique involved refining clay so that it could receive intricate impressions. Pieces of terracotta could be produced to almost any size. The result was a fashion for brick buildings finished with a truly spectacular mass of moulded and figural ornament.

Within a few years of completing Suffolk House, the duke began work to a new seat at Westhorpe in Suffolk, which incorporated the same materials in a more castle-like design. Westhorpe was demolished in the late eighteenth century, but the inner court is known to have been enclosed within a moat and possessed corner towers. Descriptions of the property record that it was battlemented, possessed fine chimneys and was entered through a gatehouse. The broad form of the façade may well have been similar to that of yet another residence he created at Henham, Suffolk, probably in the 1530s.[36]

Brandon's architectural activity in East Anglia was a spur to his chief rival in the area, the duke of Norfolk. The victor of Flodden was succeeded to the title by his son in 1524, and by 1526–7 the new duke was spending large sums on the construction of a residence in brick at Kenninghall, Norfolk. The new buildings, erected on an open site a short distance from the remains of an important castle on the manor, were commensurate in scale with some royal palaces. Today, only one subsidiary fragment of Kenninghall survives. The neighbouring church preserves pieces of terracotta from this period and it is a reasonable assumption, therefore, that the residence incorporated the material as well. Despite this new house, Framlingham Castle was not abandoned. Here the duke erected an armorial over the gate and laid out a half-moon barbican and bridge before it. As we shall see, it was from the safety of this castle in 1553 that Mary I would launch her bid for the throne of England.

THE MIDLANDS

In almost every region of England, familial rivalry encouraged very similar patterns of building. The three dominant families in the Midlands, for example, engaged in intense architectural competition over the 1520s. Thomas Grey, marquis of Dorset (d. 1530), shared with Charles Brandon the distinction of being one of the king's regular jousting partners. To this he added the advantage of close ties with Cardinal Wolsey, who may have taught him as a young boy. During the 1520s Thomas is credited by the Tudor antiquarian John Leland with having greatly expanded Bradgate, an encastellated mansion on the outskirts of Leicester. The ruins of Bradgate still survive in a superb parkland setting and their architectural quality speaks of the resources he enjoyed: they are built in diapered brick with stone detailing.

Thomas also worked on nearby Groby Castle. According to Leland, his father – also called Thomas (d. 1501) – had begun here: 'the fundation and waulles of a great gate house of brike, and a faire tour, but that was left half on finished of him, and so it standeth yet. This lorde Thomas erected also and almost finishid ij toures of brike in the front of the house, as respondent on eche side of the gatehouse.'[37]

Enough survives of this pre-1501 brick façade at Groby to be confident that it was regularly planned with the classic rhythm of elements: tower, turret, gatehouse, turret, tower. Thomas probably resumed his father's building operations at Groby but also laid out a new garden, filling in the moat around the motte 'to make an herbare there'. He must have become interested in the site just before his own death in 1530, because Leland describes all the works to the castle as incomplete. The creation of a castle garden around 1530 precisely reflects the contemporary activities of his local rivals.

Foremost of these was George, Lord Hastings, grandson of William Hastings (d. 1483), the builder of Ashby de la Zouch and Kirby Muxloe. Between the Greys and Hastings there raged an intense feud over the control of various Midland interests. So bitter was this rivalry that an altercation between family servants in Leicester in 1524 rapidly escalated into a major disturbance requiring royal intervention.[38] Hastings was desperately hungry for a title, which was finally granted on the eve of parliament in 1529. The earldom of Huntingdon was almost certainly offered by the king as encouragement for Hastings's support in the approaching trial of strength over the divorce with Katherine of Aragon. There is no documentary proof of the fact, but it is likely that Huntingdon completed his grandfather's castle at Ashby in brick at this time. Of the brick domestic buildings he probably created, no trace today remains, but his activity at the castle is suggested by the impressive surviving remains of the garden laid out immediately beneath his grandfather's great tower (pl. 308). The whole site was enclosed by a wall with a banqueting tower at each outer corner. These were battlemented structures on complex geometric plans, like compass windows.

The garden at Ashby may have been connected not only to the work of the marquis of Dorset at Groby and Bradgate but also by the activities of the third power in the area, Thomas Manners. Another of the king's young jousting companions, Thomas not only inherited a substantial landed interest in the Midlands based on Belvoir but also the barony of Roos, with extensive northern estates and the castle of Helmsley. Though he was politically active in the north, it was on the former castle that he appears to have focused his attention following his creation as first earl of Rutland in 1525. Belvoir had reputedly been deliberately ruined by William, Lord Hastings, in the 1460s as part of the Yorkist reorganisation of power in the Midlands.[39] To resurrect it as his seat, therefore, was to celebrate his return to regional power in architecture.

The repair of Belvoir was under way by 1528 and was completed by the son of the first earl. It continued to be one of the major residences of the Midlands and was further enlarged for numerous royal visits in the seventeenth century. A disastrous Civil War and a sumptuous reconstruction from 1800–c.1830 have rendered this building very problematic to reconstruct. A late sixteenth-century tapestry view suggests that it comprised a fortified court and a great tower set on a motte.[40] This would agree with Leland's description of 1540: 'In the castel be 2. faire gates. And the dongeoun is a fair rounde tour, now turnid to pleasure, as a place to walk yn, and to se the country aboute, and raylid aboute the round waull and, and a garden plot in the midle.'[41] From this description (and the tapestry illustration) it is clear that the great tower of Belvoir was not just a garden folly but remained the visual centrepiece to the castle. It also preserved its character as a fortification; just like the garden towers at Ashby de la Zouch, this was an important element of its appeal.

Political feuding aside, the bestowal of a peerage early in the reign encouraged at least one truly exceptional work of castle architecture. In February 1512 Margaret Pole, the daughter of George, duke of Clarence, was granted the lands and title of her brother, who had been executed by Henry VII in 1499 as a dynastic competitor to the throne. Restored to his possessions as countess of Salisbury in her own right in February 1512, she enjoyed unique powers for a Tudor woman and in architectural complement to her position built a seat at Warblington in Hampshire. Begun in 1517, this is the only castle of the English Middle Ages unambiguously created in its entirety by a woman (pl. 309). As adjuncts to the castle she also established an almshouse in the village and built an impressive chantry chapel, smothered in grotesque ornament, at the nearby Benedictine priory of Christchurch, Dorset.[42] Her tragic later life, however, denied her this burial place: the mother of Cardinal Reginald Pole and a supporter of Katherine of Aragon after Henry VIII's divorce, she was attainted and then executed in 1541 at the age of sixty-eight.

THE DUKE OF BUCKINGHAM

For all the building it encouraged, the distribution of titles by Henry VIII prior to the 1530s was a relatively neutral activity in political terms for a simple reason: very little land was provided to maintain these new dignities. Indeed, nearly all the figures involved came from established noble families. Meanwhile, most of the perquisites of government were increasingly being diverted to serve the king's immediate circle and the growing power of Cardinal Wolsey. Prominent amongst the critics of this situation was the duke of Buckingham. With a massive income of around £5,000 per annum and descended from Edward III, he was in both financial and dynastic terms the premier peer of England. It was a role he acted out to perfection during major court events, wearing clothing of breathtaking value and performing well in the jousting lists.

Buckingham's high birth, his dislike of Wolsey and a careless tongue made him an easy victim of court intrigue. The king became suspicious of his loyalty and the duke fell from grace with alarming speed. Arrested on his barge in the Thames in April 1519, he was tried and executed for high treason within a month. Buckingham was the first in a long line of notable victims of Henry's political jealousy, a trait that was to become steadily more exaggerated as time progressed.

308 A conjectural reconstruction by Phil Kenning of the inner garden enclosure at Ashby de la Zouch, Leicestershire, around 1630. The garden was rectangular in plan with banqueting towers at the angles. That to the bottom left is planned in the shape of a four-leafed clover and is similar to those erected by Henry VIII at Hampton Court in 1538. Its upper rooms commanded fine views over the surrounding parkland. The tower also served as a means of access between the main garden compartment and the wider garden surrounds. This enclosed area was broken up into sections by high banks of earth. Those to the right are shaped like cannon bastions, perhaps an early English instance of modern military forms becoming absorbed into garden design. The passage of the forms of fortification into gardens was encouraged both by the prestige they enjoyed and also by a connection of technical expertise: the need to move large quantities of earth. For this reason, the same men might undertake both types of work.

309 The remaining gatehouse turret of Warblington, Hampshire, begun in 1517 by Margaret Pole, countess of Salisbury. Warblington is the only castle of the English Middle Ages unambiguously created in its entirety by a female patron. The building was almost completely destroyed after the Civil War, but this seven-storey turret and the surviving outline of the moat hint at its scale. The tower is built in brick and stone, but the former was covered over in render to create an unusual polychromatic effect of grey walls with white facings. This treatment and other technical details of the building are paralleled at Cowdray and Camber in Sussex.

The fall of Buckingham brought into crown possession the single greatest inheritance that remained outside royal control, those of the church excepted. It was immediately surveyed by royal servants, and their report provides a fascinating snapshot of the duke's suite of residences, as well as an insight into contemporary judgements about their qualities and points of interest.[43]

When they are expressed at all, a small group of aesthetic responses recur in this official survey. 'Old' tends to be used in a derogatory sense, while 'new' implies that the work is good and conforms to current taste. Its synonym, used more occasionally, is 'uniform', one of the most important qualities of the Perpendicular style. The third response is positive but not framed in terms of fashion or time: it is strength. This is the aesthetic of the castle.

In many of the duke's peripheral properties, the manors he owned were maintained only as the operating centres of estates and were sometimes neglected. Amongst these were the castles of Hay, Caus and Huntingdon, which, excepting a tower used as a jail, were all described as ruinous. Oakham in Rutland, too, was in disrepair apart from the castle hall, built 'of an old fashion', which was used as a courtroom. Here, the surveyor notes, no nobleman can pass through the lordship without rendering a horseshoe. Besides those nailed to the door, he describes one set at one end of the hall a yard broad with the arms of England attached given by Edward IV. Famously, this building still preserves this remarkable collection of horseshoes (see pl. 95).

At Newport, Monmouthshire, only the castle exchequer and prison in the main gate were maintained, though there were good lodgings adjacent in need of repair. By contrast, Kimbolton Castle, Huntingdonshire, was in repair but threatened with decay through the fault of an old mantle wall that enclosed it. Likewise, Penshurst, Kent, and Maxstoke, Warwickshire, the latter described as 'a proper thing after the old building, standing within a fair and large moat full of fish'. That said, the duke had evidently not troubled to complete an extensive rebuilding campaign attributed by the surveyor to Lady Margaret Beaufort. At Stafford, the castle and its park were in repair and recommended as a stopping-off point for the king on his progress. The views from the 'uniformly built' fourteenth-century great tower of the castle for a radius of 20 or 30 miles were particularly admired and mention is specifically made of a 'surveing place' from which to enjoy them.

310   The main front of the inner court at Thornbury, Gloucestershire, viewed from the base court. Only the tower and turret to the right were ever raised to their full height. The façade was planned with a regular rhythm of elements – tower, turret, gatehouse, turret and tower – in the manner of Herstmonceux. The central gatehouse is almost unique in England for possessing a small as well as a large gate, an arrangement more common in monastic and town entrances and in France. An inscription over the entrance records that work to the buildings began in 1511. This building with its high-quality cut stonework, polygonal towers and heavy machicolis breathes the spirit of works of the 1460s at Raglan.

Brecon Castle, the birthplace of the duke, was in good repair with its lodgings and houses built in 'the old fashion'. To this, however, there had recently been added 'a goodly hall set on height, only with lights [windows] in either end and none upon the sides. And as unto the roof of the said hall, it is newly and costly made with costly pendants, after a goodly fashion.' Evidently, this followed such grand new buildings as Edward IV's hall at Eltham. Around it were fine woods and a large mere stocked with fish.

Tonbridge Castle, Kent, greatly impressed the surveyor as 'the strongest fortress, and most like unto a castle of any other that the duke had in England or Wales'. He marvelled particularly at its thirteenth-century gatehouse, which was 'as strong a fortress as few be in England'. In 1521 a complete new range of lodgings was under construction along the southern side of the castle and by implication work was also under way to the 'dungeon' on the motte, which was only partially covered by a newly laid roof. All its towers were large and fair in appearance. Nearby, at Bletchingley, Surrey, the manor place had been 'properly and newly built', presumably by the duke. All its interiors were ceiled and wainscoted in timber, so that 'they might be used at pleasure without hangings', an interesting reflection on the emerging fashion for interior panelling.

But the duke's chosen seat was the 'lordship' of Thornbury, Gloucestershire, where he chose to rebuild what is variously described as its new manor or castle with its 'stately lodgings'. Work to this building was still under way when Buckingham was executed, and the castle survives as a partially completed structure. According to an inscription over the gate, it was begun in 1511. The intention was to create a new residence around two courts and environed by an elaborate planned landscape. This included hunting parks, gardens and a new college of priests attached to the neighbouring parish church. Everything about the new buildings speaks of the duke's pretensions.

The castle was planned on a vast scale. Its outer court was to comprise a series of lodging ranges and the surviving foundations show that their exterior walls were to be set with towers and turrets. The main front of the inner court was symmetrically planned (pl. 310). Such parts of this façade as were completed evoke the work of the 1460s at Raglan Castle, itself an architectural importation from precisely this region of England. The rebuilt elements of the proposed collegiate church reflect similar connections with the Perpendicular style of the south-west: the tower is modelled on that of Gloucester Abbey (now the cathedral) and the nave window tracery relates to the tomb of the so-called Wakeman Cenotaph at Tewkesbury Abbey, Gloucestershire.

311 (*top*) Thornbury, Gloucestershire, begun in 1511. The withdrawing apartments from the Privy Garden are lit by a spectacular pair of compass windows. In an arrangement copied from Henry VII's Richmond, the more complex upper windows lit the duke's apartments while those below were for the duchess. Some features of the enclosed garden they overlook are known from documentary and archaeological evidence. Two galleries were built up against the battlemented outer wall and gave access to the adjacent collegiate church. The lower gallery walks were laid with tiles decorated with the Stafford family emblem of a knot. This device also appears sculpted throughout the interior and was even planted as a pattern in the garden itself.

312 (*bottom*) One of the brick chimneys at Thornbury, Gloucestershire. A small scroll on the base of the stack is carved with the date 1514. The chimneys at Thornbury are probably modelled on those created for Henry VII at Richmond Palace (see pl. 296). They follow, however, in a longer tradition of complex chimneys carved in red brick that developed in the fifteenth-century works at Eton and – probably – at Syon before that. The top of the side stacks echo the lobed form of the largest compass window in the withdrawing rooms, a fascinating example of the continued relationship between miniature and full-scale architectural design. As befits a castle chimney, the rim of the stack is carved with arrow loops. The chimney also bears several carvings of the family device, the Stafford knot.

But while the mason responsible for Thornbury was trained in the south-west, he also had an intimate knowledge of the royal works. The one completed range appears to take its form and detailing from Henry VII's palace at Richmond, in the 1510s still the most splendid royal residence in England. Arranged within this on two consecutive floors were the apartments of the duke and duchess, each lit by a dazzling pair of compass windows (pl. 311). Projecting above the crown of battlements are preserved a series of sumptuously carved chimneys, one of stone but the remainder in brick (pl. 312). In 1521 the remaining buildings in the inner court belonged to the older manor house and were damned by the surveyor as 'homely'. Such architectural modesty is curious given the favour in which this house had been held by Jasper Tudor, the uncle of Henry VII.

COURTIERS AND MERCHANTS

The massive estates and multiple residences of the duke of Buckingham represent one extreme of landholding and wealth in this period. But there also existed a number of individuals who through trade or service at court acquired the money to build one residence of pretension. There is always an architectural

313 Hengrave, Suffolk, begun in the 1520s. It is built of locally made grey brick detailed in stone. As fashion demanded, the chimneys were constructed of specially imported red bricks. The façade was originally symmetrical but the right-hand side was demolished in 1775 and rebuilt in its present form. At the same time a dominating tower in the far corner of the building, known from engravings, was also pulled down. The plan of this quadrangular building with an internal cloister is directly connected to works of the 1440s at Eton and Herstmonceux. A map of 1588 shows the building encircled by a moat and approached through a service court. The court was swept away in the eighteenth century.

gulf between such buildings and those of the nobility or the king, a simple expression of relative incomes. And by extension, the more modest of these graduate outside the strict category of the castle. Nevertheless, all make use of the trappings of fortification and incorporate individually, or in combination, the two architectural features long distinctive of castle design: the gatehouse and the tower. Many were also enclosed by moats and recreated in an appropriately modest fashion all the features of contemporary noble seats, including parks, gardens and burial churches. In terms of design, most are clearly connected to London masons well versed in the Perpendicular canon.

A case in point is Hengrave in Suffolk, one of the most ambitious merchant residences of Henry VIII's reign and a clear aspirant for castle status. Hengrave was purchased from the duke of Buckingham shortly before his arrest by Thomas Kytson, a wealthy London merchant eager to create a country seat, and in 1525 he received a licence to fortify this new building with battlements and turrets. The manor was laid out with a principal and base court and many of its features echo those of Thornbury but on a more modest scale. Its façade, for example, had the same distinctive rhythm of elements with turrets and domes in place of corner towers (pl. 313). The inner court at Hengrave was enclosed on three sides by a two-storey gallery, a detail that links it back with the royal works of Henry VI's

reign and the design of Eton College. In the manner of a castle, its main court incorporated a grand gatehouse and a high tower. Only the former survives, but it incorporates a fabulous first-floor compass window dated 1538 (pl. 314).

A surviving contract sheds light on the circumstances in which Hengrave was built. The mason responsible was a certain John Eastawe, of whom nothing is otherwise known. He agreed to complete the work for £200 'according to a frame which the said John was shown at Comby', a nearby manor.[44] That Eastawe was working from a frame – presumably a model – is itself a remarkable circumstance. Architectural models had long been in use on the Continent but this is the first documentary reference to one in England. His use of the frame makes it clear that he was not the designer of the building. So too does the agreement in the contract that Thomas Kytson would supply whole elements of the building – including the bay window of the hall and the gatehouse – for Estawe to incorporate in the structure.

Given the comparisons between Hengrave and buildings produced by the fifteenth-century royal works, the likelihood must be that the mason responsible for designing the house and executing these display pieces of architecture was based in London. Certainly, there is documentary evidence that Kytson otherwise employed many specialist craftsmen from the

capital. Such delivery of designs and architectural elements from London is otherwise typical of the period.

One further curiosity of the contract is that by its terms the only architectural decoration John Eastawe was required to create at Hengrave was a series of chimneys in red brick with rubbed decoration. The local clay fired to a yellow-grey colour, so these chimney bricks had to be specially created. This requirement underlines the continued importance of prominent chimney stacks as a mark of a grand residence. It also illustrates that, since the 1440s, red brick chimneys had developed into an essential feature of a grand residence. Nothing could show more clearly the extent to which brick had become naturalised within the English architectural tradition.

Meanwhile, the pioneering use of terracotta by the high nobility in the Thames valley and East Anglia over the 1510s and 1520s was also widely copied by those eager to cut an architectural figure for themselves. Henry, first Baron Marney (d. 1523), was another figure catapulted to power through his intimacy with the young king. He began, but left incomplete at his death, a substantial new seat at Layer Marney in Essex.[45] Fundamentally, this was conceived as a conventional building within the tradition of grand English residential architecture: a courtyard house of brick dominated by a gatehouse. In this case, however, the battlements and Gothic window tracery have been rendered in terracotta moulded with grotesque detailing. The forms used appear to have compared to those at Charles Brandon's residence in Southwark, Suffolk Place, discussed above. Another terracotta house of the mid-1520s that also reflects close connections with court craftsmen is Sutton Place, Surrey, built by Richard Weston, a member of the Privy Chamber who collected several lucrative posts.

Not all terracotta architecture, however, was necessarily the product of such sophisticated connections. The Pelham family, now withdrawn from Pevensey Castle, created a new residence for themselves at Laugh- ton Court, Sussex, a moated site near Lewes. This incorporated at its heart a tall tower of brick ornamented with terracotta panels.[46] And in East Anglia, Sir Henry Fermor, who was identified in a return of 1523 as the wealthiest merchant in Norfolk, erected for himself a fantastical manor house at East Barsham, Norfolk. In true, castle-like fashion this is replete with a dominating tower and a gatehouse. Every feature of the house, including its windows, chimneys and battlements, incorporates a wealth of terracotta decoration.

The fashion for terracotta was relatively restricted and short-lived. In many other parts of the kingdom local building materials often proved more attractive to patrons. At Coughton in Warwickshire, for example, a great gatehouse of stone was erected by Sir George Throckmorton around 1520, possibly as one element of an uncompleted house (pl. 315). Its upper three storeys dissolve into glass in a manner reminiscent of Henry VII's tower at Windsor. At Kirtling in Cambridgeshire, Lord North built a new residence of stone and brick after his purchase of this moated site in 1533. All that survives of this today is an elegant gatehouse with a veneer of classical detailing applied to its centrally placed compass window (pl. 316). Beyond the gatehouse there formerly stood an imposing residence that possessed a tower placed asymmetrically on one wing. Kirtling gatehouse is a version of the types of gatehouse erected by Cambridge colleges early in the century, but it compares more closely to such southeastern buildings as the gatehouse built in the 1520s at Eton College by Provost Lupton.

315 The gatehouse of Coughton, Warwickshire, erected around 1520 as the entrance to a residence that was never completed. During alterations in 1780 it was converted into the hall of the present house. The complex planning of the upper storeys of the building and the idea of breaking through the walls to create a lattice of windows are evocative of compass window design. Many details of the gatehouse, such as the form of the projecting central bay, are loosely paralleled throughout the mid-sixteenth century at such widely separated sites as Titchfield, Hampshire, in the 1530s and Kenilworth, Warwickshire, in the 1570s. Presumably it is derived from a standard gatehouse design that had wide currency amongst London masons.

Such resemblances between widely located buildings is a product of the monopoly enjoyed by London masons on architectural practice in this period. As a group these gatehouses are like distorted reflections in a gallery of mirrors. Each is a slight variation on its neighbour but the original design is invisible in the confusion of images.

THE BREAK WITH ROME

The Act of Supremacy in 1534 formally set in motion the reformation of the English church, a process that was to touch every aspect of life in the kingdom. By the terms of the act Henry VIII implicitly repudiated the authority of the pope and assumed to himself complete control of the church within his imperial realm.

England had received by Act of Parliament a royal heir to St Peter. The primary motive for Henry VIII's action was to allow him to divorce a wife who had produced no male heir. One of its added incentives was that it laid the accumulated riches of the church open to exploitation. Many of Henry's predecessors had confronted and squeezed the English church, but none had challenged its institutions so fundamentally. Nor had they acted at such a politically explosive moment, when Christendom itself was riven by religious differences and externally threatened by the expanding Ottoman Empire.

The first objects of the king's cupidity were the monasteries, of which more than 600 existed across England in the 1530s. At the direction of Thomas Cromwell, the king's secretary, royal agents were sent out to visit all the monasteries in the kingdom, valuing their property and assessing their religious condition. Their

316 The gatehouse at
Kirtling, Cambridgeshire,
built by Edward North (later
Lord North) soon after he
had purchased the manor and
its castle in 1533. It stands in a
moated enclosure that was
fortified in timber as late as
1309. The fine bay window,
crowned with miniature
battlements, is built of cut
stone and combines intricate
Gothic and antique detailing.
As at Hadleigh (see pl. 303),
the decoration of all the inner
faces of the gatehouse with
diaper shows that it was
originally free-standing. The
gatehouse became
incorporated within a larger
house encircled by a moat
that was largely demolished in
1801. Early depictions of the
building show that the turrets
were formerly capped by
domes.

reports on the standards of monastic life were –
undoubtedly at royal instruction – almost universally
damning. Armed with this justification for reform, all
monasteries with an income of less than £200 per
annum were suppressed in 1536 and their possessions
passed into the royal coffers. The monks and nuns
from these institutions were moved to larger monasteries, but two years later these in turn began to be
suppressed. Soon afterwards, Henry VIII's agents began
to destroy the shrines of England's saints, enriched
with centuries of pious bequests. St Thomas Becket's
shrine and the high-altar reredos at Canterbury alone
filled twenty-six carts with bullion.[47]

The dissolution of the monasteries marked a decisive turning point in the history of English art. Besides
the massive destruction of churches, their contents and
associated possessions that it brought about, the
Reformation overthrew the artistic dynamics of the
Middle Ages. By virtue of its wealth and interests, the
church had always been the principal patron of the arts
in the kingdom, consistently training and maintaining
the vast majority of skilled craftsmen in every sphere
of artistic endeavour. Its relative vitality and dominance over the secular sphere was scarcely less complete in the 1530s than it had been a century before.

Virtually overnight whole classes of artisan and spe-
cialists in England lost all but a fraction of their trade,
from embroiderers to singers and from glaziers to mas-

ons. In addition, the inventive mechanism that had
sustained the arts was transformed. Because it had conventionally been within the orbit of the church that
daring artistic experimentation had taken place, it was
as if the engine of invention was simply switched off.
Nevertheless, the English medieval architectural tradition did not collapse. In part, this is a reflection of its
extraordinary vigour but also the intense and sustained
demand for new secular building. As the wealth of the
church was transferred to new hands, it was turned
to new ends by new masters. Their activities were
shaped by a very fast-moving and tumultuous political situation.

HENRY VIII AND THE DEFENCE OF THE THRONE

The first serious opposition to Henry VIII's religious
changes was a series of related uprisings across England
north of the Wash. These began in Lincolnshire on 1
October 1536 but spread northwards within a week
when the lighting of beacons roused popular revolt in
Yorkshire, Westmorland, Cumberland, Richmond-
shire and Durham. Order was restored relatively quickly in Lincolnshire, and Henry installed Charles Brandon, duke of Suffolk, as a trusted royal governor of the
area. Brandon was provided with the castle of Tatter-

shall as his seat in the county, a fascinating indication of the continued prestige enjoyed by this building as remodelled by Lord Cromwell in the mid-fifteenth century. Suffolk's move to Tattershall was permanent, and over the next few years he transferred his entire landed interest from East Anglia to Lincolnshire by selling up and exchanging property. His estates were further augmented by the lands of dissolved religious houses, including Tattershall College. If he worked on the buildings at Tattershall, there is unfortunately no clear evidence of the fact.[48]

In Yorkshire and the north, meanwhile, the situation had turned very sour for the king. Religious communities returned to their houses and royal authority broke down completely. Henry denounced his opponents as rebels, but those involved described themselves as partaking in a 'pilgrimage for grace' on behalf of the commonwealth. Up to 30,000 pilgrims divided into nine 'hosts' controlled the north of England for several months in what was probably the largest peacetime uprising in English history. During this time, the only outposts of royal authority were the castles of Skipton and Scarborough, held respectively by the earl of Cumberland and Sir Ralph Eure. Both castles were besieged, and at Scarborough there was damage to the fabric by gunfire.[49] Faced with such overwhelming odds the royal forces were unable to suppress the rising by force. The duke of Norfolk, acting for the king, was forced to agree to a series of measures, including the restoration of the abbeys.

Of course, the promises were not kept and complaint of the fact was used as a pretext for bloody revenge. While suppressing smaller and uncoordinated resurgences of discontent under the unfurled royal banner (a symbol of open war upon the inhabitants), the duke of Norfolk was encouraged by the king in his passage through Yorkshire to:

> . . . . cause suche dredfull execution to be doon upon a good nombre of thinhabitauntes of every towne, village and hamlet that have offended in this rebellion, as well by hanging of them uppe in trees, as by the quartering of them and the setting of their heddes and quarters in every towne, greate and small, and in al suche other places as they may be a ferefull spectacle . . . without pitie or respecte.[50]

Henry VIII, meanwhile, was profuse in his thanks to those who had supported him. Eure received guardianship of Scarborough Castle for life and the earl of Cumberland was made a knight of the Garter.

No sooner had the domestic threat in the north of England been so brutally suppressed than Henry faced new difficulties. With the encouragement of the pope and against all diplomatic probability, Charles v, Holy Roman emperor, king of Spain and ruler of the Netherlands, buried his differences with Francis I of France to forge a powerful Catholic alliance against England. The growing political tension at court is reflected in a spate of executions. By January 1539 the French ambassador was pleading with Francis I to be recalled. According to him, Henry was acting with great pride and losing his political senses. He was fearful, moreover, of some ill turn, the king being the 'most cruel and dangerous man in the world' and acting in a rage with 'neither reason nor understanding left'.[51] The following month England was in the grip of an invasion scare. There were musters of all men between the ages of sixteen and sixty; trade was suspended; beacons were built; and all constables were sent from court to defend their castles.[52] It was not an instruction that many comfort-loving courtiers relished. In his reports from the fastness of Dover, Sir Thomas Cheyne wrote ever more plaintively for permission to return to court.[53]

In February 1539 Henry additionally commissioned a survey of fortifications in the Pale of Calais, and along the southern coasts of England and Wales. To the works in Calais were sent the king's most experienced experts in fortification, but the defence of England was scarcely less urgent. On the basis of the survey a massive building programme was initiated, funded and supplied largely by the proceeds from dissolved religious houses. Within two years about thirty new coastal fortifications had been commenced in England and twenty-four of these were sufficiently advanced to be garrisoned. Many of the new buildings were small gun towers or blockhouses, but they included a group of ten larger castles or forts (as they were variously termed) along the length of the south coast of England at Sandown, Deal, Walmer, Camber, Sandgate, Calshot, Portland, Pendennis and St Mawes.[54] In terms of military architecture, these latter buildings are without obvious European parallel: all are centrally planned and most make use of radiating groups of broad, semicircular platforms for cannon termed bastions. In one case, at St Mawes, a town was subsequently established in 1562 beside the fort, making it the last planted castle borough in England.

These castles develop directly from a tradition of free-standing artillery towers running back to such

317 The Cow Tower or *Dungeon* at Norwich, Norfolk, built in 1398–9. This free-standing gun tower is faced in brick but incorporates a decorative band of knapped flint just above the plinth. A stair turret projects to the rear. As with many early brick buildings its masonry is laid using different sizes of bricks – purchased from six different suppliers – and with little attempt at regular bonding. The bulging walls are evidence for its relatively crude construction. Henry VIII's coastal artillery forts look back to the tradition of English gun-tower architecture exemplified by this building.

buildings as the late fourteenth-century Cow Tower at Norwich (pl. 317). Where they differ from their predecessors is in the relative complexity of their wider planning. The three castles of Deal, Walmer and Sandown in Kent, for example, commanded the broad anchorage created by Goodwin Sands north of Dover. Work began in April 1539, and within a month more than 1,400 men were at work on site, an extraordinary indication of the perceived urgency of the project.[55] The three castles stood on the foreshore roughly a mile apart. At this distance, the fields of fire from the cannon in each could command the whole extent of the natural harbour and just overlap with each other. Henry VIII was personally very interested in the operation and is recorded as having produced a 'device' or plan for the works. He may even have commented on the final drawings during a hurried visit to Dover in March, where he was also engaged in a projected – and unsuccessful – expansion of the harbour on an astonishing scale. The detailed designs, however, were al-

most certainly produced by craftsmen seconded from the works at Hampton Court Palace.

Evidence for their direct involvement is provided by the survival of one very fine drawing for a castle that closely resembles Deal, the largest building in the series (pl. 318). It is the connection with Hampton Court that perhaps best explains the regular, lobed designs of the castles on the Downs. This form is anticipated in a generic sense in the designs of compass windows and chimneys, as at Windsor and Thornbury. Its most immediate precedent, however, was in a series of battlemented banqueting towers erected in the gardens of Hampton Court in 1538. In view of this architectural parallel, it is fitting that Henry VIII's fourth wife, Anne of Cleves, was banqueted in the incomplete shell of Deal Castle when she first landed on English soil in December 1539.[56] The event suggests that, despite its gaunt appearance, this building was admired both as a fortification and as a work of ingenious design suitable for royal entertainment.

Connecting the castles was a series of earthwork defences running along the foreshore. These were created under the direction of a man called Stephan von Haschenperg, clearly a foreigner, who seems to have claimed specialist knowledge of fortification as an engineer. Quite what Haschenperg's experience was remains something of a mystery, because all his known work looks highly idiosyncratic in a contemporary European context.[57] The most important project he undertook was at Carlisle in Cumberland, where he created a half-moon barbican to the inner gate of the castle (see pl. 81) and refortified one city gate as a substantial and free-standing cannon fortification. Set beside the types of diamond-shaped cannon bastion designs pioneered in Italy at this time, these designs look bizarre. Whether he was condemned as a fraud or simply outmanoeuvred in local politics, the mysterious Haschenperg was dismissed from office while at Carlisle and disappears from all records without further documentary trace.[58]

While new fortifications were being created around the coast, older buildings were also being pressed into service for the defence of the realm. Dover Castle, still an intermittent port of call for the king on progress, became the administrative centre of the new building works for the castles at Goodwin Sands. Portchester Castle, meanwhile, was provided with a munitions shed. In the north of England, the priories of Tynemouth and Lindisfarne were both commandeered as fortifications and numerous of the castles along the

318　This coloured drawing, labelled 'Castle in the Downes', is a presentation design resembling Deal. English architectural drawings or plats begin to survive in small quantities from around 1500 and this gives some idea of the conventions used in the most sophisticated. The use of distorted perspective allows the onlooker an aerial view that simultaneously indicates elevation and plan. Excitingly depicted with roaring guns (but without gunners), this drawing is precisely the kind of architectural presentation likely to catch the eye of Henry VIII. As constructed, the castle at Deal had stone parapets rather than gabions. Viewed in a European context, the semicircular bastions of Henry VIII's coastal forts were a military anachronism before they were begun in 1539.

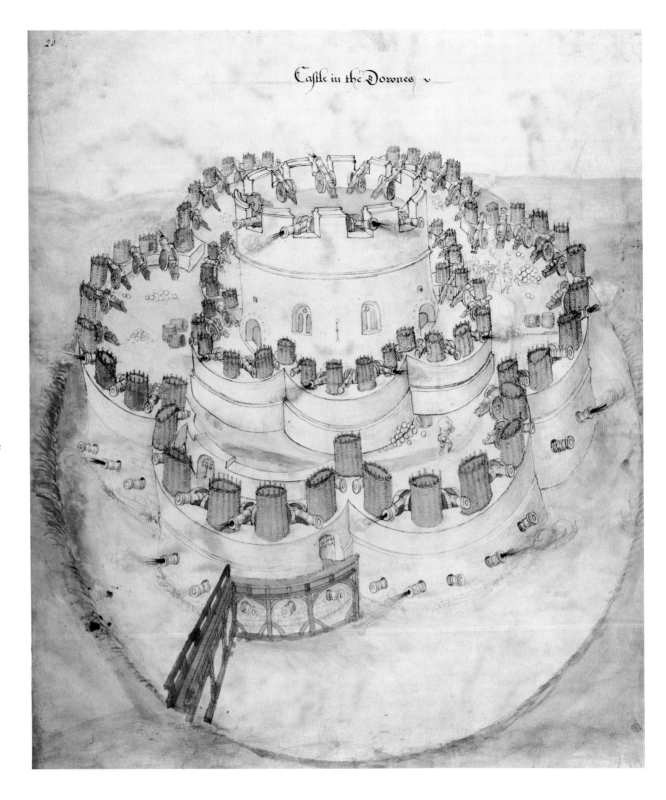

border, including Wark, Norham and Berwick, were once again repaired for war.[59] At the same time, effort was also made to survey some royal castles and assess their condition.[60]

The picture painted by the surviving returns of this survey is one of neglect, decay and defensive inadequacy. As such, they might be thought to constitute clear evidence that castles across the kingdom were increasingly dilapidated and militarily useless. But royal residences of all kinds, including castles, had always been neglected by the crown when they were not in use. What these surveys properly reflect are the breathtaking scale of the royal estate as accumulated by Henry VIII and the fact that by 1539 the king very rarely travelled beyond a tiny core of favoured residences in the south-east of England. Far from representing the decline of the castle, the ruins of castles such as Knaresborough, Middleham and Pontefract were, like England's abbeys and priories, gigantic monuments to the greed of Henry VIII and his willing servants.

MONASTIC SPOIL

By far the greatest beneficiary of church money was the king himself, who emerged through the 1530s as an eager builder. Not only did he evidently take a direct interest in architecture but he was also impatient of results. The statistics here tell an important story. Between 1530 and 1547 he more than doubled the number of residences that he owned (including castles) from approximately thirty to well over sixty. The vast majority of these were rarely used, but a small core was transformed by the king. His greatest documented expenditure fell on Hampton Court, where in the ten years following his acquisition of the palace from Cardinal Wolsey he spent £62,000.[61] This stands in comparison with the approximate expenditure by the wealthy London merchant Thomas Kytson on Hengrave of £3,500.[62] This vast gulf in architectural expenditure needs also to be set in the context of the other costs for which the crown was liable. War, in particular, then as now, guzzled bewildering quantities of money. The castles on the Downs alone, for example, consumed £27,000,[63] and the wider expenses of war were as far beyond the ordinary as defence budgets today: the king's campaigns of 1544–55 cost nearly one and a quarter million pounds.[64]

Most of Henry VIII's building was extremely conservative in form, looking back to the types of courtyard design developed in castle and collegiate architecture more than a century previously. Where these buildings chiefly differed from their predecessors was in their superficial ornament. The culminating creation of his reign makes the point well. On 22 April 1538, the eve of the feast of St George and the twenty-ninth anniversary of his accession, Henry VIII determined to found a new palace. Nonsuch was by its very name a palace beyond compare. Along with Oatlands, near Weybridge in Surrey, it was one of two subsidiary residences created within a new 10,000-acre honour attached to the recently completed palace of Hampton Court. The creation of an honour in this way is a fascinating evocation of castle endowment and it was not

isolated: in 1540 Ewelme was likewise created the seat of an honour comprising the land recently amassed in Oxfordshire by the crown.[65]

A village was razed to the ground to receive Nonsuch and its buildings were erected on foundations that were packed with imported rubble from Merton Priory, an Augustinian house suppressed in 1537. Its inner court was of timber frame and this doubtless helped accelerate the rapid process of the building, which was largely complete by 1541.[66] From the evidence of surviving views, the exterior looks astonishing (pl. 319). Its outline, dissolving into an array of pinnacles and royal beasts, was fantastic in every sense of the word. The wall surfaces were quite as spectacular: they were broken up into grids by gilded slates laid over the timber structure. Framed within this grid were stucco panels with three-quarter-life-size figures. Besides numerous classical subjects there also appeared in this display figures of Henry VIII and his heir, Prince Edward.

A body of foreign craftsmen, led by an Italian, Nicholas Bellin of Modena, executed this extraordinary cycle of decoration. Bellin had previously worked at the place of Fontainebleau, near Paris, for the French king, Francis I, but had been discovered in some dishonest practice and was forced to flee from there. Henry VIII gave him shelter and set him to work on his own palaces. It is to the decoration of Fontainebleau, particularly the Gallerie François 1er, that the Nonsuch scheme is indebted. With its deeply modelled figures, idiomatically executed architectural detailing and the kind of ornamental framing device called strapwork, it introduced to England a new idiom of classical ornament termed cartouche work. Besides Bellin, a number of other outstanding figures from the Continent were involved at Nonsuch, including Nicholas Cure, Giles Gering and Robert Lambert.[67] Most of the junior workmen were likewise foreigners, and one slate excavated from the site has working notes in French written on it.

Yet for all its novelty of ornament, Nonsuch was no more than a classic two-court English house under a wealth of cosmetic decoration. The towers and gatehouse of the inner court dignified it with the architectural character of a castle, the latter with a compass window very similar in form to that at Hengrave. Its timber-frame construction was anticipated, too, in earlier pleasure palaces, all of them lost, such as Henry V's palace at Sheen and the Pleasance at Kenilworth. Even the stucco decoration may not have been a com-

319 A view of the inner court of Nonsuch, Surrey, published by John Speed in 1611. In many respects, this extraordinary building was of completely conventional design: it was laid out on a rectangular plan with angle towers and dominated by a great gatehouse with a triple compass window on its internal face (see pl. 314). The Perpendicular grid of windows was conventional too, as was the fantastical treatment of the roofline with chimneys, battlements and heraldic beasts. What made Nonsuch unusual was the cosmetic figural and antique decoration of gilded slates and plasterwork applied to the timber-frame structure.

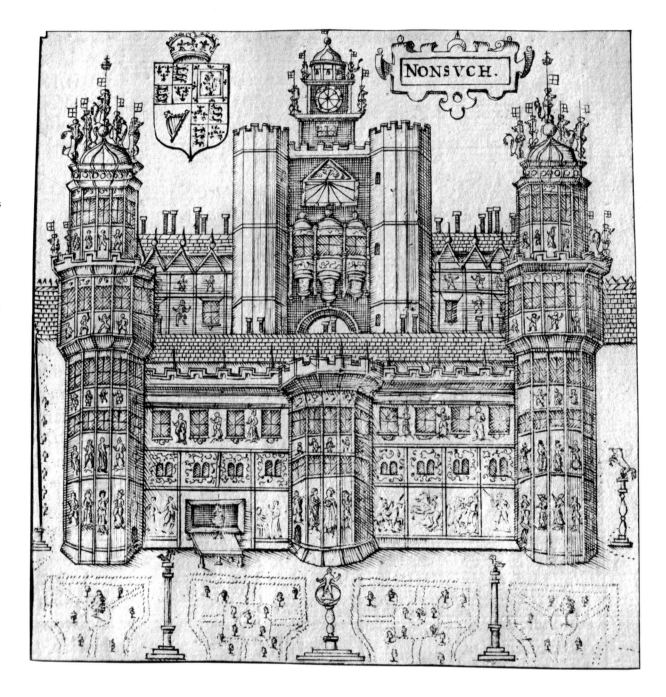

plete novelty in England; after all, the earl of Warwick's architecturally splendid stables at Warwick Castle of the 1460s were treated in some similar way.[68]

While Nonsuch was being erected, Henry VIII was involved in moulding a loyal nobility to lead his armies and uphold royal government. Titles flowed with unprecedented freedom in the latter part of the reign, and from 1537 there came with them endowments of monastic property. On occasion, the grants of complete estates allowed monasteries to pass to their new owners as fully operable concerns with defined possessions, privileges and feudal responsibilities.

A similar continuity from the monastic past was possible, too, in architectural terms. Remove the church and chapter house from a monastery and you were left with a complex that conformed exactly to the needs of a great secular household with services, a hall (the refectory), household accommodation (in the monks' and corrodians' lodgings) and a series of withdrawing apartments (the abbot's or prior's lodging). The last could be very splendid indeed: at Glastonbury, the royal commissioners, overwhelmed by the splendour of the abbot's house, concluded that it was 'mete for the king and noone else'.[69] For this reason, in most

424

cases monastic buildings were turned to secular purpose with a minimum of physical alteration in the decade after the Dissolution. Where it occurred, their architectural transformation usually waited until the relative peace of the 1550s or the 1570s and will be dealt with in the next chapter.

In some cases, however, there was pressure for fast and radical architectural change to mark the end of monastic life. A handful of monasteries were spectacularly ruined: at the great Cluniac monastery of Lewes in Sussex, for example, an Italian fortune-hunter, Giovanni Portinari, rapidly levelled the principal monastic buildings with gunpowder.[70] Perhaps the most common means of signalling the end of monastic life was simply to destroy the monastic church. The politics of such destruction are complex to unravel, but there is a broad relationship apparent between discontented regions – for example, Lincolnshire – and this last, most radical solution to fast architectural transformation.

In one area, the south-east, a distinctive pattern of monastic conversion emerges. This was almost certainly a reflection of its vulnerability to invasion and the need quickly to create in this region new governing interests sympathetic to the king's cause. Here, a group of major monasteries – along with a few other existing castle sites – were developed by a group of closely connected individuals, all of whom enjoyed the particular trust of the king. Foremost of these was Sir Anthony Browne, a lifelong intimate of the king. He was granted Battle Abbey in August 1538, the monastery founded by William the Conqueror to celebrate his victory at Hastings. Battle enjoyed very special privileges and its abbot had historically played a leading role in the defence of the coast.

By the summer of 1539 Sir Anthony was already involved in converting the abbey buildings into a suitable residence.[71] The first evidence for the operation is a letter referring to a mass walkout by the workmen, which was possibly provoked by the forced circumstances in which they laboured. After demolishing the abbey church, Sir Anthony occupied the abbot's house and began a new guest range. All these buildings were integrated visually by the addition of battlements, a finish in keeping with the imposing monastic gatehouse and the fortified precinct wall. In 1544, either in celebration of what he had achieved, or in prospect of more work, he received a licence to crenellate his new house.[72] This last detail is very surprising – there are only three other monastic conversions dignified in this way. They form part of a wider group of buildings (including artillery forts) directly connected to Browne's political and family circle.

In the same year that Browne received the licence for Battle, he also inherited a large new residence from his half-brother, William Fitzwilliam, at Cowdray in Sussex. Up until 1535 Cowdray was the seat of Owen Tudor, a distant relative of the king. As early as 1529, however, Tudor sold the reversion of the property (in other words, the title on his death) to Fitzwilliam. Soon afterwards, in 1533, a licence to crenellate Cowdray and create a park beside it was procured on Fitzwilliam's behalf. This licence seems to prove that a new residence was planned at Cowdray by its future owner, Fitzwilliam, in the early 1530s. When work to the present buildings was actually begun, however, is not clear (pl. 320).[73] Most were probably erected according to a coherent design between Fitzwilliam's elevation to the title of earl of Southampton in October 1537 and his death in 1542.[74] This period coincided with the height of his prosperity: in 1536 he was appointed high admiral and the following year he resigned as treasurer of the household, doubtless having amply lined his pockets in office.[75]

It is just possible that Sir Anthony Browne completed Cowdray after he inherited it in 1544. Certainly he oversaw the furnishing of the house in the later 1540s, commissioning a remarkable series of panel paintings recording several military expeditions and the coronation of Edward VI. These hung as a cornice frieze in the room beyond the hall dais and were destroyed when the house burnt down in 1793.[76]

The new buildings at Cowdray bear architectural comparison to two monastic conversions on the adjacent south coast. At Netley, Hampshire, the small Cistercian monastery was passed to Sir William Paulet in 1537, then the treasurer of England, and remodelled for him.[77] At the time he was involved in work to his own dynastic castle at Basing, Hampshire, more of which in the next chapter. In 1545 Sir William additionally built at Netley a 'tower and two barbicans' just beside the converted monastic buildings, which overlooked the Southampton shipping channel. He received a pardon for creating these fortifications in 1547 and was permitted to employ a professional team of gunners to serve the defences and train his tenants for war. According to this document, the tower had been begun specifically at Henry VIII's request.[78]

Finally, just a few miles down the coast, a sister religious foundation to Netley was also being converted. Titchfield, a house of Augustinian canons, was granted

320 Cowdray, Sussex, constructed around 1540 and left to ruin following a fire in 1793. It was entered though a symmetrically arranged façade with a tall central gatehouse and two angle towers, the former decorated with cross loops and arrow slits. As originally completed, there was a chimney stack between the gatehouse and each tower, creating a rhythm of elements across the façade that looks back to fifteenth-century designs such as Herstmonceux. The facings of the building are executed in a light-coloured stone, a peculiarity also found at Warblington (see pl. 309). The great hall stood opposite the gatehouse entrance. Inside its porch is an exquisite terracotta fan vault ornamented with anchors in emblem of Fitzwilliam's office as admiral and the initials ws for William Southampton. To either end of the hall range were polygonal towers, one containing kitchens and the other a series of withdrawing apartments. Projecting from the range between them was a chapel tower.

to Sir Thomas Wriothesley, the lord chancellor and future earl of Southampton.[79] Wriothesley received the property in 1537 and had already imported stone from Caen to aid in its conversion into the seat of a new barony.[80] What makes this work particularly interesting is that a correspondence survives describing affairs on the site to its patron at court. Several proposals were put forward for adapting the buildings, all of which involved reusing the cloister as the central court of the new residence. In the end, it was decided to build a gatehouse through the nave of the church, convert the refectory into a hall and the ranges to either side into withdrawing chambers, a chapel and lodgings. In the centre stood a battlemented conduit.[81] A licence to crenellate the new residence was obtained in 1542, by which time building was probably complete (pl. 321).

From the correspondence with Wriothesley, it is known that two figures were involved in advising on the conversion of Titchfield. The first was an engineer active in the construction of fortifications in France called Richard Lee. He appears to have put forward proposals that were then set aside by another mason

from Winchester, Thomas Berty. It was Berty who subsequently dominated the project. Berty was a senior mason and in 1538, while active at Titchfield, was also engaged by the prior of Winchester Cathedral Priory (now the cathedral). From 1539, moreover, he became involved in the royal programme of coastal fortification and worked at the castles of Calshot, Southsea, Hasilworth and Hurst. In the last case he was appointed the captain of the castle. This catholic employment in engineering and church work is typical of a medieval mason, a breadth of experience that was to be denied to later generations of masons by the events of the Reformation.

Berty's importance and wide employment in the region is itself strong circumstantial evidence that he was involved additionally at Netley and Cowdray (and possibly even at Warblington). That there was some overlap of personnel is additionally suggested by the detailed knowledge that the officials at Titchfield evidently enjoyed of operations in these other places. So, for example, one letter tried to shame Wriothesley into visiting his new baronial seat by force of example: 'Mr

321 Titchfield, Hampshire. This Augustinian abbey was surrendered to Sir Thomas Wriothesley, who was created Baron Wriothesley of Titchfield. He converted it into a residence from 1537. The gatehouse was built through the centre of the church nave and led to a court created within the cloister ranges. It was designed with a central oriel window (slightly recessed into the wall plane) and decorated with arrow loops. As remodelled, the buildings were battlemented throughout and supplied with superbly detailed brick gables and chimneys.

treasurer [Paulet] is now at Netlee and lately my lord Admiral [Fitzwilliam] was at his own [Cowdray], and you may not be spared to see that you never saw and correct all [?].'[82] Whether or not this attribution to Berty is correct, it is well within the evidence to observe that Cowdray, Netley, Titchfield (and Warblington) are very closely related buildings. Also that they exemplify a common design type: all are courtyard residences ornamented with the trappings of fortification, entered through gatehouses of similar form and making use of an identical (and unusual) type of lightly coloured stone dressing. Furthermore, that the provision of licences to crenellate for Battle, Titchfield and Netley set them aside from all other monastic conversions in the kingdom.

WALES

Upon the accession of Henry VIII in 1509, the principality of Wales comprised about forty-five quasi-independent marcher lordships.[83] A legacy from the thirteenth-century conquest, they gave Wales an unusually complex political geography. The crown had, over time, absorbed a number of these lordships both through the natural process of inheritance and the windfalls that came from such seizures of property as the attainder of the duke of Buckingham in 1520.

In 1525, as heir apparent to the throne, Princess Mary was sent to oversee the Council of the Marches. She spent nineteen months based in Ludlow Castle and its surrounds. But this solution was not satisfactory for many reasons, and in 1534 Rowland Lee, bishop of Coventry and Lichfield, was appointed president of the marches in her stead.

Lee proved a determined governor of Wales, repairing castles including Wigmore in an attempt to enforce law and order.[84] He chose as his 'second key to Wales' the castle of Montgomery. Not only did he repair the walls but he also created new domestic buildings within the middle ward of the castle. Materials from the nearby Augustinian priory at Chirbury were carted in wholesale as foundation material, and in June 1538 Lee reported gloatingly that a small hoard of silver utensils hidden in a ditch by friars in Ludlow had been surrendered. He hoped to turn the money towards the building at Montgomery, where he had 100 men at work.[85]

Even before Lee had begun his work at Montgomery, royal policy in Wales had undergone a radical transformation. In 1536 all local jurisdictions in the principality were abolished, thus consigning all the surviving marcher lordships and the palatinate of Chester to oblivion. A separate Act further directed that Wales be broken up into shires and return MPs to parliament. The new measures took time to implement, but they were to affect the architectural map of Wales, render-

ing some castles irrelevant for the future.[86] A case in point is Llawhaden, Pembrokeshire, which was deliberately stripped of lead by William Barlow, bishop of St Davids (1536–48), in anticipation of a move to Carmarthen, the centre of the new county. Llawhaden was never occupied again, and in 1616 the bishop received a licence to demolish the ruins.[87] As Wales was settled more firmly within the orbit of English government there were laid the foundations for a new round of castle building in the reign of Elizabeth I, which will be considered in the next chapter.

DOVER AND THE FIELD OF CLOTH OF GOLD

In the summer of 1520 England was preparing for two blockbuster diplomatic occasions. The first of these began on the evening of Sunday, 26 May, when the Holy Roman emperor, Charles V, arrived at Dover for a meeting with Henry VIII. According to a herald's contemporary account, he was received on the shore and conveyed in torchlight procession to the castle above. There he was met by the lord warden of the Cinque Ports, Sir Edward Poynings, and offered the keys to the fortress. But these he refused in most princely manner,

observing that he felt completely safe, and was conducted to his lodgings in the castle.

Meanwhile, Henry VIII, who had been at Canterbury for the last week awaiting the visit, immediately set off for Dover by torchlight. He made impressive time and arrived at two in the morning. Charles V returned the compliment of Henry's impetuous eagerness:

> As sone as the emperor hard of his coming he arose and mett with the king at the staire hedd whereas eyther of them embrased other in arms full lovinglie so that it was aright honorable sight to see the meeting of theis ij excellent princes and their them talked familiarlie a long tyme together and alwaies the king our master had the Emperor on his right hand.[88]

Despite the massive changes that have swept Dover Castle, the stair head on which Henry VIII and Charles V embraced in the early hours of that summer morning still survives. Since Edward IV's repair of the castle around 1480, the royal lodgings had been located in the twelfth-century great tower that still dominates the site. It was almost certainly here, in other words, that the emperor was lodged and from which he emerged to greet Henry VIII as he clambered up the great forebuilding stair.

Less than a week later, Henry VIII himself embarked from Dover harbour for a complementary meeting with Francis I, king of France. A pair of contemporary paintings records the progress of his journey. In the first, there is shown Dover Castle set above the full expanse of the harbour, which is filled with warships in martial finery. Each ship is carefully angled so as to display its stern, where the heaviest guns were placed. The second painting is divided into two parts, one showing Henry VIII processing out of the gates of Guines beneath the castle, again to the roar of cannon. In the other part of the painting are shown some of the highlights of the ensuing personal encounter between the two kings outside the city. Henry's turreted palace, in what became known for its fabulous grandeur as the Field of Cloth of Gold, occupies pride of place in the painting (pl. 322). Within its battlemented parapets are the sculpted figures of men hurling stones at imaginary attackers beneath.[89]

In diplomatic terms, neither encounter achieved a great deal. Henry VIII was out of his depth when dealing with the wily emperor and the Field of Cloth of Gold brought him to detest Francis I, a feeling amply returned by his rival. Nevertheless, as occasions they characterise the spirit of the opening decades of Henry VIII's reign, its vigour and splendour. In their different ways, they also reflect a reality at the heart of early sixteenth-century politics: whether in play (as jousting and display) or in earnest (as war), military prowess was the measure of a monarch and his court. Moreover, that the pretence and practice of war were inextricably connected.

The buildings at the heart of these two occasions make the point rather nicely. Dover, a great castle and fortress, was nevertheless a suitable palace to lodge an emperor; and a temporary palace in the most sumptuous context for Henry VIII, evoked in play a besieged fortification. The Tudor world had not turned its back on the castle. Indeed, as the buildings of the late Tudor age were to demonstrate so magnificently, its forms continued in high architectural fashion throughout the reigns of Henry VIII's three children.

15

THE CASTLE AND THE REFORMATION

EDWARD VI, MARY I AND ELIZABETH I

The early sixteenth-century conflict between Catholic and Reforming interests in England, as in so many other parts of Europe, had been played out in its early phases as an essentially provincial struggle. By the 1540s, however, Christendom as a whole was polarised by the Reformation and religious confession had reared itself as the defining issue in European politics. Henry VIII's children faced the political and religious problems it unleashed from a position of considerable personal disadvantage: Edward VI (1547–53) never achieved his majority and his two half-sisters, Mary I (1553–8) and Elizabeth I (1558–1603), were the first women in English history to be recognised as regnant queens of the kingdom in their own right. The regimes established by all three monarchs were consequently reliant for much of their strength on the circle of crown servants raised to power by the events of the 1530s and 1540s. In reward for their political support, and at the discretion of the crown, this group came increasingly to enjoy the resources of government. As a direct result, favoured courtiers and royal servants now emerged as the great architectural patrons of the late Tudor age.

Building by this group was episodic and bound up closely with rapidly changing political circumstances. It was the Reforming faction at court that seized control of the kingdom after the death of Henry VIII in 1547. This was headed until 1552 by the uncle of the nine-year-old king, Edward Seymour, the lord protector and duke of Somerset, and then by his chief rival, John Dudley, in sequence earl of Warwick and duke of Northumberland. Their government was Protestant in sympathy and strove to set the seal on Henry VIII's religious changes. As part of the continuing process of reformation, they oversaw on behalf of Edward VI the suppression of chantries and colleges, another mainstay of the institutional Catholic Church. The money released, combined with the fierce rivalries generated by the politics of the minority regime, spurred a brief but intense burst of building. As will become apparent, this included a group of French-inspired, neoclassical residences that broke away for the first time from the traditions of grand residential architecture inherited from the late Middle Ages.

Edward VI's untimely death in 1553 brought this short period of building to a close and reopened once more all the problems of unresolved religious conflict within the kingdom. John Dudley, the duke of Northumberland, attempted to secure a Protestant succession by supporting the doubtful claim of Lady Jane Grey to the throne. Events proved that he had completely misjudged the situation. Henry VIII's daughter, Mary, was proclaimed queen at Framlingham Castle in Suffolk. Her subsequent entrance into London dressed in a robe of royal purple on 3 August 1553 was accompanied by scenes of popular rejoicing. Mary's accession formally returned England to Catholicism and benefited the religiously conservative faction at court as well as those happy to trim their views appropriately. The regime, however, was necessarily accommodating to those of all persuasions. Moreover, since Mary attempted to keep the restoration of church property within politically realistic bounds, her short reign did little to affect the court interests established by the land distributions of Henry VIII and Edward VI. As a result, those sympathetic to reform were waiting to support the Protestant Elizabeth I upon her accession in 1558.

This event was ultimately to prove decisive in securing the Protestant Reformation in England, but the outcome was not clear for some time. Elizabeth I was a single woman without any obvious successor, and her celebrated marriage to her realm would have counted for nothing had it not been remarkably long. Moreover, stability only properly came to her regime and the kingdom in the 1570s, catalysed in part by the suppression of the Northern Rising in 1569 and the overthrow of some of her leading Catholic nobles. There followed more than a decade of intense building by those within the Elizabethan administration, from courtiers to lawyers. It gradually subsided in tandem with the souring of the Elizabethan political settlement from the late 1580s onwards.

To the tightly knit and intermarried circle at the heart of the Tudor regime, the issue of religion introduced a crucially important point of difference and division. It became possible directly to connect questions of private conscience, national interest and international diplomacy. One extreme product of this situation was the persecution of Catholics and Protestants, particularly in the reigns of Mary and Elizabeth. These religious upheavals also served to realign the relationship of powers within the British Isles. England and Scotland, after centuries of conflict, were encouraged by their common Protestantism first to peace and then to union. By contrast, and with tragic long-term results, the persistent Catholicism of Ireland confirmed English hostility towards its island neighbour. Meanwhile, it was the religious debate of the Reformation that helped inject vigour into late sixteenth-century intellectual life, blazing the way for a radical reappraisal of the world and man's place within it.

THE PRACTICE OF ARCHITECTURE

In the sphere of architecture, the aesthetic preferences of the Perpendicular style persisted throughout the late Tudor period, notably the desire for large windows, compact plans and a delight with spectacular outlines of chimneys and battlements (or ornamental versions of them). Such continuities are scarcely surprising given that most senior carpenters and masons were all trained up within the medieval tradition of building. But a revolution was brewing. Without church architecture as a forum for experimentation, masons of the late sixteenth century increasingly turned to architectural treatises and publications as a source of artistic inspiration. The bulk of these books were printed in France, but they included some Italian works and numerous publications from England's Protestant and trading allies, the Dutch. Patrons, too, began to indulge a fascination for architecture that transformed it into a respectable, gentlemanly pursuit.

The career of one outstanding mason of the period, Robert Smythson, well expresses these changes. He was the founder of an important dynasty of builders and we shall encounter him in this chapter as regularly as his sons in the next. Smythson was probably born in Westmorland in 1534/5 and the circumstances of his early career remain obscure, though he is likely to have trained in the Masons' Company of London.[1] He is first documented in March 1568 as a master mason involved in remodelling Longleat House, Wiltshire, a former Carthusian monastery, for the testy and discerning patron Sir John Thynne. There he worked with one of the few senior foreign, architectural craftsmen known to have been active in late sixteenth-century England, the Frenchman Alan Maynard. He was subsequently involved in a wide variety of building projects the length and breadth of the country for many of the greatest architectural patrons of Elizabeth I's reign, including – most famously – the countess of Shrewsbury, familiar to posterity as Bess of Hardwick.

Over the course of his long and varied career, Smythson built up a considerable collection of architectural drawings. This collection, which still survives, was further augmented by his sons, who inherited and continued their father's practice. It offers insights into the sources for Smythson's architectural ideas.[2] The number of plans as opposed to elevations, for example, suggests that Smythson still regarded as natural the medieval habit of abstracting the latter from the former. Within the collection, furthermore, there remain a few architectural drawings that he must have inherited in the course of his own training and which underline his links to the medieval masonry tradition. In addition, there are also copies of such early sixteenth-century designs as Henry VII's Chapel at Westminster, a reminder of how admired and influential this building remained. Yet the collection shows the influence of Continental treatises and pattern books on architecture too, including those of Sebastiano Serlio and Vredeman de Vries.[3]

As an architectural practitioner trained in the orbit of London and working with a collection of drawings, Smythson could be compared to any important English mason from the previous two centuries; such was the means, for example, by which Henry Yevele, Thomas Mapilton and William Orchard had all worked. Like these men, Smythson was able to conduct a national career through the use of drawings. But if in practical terms Smythson was no different from his predecessors, he did nevertheless come to differ from them in his own self-assessment. Architecture became for him more than simply a mechanical and practical skill. It became an art. Quite what this means will become apparent in the concluding discussion to this chapter of what is perhaps Robert's most fantastical architectural creation, Wollaton in Nottinghamshire, and his own funeral monument nearby. In the latter, we shall see how Smythson, as a mason with his roots firmly in the medieval tradition of architecture, aspired beyond it.

DURHAM AND THE DUKE OF NORTHUMBERLAND

The course of architectural history in England after the Reformation was not only determined by the dissolution of the monasteries; it was also shaped by the collapse of power and authority wielded by bishops. Up to this point in English history, by virtue of their peculiar position as heirs to non-hereditary, feudal inheritances, and also often their experience, learning and sensibilities, bishops had consistently been a mainstay of fine architecture and its patronage. Although Henry VIII's predations on the church had robbed bishops of several important palaces, it was really the Elizabethan settlement that finally broke them as a body in material terms. In large part this was a direct consequence of the mass deprivation of Marian bishops from office.

Several of those that took their places shamelessly sold up the property of their sees to the crown or dispersed it amongst their children, now a legitimate product of clerical marriage. One of the most notorious figures in this respect was Henry Holbeach, bishop of Lincoln, who reduced his great see to poverty by these means between 1547 and 1551.[4]

The varied and complex story of bishops and their castles at the Reformation, however, is perhaps most compellingly conveyed in the experience of Durham. In 1530 Cuthbert Tunstal, then bishop of London, was elected to the see of Durham as a successor to Cardinal Wolsey. Tunstal (1474–1559) was an illegitimate son of Thomas Tunstal, a squire of the body to Richard III, and worked as a kitchen boy for two years before he was legitimised by his parents' marriage. He subsequently trained as a theologian and spent six years at Padua University. A friend of Thomas More and Erasmus, he was of a conservative religious bent and his appointment to Durham may well have been part of a calculated attempt by Thomas Cromwell to get him away from the capital at a crucial period of the early Reformation.

Over the ensuing years of religious turmoil, Tunstal's saving grace in political terms was a preparedness to enforce religious decisions that were made regardless of his own opinions. He had also a decided aversion to the persecution of heretics and on one occasion is reputed to have bought copies of Tyndale's Bible so that he could burn them in substitute for the people who illegally read them. Amongst the interests in later life of this rather sympathetic man were coin collecting and gardening.[5] Nevertheless, he was imbued with a strong sense of his own dignity when it came to architecture and once rebuked a group of his workmen for constructing a building using rubble as opposed to tooled blocks of masonry. Angrily, he enquired, could the bishop of Durham not afford cut stone?[6]

Soon after his appointment to Durham there followed two body blows to the prestige of the bishopric. The first of these was the 1536 Act of Resumption, by which the king assumed authority over the previously independent palatinate of Durham. Two years later, the shrine of St Cuthbert, the defender of the see and Tunstal's own namesake, was despoiled. Stripping away the precious outer cover of the shrine, the hard-headed royal agents were alarmed to find the body of the saint uncorrupted within its coffin. After accidentally breaking one of Cuthbert's legs, they left it unmolested.[7] At this time the bishop was under close surveillance by

323 The north range of Durham. Bishop Tunstal added a gallery range (1) across the front of the earlier twelfth-century hall block (2), which was probably remodelled internally at the same time to form a series of withdrawing chambers. He also rebuilt the chapel to the right (3). The balcony closet for his personal use was accessible up a new stair turret, which is shown centre left (4). Throughout, Tunstal's works employ plain windows of a type that would remain popular across the north of England into the late seventeenth century. The gallery carefully accommodates the superb twelfth-century door to Bishop Puiset's hall, a tacit mark of admiration for this object from a different architectural age. The renovation of the great tower (5) initiated by Bishop Fox was also completed by Tunstal. The building has subsequently been much reduced in height.

Cromwell, who had his lodgings at Stockton, Auckland and Durham searched for incriminating evidence of opposition to the king's supremacy. When the Pilgrimage of Grace erupted in 1536, however, Tunstal was not prompted into opposition. Instead, he avoided any declaration of sympathy by taking refuge at Norham. Incidentally, he is credited with having much repaired this castle, but of his works or their date, nothing is securely known. From this security he refused to emerge even when summoned by the king.

This performance just saved Tunstal from disgrace, but his sphere of influence was henceforth circumscribed to the north. It is probably in recognition of his increasingly provincial role that in 1537 – in the immediate aftermath of the Pilgrimage of Grace – he began the last significant alterations to Durham before the Civil War. These operations involved the addition of a new gallery, porch tower and chapel along the front of the north side of the castle (pl. 323).[8] The new chapel was evidently completed by 1547–8, when a fine series of choir stalls was moved from the chapel at Auckland to furnish this new building.[9] Meanwhile,

Tunstal further completed the great tower on the motte with four storeys of lodgings (an operation begun by his predecessor Bishop Fox) and hung new iron gates at the entrance of the castle.[10] It was probably in the course of these changes that Tunstal also provided the castle with a running water supply with a cistern fed by lead pipes.

The death of Henry VIII, which coincided with the completion of these alterations, introduced Tunstal to new political difficulties. Although he managed initially to remain on good terms with the lord protector of the young king, the duke of Somerset, he soon came into conflict with the other leading figure in the minority government, John Dudley. And here it is necessary to digress into the career of Tunstal's archenemy. The son of a loyal servant of Henry VII, Dudley was a courtier swept to power by the politics of the Reformation. It is likely that Thomas Cromwell helped him secure his first office in 1532, the constableship of Warwick Castle. As such, it must have been under Dudley's direction that in 1538 the roof of the Blackfriars in Warwick was appropriated for the new royal

434

kitchen in the castle and also that substantial repairs were undertaken around 1542 to prevent subsidence in the cliff beneath the walls.[11]

Through Cromwell's agency, this office was followed by other small appointments, and in 1540 Dudley foreclosed on a large debt owed to him by a kinsman, Lord Dudley. This allowed him to take control of Dudley Castle, Warwickshire, which he adopted as his principal residence. He evidently improved the castle buildings and a letter of 1553 identifies one of the masons involved as a certain John Chapman. Possibly one in a dynasty of masons with connections to the king's works, Chapman was also involved in the remodelling of the former monasteries of Longleat and Lacock.[12] Dudley navigated the fall of Cromwell, and his continued royal favour is reflected by his creation as Viscount Lisle in 1542. He was subsequently active in Henry's later wars in Scotland and France, and at the death of Henry VIII was part of the inner governmental circle.

Dudley's importance in the minority government of Edward VI was at once acknowledged in the batch of titles distributed at the outset of the reign: on 31 March 1547 he was created earl of Warwick. Dudley claimed his right to the title through a family link with the Beauchamp family, whose heraldic devices of a bear and ragged staff he adopted.[13] This startling consolidation of his existing interest in Warwick Castle was sealed by his grant of the manor, castle and town, besides other lands, to the value of £548 per annum.[14] In a far from disinterested letter justifying this acquisition, he complained that 'the castle of itself is not able to lodge a good baron with his train, for all one side of the said castle with also the dungeon tower is clearly ruinated and down to the ground'.[15] If the buildings were damaged, they did not long remain so, and Warwick superseded Dudley as his principal seat.

In political terms, Dudley proved a brilliant manager of the young king, and eventually succeeded in outmanoeuvring the lord protector entirely. His elevation on 11 October 1551 to the title of duke of Northumberland signalled his emergence as the principal power in the realm. This choice of title was pointed: there immediately followed on 20 October his appointment as warden general on the marches of Scotland. This latter office came with a fee of £1,333 per annum, but this was not sufficient either for his office or new estate. Indeed, his eye seems to have fallen on a yet richer prize: the remaining possessions of the see of Durham.

Cuthbert Tunstal's opposition to the religious reforms of Edward VI's government had already led to friction between him and John Dudley. This had culminated on 20 May 1551, when the bishop was thrown into prison and Dudley tried to manage his execution through an act of attainder. Although this plot was frustrated, Tunstal was deprived of his see on 14 October 1552. Two weeks later Northumberland wrote to the king's secretary:

> . . . if his majesty make the dean of Durham bishop of that see, and appoint him one thousand marks more to that which he hath in his deanery, – and the same houses which he now hath, as well in the city as in the country, will serve him right honourably, – so may his majesty receive both the castle, which hath a princely site, and the other stately houses which the bishop had in the country . . .'[16]

In April 1553 the king followed this advice: the see was suppressed and a suffragan bishop established at Newcastle. Immediately afterwards, the palatine of Durham with its unparalleled powers was revived as a secular entity, almost certainly for Dudley's benefit.[17] The castle of Durham was probably not to be a seat for the bishop, or even the king, but of the new duke of Northumberland.

In the same year and at the very same time that Dudley was looking to establish his interest in the north, he was also consolidating his Warwickshire possessions. In 1553 he received a grant of the great castle of Kenilworth, the sister foundation to his former titular seat at Warwick. From the evidence of a survey of the castle made around 1563–9, it is apparent that within the next few months Dudley completed a new stable in the outer bailey of the castle.[18] The timber-frame braces of the building are shaped to represent the Dudley emblem of the ragged staff and its scale is a reminder of the importance of horses and the prestige attached to them. This building precisely copies the plan of the stable erected at Warwick Castle by Richard Beauchamp, earl of Warwick (d. 1439).[19] The mason responsible may have been a certain Robert Cock, who received the appointment of chief mason at Kenilworth in 1552.[20]

Unfortunately for Dudley, these astonishing prizes were all snatched from him by the death of the king, Edward VI, on 6 July 1553. Dudley overextended himself in support of a Protestant succession and was executed. Two of his children, Ambrose and Robert, we will encounter again later. Meanwhile, Tunstal was released by Queen Mary and restored to his revived see in April 1554. But even after these adventures Tunstal was not long to remain bishop of Durham. On Elizabeth's accession, like many other Marian bishops, he refused to take the oath of supremacy and was deprived of the see once more. He eventually died in his late eighties as a guest of the archbishop of Canterbury in 1559. His deprivation once more left the see of Durham open to exploitation.

Tunstal's successor from 1560 to 1575, Bishop Pilkington, seems to have faced insuperable problems as a Reformer in a very Catholic diocese. These difficulties were compounded when the government seized the property of several of those involved in the Northern Rising in 1569, including that of the earl of Westmorland. Much of this was held by the earl from the bishop, who consequently lost control of it for the future.[21] In combination, these circumstances had a disastrous effect on the bishop's residences, and when Richard Barnes succeeded to the see in 1577, he took Pilkington's widow to court over the dilapidations to them.[22]

Barnes himself loathed Durham and its people and offloaded episcopal property onto the crown to curry favour. This haemorrhaging of land and property from Durham was forever to remove its bishops from the forefront of architectural patronage in the north of England. Barnes, however, did at least restore the buildings of his castles at Durham and Bishop Auckland. In the two-year vacancy that followed his death in 1587, further land was pruned off the bishopric, by coincidence, at the instigation of the duke of Northumberland's son, Robert Dudley.[23] This final loss behind it, the see of Durham miraculously emerged from the Reformation greatly reduced but intact as a palatinate. So too did its principal seat remain at Durham and Bishop Auckland continue as a favoured country retreat. These buildings were in truth, however, now vestiges of past greatness rather than current power.

ANTIQUARIANISM AND THE BIRTH OF ARCHITECTURAL HISTORY

Before delving further into the architectural development of castles in this period, it is necessary to say something about the changing intellectual backdrop against which they were being viewed. It was in the sixteenth century that there appeared for the first time full descriptions of English castles as monuments with histories rooted in a consideration of their documentation and fabric. So, for example, in the 1570s the scholar Stow was able to write that Windsor was: 'buylded (as is sayd), but withowt any auctorie yt I have herd, by Kynge Arthure: so both the credit of some auncient records, and the constant fame and newyns of the worke, declare the same to have been augmentyd and amplified with the two higher wardes long since'.[24] Here was a man using his ears, his learning and his eyes to unpack the history of a castle.

Such analysis was not entirely a new development. Since the late fifteenth century, the interest in topographical and historical accounts of England had been rapidly intensifying. The scholar William Worcester (d. *circa* 1480–85) had compiled antiquarian and architectural descriptions in his travels around England.[25] Similarly, his near contemporary John Rous (d. 1492) wrote at length about the buildings, personalities and history of Warwick.[26] In the 1530s an anonymous canon of Thornton Abbey in Lincolnshire even wrote an architectural and institutional history of his own church, precisely quoting lost building accounts.[27] Were his name known or the buildings and furnishings of Thornton better preserved, such an extraordinary undertaking would surely have attracted much greater attention.

Undoubtedly the most celebrated figure in this tradition is John Leland. A self-styled 'antiquarius' (or antiquarian), a title borrowed from Continental humanist usage, Leland toured the monastic libraries of England during the 1530s in pursuit of manuscripts. Around 1540, however, he became additionally interested in the topography of England. As well as striving to rescue the forgotten works of English authors – to refute the authority of the pope – and rescue books from the effects of the Dissolution, he also travelled widely across the kingdom taking notes about the landscapes, towns, curiosities and buildings that he saw. As Leland himself stated:

> . . . there is almost neyther cape nor baye, haven, creke or pere, ryver or confluence of ryvers, breches, washes, lakes, meres, fenny waters, mountaynes, valleys, mores, hethes, forestes, woodes, cyties, burges, castels, pryncypall manor places, monasteryes and colleges, but I have seane them and noted in so doynge a whole worlde of thynges verye memorable.[28]

Leland unfortunately went mad around 1547 and his notes, written in English and Latin, have only partially survived. Nevertheless, the geographic extent of his labour, although it was never completed, marks it out as a new departure: his was an attempt to create a portrait of the whole kingdom in the 1540s, its history, institutions and physical appearance.

Castles figure frequently in Leland's notes, a mark both of their continued prominence in the landscape and their conceived importance. Some of these are described as being partially or totally ruined, but many others were in use as residences and administrative centres.[29] In architectural terms, his descriptions reflect much less technical understanding than those – for example – of his predecessor William Worcester. They also employ a magnificently catholic vocabulary that makes no attempt at consistency or descriptive precision. Just to compound the difficulties of evaluating his descriptions, Leland can additionally be grossly inaccurate on occasion, both in reported historical detail and in points of observation. How, for example, could anyone describe the great tower of Berkeley (see pl. 76) as a square building?[30] He is – in short – a source too valuable to be ignored but to be quoted with care.

The strongly historical slant of Leland's topographical interests was widely paralleled in the generation of scholars that succeeded him. One of Elizabeth I's chaplains, William Darell, compiled a treatise on the castles of Kent, *Castra in campo Cantiano ab antiquo aedita nobilium ope et diligentia*, dedicated in sycophantic strains to William Brooke, Lord Cobham, constable of Dover and lord warden of the Cinque Ports.[31] His treatment of Dover is the first architectural account of the buildings, and was written in Latin, as the preface explains, in order to appeal to an international audience.[32] Darrell may also have begun the scrapbook of medieval manuscripts relating to the castle that now survives at Knole.[33] Such architectural descriptions graduated into the related study of ancestry, which further offers valuable information about the development of castles.

HERALDRY, ANCESTRY AND THE CASTLE

A great deal of architectural research in this period was driven by an interest in family history and pedigree. During the last years of Elizabeth's reign, for example, a certain John Smyth of Nibley compiled the *Lives of the Berkeleys*, a compendious family history that incidentally unravels much of the development of the castle at Berkeley, Gloucestershire.[34] This genealogical interest was also expressed in the changing use of heraldry, still the distinguishing mark of those of gentle birth. The desire to show the descent of families and their marriages over long periods of time encouraged the division of individual shields into literally scores of subdivisions termed quarterings. By the mid-sixteenth century there were beginning to appear a complexity and variety of armorial bearing beyond the dreams of heralds a century before. At the same time heraldry began to be policed and researched with new vigour as heralds made visitations to churches and houses across the land, recording the arms they saw.

In this way, the late medieval and early Tudor love for heraldic displays that incorporated a small number of repeated devices began to give way in favour of armorial celebrations of histories or dynasties. Decorative displays of this kind were not exclusive to castles, but the antiquity of these buildings – amongst the oldest inhabited buildings in the English landscape – and their martial character made them particularly appropriate for such schemes. The most magnificent to sur-vive from the Elizabethan period is in the great chamber of Gilling, Yorkshire, created by Sir William Fairfax (pl. 324). A leading figure in the East Riding, Sir William probably began the work of rebuilding his family castle in the late 1570s, erecting new chambers on the basement of a fourteenth-century tower. It is likely to have been his appointment as sheriff of Yorkshire in 1577 that inspired him to create a complete record of the county's arms painted around the cornice of his new great chamber. In the stained-glass windows of the same room are heraldic family trees relating to the ownership of the castle since the thirteenth century.[35]

The heraldic display at Gilling followed long-established artistic conventions that find parallel in earlier buildings such as the fifteenth-century wall paintings of Belsay, Northumberland, with the arms supported on trees against a background of grass and flowers. What is new about it is the sheer wealth of heraldry and its coherent arrangement. Sir William even had amongst his books 'a register of all the gentlemen's arms in the great chamber', which presumably allowed visitors to unpack the logic of the display and identify shields within it. Other grand collections of heraldry of this kind are known from the period, for example, that in the council chamber at Ludlow (discussed below). In Queenborough, Kent, the hall was decorated with the arms of the gentry and nobility of Kent. Set amidst them were the arms of the queen with a laudatory inscription and the date 1592.[36]

324 A photograph taken in 2019 of the great chamber at Gilling, Yorkshire. The interior was probably created after 1577 and completed in 1585. Painted on boards around the cornice of the room are trees bearing the arms of leading families arranged by the county wapentakes in which they lived. In the windows are displayed the arms of the owners of Gilling from the reign of Edward 1. These are grouped by family in separate windows and set within plain glass quarries of different patterns. The whole interior is alive with visually implied narratives and hierarchies, a treatment most familiar to a modern audience in the decoration of medieval churches. The marquetry panelling was probably made by Continental craftsmen and compares to work found at nearby Helmsley and also Sizergh, Westmorland.

Incidentally, the interior of the great chamber at Gilling with its fine glass and marquetry panelling also illustrates the growing influence of Continental craftsmen and their working patterns. One panel of the glass is signed 'Bærnard Dininckhoff 1585', a German settled in York who also had a northern architectural practice.[37] Evidence for this includes surviving plans for a 'Kastel' at Sheriff Hutton in Yorkshire, a residence designed for the landowner Sir Andrew Lumsden.[38] The only properly English thing about the Gilling interior is the superb pendant vault. It is noteworthy that the craftsmen at work here were active in a number of other sites: the work of both plasterers and joiners can be paralleled at nearby Helmsley Castle, which was expanded and refurnished between 1577 and 1582 for Edward Manners, third earl of Rutland.

At Wolfeton in Dorset the Trenchard family depicted the arms of all their ancestors in the windows of the great chamber. This glazing scheme was probably first created in the 1530s but continued to be updated into the seventeenth century.[39] A similar scheme is recorded at Newnham, Warwickshire, where the different members of the family were shown as figures in appropriate period dress.[40] Figural displays of this kind continued to be created right up to the Civil War and in a variety of contexts. In 1633, for example, Lady Abigail Sherrard extended a wing of her family seat at Stapleford in Leicestershire and decorated the façade with sculptures of historical figures. This particular display, which incorporates religious panels probably copied from alabaster originals, may derive from the genealogies of English kings found on the pulpitum screens of several major churches (such as the cathedrals of Old St Paul's, Canterbury and York) and the entrance front of Westminster Hall.

The obsession of the late Tudor world with lineage is most spectacularly illustrated, however, by the work

325 The hall of Lumley Castle, Co. Durham, photographed in 1910. It shows the dynastic portraits commissioned by John, Lord Lumley, on the walls and the large equestrian figure of Edward III that stood above the dais (all now at Leeds Castle). An inventory of 1590 records that there were formerly displayed in addition marble busts of Lord Lumley's six sons and also the four Tudor monarchs who ruled in his lifetime: Henry VIII, Edward VI, Mary and Elizabeth I. Some later sources also claim that the equestrian figure represents Liulph, a fictional and remote ancestor of the family. Where appropriate, Lumley introduced sophisticated classical detailing, as is represented here by the hall fireplace. A castle overflowing with evidence of ancestry, but nevertheless touched by modern fashions, Lumley was a perfect seat for an Elizabethan nobleman.

of John, Lord Lumley (d. 1609), to his family castle at Lumley in Co. Durham. For Lord Lumley the possibilities of a political career were ended by his implication in the Ridolfi Plot of 1571 to restore Catholicism to England. He narrowly escaped execution and, following his release from the Tower of London in 1573, spent an increasing amount of time at his family seat. Lumley was himself a determined Catholic and a distinguished patron of a bewildering variety of pursuits from gardening to medicine. Amongst his most passionate interests was ancestry, which he celebrated in a variety of ways in the furnishing and fabric of the castle.

The fourteenth-century gatehouse was ornamented in 1577 with a series of shields that traced Lumley's descent back to the reign of William the Conqueror. In complement to this, the portraits of sixteen forebears were hung in the great chamber along with a 'pillar of his pedigree'.[41] There was also a painting of Richard II granting Lumley's ancestor his title of nobil-

ity and, in the hall, a large equestrian statue of Edward III, in whose reign the castle had been largely built (pl. 325). The scope of the Lumleys' ancestral display at the castle, when presented in tedious detail to James I during a visit in 1603, prompted the king to observe 'I didna' ken Adam's ither nam was Lumley'.[42]

Beyond the castle walls Lord Lumley was also involved in constituting an appropriate dynastic mausoleum. Between 1594 and 1597 he created or collected fourteen tombs of his ancestors, many of them medieval effigies, which were arranged as formidable evidence of his genealogy in the church of Chester-le-Street, Co. Durham. Over exactly the same period, and as the kinsman of Henry Fitzalan, twelfth earl of Arundel (d. 1580), Lord Lumley also restored the medieval family mausoleum in the chancel of the collegiate church at Arundel. In all his work, Lord Lumley worked in two very different artistic idioms. Many of the tombs he created evoked or copied Gothic design, as was appropriate to their antiquity. Where more fashionable magnificence was required – as in fireplaces and conduits in the castle courtyard – he switched seamlessly into the most sophisticated neo-classical detailing.

Families across the kingdom repaired and reorganised collections of tombs to draw public attention to the antiquity of their lineage. In the parish church beside their castle at Muncaster, Cumberland, for example, the Pennington family created memorials to their ancestors as far back as the reign of Edward I. This scheme of brass and stone plaques was probably created – to judge from the epigraphy – in the early seventeenth century, but was remade in the nineteenth (which makes it problematic to date). At the same time in Dorset there appears to have been a workshop producing numerous funeral effigies in medieval-style armour, a pair of which to Sir John Horsey (d. 1546) and his son (d. 1564) survives at Sherborne Abbey. There are pre-Reformation antecedents for the creations of sets of tombs in this way, of which the most impressive surviving example is the series of sarcophagi of saints and kings erected around the choir screen at Winchester Cathedral.[43]

WINDSOR AND KENILWORTH AND THE CELEBRATION OF DYNASTY

For all the undoubted grandeur and ambition of new building in England during the later sixteenth century, no newer residences approached the scale of the very greatest medieval castles. Pre-eminent amongst these remained the royal seat of Windsor, still enclosed by its huge parks created in the eleventh century. By comparison with other more recent royal residences, it was not a particularly comfortable home. Indeed, when Edward VI was compelled to move here for safety from Hampton Court during the culminating crisis of Protector Somerset's government in October 1549, he complained that the castle was like a prison with 'no galleries nor no gardens to walke in', and caught a cold.[44]

Nevertheless, Windsor remained an outstanding symbol of royal identity and prestige. Amongst other things, the direct link between the Order of the Garter and the chapel of St George made it the scene of one of the most important court festivals of the year. Quite as significant, in terms of the profile of the castle, was the choice of Windsor by Henry VIII as a burial place.

It was a decision that was materially to affect the development of the buildings. To judge by the megalomaniac proportions of the various monuments he planned, Henry VIII's intention was not so much to be buried in St George's as to make the chapel a memorial to himself: one proposal involved erecting an equestrian statue of bronze spanning the choir. Such ambition of conception perhaps dissuaded Henry's children from completing the project. In their other works at Windsor, however, the three half-siblings went to considerable lengths to honour their father's memory.

By his last will and testament Henry VIII had requested that a community of thirteen poor knights be attached to St George's College. This was to fulfil in part the unrealised direction in Edward III's original foundation statutes that twenty-four such poor knights be supported by the foundation. Edward VI secured the money for this endowment and Mary erected the new buildings for the community between 1557 and 1558. These survive against the south wall of the lower castle ward. In a neatly symmetrical arrangement, Elizabeth I then sorted out the practicalities of staffing this branch of the college.[45] All Henry's children were ultimately buried at Westminster, but around 1573 there were plans to bury Edward VI beside his father beneath a grand monument by Cornelius Cure and – in effect – turn the chapel into a shrine to the new Protestant dynasty of England.[46]

These attentions to St George's ensured that the residential buildings in the upper ward underwent small but significant alterations throughout the sixteenth century. Edward VI, for example, reorganised the castle water supply in 1542 by installing pipes and a conduit in the castle, an essential centrepiece to any Tudor palace. The creation of this water system in the upper ward was completed by Mary.[47] Much more significant, however, were the extensive repairs undertaken by Elizabeth I from 1570 onwards. Upon her accession the buildings – as always with royal castles – were reported to be in an unaccountably bad state: there was widespread dilapidation and even timber propping throughout the chapel and hall to hold up the roofs. Over the next four years, despite her legendary dislike of any expenditure on building, the queen sank more than £6,000 into the thorough repair of her lodgings. At the same time she rebuilt and enlarged the terrace walk above the Thames erected by Henry VIII and erected a bridge leading from it to a new banqueting house at the eastern end of the castle. In 1580 the great

326 Detail from Marcus Gerard's *Proceeding of the Sovereign and Knights Companions of the Order of the Garter at St George's Feast in 1578*. Behind Elizabeth I is a north view of Windsor, Berkshire. It shows the terrace and banqueting house constructed by the queen beneath the castle walls. The works to Windsor were amongst the most costly architectural projects she ever undertook. The engraving underlines the importance of Garter Day as a state celebration and its association with Windsor Castle.

tower or 'keep' to the castle was repaired and a new tennis court created beneath it with gallery access from the royal lodgings (pl. 326).[48]

Windsor was the grandest dynastic castle of this kind, but it had imitators on a scarcely less splendid scale. It was noted as early as April 1559 that the young Queen Elizabeth showed a particular fondness for Robert Dudley, son of John Dudley, the late duke of Northumberland. That year he was elected a knight of the Garter and lieutenant of Windsor, an appointment subsequently converted to the constableship of the castle. In 1560 his wife, Amy Robsart, died (or, as some suppose, was murdered) and he became a serious contender for Elizabeth's hand. His elder brother, Ambrose, received the earldom of Warwick in 1561 and the lordship of the town and castle soon afterwards. As a mark of this creation both brothers, who remained very close, adopted the ragged staff of the Beauchamp earls of Warwick as their symbol. The following year Robert Dudley received the historic partner of his brother's castle, Kenilworth, along with the lucrative baronies of Denbigh and Chirk in Wales. These grants

were crowned with the titles of baron of Denbigh and earl of Leicester in September the following year. The estates and residences included in the gifts did not at first attract Leicester away from the court, though both brothers used their Midland castles to receive the queen while on progress in 1566 and 1568.[49]

From 1570, however, Leicester began to visit Kenilworth every year and remarkable changes ensued. In 1571 he founded an almshouse at Warwick for twelve men called Lord Leycester Hospital and converted the buildings of various suppressed guilds to serve it.[50] The hospital, which by 1585 had been specifically constituted to maintain veterans from the wars, may have been part of a wider programme of religious endowment in the town that also included the proposed conversion of the collegiate church of St Mary in Warwick into a preaching centre.[51] The same year, his master mason, Robert Spicer, corresponded about a major new addition to Kenilworth Castle. Plans were drawn up for the creation of a grand new façade to the castle probably incorporating two storeys of lodging.[52] These were abandoned, however, and work began instead to

327 A reconstruction and cut-away by Chris Jones-Jenkins of Leicester's Building, Kenilworth, Warwickshire, built in 1571 and further adapted prior to 1575. It was designed to form a visual counterbalance to the great tower of the castle. Boldly conceived and with a crown of battlements, the tower contained a suite of lodgings for the queen including a privy chamber (1), a withdrawing chamber (2), a bedchamber (3), a dancing chamber (4) and an anteroom (5), with convenient access to the leads of the lower roof (6). It was designed with large grids of windows and was sumptuously furnished internally. The most important rooms were on the uppermost two floors of the four-storey building. This arrangement derived directly from great tower architecture of the Middle Ages and subsequently enjoyed great favour in numerous grand Elizabeth residences, such as Hardwick New Hall, Derbyshire.

At the same time, the old great tower was renewed, possibly as a gallery or loggia offering fine prospects over the neighbouring gardens. As part of this operation the entrance and forebuilding were rebuilt with heraldic ornament and an inscription in which the date 1570 is still discernible. Probably in conjunction with these alterations, the fourteenth-century great chamber built by John of Gaunt was given a new front and provided with large compass windows. A further visit by the queen in 1572 appears to have provoked more alterations, notably the construction of a new gatehouse on the north side of the castle. In its design, this building compares to a widespread family of earlier gatehouses and demonstrates the extraordinary continuities possible within the Perpendicular idiom (pl. 328).

As completed in the 1570s, Kenilworth was a fascinating architectural hotchpotch with surviving elements from every period of its architectural development from the 1120s onwards. Such depth of architectural history was undoubtedly admired and was consequently exaggerated in several ways. The foundation of the castle, for example, was attributed to a fictional king of Mercia called Kenelm, who was reputedly crowned in 798. Moreover, the great tower of the castle also came to be known as 'Caesar's Tower'. It is possible that the intention was to present the tower as a Roman building, but at least one contemporary thought that it was 'rather (az I have good cauz to think) for that it is square and high formed after the maner of Caesars footrz then that ever he bylt it'.[53]

Incidentally, it is indication of Dudley's admiration for historic architecture that he probably also took Romanesque sculptural fragments from the dissolved priory at Kenilworth and re-erected them in the 1570s as the main door to the parish church, where the queen attended divine service during her visits.[54] This remarkable instance of architectural recycling is a reminder of the sophisticated ways in which the buildings of the distant past could be viewed and treated in this period (pl. 329).

Elizabeth's final visit to Kenilworth lasted between 9 and 27 July 1575. This was the longest halt of any royal progress in the reign and it reflects the high favour in which Dudley basked at this time. Dudley himself may have been engaged in a last desperate bid to woo the forty-two-year-old queen and father an heir to the

328 The gatehouse at Kenilworth, Warwickshire, erected between 1570 and 1575. The gabled ranges to the right were added in the 1650s when the gatehouse was converted into a self-contained house following the destruction of the castle.

At this date the passage running through the length of the building was also blocked. The outer façade – not visible here – bears a close resemblance to the inner façade of the gatehouse erected in the mid-fourteenth century at Warwick Castle.

The composition of the inner façade, meanwhile, has several earlier sixteenth-century parallels such as Coughton, Warwickshire, and Titchfield, Hampshire. Such similarities underline the centralisation of architectural design in the Perpendicular style.

a new lodging tower, now called Leicester's Building. It balanced the massive bulk of the great tower and created a roughly symmetrical façade to the inner bailey (pl. 327).

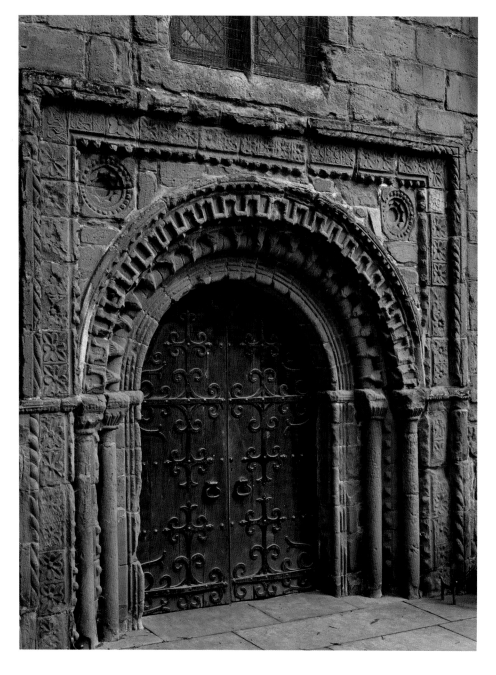

throne. The celebrations at Kenilworth, which probably emulated contemporary French court occasions, are known from a pair of contemporary descriptions. While contradictory in some points of detail, these give a good overall impression of events. According to the longer of the two, an open letter by a junior official called Robert Laneham (or Langham), keeper of the council chamber door, they were 'for the parsons, for the place, time cost, devizes, straungeness and the aboundance of all [the greatest] that ever I saw'.[55] Whether the spectacles of the visit were transporting to witness – as such adulators would wish us to believe – or more in the character of amateur dramatics must remain an open question. Whatever the case, they were fantastical in the extreme and charged with metaphor.

The queen approached the outer gates of Kenilworth Castle at eight in the evening on 19 July and was welcomed in verse by a sibyl dressed in white silk. She then rode to the main gate of the castle where a huge porter with a staff and keys burst forth and complained of the noise and bother he had suffered over the course of the day. Catching sight of the monarch, however, the porter was struck with amazement. Falling to his knees, he yielded up his keys and club to the majesty before him. After receiving a pardon from the queen for his impertinence, he called for a fanfare of welcome. At once, six trumpeters dressed in silk sounded their instruments from the walls. Each trumpeter stood 8 feet tall (presumably they stood on stilts or were otherwise dressed to appear as giants), a reference to the manly stature of Englishmen in the age of King Arthur, and their silver trumpets were of exceptional size: 5 feet long and splaying to bells 16 inches broad. By this welcome Elizabeth was understood to be entering the Arthurian universe, a universe in which her royal predecessors had so long delighted. Throughout her stay, to underline the special quality of her visit, the hands on the clock dials of the great tower were frozen at two o'clock (see pl. 49), a perfect hour for the hospitable reception of guests.

As the queen rode along the tiltyard the trumpeters on the walls accompanied her progress with melodious music. Meanwhile, from the mere, a floating island lit with torches appeared in the twilight. On it rode the Lady of the Lake (played, as all such female figures were, by a man), the keeper of King Arthur's sword, Excalibur, accompanied by two nymphs. She met the queen and in verse declaimed that since Arthur had resided here she had remained in restless pain concealed in the lake. None of the great figures associated

329 The west door of St Mary's church, Kenilworth, Warwickshire. The rich Romanesque doorway is set in a decorative frame of sculpture in a manner that is hard to parallel in surviving twelfth-century architecture. Similar compositions of elements are found, however, in Dudley's works to the castle, such as the surviving porch to the Great Hall stair. The implication is that the Romanesque door and some of its accompanying sculpture were looted from the ruins of the neighbouring abbey and re-erected here for Elizabeth I's visit. A grant of the abbey property in December 1572 that excepts buildings 'which the Queen shall order to be removed' may date the work. The reuse or imitation of ancient architecture in this way may be an Elizabethan commonplace that has received little attention.

with the castle had ever tempted her forth except Elizabeth, to whom she proffered her lake, the castle and its lord. Elizabeth accepted her homage and then declared as a humorous aside that she had always presumed the lake to have been hers anyway and would have to have words with the lady later on the matter. Her attendants were delighted by the joke.

To the sound of wind instruments the queen now moved into the castle proper. Spanning the dry ditch that divided the inner and outer baileys was a bridge with fourteen posts, each one set with gifts symbolic of certain deities of the Roman pantheon of gods: caged birds for Sylvanus, fruits for Pomona, wheat and corn for Ceres, wine for Bacchus, fish for Neptune, arms for Mars and instruments for Phoebus. Over the gateway at the head of the bridge was fastened a plaque with the royal arms and an inscription with letters of gold by which Jupiter gave these gifts to the queen. It was by now so dark, however, that the inscription was not legible and the text had to be read out. Elizabeth passed through the gate to the sound of flutes, and she dismounted at her lodgings to the roar of guns and fireworks.

Over the next two and a half weeks, and through some very hot weather, the queen entertained herself in a variety of ways. Hunting was one of her principal pastimes and she evidently took particular delight in watching the deer chased through the mere by the hounds. One stag was caught in the water alive by the huntsmen and, at the command of the queen, lost its ears as a ransom for life. The hunting trips were punctuated by carefully staged entertainments. During one, for example, the queen was confronted by a wildman of the wood who discoursed with Echo, the companion of his loneliness, in celebration of the queen and her glittering entourage.

On another occasion, as Elizabeth rode back to the castle across the great bridge that crossed the mere to the park, she was accosted from the water by a messenger from Neptune, the god of the sea and water. The Lady of the Lake, explained the messenger, was held in thrall by Sir Bruce Sans Pitee (without pity) and his bands. Would but the queen look into the water, the power of this evil knight would be broken and the Lady of the Lake be free of his powers. The queen obliged, and the Lady of the Lake appeared and gave Elizabeth a gift of the musician Orion. At that moment Orion appeared riding a dolphin in the water and sang to the accompaniment of hidden instruments in the belly of his vehicle.

It was not in the park alone, however, that the queen was regaled by such displays. There were entertainments laid on in the castle as well. These included a fight between a team of bears and dogs, a performance by an Italian acrobat, the enacting of a play, a firework display with incendiaries that burnt beneath the water of the mere, and a ludicrous bride-ale. The last was a mock wedding celebration between a hideous couple: the bridegroom was lame from a childhood football accident and the bride was reputedly a vain and ugly thirty-five-year-old woman. The wedding party danced and made itself ridiculous to the assembled courtiers with such sports as tilting at the quintain: riding with a pole at a revolving target that span to dismount its assailant.

This bride-ale coincided with the enactment by the men of Coventry – a city long famed for its plays – of a pageant in the form of a battle between the English and the Danes. Curiously, according to Laneham, the battle was a long-standing entertainment that had fallen under suspicion following the Reformation. This performance before the queen was part of an attempt to lend it respectability for the future and to demonstrate that it was without 'ill example of mannerz, popery or ony superstition'.

The English team were led into the field by Captain Cox, a mason of Coventry, who reputedly possessed a great knowledge of chivalric romances. He was probably mounted on a hobbyhorse and led the assault against the Danes flourishing his sword. In the ensuing mêlée both sides manoeuvred elaborately and fought vigorously both on foot and 'on horse'. The Danes were victorious, but after the battle were carried off by English women. Unfortunately both for the wedding party and the men of Coventry, who were busy performing beneath the windows of the queen's chamber, Elizabeth saw little of the spectacle. Instead, she was in her chamber watching 'delectable dancing' – an interesting comment on the realities of the queen's public and private life. Having missed all but the conclusion of their entertainment, Elizabeth requested that the men of Coventry should appear again on another day. Captain Cox and his followers returned once more and their performance evidently went down in legend: more than fifty years later another royal entertainment at Kenilworth was prefaced by the appearance of the 'ghost' of this remarkable Coventry mason.[56]

As a background to these spectacular occasions, food was provided in lavish quantities for the queen. On one evening a Heliogabalan feast of 300 dishes was served by way of a banquet. The queen ate little or nothing of this exquisitely prepared food, which was hungrily devoured by those of less-elevated status. Efforts were also made to beautify the gardens. These are described in some detail by Laneham, whose account has broadly been corroborated by archaeological excavation and recreated in 2008–9.[57] The gardens were divided into a regular grid of beds set with obelisks around a central fountain.[58] Facing the castle along one side of the garden was an aviary, richly decorated and filled with exotic birds. No expense was spared to entertain and amuse the queen.

The redevelopment of Kenilworth was undoubtedly the most important undertaken by Dudley on his estate, but it was not his only such project. Although he first visited Denbigh in 1584, he not only occupied and repaired the thirteenth-century castle, but also erected two important buildings in the town. In 1571 he was involved in the construction of a new town hall and in 1578 began work to a church just beyond the castle walls. Designed in a loosely Gothic style and on a huge scale, it is possible that it was intended as a new cathedral. Committed Reformers by persuasion, Dudley and his brother were both active in their support of Protestantism in this Catholic part of Wales. It may be an indication of local hostility or shortages of money that the building was never completed.[59] Whether Dudley additionally worked at the castle of his third barony of Chirk is not known. A survey of the building conducted for him around 1563 simply states: 'The castle though yt doth seeme very fayre as the walles and towers . . . yet standeth yet yt is utterly ruinous, the tymber rotten and without hope of all repairing; yet hath the fairest prospect of all the castles and houses your honour hath.'[60]

Dudley and his brother Ambrose were both buried in the great fifteenth-century Lady Chapel of St Mary's, Warwick. In this final detail the continuity of patterns of noble patronage from the Middle Ages is absolutely complete: the two men restored their respective castles and were engaged in the establishment of religious foundations in direct relation to them. In death, they lie amidst their assumed ancestors, the Beauchamp earls of Warwick. They are shown in effigy just like them, dressed in armour surrounded by the trappings of war and heraldry. A visitor might fairly wonder what exactly the Renaissance and the Reformation had changed for the nobility of Protestant England.

THE RENOVATION OF CASTLES

The earls of Leicester and Warwick were exceptional patrons, but they were not alone amongst prominent courtiers to improve medieval castles. Sir Christopher Hatton, for example, was a trusted servant and intimate of the queen who rose to become lord chancellor in 1587. He reputedly first caught her attention by virtue of his skill as a dancer, and over the 1570s became her courtly lover, writing to her in strains of improbable devotion. As a lasting symbol of his affection and loyal service he rebuilt his family seat at Holdenby in Northamptonshire, one of the largest buildings of the Elizabethan period. This he gallantly refused to occupy until the 'saint' to whom it was dedicated (Elizabeth) had visited. But the queen never came to Holdenby, which was largely demolished in the Civil War. Holdenby has rightly attracted considerable scholarly attention, as has Hatton's reworking of his London house, Ely Place, another episcopal palace extracted from a reluctant clerical owner.[61]

Yet these building operations had an important counterpart that has received much less attention. In 1572 Elizabeth sold Corfe Castle to Christopher Hatton for more than £4,000. To judge from the annotations and details of a survey drawn up by Ralph Treswell in 1586, Hatton intended to reorganise the eleventh-century great tower, known as King's Tower, as the principal set of lodgings in the castle.[62] The physical evidence of the tower would suggest that at least some of this work took place, though later alterations to it and demolition after the Civil War make it hard to be certain of this. Hatton's plans for Corfe reflect the great prestige of this castle, a status enhanced by the feudal powers enjoyed by its owner over the Dorset coast. These were powers, moreover, that Hatton apparently exploited ruthlessly in partnership with notorious pirates.[63]

Another Elizabethan favourite who transformed an important castle was the celebrated captain and privateer Sir Walter Raleigh. In 1592 he secured the lease of Sherborne, the former castle of the bishops of Salisbury, and adapted the twelfth-century towers around the perimeter wall as lodging blocks. He also recast the domestic quadrangle in the heart of the building. As part of this latter process, the great hall was demolished to make the great tower of the castle stand in grand isolation. He then rebuilt the main front of the tower on an enlarged plan, with a colossal compass window. Curiously, these works took place at about the same

330 Sherborne Lodge, Dorset. As begun around 1593, the lodge originally comprised a central block with four angle towers and a walled forecourt. It was later extended with the projecting wings in the 1620s. The parapets are starkly ornamented with chimneys. A sixteenth-century plan of the building by Simon Basil, a leading figure in the royal works and surveyor of the king's works from 1606 to 1615, still survives. It is annotated with lines of fire in the manner of a design for an artillery fort, clear evidence that the building was inspired by fortifications. An engraved plan in a French treatise by Philibert de l'Orme, *Premier tome de l'architecture* (Paris, 1568), has been suggested as a possible source for the design.

time that Raleigh also began another castle-like building just a few hundred yards away. Sherborne Lodge, as it was then known, was a compactly planned tower with four corner turrets and a crown of tall chimneys (pl. 330). Raleigh appears to have used both buildings simultaneously: his elder son was born in the castle proper in 1594 and a graffito of the same year was scratched into a window in the Lodge, evidence that it was occupied at that date. The Lodge, with its more intimate domestic arrangement, was probably intended for private recreation away from the great household.

Across the kingdom at large, the alterations made to existing castles follow clear patterns. Most frequently and importantly, domestic apartments were modernised in keeping with changing fashions of display and grand domestic living. So, for example, there are many instances of great stairs and long galleries being inserted and of great chambers being refurnished. In the case of castles specifically, work often additionally focused on entrances, where modernisation would be most readily noticed by visitors. Instances of such improvements can be found throughout the period, but there was a particular burst of activity during the decade or more of relative peace and prosperity from 1569 onwards.

Such was the case, for example, when Helmsley Castle in Yorkshire was reordered from 1577 on behalf of its owner, Edward Manners, third earl of Rutland (d. 1587). The earl, a celebrated jouster and breeder of horses, generally resided in great state at Belvoir Castle, and the work at Helmsley was undertaken by his brother, John, who oversaw his extensive northern interests.[64] The changes to the castle of the 1570s included new withdrawing apartments within the west tower and its adjacent range, both twelfth-century structures already once remodelled in the fourteenth century. The principal rooms within the latter were set on the upper floor and lit by oriel windows. In conjunction with these works a long gallery was also built across the inner bailey and the medieval castle chapel converted into a new kitchen. Most curious of all, however, was the remodelling of the southern gate to the castle in a combination of classical and Gothic detailing (pl. 331). Stone for these operations was robbed from nearby Rievaulx Abbey and, according to surviving correspondence, construction was attended by some practical difficulties.[65]

More recently created castles than Helmsley could be adapted along similar lines with a much lighter architectural touch. At Herstmonceux in Sussex, for exam-

ple, a new great stair was ingeniously contrived within one of the smaller courts of the compact plan of the 1440s, and the withdrawing apartments were completely overhauled with new fireplaces and panelling. These alterations could be ascribed – either together or variously – to two different periods. A royal survey of the nearby castle at Pevensey records that lead was removed from the buildings and taken to supply unspecified works at Herstmonceux in August 1559. Alternatively, it is known that Samuel Lennard, owner of the castle by right of his wife between 1593 and 1611, decorated at least one of the withdrawing rooms with an elaborate heraldic display.[66]

But a much more radical approach could also be adopted. Perhaps the most ambitious reconstruction of an ancestral castle in the sixteenth century was undertaken by Sir William Paulet, Baron St John, who was created marquess of Winchester in 1551, at Basing in Hampshire. This important castle suffered particularly badly in the Civil War when, as a crucial royalist stronghold, it was stormed in 1645 after a long siege, looted, burnt out and its ruins demolished. From the extant remains it is hard today to recognise what Thomas Fuller described as 'the greatest of any subject's house in England, yea larger than most (Eagles have not the largest nests of all birds) of the King's palaces'.[67]

The castle, which is first documented in the mid-twelfth century, comprised a large circular earthwork and a bailey. These two elements were respectively developed in the sixteenth century as the 'Old House' and 'New House'. Each was enclosed by ditches and possessed an imposing circuit of towers, as well as a turreted gatehouse. The windows of the principal apartments are reported to have been glazed with the repeated motto 'Love Loyaltie'.[68] Excavation of the ruins in the 1920s revealed numerous fragments of high-quality architectural detailing including Caen stone roundels of Roman emperors, which were possibly carved and imported from abroad. With the evidence available it is impossible accurately to reconstruct the progress of works to Basing but Sir William received a licence from the king to fortify the site in 1531. He was involved in expanding the neighbouring church sometime after 1540, and a date plaque recovered from the ruins records the completion of a building there in 1561.[69]

There are numerous other impressive examples of similar castle renovation projects. Between 1573 and his death from the plague in 1583, for example, Robert Corbett transformed his family castle at Moreton Cor-

331　The south gate at Helmsley, Yorkshire.
In the 1570s or 1580s a new façade was inserted between the thirteenth-century drum towers that flanked the gate passage. The new façade was ornamented with a stylised pediment. Within the vault of the gateway is a pair of openings, possibly false murder holes. The work incorporates a curious combination of classical and Gothic detailing typical of modifications to castles in this period.

448

332 The garden façade of Moreton Corbet, Shropshire, begun after 1573, in an anonymous drawing of around 1700. This façade was a high-built structure with a regular grid of windows. It was crowned by gables and an ornamented parapet – possibly part of the original design – that might pass for battlements in the classical style. The whole range was also covered in a profusion of sculpted ornament. In overall conception the design appears to be French, but it may also incorporate decorative motifs derived from the popular Flemish architectural patterns published by Vredeman de Vries in Amsterdam in 1565. That the herald and antiquarian Camden in 1610 could describe such wonderfully flamboyant and eccentric detailing as 'Italian' underlines simultaneously the aspirations of English artistic taste in this period and its limited discernment.

bet in Shropshire with the addition of a grand new residential block. Corbet had travelled widely in Europe and was a distant relation of Robert Dudley, earl of Leicester. He was also a friend of the poet and soldier Sir Philip Sidney. In the spirit of the times he was fascinated by architecture and, as the antiquarian William Camden noted in 1610, being 'carryed away with the affectionate delight of Architecture began to build in a barraine place a most gorgeous and stately house after the Italian model: but death prevented him, so he left the new work unfinished and the old castle defaced'. In fact, the castle was completed in the early seventeenth century by one of Robert's younger brothers and further repaired in the aftermath of the Civil War. It finally fell to ruin in the eighteenth century. Nevertheless, it is possible to reconstruct the essentials of Robert's plan from the evidence of the surviving ruins, several early drawings and other documentary evidence.[70]

The intention was to create a large and compactly planned residential block within the castle. This was laid out on an L-shaped plan and its principal façade overlooked a formal garden (pl. 332). Although divorced stylistically from the castle in which it stands, Robert's range related to earlier structures on the site: it was approached across the castle ditch and screened by the medieval curtain wall with its gatehouse and great tower. The deliberate juxtaposition of old and new buildings was a means of celebrating the archi-

tectural ancestry of the castle and the history of its owning family. Virtually identical arrangements were created at other modernised castles of the period, for example, at Berry Pomeroy, Devon. Here the fifteenth-century curtain wall defined the forecourt of a residence expanded in two stages by the son and grandson of Protector Somerset, Edward Seymour. Meanwhile, at Chipchase, Northumberland, a fourteenth-century great tower was preserved behind a splendid new series of domestic apartments (pl. 333).

It is in relation to such juxtaposition of medieval and modern buildings that another related, but easily overlooked, phenomenon should be viewed: the preservation of castle remains or ruins in close proximity to entirely new residences. Examples of this are to be found across the kingdom at sites such as Tickhill (Yorkshire), Codnor (Derbyshire), Barnwell (Northamptonshire) and Berkhamsted (Hertfordshire). As a survey of the latter site of 1606 noted:

. . . we take the castell to be the capitall or mansion house belonging to the lord of this Mannor. And we saie that the same is nowe in ruyne and soe hath beene and continued for a long tyme beyond our memories. But by what defaulte we knowe not. And that the same with in the scite thereof is nowe occupied by Sir Edward Cary Knight. And that the said Sir Edward Cary hath builded certain howses for his necessary use within the precinct of the said castle.[71]

333 A view of Chipchase, Northumberland. The great tower of this castle – visible to the left – is very similar in detail to nearby Belsay, built in the years 1391–6. It was incorporated in 1621 within a fine Jacobean house. The new building was martial in character with towers and battlements. Its parapets were also enlivened with prominent chimneys set at the angles of the towers. In the north of England there are numerous examples of great towers being incorporated within new buildings in this way. The effect of a great tower presiding over a regularly planned house was also occasionally recreated in entirely new buildings, such as Gawthorpe, Lancashire, built between 1600 and 1605.

By such means a new owner could usurp to himself and his new residence the prestige and status of an existing castle. Incidentally, the practice of preserving adjacent ruins is paralleled in several converted monastic sites, as at Newstead in Nottinghamshire. In such cases, the substantial survival of abandoned buildings demands some more convincing explanation than chance. The likelihood must be that owners felt the ruins lent dignity to the modern houses that stood beside them.

Finally, there are a few instances of strategically important castles being renewed for military purpose in this period. On the northern march with Scotland, the intense interest of central government in the state of major castles is reflected in the numbers of surveys these buildings underwent. At sites such as Berwick (along with the town), Wark, Harbottle, Carlisle and Norham, to name but a handful, royal money was regularly invested to improve the defences. To prevent the Isle of Wight being used as a stepping stone for the invasion of England, meanwhile, Carisbrooke was extensively reworked with new artillery fortifications between 1583 and 1603.[72] At the same time, the med-

ieval buildings in the castle were modernised for the use of the governor. On the facing shore of the mainland, the defences of Portchester were also slightly improved and the buildings repaired, of which more will be said in the next chapter.

THE MAINTENANCE OF CASTLES

Renovation and complete abandonment in favour of a new residence were two extremes of approach towards castles in the Tudor period. There was also a more modest alternative that is very easy to overlook simply because it is never accompanied by impressive new architecture: basic maintenance. In 1561, for example, the chancellor of the duchy of Lancaster was asked to draw up a report on the state of the 'castles and mansions' in this vast royal inheritance. His report, which was presented with a remarkable series of drawings showing the buildings in question, was considered by several powerful officers of state who had been charged by the queen to decide on their fate. This included the lord treasurer, a figure unlikely to be sentimental where

450

334 A view of Pontefract, Yorkshire, drawn up to illustrate the survey of castles in the duchy of Lancaster in 1561. This great castle, consistently admired and actively repaired by monarchs up to the Civil War, was almost totally destroyed in the aftermath of a long and bitter siege. Accounts for the demolition work in 1649 survive. The drawing clearly shows the series of rectangular towers erected around the castle from the late fourteenth century onwards. To the left is the huge foiled great tower that was probably begun in the mid-thirteenth century. In 1374 John of Gaunt ordered that this 'ancient' tower be raised in height using stone cut from the ditches. He presumably created the fabulously rich upper section of the building. The ruined building in the top right of the view is likely to represent Pontefract Priory, the burial place of Thomas of Lancaster, Edward II's bitter enemy, who was executed in the castle great hall in 1322.

money was concerned. The judgements they delivered on this collection of buildings are a fascinating testimony to the perceived importance of castles.

Only two of the Lancastrian estate castles, already in an advanced state of decay, were to be abandoned: Peveril and Donnington. All the others were worth saving for one reason or another: Pontefract, because it was 'an honourable castle to be maintained and kept for the goodliness of the house and for the defence of the Cuntrey' (pl. 334); Lancaster, 'because it is a great strengthe to the Contrie and succour to the Quene's justices and officers'; the dilapidated Tutbury, because it was 'an old and statly Castle' with 'a great seignory furnished with forests, parks and chases' (pl. 335); Tickhill, because it was 'an ancient monument'; Halton, 'because the howse is in good repaire and standeth pleasantly and defensible for the Contrie'; Sandal, 'because it standith in a stronge countrie of men amongst whome (if any rebellion shulde happen, as God forbid) this castle must be the staie of it' (pl. 336); and Clitheroe, simply 'because there is a gaiole in the same'.[73] These are precisely the kinds of reasons – prestige, security, administrative use, pleasure and comfort – for which castles had been maintained throughout the Middle Ages.

Of the castles owned by the duchy of Lancaster, however, only one was ever used to any extent by the queen or her administration. Hertford Castle had been neglected during the reigns of Edward VI and Mary, and after Elizabeth's accession was described by royal surveyors in familiar terms: it was in 'great decaye . . . and will yf spedye remeadye be not provyded fall into utter ruyn'.[74] Repairs were put in hand and in 1561 the

queen stayed at Hertford for sixteen days while on her summer progress. During an outbreak of plague in 1564, the castle, which was in easy reach of London, was used for a term as the seat of the Westminster law courts. The arrangements of courts and the council chamber within the domestic buildings were recorded in a plan drawn up by the surveyor Henry Hawthorne (see pl. 224). Hertford again served as a royal residence in 1576 and as a seat of government in time of plague in 1582 and 1592. Less than twenty years later, the financially pressed administration of James I demolished most of the buildings for the value of their materials, an estimated £685 principally in brick, timber, lead and tiles.[75]

Some noble families can similarly be shown to have valued castles without – as far as we know – developing them on a grand scale. In 1554, for example, Walter Hungerford (d. 1597) bought back the family castle of Farleigh Hungerford and its estates from the crown for £5,000. The high price of the purchase possibly reflects as much the value of the property as the depth of disgrace into which the Hungerfords had fallen: Walter's father had been attainted and executed by Henry VIII in 1540, the culminating indignity for a family embroiled for nearly thirty years in episodes of extreme domestic cruelty and murder.[76]

In some cases, existing castles already answered almost every fashionable need without substantial change. Matthew Arundell's remodelling of Wardour in Wiltshire before 1576, for example, illustrates how the essential continuities of the Perpendicular style allowed a building to be updated with only very superficial

changes (see pl. 242). The late fourteenth-century great tower was designed on a hexagonal plan around a small courtyard at the heart of the castle, and its regularity and ingenuity were qualities still admired by the Elizabethans. Where it diverged from the tastes of the Tudor Perpendicular was in its irregular fenestration and a complete absence of classical detailing. What Arundell did was to create a symmetrical arrangement of windows and to introduce two new classical doorways: one at the entrance flanked by stone niches and overlooked by a dating plaque and a bust of Christ, and a second at the foot of the great hall stairs.

WALES AND IRELAND

On the subject of adapted castle buildings, some special word needs to be said about the works of this period in Ireland and Wales, both regions uneasily tied into the orbit of English interests. Political authority within them was exercised by a small circle of families with close links to each other and the court. For this group – as in other parts of the British Isles – castles continued to serve both as architectural expressions of power and dynastic might. To a much greater degree than in England, however, castles were also perceived as serving a continued role in maintaining royal government in the face of hostile interests.

In 1560 Sir Henry Sidney was appointed president of the Council of the Marches in Wales. It was a post he was to hold until his death in 1584 and brought wide-ranging judicial and administrative powers over the region. Sir Henry had grown up as a close companion of Edward VI; indeed, the young king had died in his arms in 1553. The royal friendship encouraged John Dudley to arrange a match between his daughter, Mary, and Henry Sidney in 1551. The accession of Mary Tudor briefly compromised the political value of the marriage, but it turned to Henry's advantage once more when his brother-in-law, Robert Dudley, earl of Leicester, emerged as the outstanding favourite of Elizabeth I. It was in fact to Leicester that Sir Henry owed his new appointment and in May 1561 he travelled to Ludlow Castle, the official seat of royal government in Wales. His principal residence was Penshurst in Kent, but particularly from the 1570s onwards he spent a great deal of time at Ludlow and extensively modified the castle buildings. He also appears to have repaired Wigmore, though the nature of his work to this castle is not clear.[77]

At Ludlow Sir Henry's work reflected both the judicial and the residential functions of the castle. It extended from the creation of a walled enclosure for prisoners to walk in to the construction of a new tennis court. Principal amongst his additions were the construction of a stone bridge between 30 and 40 yards (27–37 m) in length to span the outer moat (now lost); alterations to the outer gatehouse; the conversion of so-called Mortimer's Tower into a storeroom for papers or muniments; and substantial changes to the domestic buildings of the inner bailey. In 1577, moreover, preparations were in hand for the installation of a clock to regulate the life of the castle.[78] Lodgings for judges were erected over the inner gate, an operation dated by a plaque to 1581, and some buildings were refenestrated. In the centre of the court, a new fountain was constructed, fed by piped water. The round nave of the twelfth-century chapel in the inner bailey was split into two floors, of which the uppermost served as a closet for the president. Both the chapel and the council chamber were ornamented with the arms of those on the council.[79] In the parish church, Sidney additionally created an elegant monument for his daughter, Ambrosia, who died at Ludlow in 1580.

It was also through the connection with the earl of Leicester that Sir Henry was subsequently twice appointed to the deputy lieutenancy of Ireland. His terms of office, 1566–71 and 1575–8, coincided with an attempt by the Elizabethan regime to anglicise the administration and political elite of Ireland. It was not an attractive or happy experiment. The seat of royal government was Dublin Castle, which Sir Henry occupied throughout his periods in office. A print of 1581 vividly captures the flavour of his martial government (pl. 337). Besides maintaining the castle he also became involved in repairs to Christ Church Cathedral in Dublin, an undertaking with a strong political undertone.

Christ Church was the seat of the Reformed church in Ireland and the setting for state ceremonial, such as the annual celebration of St George's Day. On 3 April 1562 the church nave came crashing to the ground, leaving half the building in ruin. As befitted his office, Sir Henry played a prominent role in the ensuing restoration. He provided a new floor for the nave in 1570 and – significantly – restored the tomb of Richard fitz Gilbert de Clare, the earl of Pembroke and lord of Leinster (d. 1176), which was destroyed in the collapse. De Clare, also known as Strongbow, was the first Anglo-Norman invader of Ireland, and by attending to his tomb the modern representative of the

337 A woodcut from John Derrick's *The Image of Irelande* (London, 1581). It shows Sir Henry Sidney leaving Dublin Castle, the seat of English government in Ireland, preceded by soldiers and trumpeters. The view accurately shows the thirteenth-century castle with drum towers. Above the gate are the impaled heads of bearded Irishmen. The gateposts display banners with the arms of England and Sir Henry. It is unclear how the buildings in the castle were adapted for domestic use in the sixteenth century. The print captures the brutal spirit of Tudor rule in Ireland. Whatever the experience of her English subjects, in Ireland the reign of Gloriana was anything but a golden age.

crown paid respect to the founding figure of the English conquest of Ireland. It may have been conscious antiquarianism, therefore, rather than mere penny-pinching, that encouraged Sir Henry to recycle an effigy of the 1330s for the monument.[80]

Something of the wider importance of castles in Irish affairs of this period is reflected in such episodes as the suppression during 1601–2 of the long-running rebellion of Hugh O'Neill, baron of Dungannon and earl of Tyrone. Hugh O'Neill was probably educated in the household of Henry Sidney during the 1550s and early in his life was notable amongst Gaelic lords for his support of the crown in Ireland. His rebellion in 1595 was inspired by his desire to establish palatine powers for himself in the face of English administrative and legal innovations in Ulster. It was finally suppressed by the combined effects of a brutal war of attrition waged by the deputy lieutenant, Charles Blount, Lord Mountjoy, and the crushing defeat of O'Neill's army at Kinsale on Christmas Eve 1601.[81] Mountjoy pressed home his victory ruthlessly. Early the following year, he entered the smouldering and abandoned ruins of O'Neill's seat at Dungannon Castle before pressing on to Tullahogue, where he symbolically destroyed the ancient coronation throne of the O'Neill family. The events of the campaign were recorded in detail by an English cartographer called Bartlett in Mountjoy's retinue.[82]

The affairs of southern Wales were closely bound up with those in Ireland and there too during the 1570s and 1580s castles were important as symbols of authority and power.[83] Henry Herbert, who acceded to the earldom of Pembroke in 1570 and was Sir Henry Sidney's son-in-law from 1577, was the leading magnate of the region. He invested in the development of Cardiff and is recorded around 1580 to have 'repaired and translated the form of all the rooms within the castle'.[84] This operation probably involved the reorganisation of the 1420s residential range and the construction of an adjacent tower projecting outside the curtain wall. In the years 1588–90 further works were undertaken, including the repair of chambers on the motte. Stone for both operations was robbed from two dissolved friaries in the town.[85] Meanwhile, the earl's younger brother purchased Powis Castle, which he splendidly developed as his seat.

The activity of the Herberts compares in turn with that of an ally and associate, the soldier Sir John Perrot. A man of strongly Protestant sympathy, it was probably through the earl of Pembroke's agency that he was granted governorship of Carew, Pembrokeshire, in the reign of Mary. Following Elizabeth's accession his political standing improved and he undertook two separate tours of duty in Ireland. During the latter, as deputy lieutenant between 1584 and 1588, he stormed Dunluce Castle in Antrim and carried off substantial

338 A view of Carew,
Pembrokeshire. Sir John
Perrot's work to the castle, cut
short by his death in 1592,
involved the construction of
the tall range visible to the
right with a gallery running
the full length of the upper
floor. It compares in form to
the roughly contemporary
works at both Raglan and
Powis. To the extreme right is
visible one of the spur-based
towers probably erected in the
1280s by Sir Nicholas de
Carew. He held the castle as a
baron within the honour of
Pembroke. This suggests a
connection with William de
Valence's work as self-styled
earl of Pembroke at Goodrich
and Kidwelly.

quantities of booty. The money he earned in various
offices, his rack-renting and possible complicity with
pirates, was invested in the reconstruction not only of
Carew but also of nearby Laugharne Castle, which he
received from Elizabeth I in 1575. A survey of Laugharne in 1592 describes his repairs as having begun about
fourteen years previously (i.e. in 1578).[86] At Carew, his
alterations included the reconstruction of the north
range of the quadrangular castle to create a gallery on
the upper floor (pl. 338).[87] In neither case was the work
finished, Sir John being indicted for treason and dying
in prison in 1592.[88]

Sir John Perrot's work to Carew forms an interesting parallel to perhaps the grandest castle project of the
period in Wales, the reorganisation of Raglan Castle
by William Somerset, third earl of Worcester. As a
young man, Somerset had served in Henry VIII's last
Continental campaigns and even carried the spear and
helmet of the aged king outside Calais on 25 July 1544.
His subsequent career under Henry's children was
somewhat mixed and he failed to secure royal offices
under Edward VI that would have turned his inherited
landholdings in south Wales to proper political account. This political marginalisation was almost cer-

tainly a reflection of his strong Catholic sympathies.
Under Elizabeth I, however, his situation improved and
in the 1560s he moved his seat from Chepstow Castle,
where he had previously resided, to Raglan.[89] In 1570
he was elected to the Order of the Garter and it was
probably in the 1580s that he extensively reworked the
castle there. His additions externally evoke the existing
fifteenth-century buildings, copying, for example, the
form of the polygonal castle towers. Amongst other
changes he reconstructed the great hall range and
created a new long gallery. It was probably also at this
time that the so-called White Horse Fountain, which
continually flowed with fresh water, was erected in the
inner court.

Internally, the new buildings at Raglan were very
cosmopolitan in character. The roof of the great hall
was a double-hammer-beam structure, a form that
suggests a London provenance for the design. It may
well have been similar to the surviving roof at Middle
Temple Hall, London. Similarly, one of the long
gallery fireplaces preserves caryatid figures directly
derived from an engraved plate in a French architectural work, *La Diversité des Termes* by Hugues Sambin,
published in 1572. Remarkably, a copy of this book sur-

339　Syon, Middlesex.
The house was built
after 1547 by the lord
protector and duke of
Somerset, Edward Seymour,
on the site of the Bridgettine
nunnery founded by Henry V
in 1415. With its turrets and
battlements, the building is
evidently inspired by castle
design. Archaeological
excavation suggests that the
house sits over the west end
of the monastic church, which
was entirely demolished to
receive it. The two turrets
with battlements in the
foreground stood at the
corners of an enclosed
sixteenth-century court that
was swept away in the course
of eighteenth-century
improvements. They are first
shown on a plan of 1607.

vives endorsed in Worcester's own hand, which he probably picked up while in Paris during a diplomatic visit in 1573.[90] This particular link offers a remarkably precise instance and explanation for the passage of ideas from France to England through the medium of a patron and his travels.

Concurrent with the architectural changes to the castle, grand new gardens were laid out at Raglan, possibly adaptations of predecessors created in the fifteenth century. Two formal terraces were created beneath the windows of the long galley dropping down to 'the great poole' and its associated water garden. There was also 'a garden plot, answerable in proportion to the tower', perhaps suggesting a design deliberately related in some way to the existing architecture. Whatever the case, a poem of 1587 admired the whole scene in a tidy nutshell, describing Raglan as 'the stately tower that looks ore pond and poole'.[91] It is a description that might apply to a major castle at any period over the Middle Ages in England and expresses in one sense how little the fundamental perceptions of these buildings had changed over the centuries.

THE SHADOW OF THE CASTLE

It is against this background of maintenance, repairs and alterations to existing castles that the vast majority of grand Tudor residential architecture is to be understood. Most of those raised to high office by the politics of the Reformation desired homes that con-

formed to established architectural conventions; in short, they wanted buildings that incorporated the trappings of fortification. Changing fashions made it desirable to transform towers and turrets into delicate structures of glass and battlements into fantastical subclassical ornament. Nevertheless, the intention was to create buildings in which the castle and its forms were both implicit and immediately recognisable.

Amongst those elevated to positions of power at the start of Edward VI's reign, several began new houses in an uncompromisingly castellated form. One such was the new residence built by the lord protector and duke of Somerset, Edward Seymour, on the site of the royal nunnery at Syon in Middlesex. It was granted to him in 1547 and he spent £5,000 creating a four-square courtyard residence with corner turrets and a crown of battlements over the site of the church nave and part of the cloister (pl. 339). Syon appears to have been relatively unusual in that it was built with little or no accommodation for the earlier monastic buildings. More commonly, church or claustral buildings were cannibalised to similar overall effect. At Wilton in Wiltshire, for example, the cloister of another nunnery was turned into the courtyard of a house by the earl of Pembroke. In the process, the exterior was completely recast to create an imposing residence with angle turrets and a great gatehouse.

In other cases, the process of monastic conversion involved the construction of a single dominating tower. Such was the case at Lanercost Priory in Cumberland, which was reordered by Sir Thomas Dacre in the 1550s.

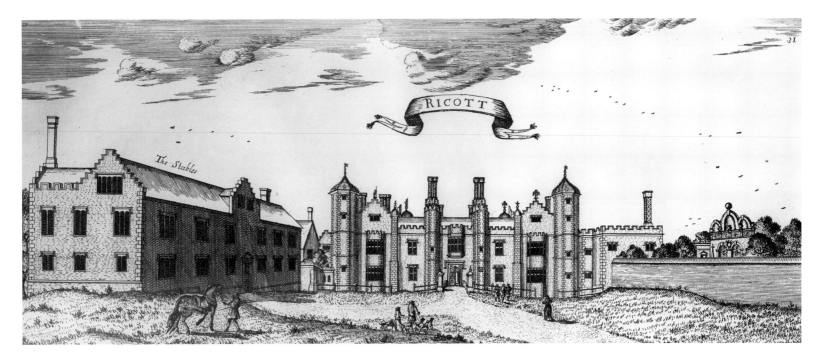

RICOTT

The Stables

340 A view of Rycote, Oxfordshire, engraved by Winstanley around 1695. The house was probably built by John Williams, a kinsman of Henry VIII's powerful secretary Thomas Cromwell, during Mary's reign. To either side of the entrance are the stables and walled gardens. The main façade, apparently unchanged from its first construction, was symmetrical and built of a combination of brick and stone. Its entire central section was projected out to form a huge gatehouse block. Like a castle entrance this incorporated turrets and battlements. The parapets of the building were enlivened with heraldic figurines and brick chimneys. Some of the detailing, such as the door in the stable range to the left, is classical and might corroborate a date in the 1550s for the building.

He had been granted the priory with its estates over the head of his half-brother, an attempt by Henry VIII to undermine the local hegemony of this great northern family.[92] The new tower, which was added to one corner of the claustral ranges, was battlemented and accommodated the principal withdrawing chambers of the new residence in exactly the manner of a great tower. It put Lanercost on an equal architectural footing with most small castles of the region.

No less than monastic conversions, most newly constructed residences of the 1550s and '60s incorporated the classic forms of castle architecture – in particular, the turreted courtyard, grand gatehouses and parapets busy with battlements and chimneys. Such is the case, for example, with Rycote in Oxfordshire, probably built in the 1550s (pl. 340); The Lordship at Standon in Hertfordshire, which preserves two dating stones inscribed 1546 and 1549; and Chatsworth in Derbyshire, a huge battlemented residence also begun in the 1550s for Sir William Cavendish, first husband of Bess of Hardwick.

It is important to appreciate that these buildings were not merely superficially similar to castles of earlier generations. In many cases they also reflect close technical knowledge of them. For example, the type of symmetrical façade with towers and turrets flanking a central gateway that is first found at Herstmonceux in Sussex in the 1440s (see pl. 277) remained current throughout the sixteenth century. One exceptionally grand and late example of the form is to be found at Burghley in

Northamptonshire, begun in 1577 by Elizabeth I's chief minister, William Cecil, Lord Burghley (pl. 341). Explanation for this continuity probably lies in the London connections of the small circle of senior masons that enjoyed a monopoly on grand commissions.

But Burghley, which conceals its links to castle design beneath a thick layer of classical ornament, was built at a moment when the character of grand domestic architecture was changing fundamentally. In the 1560s and 1570s there was articulated for the first time, largely through French example, what might be thought of as a new kind of nobleman's house. In place of the trappings of fortification, it used classical detail as a mark of status and display. It is no coincidence that this alternative tradition initially developed in the context of town houses and monastic sites, types of building for which there were no architectural conventions of detailing.

Longleat in Wiltshire, for example, was completed in the same decade as the main front of Burghley. It was built by Sir John Thynne, a prop of the Edwardian regime. He had begun rebuilding the former charterhouse at Longleat as his seat in the 1550s and then again in the years 1572–80. In this later period he employed a French mason, Alan Maynard, and also Robert Smythson. The surviving façades of Longleat, dating from this period, comprise regular tiers of windows and bay windows divided by horizontal courses of decoration in a sophisticated classical style. Longleat was deeply indebted to contemporary devel-

341 Burghley,
Northamptonshire, begun in
1577. The main front
incorporates the distinctive
rhythm of elements – tower,
turret, gatehouse, turret, tower
– that looks back to buildings
designed in the orbit of the
king's works under the
Lancastrian kings. Burghley
clothes its architectural
ancestry in castle design
beneath an impressive veneer
of classical detailing: its
battlements dissolve into rich
ornament and the astonishing
array of chimneys are treated
as columns. Each chimney
within its spectacular
roofscape, it should be noted,
culminates in a miniature
castle. These are nineteenth-
century copies of the
miniature Elizabethan copies
that ornament the parapet.

opments in town-house architecture, in particular to
the work of Protector Somerset at his London house
on the Strand, completed between 1547 and 1552.

Neither Longleat nor the tradition of French classical design it reflects is of direct relevance to the narrative of this book except as a means of focusing its
attention. Up to this moment the castle and its forms
were implicit in all grand domestic architecture. Now
there came to maturity in England a tradition of grand
residential architecture that was effectively independent of castle design. Yet even when confronted for the
first time by a meaningful choice of architectural idiom
– what might be termed castellar or French classical
design – few patrons decisively chose one or the other.
Rather, they continued to combine them.

A preference for erring towards more castle-like
buildings extended a considerable way down the social
scale to incorporate figures of county standing – lawyers, MPs or merchants with London connections. A
wide geographic spread of such buildings would
include Stiffkey (Norfolk), built 1576–81; Howley
(Yorkshire), around 1585; Thorpe Salvin (Yorkshire),
before 1582; Little Hadham (Essex), 1572–8; Torksey
(Lincolnshire), after 1559; and Brereton (Cheshire), of

the 1580s (pl. 342). The comptroller of works for the
fortifications of Berwick, Thomas Jennyson, also
created an imposing castle for himself with large drum
towers flanking the main façade at Walworth, Co.
Durham, probably around 1570.

One particularly resilient and widespread castle-
inspired feature in grand domestic buildings of every
kind was the walled forecourt articulated by a gatehouse
and turrets. Quadrangular courts of this kind may ultimately derive from the example of Gothic quadrangular castles. Whatever the case, they were clearly miniature imitations of full-scale architecture: the mid-sixteenth-century forecourt at Roydon in East Peckham,
Kent, for example, actually adopts the rhythm of Herstmonceux with a tower, a turret and a gatehouse, a turret
and a tower (pl. 343). In time-honoured fashion, the
gatehouse usually received the greatest attention. It
could even be turned into a miniature virtuoso work in
its own right, as at Tixall (Staffordshire), Madeley
(Shropshire) and Llanhydrock (Cornwall).

In some cases, as at Shute, Devon, built after 1559,
the language of such architecture was straightforwardly
inspired by the castle. There are, however, many instances of more abstracted designs. Forecourt towers,

458

for example, might be treated as pinnacles, an idea possibly inspired by the buttresses of Henry VII's Chapel, Westminster. An early example of this is to be found in the 1520s design of the inner court at Hengrave in Suffolk, and it subsequently remained popular in East Anglia. There are mid-sixteenth-century examples of the same idea at Beckingham Hall and Killigrews Margaretting in Essex and Waxham in Norfolk, for example, where the towers have been reduced to the form of ornamented pinnacles (pl. 344). In the case of Killigrews, it is possible to stand inside these pinnacles, each of which possesses arrow loops, a clear indication that these structures were intended to evoke towers.

One distinctive tower form that enjoyed particular popularity in the sixteenth century was the turret on a triangular plan. In England, it probably derived from late fifteenth-century precedents at castles such as Raglan and Berry Pomeroy in Devon, though there are much earlier French antecedents for it, as at Fère-en-Tardenois (Aisne) in the thirteenth century. The high stone wall that defines the court to Hardwick New Hall in Derbyshire, for example, is punctuated by beaked towers and crowned by curious obelisk and strapwork projections, a fashionable alternative to battlements (pl. 345). The idea at Hardwick may in fact be lifted from the towered gatehouse set in the main façade of Chatsworth, built by Bess and her first husband, Sir William Cavendish, from 1549.

Another castle form that remained popular in new architecture of this period was the great tower. There are some examples of great towers that follow closely in the idiom of their medieval predecessors. The earl of Shrewsbury, for example, constructed a tower house by 1572 beside the newly fashionable springs at Buxton (pl. 346).[93] A smaller version of this structure also built by the earl in 1574, still survives at Sheffield Manor in Yorkshire.[94] A series of related buildings of this type were further created by Robert Smythson for wealthy figures of county stature. Amongst the earliest in this series is a pair of houses at Barlborough, Derbyshire, begun in 1584 (pl. 347), and the contemporary Old Hall at Heath, Yorkshire.[95]

342 The gatehouse of Brereton, Cheshire, dated by an inscription to 1585, was built by Sir William Brereton (later first Lord Brereton). It formed the entrance to a courtyard house, much reduced in the 1720s and 1830s. Built of brick with stone facings and incorporating a stone bridge spanning the space between the two towers (probably an original feature), the building may well belong to a family of designs that descend from the early Perpendicular and the Lancastrian king's works. The same detail is also found, for example, in the main gatehouse at Warwick (see pl. 205) and a related one, perhaps, in the bridges that rise to the towers of the gatehouse of Herstmonceux, Sussex. There is rich classical detailing across the façade. The circular openings are perhaps intended to read as cannon loops.

ELIZABETHAN CASTLES

The Elizabethans did not only create new residences that simply evoked castles; occasionally they were inspired to build them too. Perhaps the most ambitious late sixteenth-century castle in England is Long-

343 (*top*)   The house and forecourt of Roydon Hall, East Peckham, Kent in 1968. The present house was begun by Thomas Roydon in the reign of Henry VIII; according to an inscription above the door to the house, it was built in 1535. Roydon was much adapted around 1600 and again in the nineteenth century. The forecourt is essentially a miniaturised range with a Herstmonceux-type façade and its familiar rhythm of elements: tower, turret, gatehouse, turret, tower. As the sixteenth century progressed, it became increasingly common to reduce the castle elements of houses to an architectural skirting in this way.

344 (*bottom*)   The forecourt of Beckingham Hall, Tolleshunt Major, Essex, built by the courtier Stephen Beckingham (d. 1558). It illustrates the degree to which castle forms could be abstracted for decorative effect. Here the turrets at the corners of the forecourt have been reduced to the form of pinnacles. The white flecking on the gatehouse is the remains of plasterwork, which was painted with patterns and arrow loops. The date of the building is uncertain, but a fragment of panelling from the house (now in the Victoria and Albert Museum, London) is dated 1546.

345 (*top*) The main front of Hardwick New Hall, Derbyshire, built by Bess of Hardwick between 1590 and 1597. The tall and compactly planned house in the background with its attached towers is evocative of a castle building, as is the forecourt with its turrets and classicised battlements. The beaked form of the forecourt turrets is particularly noteworthy. Turrets of this kind remained common into the seventeenth century in the forecourts of residences such as Raglan (Monmouthshire), Cranborne (Dorset) and Welbeck Abbey (Nottinghamshire). The form was also found on the façade of Bess's first great home, Chatsworth, in the design of the main gatehouse.

346 (*bottom*) A view of the tower at Buxton, Derbyshire, published by John Speed in 1611. It was built by the earl of Shrewsbury by 1572 at this fashionable spa town. The tower was an imposing four-storey structure with its principal withdrawing chambers on the uppermost floor. Its parapets are battlemented and studded with chimneys. On the face of the tower overlooking the town, there was a large heraldic achievement displaying the earl's arms. Set within a battlemented wall, it is to all intents and purposes a castle in the tradition of buildings such as Hunsdon, Hertfordshire.

ford in Wiltshire, which was constructed by Sir Thomas Gorges at some time between 1578 and 1591 (pl. 348). Sir Thomas was reputedly driven to build on this scale by his wife Helena, a Swedish noblewoman, the widow of the earl of Northampton and the leading lady of the queen's bedchamber. Highly advantageous to him, this match to Helena must have been the product of intrigue in the privy chamber, where Sir Thomas served for thirty-one years. It was not sanctioned by the queen, and its precise date around 1580 is therefore uncertain.[96] When the news of it broke, Sir Thomas was fortunate that the queen's displeasure extended only to a short term in prison.

Plans for the building drawn up by the surveyor John Thorpe label the three towers 'Father', 'Son' and 'Holy Ghost', an indication that the unusual triangu-

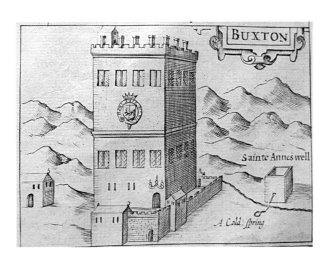

lar form of the building was intended to evoke the Trinity. As a matter of fact, it is also the shape of the artillery fort at Hurst Castle, Hampshire, where Gorges acted as keeper in the 1580s.[97] Whatever inspired the plan, Sir Thomas was evidently fascinated by complex geometry and his astonishing monument in nearby Salisbury Cathedral incorporates numerous complex figures including skeletal polyhedrals.

Longford incorporates a great deal of sophisticated classical detailing for its date. A tiered gallery termed a loggia extends between the two angle towers on the main façade and the battlements are treated as classical ornaments. Yet the building shows its Gothic connections, too, as in the superb pendant vault of the great chamber in one of the towers. In a period where large windows were fashionable, the fenestration is remarkably restrained, and one visitor in September 1603 wrote: 'all his windowes are but two lights with a transom, and yet being sette thick and uniforme shew well and faire'.[98] In this detail, and the heavy treatment of the masonry in the towers, the design is consciously evoking the solidity of a castle.

Castles could also be created on a much more modest scale by those of county standing. One of the most surprising instances of this was bound up with an extremely dark tale of greed and ambition. On 28 October 1567 Ludovic Greville, a Warwickshire gentleman and kinsman of Fulke Greville, lord of Warwick, petitioned for a royal licence 'to build a new mansion house in their manor of Mylcote, County Warwick, to embattle the said house and call it Mount-

347 (*top*) Barlborough, Derbyshire, begun in 1584, in a photograph of 1900. The building is conceived as a courtyard drawn tight to create a tower: its main façade is articulated by a pair of turrets and a prominent porch like an engaged gatehouse. The parapets are battlemented and set with numerous false chimneys. Barlborough is one in a group of compactly planned buildings of the period that are clearly inspired by castle architecture. One of these, Gawthorpe, Lancashire, was built between 1600 and 1605. It additionally incorporates a stair turret to the rear that rises like a great tower over the building.

348 (*bottom*)   A view of Longford, Wiltshire, one in a series of views depicting this castle on a triangular plan by R. Thacker made around 1680. With its towers, turrets, ornamental battlements, rusticated masonry patterns and – by the standards of the day – a low ratio of window to wall surface, this spectacular building makes unmistakable architectural claim to the title of a castle. It was built by Sir Thomas Gorges between 1578 and 1591, reputedly in response to the demands of his aristocratic Swedish wife. The main front incorporates an arcaded loggia. Behind it rise three stair turrets with bell-shaped roofs that stand at the inner angles of the central court. Drawings of the castle in the collection compiled by the surveyor John Thorpe (d. 1655) name the three castle towers after the persons of the Trinity.

349 Newark Park, Ozleworth, Gloucestershire, probably built by Sir Nicholas Poyntz in the 1540s. It was executed in the highest architectural fashion with broad grids of windows and classical detailing. With its compact plan and battlemented outline, this lodge looks like a miniaturised great tower. It is possible that such buildings belong to a much longer tradition of hunting towers. Medieval buildings of this kind, however, were usually constructed in timber and there is very little evidence for their appearance. The inclusion of buttresses in secular buildings – seen here at the angles of the building – became increasingly uncommon as the sixteenth century progressed.

grevell. Also license to impark and enclose their manor of Weston upon Avon . . . also to have free warren and a separate fishery there'.[99] The new building, constructed of brick and set on a hill a quarter of a mile from the earlier manor house, was an architectural expression of his wealth and standing.[100] It later emerged that a substantial part of his landholding came to him through the forged will of a rich tenant called Richard Webb, who was murdered on Greville's instructions. One of his henchmen confessed to the murder while drinking and was in turn killed. Greville was then taken to court for the latter murder. He refused to plead and was pressed to death with weights in 1589, his silence ensuring that his son would succeed to the inheritance.[101]

LODGES AND GARDENS

The architectural forms of castles and fortification also found application in several ways within the estates of great residences. Amongst other things they proved particularly popular in the inspiration for lodges, compactly planned buildings with small sets of domestic apartments designed for retreat and recreation. Lodges

were commonly architectural showpieces and looked back to the medieval tradition of park buildings such as Henry V's Pleasance at Kenilworth and John of Gaunt's Bird's Nest on the outskirts of Leicester. They also commonly reflect the Perpendicular fascination for ingenious geometric planning.

The most important lodges in a castle-like idiom are evocative of great tower design. Such, for example, is the battlemented tower at Newark Park, Ozleworth, Gloucestershire, probably built by Sir Nicholas Poyntz in the 1540s (pl. 349). The idea of four-square lodges remained common throughout the Tudor period. Often designs of this kind additionally incorporated corner towers, as at Sherborne (see pl. 330) and Wothorpe, a spectacular and fantastical lodge for Burghley. In some cases, lodges occupied much earlier fortified sites: Beckley Park, the lodge for Rycote, Oxfordshire, stood in the triple moat of a thirteenth-century predecessor.[102]

On occasion, the forms of the castle also spilled into other estate buildings. The Hunting Tower at Chatsworth, for example, probably built in the 1570s, is a battlemented tower in the plan of a four-leafed clover (pl. 350).[103] It probably follows in the tradition of banqueting houses constructed at Hampton Court

in 1538 and may also relate to the designs of Henry VIII's artillery forts. More advanced fortifications certainly came to be incorporated in buildings of this kind: the Banqueting House at Nonsuch, for example, takes the form of a small artillery fort with bastions. Even gardens themselves could assume the forms of fortifications. At Charborough House, Dorset, in the late sixteenth century Sir Walter Erle's garden 'was cut into redoubts and works representing these places'.[104]

ROBERT SMYTHSON AND WOLLATON

There is no more perfect expression of the Elizabethan fascination with castle architecture than the residence created by Sir Francis Willoughby at Wollaton, just outside Nottingham. Sir Francis was a highly educated and well-connected figure, with a long ancestry (of which he was intensely proud). He was also a great collector of books and numbered the discerning patron Matthew Arundell – the rebuilder of Wardour Castle, Wiltshire – as a cousin and brother-in-law. It was doubtless through this latter connection that he employed Robert Smythson to oversee a gigantic new residence that would be appropriate both to his estate and his wealth. Several drawings for the building survive within the Smythson collection of drawings.

Viewed from a distance Wollaton looks unambiguously like a massive castle with a great tower set in the centre of a regular, turreted bailey (pl. 351). In overall conception, indeed, it bears formal comparison to such castle buildings as Middleham, Yorkshire, or even the twelfth-century plan of the inner bailey and great tower at Dover with its multiple turrets. Yet unlike these remote precursors, Wollaton fuses the bailey and the great tower into a single and regularly planned architectural unit. That idea is presumably informed by the Perpendicular fascination for compact planning. Perpendicular, too, are the huge grids of windows that extend across the walls and the boxy outline of the structure with its busy parapets. The detailing of the building, however, is informed by a wealth of designs from published architectural treatises published on the Continent.[105]

Smythson created here a brilliantly idiosyncratic essay in castle design, made fashionable by the superficial application of Continental decoration known to him from books. And it was towards the outside world,

350 The Hunting Tower or Stand at Chatsworth, Derbyshire, built in the late sixteenth century on the plan of a four-leaved clover. Set high above the house and with large windows, it was perfectly designed for watching the hunt in the surrounding park. The building is relatively conservative in design, looking back to precedents such as the garden towers of Ashby de la Zouch, Leicestershire, and the banqueting houses of Hampton Court, Middlesex, erected around 1540. It reflects the fascination of masons working in the Perpendicular idiom with complex planning.

351 A view of Wollaton, Nottinghamshire, from the south. Wollaton was built by Robert Smythson between 1580 and 1588 for Sir Francis Willoughby, a landowner who enjoyed enormous revenues from coal mining. In overall form and detail, the building is undoubtedly informed by architectural pattern books published on the Continent. Nevertheless, it also unmistakeably evokes a classic English castle with a great tower and turreted bailey compacted into a single and symmetrical structure. The great hall forms the lower three storeys of the central tower, which is surmounted by a prospect chamber with fine views over the surrounding park. All the surfaces of the building dissolve into huge grids of glass. Adding drama to the composition is the three-fold recession of the façade in great steps, a treatment found in other compactly planned buildings of the period with connections to London or Smythson (see pl. 359). The house was designed to stand in the centre of a square enclosure divided into courts and gardens. This had service buildings centrally placed on three sides and a gatehouse on the fourth.

rather than the inherited tradition of medieval masonry practice, that Smythson wished to identify. On his elegant funerary monument in the parish church at Wollaton, which he undoubtedly designed, there appears the following inscription:

> HERE LYETH THE BODY OF MR ROBERT SMYTHSON, GENT ARCHITECTOR AND SURVAYOR UNTO THE MOST WORTHY HOUSE OF WOLLATON WITH DIVERSE OTHERS OF GREAT ACCOUNT. HE LIVED IN THE FAYTH OF CHRIST 79 YEARES AND THEN DEPARTED THIS LIFE THE XVTH OCTOBER ANO DNI 1614.

In describing himself as an 'architect', Smythson, like other senior figures in his profession in the early seventeenth century, was consciously reviving a Roman title. Contrary to what is sometimes claimed, there is no practical difference between the work of a late medieval master mason and an architect of the seventeenth century; but in terms of self-perception there was a deep gulf. One was the master of a craft, the other had aspirations to be regarded as an artist of

architecture and by extension as something more than a mere craftsman – in Smythson's own word, a 'gentleman'. By extension, too, the training of an architect is not to be found on the masons' floor cutting stone or in practical experience.

In this formal separation between the menial and inventive aspects of architecture, still in embryo around the death of Elizabeth I, were laid the foundations for the final overthrow of the medieval tradition of building in England. Curiously, the history of the English castle might not have been profoundly affected by this. As we shall see, in the opening decades of the seventeenth century, many of these buildings continued to enjoy undiminished prestige and to be developed on a grand scale. The castle, in other words, could have outlived changes in the condition, practice and status of its builders. What ultimately destroyed the inherited patterns of castle occupation and made this change of artistic practice revolutionary was a long and painful civil war that was to transform the architectural face of England.

465

16

THE STUART CASTLE

JAMES VI AND I AND CHARLES I

Immediately following the death of Elizabeth I on 24 March 1603, the Privy Council wrote to James VI of Scotland to offer him the English crown. He was by no means the only possible candidate for this honour in dynastic terms, but he was the most convincing. Indeed, to the largely Protestant ruling circle of Elizabethan England in 1603, he came with more personal recommendations than any monarch since Henry VIII: he was a man; he was of the right religious confession; he was experienced in government; and he already possessed two sons to succeed him. The court flocked northwards to greet their new king at the border and his journey south was in the nature of a triumphal progress. This culminated in a state entry into London (delayed by an outbreak of plague), and a joint coronation of the king and his wife, Anne of Denmark, at Westminster Abbey on 25 July. Not only had the Tudor dynasty been superseded without bloodshed by the Stuarts, but a Scottish king had at last achieved peacefully what force of arms had failed to do over preceding centuries: the union of the crowns of England and Scotland.

James VI and I's vision was to create a single realm with one king, one law and one people. To this end on 20 October 1604 he assumed the title of king of Great Britain, the name chosen to distinguish his domain from Brittany. Two years later he also demanded that British shipping fly a composition of the flags of Scotland and England. After much unseemly wrangling between English and Scottish heralds, a design was agreed and named the 'Union Jack' after the king. These gestures towards integration were about as far as James ever got towards realising his political ambition for a unified realm. Anglo–Scottish rivalry remained a constant irritant in the affairs of his reign and very little was achieved in overcoming the cultural and political divisions between Scotland and England. In Ireland, meanwhile, circumstances permitted for the settlement of the northern province of Ulster with English and Scottish settlers. The so-called Plantation of Ulster from 1610 followed on from earlier but smaller-scale Elizabethan plantations in Ireland. It was accompanied by the last major phase of peacetime castle construction in British history, an episode funded largely with English money. Quite how fragile the Stuart union of kingdoms remained was dramatically illustrated during the Civil War (in fact a series of wars) fought by James's son Charles I (1625–49) in the 1640s.

No less important than these political changes was an ongoing transformation of economic life in the

Facing page: Bolsover, Derbyshire.

realm. For centuries, England had chiefly been dependent on the Low Countries, selling wool in return for the luxuries it offered. Now the English economy began to develop an integrity of its own and to command a dependent European market. As part of this process, the kingdom's towns – so long the backbone of its economy and trade – were growing bigger, wealthier and more powerful than ever before. London in particular was emerging as the largest city in Europe, with a population approaching half a million by 1650. The ranks of its merchant and legal classes included figures with fortunes to rival those of the greatest noble families.

To this group, the ownership of land had lost nothing of its appeal and those with city money bought up estates and grand residences as passports to gentility. As we shall see, their interest extended to castles ancient and modern. But the court too cashed in on the gathering wealth of cities, for example, by securing from the king monopolies on the sale of particular goods. In crude terms, this shift of attention towards mercantile interest, which is already discernible in the later years of Elizabeth I's reign, had two important repercussions. It focused the attention of the nobility on the court and capital at the expense of their estates, the traditional seat of their wealth and support. At the same time, it reinforced the overriding importance of royal patronage as a means to success, wealth and political power.

THE NEW CLASSICISM

Within the orbit of the court and London during James I's reign (1603–25) the foundations were laid for another revival of classical forms. This episode is central to understanding the reformulation of the English architectural tradition in the later seventeenth century and – in the long term – informed a remarkable revival of castle architecture beyond the scope of this book: Vanbrugh's great residences for the Protestant aristocracy of early eighteenth-century England. It is of relevance here, however, because it helps explain the wider context in which castles were being developed in this period.

The central figure in the early seventeenth-century classical revival was Inigo Jones, the son of a London clothworker who trained as a joiner in St Paul's Churchyard.[1] Very little is known of Jones's early life beyond the fact that he travelled to Europe in about 1601. On his return to England he was involved in the production of various court masques and eventually secured the appointment as surveyor in the glittering household of James I's eldest son, Prince Henry, an appointment terminated by the early death of his patron in November 1612. Following the prince's death and at the age of forty he travelled in the years 1613–14 to the Continent and Italy for the last time, in the company of the earl of Arundel, an outstanding patron of art and architecture. To his contemporaries, Jones probably remained most familiar throughout his life as the designer of spectacular sets and stage effects for court entertainments. His friends also attributed to him many other artistic skills, such as that of a painter. Yet Jones fought vigorously for recognition as something more than a craftsman and dignified his role as a designer by assuming – like Robert Smythson – the Roman title of architect.[2]

Some flavour of how fresh and different Jones's work appeared to contemporaries is apparent in the comments of James Howell in his book *Instructions for Forreigne Travell* (1642). Attributing new buildings in London designed by Jones to the credit of their patron, the earl of Arundel, he remarked that the latter:

> . . . observing the uniforme and regular way of stone structure up and down Italy, hath introduced that forme of building to London and Westminster and elsewhere, which distasteful at first, as all innovations are, For they seeme like Bug-beares, or Gorgons heads, to the vulgar; yet they find now the commodity, firmenesse and beauty thereof, the three maine principals of architecture.

Meanwhile, Jones found opportunity to apply his ideas within royal service. In 1615 he was appointed to the post of surveyor of the king's works and buildings. In this role he was involved in a series of prestigious building operations in and around London, including the construction of the Queen's House at Greenwich (from 1616), the Banqueting House at Whitehall (begun 1619), the restoration of Old St Paul's (1634–8)[3] and the layout of Britain's first town square at Covent Garden.[4] His work stands in complete contrast to the architecture of his contemporaries.

What did Jones achieve? Most Elizabethan masons had worked in an essentially late medieval tradition of architecture, enriched by admired designs lifted from architectural publications. And by the early seventeenth century some gentlemen architects were using published volumes on architecture to create for the first time sophisticated pastiches of contemporary Italian designs, a style that might be termed academic classicism. By contrast, Jones, with his first-hand knowledge of Italian and French architecture, created buildings that were thoroughly classical. By linguistic analogy, he learnt the language of classicism from those who spoke it rather than by report. This familiarity made him confident and ingenious in tailoring the style to English needs. His approach was admiring but not slavish; rigorous but not hidebound; and assured but not overblown. After the knockout blow delivered by the Civil War, it was this tradition as interpreted by his followers that would come to dominate British architecture from around 1650 onwards.[5]

But it must be emphasised that, until the Civil War, the new architecture of Jones coexisted with that of the late medieval tradition of building. This coexistence was to some degree enforced by the parlous financial situation of the Stuart court. James I and Charles I were repeatedly driven by the long-term politics of the Reformation to involve themselves in the defence of the Protestant cause in the running international conflicts that are today known as the Thirty Years War. Yet parliament consistently refused to sanction the taxation necessary to sustain military intervention in European affairs. In effect, they were compelled to fight wars abroad at the cost of disquiet at home. It was, in fact, the issue of taxation that ultimately precipitated England into civil war in the 1640s. Ironically, the Commonwealth government overcame the problem of maintaining a standing army by enforcing a very similar system of arbitrary taxation to that devised by Charles I. In artistic terms, the relative poverty of the crown denied Jones the opportunities for fresh architectural commissions on a grand scale.

It would be wrong, however, entirely to impute the persistence of the medieval tradition of architecture to poverty alone. The geometrical sophistication of late medieval design continued to be greatly admired by patrons and craftsmen in this period. In the opening years of James I's reign, indeed, the Perpendicular style underwent something of a revival. The plans produced for a new royal hunting lodge at Ampthill in Bedfordshire around 1605, for example, represent a building entirely composed of compass windows and complex figures that could have been lifted off a plan for Henry VII's Chapel at Westminster.[6] Nor is this particular comparison fortuitous. Such collections of drawings as survive from this period, including that of the Smythsons and the surveyor John Thorpe, contain drawings of the chapel.[7] Exciting though the brave new world of classicism was, the medieval architectural inheritance of early seventeenth-century England was both impressive and admired. Castles were a central part of this inheritance, and they continued to dominate the English landscape.

Above and beyond the prestige attached to these buildings as ancient seats, the continued popularity of the castle and its architectural forms into the seventeenth century is partly to be explained in ideological terms. Throughout this period there survived the ideal of a fighting, knightly class distinguished by long ancestry, land ownership and military vocation. The spirit of this ideal was captured perfectly by Jones' first patron, Prince Henry (d. 1612), whose enthusiasm for martial endeavours of all kinds and horsemanship made him a fashionable paragon of Protestant nobility.[8] There can be little doubt that this idea of a chivalric society was increasingly a matter of fantasy rather than reality, but its power in a country preserved from the realities of Continental warfare should not be underrated. Jousting, for example, remained a court pastime even into the reign of Charles I. And in death, gentlemen and noblemen still universally chose to be represented on their funeral monuments in armour. It was an innocence that the Civil War would shatter.

THE THEATRE OF THE EMPIRE OF GREAT BRITAIN

James I's creation of Great Britain was soon celebrated in visual form by the publication of the *Theatrum Imperii Magnae Britanniae* by John Speed, a landmark in the burgeoning field of English historical, antiquarian and topographical study. Completed in 1612, this was the first published atlas of the whole of Great Britain. It incorporated county maps of England and Wales, provincial maps of Ireland and a detailed overview of Scotland.[9] The *Theatrum* was produced in accompaniment to a history of the realm from Julius Caesar to the accession of James I. To such material, however, Speed added a great deal of additional information. Besides the county maps are numerous inserted vignettes of costume, heraldry, battles, antiquities, great houses, castles and towns.[10] As a whole, these maps not only present a remarkably full image of the physical appearance of Great Britain around 1600, but also a fascinating insight into what was deemed notable within it.

As a group, the inset town maps testify to the continued dominance of castles as landmarks within virtually every major city in the kingdom. Moreover, although simplified and stylised, Speed's images of castles are interesting as architectural records. In many cases, they are the earliest – and sometimes the only – visual records of these buildings. Richard II's great tower of Southampton, for example, is known only through Speed's depiction of it (see pl. 241), as is the earl of Shrewsbury's tower at the spa of Buxton (see pl. 346). Yet in considering Speed's maps as architectural records, it is also important to be aware of their limitations. There are some odd omissions: in the map of Gloucester, for example, the great tower of the castle that stood until the eighteenth century is not obviously visible at all. Moreover, since Speed self-confessedly wished to celebrate the beauty and wealth of Britain, some details of the maps are evidently idealised.

One reflection of such flattering distortion is the near-total absence of ruins from the townscapes he shows. Wherever castle fabric is shown by Speed it appears to be whole and well maintained. This is despite the fact that many of these buildings – such as Northampton – are known from documentary evidence to have been in ruin at this time. Likewise, where circuits of town walls are shown they are generally represented as being complete and in repair. In both details Speed is revealing his vision of English towns as they should be, an interesting comment on the perceived importance of both castles and walls as architectural marks of civic status and identity.[11]

The irony is that Speed is actually presenting in his *Theatrum* a group of some of the most neglected castles in the kingdom. Castles in most county towns were the seats of the king's officer or sheriff and as such almost solely maintained for the purposes of administration and justice. Virtually the only buildings of interest to crown officials at castles such as Chester, Oakham (Rutland), Lincoln, Exeter (Devon), Leicester and Lancaster were the prison and the courthouse. Moreover, such were the financial straits of the treasury that James I proved considerably more dispassionate about the fate of superfluous residences and castles than Elizabeth I. Rather than organise the repairs of the castles of the duchy of Lancaster centrally, for example, responsibility for maintenance seems to have devolved on local officers. Many spared themselves trouble and expense by neglecting their charges.

There were some important exceptions to this rule, however. In 1609, for example, it was determined to repair the twelfth-century hall of Leicester Castle, then serving as a courtroom. A list of specifications for the work states that the windows of the hall were to be raised and barred so that people could not clamber in during sessions or sit on the ledges. Locks were to be fitted to the doors to prevent cattle from wandering in during sessions and the furnishings of the interior were to be altered: a new board with the royal arms was to be erected and the whole interior whitewashed. The money for these repairs was apparently levied through the system of castle-guard, with the leading figures of the honour paying in proportion to their landholdings.[12] Such usage and repair have ensured the survival of the hall at Leicester, which remained in use as a court until the twentieth century. Similar circumstances have preserved the great halls at Winchester (Hampshire) and Oakham.

Speed in his maps focused almost exclusively on recorded castles in an urban context. It is the challenge for historians to reach behind the pictures they presents and try and understand what was happening to castles at large in the kingdom.

THE ENGLISH NOBILITY AND THE CASTLE

In May 1617 James I passed through Warkworth in Northumberland on his way to Scotland. This small town, sheltering beneath its castle, did not receive the king with any celebration or notable event. Indeed, the monarch's memory of Warkworth probably merged with that of scores of other similar settlements that he passed through on this and other long journeys through his realm. Yet the details of this unexceptional visit are notable because they are recorded by the earl of Northumberland's officer, Captain Whitehead. He attended the king as he passed through the family estates in place of the absent earl, his master. The report of events that Whitehead later wrote not only evokes vividly a day in the life of the itinerant court but also its response to a castle as a monument, ruin and work of architecture.

Warkworth Castle would have been visible to the royal party as it approached the town from the south. According to Captain Whitehead's account, it caught the king's particular attention, and as he passed beneath the walls he 'did very much gaze upon it, onely said [*sic*] when he came to the tower wher the lyone is pictured on the wall: This lyone houldes up the castle.'

352 A view of Arundel,
Sussex, by Wenceslaus Hollar
dated 1644. It was probably
produced as a visual record of
the castle in case it was
ruined; the previous year
Arundel had fallen to a
parliamentarian force after a
short siege and its future was
in doubt. When an order was
issued for the demolition of
the castle defences in 1653,
however, it seems that the
work was not very rigorously
undertaken. As a result, the
buildings were quickly
restored and reoccupied in the
1650s. The view clearly shows
the stepped gable and central
louvre of the great hall
restored in the 1630s. A visitor
to the castle in 1635, Captain
Hammond, was presented in
this particular room with a
medieval relic: the fourteenth-
century sword of Bevis, the
supposed founder of the
castle. At this date the tower
on the motte was also called
the Bevis Tower after this
founder figure.

Presumably James I stared at the building as he rode beneath its walls and made this comment at the head of the high street looking up at the fourteenth-century great tower and its sculpture of the Percy lion, defiantly displayed towards the north and Scotland. The royal entourage then evidently continued into the town and rested there, because the letter goes on to report:

> Most of the lordes went into the castle and stayed ther above an houre, where they found nothinge but goates and sheep in everye chamber . . . The lordes were much moved to se it soe spoyled and soe badly kept . . . commendinge it for the best sight that ever they had sene.[13]

Judged at face value, the ruin of Warkworth could be understood as illustrating a conventional picture: that by the seventeenth century castles around the kingdom were increasingly abandoned and ruinous. But the circumstances and details of this report repay careful analysis because they tell a very different and intriguing story.

Warkworth had first fallen into neglect during the 1570s in peculiar and unexpected fashion. In 1567 the castle had been surveyed in preparation for a remodelling programme by the seventh earl of Northumberland. Work began soon afterwards, with roofs being stripped off several buildings.[14] These operations were abruptly interrupted by the Northern Rising in 1569, in which the earl was implicated. Following the flight and execution of the earl, the castle was then pillaged by the warden of the march, Sir John Forster. That

Warkworth was not afterwards repaired was the result of another political disaster for the Percy family.

At the time of James's visit, the earl of Northumberland was languishing in the Tower of London for his connections with one of the conspirators of the Gunpowder Plot of 1605. The frustrations of his imprisonment (which was to last for more than fourteen years) were made worse by the imposition of a swingeing £30,000 fine.[15] In combination, the earl's absence and his acute financial difficulty had plunged the Northumberland estate into disarray. To make money, meanwhile, some derelict buildings at Warkworth were stripped of lead and the castle leased out to Sir Ralph Grey, the owner of nearby Chillingham, who had no interest in occupying or using it. By contrast, the principal family castle at Alnwick remained in the hands of the earl's officers, admired and in relatively good repair.[16] So too did the comparably insignificant Prudhoe, which in 1617 still had a constable employed by the earl on a salary of £10 a year and a porter on £3 0s. 8d.[17] The ruins of Warkworth were, in other words, not the product of casual neglect but of exceptional dynastic misfortune, and the royal party must have known this.

To appreciate their response in the light of this, it is further necessary to understand who the visitors in 1617 were. Amongst the courtiers specifically referred to in the steward's letter were the earl of Arundel, the earl of Rutland, Lord Walden and Lord Compton. In architectural terms this list is very intriguing. The earl of Arundel is one and the same as the companion and patron of Inigo Jones, here recently returned from his Continental travels. Besides being fascinated with classical architecture, Arundel (d. 1646) set aside money in 1627 for the maintenance of his ancestral castle at Arundel, along with that of the family burial chapel in the adjacent church.[18] He also actively maintained the buildings of the castle, for example, restoring the hall in 1635.[19] It was probably at his direction, moreover, that the celebrated Bohemian engraver and etcher Wenceslaus Hollar (d. 1677) depicted Arundel Castle in 1644 (pl. 352).

Francis, earl of Rutland (d. 1632), was a man of very similar experience to Arundel. Between 1595 and 1600 he had travelled widely for his education in Europe, returning just in time to partake in the hotheaded (and unsuccessful) rebellion against Elizabeth I led by the earl of Essex. Following his pardon, he partook enthusiastically in court masques and tournaments. With his title in 1612 came two important family castles, Helmsley in Yorkshire and Belvoir in Rutland. Set in the Midlands with its superb hunting parks, Belvoir attracted no fewer than six visits by James i. Francis as well as his son and heir, George (d. 1641), also entertained Charles i there. As a direct result the castle was in a virtually continuous state of change in the early seventeenth century, often at the hands of craftsmen loaned from the royal works. Most of the alterations undertaken, including the remodelling of the main façade by Francis, appear to have been relatively cosmetic. Unfortunately, the licensed destruction of the castle in the Civil War and its extensive rebuilding later have effaced most of the evidence for the appearance of the buildings.

Helmsley was also important to the earl, who successfully built up a profitable iron industry in the locality of the town. As part of this operation the now idyllic ruins of the nearby Cistercian abbey of Rievaulx were used for smelting iron. Something of Francis's occupation of Helmsley is known from a legal dispute: he converted to Catholicism and an attempt was made in 1631 to convict him in Yorkshire as a recusant, or absentee from church services. The case hinged on his residency in the castle. Although he was shown to visit the castle regularly, the prosecution could not prove that he had spent four consecutive Sundays in Helmsley Castle. As a result, he did not qualify as a resident and the case failed.[20]

The next in the list of courtiers at Warkworth, Lord Walden, must be Theophilus Howard, eldest son of the earl of Suffolk and in 1617 captain of the king's band of gentlemen pensioners. Walden was not himself a builder but his father was outstanding in this respect. Suffolk's most celebrated creation was Audley End in Essex, one of the largest Jacobean residences constructed in England. It was built between 1603 and 1616 and, according to the earl, along with its furnishing cost £200,000. Whether a true estimate of its value or not, it was funded through peculation and corruption on a scale sufficient to ensure the earl's dismissal from office on 19 July 1619. The final reference, to Lord Compton, is ambiguous. It probably refers to Sir William Compton (d. 1630), later the earl of Northampton, but it could conceivably identify his eldest son, Spencer (d. 1643), who was sixteen years old in 1617. Their seat was Compton Wynyates, the cannibalised castle of Fulbrooke, but both were active in the government of Wales. Sir William resided at Ludlow Castle.[21]

By their careers and architectural interest, the admiration of Warkworth by this particular group cannot be dismissed as sentimental or eccentric. These were prominent figures within the court with cosmopolitan tastes and wide experience. Their judgement is a reflection of just how admired castles remained and – by extension – how central they were to noble identity. No wonder, therefore, that their reported condemnation stung the earl of Northumberland into writing a letter to his erring tenant demanding that he look after this ancestral castle.[22] Sir Ralph Grey happily ignored the request in the knowledge that the earl was powerless to do anything about the problem. He himself, however, was just as appreciative of castles: his own residence at Chillingham was substantially altered in the late sixteenth and seventeenth centuries.[23]

PATTERNS OF CASTLE BUILDING

The story of Warkworth, then, far from illustrating a decline in the importance of the castle in England, offers evidence for the opposite understanding: that these buildings remained highly prized and admired. Moreover, that where great patrimonies remained intact, there was particularly strong incentive to restore or modernise castles competitively. The Clifford family, for example, with its holdings in the north-west, was intermittently involved in the restoration of castles. Francis Clifford, fourth earl of Cumberland (d. 1641), occupied the royal castle of Carlisle in the early years of James i's reign in his official capacity as lord warden of the marches. When the king returned from Scotland in 1617, however, the earl entertained him at his family castle at Brougham in Westmorland. There elaborate preparations had been made: food was gathered in great quantities; musicians, hangings, linen and plate were all hired or borrowed for the occasion. All told, the ensuing two-day visit with its celebrations and banqueting is estimated to have cost at least £1,200.[24]

One of those involved in the reception of James i at Brougham was Henry Clifford, the eldest son of the earl of Cumberland. He was a scholarly figure with interests in mathematics, music (he played the lute) and architecture. As a young man he was an active jouster and from 1621 took over responsibility for managing the affairs of his ageing father. At Skipton Castle, Yorkshire, the principal family seat, he undertook various improvements to the buildings, with a particular burst of work coinciding with his summons to parliament as Baron Clifford. His elevation to the peerage in 1628, for example, coincided with his creation of a grotto in the outer gatehouse.[25] As lord lieutenant of Cumberland, Henry was closely involved in the bishops' wars. Despite quarrelling with other commanders and even refusing to submit his charge of Carlisle Castle in Charles I's presence, he remained royalist in the Civil War and prepared the principal castles of Yorkshire – including Skipton – in defence of the king's cause.

Meanwhile, the chief rival of the Cliffords in the affairs of the north-west, Lord William Howard, was likewise occupied with castle building. He took the unusual course of stripping one of his family castles to furnish another: gutting Kirkoswald, which had been lavishly reordered in the mid-sixteenth century, and transferring its contents to Naworth. There glass, paintings, sculpture and ceilings were re-erected. The operation is documented piecemeal between 1602 and 1628, but may have been under way for longer.[26]

The improvement of inherited castles can be paralleled at the opposite extreme of the kingdom. In October 1617 George Luttrell contracted with the master mason William Arnold for a plan and 'upright' of 'a house or parcel of building to be sett up and built within the castle of Dunster'. Arnold had previously worked on the rebuilding of the medieval hunting lodge of Cranborne for Robert Cecil, first earl of Salisbury, between 1608 and 1612. He also probably designed Montacute House in Somerset and worked on the new Oxford college of Wadham between 1610 and 1612 (see below).[27] The new building at Dunster, Somerset, ingeniously incorporated various medieval structures, including a tower, behind an almost-symmetrical façade. It was turreted in the manner of a castle and crowned with battlements pierced by arrow loops. There was also a strikingly low ratio of window to wall-surface area, which emphasised the character of the building as a castle. In the course of the work Luttrell quarrelled with Arnold, alleging that the work had been poorly done and that the cost had escalated from £462 to £1,200: an everyday story of architectural wrangling.

Other patrons were encouraged to purchase and restore castles as attributes of nobility. In 1613 Edward Herbert bought the castle of Montgomery. He acquired it in a state of disrepair from his kinsman, the earl of Pembroke, who had been granted it by the king in 1607. At the time, Herbert was pursuing a successful career at court, which culminated in his appointment as ambassador to Paris. Between 1622 and 1625, shortly before his return to England, he began a new,

brick residence within the inner ward of the castle. The material was a complete novelty in the area and he brought in the expertise of a family from the area of Essex and Hertfordshire called Scampion for moulding and firing its 600,000 constituent bricks. In 1629 Herbert was created first baron of Chirbury, the nearby town to the castle. A noted bibliophile, he brought to the castle a large collection of books. Following the resistance of his heir to parliament, Montgomery Castle – along with these new buildings – was razed to the ground between June and October 1649 by a group of more than 150 workmen. Unusually, directions were issued for the building to be drawn before it was demolished, but if any pictures were made they are not known to survive.[28]

Another Welsh castle to become the focus of attention for the ambitions of a rising family was Conwy. In 1627, following a depressing account of dilapidations, the castle was sold by the crown for £100 to Charles I's Secretary of State, Edward, Viscount Conway of Conwy Castle.[29] He assumed this title shortly before the purchase and it is possible that he had plans to restore the building as his seat. If so, he died in 1631 before any work was done. His son and heir, the erudite second Viscount Conway, certainly intended to occupy the castle. Writing to his cousin in 1635, he rejoiced in the strength of the castle walls and the quantity of lead available that could be turned towards repairs. He also asked what special rights attended the ownership of the castle and proposed to import timber from his Irish estates to supply the rebuilding work.

Whether or not any work was done is not clear, but in 1645 during the Civil War the castle was occupied for the king by the archbishop of York, John Williams (d. 1650). He was locally born and claimed to have repaired it 'from the bare walls'. Conwy fell after a siege in 1646 and was held by a parliamentarian garrison until an order was issued in 1655 that its defences, along with those of Caernarfon, be demolished. After the Civil War the work of destruction was completed by the third Lord Conway. Curiously, the local populace appear to have been resistant to this final attack on the castle and the exasperated agent insultingly told one man who confronted him about the demolition work that 'your Lordship did not like it should stand in such a beggarly cuntrye, you would pulld downe [sic] and sett it upp in another place'.[30]

The occupation of castles by successful state officers was by no means geographically restricted to the more remote areas of the kingdom. Following his creation as

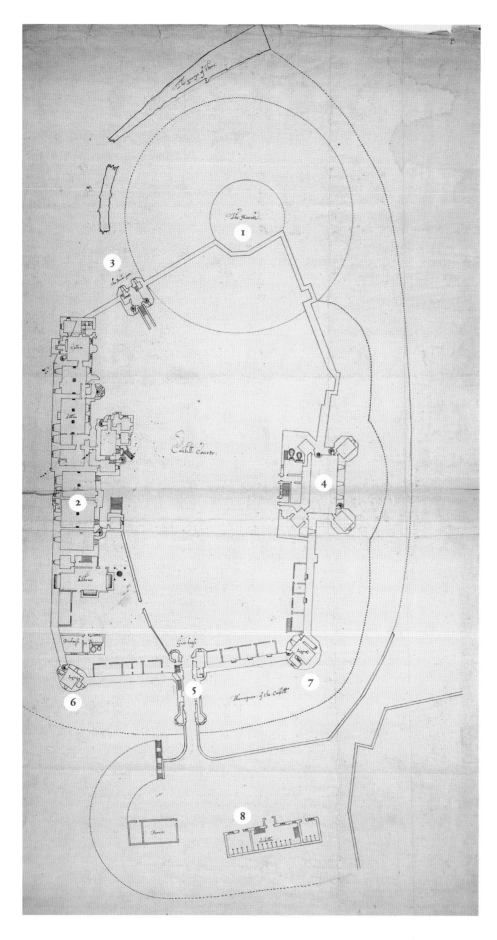

first earl of Manchester, the royal administrator Sir Henry Montagu bought Kimbolton Castle in 1615, a building probably little altered since the mid-sixteenth century. Undoubtedly the most ambitious restoration of the period, however, was undertaken by the courtier and writer Fulke Greville (d. 1628) at Warwick. Following the death of Ambrose Dudley, earl of Warwick, the castle had fallen into neglect and Fulke's father had actually petitioned to remove stone from the castle in 1601, writing to Sir Robert Cecil in forthright terms:

> I have a house much older than I, and . . . it threateneth every day to fall upon me. Now, Sir, the Queen hath the ruins of a house in this country, which hath been a common gaol these ten or twelve years; the walls down in many places hard to the ground; the roof open to all weathers; the little stone building there was mightily in decay; the timber lodgings built thirty years agone for herself, all ruinous; the garden let out for forty-four years, the barns fallen and stolen away . . . so as in very short time there will be nothing left but a name of Warwick. This, sir, I beg not, but desire to buy for as much as it is worth; because the stone is already cut and the love of my country will give me carriage . . .[31]

The petition was unsuccessful, but in 1604 Fulke received a grant of the castle. His motives for doing so are difficult to explain but most probably he wished to acquire it because of his family links with the Beauchamps, formerly earls of Warwick. At the time of the grant a royal survey confirmed the parlous state of the buildings and valued its materials in the event of demolition at £470.[32]

It was probably at about this time that Fulke commissioned Robert Smythson to undertake a survey of the castle with a view to repairing it (pl. 353). The repairs to the castle seem to have involved the renovation and extension of the medieval domestic apartments. At the same time the gardens and surrounds were reorganised and the motte converted into a garden feature. Work was well under way by 1610, when £450 was spent on the buildings, and it was apparently nearing completion in 1614.[33] Writing in 1656, the antiquary Sir William Dugdale reported that Fulke spent:

> . . . more than 20,000l. cost (as I have heard) in repairing and adorning it, [and] made it a place not only of great strength, but extraordinary delight, with most pleasant gardens walks and thickets, such

as this part of England can scarcely parallel, so that now it is the most princeply seat that is within these midland parts of the Realm.[34]

The combination of strength and beauty at Warwick – qualities peculiar to the castle – were also praised in the 1630s by Richard Corbet:

> The orchards, gardens rivers and the aire,
> Doe with the trenches, rampirs, walls, compare:
> It seems nor art nor force can intercept it,
> As if a lover built, a soldier kept it.[35]

Incidentally, the fashion for pleasure grounds in the form of castles and fortifications continued throughout this period. Sir Henry Fanshawe, a trusted crown servant, created one such in his celebrated garden at Ware Park, Hertfordshire. One visitor in October 1606 reported:

> . . . here have ben every day since my coming above forty men at worke, for the new garden is wholly translated, new levelled, and in a manner transplanted, because most of the first trees were dead with being set too deepe, and in the middest of yt in steede of a knot he is making a fort, in perfect proportion,

with his rampars, bulwarkes, counterscarpes and all other appurtenances, so that when [finished] yt is like to prove an invincible peece of worke.[36]

Castles appeared in other forms within great estates. At Walton in Somerset, an octagonal castle with a central tower was created as a landscape feature by first Lord Poulett. Meanwhile, at Hatfield, the newly built residence of the earl of Salisbury, there were payments in 1612 for erecting and painting small timber castles on top of the lodges that flanked the entrance. Presumably these resembled the kinds of miniature castles found in the battlements of Burghley in the 1570s. The castle chimney pots are nineteenth-century.[37]

One alternative to reconstructing a family castle was to build a new house that echoed in more fashionable form the design of its predecessor. This was the approach adopted by Sir Dudley Digges at Chilham in Kent. Sir Dudley was a well-connected gentleman and diplomat who wrote a treatise on military discipline in 1604. He appears to have erected the new house at Chilham after 1610, when his three sisters-in-law conveyed the property with its twelfth-century castle to him. And the building was apparently sufficiently complete for him to take up residence in 1616.[38] Chilham

355 The great tower on the motte of Tamworth, Staffordshire, in a detail from an engraving by Wenceslaus Hollar published in 1656. By the seventeenth century the buildings on the motte were already a complex patchwork of different periods of building. The surviving timber-frame hall, for example, is thought to have been erected soon after 1423 and there is record of the motte buildings being repaired in the 1540s. It was probably in anticipation of a royal visit in 1619 that the motte was again modernised by Sir John Ferrers. His work included the construction of the two projecting wings shown in the engraving. These were demolished in a restoration of the castle between 1807 and 1811.

is laid out on a polygonal plan that is almost certainly inspired by the design of the medieval great tower that stands beside it. Above the door is inscribed: 'The Lord is my house of Defense and my Castle' (pl. 354).

For those successful in the law, administration or business, castles might similarly lend respectability to success. Chirk Castle in Flintshire was bought in 1595 by Thomas Myddleton, a future lord mayor of London, who repaired it and then granted it to his son as a base for a county career in 1612.[39] Similarly, the well-connected Ferrers family of Staffordshire chose to reside at Tamworth and enlarged the residential buildings on the motte, probably in anticipation of James I's visit in August 1619 (pl. 355).[40] Meanwhile, Stokesay in Shropshire, itself built by a thirteenth-century merchant, was owned from 1620 by William Craven, the son of a lord mayor of London. Concerned with a more glamorous court career, Craven leased it in turn to a local MP, Charles Baldwyn. It was probably Baldwyn around 1620 who built a new kitchen and the fine surviving gatehouse to the castle.

All the castles discussed so far were remodelled in a manner that substantially preserved their medieval character. In one instance, however, at Caverswall in Staffordshire, the buildings were recast in more radical fashion around 1611 by a certain Matthew Cradock, a wool merchant who rose to become both an MP and mayor of Stafford.[41] Here the bailey of the quadrangular castle begun in the late thirteenth century was turned into the forecourt of a tower residence (pl. 356). Caverswall – which was possibly designed by one of

the Smythson dynasty of masons – is evidence of the way in which it was possible to play with the tradition of castle architecture in the light of new architectural fashions. There were individuals amongst the nobility who also created castles in a more modern idiom to similarly brilliant effect.

BOLSOVER CASTLE AND THE CAVENDISH FAMILY

Bolsover in Derbyshire is perhaps the most celebrated and spectacular castle of the early seventeenth century. It stands on the edge of a high escarpment overlooking a broad valley, now the route of the M1, the principal motorway connecting the north and south of England. By the late sixteenth century this valley had emerged as a millionaires' row that included three great houses associated with the formidable Bess of Hardwick, countess of Shrewsbury: the two halls at Hardwick and the lost house at Owlcotes. In this glittering company was one substantial medieval castle dating back to at least the twelfth century. Whether it was ruinous from the late Middle Ages onwards – as is commonly assumed – is not clear: when the antiquarian Leland passed the site in the 1540s several decades earlier he simply noted 'a great building of an old castle'.

In 1613 the medieval castle of Bolsover passed into the possession of one of Bess's younger sons, Charles

356 A view of Caverswall, Staffordshire, from the west in 1911. The quadrangular castle with polygonal angle towers was built by Sir William de Caverswall (d. 1292), whose lost monument in the parish church was reported in the seventeenth century to bear the legend 'Castri structor eram, domibus fossisque cemento / Vivus dans operam, nunc claudor in hoc monumento' (Of the castle I was builder, with its houses, ditches and stone / while alive giving this work, now I am enclosed in this monument). The work was also associated with a licence to crenellate dated 1275. A certain Matthew Cradock, a merchant, MP and mayor of Stafford, remodelled the castle around 1611. He erected a residential tower on one side of the quadrangular medieval bailey (visible in the centre). It stands like a great tower in a castle enclosure and creates a composition strongly reminiscent of such late Tudor buildings as Hardwick New Hall.

Cavendish. He began work to what is known as the Little Castle at Bolsover in 1612 (pl. 357). As a matter of fact, this was not the first castle Cavendish had attempted to build. In the 1590s he had planned a new residence for himself at Slingsby in Yorkshire. This was similarly the site of a medieval castle and the surviving plans for the building, drawn up by Robert Smythson, show that it was to be a compact and high-built residence enclosed within a turreted court much like Caverswall.[42] At Bolsover, Charles created a self-contained house cast unmistakably in the form of a great tower. Work to the Little Castle was overseen by the mason John Smythson. It is a matter of debate, however, as to whether he or his father, Robert (d. 1614), actually designed the building. Moreover, since Charles Cavendish enjoyed a reputation for architectural expertise, his own contribution and role in the operation are also in question.[43]

Charles died in 1617 before the Little Castle was complete, and the building was finished and fitted out by his son, William. An intimate of James I's heir, Prince Henry, William had been encouraged in his interest of music and the patronage of art since his youth. The interiors he created are very beguiling – at once grand but intimate. Several contain elaborate painted decoration, the most complete domestic sequence to survive from the early seventeenth century.

Having finished the Little Castle, William Cavendish began to remodel the wider castle around 1627. These works may have been intended to celebrate his growing political stature: he had been created Viscount Mansfield in 1620 and in 1628 was raised to the dignity of earl of Newcastle. A second set of residential buildings was created along a terrace beside the Little Castle at Bolsover. Such a duplication of lodgings is a fascinating throwback to the kinds of architectural arrangements made for the great and riding households in the fifteenth century at such castles as Warkworth and Ashby de la Zouch (Leicestershire). Battlemented and with buttresses in the form of cannon barrels, the new buildings at Bolsover made conscious architectural reference to their place in a castle.

When work to the terrace was being completed in May 1633, the earl was visited in his new home by the king and queen. Following a banquet in the Little Castle the royal couple were entertained with a masque by Ben Jonson which involved a certain Colonel Vitruvius – a portrait of Jonson's architectural rival Inigo Jones – and a group of the workmen involved in the building.[44] It was probably shortly after this event that the earl added to the castle a new riding school range. Riding was one of his particular pleasures and he had been trained in the art of dressage since he was ten. For those within the court circle, the fashion for this

357 (*facing page*) The Little
Castle, Bolsover, Derbyshire,
begun by Charles Cavendish
in 1612 within the walls of a
medieval castle. Its military air
is reinforced by the smallness
of the windows and its
turreted entrance forecourt.
There is an impressive array of
battlements, chimneys and
cupolas crowning the
building. On two sides are
balconies, one overlooking the
forecourt and the other an
adjacent garden and fountain.
Bolsover must have appeared
quite similar to the medieval
great towers that were being
renovated in this period, as at
Corfe and Dover. To the right
of the Little Castle is a series
of seventeenth-century
buildings in the bailey that
duplicated the
accommodation provided by
the great tower, a common
medieval arrangement. Just
visible at the right-hand edge
of the photograph is a buttress
in the form of a canon barrel.

style of riding encouraged the construction of several
such buildings at residences including Welbeck, St
James's Palace and – possibly – at Wolfeton (Dorset).
In this sense, the new range was really a fashionable
version of the grand stables that had been built at castles such as Warwick and Kenilworth by Richard Beauchamp (d. 1439) and John Dudley (d. 1553) as advertisements respectively of chivalry and high office.

Bolsover is the most famous of three castles that
are directly connected to William Cavendish and the
Smythsons. William's younger brother, Charles, a dwarf
who was to prove a gallant commander in the Civil
War, fulfilled his father's intention of building a new
house in the fortified style on the site of the medieval
castle at Slingsby. Only the decaying ruins of this compactly planned building now survive, but its form is
known from a plan and elevation of around 1700. Set
on a podium after the fashion of Wollaton, the building possessed four corner towers and a crown of battlements. Circumstances dictate that it was probably
erected around 1630.

Similarly exiguous is the medieval castle of Ogle,
Northumberland, which William Cavendish inherited
from his mother along with the barony of Ogle in 1629.
This building is represented in an accomplished engraving of the 1660s, which shows it as a four-square courtyard residence with angle towers and encircled by a
moat. Very unusually for an English castle, the main
ranges are covered by steeply pitched roofs and the
corner towers are capped by onion domes. The detail is
unlikely to be correct, but the architecture of the castle
cannot be properly assessed with the evidence available.

It is conventional to treat buildings such as Bolsover
and Slingsby as 'mock' castles, simply because they are
not defensible, and also to look for their inspiration
in the theatrical sets created for contemporary court
entertainments, such as masques and tournaments.[45]
Such comparisons are useful, but they miss the full
spirit of these buildings. By creating castles that incorporated towers and which were decked in the trappings
of fortification, the Cavendish family were advertising
in architecture their status and military vocation. It
was a vocation both brothers took very seriously in the
Civil War. William played a particularly prominent
role, commanding the royalist army at the catastrophe
of Marston Moor in 1644. His role as a patron of castle
architecture actually resumed after the Civil War in his
repair of the demolished castle at Nottingham.

To view the Cavendish castles purely in the context
of seventeenth-century court life is also to miss their
architectural context amongst England's inherited castles. Throughout the seventeenth century these were
in the process of alteration and provide much more
immediate comparisons for the design of the Little
Castle than any stage set.

DOVER AND THE ENGLISH
GREAT TOWER

In 1624 George Villiers, duke of Buckingham, was
appointed constable of Dover Castle and warden of the
Cinque Ports by James I. The post was a mark of the
exceptional trust and favour the duke enjoyed. Dover
not only remained an important fortress controlling
the shortest crossing between England and the Continent, but it also enjoyed considerable prestige as a
castle. In celebration of his appointment, a special roll
listing the shields of arms of all his predecessors was
presented to him.[46] Buckingham's subsequent work to
the buildings at Dover reflects both its strategic and
residential importance. Besides repairing the defences,
he spent nearly £1,850 on the domestic accommodation in the inner bailey of the castle. This included the
repair of Arthur's Hall and the renovation of the great
tower with a set of royal apartments for the king and
queen respectively on the top and first floors as well as
six connected bedchambers. A surviving account dated
between 1 October 1625 and 30 September 1626 offers
good information about what was done.[47]

A new doorcase with rusticated pilasters and an
escutcheon of the king's arms was erected at the entrance to the tower and new windows were inserted to
light the forebuilding stair. These windows were probably added because the whole structure was roofed
over at this time. Meanwhile, two chambers in the
tower, identified in the building accounts as the presence and privy chamber, were plastered to create barrel
vaults. These were then painted with 'freetworke in
distemper' – presumably a type of imitation coffering
– by the king's sergeant painter, who was paid extra in
consideration of carrying materials 'the farre distance
betwixt London and Dover'. To keep out draughts the
windows were sealed with plaster and the floors were
laid with plaster of Paris. Where it was damaged, the
woven matting that lay in many of the principal chambers was repaired or relaid. At the same time, a great
deal of new wainscoting was erected, fixing sockets for
which are still visible in the fabric of the building, and

painted in distemper. A balcony was also erected somewhere on the building, probably overlooking the base of the forebuilding stair.

Much of this work must have been completed after Dover served as the setting of an important state occasion. In 1625 Northampton was instructed to receive the new wife of Prince Charles at Dover Castle. In fact, by the time Henrietta Maria arrived at Dover in June her husband had succeeded to the English throne as Charles I. He came as a monarch, therefore, to entertain her in the great tower. The queen's chamberlain, Leveneur de Tillières, was not impressed by this reception. 'The castle', he wrote in his memoirs, 'is an old building made *à l'antique*, where the queen was badly lodged with worse furnishing and her train treated with much less magnificence than was appropriate considering the importance of the occasion.'[48] Given what we know of Charles I's fastidious tastes, it is quite possible that he would have agreed. The fact that Northampton persevered with his modernisation of the tower after this event suggests that he hoped to welcome the king and queen there again and lodge them more appropriately. Political difficulties intervened, however, and this wish was never fulfilled. Four hundred and fifty years after its first construction by Henry II, this was the last time that the great tower at Dover was to be used as a royal residence.

That Northampton hoped to flatter the royal couple on their return, however, is shown by one remarkable recorded detail of the new decoration in the tower described by the admiring Captain Hammond when he visited Dover Castle in 1635:

From hence wee march'd up againe to the great Castle [i.e. the great tower], and there mounted up 120. Stayres to the Leads, wheron I had a full view of the Towne, standing underneath me in a deep hole; of all the Towers within her [the castle], which shew'd like a Towne, within it Selfe; of all her owne and neighbouring Bulwarks within the Towne; of the stately Shipps sayling through and riding in that brave Road : nay further, I saw part of our neighbouring Kingdome, Callice [Calais] and Bullen [Boulogne], enough I think to see in one place; and descending downe againe I pass'd by the Guard Chamber; the Chamber of Presence, and the Bed Chambers for both their Majesties. And by the way, where our now gracious Soveraigne first met and saluted his Royall Spouse, I mett with these two verses written on a little Tablet:

All places of this Castle, onelie this
Where Charles and Mary, shar'd a Royall kisse.[49]

As it stood in 1626, the great tower of Dover and the adjacent inner bailey apartments echoed Bolsover very closely. Such points of formal comparison between contemporary and ancient architecture deserve more attention than they have conventionally received. Particularly intriguing is the evident prestige enjoyed by the form of the great tower. These buildings are commonly characterised today as 'medieval' or – inaccurately – as 'Gothic' structures. Yet in the seventeenth century most ancient great towers continued to be viewed as Roman, and perhaps therefore as home-grown examples of classical design. As the doomed Prince Edward V commented of the Tower of London in Shakespeare's play of the 1590s, *Richard III*:

Gloucester: . . . Your Highness shall repose you
    at the Tower;
Then where you please, and shall be thought
    most fit
For your best health and recreation.
Prince: I do not like the Tower, of any place.
Did Julius Caesar build that place, my lord?
Buckingham: He did, my gracious lord, begin
    that place,
Which, since, succeeding ages have re-edified.
Prince: Is it upon record, or else reported
Successively from age to age, he built it?
Buckingham: Upon record, my gracious lord.
Prince: But say, my lord, it were not regist'red,
Methinks the truth should live from age to age,
As 'twere retailed to all posterity,
Even to the general all-ending day.

This perceived connection with the Roman past may have informed the restoration of the White Tower on the eve of the Civil War between 1638 and 1640. The work was the responsibility of Inigo Jones in his post of surveyor of the king's works, and it respects the original design of the building.[50] Here the Stuart vision of the Roman world elides almost seamlessly into the Norman one.

The White Tower, of course, has long enjoyed exceptional prestige as the seat of royal authority in the capital and has figured large in the foundation myths of London. Nevertheless, other patrons may also have been encouraged to imply that their own great towers had similar claims to antiquity and deserved to be set off with classical ornament or decoration. At Raglan,

358 Lulworth, Dorset, completed between 1608 and 1610. The castle is laid out on a compact, rectangular plan with a drum tower at each corner. It is fronted by a stone terrace, and the main façade, built throughout in cut stone, is sparingly detailed with tiers of windows. These diminish in height as they rise up the building and are divided on each storey by string courses. The walls are crowned with battlements and the parapets of the towers are additionally ornamented with arrow loops and bands of decorative brickwork. Incorporated within this tower were all the principal apartments of a great house in a familiar format. The building was entered through an internalised porch, which led into the screens passage and hall. There were services and kitchens in the basement, as well as a buttery in one of the angle towers. At the upper levels of the building were withdrawing rooms and bedchambers. Connecting all the floors was a great stair. The plan that is revealed looks very similar in some points of formal detail to a Romanesque great tower with a central spine wall. An engraving of 1721 shows the castle in its former surrounds, including a seventeenth-century walled forecourt and gatehouse.

for example, probably around 1610, the great tower was encircled by a garden walk countersunk into the ground beside the moat. Around it were placed niches decorated with shells and set with the statues of Roman emperors. Curiously, an almost identical arrangement of sculpture was created in the garden fountain overlooked by the Little Castle at Bolsover. At Warwick, one of the mid-fourteenth-century towers of the castle was entitled Caesar's Tower by the mid-seventeenth century, as was the neighbouring great tower of Kenilworth (see previous chapter).

Even later patrons were sometimes tempted absolutely to assert the classical origins of such buildings. Lady Anne Clifford, a noted restorer of her family castles in the 1650s, respectively entitled the great towers in her castles of Brough, Brougham and Appleby, the Roman Tower, the Pagan Tower and Caesar's Tower, in celebration of their supposed depth of history. Moreover, she wrote of the last:

> And though Appleby Castle was built before William the Conqueror's time, for the great tower called Caesar's Tower was undoubtedly built by the Romans when they were masters of Great Britaine, yet the greatest part of the building of the castle was often defaced and broken down by the wars between England and Scotland.[51]

This mistaken attribution of great towers to the Roman period continued popularly even into the nineteenth century. In his introduction to *The Antiquities of England and Wales* (London, 1787), for example, Francis Grose explains that one type of great tower was known as a Juliet after Julius Caesar, the reputed builder.

The architecture of the great tower, however, was not merely popular because of its associations with the Roman world. It also suited the contemporary fashion for compact and symmetrical design. As such, the great tower remained the ultimate source of inspiration for a substantial group of early seventeenth-century lodges and grand residences. It was probably with a view to satisfying James I's love of hunting, for example, that Thomas, third Lord Bindon, built Lulworth Castle, Dorset. The new building was completed between 1608 and 1610 as the centrepiece to a 1,000-acre park that Bindon had created and stood just 4 miles from his house at Bindon Abbey (pl. 358). According to Bindon's own admission, inspiration for the new building had come from James I's principal minister, Robert Cecil, first earl of Salisbury, who managed 'in a powerful speche to me at Byndon to have layde the first foundatiyon of the pyle in my mind'.[52] Lulworth survived as a country house until the early twentieth century and was much altered internally in the eigh-

359 Plas Teg, Flintshire, built from about 1610 onwards by an MP and senior naval administrator, John Trevor. In the manner of a castle it is prominently sited. The circular openings above the upper windows are perhaps intended to represent gun embrasures. The plan of the building with its recessed planes is comparable to that of Wollaton (see pl. 351). Designs for this building – or one very similar to it – survive in the collection of drawings owned by the London-based surveyor John Thorpe, evidence for the wide-ranging influence of figures and architectural fashions from the capital in this period.

teenth. A disastrous fire in 1929, however, revealed evidence for the original arrangement of rooms once more.

In both its form and castellated character, Lulworth bears close resemblance to another castle begun in 1626 by Sir Thomas Morgan, steward of the earl of Pembroke, at Ruperra in Glamorgan – so close, indeed, that a common link with the Smythsons has plausibly been suggested.[53] Not exclusive of this attribution, the plans for buildings in the form of Ruperra and Lulworth were also circulating widely in connection with a developing tradition of suburban houses around London by the 1610s.[54] It is probably from the capital, for example, that the designs of other related buildings derive. In the case of Plas Teg, Flintshire, built around 1610 (pl. 359), or the even grander Westwood, Worcestershire, built by Sir John Packinton *circa* 1600, explanation for compact and four-square designs can be found without recourse to the Smythsons. In the

former case, for example, a plan for the house – or a building very like it – survives in the drawing collection of the royal surveyor John Thorpe (d. 1655).[55]

Some patrons chose to add new great towers to existing residences. The enthusiastic antiquarian and historian Sir Thomas Brudenell, for example, created a great tower for his house at Deene Park in Northamptonshire around 1622.[56] Battlemented and with heraldic decoration inside and out, it proclaimed the dynastic pretensions of his family. Other lost buildings might also belong to this late tradition of great tower architecture, for example, the high tower erected by James I at Eltham in Kent.

Throughout this period, the form of the great tower was also popular in the decorative arts and found some surprising applications. One such is the great seventeenth-century silver centrepiece for a table in the form of a tower with cannon that survives amongst the crown jewels.[57] Valuable table ornaments in the form

360 Inigo Jones's design for Oberon's Palace in a stage set for Scene 2 of Jonson's *Oberon, The Fairy Prince* (1611). In the directions, the palace is described as being within a cavern. It takes the form of a great tower with angle turrets and a dome. The tower is battlemented and the turrets possess tall arrow loops, a comment on the perceived connection between high estate and the trappings of fortification. Designs like this have been represented as the inspiration for buildings such as the Little Castle at Bolsover. In fact, remodelled great towers such as Dover and the White Tower (repaired under Jones's direction in the years 1638–40) offer far more immediate parallels for the castle architecture of the Stuart nobility. Oberon's castle has been splendidly recreated in timber in the new gardens at Arundel Castle, completed in 2009.

sational costumes, music and stage sets, the rather florid texts of masques must have been fantastic fun to perform for the tiny circle that partook in them.

CHARITABLE AND COLLEGIATE FOUNDATIONS

It was not only in great residences that the influence of castle design continued to be apparent in Stuart England. In their generosity to charitable foundations – usually almshouses and schools – in the shadow of their homes, the nobility and gentry created institutions in clear succession to the chantry foundations of the Middle Ages. On occasion, these buildings were also connected – both physically and in their architecture – to castles.

Henry Howard, earl of Northampton (d. 1614), was one outstanding political figure who established foundations in this tradition. He was a scholar, a herald and an antiquarian, and as constable of Dover Castle and warden of the Cinque Ports chose to be buried in St Mary in Castro in Dover (although his monument by Nicholas Stone was moved to Greenwich by the Mercers' Company in 1696).[60] At the same time, the earl also established three hospitals dedicated to the Holy and Undivided Trinity. These stood at Greenwich and beside his ancestral castles of Clun, Shropshire, and Castle Rising, Norfolk. The last is perhaps the best preserved and in its modest way clearly shows the influence of medieval planning with a gatehouse and prominent chimney stacks.

A grander building in the same idiom is the gatehouse of Abbot's Hospital, Guildford, built between 1619 and 1622 by George Abbot, archbishop of Canterbury, who was born in the town. The foundation celebrates in architecture the success of a poor local boy who did well for himself and wished to offer future benefits to its population. This is exactly the spirit in which such late medieval bishops as Waynflete and Rotherham built colleges in their birthplaces. The design of the gatehouse and the layout of the hospital similarly look back to late medieval example. Yet even this building is relatively modest when compared with the ambition of major university college buildings in the early seventeenth century.

At Oxford, the medieval tradition of collegiate design survived the Reformation. Wadham College, founded by a Somersetshire couple, Nicholas and Dorothy

of castle towers are documented in England from at least the fifteenth century, for example, a huge gilt salt owned by Sir John Fastolf of Caister Castle, Norfolk, in 1459.[58] In 1611, meanwhile, a recusant barrister called Robert Dover settled in the Cotswolds and established an early revival of the 'Olimpic Games'. This immensely popular sporting event included such varying competitions as running, fencing, horse racing, wrestling, leaping, throwing the hammer, dancing and even chess. The frontispiece to a series of poems celebrating these annual games entitled *Annalia Dubrensia*, published in 1636, shows a scene of the games with Dover on horseback in control of events and a stage-set great tower with guns firing behind him.[59]

Dover's castle that presided over his games was certainly related to the tradition of temporary buildings created for public, royal and court entertainments that stretches back at least into the fourteenth century. Drawings of a few such seventeenth-century castles still survive, including that erected as the stage for a firework display to celebrate the marriage of Princess Elizabeth, James I's daughter, to the elector palatine in 1613. There is also a design by Inigo Jones for a stage set of Oberon's Palace (pl. 360). This was to be used in a masque, a genre of private entertainment performed by courtiers themselves. Accompanied by sen-

361 The courtyard façade of the hall and chapel at Wadham College, Oxford. Wadham was built between 1610 and 1612 by the Somerset mason William Arnold, who also worked at Dunster Castle. The design he produced – with a courtyard comprising three lodging ranges and an integrated hall and chapel – follows in the fourteenth-century tradition of Edward III's upper ward at Windsor and its architectural follower, New College, Oxford. Here, symmetry has been imposed on the hall and chapel range by creating a second and false door to the former (right). The whole composition is lent dignity by a tall central porch and crown of battlements. This was no provincial work of architecture: the design of the college was approved as a plat or drawing by the king, the archbishop of Canterbury, the lord chancellor and the lord treasurer.

Wadham, for example, is a symmetrical reworking of the classic Oxford design in which the hall and chapel form the principal range of a quadrangle enclosed on three sides by lodgings. Battlemented throughout and entered through an imposing gatehouse, Wadham is in a very real sense the descendant of Edward III's upper ward at Windsor Castle and William Wykeham's foundation of the 1380s at New College, Oxford (pl. 361). It was designed and executed, however, by a figure with no demonstrable connection with Oxford: a shortage of masons encouraged the executors of Nicholas Wadham to send up a group of masons from Somerset. They were under the direction of William Arnold, whom we have already encountered at Dunster Castle.[61]

Arnold was not alone amongst contemporary masons at Oxford capable of conforming to the medieval tradition of collegiate architecture. The same shortage of masons also introduced to Oxford the Yorkshire mason John Akroyd. In 1609 he contracted to build the Fellows' Quadrangle of Merton College for £570.[62] With its novel, inward-facing gatehouse façade, this building was the antecedent for his most dazzling creation and the new architectural heart to the Jacobean university: the Schools Quadrangle, begun in 1613, and the new front of the Divinity Schools (1610–12). The catalyst for this extraordinary undertaking was the

agreement reached in 1610 between the namesake of the library, the diplomat and bibliophile Sir Thomas Bodley, and the Stationers' Company in London. By this it was agreed that every book entered at Stationers' Hall should come to Oxford's university library, the origin of the Bodleian's status as a copyright library.

Even as the Civil War loomed, the fascination of Oxford with castle and Perpendicular forms remained strong. William Laud, archbishop of Canterbury, created Canterbury Quad at his former college of St John's between 1631 and 1636. On two sides the courtyard is faced with arcaded loggias and gateway façades superbly detailed in the classical style. All the ranges, however, are crowned with battlements and incorporate Gothic window forms. Within the gateways, moreover, the passages are covered with sophisticated fan vaults, a form unique to the Perpendicular style. And in 1642–3 the college further expanded its buildings with a new lodging range incorporating a centrally placed and battlemented gatehouse called Cook's Building.

As has often been commented, there is a great deal that is wilfully conservative about these buildings, as if the university were concerned to celebrate its medieval origins. Nevertheless, they also illustrate the degree to which the Perpendicular remained a living architectural tradition, practised by the best masons and admired by the most sophisticated patrons. Indeed, these continuities are apparent in institutional architecture across the country. The Inns of Court in London, for example, were housed in what are in effect collegiate complexes with battlemented gatehouses, halls and chapels.

THE PLANTATION OF ULSTER

Castles were understood as one means by which royal power might be extended in seventeenth-century Ireland. As a result, there was a great deal of official encouragement for loyal supporters of the English administration to engage in their construction. Randall McDonnell, for example, a son of the Scots-Irish chieftain Sorley Boy McDonnell, was knighted by Lord Mountjoy in 1602 for his support in crushing the earl of Tyrone's rebellion.[63] The following year James I issued a confirmation of his family lands in Ulster, and three years later, in July 1606, this property was regranted on condition that he build a 'a fort or garrison' at Dunluce – his principal seat – and a 'castle or mansion house' at Glenarm (both Co. Antrim).[64] At Glenarm there survives an inscription, dated to the year of his death, recording his work to the castle (of which nothing now survives).[65] Of Dunluce, meanwhile, two official English visitors reported in 1610 that:

> . . . Sir Randall McDonnell hath buylte a fayre stone walle about the whole rock within which he hath erected a good house of stone with many lodgings and other rooms. The towne of Dunluce consists of many tenements after the fashion of the Palle [the Pale] peopled for the most part with Scotishmen.[66]

This process of constructing castles was massively accelerated following one of the most celebrated episodes of early modern Irish history. Frustrated by their treatment at the hands of the English government in Ireland, four Gaelic earls set sail from Ireland on 4 September 1607, in the hope of Spanish support against the crown. The so-called Flight of the Earls proved a disastrous political miscalculation. James I declared the estates of the refugee earls forfeit and prepared to colonise the province with a new population. There had been several Elizabethan plantations established in Ireland, but none on this scale. This was intended, moreover, as a commercial operation similar in character to the settlement underpinning British colonial expansion in America and came to be sub-stantially underwritten financially by the City of London. It was an undertaking – in short – that breathed the future spirit of British imperialism.

In April 1610 there was published in London a book of successful applicants for land in Ulster. The confiscated estates in the king's hand had been broken down into 'baronies', each of which was further divided up into small, medium and large holdings. Two groups of settlers were created to occupy these. The most important were undertakers, who held their land in knight service to the king. They were obliged to take the Oath of Succession – in other words demonstrate their Protestantism – and agreed to displace all the native Irish from their estates. In addition, they agreed to settle at least twenty-four English or Scottish Protestants for every 1,000 acres that they held. To safeguard their property, undertakers were obliged to construct castles and bawns (fortified enclosures around houses) in proportion to their landholding. An undertaker with 2,000 acres, for example, was responsible for constructing a castle and a bawn.

Mixed up with the undertakers in each barony were a certain number of servitors, who were exempt from the oath and the obligation to settle outsiders on the land. Those who received 1,500 acres held them by knight's service to Dublin Castle and agreed to build a stone or brick house with a bawn. Undertakers with 1,000 acres, by contrast, were to build a bawn within two years of occupying the land. In addition, numerous new towns were established across the province, all of them laid out on formal plans and several with impressive fortifications, as at Derry (or Londonderry, after the home of the investors who financed it).

The ensuing colonisation was neither as clean nor as tidy as planned. It did, however, prompt a great deal of building. Some sense of this is provided by contemporary records of the settlement made by officials concerned to check on the progress of plantation. The notes of one commissioner in 1622 record a broad spectrum of work. At one extreme was the exemplary

> William Brownlow Esq. Hath 2 proporcons, viz Dewcorran containing 1500 acres, upon which is built a good howse or castle of stone, and brick, lay'd with lime, 3 stories high, wherin himself, his wife and Familie, now inhabite. This howse is compassed with a strong Bawne of lyme and stone 159 foot long, 93 foot broad, and 14 foot in height, with a fair Flancker [a projecting bastion that offers flanking fire along a wall] square to the South East; and he is purposed

to make another opposite. He hath made neer adioyning a good village, consisting of 40 howses, inhabited with English tenants, on both sides of the streets, in which a good windemill stands.

Other undertakers lived in half-completed buildings or in ones that were already ruinous. In one case, no buildings had been begun at all, though the owner promised to build 'a Bawne and Castle according to the Pattene of the Ld Grandizon at Ballymore'.[67]

Some Irish bishops were likewise involved in the construction of castles. John Leslie, bishop of Raphoe, for example, began a castle close to his cathedral church. It cost approximately £3,500 to build and may well have been designed by a London mason. The details of its construction can be reconstructed from a pair of inscriptions and a note in the family Bible: 'In the year 1636, on Tuesday, 17th May the foundation of the castle of Raphoe was laid; the building was completed 19th August 1637; the fifth year of our translation, with the beneficence of God, we moved into the new house Thursday, 14th December 1637.'

The Plantation of Ulster encouraged exactly the same kinds of building as earlier English imperial endeavours, such as Edward 1's conquest of Wales. Indeed, there is something very medieval about the whole conception of the plantation – the structure of its society and the network of castles, towns and churches that James 1 attempted to impose on the province. His experiment was to prove profoundly unhappy. The plantation established deep-seated tensions between the native Irish and the planters, which were to explode with horrifying ferocity in the 1640s.

THE ROYAL ESTATE

It was James 1 who made the first serious reductions to the vastly disproportionate body of residences collected by the Tudors. A wave of surveys in 1603–4 followed his accession to the throne, a reflection of his attempt to grasp what he had inherited. Many of the most attractive and valuable properties were parcelled out to his circle of favourites as part of the round of gifts that followed his accession. The great Yorkist castle of Fotheringhay in Northamptonshire, for example, was granted to Lord Mountjoy in 1603, but was demolished twenty years later after passing through the hands of several further owners. This demolition may have resulted directly from its role in the

final imprisonment and execution of Mary, queen of Scots, which tarnished the buildings in some people's eyes. Captain Hammond, a tourist in 1635, wrote of it:

. . . I hastened to visite a sickly and dying castle, not able to hold up her head, which never left aking, ever sithence that heroicke spirited Queen left aking hers there . . . Her stately hall I found spacious, large and answerable to the other Princelike Roomes, but drooping and desolate, for that there was the Altar, where that great Queen's head was sacrific'd; as all the rest of those precious, sweet Buildings doe sympathize, decay, fall, perish and goe to wracke, for that unluckie and fatal blow.[68]

Some of the castle materials were reputedly acquired by the antiquarian Sir Robert Cotton in the restoration of his own castle at Conington, Huntingdonshire.

In the north of England, where there was now prospect of lasting peace along the border, the process of alienating castles was very rapid. It can be difficult to trace accurately what happened to buildings after they were sold off. The conventional wisdom is that they were already ruins and were now left to moulder away. In reality, the history of these buildings was often much more complicated and intriguing. Two determining factors in the future history of the castle were whether the new owner needed a residence and whether the castle came with any land; a great building with no estate was neither inviting nor economically viable.

Some buildings were indeed probably abandoned. Dunstanburgh Castle in Northumberland, for example, was sold by James 1 in August 1604 and bought the following year by Sir Ralph Grey. There is no evidence that it was ever again occupied by anyone of social standing.[69] Similarly, Bamburgh was granted in 1610 to an illegitimate child of Sir John Forster, previously warden of the marches and earlier responsible for having ruined the castle for the value of its materials in 1584.[70] The fate of other castles is more difficult to trace. Middleham in Yorkshire, for example, was granted to a local landowner, Sir Henry Linley, in 1604 along with much of its associated property. He evidently lived in the buildings because he is described in the register of his burial on 8 November 1609 as being of Middleham Castle, though whether he undertook any work to them is not clear.[71] His heirs may have occupied the castle, too, but by the time it was drawn by Francis Place in 1711 Middleham was in an advanced state of ruin.[72]

In some cases, castles were granted away in conjunction with titles, clear evidence of the close perceived connection between the two. When Ludovic Stuart, Lord Lennox, for example, was created duke of Richmond in 1623, he also received a grant of the castle. Significantly, it came without its valuable honour, so the gift was of very small value. Moreover, the new duke died almost immediately and the castle reverted to the crown.[73] Had he lived, it is possible that some architectural changes might have resulted from this grant. It may also have been in celebration of title that James granted the castle of Scarborough to John, earl of Holderness, in 1619. When John died soon afterwards in 1626, it was conveyed to one Francis Thompson of Humbleton, who leased the castle for pasture.[74] There is no reason for supposing that the buildings were well kept in this period, but it is remarkable that the floors and roof of the great tower remained intact. As a result, when the castle was besieged in 1644–5 it became the residence of 'the Governor, his laddie, and most of the gentlemen and officers of qualitie', though when it was split in half by cannon fire they were forced to use the other available accommodation, 'poore cabbins reared against the walls and banckes in the castle yearde'.[75]

There were also individuals who purchased royal castles as an attribute of nobility. Barnard Castle and Raby, after a complex passage through the hands of James I's favourite Robert Carr, earl of Somerset, and the prince of Wales, finally ended up in the possession of a courtier and an outsider to the affairs of the region, Sir Henry Vane. The despoliation of Raby at some stage in this process provoked an outraged response from one anonymous native of Co. Durham: 'O madnesse! Can forty poundes worth of leade be worthe more then a tower, whose buildinge cost above two thousande? Shall such a princely building (which might have bene the seate of the greatest Emperour of the worlde) be made a dawes nest?'[76] Sir Henry settled upon Raby as his future seat in 1630 and completely remodelled the buildings. He was obviously not so enamoured of Barnard Castle, however, which he stripped of materials to help in the work.

It is a curious footnote to this episode that in 1640 when the much-hated royal servant Thomas Wentworth assumed the title of earl of Strafford he also chose to be created baron of Raby, probably a reference to his remote Neville ancestry. Vane was deeply insulted: he regarded the award of the title as an infringement of his dignity. He never forgave Strafford

the affront, and played a prominent role in the parliamentary attempt to have the earl impeached.[77]

To a very limited extent, some English castles continued to serve some military role. At Portchester Castle in Hampshire, the newly appointed constable, Sir Thomas Cornwallis, attempted to restore the castle for his own use. With a grant of oaks from the king's forest he restored the residential apartments of the inner bailey and strengthened the fortifications of the gate into it. In a royal survey of 1609 the works were estimated to have cost the relatively modest sum of £300 and were incomplete. The same survey further reported that the other apartments were verging on ruin and recommended that the great tower be reduced in height to stop the castle chimneys from smoking. The latter operation was never set in hand and Portchester was placed under the custodianship of the governor of Portsmouth and then apparently neglected. Cornwallis must have retained some connection with or affection for the castle, however, because in 1618 he was buried in the church within the walls of the Roman fort that continued to define its outer defences. In 1632 Charles I sold Portchester to a local landowner, Sir William Uvedale, but nothing further is known of what happened to the buildings before the Civil War.[78]

Carlisle, meanwhile, was pressed into service in the restoration of order in the Borders – what James I liked to think of as the middle shires of his kingdom. Francis Clifford, fourth earl of Cumberland (d. 1641), was appointed lord warden to pacify the western march and offered Carlisle as his base in 1605. He initially used the castle a great deal and restored its buildings, but his residence at Carlisle diminished as the area became more peaceful. As a consequence, both the castle and town languished. It is a fascinating comment on the perceived importance of the castle to the region that when James I visited the city in 1617 he was petitioned by the town for 'a nobleman to lye in Karliell Castle'.[79] Nevertheless, the castle passed by stages into neglect and was even stripped of its guns. The earl, meanwhile, preferred to spend his money and time on his own family castles: rather than entertain the king at Carlisle, he escorted him to nearby Brougham in Westmorland to be entertained.

There were some interesting exceptions to the widespread neglect of royal castles. The most obvious is Windsor, which by virtue of its size and prestige remained the principal seat of the English kings and the Order of the Garter. In 1626 Nicholas Stone was appointed 'master mason and architect' of the castle by

Charles I. The latter title was an innovation in a royal patent of this kind, an indication of how this Roman denomination was gradually gaining ascendancy. Stone (1587–1647) was the son of a Devon quarryman who became apprenticed to a Dutch sculptor in London. As a result of this connection he travelled to Amsterdam and on his return set up a very successful tomb-making workshop. He also worked as a master mason in such operations as the Whitehall Banqueting House, designed by Inigo Jones.

The works he oversaw at Windsor included alterations to the chapel, the erection of a new balcony in the royal apartments, 'in the room where King Henry VI was born', and the creation of an ornamental gate at the eastern extreme of the castle.[80] Like Windsor, the castle of Tutbury provided excellent hunting and was also the site of a royal stud. James I visited here on several occasions and in the 1630s Charles I built a new lodging range in the castle. Few traces of this building survive today, but an elegant classical doorway leading from the moat still remains from this period.[81]

The assets of most remaining royal castles not in residential use presented too tempting a target for monarchs increasingly strapped for cash. Gradually, the buildings of redundant manors and castles were surveyed and either sold off or demolished for the value of their materials. Such castles as remained in royal hands were, even by the time of a survey in 1609, largely in a bad state of repair. By the 1630s formerly important castles such as Nottingham were being stripped of materials. There was, however, one startling and surprising exception to this rule. At Pontefract, the greatest royal castle of the north, active attempts were made to keep the fabric in repair. In 1616 James I entered into a covenant to maintain the castle and in 1618 ordered that it be surveyed, observing that it was his duty 'to prevent the Ruynes of a Monument of such antiquity and goodly building'. The result was the release of an impressive £3,000 for repairs between 1618 and 1620. Charles, as prince of Wales, inherited the building from his mother in the course of these works, and also appears to have shown an interest in the fabric.[82]

During the early seventeenth century a number of castles were also resumed by the crown. In 1619, for example, Goodrich in Herefordshire came into the king's hands in part satisfaction for a debt. It was later granted to the earl of Kent, who restored the buildings at his own cost in 1631–2. The castle was then leased out to Richard Tyler, who became the nominal con-

stable. In one instance, the crown actively engaged in trying to get hold of a castle. James I exploited the doubtful legitimacy of Robert Dudley, the earl of Leicester's son, to secure possession of Kenilworth in 1603. A survey taken in the same year emphasises repeatedly the extraordinary scale and magnificence of the buildings. The castle interiors were sufficient – so the report ran – to receive the king, the queen and their heir, Prince Henry, at one time and were 'built with as much uniformity and conveniency as any houses of later time, and with such stately cellars all carried upon pillars and architecture of freestone carved and wrought as the like are not within this kingdom'. Viewed as a whole with its buildings, parks and wider estate, the surveyor declared: 'the like both for strength, state and pleasure not being within this realm of England'.

In 1611 Prince Henry offered the vast sum of £14,600 for the title to Kenilworth, but died before the purchase was complete. His brother and the future king, Charles, received the castle in his stead, for some reason paying only £4,000 for it. There is no evidence that Charles altered the castle buildings, though they remained in good repair. In 1624 the castle was the setting for an entertainment written by Ben Jonson called *The Masque of Owls*. Two years later it was made part of the marriage portion of Charles I's bride, Henrietta Maria, and passed into the custody of Robert Carey, earl of Monmouth.

In an assessment of the state of royal castles in 1640, as with their state in the kingdom at large, it would be as inaccurate to treat either the barren ruins of Fotheringhay or the splendours of Kenilworth as representative. Yet it is almost exclusively the image of the ruined and neglected castle that continues to dominate the popular perception of these buildings in this period. The example of Kenilworth is an important antidote to this vision. Castles were being wasted; patrons were interested in new and exciting forms of architecture; yet at the same time these buildings constituted some of the grandest residences in seventeenth-century England. They were, moreover, admired for their architecture, their great attendant estates and their historical associations. Castles were exclusive and desirable residences, demonstrative of nobility and power. And though they might be ruined and laid low, they could also be resuscitated to breathe grandeur into new political careers.

What happened in the 1640s, however, was finally to remove the vast majority of castles from the English landscape and in so doing to change fundamentally the established course of English architecture.

THE CIVIL WAR

It is impossible to summarise satisfactorily here the dramatic and varied history of many castles during the Civil War. Nor is it desirable, considering how many compelling, contemporary accounts of the conflict survive, including letters, broadsheets and memoirs. The fighting caused the widespread destruction of property, but when it ceased a deliberate programme of castle demolition began, much of this focused between 1648 and 1650.[83] In view of the continuing instability of the kingdom and parliament's limited resources, the surest protection against armed opposition was to remove all unnecessary fortifications wherever they existed.

The extent of the destruction varied markedly from place to place. Sometimes it was little more than symbolic, as in the case at Berkeley in Gloucestershire, where the staunchly parliamentarian family was required to create a small breach in the great tower of the castle. In others it was malicious and tinged by a desire to efface the physical trappings of the social order that these buildings represented. When this happened, as at Raglan, not only fortifications but also whole castles were ruined, including parks, gardens and lakes. Yet generalisations do not do this subject justice and perhaps the best way of providing a flavour of what occurred is to summarise briefly the experience of the four buildings at the heart of this narrative.

Windsor Castle was occupied by parliamentary troops on 23 October 1642 after the battle of Edgehill and became an important military headquarters. The only particular target for damage was the royal college of St George, so long a symbol of the English monarchy. In a spirited act of defiance, the dean, Christopher Wren (the father of the architect), refused to surrender the keys of the college to the parliamentary troops. In response, the chapel and treasury were broken open and plundered. With the exception of the community of poor knights, the whole college was then turned out of its quarters. An attempt by Prince Rupert to storm the castle in November 1642 was beaten off and in 1643 another round of destruction followed. Again, this focused on the college, where several buildings were destroyed, including the chapter house. What remained of Henry VIII's intended tomb

was sold off and lead and glass were stripped from the chapel. The other castle buildings seem not to have been too badly affected, however, and the king returned here both in 1647 and then in December 1648, on the latter occasion journeying towards his trial at Westminster.

Following the king's execution, the royal corpse was brought back to Windsor for burial in St George's Chapel. The ceremony was hurriedly conducted during a snowstorm on 9 February 1649 in what must have felt like a derelict building. His decapitated body was laid to rest beside the coffin of Henry VIII and his queen Jane Seymour. In 1652 the castle was proposed for 'slighting' or demolition, but it was saved by opposition in parliament, an interesting comment on its perceived importance and significance. The Great Park, however, was broken up into lots and sold off. Windsor, of course, was to bounce back as a major royal seat after the Restoration precisely because it symbolised the return of the monarchy. It deserves mention, however, that even in this nadir of its fortunes, by a strange turn of events there was building in the castle during the Commonwealth: the resolution of a protracted legal case released funds to extend the residential apartments of the poor knights.[84]

Kenilworth Castle suffered the worst of all the four castles treated here. On 24 July 1649 it was directed that the defences of Kenilworth be demolished. The parliamentary commander of the castle, a certain Colonel Hawkesworth, used the instruction as a means of paying his men and officers, who were owed substantial arrears of pay. Besides destroying the defences and blasting open with gunpowder the massively constructed twelfth-century great tower, Hawkesworth also stripped all the fittings of the principal buildings. Of the magnificent suite of royal apartments, residential towers and service buildings, only the stables and gatehouse were preserved. The castle estates and the great lake or mere that enclosed it were similarly treated. In the words of William Best, vicar of Kenilworth, writing within living memory in 1717:

These new lords of the manor . . . pulled down and demolished the castle, cut down the king's woods, destroyed his parks and chase, and divided the lands into farms, amongst themselves, and built them houses to dwell in. Hawkesworth seated himself in the gatehouse of the castle and drained the famous pool, consisting of several hundred acres of ground.[85]

The castle remains a ruin of breathtaking splendour to the present day.

For Durham the traumas of civil war began early: in 1640 the city was twice occupied by troops during the so-called Bishops' War. An English army was first to be billeted in the city, but it was quickly replaced by a victorious Scottish one. Besides exacting a large indemnity from the populace, the Scottish troops reputedly damaged the cathedral, destroying the organ and font. The Scots left the city in August 1641 but returned in 1644 as the royalist cause collapsed. Their visit was accompanied by a serious outbreak of plague. Soon afterwards, the see of Durham, like all other bishoprics, was suppressed and its property sold off by the state. The castle was bought for £1,267 by Sir Thomas Andrews, a draper and lord mayor of London.[86] It subsequently served as a hospital for prisoners captured in Cromwell's Scottish campaign. Most of the captives, however, were held in the cathedral. Without firewood or proper supplies the fabric and furnishings of both buildings were badly damaged. Following the Restoration, a massive repair programme was begun by the new bishop, John Cousin. As they survive today, both buildings bear the mark of his carefully documented endeavours.

The strategic importance of Dover made the castle an important object for both sides. It was initially held for the king by its small garrison but a merchant called Drake plotted to capture it by surprise. On the night of 1 August 1642 he and about ten men scaled the cliffs with ladders and ropes. The ascent was believed to be impossible and the party was not spotted. Confused by this completely unexpected night-time assault, the garrison was persuaded to surrender. Next day a larger parliamentary force was marched from Canterbury to hold the castle. Various royalist attempts were made to recapture Dover but with no success.[87] At the end of the hostilities the castle was preserved for its strategic value, though it is unclear exactly what – if anything – happened to the buildings. Even the documented account of Drake's exploit begs many questions, not least where the royalist garrison were lodged when they were surprised. Whatever the case, Dover continued in unbroken military occupation until 1958.[88]

As the experiences of these four buildings in the Civil War well illustrate, the history of the castle in England did not come to an end in the 1640s. Yet in almost every sense, the castle was to enjoy a completely different place in England and the minds of its people after these momentous events. Castles before the hos-tilities of the Civil War had been an accepted part of the landscape, both as ancient monuments and as heirlooms of nobility. Now they were hunted down, architectural enemies of peace and the Commonwealth. Even some owners were prepared to acknowledge in the 1650s that the sting of their fortifications needed to be drawn. The earl of Huntingdon, was one such. Having witnessed the demolition of his residence at Ashby de la Zouch, Leicestershire, he wrote a petition to parliament demanding redress for his financial loss:

Ashby Towers
By Order of Parliament bearing the date 1648 Ashby howse the oneley convenient mansion of the said earl of Huntingdon (and standing monument of his worthy ancestors) was to be slighted. To which order the said earle consented and submitted: And out of his tender affection to the countrys quiet and benefit (which he foresaw providing for) did not so much interrupt the Authorities that commanded it . . . Hoping always the intent of the order had been such as the letter thereof held forth, the slighting and onelie making untenable of the said hows: and not the demolishers men willing to understand (for their easesye dispatches) the raceing [razing] and utter ruine, not onelie of the piles themselves but of the very ruins of them: so the unexpected detriment of the materials and untollerable losse of the said earle . . .[89]

In a national sense, the scale of such destruction is difficult to quantify, but it can probably claim to be the single most radical change inflicted violently on the architectural landscape of England between the Reformation of the 1540s and the Second World War. Bound up with it, moreover, was the brief overthrow of the political order of medieval monarchy and nobility in the kingdom. The axe blow that beheaded Charles I on the scaffold outside Whitehall on 30 January 1649 cut more than the sinews and bones of a king. Usurpation and the murder of a monarch were nothing new to English politics, but this execution publicly discredited the very ideals of heredity and divinely ordained rule that were so central to the legitimacy of the crown. Indeed, the deep groan that famously escaped the onlooking crowd after the axe fell might have been the dying breath of the Middle Ages. Nor is it sentimental to see in the aftermath of the fighting a disenchantment with the martial ethos of nobility and knighthood. After a decade of dissent, bloodshed and suffering, chivalry and war were decidedly out of fashion.

362 The ruins of Kenilworth still speak of the former majesty of this great castle. Before the destruction of 1649 these buildings would have been reflected in the water of a broad mere and approached through a great park.

When Britain began to recover from its effects in the 1660s, it wished to turn its back on the immediate past. For those in the court of Charles II this was not difficult to do. His close circle was largely formed by a young generation, many of whom had had their tastes formed in exile. They returned to England faced with the task of restoring their fortunes, buildings and estates. Old residences of all kinds, laid open to the weather for more than a decade, were not likely to constrain their efforts to start afresh. The imported vision of the baroque palace briefly captivated England, and although the ideal of the castle was to haunt patrons

and architects throughout the later seventeenth century, it was not until Vanbrugh and Hawksmoor played with these ideas again that the two ideals were meaningfully integrated. That story – the creation of a new and distinctive classical architecture for a Protestant English aristocracy – in many details picks up on themes that have been central to this narrative. Nevertheless, it lies beyond the compass of this history. To all intents and purposes, the long medieval history of the castle as a living architectural tradition in England may be considered to end with the execution of Charles I.

NOTES

INTRODUCTION

1   E. Kite, *The Monumental Brasses of Wiltshire*, London, 1860, 14–19.

2   The Latin text is recorded in R. Symonds, *Diary of the Marches of the Royal Army during the Great Civil War*, ed. C. E. Long, Camden Society, old series, 74, London, 1859, 136–7.

3   R. A. Brown, *English Castles*, third rev. edn, London, 1976, 128.

4   For castle synonyms in the twelfth century, see, for example, *The Ecclesiastical History of Orderic Vitalis*, ed. and trans. M. Chibnall, vol. I, Oxford, 1980, *index verborum*, 244–386.

5   *Regesta Regum Anglo-Normannorum, 1066–1154*, vol. III: *1135–1154*, ed. H. A. Cronne and R. H. C. Davis, Oxford, 1968, 98: 'turris Lundoniensis, mota Windlesores, motam Oxeneford, firmitatem Lincolie, castra Wintonie, munitione Hamtone'.

6   R. A. Brown, 'An Historian's Approach to the Origins of the Castle in England', *Archaeological Journal*, 126 (1969), 131–46.

7   Most recently in R. Liddiard, *Castles in Context: Power, Symbolism and Landscape, 1066–1500*, Macclesfield, 2005; and O. Creighton, *Castles and Landscapes: Power, Community and Fortification in Medieval England*, London, 2002.

8   The National Archives, E36/150, 4.

9   *Calendar of Inquisitions Miscellaneous (Chancery) Preserved in the Public Record Office*, vol. II: *1307–1349*, London, 1916, 418–20. For a general discussion of this point, see C. Coulson, *Castles in Medieval Society: Fortresses in England, France and Ireland in the Central Middle Ages*, Oxford, 2003, 60–1.

10   *The Paston Letters, 1422–1509 AD*, ed. J. Gairdner, vol. V, London, 1904; reprinted Gloucester, 1986, 302.

11   J. H. Harvey, *The Perpendicular Style*, London, 1978, which concludes in 1485.

12   J. Roberts, *Royal Landscape: The Gardens and Parks of Windsor*, London, 1997, 7–16.

13   P. Chaplais, *English Diplomatic Practice in the Middle Ages*, Hambledon and London, 2003, 73.

14   London, Lambeth Palace, MS 1212, fol. 188, enrolled in *Regesta Regum Anglo-Normannorum, 1066–1154*, vol. II: *1100–1135*, ed. C. Johnson and H. A. Cronne, Oxford, 1956, 203, no. 1475.

15   C. Coulson, 'Freedom to Crenellate by Licence: An Historiographical Revision', *Nottinghamshire Medieval Studies*, 38 (1994), 1–61.

16   T. H. Turner and J. H. Parker, *Some Account of Domestic Architecture in England*, vol. III: *From Richard II to Henry VIII*, Oxford, 1859, part 2, 401–22.

17   *Calendar of Patent Rolls: Elizabeth I, 1566–1569*, 33.

18   J. F. Curwen, *The Castles and Fortified Towers of Cumberland, Westmorland and Lancashire North-of-the-Sands*, Cumberland and Westmorland Antiquarian and Archaeological Society, extra series, 13, Kendal, 1913, 212, where the reference is cited as *Calendar of Patent Rolls: James I, 1619–1623*, 357.

19   My research is indebted to the manuscript hand list drawn up by Charles Coulson, of which a copy may be found in the library of the Society of Antiquaries of London. More recently, a similar interpretative list has appeared in print: P. Davis, 'English Licences to Crenellate, 1199–1567', *Castle Studies Group Journal*, 20 (2006–7), 226–45 and http://homepage.mac.com/philipdavis/Indexs/Locindex.html.

20   Coulson, *Castles in Medieval Society*, 98–188; and C. Coulson, 'Structural Symbolism in Medieval Castle Architecture', *Journal of the British Archaeological Association*, 132 (1979), 73–90.

21   C. Platt, 'Revisionism in Castle Studies: A Caution', *Medieval Archaeology*, 51 (2007), 83–102.

22   British Library, Cotton MS Faustina B VII, fol. 72v.

23   W. Dugdale, *The Antiquities of Warwickshire*, second edn, vol. II, London, 1730, 1138.

24   See Chapter Thirteen below.

1   C. Wilson, 'Henry, *fl.* 1243–1253', in *Oxford Dictionary of National Biography*, Oxford, 2004: www.oxforddnb.com/view/article/42254 (accessed 25 September 2007).

2   A. J. Taylor, 'The Date of Clifford's Tower, York', *Archaeological Journal*, III (1955), 157, quoting *Close Rolls of the Reign of Henry III, 1242–1247*, London, 1963, 293.

3   *History of the King's Works*, vol. I, 57–64.

4   Harvey, *English Mediaeval Architects*, 202.

5   *History of the King's Works*, vol. IV, 464.

6   F. Bucher, 'Medieval Architectural Design Methods, 800–1560', *Gesta*, II/2 (1972), 37–51.

7   See L. R. Shelby, *Gothic Design Techniques*, London and Amsterdam, 1977, and the most recent thoughts on the subject: P. Kidson, 'Roriczer's Iceberg', *Journal of the Courtauld and Warburg Institutes*, 71 (2008), 1–20.

8   *History of the King's Works*, vol. I, 157.

9   *History of the King's Works*, vol. I, 113.

10   *History of the King's Works*, vol. II, 890.

11   For a more considered overview, see R. K. Morris, 'The Development of Later Gothic Mouldings in England, *c.*1250–1400, part I', *Architectural History*, 21 (1978), 19–21.

12   M. Whiteley, 'Deux escaliers royaux du XIVᵉ siècle: les "Grands Degrez" du Palais de la Cité et les "Grande Viz" du Louvre', *Bulletin Monumental*, 147 (1989), 133–54.

13   C. M. Woolgar, *The Great Household in Late Medieval England*, New Haven and London, 1999, 8–29.

14   In addition to the published works cited below are *The Household of Edward IV: The Black Book and the Ordinance of 1478*, ed. A. R. Myers, Oxford, 1959; and the Eltham Ordinances published in *A Collection of Ordinances and Regulations for the Government of the Royal Household*, London, 1790, 109–61.

15   For a detailed case study of this household division, see M. Hayward, *Dress at the Court of King Henry VIII*, Leeds, 2007, 275–87.

16   *William Worcestre: Itineraries*, ed. J. Harvey, Oxford, 1969, 218–19.

17   G. Worsley, *The British Stable*, New Haven and London, 2004, 9 and 25.

18   J. Smyth, *The Lives of the Berkeleys*, ed. J. Maclean, vol. I, Gloucester, 1883, 324.

19   'Constitutio Domus Regis', in R. Fitz Nigel, *Dialogus de scaccario*, ed. and trans. C. Johnson, rev. edn, ed. F. E. L. Carter and D. E. Greenaway, Oxford, 1983, 129–35.

20   A. Bryant, ed., *Letters, Speeches and Declarations of King Charles II*, London, 1935, 146. I am grateful to Anna Keay for this reference.

21   Woolgar, *The Great Household*, 31–2 and 172–4; F. Lachaud, 'Liveries of Robes in England,

*c.*1200–*c.*1300', *English Historical Review*, III (1996), 279–98; D. Starkey, 'The Age of the Household', in *The Later Middle Ages*, ed. S. Medcalf, London, 1981, 225–90; and Hayward, *Dress at the Court of King Henry VIII*, 253–9.

22   *The Earl of Northumberland's Household Book*, ed. B. T. Percy, London, 1905, 45 and 150–1.

23   *History of the King's Works*, vol. II, 935.

24   Leland, *Itinerary*, vol. I, 53.

25   J. Blair, 'Hall and Chamber: English Domestic Planning, 1000–1250', in *Manorial Domestic Buildings in England and Northern France*, ed. G. Meirion-Jones and M. Jones, Occasional Papers from the Society of Antiquaries of London, new series, 15, London, 1993, 1–21.

26   Bede, *Ecclesiastical History of the English People*, trans. L. Sherley-Price, revised L. E. Latham, rev. edn, London, 1990, 129–30.

27   Hammond, *A Relation of a Short Survey of the Western Counties*, ed. L. G. Wickham Legg, Camden Miscellany, 16, London, 1936, 71.

28   J. Heywood and T. Wright, *The Ancient Laws of the 15th Century for King's College, Cambridge, and for the Public School of Eton*, London, 1850, statute 16: 'Of the manner of sitting . . . at table'.

29   J. Nichols, *The History and Antiquities of the County of Leicester*, vol. II, part ii, London, 1804, 596.

30   J. Blair, 'The Twelfth-century Bishop's Palace at Hereford', *Medieval Archaeology*, 31 (1987), 59–72.

31   L. F. Salzman, *Building in England down to 1540* [1952], reprinted with additions and corrections, Oxford, 1967, 260.

32   The 'tres espeeres', for example, commissioned for the hall of Kenilworth in 1347. See The National Archives, DL 42/11, fols 52–3, as transcribed in M. W. Thompson, 'Three Stages in the Construction of the Hall at Kenilworth Castle, Warwickshire', in *Ancient Monuments and their Interpretation*, ed. M. R. Apted, R. Gilyard-Beer and A. D. Saunders, London and Chichester, 1977, 217. Also the hall screens mentioned at Leicester in 1377–8: The National Archives, DL Min. Acc. 212/3247 m.5, cited in L. Fox, *Leicester Castle*, Leicester, 1944, 17.

33   J. Goodall, 'Cheynegates, Westminster Abbey', *Country Life*, 204 (6 January 2010), 38–44.

34   P. Brears, *Cooking and Dining in Medieval England*, Totnes, 2007.

35   John McNeill, personal communication.

36   T. J. Miles and A. D. Saunders, 'The Chantry Priest's House at Farleigh Hungerford Castle', *Medieval Archaeology*, 19 (1975), 176–8.

37   Hayward, *Dress at the Court of King Henry VIII*, 129–33.

38   J. Ashbee, 'The Function of the White

Tower under the Normans', in *The White Tower*, ed. E. Impey, New Haven and London, 2008, 133–4.

39   P. Binski, *The Painted Chamber at Westminster*, Occasional Papers of the Society of Antiquaries of London, new series, 9, London, 1986, 13–15.

40   The standard work on this subject is A. Ricketts, *The English Household Chapel: Building a Protestant Tradition*, Reading, 2007.

41   C. Gapper, J. Newman and A. Ricketts, 'Hatfield: A House for a Lord Treasurer', in *Patronage, Culture and Power: The Early Cecils*, ed. P. Croft, New Haven and London, 2002, 88–93.

42   I am grateful to Jane Watkins for this point.

43   Repairs listed in Oxford, Bodleian Library, MS Rawlinson D.775, fols 156–8.

44   David Robinson, personal communication.

45   S. Thurley, *The Royal Palaces of Tudor England*, New Haven and London, 1993, 174–5.

46   C. Wilson, 'The Royal Lodgings of Edward III at Windsor Castle', in *Windsor: Medieval Archaeology, Art and Architecture of the Thames Valley*, ed. L. Keen and E. Scarff, British Archaeological Association Conference Transactions, 25, Leeds, 2002, 30.

47   Bodleian Library, MS Rawlinson D.776, fol. 203v, cited in Thurley, *Royal Palaces of Tudor England*, 174.

48   C. H. Hartshorne, ed., 'Kenilworth Castle', *Royal Archaeological Institute of Great Britain and Ireland Proceedings (Northumberland)*, 2 (1852), appendix 8, cxxxvi–cxxxix.

49   *Middle English Dictionary*, ed. H. Kurath, vol. II, Ann Arbor, MI, 1963, 343–4.

50   For general discussions of this subject, see P. Brears, *Cooking and Dining in Medieval England*, Totnes, 2007, 69–78, and Salzman, *Building in England down to 1540*, 262–85.

51   R. Turner, 'The Sub-tidal Cistern', in *Chepstow Castle: Its History and Buildings*, ed. R. Turner and A. Johnson, Almeley, 2006, 119–26.

52   R. Liddiard, *Beeston Castle*, London, 2007 [English Heritage guidebook], 16–17.

53   Salzman, *Building in England down to 1540*, 267.

54   M. Sparks, *Canterbury Cathedral Precincts: A Historical Survey*, Canterbury, 2007, *passim*.

55   E. R. Macpherson and E. G. J. Amos, 'The Norman Waterworks in the Keep of Dover Castle', *Archaeologia Cantiana*, 43 (1931), 167–72.

56   Brears, *Cooking and Dining in Medieval England*, 74.

57   E. Venables, 'The Castle of Herstmonceux and its Lords', *Sussex Archaeological Collections*, 4 (1851), 199.

58   Thurley, *The Royal Palaces of Tudor England*, 163–71.

59 M. Wood, *The English Medieval House*, London, 1965, 279.

60 T. H. Turner, *Some Account of Domestic Architecture in England*, vol. 1, Oxford, 1851, 194.

61 M. Biddle et al., *Henry VIII's Coastal Artillery Fort at Camber Castle, Rye, East Sussex: An Archaeological, Structural and Historical Investigation*, Oxford, 2001.

62 I am grateful to John McNeill for advice on this point.

63 A. Maguire and A. Gomme, 'Who Needs Two Kitchens? And Who Parleyed in the Winter Parlour?', *Architectural History*, 38 (1995), 58–68.

64 *Rites of Durham, Being a Description or Brief Declaration of all the Ancient Monuments, Rites and Customs Belonging or Being within the Monastical Church of Durham Before the Suppression, Written 1593*, ed. J. T. Fowler, Surtees Society, 107, Durham, 1903, 86–7.

65 Most recently P. Purton, *A History of the Early and Late Medieval Siege*, 2 vols, Woodbridge, 2010. See also J. Bradbury, *Medieval Siege*, Woodbridge, 1992; and C. Duffy, *Siege Warfare: The Fortress in the Early Modern World, 1494–1660*, London, 1979.

66 For a history of this weapon, see J. Bradbury, *The Medieval Archer*, Woodbridge, 1996.

67 See p. 371 below.

68 R. Turner, C. Jones-Jenkins and S. Priestley, 'Roger Bigod's Great Tower', in *Chepstow Castle*, ed. R. Turner and A. Johnson, 168.

69 Two in particular have attracted detailed study in A. Taylor, 'Master Bertram, "Ingeniator regis"', in *Studies in Medieval History Presented to R. Allen Brown*, ed. C. Harper-Bill, C. Holdsworth and J. Nelson, Woodbridge, 1989, 289–315; and R. Turner, 'The Life and Career of Richard the Engineer', in *The Impact of the Edwardian Castles in Wales*, ed. D. M. Williams and J. R. Kenyon, Oxford, 2010, 46–58.

70 See p. 170.

71 See pp. 241–2.

72 http://classes.bnf.fr/villard/feuillet/index.htm. The drawing is on fol. 59.

73 See 190.

74 R. Avent, *Criccieth Castle*, Cardiff, 1989 [CADW guidebook], 7.

75 J. Murray Kendall, 'The Siege of Berkhampstead Castle in 1216', *Antiquaries Journal*, 3 (1923), 37–48.

76 See p. 180.

77 See p. 170.

78 See p. 157.

79 J. Goodall, 'The Siege of Dover 1216', *Château Gaillard*, 19 (2000), 91–102.

80 D. Renn, 'The Avranches Traverse at Dover Castle', *Archaeologia Cantiana*, 84 (1969), 79–92.

81 P. N. Jones and D. Renn, 'The Military Effectiveness of Arrow Loops: Some Experiments at White Castle', *Château Gaillard*, 9–10 (1982), 450–1.

82 As in the classic English study, T. E. Lawrence, *Crusader Castles*, ed. D. Pringle, Oxford, 1988 edn.

83 H. Kennedy, *Crusader Castles*, Cambridge, 1994, 201.

84 J. R. Kenyon, 'Early Artillery Fortifications in England and Wales: A Preliminary Survey and Reappraisal', *Archaeological Journal*, 138 (1981), 205–41.

85 See below, p. 383.

86 A. D. Saunders, 'The Cow Tower, Norwich: An East Anglian Bastille?', *Medieval Archaeology*, 29 (1985), 109–19; and B. S. Ayers, R. Smith and N. Tillyard, 'The Cow Tower, Norwich: A Detailed Survey and Partial Reinterpretation', *Medieval Archaeology*, 32 (1988), 184–207.

87 Salzman, *Building in England down to 1540*, 462.

88 J. H. Harvey, *William Worcestre Itineraries*, Oxford, 1969, 190–1.

89 See p. 367.

2 THE CASTLES OF
THE CONQUEST

1 *The Ecclesiastical History of Orderic Vitalis*, ed. and trans. M. Chibnall, vol. 11, Oxford, 1968, 184–5.

2 See such classic works as J. H. Round, *Feudal England*, ed. F. Stenton, London, 1964.

3 For a full discussion of this building, see J. Mesqui, 'La Tour maîtresse du Donjon de Loches', in *Deux donjons construits autour de l'an mil en Touraine*, Société française d'archéologie, Paris, 1998, 5–125.

4 B. Davison, 'Early Earthwork Castles: A New Model', *Château Gaillard*, 3 (1966), 37–46, though his model is in many points hard to accept.

5 The subject is concisely discussed in D. J. C. King, *The Castle in England and Wales: An Interpretative History*, London, 1988, 36–40.

6 Its use in reference to stone towers is common into the sixteenth century. An example of its application to a motte occurs in a reference to the creation at Ardres in 1060 of 'a motte of the greatest height or a tall donjon' (*motam altissimam sive dunjonem eminentem*). *Chronique de Lambert d'Ardres*, in *Receuil de textes relatifs à l'histoire de l'architecture*, ed. V. Mortet, vol. 1, Paris, 1911, 182; as quoted in R. A. Brown, *English Castles*, third rev. edn, London, 1976.

7 C. Coulson, *Castles in Medieval Society: Fortresses in England, France and Ireland in the Central Middle Ages*, Oxford, 2003, 69. I am otherwise indebted to Charles Coulson for correspondence on this point.

8 P. Siguret, 'Trois mottes de Bellême, Orne', *Château Gaillard*, 1 (1962), 135 n. 4.

9 J. R. Kenyon and M. W. Thompson, 'The Origin of the Word "Keep"', *Medieval Archaeology*, 38 (1994), 175–6.

10 *Ecclesiastical History of Orderic Vitalis*, vol. 11, 218.

11 R. Gem, 'The Romanesque Rebuilding of Westminster Abbey', *Anglo-Norman Studies*, 3 (1981), 61–4.

12 R. A. Brown, 'The Norman Conquest and the Genesis of English Castle Building', *Château Gaillard*, 3 (1969), 131–46.

13 E. Fernie, *The Architecture of the Anglo-Saxons*, London, 1983, 90–111.

14 See M. Chibnall, *The Debate on the Norman Conquest*, Manchester, 1999.

15 E. Fernie, *The Architecture of Norman England*, Oxford, 2000, 24.

16 Brown, *English Castles*, 16–20.

17 A. Williams, 'A Bell House and a Burh-Geat: Lordly Residences in England before the Conquest', in *Anglo-Norman Castles*, ed. R. Liddiard, Woodbridge, 2003, 23–8.

18 For Portchester, see B. Cunliffe, *Excavations at Portchester*, vol. 11: *Saxon*, London, 1976. For Goltho, see G. Beresford, 'Goltho Manor, Lincolnshire: The Buildings and their Surroundings', *Anglo-Norman Studies*, 4 (1982), 13–36; and for a suggested alternative dating, P. Everson, 'What Is in a Name? "Goltho", Goltho and Bullington', *Lincolnshire History and Archaeology*, 23 (1988), 93–9.

19 R. Eales, 'Royal Power and Castles in Norman England', in *Anglo-Norman Castles*, ed. Liddiard, 64.

20 C. W. Hollister, *Anglo-Saxon Military Institutions on the Eve of the Norman Conquest*, Oxford, 1962, 138–9.

21 H. M. Colvin, 'An Iron Age Fort at Dover?', *Antiquity*, 33 (1959), 125–7.

22 For a recent survey, see K. Booth, 'The Roman Pharos at Dover', *English Heritage Historical Review*, 2 (2007), 8–20.

23 *The Anglo-Saxon Chronicles*, trans. and ed. M. Swanton, London, 2000, 172–3.

24 *Anglo-Saxon Chronicles*, 175.

25 *The Gesta Guillelmi of William of Poitiers*, trans. and ed. R. H. C. Davis and M. Chibnall, Oxford, 1998, 70–1.

26 *Gesta Guillelmi of William of Poitiers*, 142–5.

27 R. A. Brown, 'An Historian's Approach to the Origins of the Castle in England', *Archaeological Journal*, 126 (1969), 131–46.

28 Williams, 'A Bell House and a Burh-Geat', 29–30.

29 Wace, *The Roman de Rou*, ed. A. J. Holden and trans. G. S. Burgess, St 240–1.

30 The motte in the present castle at Hastings, however, showed no evidence of such construction. P. A. Barker and K. J. Barton, 'Excavations at Hastings Castle, 1968', *Archaeological Journal*, 134 (1977), 88.

31 M. Biddle, 'Excavations at Dover', *Medieval Archaeology*, 6–7 (1962–3), 322; 8 (1964), 254–5; and Brown, *English Castles*, 46.

32 F. H. Baring, *Domesday Tables*, London, 1909, 212–13.

33 *Gesta Guillelmi of William of Poitiers*, 161–3.

34 B. Watson, 'The Norman Fortress on Ludgate Hill in the City of London, England: Recent Excavations, 1986–1990', *Château Gaillard*, 15 (1990), 335–45; and E. Impey, 'London's Early Castles and the Context of their Creation', in *The White Tower*, ed. E. Impey, New Haven and London, 2008, 13–26.

35 Impey, 'London's Early Castles'; and E. Impey and G. Parnell, *The Tower of London: The Official Illustrated History*, London, 2000, 15.

36 D. Stocker, 'The Two Early Castles of Lincoln', in *The Early History of Lincoln Castle*, ed. P. Lindley, Occasional Papers in Lincolnshire History and Archaeology, 12, Lincoln, 2004, 9.

37 E. Armitage, *Early Norman Castles of the British Isles*, London, 1912; and D. F. Renn, *Norman Castles in Britain*, second edn, London, 1973, 13 (map B).

38 *Gesta Guillelmi of William of Poitiers*, 161–5.

39 F. Barlow, 'Guenta', *Antiquaries Journal*, 44 (1964), 217–19.

40 *Anglo-Saxon Chronicles*, 200.

41 C. P. Lewis, 'William fitz Osbern, Earl (d. 1071)', in *Oxford Dictionary of National Biography*, Oxford, 2004: www.oxforddnb.com/view/article/9620 (accessed 8 August 2007); D. Douglas, 'The Ancestors of William fitz Osbern', *English Historical Review*, 59 (1944), 62–79; and D. Bates, 'The Conqueror's Adolescence', *Anglo-Norman Studies*, 25 (2003), 1–18.

42 *The Chronicle of Battle Abbey*, ed. and trans. E. Searle, Oxford, 1980, 34–5.

43 S. Rigold, 'Recent Investigations into the Earliest Defences of Carisbrooke Castle, Isle of Wight', *Château Gaillard*, 3 (1966), 128–37.

44 C. P. Lewis, 'The Norman Settlement of Herefordshire under William I', *Anglo-Norman Studies*, 7 (1984), 195–213; and T. Purser, 'William Fitz Osbern, Earl of Hereford: Personality and Power on the Welsh Frontier, 1066–1071', in *Armies, Chivalry and Warfare in Medieval Britain and France: Proceedings of the 1995 Harlaxton Symposium*, ed. M. Strickland, Stamford, 1998, 133–46.

45 The authoritative recent treatments of the building are R. Turner, C. Jones-Jenkins and S. Priestley, 'The Norman Great Tower', in *Chepstow Castle: Its History and Buildings*, ed. R. Turner and A. Johnson, Almeley, 2006, 23–42; and R. Turner et al., 'The Great Tower, Chepstow Castle, Wales', *Antiquaries Journal*, 84 (2004), 223–318.

3 THE CASTLES OF SETTLEMENT

1 G. Lapsley, 'Some Castle Officers in the 12th Century', *English Historical Review*, 33 (1918), 353–5; J. H. Round, 'The Staff of a Castle in the 12th Century', *English Historical Review*, 35 (1920), 95–7; and N. J. G. Pounds, *The Medieval Castle in England and Wales: A Social and Political History*, Cambridge, 1990, 49–50.

2 See, for example, L. F. Salzman, 'Documents Relating to Pevensey Castle', *Sussex Archaeological Collections*, 49 (1906), 3–4.

3 R. J. Ivens, 'Deddington Castle, Oxfordshire, and the English Honour of Odo of Bayeux', *Oxoniensia*, 49 (1984), 101–7.

4 R. Mortimer, 'The Beginnings of the Honour of Clare', *Anglo-Norman Studies*, 3 (1980), 119–41.

5 W. J. Corbett, 'The Development of the Duchy of Normandy and the Norman Conquest of England', in *Cambridge Medieval History*, vol. v: *Contest of Empire and Papacy*, ed. J. R. Tanner et al., Cambridge, 1926, 507–20.

6 R. Liddiard, *'Landscapes of Lordship': Norman Castles and the Countryside in Medieval Norfolk, 1066–1200*, British Archaeological Reports British Series, 309, Oxford, 2000, 28–30.

7 *The Metrical Chronicle of Robert of Gloucester*, ed. W. A. Wright, Rolls Series, 86, vol. II, London, 1887, 507; and *VCH: Berkshire*, vol. II, London, 1907, 122.

8 M. Biddle, 'Seasonal Festivals and Residence: Winchester, Westminster and Gloucester in the 10th–12th Centuries', *Anglo-Norman Studies*, 8 (1986), 51–63.

9 T. E. Harwood, *Windsor Old and New*, London, 1929, 81.

10 F. Barlow et al., *Winchester in the Early Middle Ages: An Edition and Discussion of the Winton Domesday*, ed. M. Biddle, Winchester Studies, 1, Oxford, 1976, 289–95.

11 *History of the King's Works*, vol. I, 43.

12 J. F. A. Mason, 'The Rapes of Sussex and the Norman Conquest', *Sussex Archaeological Collections*, 102 (1964), 68–93.

13 F. W. Hardman, 'Castleguard Service at Dover Castle', *Archaeologia Cantiana*, 49 (1937), 98–100.

14 *The Chronicle of Battle Abbey*, ed. and trans. E. Searle, Oxford, 1980, 48–51 and notes.

15 *The Gesta Normannorum ducum of William of Jumièges, Orderic Vitalis and Robert of Torigni*, ed. and trans. E. M. C. van Houts, vol. II, Oxford, 1995, 229.

16 J. C. Ward, 'The Lowry of Tonbridge and the Lands of the Clare Family in Kent, 1066–1217', *Archaeologia Cantiana*, 96 (1980), 119–31.

17 C. P. Lewis, 'The Early Earls of Norman England', *Anglo-Norman Studies*, 13 (1990), 207–23.

18 J. Blair, 'D'Oilly, Robert (d. c.1092)', in *Oxford Dictionary of National Biography*, Oxford, 2004: www.oxforddnb.com/view/article/23719 (accessed 8 August 2007).

19 *Cartulary of Oseney Abbey*, ed. H. E. Salter, Oxford Historical Series, 97, Oxford, 1934, 1.

20 A. Dodd, ed., *Oxford before the University*, Thames Valley Landscapes Monographs, 19, Oxford, 2003, 50.

21 Julian Munby, personal communication.

22 B. Durham, 'The Thames Crossing at Oxford: Archaeological Studies, 1979–82', *Oxoniensia*, 49 (1984), 87–95.

23 K. S. B. Keats-Rohan, 'The Devolution of the Honour of Wallingford, 1066–1148', *Oxoniensia*, 54 (1989), 311–18.

24 *The History of the Church of Abingdon*, ed. and trans. J. Hudson, vol. II, Oxford, 2002, 328–31.

25 J. Green, 'The Sheriffs of William the Conqueror', *Anglo-Norman Studies*, 5 (1982), 129–45.

26 C. G. Harfield, 'A Hand-List of Castles Recorded in the Domesday Book', *English Historical Review*, 106 (1991), 371–92.

27 R. Eales, 'Royal Power and Castles in Norman England', in *Anglo-Norman Castles*, ed. R. Liddiard, Woodbridge, 2003, 48–51.

28 E. Fernie, *The Architecture of Norman England*, Oxford, 2000, 26–7.

29 P. Barker and R. Higham, *Timber Castles*, London, 1992.

30 '. . . novo edificandi genere consurgere', in William of Malmesbury, *Gesta Regum Anglorum*, ed. and trans. R.A.B. Mynors, R. M. Thomson and M. Winterbottom, vol. I, Oxford, 1998, 460–1; and R. A. Brown, 'William of Malmesbury as an Architectural Historian', in *Mélanges d'archéologie et d'histoire médiévale en l'honneur du Doyen Michel de Boüard*, Mémoires et documents publié par la Société de l'Ecole des Chartes, 27, Geneva, 1982, 9–16.

31 J. Bony, 'The Stonework Planning of the First Durham Master', in *Medieval Architecture and its Intellectual Context: Studies in Honour of Peter Kidson*, ed. E. Fernie and P. Crossley, London and Ronceverte, 1990, 19–34.

32 Pounds, *The Medieval Castle in England and Wales*, 18–19. There are errors apparent in the map presented here, as, for example, in the low estimate for the motte at Thetford.

33 D. J. C. King, *The Castle in England and Wales: An Interpretative History*, London, 1988, 53–6; though even this assumes a questionable consistency of usage.

34 King, *The Castle in England and Wales*, 49 and 59. No report of this excavation has ever been published or can be expected: Derek Renn, personal communication.

35 For a full treatment of the White Tower, see E. Impey, ed., *The White Tower*, New Haven and London, 2008.

36 *Textus Roffensis*, ed. T. Hearne, Oxford, 1722, 212.

37 'Vita Sancti Thamae Cantuarensis Archiepiscopi et martiris auctore Wilelmo filii Stephani', in *Materials for the History of Thomas Becket, Archbishop of Canterbury*, ed. J. C. Robertson, vol. III, London, 1877, 3. As translated by Jeremy Ashbee.

38 *History of the King's Works*, vol. I, 31.

39 P. J. Drury, 'Aspects of the Origins and Development of Colchester Castle', *Archaeological Journal*, 139 (1982), 400; and Drury et al., 'The Temple of Claudius at Colchester Reconsidered', *Britannia*, 15 (1984), 7–50.

40 E. Impey, 'The *Turris famosa* at Ivry-la-Bataille, Normandy', in *The Seigneurial Residence in Western Europe, AD c800–1600*, ed. G. Meirion-Jones, E. Impey and M. Jones, British Archaeological Reports International Series, 1088, Oxford, 2002, 189–210.

41 *The Ecclesiastical History of Orderic Vitalis*, ed. and trans. M. Chibnall, vol. IV, Oxford, 1973, 290–1.

42 Symeon of Durham, *Libellus de Exordi*, ed. and trans. D. Rollason, Oxford 2000, 183–5 and note.

43 W. M. Aird, *St Cuthbert and the Normans*, Woodbridge, 1998, 82–5.

44 B. English, *The Lords of Holderness, 1086–1260*, Oxford, 1979, 6–9.

45 P. Dalton, *Conquest, Anarchy and Lordship: Yorkshire, 1066–1154*, Cambridge, 1994, 39–49.

46 *The Anglo-Saxon Chronicles*, trans. and ed. M. Swanton, London, 2000, 17; though in 651 it was also described as a royal city (*urbem*) by Bede. Bede, *Ecclesiastical History of the English People*, trans. L. Sherley-Price, revised L. E. Latham, rev. edn, London, 1990, 168.

47 William of Malmesbury, *Gesta Pontificum Anglorum*, ed. and trans. M. Winterbottom, vol. I, Oxford, 2007, 412–15.

48 'Eodem tempore, scilicet quo rex reverses de Scotia fuerat, in Dunelmo castellum condidit, ubi se cum suis episcopus tute ab incursantibus habere potuisset', in Symeon of Durham, *Historia Regum*, ed. T. Arnold, Rolls Series, 75, vol. II, London, 1884, 199–200. From this sentence one authority has understood the bishop to be the builder

of the castle: *VCH: Durham*, vol. II, London, 1907, 10 n. 57. This is not my reading of it.

49 Manuscript cited in W. Hutchinson, *The History and Antiquities of the County Palatine of Durham*, vol. II, Newcastle, 1787, 279.

50 C. Hart, ed. and trans., *The Early Charters of Northern England and the North Midlands*, Leicester, 1975, 147.

51 E. Cambridge, 'Early Romanesque Architecture in North-East England: A Style and its Patrons', in *Anglo-Norman Durham, 1093–1193*, ed. D. Rollason, M. Harvey and M. Prestwich, Woodbridge, 1994, 141–60.

52 *Lestorie des Engles*, ed. T. D. Hardy and C. T. Martin, Rolls Series, 90, vol. I, London, 1888, lines 5315–30.

53 *Early Yorkshire Charters*, vol. IV: *The Honour of Richmond, 1*, ed. C. T. Clay, Leeds, 1935, 94–5.

54 *Domesday Book*, vol. XXX: *Yorkshire*, ed. M. L. Faull and M. Stinson, vol. II, Chichester, 1986, SN Ct.A 45.

55 *Early Yorkshire Charters*, vol. IV: *The Honour of Richmond, 1*, 22, no. 21.

56 Leland, *Itinerary*, vol. IV, 79.

57 *Early Yorkshire Charters*, vol. I, ed. W. Farrer, Edinburgh, 1914, 264–5, no. 350, and 270, no. 354; and *Early Yorkshire Charters*, vol. IV: *The Honour of Richmond, 1*, 4–5, no. 4, and 8–11, no. 8.

58 C. Clarkson, *The History of Richmond in the County of York*, Richmond, 1821: forty-eight recorded 'sketches of figures drawn with red paint, some colours appearing yet very fresh'.

59 *Early Yorkshire Charters*, vol. IV: *The Honour of Richmond, 1*, 6 and 18; and vol. V: *The Honour of Richmond, 2*, 201.

60 '. . . giardinum pertinens ad castrum Rich . . .', in R. Gale, *Registrum Honoris de Richmond*, London, 1722, appendix, 50.

61 L. Butler, 'The Origins of the Honour of Richmond and its Castles', *Château Gaillard*, 16 (1992), 69–80.

62 A. Ballard, 'Castle Guard and Barons' Houses', *English Historical Review*, 25 (1910), 712–15.

4 THE AGE OF MAGNIFICENCE

1 *The Ecclesiastical History of Orderic Vitalis*, ed. and trans. M. Chibnall, vol. III, Oxford, 1972, 248–9.

2 G. Henderson, 'Giraldus Cambrensis: A Note on his Account of a Painting in the King's Chamber at Winchester', *Archaeological Journal*, 118 (1961), 175.

3 R. Bartlett, *England under the Norman and Angevin Kings, 1075–1225*, Oxford, 2000, 12, and Anglo-Norman relations, 13–25.

4 H. A. Cronne, *The Reign of Stephen, 1135–54*, London, 1970, 27 and 71.

5 *The Anglo-Saxon Chronicles*, trans. and ed. M. Swanton, London, 2000, 264–5.

6 G. H. White, 'King Stephen's Earldoms', *Transactions of the Royal Historical Society*, fourth series, 13 (1930), 51–82; and Cronne, *The Reign of Stephen*, 139–47.

7 William of Malmesbury, *Gesta Regum Anglorum*, ed. and trans. R. A. B. Mynors, R. M. Thomson and M. Winterbottom, vol. I, Oxford, 1998, 546–9.

8 *The Ecclesiastical History of Orderic Vitalis*, ed. and trans. M. Chibnall, vol. IV, Oxford, 1973, 132–5.

9 D. Bates, 'Odo, Earl of Kent (*d.* 1097)', in *Oxford Dictionary of National Biography*, Oxford, 2004: www.oxforddnb.com/view/article/20543 (accessed 13 January 2009).

10 *The Anglo-Saxon Chronicles*, 231.

11 W. M. Aird, 'Mowbray, Robert de, Earl of Northumbria (d. 1115/1125)', in *Oxford Dictionary of National Biography*: www.oxforddnb.com/view/article/19457 (accessed 15 October 2007).

12 For an expression of these ideas, see R. A. Brown, 'A List of Castles, 1154–1216', *English Historical Review*, 74 (1959), 249–80. The debate is nicely summarised and discussed in R. Eales, 'Royal Power and Castles in Norman England', in *Anglo-Norman Castles*, ed. R. Liddiard, Woodbridge, 2003, especially 53–67.

13 N. J. G. Pounds, *The Medieval Castle in England and Wales: A Social and Political History*, Cambridge, 1990, 29.

14 P. A. Stamper, 'Excavations on a Mid-Twelfth Century Siege Castle at Bentley, Hampshire', *Proceedings of the Hampshire Field Club and Archaeological Society*, 40 (1984), 81–9.

15 B. English, *The Lords of Holderness, 1086–1260*, Oxford, 1979, 21–2.

16 *Gesta Stephani*, ed. K. R. Potter, Oxford, 1976, 108–11. I am grateful to Richard Plant for this reference.

17 M. Rylatt and P. Mason, *The Archaeology of the Medieval Cathedral and Priory of St Mary, Coventry*, Coventry, 2003, 16–18.

18 Henry of Huntingdon, *Historia Anglorum*, ed. A. Thomas, Rolls Series, 74, London, 1879, 237.

19 For the most recent discussion of the fabric, see S. Thurlby and R. Baxter, 'The Romanesque Abbey Church at Reading', in *Windsor: Medieval Archaeology, Art and Architecture of the Thames Valley*, ed. L. Keen and E. Scarff, British Archaeological Association Conference Transactions, 25, Leeds, 2002, 282–301.

20 T. E. Harwood, *Windsor Old and New*, London, 1929, 101.

21 G. Astill, 'Windsor in the Context of Medieval Berkshire', in *Windsor: Medieval Archaeology*, ed. Keen and Scarff, 5.

22 *Chonicon Abbatiae de Evesham*, ed. W. D. Macray, Rolls Series, 29, London, 1863, 98.

23 D. Crouch, 'Geoffrey de Clinton and Roger, Earl of Warwick: New Men and Magnates in the Reign of Henry I', *Bulletin of the Institute of Historical Research*, 55 (1982), 113–24.

24 P. B. Chatwin, 'Brandon Castle, Warwickshire', *Birmingham Archaeological Society Proceedings and Transactions*, 73 (1955), 63–83.

25 E. Mason, 'The Maudits and the Chamberlainship of the Exchequer', *Bulletin of the Institute of Historical Research*, 49 (1976), 1–23; Mason, 'The King, the Chamberlain and Southwick Priory', *Bulletin of the Institute of Historical Research*, 53 (1980), 1–10; and *VCH: Hampshire and the Isle of Wight*, vol. III, London, 1908, 151–8.

26 *The Waltham Chronicle*, ed. L. Watkiss and M. Chibnall, Oxford, 1994, 76–9.

27 A. Wareham, 'The Motives and Politics of the Bigod Family, 1066–1177', *Anglo-Norman Studies*, 17 (1994), 231–2.

28 R. Liddiard, 'Castle Rising, Norfolk: "A Landscape of Lordship"?', *Anglo-Norman Studies*, 22 (1999), 169–86.

29 For a consideration of depictions of castles on seals, see J. Cherry, '*Imago Castelli*: The Depiction of Castles on Medieval Seals', *Château Gaillard*, 15 (1992), 83–90.

30 B. R. Kemp, 'Salisbury, Roger of (d. 1139)', in *Oxford Dictionary of National Biography*: www.oxforddnb.com/view/article/23956 (accessed 16 October 2007).

31 See J. McNeil, *Old Sarum*, London, 2006 [English Heritage Red Guide].

32 R. A. Stalley, 'A 12th-century Patron of Architecture: A Study of the Buildings Erected by Roger, Bishop of Salisbury, 1102–39', *Journal of the British Archaeological Association*, third series, 34 (1971), 62–83.

33 D. M. Smith, 'Alexander (d. 1148)', in *Oxford Dictionary of National Biography*: www.oxforddnb.com/view/article/324 (accessed 16 October 2007); P. Marshall and J. Samuels, *Guardian of the Trent: The Story of Newark Castle*, Newark, 1997; and P. Marshall, 'The 12th-century Castle at Newark', in *Southwell and Nottinghamshire: Medieval Art, Architecture and Industry*, ed. J. Alexander, British Archaeological Association Conference Transactions, 21, Leeds, 1998, 110–25.

34 M. Biddle, *Wolvesey*, London, 1986, 10 [English Heritage guidebook]; and Biddle, 'Wolvesey: The *domus quasi palatium* of Henry of Blois in Winchester', *Château Gaillard*, 3 (1966), 28–36.

35 *Annales Monastici*, vol. II: *Annales Monasterii de Wintonia, AD 519–1277*, ed. H. R. Luard, Rolls Series, 36, London, 1865, 51.

36 William of Malmesbury, *De Gestis Regum Anglorum*, ed. W. Stubbs, Rolls Series, 90, vol. II, London, 1889, 484.

37 J. Ashbee, 'Cloisters in English Palaces in the 12th and 13th Centuries', *Journal of the British Archaeological Association*, 159 (2006), 71–90.

38 J. O. Prestwich, 'The Career of Ranulf Flambard', in *Anglo-Norman Durham, 1093–1193*, ed. D. Rollason, M. Harvey and M. Prestwich, Woodbridge, 1994, 299–310; and J. F. A. Mason, 'Flambard, Ranulf (c.1060–1128)', in *Oxford Dictionary of National Biography*: www.oxforddnb.com/view/article/9667 (accessed 13 January 2009).

39 *The Ecclesiastical History of Orderic Vitalis*, ed. and trans. M. Chibnall, vol. v, Oxford, 1975, 310–12.

40 Symeon of Durham, *Libellus de Exordi*, ed. and trans. D. Rollason, Oxford, 2000, 276–7.

41 M. G. Snape, 'Documentary Evidence for the Building of Durham Cathedral and its Monastic Buildings', in *Medieval Art and Architecture at Durham Cathedral*, ed. N. Coldstream and P. Draper, British Archaeological Association Conference Transactions, 3, Leeds, 1980, 22.

42 Laurence of Durham, *Dialogi Laurentii Dunelmensis Monachi ac Prioris*, ed. J. Raine, Surtees Society, 70, Durham, 1878, 11–12. Translated and discussed in P. Barker and R. Higham, *Timber Castles*, London, 1992, 118–19.

43 H. L. Janssen, 'The Archaeology of the Medieval Castle in the Netherlands: Results and Prospects for Future Research', in *Medieval Archaeology in the Netherlands: Studies Presented to H. H. van Regteren Altena*, ed. J. C. Besteman, J. M. Bos and H. A. Heidinga, Assen and Maastricht, 1990, 230.

44 M. W. Thompson, 'Recent Excavations in the Keep of Farnham Castle, Surrey', *Medieval Archaeology*, 4 (1960), 81–94.

45 'The entrance was flanked by two drum towers, from which all the ashlar had been stripped, and consisted of one wide archway of some 9 ft span': *Proceedings of the Society of Antiquaries*, 23 (1909–11), 195–6. This detail has been edited out in all recent plans of the castle on the authority of the Royal Commission on Historical Monuments of England in *Ancient and Historical Monuments in the City of Salisbury*, vol. I, London, 1980, 6: 'there is no evidence for the rounded outer ends shown on the excavators' plan; more probably they were square'. The explicit statement of the excavators to the contrary should surely be taken more seriously.

46 T. A. Heslop, *Norwich Castle Keep*, Norwich, 1994.

47 The ideas put forward by Heslop (*Norwich Castle Keep*) have been challenged in certain points in P. J. Drury, 'Norwich Castle Keep'; and in P. Dixon and P. Marshall, 'Norwich Castle and its Analogues', in *The Seigneurial Residence in Western Europe, AD c800–1600*, ed. G. Meirion-Jones, E. Impey and M. Jones, British Archaeological Re-

ports International Series, 1088, Oxford, 2002, 211–34 and 235–43 respectively.

48 Malcolm Thurlby, personal communication. I am much indebted to Pam White for the opportunity to inspect the remains of the tower from a scaffold in 2007.

49 E. Fernie, *The Architecture of Norman England*, Oxford, 2000, 78.

50 J. Goodall, 'The Great Tower of Rochester Castle', in *Medieval Art, Architecture and Archaeology at Rochester*, ed. T. Ayers and T. Tatton-Brown, British Archaeological Association Conference Transactions, 28, Leeds, 2006, 274. For the castle, see W. H. Butcher, 'Historical Sketch of the Castle of Devizes', *Journal of the British Archaeological Association*, 40 (1884), 133–51.

51 J. Goodall, 'The Great Tower of Carlisle Castle', in *Carlisle and Cumbria: Roman and Medieval Architecture, Art and Archaeology*, ed. M. McCarthy and D. Weston, British Archaeological Association Conference Transactions, 27, Leeds, 2004, 46–52.

52 P. Dixon and P. Marshall, 'Norwich Castle and its Analogues', in *The Seigneurial Residence in Western Europe*, ed. Meirion-Jones, Impey and Jones, 238 and 242.

53 J. H. Spencer, 'Structural Notes on Taunton Castle', *Proceedings of the Somersetshire Archaeological and Natural History Society*, 56 (1910), 38–49; W. Vivian-Neal and H. St John Gray, 'Materials for the History of Taunton Castle', *Proceedings of the Somersetshire Archaeological and Natural History Society*, 86 (1940), 45–78; and T. J. Hunt, 'Some 13th-century Building Accounts for Taunton Castle', *Proceedings of the Somersetshire Archaeological and Natural History Society*, 114 (1969–70), 39–44.

54 G. L. Good, 'Bristol Castle Keep: A Re-Appraisal of the Evidence and a Report on the Excavations in 1989', *Bristol and Avon Archaeology*, 13 (1996), 17–45; and William Worcester, *The Topography of Medieval Bristol*, ed. F. Neal, Bristol Record Society, 51, Bristol, 2000, 222–3 and 240–1.

55 *VCH: Gloucester*, vol. IV, Oxford, 1988, 245–7.

56 *Regesta Regum Anglo-Normannorum, 1066–1154*, vol. II: *1100–1135*, ed. C. Johnson and H. A. Cronne, Oxford, 1956, 203, no. 1475.

57 Gervase of Canterbury, *Opera Historica*, ed. W. Stubbs, Rolls Series, 73, vol. II, London, 1880, 382.

58 J. Goodall, 'The Great Tower of Rochester Castle', in *Medieval Art, Architecture and Archaeology at Rochester*, ed. Ayers and Tatton-Brown, 265–99.

59 D. Crouch, 'Vere, Aubrey (III) de, Count of Guînes and Earl of Oxford (d. 1194)', in *Oxford Dictionary of National Biography*: www.

oxforddnb.com/view/article/28204 (accessed 18 October 2007).

60 M. North, 'St Leonard's Tower: Some Aspects of Anglo-Norman Building Design and Construction', *Archaeologia Cantiana*, 121 (2001), 269–86, pushes the date back and is non-committal about its function.

61 J. Ashbee, *Goodrich Castle*, London, 2005, 16–19 [English Heritage Red Guide], offers the most recent published consideration of this building. See also M. Thurlby, *Romanesque Architecture and Sculpture in Wales*, Almeley, 2006, 91–2.

62 Biddle, *Wolvesey*; and Biddle, 'Wolvesey: The *domus quasi palatium* of Henry of Blois', 28–36.

63 P. Dixon and P. Marshall, 'The Great Tower at Hedingham Castle: A Reassessment', *Fortress*, 18 (1993), 16–23.

64 *Pipe Rolls*, 13 Henry II (1166–7), vol. XI, I. I am grateful to Jeremy Ashbee for this reference.

65 P. Marshall, 'The Ceremonial Function of the Donjon in the 12th Century', *Château Gaillard*, 20 (2000), 141–51.

66 D. Crouch, 'Geoffrey de Clinton and Roger, Earl of Warwick: New Men and Magnates in the Reign of Henry I', *Bulletin of the Institute of Historical Research*, 55 (1982), 120–3.

67 This narrative is set out in detail in A. Young, 'The Bishopric of Durham in Stephen's Reign', in *Anglo-Norman Durham, 1093–1193*, ed. D. Rollason, M. Harvey and M. Prestwich, Woodbridge, 1994, 353–68; and Young, 'William Cumin: Border Politics and the Bishopric of Durham, 1141–4', *Borthwick Papers*, 54 (1979), 1–37.

68 Symeon of Durham, *Libellus de Exordi*, 318–19.

69 Symeon of Durham, *Libellus de Exordi*, 315.

70 Symeon of Durham, *Libellus de Exordi*, 306–9.

5   THE EARLY ANGEVIN CASTLE

1 R. A. Brown, 'Royal Castle Building in England, 1154–1216', *English Historical Review*, 70 (1955), 353–98.

2 'Epistolae ad Historiam Thomae Cantuarensis Archiepiscopi Pertinens', in *Materials for the History of Thomas Becket, Archbishop of Canterbury*, vol. VI: *Epistles*, ed. J. C. Robertson, Rolls Series, 67, London, 1882, 72; quoted in R. Bartlett, *England under the Norman and Angevin Kings, 1075–1225*, Oxford, 2000, 48.

3 L. Grant, *Architecture and Society in Normandy, 1120–1270*, New Haven and London, 2005, 42–61.

4 For the excavation of this building, see H. Braun, 'Some Notes on Bungay Castle', *Suffolk Institute of Archaeology*, 22 (1936), 109–19, 201–23 and 334.

5 *Royal Commission on Historical Monuments of England: Essex*, vol. I, London, 1916, 233–4.

6 R. A. Brown, 'Framlingham Castle and Earl Bigod, 1154–1216', *Proceedings of the Suffolk Institute of Archaeology*, 25 (1951), 127–48.

7 A. Wareham, 'The Motives and Politics of the Bigod Family, 1066–1177', *Anglo-Norman Studies*, 17 (1994), 239.

8 For an analysis of the building, see V. Potter, M. Poulter and J. Allen, *The Building of Orford Castle: A Translation from the Pipe Rolls*, Woodbridge, 2002.

9 *History of the King's Works*, vol. I, 77.

10 *History of the King's Works*, vol. II, 613.

11 *History of the King's Works*, vol. I, 76–7.

12 M.-P. Baudry, *Les Fortifications des Plantagênets en Poitou, 1154–1242*, Mémoirs de la section d'archéologie et d'histoire de l'art, II, Paris, 2001, 77.

13 T. A. Heslop, 'Orford Castle: Nostalgia and Sophisticated Living', *Architectural History*, 34 (1991), 36–58.

14 P. J. Drury and E. C. Norton, '12th-century Floor- and Roof-Tiles at Orford Castle', *Proceedings of the Suffolk Institute of Archaeology and History*, 36 (1985), 1–7.

15 *History of the King's Works*, vol. II, 830.

16 William of Newburgh, *Historia Rerum Anglicarum*, in *Chronicles of the Reigns of Stephen, Henry II and Richard I*, ed. R. Howlett, Rolls Series, 82, vol. I, London, 1884, 104.

17 Reginald of Durham, *Libellus de Admirandis Beati Cuthberti Vertutibus quae novellis patratae sunt temporibus*, ed. J. Raine, Surtees Society, I, London, 1835, 82–3.

18 As, for example, on J. Forster's map of the city of 1754, which shows the wall with a series of open-backed towers on a rectangular plan.

19 Symeon of Durham, *Libellus de Exordi*, ed. and trans. D. Rollason, Oxford, 2000, 323.

20 *Historiae Dunelmensis Scriptores Tres*, ed. J. Raine, Surtees Society, 9, Newcastle, 1839, 12.

21 J. Cunningham, 'Hugh of Le Puiset and the Church of St Cuthbert, Darlington', in *Medieval Art and Architecture at Durham Cathedral*, ed. N. Coldstream and P. Draper, British Archaeological Association Conference Transactions, 3, Leeds, 1980, 166–7; and Cunningham, 'Auckland Castle: Some Recent Discoveries', in *Medieval Architecture and its Intellectual Context: Studies in Honour of Peter Kidson*, ed. E. Fernie and P. Crossley, London and Ronceverte, 1990, 81–90.

22 Reginald of Durham, *De Admirandis Beati Cuthberti*, 111–12.

23 J. Goodall, 'The Great Tower of Carlisle Castle', in *Carlisle and Cumbria: Roman and Medieval Architecture, Art and Archaeology*, ed. M. McCarthy and D. Weston, British Archaeological Association Conference Transactions, 27, Leeds, 2004, 39–62.

24 M. McCarthy, H. Summerson and R. Annis, *Carlisle Castle*, English Heritage Archaeological Report, 18, London, 1990, 57.

25 *Pipe Rolls*, 16 Henry II (1169–70), vol. XV, 51–2.

26 *History of the King's Works*, vol. II, 746. For drawings of the building before its restoration, see the series of drawings of 1817 engraved in *Vetusta Monumenta*, vol. V, London, 1835. The originals are in the library of the Society of Antiquaries of London.

27 W. H. D. Longstaffe, 'The New Castle upon Tyne', *Archaeologia Aeliana*, new series, 4 (1860), 63–98; W. H. Knowles, 'The Castle of Newcastle-upon-Tyne', *Archaeologia Aeliana*, fourth series, 2 (1926), 8–36. For pre-restoration views of the interiors, see J. C. Brown, *A Guide to the Castle of Newcastle upon Tyne*, Newcastle, 1847. I am very grateful to John Nelson for his help researching this building.

28 Symeon of Durham, *Libellus de Exordi*, 276–7.

29 P. Dixon, 'The Great Tower in the 12th Century: The Case of Norham Castle', *Archaeological Journal*, 150 (1993), 410–32.

30 For a detailed discussion of this dating, see Goodall, 'The Great Tower of Carlisle Castle', 39–62.

31 *Jordan Fantosme's Chronicle*, ed. R. C. Johnstone, Oxford, 1981, verse 152.

32 R. S. Ferguson, 'The Earthworks and Keep of Appleby Castle', *Transactions of the Cumberland and Westmorland Antiquarian and Archaeological Society*, 8 (1886), 386–93.

33 *History of the King's Works*, vol. II, 853; and C. H. Blair, 'The Castle of Wark-upon-Tweed', *Berwickshire Naturalists' Club*, 29 (1935–7), 79.

34 *Royal and Other Historical Letters Illustrative of the Reign of Henry III*, ed. W. Shirley, Rolls Series, 27, vol. I, London, 1862, 141.

35 L. Keen, 'The Umfavilles, the Castle and the Barony of Prudhoe, Northumberland', *Anglo-Norman Studies*, 5 (1982), 177–81; and S. West, *Prudhoe Castle*, London, 2006, 21–4 [English Heritage Red Guide].

36 *A History of Northumberland*, vol. XI, 47.

37 *Jordan Fantosme's Chronicle*, ed. Johnstone, verse 128.

38 *Jordan Fantosme's Chronicle*, ed. Johnstone, verse 151.

39 *Jordan Fantosme's Chronicle*, ed. Johnstone, verse 155.

40 P. Turnbull and D. Walsh, 'Recent Work at Egremont Castle', *Transactions of the Cumberland and Westmorland Antiquarian and Archaeological Society*, 94 (1994), 77–89; and M. Thurlby,

'Romanesque Architecture and Architectural Sculpture in the Diocese of Carlisle', in *Carlisle and Cumbria*, ed. McCarthy and Weston, 284–7.

41   L. Keen, 'The Umfravilles, the Castle and the Barony of Prudhoe, Northumberland', *Anglo-Norman Studies*, 5 (1982), 173.

42   R. Eales, *Peveril Castle*, London, 2006, 21 [English Heritage Red Guide].

43   For all these details, see *History of the King's Works*, vol. II, 865; and T. Tatton-Brown, 'Windsor Castle before 1344', in *Edward III's Round Table at Windsor*, ed. J. Munby, R. Barber and R. Brown, Woodbridge and Rochester, NY, 2007, 20–4.

44   R. W. Eyton, *Court, Household and Itinerary of Henry II*, London, 1878, 228.

45   For one of several recent accounts of the reconstruction of Canterbury, see P. Draper, *The Formation of English Gothic*, London and New Haven, 2006, 13–33.

46   This expenditure is tabulated in Brown, 'Royal Castle Building in England'.

47   *Pipe Rolls*, 32 Henry II (1185–6), vol. XXXVI, 187.

48   *Pipe Rolls*, 28 Henry II (1181–2), vol. XXXI, 150; and 32 Henry II (1185–6), vol. XXXVI, 186.

49   *Pipe Rolls*, 10 John (1208), new series, vol. XXIII, 171.

50   C. M. Burrell, 'Documents Relating to Knepp Castle', *Sussex Archaeological Collections*, 3 (1850), 4–5.

51   The National Archives, E101/462/11. This account for 1286 records the repair of leads over St Thomas's Chapel, which proves that it was the upper of the two chambers.

52   W. Hutchinson, *The History and Antiquities of the County Palatine of Durham*, vol. I, Newcastle, 1787, 176.

53   Brown, 'Framlingham Castle and Earl Bigod'; and N. Stacey, *Framlingham Castle*, London, 2009 [English Heritage Red Guide].

54   *The History of William Marshall*, ed. A. J. Holden et al., Anglo-Norman Text Society, Occasional Publications Series, 4, London, 2002, 27–33; and D. Crouch, *William Marshal: Court, Career and Chivalry in the Angevin Empire, 1147–1219*, Harlow, 1990.

55   R. Avent and D. Miles, 'The Main Gatehouse', in *Chepstow Castle: Its History and Buildings*, ed. R. Turner and A. Johnson, Almeley, 2006, 51–62.

56   For an attempt, see J. Goodall, *Pevensey Castle*, London, 1999, 23 [English Heritage guidebook].

57   P. Barker and R. Higham, *Timber Castles*, London, 1992, 326–52.

58   Barker and Higham, *Timber Castles*, 115–16.

59   *Chronica Magistri Rogeri de Houedene*, ed. W. Stubbs, Rolls Series, 51, vol. III, London, 1870,

33–4. I am grateful to Jeremy Ashbee for this reference.

60   *History of the King's Works*, vol. II, 836.

61   M. W. Thompson, *Farnham Castle*, London, 1961, 14; and N. W. Alcock and R. J. Buckley, 'Leicester Castle: The Great Hall', *Medieval Archaeology*, 31 (1987), 73–9.

62   D. J. C. King, *The Castle in England and Wales: An Interpretative History*, London and Sydney, 1988, 53–5.

63   Barker and Higham, *Timber Castles*, 125.

64   P. Dalton, *Conquest, Anarchy and Lordship: Yorkshire, 1066–1154*, Cambridge, 1994, 33–4 and 298–9.

65   H. Sands, H. Braun and L .C. Loyd, 'Conisbrough and Mortemer', *Yorkshire Archaeological Journal*, 32 (1936), 147–59.

66   Stuart Harrison and Karen Impey, personal communication.

6   THE GOTHIC CASTLE

1   J. W. Baldwin, *The Government of Philip Augustus*, Berkeley, CA, 1986, 298–301.

2   F. M. Powicke, *The Loss of Normandy*, Manchester, 1913.

3   L. Grant, *Architecture and Society in Normandy, 1120–1270*, New Haven and London, 2005, 7–17.

4   D. Crouch, *The Image of Aristocracy in Britain, 1000–1300*, New York and London, 1992, 220–51.

5   *Scrope and Grosvenor Roll*, ed. N. H. Nicholas, London, 1832.

6   Cambridge, Corpus Christi College, MS 16, fol. 88b; and *Rolls of Arms of Henry III: The Matthew Paris Shields, c.1244–59*, ed. T. D. Tremlett, London, 1967, 65 and 82.

7   For an introduction to this subject, see R. Barber and J. Barker, *Tournaments: Jousts, Chivalry and Pageants in the Middle Ages*, Woodbridge, 1989; and J. R. V. Barker, *The Tournament in England, 1100–1400*, Woodbridge, 1986.

8   R. Bartlett, *England under the Norman and Angevin Kings, 1075–1225*, Oxford, 2000, 241–4.

9   For one of many introductions to this subject, see M. Keen, *Chivalry*, London and New Haven, 1984.

10   My namesake John Goodall kindly pointed out the earliest reference to the arms of peace and war known to him: the will of John de Warenne, eighth earl of Surrey, dated 24 June 1347. *Testamenta Eboracensia I*, ed. J. Raine, Surtees Society, 4, London, 1836, 42. Another instance occurs in Viscount Dillon and W. H. St John Hope, 'Inventory of the Goods and Chattels Belonging to Thomas Duke of Gloucester and Seized in his Castle at Pleshey, Co. Essex, 21

Richard II (1397)', *Archaeological Journal*, 54 (1897), 305–8.

11   For an introduction to this, see R. Barber, *King Arthur: Hero and Legend*, third rev. edn, Woodbridge, 1986.

12   Bartlett, *England under the Norman and Angevin Kings*, 251.

13   R. S. Loomis, 'Edward I, Arthurian Enthusiast', *Speculum*, 28 (1953), 114–27.

14   M. Biddle et al., *King Arthur's Round Table*, Woodbridge, 2000, 182.

15   The National Archives, C62/15 m19. I am grateful to Jeremy Ashbee for this reference.

16   'Be it recorded that the lord king ordered William of Norwich, acting treasurer, through the mouth of the constable of the Tower, John of Cromwell, to make five springalds as quickly as he could for the defence of Warenne's Tower in the said Tower of London. And be it further recorded that because of this command, there was no hope of peace between the king and the earls'; The National Archives, E101 468/20, fol. 4v. I am indebted to Jeremy Ashbee for this reference.

17   The National Archives, E101 468/20, fol. 4v.

18   Summarised in R. A. Brown, 'Royal Castle Building in England, 1154–1216', *English Historical Review*, 70 (1955), 353–98.

19   *VCH: Hampshire and the Isle of Wight*, vol. IV, London, 1911, 88–90; and *History of the King's Works*, vol. II, 766–8.

20   *History of the King's Works*, vol. II, 766.

21   *History of the King's Works*, vol. II, 830; and J. Goodall, *Scarborough Castle*, London, 2000, 24–5 [English Heritage guidebook].

22   The National Archives, *Pipe Roll*, 13 Henry II (1166–7), vol. XI, 1. I am grateful to Jeremy Ashbee for this reference.

23   S. C. Barber, 'Archaeological Excavations at Knaresborough, 1925–28', *Yorkshire Archaeological Journal*, 30 (1931), 221.

24   St John Hope, *Windsor Castle: An Architectural History*, vol. I, London, 1913, 17.

25   Barber, 'Archaeological Excavations at Knaresborough', 217–20.

26   M. Reeve and M. Thurlby, 'King John's Gloriette at Corfe Castle', *Journal of the Society of Architectural Historians*, 64 (2005), 168–85.

27   J. Goodall, 'The Siege of Dover, 1216', *Château Gaillard*, 19 (2000), 98–100.

28   J. Kenyon, *Medieval Fortifications*, Leicester, 1990, 78–82.

29   D. J. C. King, 'Pembroke Castle', *Archaeologia Cambrensis*, 127 (1978), 98–105; and I. W. Rowlands, 'William Marshal, Pembroke Castle and the Historian', *Château Gaillard*, 17 (1994), 151–5.

30   M. Fleury, 'Le Louvre des rois: les fouilles de la Cour Carrée', *Dossiers histoire et archéologie*,

110 (November 1986), 14. I am grateful to Mary Whiteley for this reference.

31 J. Mesqui, *Châteaux et enceintes de la France médiévale*, vol. I, Paris, 1991, 162–6; and Mesqui, *Châteaux forts et fortifications en France*, Paris, 1997, 290–1.

32 R. Avent, 'William Marshal's Castle at Chepstow and its Place in Military Architecture', in *Chepstow Castle: Its History and Buildings*, ed. R. Turner and A. Johnson, Almeley, 2006, 89.

33 H. Summerson, M. Trueman and S. Harrison, 'Brougham Castle, Cumbria', *Cumberland and Westmorland Antiquarian and Archaeological Society Research Series*, 8 (1998), 9.

34 *A History of Northumberland*, vol. V, 23–5.

35 J. Goodall, *Warkworth Castle*, 2006, 35 [English Heritage guidebook].

36 Matthew Paris, *Historia Anglorum*, ed. F. Madden, Rolls Series, 44, vol. III, London, 1869, 67.

37 For a contemporary perspective, see Giraldus Cambrensis, *Expugnatio Hibernica*, ed. and trans. A. B. Scott and F. X. Martin, Dublin, 1978.

38 T. E. McNeill, 'The Great Towers of Early Irish Castles', *Anglo-Norman Studies*, 12 (1989), 99–117.

39 P. D. Sweetman, 'The Development of Trim Castle in the Light of Recent Research', *Château Gaillard*, 18 (1998), 223–30.

40 M. Potterton, *Medieval Trim: History and Archaeology*, Dublin, 2005, 235.

41 Potterton, *Medieval Trim*, 212.

42 T. McNeill, *Castles in Ireland: Feudal Power in a Gaelic World*, London and New York, 1997, 34–7.

43 B. H. St John O'Neil, *Castle Rushen, Isle of Man*, London 1960, 5 [Ministry of Works guidebook].

44 T. McNeill, *Carrickfergus Castle*, Belfast, 1981, 3.

45 O. Davies and D. B. Quinn, eds, *The Irish Pipe Roll of 14 John, 1211–12*, supplement to *Ulster Journal of Archaeology*, 4 (1941), 61.

46 G. H. Orpen, 'Athlone Castle: Its Early History, with Notes on Some Neighbouring Castles', *Journal of the Society of Antiquaries of Ireland*, 37 (1907), 262–5.

47 G. H. Orpen, *Ireland under the Normans, 1169–1216*, vol. II, Oxford, 1911, 307–8.

48 Davies and Quinn, eds, *Irish Pipe Roll of 14 John, 1211–12*, in the supplement to *Ulster Journal of Archaeology*, 4 (1941), 69.

49 For a clear overview of what follows, see D. A. Carpenter, *The Minority of Henry III*, London, 1990, 5–49.

50 *Memoriale fratris Walteri de Coventria*, ed. W. Stubbs, Rolls Series, 58, vol. II, London, 1873, 226–7; other accounts of the siege also appear in *Radulphi de Coggeshall Chronicon Anglicanum*, ed.

J. Stevenson, Rolls Series, 66, London, 1875, 175–6; and *Chronica Rogeri de Wendover*, ed. H. Hewlett, Rolls Series, 84, vol. II, London, 1887, 148–51.

51 *Calendar of the Liberate Rolls Preserved in the Public Record Office: Henry III*, vol. IV: *1251–1260*, London, 1959, 304 and 452.

52 W. L. Warren, *King John*, second edn, London, 1978, 249–50.

53 *Matthaei Parisiensis Monachi Sancti Albani: Chronica Majora*, ed. H. R. Luard, Rolls Series, 57, vol. II, London, 1874, 655.

54 *Calendar of Patent Rolls: Henry III, 1216–1225*, 62.

55 For a more detailed account of what follows, see Goodall, 'Siege of Dover', 91–102.

56 *Histoire des ducs de Normandie et des rois d'Angleterre*, ed. F. Michel, Paris, 1840, 170.

57 M. Weiss, 'The Castellan: The Early Career of Hubert de Burgh', *Viator*, 5 (1974), 244.

58 *Histoire des ducs de Normandie et des rois d'Angleterre*, ed. Michel, 178.

59 *Radulphi de Coggeshall Chronicon Anglicanum*, ed. Stevenson, 182.

60 'Lors fist Looys drecier ses perieres et ses mangounnais pour jeter a la porte et au mur; si fist j. Castel de cloies moult haut et un cat por mener au mur', *Histoire des ducs de Normandie et des rois d'Angleterre*, ed. Michel, 178.

61 *Histoire des ducs de Normandie et des rois d'Angleterre*, ed. Michel, 178–9.

62 '. . . iussit Ludowicus petrarias et alias belli machinas circa castri ambitum erigere, quibus undique collocatis damnosos lapides emittere non cessabant', Rogeri de Wendover, *Chronica sive Flores Historiarum*, ed. H. O. Coxe, Rolls Series, 84, vol. II, London, 1842, 201.

63 *Histoire des ducs de Normandie et des rois d'Angleterre*, ed. Michel, 192 and 195–6.

64 H. L. Cannon, 'The Battle of Sandwich, and Eustace the Monk', *English Historical Review*, 27 (1912), 649–70.

65 *History of the King's Works*, vol. I, 109.

66 See, for example, T. Borenius, 'The Cycles of Images in the Castles and Palaces of Henry III', *Journal of the Warburg and Courtauld Institutes*, 6 (1943), 40–50.

67 The National Archives, c62/15 m19. I am grateful to Jeremy Ashbee for this reference.

68 *Calendar of the Liberate Rolls: Henry III*, vol. I: *1226–1240*, London, 1916, 482: 'And to cause the tower to be whitewashed in the places (*per loca*) that were not whitewashed before.' Checking this entry against the manuscript (The National Archives, c62/14 m8), Jeremy Ashbee has pointed out that the great tower in question is at Rochester, not Dover, as the printed calendar states.

69 F. J. West, 'Burgh, Hubert de, Earl of Kent

(c.1170–1243)', in *Oxford Dictionary of National Biography*, Oxford, 2004: www.oxforddnb.com/view/article/3991 (accessed 27 January 2009).

70 H. M. Colvin, ed., *Building Accounts of Henry III*, Oxford, 1971, 20–87.

71 M.-P. Baudry, *Les Fortifications des Plantagênets en Poitou, 1154–1242*, Mémoirs de la section d'archéologie et d'histoire de l'art, 11, Paris, 2001, 56–8.

72 G. Home, *Old London Bridge*, London, 1931, 116–17.

73 C. Wilson, 'Lausanne and Canterbury: A Special Relationship Reconsidered', in *Die Kathedrale von Lausanne und ihr Marienportal im Kontext der europäischen Gotik*, ed. P. Kurmann and M. Rohde, Berlin and New York, 2004, 121.

74 Baudry, *Les Fortifications des Plantagênets en Poitou*, 74–8.

75 E. E. Viollet-le-Duc, *An Essay on the Military Architecture of the Middle Ages*, trans. M. MacDermott, third edn, Oxford and London, 1907, 10–13.

76 M.-P. Baudry, 'La Politique de fortification des Plantagênets en Poitou', *Anglo-Norman Studies*, 24 (2001), 57.

77 *Close Rolls of the Reign of Henry III, 1247–1251*, London, 1922, 8.

78 Pipe Rolls: 13 Henry III, The National Archives, E372/73, m.1, cited with a complete listing of costs in S. Brindle and S. Priestley, 'Windsor Castle, Appendix One: Castle, Payments and Supply of Materials in the Reign of Henry III', unpublished English Heritage draft report. I am grateful to Stephen Brindle for this information.

79 T. Tatton-Brown, 'Windsor Castle before 1344', in *Edward III's Round Table at Windsor*, ed. J. Munby, R. Barber and R. Brown, Woodbridge and Rochester, NY, 2007, 13–28.

80 *History of the King's Works*, vol. II, 710–11.

81 D. Renn, 'Cob Hall Tower', in *The Early History of Lincoln Castle*, ed. Phillip Lindley, Occasional Papers in Lincolnshire History and Archaeology, 12, Lincoln, 2004, 79–86.

82 D. Baker and E. Baker, 'Bedford Castle', *Bedfordshire Archaeological Journal*, 13 (1979), 13–17.

83 Carpenter, *The Minority of Henry III*, 363–6; G. H. Fowler, 'Munitions in 1224', *Bedfordshire Historical Record Society*, 5 (1920), 117–32; and E. Amt, 'Besieging Bedford: Military Logistics in 1224', *Journal of Medieval Military History*, 1 (2002), 101–24.

84 P. Mayes and L. Butler, *Sandal Castle Excavations, 1964–73*, Wakefield, 1983, 3–4 and 27.

85 M. W. Thompson, 'The Origins of Bollingbroke Castle, Lincolnshire', *Medieval Archaeology*, 10 (1966), 152–6.

86 Carpenter, *The Minority of Henry III*, 311.

87 R. Turner, S. Priestley and C. Jones Jen-

kins, 'The Marshals' Use of the Great Tower', in *Chepstow Castle*, ed. Turner and Johnson, 91–2.

88 N. Coldstream and R. K. Morris, 'The Architecture and Decoration of the Marshal's Great Tower', in *Chepstow Castle*, ed. Turner and Johnson, 101–12.

89 K. J. Barton and E. W. Holden, ' Excavations at Bramber Castle, Sussex, 1966–7', *Archaeological Journal*, 134 (1977), 19–20.

90 *History of the King's Works*, vol. II, 866 and 859. See also Colvin, ed., *Building Accounts of Henry III*.

91 D. Park and R. Pender, 'Henry III's Wall Paintings of the Zodiac in the Lower Ward of Windsor', in *Windsor: Medieval Archaeology, Art and Architecture of the Thames Valley*, ed. L. Keen and E. Scarff, British Archaeological Association Conference Transactions, 25, Leeds, 2002, 125–31.

92 The National Archives, c62/42 m.4 and E101/491/17 m.3 and m.4. I am grateful to Jeremy Ashbee for these references. See also *Calendar of Patent Rolls: Elizabeth I, 1575–1578*, 341; and Hammond, *A Relation of a Short Survey of the Western Counties*, ed. L. G. Wickham Legg, Camden Miscellany, 16, London, 1936, 51.

93 I. Roberts, *Pontefract Castle: Archaeological Excavations, 1982–86*, Yorkshire Archaeology, 8, Leeds, 2002, 17–27. It is possible that an order to cover the 'tower' with lead in 1244 marks its completion. *Calendar of the Liberate Rolls: Henry III, vol. III: 1240–1245*, London, 1930, 256.

94 L. F. Salzman, 'Documents Relating to Pevensey Castle', *Sussex Archaeological Collections*, 49 (1906), 18.

95 Salzman, 'Documents Relating to Pevensey Castle', 3–4.

96 W. Lambarde, *A Perambulation of Kent Written in 1570*, London, 1826, 140–1.

97 Barton and Holden, 'Excavations at Bramber Castle', 20.

98 *Knights of Edward I*, ed. C. Moor, Harleian Society, 80, vol. I, London, 1929, 57.

99 T. H. Baker, 'Notes on the History of Mere', *Wiltshire Archaeological and Natural History Magazine*, 30 (1896), 230–1.

100 R. Radford, 'Tintagel: The Castle and the Celtic Monastery: Interim Report', *Antiquaries Journal*, 15 (1935), 401–19; W. Borlase, *Antiquities, Historical and Monumental of the County of Cornwall*, London, 1769, 352–3 and pl. xxx; and English Heritage Red Guide, 2010.

101 S. Toy, 'The Round Castles of Cornwall', *Archaeologia*, 83 (1933), 207–17.

102 *History of the King's Works*, vol. II, 562.

103 N. Vincent, 'Richard, First Earl of Cornwall and King of Germany, 1209–1272', in *Oxford Dictionary of National Biography*: www.oxforddnb.com/view/article/23501 (accessed 23 March 2007).

104 'Chronicon Vulgo Dictum Chronicon Thomae Wykes', in *Annales Monastici*, ed. H. R. Luard, Rolls Series, 36, vol. IV, London, 1869, 178.

105 *VCH: County of Warwick*, vol. II, London, 1908, 429–30.

106 *The Metrical Chronicle of Robert of Gloucester*, ed. W. A. Wright, Rolls Series, 86, vol. II, London, 1887, 771–2.

107 *Matthaei Parisiensis Monachi Sancti Albani: Chronica Majora*, vol. III, London, 1876, 80.

108 *Matthaei Parisiensis Monachi Sancti Albani: Chronica Majora*, vol. III, 93–4.

109 G. Keevill, *The Tower of London Moat: Archaeological Excavations, 1995–9*, Oxford, 2004, 45–78; and E. Impey, 'The Western Entrance to the Tower of London, 1240–1241', *Transactions of the London and Middlesex Archaeological Society*, 48 (1998), 59–75.

110 E. King, 'Observations on Ancient Castles', *Archaeologia*, 6 (1782), 267, pl. 31.

111 P. H. Humphries, *Llanstephan Castle*, rev. edn, Cardiff, 1996 [CADW guidebook]. The fullest account of the building is D. J. C. King, *Llanstephan Castle*, London, 1963 [Ministry of Works guidebook], but see also R. Avent, 'The Development of Three Coastal Castles', in *Sir Gâr: Studies in Carmarthenshire History*, ed. H. James, Carmarthen, 1991, 167–88.

112 D. Renn, *Caerphilly Castle*, rev. edn, Cardiff, 1997 [CADW guidebook].

7 THE KING'S WORKS AND WALES

1 For the details of the reign, see M. Prestwich, *Edward I*, London, 1988.

2 For example, R. A. Brown, *English Castles*, third rev. edn, London, 1976, 128.

3 R. M. Haines, *King Edward II*, Montreal, 2003; and J. R. S. Phillips, 'Edward II (1284–1327)', in *Oxford Dictionary of National Biography*, Oxford, 2004: www.oxforddnb.com/view/article/8518 (accessed 31 October 2007).

4 Phillips, 'Edward II' (accessed 10 February 2009).

5 M. Biddle, 'A 13th-century Architectural Sketch from the Hospital of St John the Evangelist, Cambridge', *Proceedings of the Cambridge Antiquarian Society*, 54 (1961), 99–108.

6 R. Branner, 'Drawings from a 13th-century Architect's Shop: The Reims Palimpsest', *Journal of the Society of Architectural Historians*, 17 (1958), 9–21; S. Murray, 'The Gothic Façade Drawings in the "Reims Palimpsest"', *Gesta*, 17 (1978), 51–5; and for Villard de Honnecourt's sketchbook, http://classes.bnf.fr/villard/feuillet/index.htm.

7 J. Bony, *French Gothic Architecture of the 12th and 13th Centuries*, Berkeley, CA, and London, 1983, 388–401.

8 Cited in P. Binski, *Westminster Abbey and the Plantagenets*, New Haven and London, 1995, 45–6. The poem is of *circa* 1260.

9 The core literature on the chapel is F. Mackenzie, *The Architectural Antiquities of the Collegiate Chapel of St Stephen*, London, 1844; J. M. Hastings, *St Stephen's Chapel*, Cambridge, 1955; *History of the King's Works*; and C. Wilson, 'The Origins of the Perpendicular Style and its Development to c.1360', unpublished ph.D thesis, University of London, 1980, 34–80.

10 C. Wilson, *The Gothic Cathedral*, London, 1992, 194.

11 The two principal published surveys are J. Bony, *The English Decorated Style*, Oxford, 1979; and N. Coldstream, *The Decorated Style: Architecture and Ornament, 1240–1360*, Toronto and Bath, 1994.

12 M. Prestwich, 'Edward I (1239–1307)', in *Oxford Dictionary of National Biography*: www.oxforddnb.com/view/article/8517 (accessed 31 October 2007).

13 W. H. St John Hope, *Windsor Castle: An Architectural History*, vol. I, London, 1913, 86 and 98 n. 20.

14 C. Wilson, 'Beverley, Robert of (d. 1285)', in *Oxford Dictionary of National Biography*: www.oxforddnb.com/view/article/42212 (accessed 31 October 2007).

15 The National Archives, E163/2/39, cited in H. G. Richardson's review of the *History of the King's Works*, in *English Historical Review*, 80 (1965), 553–6.

16 *History of the King's Works*, vol. II, 716–17.

17 *History of the King's Works*, vol. II, 836.

18 E. Impey and G. Parnell, *The Tower of London: The Official Illustrated History*, London, 2000, 38.

19 S. G. Priestley and R. C. Turner, 'Three Castles of the Clare Family in Monmouthshire during the Thirteenth and Fourteenth Centuries', *Archaeologia Cambrensis*, 152 (2003), 9–52.

20 *Close Rolls of the Reign of Henry III, 1264–1268*, London, 1937, 190. In April 1260 Roger de Leybourne was ordered to desist from strengthening his castle at Leybourne or risk its demolition: *Close Rolls of the Reign of Henry III, 1259–1261*, London, 1934, 283–4.

21 *H: Northamptonshire*, vol. III, London, 1930, 71 n. 2a. See also C. A. Markham, 'Barnwell Castle, Northamptonshire', *Associated Architectural Society Reports and Papers*, 31 (1911–12), 525–39; B. L. Giggins, 'Barnwell Castle Survey, 1980–5', *South Midlands Archaeology*, 16 (1986), 79–84; and M. Audouy, 'Excavations at Barnwell Castle, Northants, 1980', *Northamptonshire Archaeology*, 25 (1993–4), 123–6.

22 R. Turner et al., 'The 'Gloriette in the Lower Bailey', in *Chepstow Castle: Its History and Buildings*, ed. R. Turner and A. Johnson, Almeley, 2006, 135–50.

23   R. Turner et al., 'The New or Marten's Tower', in *Chepstow Castle*, ed. Turner and Johnson, 151–66.

24   '. . . painting in colour the figures of stone mounted over the great chamber facing the Thames' (*ymaginibus de petro assisis super magnam cameram versus Thamisiam depigendis coloribus*), 1277–8; The National Archives, E372/121 rot.22. I am grateful to Jeremy Ashbee for this reference.

25   C. Wilson, 'Not Without Honour Save in its Own Country? Saint-Urbain at Troyes and its Contrasting French and English Posterities', in *The Year 1300 and the Creation of a New European Architecture*, ed. A. Gajewski and Z. Opacic, Turnhout, 2007, 114–18.

26   David Park has kindly pointed out the existence of this motif in the twelfth-century crypt paintings at Chartres Cathedral. A source in ivory has also been suggested for the sedilia at Troyes: Wilson, 'Not Without Honour?', 120 n. 26.

27   N. Ludlow, 'Pembroke Castle', *Fortress*, 8 (1991), 25–30.

28   J. Ashbee, *Goodrich Castle*, London, 2005, 32–5 [English Heritage Red Guide]. More detailed analysis is presented in an important but as yet unpublished monograph on the castle produced for English Heritage by Ron Shoesmith, Bruce Copplestone-Crow and Pat Hughes. I have had sight of a draft manuscript of this.

29   D. J. C. Cathcart-King and J. C. Perks, 'Carew Castle, Pembrokeshire', *Archaeological Journal*, 119 (1962), 270–307.

30   'et conducen' D Carpent' ad Rege' ap' Sileha'', *Pipe Rolls*, 20 Henry II (1173–4), 38.

31   *History of the King's Works*, vol. I, 293–9.

32   *History of the King's Works*, vol. I, 299–307.

33   G. Hughes, 'Note on the Proposed Excavations at Aberystwyth Castle', *Archaeologia Cambrensis*, sixth series, 3 (1903), 272; and Hughes, 'Aberystwyth Castle Excavations Carried Out in 1903', *Archaeologia Cambrensis*, sixth series, 4 (1904), 317.

34   J. G. Edwards, 'The Name of Flint Castle', *English Historical Review*, 29 (1914), 315–17.

35   *History of the King's Works*, vol. I, 308–18; and J. G. Edwards, 'The Building of Flint', *Flintshire Historical Society*, 12 (1951), 5–20.

36   T. J. Miles, 'Flint: Excavations at the Castle and on the Town Defences, 1971–4', *Archaeologia Cambrensis*, 145 (1996), 67–120.

37   A. J. Taylor, 'The Building of Flint: A Postscript', *Flintshire Historical Society*, 17 (1957), 34–41; and D. J. C. King, 'The Donjon of Flint Castle', *Chester and North Wales Architectural and Archaeological and Historical Society Journal*, 45 (1958), 61–9.

38   A. Taylor, *Rhuddlan Castle*, fourth rev. edn, Cardiff, 1987, 12 [CADW guidebook].

39   *History of the King's Works*, vol. I, 318–27.

40   *History of the King's Works*, vol. I, 324.

41   *History of the King's Works*, vol. I, 357–65.

42   J. Ashbee, *Conwy Castle*, Cardiff, 2007, 60–1 [CADW guidebook]; and R. B. White, 'Llywellyn's Hall, Conwy', *Caernarvonshire Historical Society Transactions*, 56 (1995), 29–34.

43   As shown in the survey of the Tower of London of 1597. See A. Keay, *The Elizabethan Tower of London: The Haiward and Gascoyne Plan of 1597*, London Topographical Society Publication, 158, London, 2001, 45–7.

44   C. Kightly, *A Royal Palace in Wales: Caernarfon*, Cardiff, 1991, 5–9.

45   *History of the King's Works*, vol. I, 370.

46   A. Wheatley, *The Idea of the Castle in Medieval England*, Woodbridge, 2004, 143–4.

47   R. K. Morris, 'The Development of Later Gothic Mouldings in England, *c.*1250–1400, part I', *Architectural History*, 21 (1978), 27.

48   British Library, Harley MS 2073, fol. 110/1. For published facsimiles, see the frontispiece of R. Newcombe, *An Account of the Castle and Town of Ruthin*, Ruthin, 1829. I am grateful to Diane Williams for her help tracking the manuscript down.

49   *History of the King's Works*, vol. I, 333.

50   Leland, *Itinerary*, vol. III, 98.

51   T. McNeill, *Castles in Ireland*, London and New York, 1997, 103; and D. M. Waterman, 'Greencastle, Co. Donegal', *Ulster Journal of Archaeology*, 21 (1958), 74–88.

52   S. Duffy, 'Burgh, Richard de, Second Earl of Ulster (b. in or after 1259, d. 1326)', in *Oxford Dictionary of National Biography*: www.oxforddnb.com/view/article/3995 (accessed 28 October 2007).

53   Kightly, *A Royal Palace in Wales*, 12–14.

54   *History of the King's Works*, vol. I, 398–402.

55   A. J. Taylor, 'Master James of St Georges', *English Historical Review*, 65 (1950), 433–57; and Taylor, 'Castle Building in 13th-Century Wales and Savoy', *Proceedings of the British Academy*, 63 (1977), 265–92.

56   See, for example, the list in Taylor, 'Castle Building in 13th-Century Wales and Savoy', 267.

57   N. Coldstream, 'Architects, Advisers and Design at Edward I's Castles in Wales', *Architectural History*, 46 (2003), 19–36.

8   THE KING'S SERVANTS AND THE ARCHITECTURE OF WAR

1   C. M. Fraser, 'Bek, Antony (I) (c.1245–1311)', in *Oxford Dictionary of National Biography*, Oxford, 2004: www.oxforddnb.com/view/article/1970 (accessed 28 October 2007).

2   *Historiae Dunelmenses Scriptores Tres*, ed. J. Raine, Surtees Society, 9, Newcastle, 1839, 60.

3   *VCH: Durham,* vol. II, London, 1907, 126–7 and 128–9.

4   J. Cunningham, 'Auckland Castle: Some Recent Discoveries', in *Medieval Architecture and its Intellectual Context: Studies in Honour of Peter Kidson*, ed. E. Fernie and P. Crossley, London and Ronceverte, 1990, 81–90.

5   J. Raine, *A Brief Historical Account of the Episcopal Castle or Palace at Bishop Auckland*, Durham, 1852, 84–90.

6   H. Woods, 'Excavations at Eltham Palace, 1975–9', *London and Middlesex Archaeological Society*, 33 (1982), 215–65.

7   N. J. Tringham, 'The Palace of Bishop Walter Langton in Lichfield Cathedral Close', in *Medieval Archaeology and Architecture at Lichfield*, ed. J. Maddison, British Archaeological Association Conference Transactions, 13, London, 1987, 85–100; and J. Maddison, 'Building at Lichfield Cathedral during the Episcopate of Walter Langton, 1296–1321', in *Medieval Archaeology and Architecture at Lichfield*, ed. Maddison, 66–70.

8   P. Marshall and J. Samuels, *Guardian of the Trent: The Story of Newark Castle*, Newark, 1997, 32.

9   J. Cherry and P. Draper, 'Excavations in the Bishop's Palace, Wells', in *Medieval Art and Architecture at Wells and Glastonbury*, ed. P. Draper and N. Coldstream, British Archaeological Association Conference Transactions, 4, Leeds, 1981, 52–3.

10   J. West, 'Acton Burnell Castle, Shropshire: A Re-interpretation', in *Collectanea Historica: Essays in Memory of Stuart Rigold*, ed. A. Detsicas, Maidstone, 1981, 85–92.

11   E. Martin, 'Little Wenham Hall: A Reinterpretation', *Proceedings of the Suffolk Institute of Archaeology and History*, 39 (1998), 154–8.

12   E. Hasted, *The History and Topographical Survey of the County of Kent*, vol. II, Canterbury, 1782, 182; and M. Conway, 'Allington Castle', *Country Life*, 43 (1919), 386–91, 404–8, 424–9.

13   H. Summerson, ''Most Renowned of Merchants': The Life and Occupations of Laurence of Ludlow, d. 1294', *Midland History*, 30 (2005), 20–36.

14   M. Prestwich, *The Three Edwards: War and State in England, 1272–1377*, London, 1980, 105.

15   N. C. Vincent, 'The Origins of the Chancellorship of the Exchequer', *English Historical Review*, 108 (1993), 105–21.

16   Notably by the late Andor Gomme in lectures. For my own perspective on the building, see J. Goodall, 'Markenfield Hall', *Country Life*, 25 (18 June 2008), 116–21.

17   W. M. Palmer, *Cambridge Castle*, Cambridge, 1928; and *History of the King's Works*, vol. II, 584–7.

18   *History of the King's Works*, vol. II, 815–18.

19   *VCH: County of York: North Riding*, vol. I, London, 1914, 12.

20   The National Archives, E101/462/11.

21 *History of the King's Works*, vol. II, 755.

22 *History of the King's Works*, vol. II, 822.

23 *History of the King's Works*, vol. II, 695–9.

24 *History of the King's Works*, vol. II, 846–7.

25 S. Toy, 'The Round Castles of Cornwall', *Archaeologia*, 83 (1933), 205.

26 *History of the King's Works*, vol. II, 563–5.

27 *History of the King's Works*, vol. II, 566.

28 Prestwich, *The Three Edwards*, 42.

29 M. Prestwich. *Edward I*, London, 1988, 469–516.

30 *History of the King's Works*, vol. I, 413–15; and A. J. Taylor, 'Documents Concerning the King's Works at Linlithgow, 1301–3', in *Studies in Scottish Antiquity Presented to Stewart Cruden*, ed. D. J. Breeze, Edinburgh, 1984, 187–95.

31 *History of the King's Works*, vol. I, 417.

32 W. D. Simpson, 'A New Survey of Kildrummy Castle', *Proceedings of the Society of Antiquaries of Scotland*, 62 (1927–8), 36–80; and Simpson, *Kildrummy Castle and Glenbuchat Castle*, Edinburgh, 1995 edn, 6–7 and 16 [Historic Scotland guidebook]. In the latter the labels of the comparative plans have been mistakenly exchanged. See also C. Tabraham, '*Scottorum Malleus*: Edward I and Scotland', in *The Impact of the Edwardian Castles in Wales*, ed. D. M. Williams and J. Kenyon, Oxford, 2010, 190–1.

33 J. Bain, ed., *Calendar of Documents Relating to Scotland*, vol. II, Edinburgh, 1884, 257 (no. 1005).

34 Bain, ed., *Calendar of Documents Relating to Scotland*, vol. II, 331–2 (no. 1307).

35 *The Siege of Carlaverock*, ed. H. H. Nicholas, London, 1828, 61.

36 *The Siege of Carlaverock*, ed. Nicholas, 64–5.

37 *History of the King's Works*, vol. I, 412.

38 *History of the King's Works*, vol. I, 413.

39 *History of the King's Works*, vol. I, 417–18; and Prestwich, *Edward I*, 501–2.

40 *Calendar of Patent Rolls: Edward II, 1307–1313*, 144.

41 H. Summerson, M. Trueman and S. Harrison, *Brougham Castle, Cumbria*, Cumberland and Westmorland Antiquarian and Archaeological Society Research Series, 8, Kendal, 1998, 14 and 99–104.

42 M. McCarthy, H. Summerson and R. Annis, *Carlisle Castle*, English Heritage Archaeological Report, 18, London, 1990, 96–101 and 134.

43 R. T. Spence, *Skipton Castle and its Builders*, Skipton, 2002, 47–54.

44 *Calendar of the Close Rolls Preserved in the Public Record Office: Edward II*, vol. II: *1313–1318*, London, 1897, 569–70.

45 *A History of Northumberland*, vol. V, 30.

46 *Johannis de Trokelowe et Henrici de Blaneforde . . . chronica et annales*, ed. H. T. Riley in *Chronica monasterii S. Albani*, Rolls Series, 28, vol. III, London, 1866, 91.

47 *History of the King's Works*, vol. II, 780.

48 J. Raine, *The History and Antiquities of North Durham*, London, 1852, 111–12.

49 R. Newman, 'Excavations and Survey at Piel Castle, near Barrow-in-Furness, Cumbria', *Transactions of the Cumberland and Westmorland Antiquarian and Archaeological Society*, 87 (1987), 101–16; J. F. Curwen, 'Piel Castle, Lancashire', *Transactions of the Cumberland and Westmorland Antiquarian and Archaeological Society*, 10 (1910), 271–87; W. Harrison, 'Piel Castle', *Transactions of the Cumberland and Westmorland Antiquarian and Archaeological Society*, 3 (1876–7), 232–40.

50 As the owner of the manor, the abbey is the only obvious builder of this exiguous structure. *VCH: County of Lancaster*, vol. VIII, London, 1914, 308–10.

51 J. S. Hamilton, 'Gaveston, Piers, Earl of Cornwall (d. 1312)', in *Oxford Dictionary of National Biography*: www.oxforddnb.com/view/article/10463 (accessed 10 February 2009).

52 R. M. Haines, *King Edward II*, Montreal, 2003, 82–6.

53 *Calendar of the Close Rolls: Edward II*, vol. II: *1313–1318*, 491; and *VCH: County of Worcester*, vol. III, London, 1913, 338–46.

54 J. Conway Davies, 'The Despenser War in Glamorgan', *Transactions of the Royal Historical Society*, third series, 9 (1915), 21–64.

55 *Calendar of the Close Rolls: Edward II, 1318–1323*, London, 1895, 541–2. This document of 1322 states that the mob 'in the said towns and castles . . . took and burnt all the charters, remembrances and muniments of the said Hugh, to his damage of £2,000'.

56 R. Morris, 'Later Gothic Architecture in South Wales', in *Cardiff: Architecture and Archaeology in the Medieval Diocese of Llandaff*, ed. J. R. Kenyon and D. M. Williams, British Archaeological Association Conference Transactions, 29, Leeds, 2006, 109.

57 *Calendar of Patent Rolls: Edward II, 1307–1313*, 369.

58 *Complete Peerage*, vol. IV, 266.

59 C. Valente, 'The Deposition and Abdication of Edward II', *English Historical Review*, 113 (1998), 852–81.

60 *History of the King's Works*, vol. II, 689–90; and Harvey, *English Mediaeval Architects*, 30 and 299.

61 Hamilton, 'Gaveston, Piers, Earl of Cornwall' (accessed 17 November 2007).

9   THE LION OF ENGLAND

1 *Chronicon Galfridi le Baker de Swynebroke*, ed. E. M. Thompson, Oxford, 1889, 46.

2 C. Shenton, 'Edward III and the Coup of 1330', in *The Age of Edward III*, ed. J. S. Bothwell, Woodbridge, 2001, 13–34; and B. Morley and D. Gurney, *Castle Rising Castle, Norfolk*, East Anglian Archaeology Report, 81, 1997, 3–4 and 60–70.

3 M. Keen, *England in the Later Middle Ages*, London, 1973, 107–9.

4 W. M. Ormrod, *The Reign of Edward III*, London and New Haven, 1990, 29–68.

5 C. Given-Wilson, *The English Nobility in the Late Middle Ages*, London, 1996, 55–68.

6 S. L. Waugh, 'Edmund, First Earl of Kent (1301–1330)', in *Oxford Dictionary of National Biography*, Oxford, 2004: www.oxforddnb.com/view/article/8506 (accessed 10 November 2007).

7 R. R. Davies, 'Mortimer, Roger (VI), Second Earl of March (1328–1360)', in *Oxford Dictionary of National Biography*: www.oxforddnb.com/view/article/19355 (accessed 10 November 2007).

8 J. S. Bothwell, 'Edward III, the English Peerage and the 1337 Earls: Estate Redistribution in Fourteenth-century England', in *The Age of Edward III*, ed. J. S. Bothwell, Woodbridge, 2001, 35–52; and Given-Wilson, *The English Nobility in the Late Middle Ages*, 35–9.

9 Ormrod, *Reign of Edward III*, 96.

10 J. Alexander and P. Binski, *The Age of Chivalry: Art in Plantagenet England, 1200–1400*, exhibition catalogue, Royal Academy, London, 1987, 498.

11 W. M. Ormrod, 'Ufford, Robert, First Earl of Suffolk (1298–1369)', in *Oxford Dictionary of National Biography*: www.oxforddnb.com/view/article/27977 (accessed 10 November 2007); and *Complete Peerage*, vol. XII, part I, 430.

12 The survey is The National Archives, E120/1 m.1.

13 S. Toy, 'The Round Castles of Cornwall', *Archaeologia*, 83 (1933), 208.

14 N. J. G. Pounds, 'The Duchy Palace at Lostwithiel, Cornwall', *Archaeological Journal*, 136 (1979), 203–17.

15 R. Barber, 'Edward, Prince of Wales and of Aquitaine (1330–1376)', in *Oxford Dictionary of National Biography*: www.oxforddnb.com/view/article/8523 (accessed 7 November 2007).

16 *History of the King's Works*, vol. I, 352.

17 D. Robinson, ed., *The Cistercian Abbeys of Britain*, London, 1998, 192.

18 Ormrod, *Reign of Edward III*, 96.

19 *Complete Peerage*, vol. XII, part 2, 647.

20 J. M. Lewis, *Carreg Cennen Castle*, Cardiff, 2006, 1–3 [CADW guide pamphlet].

21 *A History of Northumberland*, vol. XI, 410–25, and vol. XIV, 331–46.

22 C. Kightly, *Farleigh Hungerford*, London, 2006, 17–18 [English Heritage Red Guide].

23 *A History of Northumberland*, vol. XI, 460–70.

24 A. Emery, *Greater Medieval Houses of England and Wales*, vol. I: *Northern England*, Cambridge, 1996, 110–14; and C. J. Bates, 'The Barony and Castle of Langley', *Archaeologia Aeliana*, 10 (1885), 38–56. The latter account includes good pre-restoration photographs.

25 For summary accounts, see respectively Emery, *Greater Medieval Houses*, vol. I: *Northern England*, 337–9 and 339–44. For Gilling, see also A. Cramer, *Gilling Castle*, Ampleforth, 2008; and J. Bilson, 'Gilling Castle', *Yorkshire Archaeological Journal*, 19 (1907), 105–92.

26 J. Darlington, ed., *Stafford Castle: Survey, Excavation and Research, 1978–98. Volume I: The Surveys*, Stafford, 2001, 48–51 and 101–15; and M. J. B. Hislop, 'Master John Burcestre and the Castles of Stafford and Maxstoke', *Transactions of the South Staffordshire Archaeological and Historical Society*, 33 (1991–2), 14–20.

27 *History of the King's Works*, vol. II, 819.

28 *History of the King's Works*, vol. II, 891–2.

29 J. M. W. Bean, 'Percy, Henry, Second Lord Percy (1301–1352)', in *Oxford Dictionary of National Biography*: www.oxforddnb.com/view/article/21929 (accessed 10 November 2007).

30 *The Percy Chartulary*, ed. M. T. Martin, Surtees Society, 117, Durham, 1911 (for 1909), 481.

31 For a discussion of this subject, see J. Cherry, 'The Breaking of Seals', in *Middelalderlige Seglstamper i Norden*, ed. M. Anderson and G. Tegnér, Roskilde, 2002, 81–96.

32 In medieval usage, the terms lion and leopard are in some cases synonymous. C. Shenton, 'Edward III and the Symbol of the Leopard', in *Heraldry, Pageantry and Social Display in Medieval England*, ed. P. Coss and M. Keen, Woodbridge, 2002, 69–81.

33 J. M. W. Bean, 'The Percies' Acquisition of Alnwick', *Archaeologia Aeliana*, fourth series, 32 (1954), 309–19.

34 W. H. Knowles, 'The Gatehouse and Barbican at Alnwick Castle with an Account of the Recent Discoveries', *Archaeologia Aeliana*, third series, 5 (1909), 286–303.

35 W. Dugdale, 'Northumbrian Monuments; or, The Shields of Arms, Effigies and Inscriptions in the Churches, Castles and Halls of Northumberland', *Newcastle upon Tyne Record Committee*, 4 (1924), 10–14.

36 H. A. Ogle, *Ogle and Bothal; or, A History of the Baronies of Ogle, Bothal and Hepple*, Newcastle upon Tyne, 1902, 333.

37 C. J. Bates, *The Border Holds of Northumberland*, Newcastle, 1891, 284.

38 S. West, *Prudhoe Castle*, London, 2006, 8–11 [English Heritage Red Guide].

39 See F. Watson, 'Umfraville, Gilbert de, Seventh Earl of Angus (1244?–1307)', in *Oxford Dictionary of National Biography*: www.oxforddnb. com/view/article/27988 (accessed 10 November 2007).

40 G. Fairclough, 'Edlingham Castle: The Military and Domestic Development of a Northumbrian Manor. Excavations, 1978–80: Interim Report', *Château Gaillard*, 9–10 (1982), 373–87.

41 *A History of Northumberland*, vol. VII, 113–16; and Richard Barber, 'Felton, Sir William, the Younger (d. 1367)', in *Oxford Dictionary of National Biography*: www.oxforddnb.com/view/ article/9277 (accessed 10 November 2007).

42 'Cronica monasterii de Alnewyke', ed. W. Dickson in *Archaeologia Aeliana*, 3 (1844), appendix, 40 (where the old-style year of 1351 is given).

43 For a discussion of the monument, see N. Dawton, 'The Medieval Monuments', in *Beverley Minster: An Illustrated History*, ed. R. Horrox, Cambridge, 2000, 133–45.

44 *Calendar of Inquisitions Miscellaneous (Chancery) Preserved in the Public Record Office*, vol. III: *1348–1377*, London, 1937, 162–4 (no. 435).

45 T. Tatton-Brown, 'Rose Castle', in *Carlisle and Cumbria: Roman and Medieval Architecture, Art and Archaeology*, ed. M. McCarthy and D. Weston, British Archaeological Association Conference Transactions, 27, Leeds, 2004, 257–68.

46 M. McCarthy, H. Summerson and R. Annis, *Carlisle Castle*, English Heritage Archaeological Report, 18, London, 1990, 142.

47 *History of the King's Works*, vol. II, 788.

48 *History of the King's Works*, vol. II, 592–3.

49 *Calendar of Patent Rolls: Edward III, 1330–1334*, 517.

50 R. K. M. Morris, 'European Prodigy or Regional Eccentric? The Rebuilding of St Augustine's Abbey Church, Bristol', in *'Almost the Richest City': Bristol in the Middle Ages*, ed. L. Keen, British Archaeological Association Conference Transactions, 19, London, 1997, 41–56.

51 *William Worcestre: Itineraries*, ed. J. Harvey, Oxford, 1969, 401; and H. Brakspear, 'St Mary Redcliffe, Bristol', *Transactions of the Bristol and Gloucestershire Archaeological Society*, 44 (1922), 271–92.

52 For a discussion of this point, see P. Crossley, 'Peter Parler and England: A Problem Revisited', *Wallraf-Richartz-Jahrbuch*, 64 (2003), 53–82.

53 J. Smyth, *The Lives of the Berkeleys*, ed. J. Maclean, vol. I, Gloucester, 1883, 308–9.

54 Smyth, *Lives of the Berkeleys*, vol. I, 309.

55 Smyth, *Lives of the Berkeleys*, vol. I, 309; J. Goodall, 'Beverston Castle, Gloucestershire', *Country Life*, 202 (24 September 2008), 104–7; and T. H. Turner and J. H. Parker, *Some Account of Domestic Architecture in England*, vol. III, Oxford, 1859, part 1, plates facing 181 and 182; part 2, 253–6.

56 Smyth, *Lives of the Berkeleys*, vol. I, 304–5.

57 Smyth, *Lives of the Berkeleys*, vol. I, 306.

58 G. Williams, 'Gower, Henry (1277/8–1347)', in *Oxford Dictionary of National Biography*: www.oxforddnb.com/view/article/11174 (accessed 10 February 2009).

59 For a complete catalogue of the sculpture, see R. Turner (in the contribution by N. Coldstream), 'St Davids Bishop's Palace, Pembrokeshire', *Antiquaries Journal*, 80 (2000), 146–89.

60 *Royal Commission on the Ancient and Historical Monuments of Wales: An Inventory of the Ancient Monuments in Glamorgan*, vol. III: *Medieval Secular Monuments*, pt 1b: *Non-Defensive*, Aberystwyth, 2000, 358.

61 A. Tuck, 'Beauchamp, Thomas, Eleventh Earl of Warwick (1313/14–1369)', in *Oxford Dictionary of National Biography*: www.oxforddnb. com/view/article/53085 (accessed 10 February 2009).

62 R. K. Morris, 'The Architecture of the Earls of Warwick in the 14th Century', in *England in the 14th Century: Proceedings of the 1985 Harlaxton Symposium*, ed. W. Ormrod, Woodbridge, 1986, 161–6.

63 W. Dugdale, *The Antiquities of Warwickshire*, second edn, vol. I, London, 1730, 401.

64 M. W. Thompson, *The Decline of the Castle*, Cambridge, 1987, 75–6.

65 *VCH: Suffolk*, vol. II, London, 1907, 63.

66 A. B. Whittingham, 'Bury St Edmunds Abbey', *Archaeological Journal*, 108 (1951), 186.

67 J. N. Hare, *Battle Abbey: The Eastern Range and the Excavations of 1978–80*, Historic Building and Monuments Commission for England, 2, London, 1985, 11–14.

68 Work probably began when a new master mason was appointed by the abbey in 1377. And it was probably complete by 1389, when money was paid to build 'the wall and ditch to the south of the gate'; Oxford, Bodleian Library, MS Tanner 166, fols 31r and 22v, respectively; *Calendar of Patent Rolls: Richard II, 1381–1385*, 166.

69 For a discussion of the walls, see J. Bartlett, 'The Medieval Walls of Hull', *Kingston upon Hull Museums Bulletin*, 3 and 4 (1969–70, revised 1971).

70 J. Goodall, 'Thornton Abbey', *Country Life*, 189 (5 October 1995), 44–7.

71 *Calendar of Patent Rolls: Edward III, 1354–1358*, 574; and *VCH: Hertfordshire*, vol. II, London, 1908, 509–10.

72 *A History of Northumberland*, vol. VIII, 99–100.

73 *A History of Northumberland*, vol. VIII, 95.

74 W. M. Ormrod, 'Clinton, William, Earl of Huntingdon (d. 1354)', in *Oxford Dictionary of National Biography*: www.oxforddnb.com/view/ article/53080 (accessed 10 February 2009).

75 *Calendar of Patent Rolls: Edward III, 1334–1338*, 415; and *Calendar of the Close Rolls Preserved in the Public Record Office: Edward III*, vol. VI: *1341–1343*, London, 1902, 61.

76 Dugdale, *Antiquities of Warwickshire*, vol. II, 998; and *VCH: County of Warwick*, vol. II, London, 1908, 91–4.

77 Morris, 'Architecture of the Earls of Warwick', 161–74.

10 THE GENESIS OF THE PERPENDICULAR STYLE

1 C. Wilson, 'The Origins of the Perpendicular Style and its Development to *c*.1360', unpublished ph.d thesis, University of London, 1980; and R. K. Morris, 'Master Masons at Gloucester Cathedral in the 14th Century', *Friends of Gloucester Cathedral*, 67 (2003), 10–17.

2 C. Cragoe, 'Fabric, Tombs and Precinct, 1087–1540', in *St Paul's: The Cathedral Church of London, 604–2004*, ed. D. Keene, A. Burns and A. Saint, New Haven and London, 2004, 139.

3 For William Ramsey's career, see Wilson, 'Origins of the Perpendicular Style', 171–258. A full, but in some important points misleading, treatment is also provided in print in Harvey, *English Mediaeval Architects*, 242–5.

4 As, for example, in the side chapels of the chapel of King's College, Cambridge (from 1448 to 1515).

5 J. Vale, 'Image and Identity in the Prehistory of the Order of the Garter', in *St George's Chapel, Windsor, in the Fourteenth Century*, ed. N. Saul, Woodbridge, 2005, 47.

6 Vale, 'Image and Identity', 38–9.

7 R. Barber, 'The Round Table Feast of 1344', in *Edward III's Round Table at Windsor*, ed. J. Munby, R. Barber and R. Brown, Woodbridge and Rochester, ny, 2007, 38–43.

8 J. Munby, 'The Round Table Building', in *Edward III's Round Table at Windsor*, ed. Munby, Barber and Brown, 44–66.

9 R. Bowers, 'Music and the Musical Establishment of St George's Chapel in the Fifteenth Century', in *St George's Chapel, Windsor, in the Late Middle Ages*, ed. C. Richmond and E. Scarff, Windsor, 2001, 174–5.

10 As, for example, the golden plait of hair that was the emblem of the Gesellschaft von Zopf; see G. Brucher, ed., *Geschichte der Bildenden Kunst in Oesterreich*, vol. II: *Gotik*, Munich and New York, 2000, 581.

11 Harvey, *English Mediaeval Architects*, 280.

12 W. H. St John Hope, *Windsor Castle: An Architectural History*, vol. I, London, 1913, 86 and 107–9.

13 J. Goodall, 'The Aerary Porch and its Influence on Late Medieval English Vaulting', in *St George's Chapel, Windsor, in the Fourteenth Century*, ed. Saul, 165–202.

14 C. Wilson, 'The Medieval Monuments', in *Canterbury Cathedral*, ed. P. Collinson, N. Ramsay and M. Sparks, Oxford, 1995, 485.

15 R. A. Brown, 'King Edward's Clocks', *Antiquaries Journal*, 39 (1959), 283–6.

16 J. Munby, 'Carpentry Works for Edward III at Windsor', in *St George's Chapel, Windsor, in the Fourteenth Century*, ed. Saul, 225–37.

17 C. Burgess, 'St George's College, Windsor: Context and Consequence', in *St George's Chapel, Windsor, in the Fourteenth Century*, ed. Saul, 63–96.

18 *Calendar of Papal Registers, 1305–42*, London, 1895, 184.

19 A. H. Thompson, *The History of the Hospital and the New College of the Annunciation of St Mary in the Newarke, Leicester*, Leicester, 1937, 11–40.

20 J. Goodall, 'The College of St Mary in the Newarke, Leicester', in *Medieval Art and Architecture in Coventry*, ed. L. Monckton and R. K. Morris, British Archaeological Association Conference Transactions, in preparation.

21 Leland, *Itinerary*, vol. I, 15–16.

22 *VCH: County of Warwick*, vol. II, London, 1908, 124–9.

23 R. K. Morris, 'The Architecture of the Earls of Warwick in the 14th Century', in *England in the 14th Century, Proceedings of the 1985 Harlaxton Symposium*, ed. W. M. Ormrod, Woodbridge, 1986, 170–3.

24 A. Verduyn, 'Norwich, John, First Lord Norwich (c.1299–1362)', in *Oxford Dictionary of National Biography*, www.oxforddnb.com/view/article/20361 (accessed 8 August 2007).

25 E. Martin, 'Mettingham Castle: An Interpretation of a Survey of 1562', *Proceedings of the Suffolk Institute of Archaeology and History*, 37 (1990), 115–23.

26 *VCH: Norfolk*, vol. II, London, 1906, 457–8.

27 C. Given-Wilson, 'Wealth and Credit, Public and Private: The Earls of Arundel, 1306–1397', *English Historical Review*, 106 (1991), 1–26.

28 M. W. Thompson, 'Recent Excavations in the Keep of Farnham Castle, Surrey', *Medieval Archaeology*, 4 (1960), 92–3.

29 *History of the King's Works*, vol. II, 877; and for a detailed analysis of the figures involved, S. Brindle and S. Priestley, 'Edward III's Building Campaigns at Windsor and the Employment of Masons', in *St George's Chapel, Windsor, in the Fourteenth Century*, ed. Saul, 203–23.

30 C. Wilson, 'The Royal Lodgings of Edward III at Windsor Castle', in *Windsor: Medieval Archaeology, Art and Architecture of the Thames Valley*, ed. L. Keen and E. Scarff, British Archaeological Association Conference Transactions, 25, Leeds, 2002, 19–30.

31 *History of the King's Works*, vol. II, 797–800.

32 *History of the King's Works*, vol. II, 662–6; *Royal Commission on Historical Monuments of England: Essex*, vol. IV, London, 1923, 64–5; P. L. Drewett, 'Excavations at Hadleigh Castle, Essex, 1971–2', *Journal of the British Archaeological Association*, 38 (1975), 152–4; and M. Alexander and S. Westlake, 'Hadleigh Castle, Essex', *English Heritage Historical Review*, 4 (2009), 5–21.

33 B. Cunliffe and J. Munby, *Excavations at Portchester Castle*, vol. IV: *Medieval, the Inner Bailey*, London, 1985, 126–8 and 171.

34 *History of the King's Works*, vol. II, 639.

35 *History of the King's Works*, vol. II, 811.

36 A. J. Taylor, *The Jewel Tower, Westminster*, London, 1965 [Ministry of Works guidebook].

37 Quoted in S. Walker, 'John, Duke of Aquitaine and Duke of Lancaster, Styled King of Castile and León (1340–1399)', in *Oxford Dictionary of National Biography*: www.oxforddnb.com/view/article/14843 (accessed 8 August 2007).

38 A. Goodman, *John of Gaunt: The Exercise of Princely Power in 14th-century Europe*, London, 1992, 301–12.

39 Goodman, *John of Gaunt*, 48–9.

40 *John of Gaunt's Register*, ed. S. Armitage-Smith, 2 vols, Camden Series, third series, 20–1, London, 1911, vol. II, 122 (no. 1156).

41 Harvey, *English Mediaeval Architects*, 337–8.

42 M. W. Thompson 'Three Stages in the Construction of the Hall at Kenilworth Castle, Warwickshire', in *Ancient Monuments and their Interpretation*, ed. M. R. Apted, R. Gilyard-Beer and A. D. Saunders, London and Chichester, 1977, 217–18.

43 C. Norton, 'Le Mécénat du Duc Philippe le Hardi et de ses frères dans le domaine des Carrelages', in *Actes des journées internationales Claus Sluter*, ed. J.-P. Lecat, Dijon, 1992, 211–32.

44 Its only rival is the oriel in the Abbot's Lodgings at Westminster, which were also a product of the royal works in the 1370s. J. Goodall, 'Cheynegates, Westminster Abbey', *Country Life*, 204 (6 January 2010), 38–44.

45 R. K. Morris, *Kenilworth Castle*, London, 2006, 14–15 [English Heritage Red Guide]; and P. Brears, *Cooking and Dining in Medieval England*, Totnes, 2008, 173–201.

46 *John of Gaunt's Register*, vol. II, 259 (no. 1566). For a consideration of castle gardens in this period, see M. Whiteley, 'Relationship between Garden Park and Princely Residence in Medieval France', in *Architecture, jardin, paysage: l'environnement du château et de la villa au XVe et XVIe siècles. Actes du Colloque tenu à Tours, 1992*, ed. M. Chatenet, Paris, 1999, 91–102.

47 The National Archives, DL 43/15/7, cited in J. H. Harvey, 'Sidelights on Kenilworth Castle', *Archaeological Journal*, 101 (1944), 96 n. 3.

48 Goodman, *John of Gaunt*, 305; and *History of the King's Works*, vol. II, 901.

49 *John of Gaunt's Register*, vol. II, 242–3 (no. 1508).

50 L. F. Salzman, *Building in England down to 1540: A Documentary History*, Oxford, 1952, 459–60.

51 *History of the King's Works*, vol. III, pt 1, 254.

52 For a full discussion of Guy's Cliffe, see J. Goodall, 'Guy's Cliffe, Warwick', in *Medieval Art and Architecture in Coventry*, ed. Monckton and Morris.

53 For a short discussion of this dynastic patronage with references to further reading, see A. Payne, 'The Beauchamps and the Nevilles', in *Gothic: Art for England, 1400–1547*, ed. R. Marks and P. Williamson, exhibition catalogue, Victoria and Albert Museum, London, 2003, 219–21.

54 *The Rous Rol*, ed. W. Courthope, London, 1845, no. 57.

55 N. H. Nicholas, *Testamenta Vetusta*, vol. I, London, 1826, 79.

56 C. Fiennes, *Through England on a Side Saddle*, ed. E. W. Griffiths, London, 1888, 95.

57 Hammond, *A Relation of a Short Survey of the Western Counties*, ed. L. G. Wickham Legg, Camden Miscellany, 16, London, 1936, 31.

58 I am grateful to John Martin Robinson for the details of this sword.

59 L. L. Gee, *Women, Art and Patronage from Henry III to Edward III*, Woodbridge, 2002, 60.

60 Leland, *Itinerary*, vol. I, 75.

61 M. Hislop, 'The Castle of Ralph, 4th Baron Neville at Raby', *Archaeologia Aeliana*, fifth series, 20 (1992), 93–4.

62 J. F. Hodgson, 'Raby: In Three Chapters', *Transactions of the Architectural and Archaeological Society of Durham and Northumberland*, 3 (1880–85), 171.

63 Leland, *Itinerary*, vol. IV, 55.

64 Abbot Cummins, 'The Cave Chapels of Knaresborough', *Yorkshire Archaeological Journal*, 28 (1926), 80–8.

65 J. Goodall, *Warkworth Castle and Hermitage*, London, 2006, 28–31 [English Heritage Red Guide].

66 '. . . tapetas pro aula de antiques armis de Percy', *Testamenta Eboracensia*, ed. J. Raine, vol. I, Surtees Society, 4, London, 1836, 59.

67 R. M. Haines, 'Hatfield, Thomas (c.1310–1381)', in *Oxford Dictionary of National Biography*: www.oxforddnb.com/view/article/12598 (accessed 8 August 2007).

68 C. Wilson, 'The Neville Screen', in *Medieval Art and Architecture at Durham Cathedral*, ed. N. Coldstream and P. Draper, British Archaeological Association Conference Transactions, 3, Leeds, 1980, 98.

69 *VCH: Durham*, vol. III, London, 1928, 22

n. 60; and *Deputy Keeper of the Public Records Report*, 31 (1870), 113. Dated to the sixth year of Hatfield's pontificate.

70 J. Allibone, *Anthony Salvin: Pioneer of Gothic Revival, 1799–1881*, Columbia, MO, 1987, 132–3 and 164.

71 W. Hutchinson, *The History and Antiquities of the County Palatine of Durham*, vol. II, Newcastle, 1787, 285–6.

II THE TRIUMPH OF THE PERPENDICULAR

1 *The Anonimalle Chronicler, 1333–81*, ed. V. H. Galbraith, London, 1927, 102.

2 N. Saul, *Richard II*, New Haven and London, 1997, 339–45; and Saul, 'Richard II and the Vocabulary of Kingship', *English Historical Review*, 110 (1995), 854–77.

3 C. Wilson, 'Rulers, Artificers and Shoppers: Richard II's Remodelling of Westminster Hall, 1393–99', in *The Regal Image of Richard II and the Wilton Diptych*, ed. D. Gordon, L. Monnas and C. Elam, London, 1997, 45 and 280 nn. 55 and 56; T. Campbell, *Tapestry in the Renaissance: Art and Magnificence*, exhibition catalogue, Metropolitan Museum of Art, New York, 2002, 15–16.

4 A. Goodman, *John of Gaunt: The Exercise of Princely Power in 14th-Century Europe*, London, 1992, 79–80.

5 'Wyngefeld, Sternefelde and Huntyngfelde', *Calendar of Patent Rolls: Richard II, 1381–1385*, 555; and S. W. H. Aldwell, *Wingfield: Its Church, Castle and College*, Ipswich, 1925. A team headed by Rob Liddiard from the University of East Anglia is currently (2009–10) involved in a major reappraisal of this site.

6 *Complete Peerage*, vol. XII, pt 1, 430.

7 A. Tuck, 'Vere, Robert de, Ninth Earl of Oxford, Marquess of Dublin, and Duke of Ireland, (1362–1392)', in *Oxford Dictionary of National Biography*: www.oxforddnb.com/view/ article/28218 (accessed 8 August 2007).

8 F. Williams, *Pleshey Castle, Essex, 12th–16th Century: Excavations in the Bailey, 1959–63*, British Archaeological Reports British Series, 42, Oxford, 1977, 12.

9 [Viscount] Dillon and W. H. St John Hope, 'Inventory of the Goods and Chattels Belonging to Thomas, Duke of Gloucester', *Archaeological Journal*, 54 (1897), 275–308.

10 Leland, *Itinerary*, vol. IV, 91–2, though he elsewhere (vol. I, 5) attributes much of the work to 'Catarine of Spaine'.

11 *History of the King's Works*, vol. III, 250. An early seventeenth-century view of the castle from a map of 'The Perambulations of the Bounds of

Rockingham Forest' is displayed on information boards in the church (1999).

12 R. Marks, 'The Glazing of Fotheringhay Church and College', *Journal of the British Archaeological Association*, 131 (1978), 79–83.

13 Saul, *Richard II*, 155 n. 26.

14 Saul, *Richard II*, 154.

15 Thomas Walsingham, *Historia Anglicana*, ed. H. T. Riley, Rolls Series, 28, vol. II, London, 1864, 147.

16 S. Mitchell, 'Richard II: Kingship and the Cult of Saints', in *The Regal Image of Richard II*, ed. Gordon, Monnas and Elam, 117.

17 *History of the King's Works*, vol. I, 527–33.

18 Wilson, 'Rulers, Artificers and Shoppers', in *The Regal Image of Richard II*, 33–59.

19 Saul, *Richard II*, 381–3.

20 *VCH: County of Warwick*, vol. VI, London, 1951, 23; J. H. Edwards, 'Baginton Castle Excavations, 1933–48', *Birmingham Archaeological Society Transactions and Proceedings*, 69 (1951), 44–9; and a plan facing *Birmingham Archaeological Society Transactions and Proceedings*, 67 (1947–8), 14.

21 *History of the King's Works*, vol. I, 189–200.

22 C. Wilson, 'Yevele, Henry (d. 1400)', in *Oxford Dictionary of National Biography*: www. oxforddnb.com/view/article/30220 (accessed 8 August 2007); and Harvey, *English Mediaeval Architects*, 358–66. A thorough study that comes to a very different assessment of Yevele from that presented here is A. D. McLees, 'Henry Yevele: Disposer of the King's Works of Masonry', *Transactions of the British Archaeological Association*, third series, 36 (1973), 52–71.

23 S. Badham, 'Monumental Brasses and the Black Death: A Reappraisal', *Antiquaries Journal*, 80 (2000), 231–2.

24 R. G. Davies, 'Thomas Arundel as Archbishop of Canterbury, 1396–1414', *Journal of Ecclesiastical History*, 24 (1973), 9–21.

25 T. Tatton-Brown, 'The Abbey Precinct, Liberty and Estate', in *St Augustine's Abbey, Canterbury*, ed. R. Gem, London, 1997, 131.

26 F. Beeston, *An Archaeological Description of Saltwood Castle*, London, *circa* 1910, 51.

27 W. D. Peckham, 'The Architectural History of Amberley Castle', *Sussex Archaeological Collections*, 62 (1921), 31.

28 L. F. Salzman, 'The Property of the Earl of Arundel, 1397', Sussex Archaeological Collections, 91 (1953), 32–52; and C. Given-Wilson, 'Wealth and Credit, Public and Private: The Earls of Arundel, 1306–1397', *English Historical Review*, 106 (1991), 1–26.

29 M. T. Elvins, *Arundel Priory*, London, 1981, 7–19.

30 Harvey, *English Mediaeval Architects*, 360.

31 Elvins, *Arundel Priory*, 29–36.

32 Frustratingly little is known about this

building. See W. Hooper, *Reigate: Its Story Through the Ages*, Guildford, 1945, 44–9. J. Watson, *Memoirs of the Ancient Earls of Warren and Surrey*, Warrington, 1782, vol. I, includes a plan and engraving of the site.

33 R. Barber, 'Arundel, Sir John (c.1348–1379)', in *Oxford Dictionary of National Biography*: www.oxforddnb.com/view/article/718 (accessed 8 August 2007).

34 A 1690s drawing of Betchworth Castle survives in Aubrey's perambulation of Surrey of 1673: Oxford, Bodleian Library, MS Add. 25279, fol. 57a.

35 Goodman, *John of Gaunt*, 71 and 307.

36 *John of Gaunt's Register, 1379–1383*, ed. E. Lodge and R. Somerville, Camden third series, vol. CVI, London, 1937, xv.

37 N. Saul, *Death, Art and Memory in Medieval England: The Cobham Family and their Monuments, 1300–1500*, Oxford, 2001, 80–101.

38 Saul, *Death, Art and Memory*, 48–50. The receipt for the glass is dated 6 February 1383 (British Library, Harley Ch. 48 E 47).

39 Harvey, *English Mediaeval Architects*, 362.

40 M. J. Becker, *Rochester Bridge, 1357–1856: A History of its Early Years*, London, 1930, 13–31.

41 Leland, *Itinerary*, vol. V, 6; G. Home, *Old London Bridge*, London, 1931, 99–103. For the architectural context, see L. Monckton, 'The Collegiate Church of All Saints, Maidstone', in *Medieval Art, Architecture and Archaeology at Rochester*, ed. T. Ayers and T. Tatton-Brown, British Archaeological Association Conference Transactions, 28, Leeds, 2006, 308–12.

42 Harvey, *English Mediaeval Architects*, 76 and 273.

43 L. B. L., 'Cowling Castle', *Archaeologia Cantiana*, 2 (1859), 95–102; D. Knoop, G. P. Jones and N. B. Lewis, 'Some New Documents Concerning the Building of Cowling Castle and Cobham College', *Archaeologia Cantiana*, 46 (1934), 52–6; and W. A. Scott Robertson, 'Coulyng Castle', *Archaeologia Cantiana*, 11 (1877), 128–44.

44 N. Saul, *Scenes from Provincial Life: Knightly Families in Sussex, 1280–1400*, Oxford, 1986, 68–9.

45 *History of Parliament: The House of Commons, 1386–1421*, ed. J. S. Roskell, L. Clark and C. Rawcliffe, vol. II, Stroud, 1992, 738–41.

46 S. Walker, *The Lancastrian Affinity, 1361–1399*, Oxford, 1990, 127–41. I am grateful to Nigel Saul for this reference.

47 *VCH: County of Oxford*, vol. VIII, London, 1964, 178–83; A. Emery, *Greater Medieval Houses of England and Wales*, vol. III: *Southern England*, Cambridge, 2006, 153; and *Complete Peerage*, vol. VIII, 51–2.

48 D. J. Turner, 'Bodiam Castle: True Castle or Old Soldier's Dream House?', in *England in the 14th Century: Proceedings of the 1985 Harlaxton Symposium*, ed. W. Ormrod, Woodbridge, 1986, 267–77; and C. Coulson, 'Some Analysis of the Castle of Bodiam, East Sussex', *Ideals and Practice of Medieval Knighthood*, 4 (1992), 51–107.

49 *History of the King's Works*, vol. II, 851, 813 and 594.

50 *History of the King's Works*, vol. II, 803–4.

51 M. Jones, 'Ashton, Sir Robert (d. 1384)', in *Oxford Dictionary of National Biography*: www.oxforddnb.com/view/article/777 (accessed 13 August 2007).

52 *History of the King's Works*, vol. II, 789–90.

53 J. Kenyon, 'Early Artillery Fortifications in England and Wales: A Preliminary Survey and Reappraisal', *Archaeological Journal*, 138 (1981), 205–40.

54 J. Goodall, 'Cheynegates, Westminster Abbey', *Country Life*, 204 (6 January 2010), 38–44.

55 B. Cunliffe and J. Munby, *Excavations at Portchester Castle*, vol. IV: *Medieval, the Inner Bailey*, London, 1985, 184–205 and 304–6.

56 M. Binney, 'Penshurst Place, I', *Country Life*, 151 (9 March 1972), 554–8; A. Emery, *Greater Medieval Houses*, vol. III: *Southern England*, 386–94; C. Rawcliffe, 'Devereux, John, Baron Devereux (d. 1393)', in *Oxford Dictionary of National Biography*: www.oxforddnb.com/view/article/7564 (accessed 13 August 2007).

57 Saul, *Richard II*, 116, 120–1 and 164.

58 J. Gillespie, 'Dover Castle: Key to Richard II's Kingdom', *Archaeologia Cantiana*, 105 (1988), 187–9.

59 J. L. Leland, 'Burley, Sir Simon (1336?–1388)', in *Oxford Dictionary of National Biography*: www.oxforddnb.com/view/article/4036 (accessed 13 August 2007).

60 *History of the King's Works*, vol. II, 623.

61 C. Platt, *Medieval Southampton*, London and Boston, MA, 1973, 125–9.

62 Harvey, *English Mediaeval Architects*, 352–6.

63 *History of the King's Works*, vol. II, 842–4.

64 Leland, *Itinerary*, vol. I, 277.

65 J. N. Hare. 'Bishop's Waltham Palace', *Archaeological Journal*, 145 (1988), 222–54.

66 J. Crook and Y. Kusuba, 'The Perpendicular Remodelling of the Nave: Problems and Interpretations', in *Winchester Cathedral: Nine Hundred Years, 1093–1993*, ed. J. Crook, Chichester, 1993, 215–30.

67 *Calendar of Patent Rolls: Richard II, 1391–1396*, 261.

68 S. Walker, 'Lovell, John, Fifth Baron Lovell (c.1342–1408)', in *Oxford Dictionary of National Biography*: www.oxforddnb.com/view/article/53092 (accessed 20 August 2007).

69 L. Keen, 'Excavations at Old Wardour Castle, Wiltshire', *Wiltshire Archaeological and Natural History Magazine*, 62 (1967), 67–78.

70 One of many circumstantial pieces of evidence for this is that the probable builder, Drouet, was in the duke's household only from 1398. A. de Champeaux and P. Gauchery, *Les Travaux d'art exécutés pour Jean de France, duc de Berry*, Paris, 1894, 78.

71 Emery, *Greater Medieval Houses*, vol. III: *Southern England*, 534–49; and A. Emery, *Dartington Hall*, Oxford, 1970.

72 *History of Parliament: House of Commons, 1386–1421*, vol. II, 670–3.

73 J. A. Tuck, 'Richard II and the Border Magnates', *Northern History*, 3 (1968), 27–52; and R. L. Storey, 'The Wardens of the Northern Marches of England towards Scotland', *English Historical Review*, 72 (1957), 593–615.

74 J. M. W. Bean, 'Percy, Henry, First Earl of Northumberland (1341–1408)', in *Oxford Dictionary of National Biography*: www.oxforddnb.com/view/article/21932 (accessed 13 August 2007).

75 Harvey, *English Mediaeval Architects*, 181.

76 From his work with Stephen Priestly on the Windsor building accounts Steven Brindle has kindly passed on references to two stone layers: John Lewy, working for 30 days at 5d. in 1361–2, and 30 and 112 days at 5d. in 1362–3; and John Lewy (senior) working for 112 days in 1362–3.

77 M. J. B. Hislop, 'John Lewyn of Durham: A North Country Master Mason of the 14th Century', *Journal of the British Archaeological Association*, 151 (1998), 170–89; E. Cambridge, 'The Masons and Building Works of Durham Priory, 1339–1539', unpublished PH.D thesis, University of Durham, 1992, 254–69; and John Harvey, 'Lewyn, John (fl. 1364–1398)', rev. C. Wilson, in *Oxford Dictionary of National Biography*: www.oxforddnb.com/view/article/37675 (accessed 13 August 2007).

78 C. Wilson, 'The Neville Screen', in *Medieval Art and Architecture at Durham Cathedral*, ed. N. Coldstream and P. Draper, British Archaeological Association Conference Transactions, 3, Leeds, 1980, 90–104.

79 *History of the King's Works*, vol. II, 819–20.

80 R. Gilyard-Beer, 'De Ireby's Tower in Carlisle Castle', in *Ancient Monuments and their Interpretation*, ed. M. R. Apted, R. Gilyard-Beer and A. D. Saunders, London and Chichester, 1977, 191–210.

81 M. Hislop, 'John of Gaunt's Building Works at Dunstanburgh Castle', *Archaeologia Aeliana*, fifth series, 23 (1995), 139–44.

82 Leland, *Itinerary*, vol. V, 139.

83 *VCH: County of York*, vol. III, London, 1913, 246; and J. Goodall, *Richmond Castle and Easby Abbey*, London, 2001, 31 [English Heritage guidebook].

84 M. Hislop, 'Bolton Castle and the Practice of Architecture in the Middle Ages', *Journal of the British Archaeological Association*, 149 (1996), 10–

22, with a transcription of the contract by A. Hislop.

85 M. Hislop, 'The Date of the Warkworth Donjon', *Archaeologia Aeliana*, fifth series, 19 (1991), 79–92.

86 A. Tuck, 'Neville, Ralph, First Earl of Westmorland (c.1364–1425)', in *Oxford Dictionary of National Biography*: www.oxforddnb.com/view/article/19951 (accessed 13 August 2007).

87 Leland, *Itinerary*, vol. 1, 71–2.

88 J. Allibone, *Anthony Salvin: Pioneer of Gothic Revival Architecture, 1799–1881*, Columbia, MO, 1987, 2–11.

89 C. Surtees, *The History of the Castle at Brancepeth*, London, 1920, 6–12.

90 M. Hislop, 'The Castle of Ralph, 4th Baron Neville at Raby', *Archaeologia Aeliana*, fifth series, 20 (1992), 91–7.

91 Leland, *Itinerary*, vol. 1, 65.

92 A. L. Brown, 'Percy, Thomas, Earl of Worcester (c.1343–1403)', in *Oxford Dictionary of National Biography*: www.oxforddnb.com/view/article/21955 (accessed 30 December 2007).

93 M. Hislop, 'Lumley Castle: Its Antecedents and its Architect', *Archaeologia Aeliana*, fifth series, 24 (1996), 83–98.

94 B. Morley, 'Hylton Castle', *Archaeological Journal*, 133 (1976), 118–34.

95 *History of Parliament: House of Commons, 1386–1421*, vol. III, 731–3.

96 S. Brindle and S. Priestley, 'Edward III's Building Campaigns at Windsor and the Employment of Masons', in *St George's Chapel, Windsor, in the Fourteenth Century*, ed. N. Saul, Woodbridge, 2005, 221–2.

97 Harvey, *English Mediaeval Architects*, 275.

98 R. Morris, 'Later Gothic Architecture in South Wales', in *Cardiff: Architecture and Archaeology in the Medieval Diocese of Llandaff*, ed. J. R. Kenyon and D. M. Williams, British Archaeological Association Conference Transactions, 29, Leeds, 2006, 126.

99 W. B. Jones and E. A. Freeman, *The History and Antiquities of St David's*, London, 1856, 179–89.

100 R. Turner, *Lamphey Palace and Llawhaden Castle*, rev. edn, Cardiff, 2000, 30 and 33 [CADW guidebook].

101 S. Walker, 'Letters to the Dukes of Lancaster in 1381 and 1399', *English Historical Review*, 106 (1991), 75–9. I am grateful to Nigel Saul for this reference.

102 C. Wilson, 'The Tomb of Henry IV and the Holy Oil of St Thomas of Canterbury', in *Medieval Architecture and its Intellectual Context: Studies in Honour of Peter Kidson*, ed. E. Fernie and P. Crossley, London and Ronceverte, 1990, 181–90.

12 THE LANCASTRIAN AGE

1 Harvey, *English Mediaeval Architects*, 187–9.

2 Harvey, *English Mediaeval Architects*, 188; and C. Wilson, 'Yevele, Henry (d. 1400)', in *Oxford Dictionary of National Biography*, Oxford, 2004: www.oxforddnb.com/view/article/30220 (accessed 4 January 2010).

3 Harvey, *English Mediaeval Architects*, 330–1.

4 Harvey, *English Mediaeval Architects*, 159.

5 G. Vasari, 'Filippo Brunelleschi, scultore et architetto', *Le vite* [1568], vol. III, 155–6: http://biblio.signum.sns.it/cgi-bin/vasari/Vasari-all?code_f=print_page&work=Torrentiniana&volume_n=3&page_n=155.

6 *History of the King's Works*, vol. II, 848–9.

7 F. R. H. du Boulay, 'Henry of Derby's Expeditions to Prussia, 1390–91 and 1392', in *The Reign of Richard II: Essays in Honour of May McKisack*, ed. F. R. H. du Boulay and C. M. Barron, London, 1971, 153–72.

8 A. L. Brown and H. Summerson, 'Henry IV (1366–1413)', in *Oxford Dictionary of National Biography*: www.oxforddnb.com/view/article/12951 (accessed 4 January 2010).

9 *History of the King's Works*, vol. II, 692–3.

10 *VCH: Lancaster*, vol. VIII, London, 1914; and E. W. Cox, 'Lancaster Castle', *Transactions of the Historic Society of Lancashire and Cheshire*, 48 (1896), 106–7 and 114–16.

11 I. Roberts, *Pontefract Castle: Archaeological Excavations, 1982–6*, Leeds, 2002, 56–7.

12 *History of the King's Works*, vol. II, 703.

13 Harvey, *English Mediaeval Architects*, 275; and *History of the King's Works*, vol. II, 847–8.

14 Roberts, *Pontefract Castle*, 47–50.

15 *History of the King's Works*, vol. II, 677.

16 J. Kenyon, *Kidwelly Castle*, rev. edn, Cardiff, 2007, 17–21 [CADW guidebook].

17 J. M. W. Bean, 'Henry IV and the Percies', *History*, 44 (1959), 212–27.

18 *Proceedings and Ordinances of the Privy Council of England*, vol. I: *1386–1410*, ed. Sir Harris Nicolas, London, 1834, 215–16.

19 *Proceedings and Ordinances of the Privy Council*, vol. I, 275.

20 *History of the King's Works*, vol. II, 262.

21 J. Knight, 'Newport Castle', *Monmouthshire Antiquary*, 7 (1991), 25–6.

22 *A History of Northumberland*, vol. VI, 75–8; and A. Emery, *Greater Medieval Houses of England and Wales*, vol. I: *Northern England*, Cambridge, 1996, 62.

23 A. C. Reeves, 'Fitzhugh, Henry, Third Baron Fitzhugh (1363?–1425)', in *Oxford Dictionary of National Biography*: www.oxforddnb.com/view/article/50151 (accessed 23 December 2007).

24 M. J. Bennett, 'Stanley, Sir John (c.1350–1414)', in *Oxford Dictionary of National Biography*: www.oxforddnb.com/view/article/26275 (accessed 4 January 2010).

25 C. M. Fraser, 'Langley, Thomas (c.1360–1437)', in *Oxford Dictionary of National Biography*: www.oxforddnb.com/view/article/16027 (accessed 23 December 2007).

26 *VCH: Durham*, vol. III, London, 1928, 25; and M. Johnson, 'The Great North Gate of Durham Castle', *Durham and Northumberland Architectural and Archaeological Society Transactions*, new series, 4 (1978), 111.

27 *Historiae Dunelmensis Scriptores Tres*, ed. J. Raine, Surtees Society, 9, Newcastle, 1839, 146–7.

28 Harvey, *English Mediaeval Architects*, 194.

29 *Historiae Dunelmensis Scriptores Tres*, 146–7.

30 *Historiae Dunelmensis Scriptores Tres*, 146.

31 P. Dixon, 'The Great Tower in the 12th Century: The Case of Norham Castle', *Archaeological Journal*, 150 (1993), 426–7.

32 J. Raine, *The History and Antiquities of North Durham*, London, 1852, 287; and Harvey, *English Mediaeval Architects*, 107.

33 *Historiae Dunelmensis Scriptores Tres*, 146.

34 R. L. Storey, *Thomas Langley and the Bishopric of Durham, 1406–1435*, London, 1961, 86–92, 188 and 196–7.

35 *History of the King's Works*, vol. II, 998.

36 *History of the King's Works*, vol. II, 1000.

37 *Gothic: Art for England, 1400–1547*, ed. R. Marks and P. Williamson, exhibition catalogue, Victoria and Albert Museum, London, 2003, 283.

38 This section is much indebted to the work of Nicholas J. Moore, who kindly bequeathed his archive of research to me. One valuable, but dated, work on this subject is N. Lloyd, *A History of English Brickwork*, London, 1925.

39 A. F. Leach, 'The Building of Beverley Bar', *Transactions of the East Riding Antiquarian Society*, 4 (1896), 26–49.

40 N. J. Moore, 'Brick', in *English Medieval Industries*, ed. J. Blair and N. Ramsey, London, 1991, 227–9.

41 H. J. Böker, *Die mittelalterliche Backsteinarchitektur Norddeutschlands*, Darmstadt, 1988, 268–77.

42 See *VCH: County of Oxford*, vol. VIII, London, 1964, 141–7; and J. Goodall, 'Stonor Park, II', *Country Life*, 195 (12 April 2001), 62–5.

43 *Kingsford's Stonor Letters and Papers*, ed. C. Carpenter, Cambridge, 1996, 117–18.

44 J. Foyle, 'Syon Park: Rediscovering Medieval England's Only Bridgettine Monastery', *Current Archaeology*, 192 (June 2004), 550–5.

45 Leland, *Itinerary*, vol. II, 48.

46 The fortifications were to be built of stones, lime and 'brik'. *Calendar of Patent Rolls: Henry VI, 1422–1429*, 351.

47 M. Biddle, L. Barfield and A. Millard,

'The Excavation of the Manor, Rickmansworth, Hertfordshire', *Archaeological Journal*, 116 (1959), 136–99.

48   *Calendar of Patent Rolls: Henry VI, 1429–1436*, 250; and P. Dixon, *Excavations at Greenwich Palace, 1970–71*, London, 1972 [pamphlet report].

49   A. Smith, '"The Greatest Man of that Age": The Acquisition of Sir John Fastolf's East Anglian Estates', in *Rulers and Ruled in Late Medieval England: Essays Presented to Gerald Harriss*, ed. R. E. Archer and S. Walker, London, 1995, 137–54.

50   *The Paston Letters, 1422–1509 AD*, ed. J. Gairdner, 6 vols, London, 1904; reprinted Gloucester, 1986, vol. IV, 235 (no. 638): 'Item. Considerandum est quod, ulta dictas perquisiciones, edifficacio manerii de Castre velut fortalicium defensionis patrie constabat in triginta annis vjm li.'

51   H. D. Barnes and W. D. Simpson, 'The Building Accounts of Caister Castle, 1432–5', *Norfolk Archaeology*, 30 (1952), 178–88.

52   Harvey, *English Mediaeval Architects*, 341.

53   T. P. Smith, 'Rye House, Hertfordshire, and Aspects of Early Brickwork in England', *Archaeological Journal*, 132 (1975), 111–51; and Smith, 'The Early Brickwork of Someries Castle, Bedfordshire, and its Place in the History of English Brick Building', *Journal of the British Archaeological Association*, 129 (1976), 42–58.

54   *William Worcestre: Itineraries*, ed. J. Harvey, Oxford, 1969, 46–9; and R. T. Andrews, 'The Rye House Castle and the Manor of Rye', *East Hertfordshire Archaeological Society Transactions*, 2, pt 1 (1902), 32–45.

55   J. Goodall, *God's House at Ewelme: Life, Art and Devotion in a Medieval Almshouse*, Aldershot, 2001, 293–5.

56   T. P. Smith, *The Medieval Brickmaking Industry in England, 1400–1450*, British Archaeological Reports British Series, 138, Oxford, 1985, 32–4.

57   W. D. Simpson, 'The Building Accounts of Tattershall Castle, 1434–72', *Lincoln Record Society*, 55 (1960), 32.

58   Simpson, 'Building Accounts of Tattershall Castle', 36.

59   A detail particularly well preserved on the second-floor corridor vault. This finish remained popular in brick interiors throughout the fifteenth century and can be seen, for example, at Hunsdon (Hertfordshire) from *circa* 1450; Oxburgh (Norfolk), where it is restored; and Hadleigh (Suffolk), *circa* 1480.

60   *Calendar of Patent Rolls: Henry VI, 1441–1446*, 402–3.

61   *Calendar of Patent Rolls: Henry VI, 1446–1452*, 77. The tower is described in the licence as being made of 'stones with lime and sand', evi-dence of how indifferent a patron might be to materials.

62   An arrangement clearly apparent in a drawing dated 9 July 1773 in Oxford, Bodleian Library, Gough Herts 18, after page 252.

63   *William Worcestre*, ed. Harvey, 50–1.

64   S. J. Payling, 'Cornwall, John, Baron Fanhope (*d.* 1443)', in *Oxford Dictionary of National Biography*: www.oxforddnb.com/view/article/54423 (accessed 10 February 2009).

65   Leland, *Itinerary*, vol. I, 102–3 (and vol. V, 8).

66   *VCH: County of Bedford*, vol. III, London, 1912, 270–3; *Gentleman's Magazine*, third series, 32 (London, 1849), 479; and M. S. F. George, 'The Builder of Ampthill Castle', *Bedfordshire Magazine*, 5 (1956), 185.

67   S. J. Payling, 'The Ampthill Dispute: A Study in Aristocratic Lawlessness and the Breakdown of Lancastrian Government', *English Historical Review*, 413 (1989), 881–907.

68   J. Ashbee, *Goodrich Castle*, London, 2005, 38–9 [English Heritage Red Guide]. A drafted – but unpublished – monograph on the castle produced for English Heritage by Ron Shoesmith, Bruce Copplestone-Crow and Pat Hughes contains a detailed consideration of this.

69   C. Kightly, 'Hungerford, Walter, First Baron Hungerford (1378–1449)', in *Oxford Dictionary of National Biography*: www.oxforddnb.com/view/article/14181 (accessed 24 December 2007).

70   T. J. Miles and A. D. Saunders, 'The Chantry Priest's House at Farleigh Hungerford Castle', *Medieval Archaeology*, 19 (1975), 176–8.

71   T. Turville-Petre, 'The Persecution of Elizabeth Swillington by Ralph, Lord Cromwell', *Nottingham Medieval Studies*, 42 (1998), 174–87.

72   *Paston Letters*, vol. II, 101 (no. 88).

73   R. Turner and S. Priestley, 'The Hunting Preserves', in *Chepstow Castle: Its History and Buildings*, ed. R. Turner and A. Johnson, Almeley, 2006, 185–98.

74   M. Whiteley, 'Relationship between Garden Park and Princely Residence in Medieval France', *Architecture, jardin, paysage: l'environnement du château et de la villa au XVe et XVIe siècles. Actes du Colloque tenu à Tours, 1992*, Paris, 1999, 91–102.

75   M. W. Thompson, 'Reclamation of Waste Ground for the Pleasance at Kenilworth Castle, Warwickshire', *Medieval Archaeology*, 8 (1964), 222–3.

76   M. W. Phelps, 'The Pleasaunce, Kenilworth', *Birmingham Archaeological Society Transactions and Proceedings*, 49 (1923), 61–2.

77   M. Meiss, *French Painting in the Time of Jean de Berry: The Limbourgs and their Contemporaries*, vol. I, London, 1974, 204.

78   *VCH: County of Warwick*, vol. VIII, London, 1969, 469.

79   *History of the King's Works*, vol. II, 901; and A. Goodman, *John of Gaunt: The Exercise of Princely Power in 14th-century Europe*, London, 1992, 305.

80   M. L. Robertson, 'Court Careers and County Quarrels: George Hastings and Leicestershire Unrest, 1509–1529', in *State, Sovereigns and Society in Early Modern England: Essays in Honour of A. J. Slavin*, ed. C. Carlton et al., Stroud, 1997, 161.

81   Leland, *Itinerary*, vol. IV, 115.

82   For a more detailed consideration of what follows, see J. Goodall, 'A Medieval Masterpiece: Herstmonceux Castle, Sussex', *Burlington Magazine*, 146, no. 1217 (August 2004), 516–25.

13   THE YORKIST AND EARLY TUDOR SETTLEMENT

1   *The Paston Letters, 1422–1509 AD*, ed. J. Gairdner, 6 vols, London, 1904; reprinted Gloucester, 1986, vol. IV, no. 533.

2   John Warkworth, *A Chronicle of the First Thirteen Years of the Reign of King Edward the Fourth*, ed. J. O. Halliwell, Camden Society, old series, 10, London, 1839, 37–9.

3   Warkworth, *A Chronicle*, 25; M. Biddle, L. Barfield and A. Millard, 'The Excavation of the Manor, Rickmansworth, Hertfordshire', *Archaeological Journal*, 116 (1959), 136–99.

4   *Calendar of Patent Rolls: Henry VI, 1422–1429*, 351.

5   R. A. Griffiths, 'Herbert, William, First Earl of Pembroke (c.1423–1469)', in *Oxford Dictionary of National Biography*: www.oxforddnb.com/view article/13053 (accessed 12 January 2009).

6   Warkworth, *A Chronicle*, 3.

7   Griffiths, 'Herbert, William, First Earl of Pembroke'.

8   J. H. Parker, *The Architectural Antiquities of the City of Wells*, Oxford, 1860; and C. H. Clough, 'Gunthorpe, John (*d.* 1498)', in *Oxford Dictionary of National Biography*: www.oxforddnb.com/view/article/11752 (accessed 13 January 2009).

9   Parker, *Architectural Antiquities of the City of Wells*; and Clough, 'Gunthorpe, John'.

10   Leland, *Itinerary*, vol. I, 97–8.

11   *History of Parliament: Biographies of the Members of the Commons House, 1439–1509*, by J. C. Wedgewood and A. D. Holt, vol. I, London, 1936, 208–9.

12   *Royal Commission on Historical Monuments of England: Essex*, vol. II: *Central and South-West*, London, 1921, 208.

13   F. Grose, *The Antiquities of England and*

Wales, London, 1772–5, vol. I, no page numbers. The drawings are dated 1773.

14 M. Hicks, *False, Fleeting, Perjur'd Clarence*, Gloucester, 1992, 169.

15 Warkworth, *A Chronicle*, 8.

16 M. J. Bennett, 'Stanley, Thomas, First Earl of Derby (*c.*1433–1504)', in *Oxford Dictionary of National Biography*: www.oxforddnb.com/view/article/26279 (accessed 10 January 2010).

17 *William Worcestre: Itineraries*, ed. J. Harvey, Oxford, 1969, 186–91.

18 *The Rous Rol*, ed. W. Courthope, London, 1845, no. 59.

19 P. Henderson, 'Life at the Top: 16th- and 17th-century Roofscapes', *Country Life*, 177 (3 January 1985), 6–9; and M. Girouard, 'Feasts of Delight', *Country Life*, 203 (25 November 2009), 77–80.

20 A. J. Pollard, 'St Cuthbert and the Hog: Richard III and the County Palatine of Durham, 1471–85', in *Kings and Nobles in the Later Middle Ages*, ed. R. A. Griffiths and J. Sherborne, Stroud and New York, 1986, 109–29.

21 For the literature on the castle, see D. R. Perriam and J. Robinson, *The Medieval Fortified Buildings of Cumbria*, Cumberland and Westmorland Antiquarian and Archaeological Society, extra series, 29, 1998, 212.

22 M. McCarthy, H. Summerson and R. Annis, *Carlisle Castle*, English Heritage Archaeological Report, 18, London, 1990, 161–2.

23 P. Mayes and L. Butler, *Sandal Castle Excavations, 1964–73*, Wakefield, 1983, 5 and 18–19.

24 D. Austin, *Acts of Perception: A Study of Barnard Castle in Teesdale*, English Heritage and the Architectural and Archaeological Society of Durham and Northumberland, Research Report no. 6, vol. I, Durham, 2007, 76.

25 Philippe de Commynes, *Memoirs: The Reign of Louis IX, 1461–83*, trans. M. Jones, Harmondsworth, 1972, 360–1.

26 *Calendar of the Charter Rolls, 1427–1516*, vol. VI, London, 1927, 242. The previous page also has a licence for the establishment of markets at Ashby.

27 San Marino, CA, Huntington Library, Map Drawer II U2 (formerly HAM Box 22, [3]), fol. 14r. The operation continued until the sequence of accounts ceased in 1477–8.

28 Huntington Library, Hastings Miscellaneous Box 13 (Dugdale MSS, dated 1677), numbered page 19.

29 A. H. Thompson, 'The Building Accounts of Kirby Muxloe Castle, 1480–4', *Transactions of the Leicestershire Archaeological Society*, 11 (1913–20), 193–345.

30 Harvey, *English Mediaeval Architects*, 73.

31 Thompson, 'Building Accounts of Kirby Muxloe Castle', 333.

32 Payments to a mason, Henry Crane, for making a grate for the great pool. Huntington Library, HAM Oversize Box 6 (formerly HAM Box 58A), fol. 22h.

33 Leland, *Itinerary*, vol. I, 20.

34 Huntington Library, HAM Oversize Box 9 (formerly HAM Box 58), fols 3A and 2KV.

35 G. Moodey, 'The Restoration of Hertford Castle Gatehouse', *Hertfordshire Archaeology*, 3 (1973), 100–9; and *History of the King's Works*, vol. II, 677–81.

36 T. Tatton-Brown, 'The Constructional Sequence and Topography of the Chapel and College Buildings at St George's', in *St George's Chapel, Windsor, in the Late Middle Ages*, ed. C. Richmond and E. Scarff, Windsor, 2001, 6.

37 The very unusual panelling of the eastern aisle at Windsor, for example, is paralleled in the chancel walls and windows at Warwick.

38 C. Wilson, 'Janyns, Henry (fl. 1453–1483)', in *Oxford Dictionary of National Biography*: www.oxforddnb.com/view/article/42237 (accessed 13 July 2008); and Harvey, *English Mediaeval Architects*, 159.

39 A. F. Sutton and L. Visser-Fuchs, 'The Reburial of Richard, Duke of York, 21–30 July 1476', *The Ricardian*, 10 (1994), 122–65.

40 J. Skelton, *Complete Poems*, ed. P. Henderson, London, 1959, 2–4.

41 W. Darell, *A History of Dover Castle*, London, 1786, 26, 36, 37, 60–1.

42 M. Caviness, *The Windows of Christchurch Cathedral, Canterbury*, Corpus Vitrearum Medii Aevi, 2, London, 1981, 251–73.

43 *History of the King's Works*, vol. II, 641.

44 *History of the King's Works*, vol. II, 936–7.

45 Leland, *Itinerary*, vol. I, 95–6.

46 Huntington Library, Huntingdon Papers, Personal Papers, Box 4.

47 John Stow, *A Survey of London by John Stow . . . Reprinted from the Text of 1603*, ed. C. L. Kingsford, vol. I, Oxford, 1908, 48–9.

48 R. A. Griffiths, 'Ludlow during the Wars of the Roses', in *Ludlow Castle: Its History and Buildings*, ed. R. Shoesmith and A. Johnson, Logaston, 2000, 57–68; and W. H. St John Hope, 'The Castle of Ludlow', *Archaeologia*, 61 (1908), 304–16.

49 Thomas More, 'The History of King Richard the Thirde (1513)', in *The Works of Sir Thomas More*, London, 1557, 53–5.

50 *History of the King's Works*, vol. II, 894.

51 *The Rous Rol*, ed. Courthope, no. 17.

52 Leland, *Itinerary*, vol. II, 40.

53 Leland, *Itinerary*, vol. I, 60; *VCH: County of York: North Riding*, vol. II, London, 1923, 542 and 551.

54 *History of the King's Works*, vol. III, 5.

55 As shown in a survey of 1610, Essex Record Office, D/DMHP1. Reproduced in A. Emery, *Greater Medieval Houses of England and Wales, 1300–1500*, vol. II: *East Anglia, Central England and Wales*, Cambridge, 2000, 113.

56 W. M. Palmer *William Cole of Milton*, Cambridge, 1935, 90.

57 A transcript of the seventeenth-century manuscript describing the life of Sir Rhys appears in *The Cambrian Register for 1795*, London, 1796. The joust is described within it on pp. 123–34.

58 D. J. C. Cathcart-King and J. C. Perks, 'Carew Castle, Pembrokeshire', *Archaeological Journal*, 119 (1962), 304–5.

59 J. Lewis, 'Lathom House: The Northern Court', *Journal of the British Archaeological Association*, 152 (1999), 150–71.

60 B. Coward, *The Stanleys: Lords Stanley and Earls of Derby, 1385–1672*, Manchester, 1985, 20.

61 *VCH: County of Oxford*, vol. IX, London, 1969, 112–13.

62 *VCH: County of Oxford*, vol. IX, figure of Hanwell Castle and 114 n. 39.

63 *Gothic: Art for England, 1400–1547*, ed. R. Marks and P. Williamson, exhibition catalogue, Victoria and Albert Museum, London, 2003, 284–5.

64 *Letters and Papers: Henry VIII*, vol. III (1), 508–9. For a conjectural reconstruction by S. Conlin of the building *circa* 1680 following further sixteenth-century remodelling, see S. Thurley, 'Kimbolton Castle', *Country Life*, 200 (30 March 2006), 69.

65 J. Leland, *Iohannis Lelandi Antiquarii de Rebus Britannicis Collectanea*, ed. T. Hearne, vol. IV, London, 1770, 210.

66 *History of the King's Works*, vol. III, 258.

67 M. K. Jones and M. G. Underwood, *The King's Mother: Lady Margaret Beaufort, Countess of Richmond and Derby*, Cambridge, 1992, 71–2.

68 For a discussion of this, see D. Starkey, *The Reign of Henry VIII: Personalities and Politics*, London, 1985, 22–6.

69 Wilson, 'Janyns, Henry'.

70 C. Wilson, 'The Designer of Henry VII's Chapel, Westminster Abbey', in *The Reign of Henry VII: Proceedings of the 1993 Harlaxton Symposium*, ed. B. Thompson, Stamford, 1995, 144–5.

71 The details of the reconstruction require further elucidation. For two views, see S. Thurley, *The Royal Palaces of Tudor England*, New Haven and London, 1993, 27–32; and *History of the King's Works*, vol. IV, 224–7. If the principal lodgings of the Lancastrian palace were in the timber-frame 'Byflete', Thurley's idea that the lodgings is a recast fifteenth-century *donjon* cannot be correct.

72 Stow, *Survey of London*, vol. I, 66–7. See also P. Marsden, 'Baynard's Castle', *Medieval Archaeology*, 17 (1973), 162–3; and J. H. MacMichael, 'Baynard's Castle and Excavations on the Site',

Journal of the British Archaeological Association, 46 (1890), 173–84.

73 See V. Davis, *William Waynflete, Bishop and Educationalist*, Woodbridge, 1993.

74 R. Marks, *Stained Glass of the Collegiate Church of the Holy Trinity, Tattershall*, London and New York, 1984, 22; and Harvey, *English Mediaeval Architects*, 73–4.

75 Harvey, *English Mediaeval Architects*, 220–3.

76 Harvey, *English Mediaeval Architects*, 73–4.

77 R. Chandler, *The Life of William Waynflete*, London, 1811, 368.

78 Chandler, *Life of William Waynflete*, 369–70.

79 Oxford, Bodleian Library, MS Aubrey 4, fols 45r and 45br.

80 Leland, *Itinerary*, vol. IV, 29.

81 *Royal Commission on Historical Monuments of England: Huntingdonshire*, London, 1926, 34–7; *VCH: County of Huntingdon*, vol. II, London, 1932, 260–64; and *Gentleman's Magazine*, new series, 15 (1841), pt I, 241–7.

82 P. Marshall and J. Samuels, *Guardian of the Trent: The Story of Newark Castle*, Newark, 1997, 37.

83 C. Harper-Bill, 'Morton, John (d. 1500)', in *Oxford Dictionary of National Biography*: www.oxforddnb.com/view/article/19363 (accessed 26 February 2007).

84 For two accounts of his career, see Harvey, *English Mediaeval Architects*, 316–25; and F. Woodman, *The Architectural History of King's College Chapel*, London, 1986, 197–204.

85 A. Hussey, 'Ford Manor House and Lands in 1647', *Archaeologia Cantiana*, 26 (1904), 119–32; B. J. Bennett, 'Ford Manor', *Archaeologia Cantiana*, 45 (1933), 168–73; T. Tatton-Brown, *Lambeth Palace*, London, 2000, 55–8; and H. Gough, 'The Archbishop's Manor at Ford, Hoath', *Archaeologia Cantiana*, 121 (2001), 251–68.

86 Harvey, *English Mediaeval Architects*, 55–6.

87 A. Wood, *Athenae Oxonienses*, London, 1721, 665.

88 I am grateful to Peter Brears for his notes on the kitchen. See his analysis in *Cooking and Dining in Medieval England*, Totnes, 2008.

89 Quoted in *VCH: Durham*, vol. III, London, 1928, 27.

90 Leland, *Iohannis Lelandi Antiquarii*, vol. IV, 276–7.

91 '. . . quamvis archiepiscopus in altiori solio sedisset, se tamen in pinguiori collocatum', in *Matthaei Parker Cantuariensis Archiepiscopi de Antiquitate Britannicae Ecclesiae etc.*, ed. S. Drake, London, 1739, 461.

92 C. Tracy, 'Master William Pykenham, LL.D (c.1425–97), Scholar, Churchman, Lawyer and Gatehouse Builder', *Proceedings of the Suffolk Institute of Archaeology and History*, 41 (2007), 292–3.

1 For example, G. Vasari, 'Proemio', *Le Vite* (1568), vol. III, 5: 'o vogliamole chiamare età, da la rinascita di queste arti sino al secolo che noi viviamo': http://biblio.signum.sns.it/cgi-bin/vasari/Vasari-all?code_f=print_page&work=Giuntina&volume_n=3&page_n=5.

2 For a recent discussion of England's reception of classicism, see M. Girouard, *Elizabethan Architecture*, New Haven and London, 2009, 126–216.

3 Quoted in D. Starkey, *The Reign of Henry VIII*, London, 1985, 41.

4 Leland, *Itinerary*, vol. II, 48, and vol. V, 155.

5 J. Newman, 'Cardinal Wolsey's Collegiate Foundations', in *Cardinal Wolsey: Church, State and Art*, ed. S. Gunn and P. Lindley, Cambridge, 1991, 109.

6 W. H. St John Hope, *Windsor Castle: An Architectural History*, vol. I, London, 1913, 248.

7 F. Kisby, 'A Study of the Peripatetic Household of the Early Tudor Kings, 1485–1547', *Court Historian*, 4 (1999), 29–39.

8 The National Archives, DL 42/95, fol. 80v, cited in *History of the King's Works*, vol. III, 258.

9 *History of the King's Works*, vol. III, 259.

10 J. H. Harvey, 'Sidelights on Kenilworth Castle', *Archaeological Journal*, 101 (1944), 92.

11 S. Foister, *Holbein and England*, New Haven and London, 2004, 121–3.

12 W. Hutchinson, *The History and Antiquities of the County Palatine of Durham*, vol. I, Newcastle, 1785, 391.

13 *Rites of Durham, Being a Description or Brief Declaration of all the Ancient Monuments, Rites and Customs Belonging or Being within the Monastical Church of Durham Before the Suppression, Written 1593*, ed. J. T. Fowler, Surtees Society, 107, Durham, 1903, 94–5.

14 J. Raine, *The History and Antiquities of North Durham*, London, 1852, 292.

15 Raine, *History and Antiquities of North Durham*, 293.

16 E. Cambridge, 'The Masons and Building Works of Durham Priory, 1339–1539', unpublished PH.D thesis, University of Durham, 1992, 287.

17 Raine, *History and Antiquities of North Durham*, 294.

18 *History of the King's Works*, vol. IV, 681.

19 C. J. Bates, *The Border Holds of Northumberland*, Newcastle, 1891, 342–4.

20 Leland, *Itinerary*, vol. V, 51.

21 C. H. Hunter Blair, 'Harbottle Castle', *History of Berwickshire Naturalists' Club*, 28 (1932–4), 215–31.

22 C. J. Ferguson, 'The Barony of Gilsland and its Owners to the End of the 16th Century', *Transactions of the Cumberland and Westmorland Antiquarian and Archaeological Society*, 4 (1878–9), 489–91.

23 M. W. Taylor, 'Kirkoswald Castle', *Transactions of the Cumberland and Westmorland Antiquarian and Archaeological Society*, 2 (1874–5), 1–10.

24 *Gothic: Art for England, 1400–1547*, ed. R. Marks and P. Williamson, exhibition catalogue, Victoria and Albert Museum, London, 2003, 292–3.

25 E. Chappell, 'New Light on the "Little Men" of Naworth Castle', in *Late Gothic England: Art and Display*, ed. R. Marks, Donington, 2007, 70–80.

26 *Historiae Dunelmensis Scriptores Tres*, ed. J. Raine, Surtees Society, 9, Newcastle, 1839, 151 and 155.

27 W. H. Chippindall, *A 16th-Century Survey and Year's Account of the Estates of Hornby Castle, Lancashire*, Manchester, 1939, 27.

28 Chippindall, *A 16th-Century Survey*, 12–20.

29 Peter Brears, personal communication. The panelling survives at Burton Agnes, Yorkshire.

30 Leland, *Itinerary*, vol. I, 52–4.

31 *Letters and Papers: Henry VIII*, vol. XII, pt 2, 205–6.

32 *Medieval Framlingham: Select Documents, 1270–1524*, ed. J. Ridgard, Suffolk Record Society, 27, Woodbridge, 1985, 129–58.

33 S. J. Gunn, 'Brandon, Charles, First Duke of Suffolk (c.1484–1545)', in *Oxford Dictionary of National Biography*: www.oxforddnb.com/view/article/3260 (accessed 4 January 2010).

34 British Library, Cotton MS Caligula D. vi, fol. 186r, quoted in Gunn, 'Brandon, Charles, First Duke of Suffolk'.

35 J. Schofield, *Medieval London Houses*, London and New Haven, 1995, 230.

36 S. J. Gunn and P. G. Lindley, 'Charles Brandon's Westhorpe: An Early Tudor Courtyard House in Suffolk', *Archaeological Journal*, 145 (1988), 272–89.

37 Leland, *Itinerary*, vol. I, 17–18.

38 M. L. Robertson, 'Court Careers and County Quarrels: George Hastings and Leicestershire Unrest, 1509–1529', in *State, Sovereigns and Society in Early Modern England: Essays in Honour of A. J. Slavin*, ed. C. Carlton et al., Stroud, 1997, 153–67.

39 Leland, *Itinerary*, vol. I, 97–8.

40 M. Clayton, 'A Tapestry Map of Nottinghamshire', *Transactions of the Thoroton Society of Nottinghamshire*, 38 (1934), 65–80.

41 Leland, *Itinerary*, vol. I, 98.

42 *VCH: Hampshire and the Isle of Wight*, vol. III, London, 1908, 134–9.

43 The National Archives, E36/150.

44 J. Gage, *The History and Antiquities of Hengrave*, London, 1822, 41.

45 D. Starkey, *Henry: Virtuous Prince*, London, 2008, 269–75.

46 J. Farrant et al., 'Laughton Place: A Manorial and Architectural History, with an Account of Recent Restorations and Excavation', *Sussex Archaeological Collections*, 129 (1991), 99–164.

47 *Letters and Papers: Henry VIII*, vol. XIII, pt 2, 49 (no. 133).

48 P. Everson and D. Stocker, 'The Archaeology of Vice-Regality: Charles Brandon's Brief Rule in Lincolnshire', in *The Archaeology of Reformation, 1480–1580*, ed. D. Gaimster and R. Gilchrist, Leeds, 2003, 145–8.

49 J. Binns, 'Scarborough and the Pilgrimage of Grace', *Transactions of the Scarborough Archaeological and Historical Society*, 33 (1997), 23–39.

50 *Letters and Papers: Henry VIII*, vol. XII, pt 2, 479 [1537].

51 *Letters and Papers: Henry VIII*, vol. XIV, pt 1, 53 [1539].

52 *Letters and Papers: Henry VIII*, vol. XIV, pt 1, 152 [1539].

53 *Letters and Papers: Henry VIII*, vol. XIV, pt 1, 336, 351 [1539].

54 *History of the King's Works*, vol. IV, 369–85; A. Saunders, *Fortress Britain*, Liphook, 1989, 37–52; and M. Biddle et al., *Henry VIII's Coastal Artillery Fort at Camber Castle, Rye, East Sussex: An Archaeological, Structural and Historical Investigation*, Oxford, 2001.

55 *History of the King's Works*, vol. IV, 455–65.

56 *Letters and Papers: Henry VIII*, vol. XV, 4 [1540].

57 B. H. St John O'Neill, 'Stephan von Haschenperg, an Engineer to King Henry VIII, and his Work', *Archaeologia*, 91 (1945), 137–55.

58 M. McCarthy, H. Summerson and R. Annis, *Carlisle Castle*, English Heritage Archaeological Report, 18, London, 1990, 171–3.

59 *History of the King's Works*, vol. IV, 369–77, 607–94.

60 The National Archives, E36/159.

61 S. Thurley, *The Royal Palaces of Tudor England*, New Haven and London, 1993, 52.

62 M. Howard, *The Early Tudor Country House: Architecture and Politics, 1490–1550*, London, 1987, 37–8.

63 *History of the King's Works*, vol. IV, 455.

64 J. J. Scarisbrick, *Henry VIII*, London, 1983 edn, 453.

65 *History of the King's Works*, vol. IV, 91.

66 M. Biddle, *Nonsuch Palace*, Oxford, 2005; and S. Thurley, 'Nonsuch: A Palace Fit for a Prince?', *Country Life*, 199 (11 August 2005), 42–5, which includes a reconstruction drawing by Stephen Conlin.

67 *History of the King's Works*, vol. IV, 23–4, 179–205; and M. Girouard, *Elizabethan Architecture*, New Haven and London, 2009, 129–31.

68 *William Worcestre: Itineraries,* ed. J. Harvey, Oxford, 1969, 218–19.

69 Quoted in Howard, *Early Tudor Country House*, 139.

70 For a discussion of monastic demolitions, see R. K. Morris, 'Monastic Architecture: Destruction and Reconstruction', in *The Archaeology of Reformation*, ed. Gaimster and Gilchrist, 235–51.

71 H. Brakspeare, 'The Abbot's House at Battle', *Archaeologia*, 83 (1933), 166.

72 *Letters and Papers: Henry VIII*, vol. XIX (1), 637 (no. 1035.150).

73 W. H. St John Hope, *Cowdray and Easebourne Priory*, London, 1919, 17–23.

74 J. Goodall, 'Cowdray House, West Sussex', *Country Life*, 203 (17 June 2009), 82–5.

75 W. B. Robison, 'Fitzwilliam, William, Earl of Southampton (c.1490–1542)', in *Oxford Dictionary of National Biography*: www.oxforddnb.com/view/article/9663 (accessed 4 January 2010).

76 Their original location is described in J. Ayloff, 'An Account of Some Ancient English Historical Paintings at Cowdray in Sussex', *Archaeologia*, 3 (1775), 240–1.

77 J. Hare, 'Netley Abbey: Monastery, Mansion and Ruin', *Proceedings of the Hampshire Field Club Archaeological Society*, 49 (1993), 207–27.

78 *Calendar of Patent Rolls: Edward VI, 1547–1548*, 66–7.

79 W. H. St John Hope, 'The Making of Place House, Titchfield, near Southampton, in 1538', *Archaeological Journal*, 63 (1906), 231–44.

80 *Letters and Papers: Henry VIII*, vol. XII (1), 287.

81 Leland, *Itinerary*, vol. I, 281.

82 *Letters and Papers: Henry VIII*, vol. XIII (1), 282.

83 E. W. Ives, 'Henry VIII (1491–1547)', in *Oxford Dictionary of National Biography*: www.oxforddnb.com/view/article/12955 (accessed 5 January 2010).

84 H. M. Colvin, 'Castles and Government in Tudor England', *English Historical Review*, 83 (1968), 226–7.

85 J. D. K. Lloyd, 'Montgomery Castle and the Herberts', *Archaeologia Cambrensis*, 104 (1955), 56.

86 W. L. Williams, 'The Union of England and Wales', *Transactions of the Honourable Society of Cymmrodorion* (1907–8), 47–117.

87 R. Turner, *Lamphey Bishop's Palace and Llawhaden Castle*, second edn, Cardiff, 2000, 31 [CADW guidebook].

88 J .G. Russell, *The Field of Cloth of Gold*, New York, 1969, 209.

89 S. Anglo, 'The Hampton Court Painting of the Field of Cloth of Gold as an Historical Document', *Antiquaries Journal*, 46 (1966), 287–307.

15   THE CASTLE AND THE REFORMATION

1 M. Girouard, *Elizabethan Architecture*, New Haven and London, 2009, 378.

2 M. Girouard, 'The Smythson Collection of the Royal Institute of British Architects', *Architectural History*, 5 (1962), 23–184.

3 M. Girouard, *Robert Smythson and the Elizabethan Country House*, New Haven and London, 1983, 14–16.

4 M. Bowker, 'Holbeach, Henry (d. 1551)', in *Oxford Dictionary of National Biography*: www.oxforddnb.com/view/article/13477 (accessed 3 September 2007).

5 D. G. Newcombe, 'Tunstal, Cuthbert (1474–1559)', in *Oxford Dictionary of National Biography*: www.oxforddnb.com/view/article/27817 (accessed 4 January 2010).

6 J. Raine, *A Brief Historical Account of the Episcopal Palace or Castle of Auckland*, Durham, 1852, 64.

7 *Rites of Durham, Being a Description or Brief Declaration of all the Ancient Monuments, Rites and Customs Belonging or Being within the Monastical Church of Durham Before the Suppression, Written 1593*, ed. J. T. Fowler, Surtees Society, 107, Durham, 1903, 102–3.

8 Raine, *Brief Historical Account*, 65.

9 Raine, *Brief Historical Account*, 69.

10 Leland, *Itinerary*, vol. I, 73.

11 *VCH: County of Warwick*, vol. VIII, London, 1969, 458.

12 Harvey, *English Mediaeval Architects*, 51; and N. Pevsner, *The Buildings of England: Staffordshire*, Harmondsworth, 1974, 119.

13 S. Adams, '"Because I am of that countrye and mynde to plant myself there": Robert Dudley, Earl of Leicester, and the West Midlands', *Midland History*, 20 (1995), 24–9.

14 D. Loades, 'Dudley, John, Duke of Northumberland (1504–1553)', in *Oxford Dictionary of National Biography*: www.oxforddnb.com/view/article/8156 (accessed 4 January 2010).

15 The National Archives, SP 10/1/30, quoted in *VCH: County of Warwick*, vol. VIII, 458.

16 P. F. Tytler, *England under the Reigns of Edward VI and Mary*, vol. II, London, 1839, 142–3.

17 A letter of 7 April 1552 from Northumberland to Cecil, The National Archives: State Papers Domestic, Edward VI, vol. XIV, no. 18, cited in *VCH: Durham,* vol. II, London, 1907, 164; and H. R. Trevor-Roper, 'The Bishopric of Durham and the Capitalist Revolution', *Durham University Journal*, new series, 7 (1945–6), 45–58.

18 Chirk Castle, MS F 13310, as transcribed by Richard K. Morris and Emily Cole.

19 G. Worsley, *The British Stable*, New Haven and London, 2004, 9 and 25.

20   *Calendar of State Papers, Domestic Series, of the Reign of Edward VI*, ed. C. S. Knighton, London, 1992, 242, no. 660.

21   B. Usher, 'Durham and Winchester: Episcopal Estate and the Elizabethan Settlement: A Reappraisal', *Journal of Ecclesiastical History*, 49 (1998), 393–406.

22   W. Hutchinson, *The History and Antiquities of the County Palatine of Durham*, vol. I, Newcastle, 1785, 448.

23   J. Strype, *Annals of the Reformation*, vol. III, London, 1737, 469.

24   W. H. St John Hope, *Windsor Castle: An Architectural History*, vol. I, London, 1913, 280.

25   N. Orme, 'Worcester, William (1415–1480x85)', in *Oxford Dictionary of National Biography*: www.oxforddnb.com/view/article/29967 (accessed 4 January 2010).

26   N. Orme, 'Rous, John (c.1420–1492)', in *Oxford Dictionary of National Biography*: www.oxforddnb.com/view/article/24173 (accessed 4 January 2010).

27   Oxford, Bodleian Library, MS Tanner 166.

28   Quoted in J. P. Carley, 'Leland, John (c.1503–1552)', in *Oxford Dictionary of National Biography*: www.oxforddnb.com/view/article/16416 (accessed 4 January 2010).

29   For an abbreviated listing of all Leland's comments on English castles by place, see M. Thompson, *The Decline of the Castle*, Cambridge, 1987, 171–8.

30   'There is a sqware dungeon towre in the castle. . . ', Leland, *Itinerary*, vol. V, 101.

31   T. F. Mayer and C. B. Walters, eds, *The Correspondence of Reginald Pole*, vol. IV: *A Biographical Companion: The British Isles*, Aldershot and Burlington, VT, 2008, 174–5.

32   W. Darell, *A History of Dover Castle*, London, 1786, vii.

33   C. Shenton, 'Dover Castle's Ancient Keepers: An Antiquarian Manuscript at Knole', *Apollo* (April 2006), 62–6.

34   J. Smyth, *The Lives of the Berkeleys*, ed. J. Maclean, 3 vols, Gloucester, 1883–5.

35   J. Bilson, 'Gilling Castle', *Yorkshire Archaeological Journal*, 19 (1907), 135–6 and 144.

36   E. H. Hasted, *The History and Topographical Survey of the County of Kent*, vol. II, Canterbury, 1782, 656 (notes).

37   N. Cooper, *Houses of the Gentry*, New Haven and London, 1999, 42–4.

38   Reproduced in Cooper, *Houses of the Gentry*, 43.

39   J. Hutchins, *The History and Antiquities of the County of Dorset*, Westminster, 1863, 546–52, where the arms are engraved.

40   W. Dugdale, *The Antiquities of Warwickshire*, second edn, vol. I, London, 1730, pl. facing 89.

41   M. F. S. Hervey, 'A Lumley Inventory of 1609', *Walpole Society*, 6 (1918), 42.

42   E. Milner and E. Benham, eds, *Records of the Lumleys of Lumley Castle*, London, 1904, 92.

43   M. Biddle, 'Early Renaissance at Winchester', in *Winchester Cathedral: Nine Hundred Years, 1093–1993*, ed. J. Crook, Chichester, 1993, 264–78.

44   *Literary Remains of King Edward the Sixth*, ed. J. G. Nichols, vol. I, Roxburghe Club, 75, London, 1857, cxxxi.

45   St John Hope, *Windsor Castle*, 259–61.

46   *History of the King's Works*, vol. III, 321 and pl. 8.

47   St John Hope, *Windsor Castle*, 256–7.

48   St John Hope, *Windsor Castle*, 266–86; and *History of the King's Works*, vol. III, 319–27.

49   S. Adams, 'Dudley, Ambrose, Earl of Warwick (c.1530–1590)', in *Oxford Dictionary of National Biography*: www.oxforddnb.com/view/article/8143 (accessed 4 January 2010).

50   *VCH: County of Warwick*, vol. VIII, 423–7; and E. G. Tibbetts, 'The Hospital of Robert, Earl of Leicester, in Warwick', *Transactions of the Birmingham Archaeological Society*, 60 (1940 for 1936), 112–44.

51   Adams, '"Because I am of that countrye"', 46.

52   R. K. Morris, 'An Elizabethan Plan for Kenilworth Castle in the Archive at Longleat House', *English Heritage Historical Review*, 2 (2007), 22–35.

53   J. Nichols, *The Progresses and Public Processions of Queen Elizabeth*, vol. I, London, 1823, 428.

54   H. Sunley, 'Recent Observations on the West Doorway of St Nicholas' Church, Kenilworth', *Transactions of the Birmingham and Warwickshire Archaeological Society*, 95 (1987–8), 73–9.

55   The two accounts are published in Nichols, *Progresses and Public Processions of Queen Elizabeth*, 420–523.

56   Nichols, *Progresses and Public Processions of Queen Elizabeth*, London, 449–55.

57   R. Strong, 'Gloriana's Garden', *Country Life*, 203 (5 August 2009), 46–50. English Heritage is currently preparing a monograph on this undertaking.

58   E. Woodhouse, 'Kenilworth: The Earl of Leicester's Pleasure Grounds Following Robert Laneham's Letter', *Garden History*, 27 (1999), 127–44.

59   L. Butler, 'Leicester's Church, Denbigh: An Experiment in Puritan Worship', *Journal of the British Archaeological Association*, third series, 37 (1973), 40–62.

60   Reproduced in *Chirk Castle*, London, 2002 edn, 48 [National Trust guidebook].

61   F. Heal, 'Cox, Richard (c. 1500–81), in *Oxford Dictionary of National Biography*: www. oxforddnb.com/view/article/6526 (accessed 10 June 2010).

62   The plans were engraved for G. T. Clark, 'Corfe Castle', *Archaeological Journal*, 22 (1865), 203–5.

63   W. T. MacCaffrey, 'Hatton, Sir Christopher (c.1540–1591)', in *Oxford Dictionary of National Biography*: www.oxforddnb.com/view/article/12605 (accessed 4 January 2010).

64   S. M. Jack, 'Manners, Edward, Third Earl of Rutland (1549–1587)', in *Oxford Dictionary of National Biography*: www.oxforddnb.com/view/article/17952 (accessed 4 January 2010).

65   J. Clark, *Helmsley Castle*, London, 2004, 32 [English Heritage guidebook].

66   J. Goodall, 'A Medieval Masterpiece: Herstmonceux Castle, Sussex', *Burlington Magazine*, 146, no. 1217 (August 2004), 521.

67   T. Fuller, *The History of the Worthies of England*, London 1662, fascicule 2, 3.

68   Fuller, *History of the Worthies of England*, fascicule 2, 3.

69   C. R. Peers, 'On the Excavation of the Site of Basing House, Hampshire', *Archaeologia*, 61 (1909), 564; and *VCH: Hampshire and the Isle of Wight*, vol. IV, London, 1911, 115–27.

70   E. Harwood, 'Moreton Corbet Castle', *English Heritage Historical Review*, 1 (2006), 37–45.

71   *Two Surveys of the Manor of Berkhamstead of 1607 and 1616*, ed. Anon., London, 1868, 73.

72   *History of the King's Works*, vol. IV, 531–5; and C. J. Young, *Excavations at Carisbrooke Castle, Isle of Wight, 1921–1996*, Wessex Archaeological Report, 18, Salisbury, 2000, *passim*.

73   Quoted in *History of the King's Works*, vol. III, 179–81.

74   *History of the King's Works*, vol. III, 254–7.

75   *History of the King's Works*, vol. III, 257.

76   C. Kightly, *Farleigh Hungerford Castle*, London, 2006, 23–4.

77   T. Auden, 'Wigmore Castle', *Transactions of the Shropshire Archaeological and Natural History Society*, 39 (1909), 372, though a survey of 1584 reports the buildings to be in a parlous condition; British Library, MS Lansdowne 82, fol. 199r and v. I am grateful to Carol Davidson Cragoe for these references.

78   W. Hodges, *An Historical Account of Ludlow Castle*, Ludlow, 1794, 90.

79   Hodges, *An Historical Account of Ludlow Castle*, 32–8; and R. Shoesmith and A. Johnson, eds, *Ludlow Castle: Its History and Buildings*, Logaston, 2000, 77 and 104.

80   R. Stalley, 'The 1562 Collapse of the Nave and its Aftermath', in *Christ Church Cathedral, Dublin*, ed. K. Milne, Dublin, 2000, 231.

81   J. Bardon, *A History of Ulster*, Belfast, 1992, 75–114.

82   W. J. Smyth, *Map-making, Landscapes and*

Memory: A Geography of Colonial and Early Modern Ireland, c.1530–1750, Cork, 2006, 49–51.

83 M. Gray, 'Castles and Patronage in 16th-century Wales', *Welsh History Review*, 15 (1990–1), 481–93.

84 R. Merrick, *Morganiae archaiographica: A Book of the Antiquities of Glamorganshire*, ed. Brian Ll. James, South Wales Record Society, 1, Barry Island, 1983, 91.

85 *Royal Commission on the Ancient and Historical Monuments of Wales: An Inventory of the Ancient Monuments in Glamorgan*, vol. III: *Medieval Secular Monuments*, part Ia: *The Early Castles*, London, 1991, 171.

86 R. Avent, *Laugharne Castle*, Cardiff, 1995, 39 [CADW guidebook].

87 D. J. C. Cathcart-King and J. C. Perks, 'Carew Castle, Pembrokeshire', *Archaeological Journal*, 119 (1962), 294–5 and 306–7.

88 R. Turvey, 'Perrot, Sir John (1528–1592)', in *Oxford Dictionary of National Biography*: www.oxforddnb.com/view/article/21986 (accessed 4 January 2010).

89 W. R. B. Robinson, 'Somerset, William, Third Earl of Worcester (1526/7–1589)', in *Oxford Dictionary of National Biography*: www.oxford dnb.com/view/article/26015 (accessed 4 January 2010).

90 H. Colvin, 'Hermes, Termes and Caryatids in English Architecture', in *Essays in English Architectural History*, New Haven and London, 1999, 116; and J. Kenyon, *Raglan Castle*, rev. edn, Cardiff, 2003, 42 [CADW guidebook].

91 Thomas Churchyard, 'The Worthies of Wales' [1587], quoted in E. Whittle, 'The Renaissance Gardens of Raglan Castle', *Garden History*, 17 (1989), 84.

92 H. Summerson and S. Harrison, *Lanercost Priory, Cumbria*, Cumberland and Westmorland Antiquarian and Archaeological Society Research Series, 10, Kendal, 2000, 44.

93 Girouard, *Robert Smythson*, 118.

94 Girouard, *Robert Smythson*, 119.

95 O. J. Weaver, 'Heath Old Hall, Yorkshire', in *Ancient Monuments and their Interpretation: Essays Presented to A. J. Taylor*, ed. M. R. Apted, R. Gildyard-Beer and A. D. Saunders, Chichester, 1977, 285–301.

96 *History of Parliament: The House of Commons, 1558–1603*, ed. P. W. Hasler, vol. II, London, 1981, 208.

97 *History of Parliament: House of Commons, 1558–1603*, vol. II, 208.

98 *Journal of Sir Roger Wilbraham, 1593–1616*, ed. H. S. Scott, Camden Miscellany, third series, 10, London, 1902, 66.

99 *Calendar of Patent Rolls: Elizabeth I, 1566–1569*, 33.

100 Dugdale, *Antiquities of Warwickshire*, vol. II, 710.

101 *VCH: County of Warwick*, vol. V, London, 1949, 200.

102 *VCH: County of Oxford*, vol. V, London, 1957, 57–9.

103 J. Barnatt and T. Williamson, *Chatsworth: A Landscape History*, Macclesfield, 2005, 46–7.

104 P. Henderson, *The Tudor House and Garden*, New Haven and London, 2005, 203.

105 Girouard, *Robert Smythson*, 88–108.

16 THE STUART CASTLE

1 J. Newman, 'Jones, Inigo (1573–1652)', in *Oxford Dictionary of National Biography*: www.oxforddnb.com/view/article/15017 (accessed 4 January 2010).

2 C. Anderson, *Inigo Jones and the Classical Tradition*, Cambridge, 2007.

3 G. Higgott, 'The Fabric to 1670', in *St Paul's: The Cathedral Church of London, 604–2004*, ed. D. Keene, A. Burns and A. Saint, New Haven and London, 2004, 171–90.

4 See J. Harris and G. Higgott, *Inigo Jones: Complete Architectural Drawings*, exhibition catalogue, The Drawing Centre, New York; The Frick Art Museum, Pittsburgh; and The Royal Academy, London (New York, 1989); and D. Duggan, '"London the ring, Covent Garden the jewell of that ring": New Light on Covent Garden', *Architectural History*, 43 (2000), 140–61.

5 G. Worsley, *Classical Architecture in Britain: The Heroic Age*, London and New Haven, 1995, 1–19.

6 R. A. Skelton and J. Summerson, *A Description of Maps and Architectural Drawings in the Collection Made by William Cecil, 1st Baron Burghley, now at Hatfield House*, The Roxburghe Club, Oxford, 1971, cat. no. 173; and M. Girouard, *Elizabethan Architecture*, New Haven and London, 2009, 119–20.

7 J. Summerson, ed., *The Book of Architecture of John Thorpe in Sir John Soane's Museum*, Walpole Society, 40, Glasgow, 1966.

8 R. Strong, *Henry, Prince of Wales, and England's Lost Renaissance*, London, 1986.

9 See the annotated facsimile, J. Speed, *The Counties of Britain: A Tudor Atlas*, London, 1995.

10 R. A. Skelton, 'Tudor Town Plans in John Speed's *Theatre*', *Archaeological Journal*, 108 (1951), 109–20.

11 O. Creighton and P. Higham, *Medieval Town Walls*, Stroud, 2005, 165–73.

12 San Marino, CA, Huntington Library, Huntingdon Papers, HAF Box 7 (2), (3), (4), (5) and (6).

13 *A History of Northumberland*, vol. V, 71.

14 *A History of Northumberland*, vol. V, 61–2.

15 *Complete Peerage*, vol. XI, 734.

16 G. R. Batho, 'The State of Alnwick Castle, 1557–1632', *Archaeologia Aeliana*, fourth series, 36 (1958), 129–45.

17 C. J. Bates, *Border Holds of Northumberland*, Newcastle, 1891, 211.

18 *VCH: Sussex*, vol. V, pt I, London, 1997, 43.

19 Hammond, *A Relation of a Short Survey of the Western Counties*, ed. L. G. Wickham Legg, Camden Miscellany, 16, London, 1936, 30–1.

20 A. J. Loomie, 'Manners, Francis, Sixth Earl of Rutland (1578–1632)', in *Oxford Dictionary of National Biography*: www.oxforddnb.com/view/article/17953 (accessed 27 January 2009).

21 *Complete Peerage*, vol. IX, 677–81; and M. Bennett, 'Compton, Spencer, Second Earl of Northampton (1601–1643)', in *Oxford Dictionary of National Biography*: www.oxforddnb.com/view/article/6035 (accessed 4 January 2010).

22 *A History of Northumberland*, vol. V, 71–2.

23 *A History of Northumberland*, vol. XIV, 338–48.

24 H. Summerson, M. Trueman and S. Harrison, *Brougham Castle, Cumbria*, Cumberland and Westmorland Antiquarian and Archaeological Society Research Series, 8, Kendal, 1998, 46–9; and R. T. Spence, 'A Royal Progress in the North: James I at Carlisle Castle and the Feast of Brougham, August 1617', *Northern History*, 27 (1991), 41–89.

25 R. T. Spence, *Skipton Castle and its Builders*, Skipton, 2002, 97–101.

26 *Selections from the Household Books of Lord William Howard*, ed. G. Ornsby, Surtees Society, 68, Durham, 1878, 132 and 194.

27 H. Colvin, *A Biographical Dictionary of British Architects, 1600–1840*, third edn, New Haven and London, 1995, 78–9.

28 J. D. K. Lloyd, 'Montgomery Castle and the Herberts', *Archaeologia Cambrensis*, 104 (1955), 52–64; and Lloyd, 'The "New Building" at Montgomery Castle', *Archaeologia Cambrensis*, 114 (1965), 60–8.

29 S. Kelsey, 'Conway, Edward, First Viscount Conway and First Viscount Killultagh (c.1564–1631)', in *Oxford Dictionary of National Biography*: www.oxforddnb.com/view/article/6120 (accessed 29 November 2008).

30 A. J. Taylor, 'The Dismantling of Conway Castle', *Transactions of the Ancient Monuments Society*, 29 (1985), 81–9.

31 *Calendar of the Manuscripts of the Most Honourable the Marquis of Salisbury*, Historical Manuscripts Commission, 9, pt II, Dublin, 1906, 433–4.

32 *VCH: County of Warwick*, vol. VIII, London, 1969, 458.

33 *VCH: County of Warwick*, vol. VIII, 459.

34 W. Dugdale, *The Antiquities of Warwickshire*, second edn, vol. I, London, 1730, 427–8.

35   *Poems of Richard Corbet*, London, 1807 edn, 198–9; quoted in P. Henderson, *The Tudor House and Garden*, New Haven and London, 2005, 127.

36   *The Letters of John Chamberlain*, ed. N. E. McLure, Memoirs of the Philadelphia Philosophical Society, 12, vol. I, Philadelphia, 1939, 235.

37   Henderson, *Tudor House and Garden*, 61.

38   S. Kelsey, 'Digges, Sir Dudley (1582/3–1639)', in *Oxford Dictionary of National Biography*: www.oxforddnb.com/view/article/7635 (accessed 4 January 2010).

39   H. Middleton, *A Memoir of Chirk Castle from Original Manuscripts*, London, 1923, 17.

40   R. Meeson, 'The Timber Frame of the Hall at Tamworth Castle, Staffordshire, and its Context', *Archaeological Journal*, 140 (1983), 331–3.

41   M. E. Blizzard, 'Caverswall Castle', *North Staffordshire Field Club Transactions*, 72 (1937–8), 49–61.

42   M. Girouard, *Robert Smythson and the Elizabethan Country House*, New Haven and London, 1983, 180–1.

43   Girouard, *Robert Smythson*, 234–51.

44   Girouard, *Robert Smythson*, 265–6.

45   Girouard, *Robert Smythson*, 217–32.

46   F. W. Steer, ed., *John Philpot's Roll of the Constables of Dover Castle and the Lord Wardens of the Cinque Ports, 1627*, London, 1955.

47   The National Archives, E351/3259. I am grateful to Gordon Higgott for his ideas about these accounts. These are published in abbreviated form in 'The Great Tower in the 17th and 18th Centuries', *Research News: Newsletter of the English Heritage Research Department*, 12 (2009), 9–11.

48   *History of the King's Works*, vol. III, 248.

49   Hammond, *A Relation of a Short Survey of the Western Counties*, 24.

50   E. Impey, ed., *The White Tower*, New Haven and London, 2008, 174–7.

51   Quoted in R. S. Ferguson, 'The Earthworks and Keep of Appleby Castle', *Transactions of the Cumberland and Westmorland Antiquarian and Archaeological Society*, 8 (1886), 394. For the foundation myths of Julius Caesar, see A. Wheatley, *The Idea of the Castle in Medieval England*, Woodbridge, 2004, 142–5.

52   Quoted in J. Berkeley, *Lulworth and the Welds*, Gillingham, 1971, 24.

53   Girouard, *Robert Smythson*, 228.

54   N. Cooper, *Houses of the Gentry*, New Haven and London, 1999, 141–94.

55   P. Smith, 'Plas Teg', *Flintshire Historical Society*, 18 (1960), 157–62.

56   J. Wake, *The Brudenells of Deene*, London, 1953, 108.

57   C. Blair, ed., *The Crown Jewels: The History of the Coronation Regalia*, vol. II: *The Catalogues*, London, 1998, 395–8.

58   T. Amyot, 'A Transcript of Two Rolls Containing an Inventory of Effects Belonging to Sir John Fastolf', *Archaeologia*, 21 (1827), 240.

59   C. Whitfield, *Robert Dover and the Cotswold Games*, London and New York, 1962, pl. 5.

60   E. H. Hasted, *The History and Topographical Survey of the County of Kent*, vol. IV, Canterbury, 1799, 59.

61   Colvin, *A Biographical Dictionary of British Architects*, 78–9.

62   Colvin, *A Biographical Dictionary of British Architects*, 68.

63   *Complete Peerage*, vol. I, 174.

64   J. Lodge, *The Peerage of Ireland*, vol. I, London, 1754, 109.

65   C. E. B. Brett, *The Buildings of Antrim*, Belfast, 1996, 100.

66   Quoted in Brett, *Buildings of Antrim*, 21.

67   V. Treadwell, 'The Survey of Armagh and Tyrone, 1622', *Ulster Journal of Archaeology*, 23 (1960), 126–37.

68   Hammond, *A Relation of a Short Survey of the Western Counties*, 85.

69   *A History of Northumberland*, vol. II, 209.

70   C. J. Bates, *The Border Holds of Northumberland*, Newcastle, 1891, 80 and 266.

71   W. Atthill, *Documents Relating to the Foundation and Antiquities of the Collegiate Church of Middleham*, Camden Society, 38, London, 1847, 22.

72   British Museum, British Imp pii, 1850-2-23-825.

73   *VCH: County of York: North Riding*, vol. I, London, 1914, 11.

74   *VCH: County of York: North Riding*, vol. II, London, 1923, 542.

75   C. Firth, ed., 'Sir Hugh Cholmley's Narrative of the Siege of Scarborough, 1644–5', *English Historical Review*, 32 (1917), 583–4.

76   Anon., *A Relation of Some Abuses Which Are Committed Against the Common-Wealth*, ed. F. Madden, Camden Miscellany, 3, [London,] 1855, 12.

77   R. M. Smuts, 'Vane, Sir Henry (1589–1655)', in *Oxford Dictionary of National Biography*: www.oxforddnb.com/view/article/28085 (accessed 27 January 2009).

78   B. Cunliffe and B. Garratt, *Excavations at Portchester Castle*, vol. V: *Post Medieval, 1609–1819*, London, 1994, 130–1.

79   M. McCarthy, H. Summerson and R. Annis, *Carlisle Castle*, English Heritage Archaeological Report, 18, London, 1990, 194.

80   *History of the King's Works*, vol. III, 331.

81   *History of the King's Works*, vol. III, 297.

82   *History of the King's Works*, vol. III, 289.

83   *Parliamentary Papers, passim*.

84   W. H. St John Hope, *Windsor Castle: An Architectural History*, vol. I, London, 1913, 302.

85   E. Carey-Hill, 'The Hawkesworth Papers, 1601–60', *Birmingham Archaeological Proceedings and Transactions*, 54 (1929–30), 21–37.

86   W. Hutchinson, *The History and Antiquities of the County Palatine of Durham*, vol. I, Newcastle, 1785, 512–14.

87   Hasted, *History and Topographical Survey of the County of Kent*, vol. IV, 64.

88   J. Coad, *Dover Castle*, London, 1995, 116.

89   Huntington Library, HPP Box 19 (7).

SELECT BIBLIOGRAPHY

GENERAL SOURCES OF REFERENCE

The subject of castles has an immense bibliography and it would be pointless in a book of this kind to try and present one that aimed at completeness. The more so since two books have been published in recent years that provide an excellent overall survey of the subject: D. J. C. King, *Castellarium Anglicanum: An Index and Bibliography of the Castles in England, Wales and the Islands*, 2 vols, New York, 1983, and J. R. Kenyon, *Castles, Town Defences and Artillery Fortifications in the United Kingdom and Ireland: A Bibliography, 1945–2006*, Donington, 2008.

These volumes both offer lists of castle bibliography by site, and Kenyon additionally catalogues general literature on the subject in a short introductory section. I have also used several other topographical indexes for my research, notably the card index of the Society of Antiquaries of London, as well as its electronic catalogue http://www.sal.org.uk/museum/ prints anddrawings/ and catalogue of publications http://www.sal.org.uk/library/catalogue/; the British Library manuscript topographical index and the electronic indexes http://www.bl.uk/; and the Public Record Office – now The National

Archives – indexes and web resources http://www.nationalarchives.gov.uk/.

The long-running series of *Country Life* illustrated architectural articles that have been published weekly almost since the foundation of the magazine in 1897 has also been immensely helpful in compiling this book. Collectively – and through the medium of the published index – they constitute the single greatest survey of British architecture in existence. Three other series have served as useful points of reference for this study: *The Buildings of England* series (familiarly known as Pevsners) and the two partially completed projects of the Victoria History of the Counties of England and the Royal Commission for Historic Monuments in England.

Another outstandingly important point of reference for my research has been the new *Oxford Dictionary of National Biography*, 60 vols, Oxford, 2004. The full extent of my debt to this great scholarly undertaking and its contributors is not reflected in the notes. By using the online and searchable version of the text, http://www.oxforddnb.com, in particular, it has been possible to assemble countless important titbits of information that have materially fleshed out the text.

STRUCTURE OF THE BIBLIOGRAPHY

The bibliography that follows is headed by a listing of secondary sources relating to the architecture and archaeology of the four castles that lie at the heart of the narrative of this book: Dover, Durham, Kenilworth and Windsor. This excludes biographical and historical studies unless they have a direct bearing on the fabric.

Thereafter, the bibliography is arranged by chapter and lists the principal source texts and studies used in each. The listing for the first chapter presents a survey of general works on the subject in chronological order. There are further references listed in the notes, which offer, therefore, a more specialist bibliography to particular issues. Even so, the text is sparingly footnoted. My intention has been to acknowledge my sources and furnish the interested reader with avenues of further research. It has not been to add weight to an already long book by compiling chapter and verse citations of all relevant literature. A useful source of information for news in this field is the Castle Studies Group website: http://www.castlestudiesgroup.org.uk/

DOVER

C. S. Akers, *Historical Sketch of the Fortifications of Dover*, London, 1887

Anon., 'Stephen de Pencestre's Laws for the Government of Dover Castle', *Archaeologia Cantiana*, 3 (1860), 196–9

G. M. Atherton, *Soldiers of the Castle: Dover Castle Garrisoned*, Dover, 2004

W. Batcheller, *A New History of Dover and of Dover Castle during the Roman, Saxon and Norman Governments*, Dover, 1828

P. Bennett, T. Tatton-Brown and S. Ouditt, 'Dover Castle', in *Canterbury's Archaeology: 14th Annual Report*, 1989–90 (1991), 26–9

—, — and —, 'Interim Report on Work Carried Out in 1990 . . . Dover Castle', *Archaeologia Cantiana*, 108 (1990), 238–44

M. Biddle, 'Excavations at Dover', *Medieval Archaeology*, 6–7 (1962–3), 322; and 8 (1964), 254–5

—, 'The Earthworks around St Mary in Castro', *Archaeological Journal*, 126 (1969), 264–5

M. Binney, 'Dover Castle', *Country Life*, 174 (1983), 1902–5; 175 (1984), 18–21

T. Blashill, 'The Development of the Fortifications of Dover Castle', *Journal of the British Archaeological Association*, 40 (1884), 152–7

K. Booth, 'The Roman Pharos at Dover', *English Heritage Historical Review*, 2 (2007), 8–20

— and P. Roberts, 'Recording the Keep, Dover Castle', *Château Gaillard*, 19 (2000), 21–3

G. Bosanquet, 'Dover in 1066: Translated Extracts', *Archaeologia Cantiana*, 61 (1948), 156–9

R. A. Brown, *Dover Castle*, London, 1966 [Ministry of Works guidebook]

—, 'Dover Castle', *Archaeological Journal*, 126 (1969), 205–11, 262–4

G. T. Clark, *Mediaeval Military Architecture in England*, vol. II, London, 1884, 4–24

J. G. Coad, 'Dover Castle, 1898–1963: Preservation of a Monument: A Postscript', in *Studies in Medieval History Presented to R. Allen Brown*, ed. C. Harper-Bill, C. J. Holdsworth and J. Nelson, Woodbridge, 1989, 57–69

—, *Dover Castle*, London, 1995

—, *Dover Castle*, London, 2007 [English Heritage Red Guide]

— and P. N. Lewis, 'The Later Fortifications of Dover Castle', *Post Medieval Archaeology*, 16 (1982), 141–200

H. M. Colvin, 'An Iron Age Fort at Dover?', *Antiquity*, 33 (1959), 125–7

—, ed., *Building Accounts of Henry III*, Oxford, 1971, 20–87

A. M. Cook, D. C. Mynard and S. E. Rigold, 'Excavations at Dover Castle, Principally in the Inner Bailey', *Journal of the British Archaeological Association*, third series, 32 (1969), 54–104

H. S. Cumming, 'On Some Ancient Relics Preserved in the Keep of Dover Castle', *Journal of the British Archaeological Association*, 26 (1870), 335–40

W. Darell, *A History of Dover Castle*, London, 1786

T. Fisher, *Kentish Traveller's Companion*, Canterbury, 1779, 174–87

J. Gillespie, 'Dover Castle: Key to Richard II's Kingdom', *Archaeologia Cantiana*, 105 (1988), 179–95

J. Goodall, 'The Siege of Dover, 1216', *Château Gaillard*, 19 (2000), 91–102

—, 'The Key of England' and 'The Powerhouse of Kent', *Country Life*, 193 (18 and 25 March 1999), 44–7, 110–16

F. W. Hardman, 'Castleguard Service of Dover Castle', *Archaeologia Cantiana*, 49 (1937), 96–107

J. Harris, *The History of Kent*, vol. I, part 3, London, 1719, 371–6

C. H. Hartshorne, ed., 'Compotus Operacionis Castri Dovore', *Royal Archaeological Institute of Great Britain and Ireland Proceedings (Northumberland)*, 2 (1852), appendix 8, cxxxv

E. Hastead, *The History of Kent*, vol. IV, Canterbury, 1799, 57–60

History of the King's Works, vol. II, 629–41

History of the King's Works, vol. III, part 1, 242–488

J. Horn, *Horn's Description of Dover*, Dover, 1817

F. Hull, 'The Domesday of Dover Castle: An Archival History', *Archaeologia Cantiana*, 98 (1982), 67–75

J. T. Irvine, 'Dover Castle Church', *Journal of the British Archaeological Association*, 41 (1885), 284–8

J. B. Jones, *Annals of Dover*, Dover, 1916

A. C. Kay, 'The Dover Castle Clock', *Connoisseur*, 118 (1949), 118–19

J. Lyon, *A History of the Town and Port of Dover*, 2 vols, Dover, 1813

A. Macdonald, 'Plans of Dover Harbour in the 16th Century', *Archaeologia Cantiana*, 49 (1937), 108–26

E. R. Macpherson and E. G. J. Amos, 'The Norman Waterworks in the Keep of Dover Castle', *Archaeologia Cantiana*, 43 (1931), 167–72

W. Minet, 'Some Unpublished Plans of Dover Castle', *Archaeologia*, 72 (1922), 185–224

W. E. Peck, 'Notes on the Keep, the Roman Pharos and the Shafts at the Shot Yard Battery, Dover Castle', *Archaeologia*, 45 (1880), 328–36

J. Philipot, *John Philipot's Roll of the Constables of Dover Castle and the Lord Wardens of the Cinque Ports*, ed. F. W. Steer, London, 1956

G. T. Plunkett, 'The Development of the Fortifications of Dover Castle', *Journal of the British Archaeological Association*, 40 (1884), 373–8

C. A. Ralegh Radford, *Dover Castle*, London, 1959 [Ministry of Works guidebook]

D. Renn, 'The Avranches Traverse at Dover Castle', *Archaeologia Cantiana*, 84 (1969), 79–92

S. E. Rigold, 'Excavations at Dover Castle, 1964–66', *Journal of the British Archaeological Association*, third series, 30 (1967), 87–121

J. H. Round, 'The Attack on Dover, 1067', *The Antiquary*, 12 (1885), 49–53

G. G. Scott, 'The Church on the Castle Hill', *Archaeologia Cantiana*, 5 (1863), 1–18

C. Shenton, 'Dover Castle's Ancient Keepers: An Antiquarian Manuscript at Knole', *Apollo* (April 2006), 62–6

S. P. H. Statham, *A History of Dover*, London, 1899

—, *Dover Charters and Other Documents*, London, 1902

A. Taylor, 'Stephen de Pencestre's Account as Constable of Dover Castle for the Years Michaelmas 1272 to Michaelmas 1274', in *Studies in Castle Building*, ed. A. Taylor, London and Ronceverte, 1985, 250–56

H. A. Tipping, 'Dover Castle', *Country Life*, 51 (1922), 700–7, 743–51 and 786–92

A. Way, 'Original Documents: Accounts of the Constables of the Castle of Dover, 1344, 1361', *Archaeological Journal*, 11 (1854), 381–8

English Heritage is intending to publish the research that underpinned its representation of the great tower of the castle in 2009 as an interior furnished in the late twelfth century for Henry II. A preliminary publication with short articles by several scholars who have contributed to the work is to be found in 'Dover Castle', *Research News: Newsletter of the English Heritage Research Department*, no. 12 (Summer 2009), 3–19.

DURHAM

G. Allan, *Historical and Descriptive View of the City of Durham and its Environs*, Durham, 1824

Anon., 'Durham Castle', *Country Life*, 23 (1908), 126–35

Anon., 'Proceedings of a Meeting at Durham', *Archaeological Journal*, 65 (1908), 310–29

R. W. Billings, *Illustrations of the Architectural Antiquities of the County of Durham*, London and Durham, 1846

M. Binney, 'Durham Castle', *Country Life*, 183 (28 September 1989), 134–9

C. H. Blair, 'The Armorials upon Durham Castle' *Archaeologia Aeliana*, fourth series, 16 (1939), 109–19

R. Brickstock, *Durham Castle: Fortress, Palace, College*, Durham, 2007

G. B. Brown, 'Saxon and Norman Sculpture in Durham', *Antiquity*, 5 (1931), 438–40

D. Bythell, *Durham Castle: University College Durham*, Durham, 1985 [guidebook]

E. Cambridge, 'The Masons and Building Works of Durham Priory, 1339–1539', unpublished ph.d thesis, University of Durham, 1992

J. Charlton, 'Durham Castle', *Archaeological Journal*, 111 (1954), 202–3

G. T. Clark, *Mediaeval Military Architecture in England*, vol. 11, London, 1884, 32–5

N. Coldstream and P. Draper, eds, *Medieval Art and Architecture at Durham Cathedral*, British Archaeological Association Conference Transactions, 3, Leeds, 1980

B. Colgrave, 'The Restoration of the Norman Chapel in Durham Castle', in *Durham and Northumberland Architectural and Archaeological Society Transactions*, 10 (1946–54), 380–81

J. Davies, *The Antiquities of the Abbey or Cathedral of Durham: Also a Particular Description of the County Palatine of Durham*, Newcastle, 1767

A. Emery, *Greater Medieval Houses of England and Wales*, vol. 1: *Northern England*, Cambridge, 1996, 76–81

W. Fordyce, *The History and Antiquities of the County Palatine of Durham*, vol. 1, London, 1857

C. M. Fraser, *A History of Antony Bek, Bishop of Durham, 1283–1311*, Oxford, 1957

H. Gee, 'Discoveries in the Castle of Durham', *Proceedings of the Society of Antiquaries of London*, 20 (1903–5), 17–18

W. Greenwell, 'The Early History of Durham Castle', *Durham and Northumberland Architectural and Archaeological Society Transactions*, 7 (1934), 56–91

M. Hicks, 'The Forfeiture of Barnard Castle to the Bishop of Durham in 1459', *Northern History*, 33 (1987), 223–31

Historiae Dunelmensis Scriptores Tres, ed. J. Raine, Surtees Society, 9, Newcastle, 1839

History of the King's Works, vol. 11, 643

W. Hutchinson, *The History and Antiquities of the County Palatine of Durham*, 3 vols, Newcastle, 1785–94

M. Johnson, 'The Great North Gate of Durham Castle', *Durham and Northumberland Architectural and Archaeological Society Transactions*, new series, 4 (1978), 105–18

G. T. Lapsley, *The County Palatine of Durham: A Study in Constitutional History*, New York and London, 1900

P. Lowther et al., 'The City of Durham: An Archaeological Survey', *Durham Archaeological Journal*, 9 (1993), 27–119

G. Ornsby, 'Durham Castle', *Journal of the British Archaeological Association*, 22 (1866), 46–63

M. Roberts, *Durham*, London, 1994

D. Rollason, M. Harvey and M. Prestwich, eds, *Anglo-Norman Durham, 1093–1193*, Woodbridge, 1994

G. Simpson and V. Hatley, 'An Excavation below Tunstal's Chapel, Durham Castle', *Antiquaries Journal*, 33 (1953), 56–63

R. L. Storey, *Thomas Langley and the Bishopric of Durham, 1406–1435*, London, 1961

R. Surtees, *The History and Antiquities of the County Palatine of Durham*, vol. 1v, London, 1840

H. R. Trevor-Roper, 'The Bishopric of Durham and the Capitalist Revolution', *Durham University Journal*, new series, 7 (1946), 45–58

B. Usher, 'Durham and Winchester Episcopal Estate and the Elizabethan Settlement: A Reappraisal', *Journal of Ecclesiastical History*, 49 (1998), 393–406

VCH: A History of the County of Durham, vol. 11, London, 1907

C. E. Whiting, 'The Castle of Durham in the Middle Ages', *Archaeologia Aeliana*, fourth series, 10 (1933), 123–32

A. Young, 'William Cumin: Border Politics and the Bishopric of Durham, 1141–4', *Borthwick Papers*, 54 (1979)

KENILWORTH

S. Adams, '"Because I am of that countrye and mynde to plant myself there": Robert Dudley, Earl of Leicester and the West Midlands', *Midland History*, 20 (1995), 21–74

R. A. Brown, 'A Note on Kenilworth Castle: The Change to Royal Ownership', *Archaeological Journal*, 110 (1953), 120–24

G. T. Clark, *Mediaeval Military Architecture in England*, vol. 11, London, 1884, 130–53

C. R. Denton, 'The Medieval Meres of Kenilworth', *Country Life*, 126 (29 October 1959), 714–15

J. H. Drew, 'Notes on the Water System at Kenilworth Castle', *Birmingham Archaeological Society Transactions and Proceedings*, 81 (1963–4), 74–7

—, 'Kenilworth Castle: A Discussion of its Entrances', *Birmingham Archaeological Society Transactions and Proceedings*, 84 (1967–70), 148–59

W. Dugdale, *The Antiquities of Warwickshire*, vol. 1, London, 1730 edn, 236–65

A. Emery, *Greater Medieval Houses of England and Wales, 1300–1500*, vol. 11: *East Anglia, Central England and Wales*, Cambridge, 399–408

C. H. Hartshorne, ed., 'Kenilworth Castle', *Royal Archaeological Institute of Great Britain and Ireland Proceedings (Northumberland)*, 2 (1852), appendix 8, cxxxvi–cxxxix

J. H. Harvey, 'Sidelights on Kenilworth Castle' *Archaeological Journal*, 101 (1944), 91–107

History of the King's Works, vol. 11, 682–5

History of the King's Works, vol. 111, part 1, 258–60

E. H. Knowles, *The Castle of Kenilworth*, Warwick, 1872

N. Molyneux, 'Kenilworth Castle in 1563', *English Heritage Historical Review*, 3 (2008), 46–61

B. Morley, P. Brown and T. Crump, (compiled by P. Ellis), 'The Elizabethan Gardens and Leicester's Stables at Kenilworth Castle', *Birmingham and Warwickshire Archaeological Society*, 99 (1995), 81–119

R. K. Morris, *Kenilworth Castle*, London, 2006 [English Heritage Red Guide]

—, 'A Plan for Kenilworth Castle at Longleat', *English Heritage Historical Review*, 2 (2007), 22–35

—, ' "I was never more in Love with and olde howse nor never newe worke coulde be better bestowed": The Earl of Leicester's Remodelling of Kenilworth Castle for Queen Elizabeth 1', *Antiquaries Journal*, 89 (2009), 241–305

M. W. Phelps, 'The Pleasaunce, Kenilworth', *Birmingham Archaeological Society Transactions and Proceedings*, 49 (1923), 61–2

P. Rahtz, 'Kenilworth Castle, 1960', *Birmingham Archaeological Society Transactions and Proceedings*, 81 (1963–4), 55–73

R. Strong, 'Gloriana's Garden', *Country Life*, 203 (5 August 2009), 46–50

H. Sunley, 'Recent Observations on the West Doorway of St Nicholas' Church, Kenilworth', *Transactions of the Birmingham and Warwickshire Archaeological Society*, 95 (1987–8), 73–9

M. W. Thompson, 'Reclamation of Waste Ground for the Pleasance at Kenilworth Castle, Warwickshire', *Medieval Archaeology*, 8 (1964), 222–3

—, 'Two Levels of the Mere at Kenilworth Castle, Warwickshire', *Medieval Archaeology*, 9 (1965), 156–61

—, 'Three Stages in the Construction of the Hall at Kenilworth Castle, Warwickshire', in *Ancient Monuments and their Interpretation*, ed. M. R. Apted, R. Gilyard-Beer and A. D. Saunders, London and Chichester, 1977, 211–18

—, *Kenilworth Castle*, London, 1987 edn [English Heritage guidebook]

VCH: Warwick, vol. VI, Oxford, 1951, 132–8

E. Woodhouse, 'Kenilworth: The Earl of Leicester's Pleasure Grounds Following Robert Laneham's Letter', *Garden History*, 27 (1999), 127–44

The research that informed the reconstruction of the Elizabethan garden at Kenilworth that opened in 2009 is to be published in an edited volume on the castle by English Heritage.

WINDSOR

R. Barber, R. Brown and J. Munby, eds, *Edward III's Round Table at Windsor*, Woodbridge and Rochester, NY, 2007

B. Baud, J. Britton and M. Gandy, *Architectural Illustrations of Windsor Castle*, London, 1842

C. R. Beard, *The Tomb and Achievements of King Henry VI at Windsor*, Frome, 1936

J. Bond, 'The Medieval Constables of Windsor Castle', *English Historical Review*, 82 (1967), 225–59

S. Brindle and B. Kerr, *Windsor Revealed: New Light on the History of the Castle*, London, 1997

P. E. Curnow, 'Royal Lodgings of the 13th Century in the Lower Ward at Windsor Castle: Some Recent Archaeological Discoveries', *Friends' Annual Report to 30th September 1965* (1965), 218–28

T. E. Harwood, *Windsor Old and New*, London, 1929

History of the King's Works, vol. II, 864–88

History of the King's Works, vol. III, part 1, 302–33

L. Keen and E. Scarff, eds, *Windsor: Medieval Archaeology, Art and Architecture of the Thames Valley*, British Archaeological Association Conference Transactions, 25, Leeds, 2002

C. Richmond and E. Scarff, eds, *St George's Chapel, Windsor, in the Late Middle Ages*, Windsor, 2001

J. Roberts, *Views of Windsor: Watercolours by Thomas and Paul Sandby from the Collection of Her Majesty the Queen*, London, 1995

—, *Royal Landscape: The Gardens and Parks of Windsor*, London, 1997

N. Saul, ed., *St George's Chapel, Windsor, in the Fourteenth Century*, Woodbridge, 2005

W. H. St John Hope, *Windsor Castle: An Architectural History*, 2 vols and plans, London, 1913

PREFACE

General Works in Chronological Order of Publication

F. Grose, *The Antiquities of England and Wales*, London, 6 vols, 1772–87

E. King, 'Observations on Ancient Castles', *Archaeologia*, 4 (1778), 364–413

—, 'Sequel to the Observations on Ancient Castles', *Archaeologia*, 6 (1782), 231–380

F. Grose, *Military Antiquities Respecting a History of the English Army from the Conquest to the Present Time*, 2 vols, London, 1786–88

—, *The Antiquities of Ireland*, 2 vols, London, 1791–5

E. King, *Munimenta Antiqua; or, Observations on Ancient Castles including Remarks on the Whole Progress of Architecture, Ecclesiastical as well as Military, in Great Britain: and on the Corresponding Changes in Manners, Laws and Customs etc.*, 4 vols, London, 1799–1804

J. Nash, *The Mansions of England in the Olden Time*, 4 vols, London, 1839–49

Archaeological Journal, published from 1844

G. T. Clark, 'On Military Architecture', *Archaeological Journal*, 1 (1844–5), 93–107

Journal of the British Archaeological Association, published from 1846

T. H. Turner and J. H. Parker, *Some Account of Domestic Architecture in England . . . From the Conquest to Henry VIII*, 3 vols in 4, Oxford, 1851–9

E. E. Viollet-le-Duc, *Dictionnaire raisonné de l'architecture française du XIe au XVIe siècle*, 10 vols, Paris, 1854–70

—, *An Essay on the Military Architecture of the Middle Ages*, trans. M. Macdermott, London, 1860

—, *Annals of a Fortress*, trans. B. Bucknall, London, 1875

G. T. Clark, *Mediaeval Military Architecture in England*, 2 vols, London, 1884

T. MacGibbon and D. Ross, *The Castellated and Domestic Architecture of Scotland from the 12th to the 18th Centuries*, 5 vols, Edinburgh, 1887–92

C. J. Bates, *The Border Holds of Northumberland*, Newcastle, 1891

J. H. Round, *Geoffrey de Mandeville: A Study of the Anarchy*, London, 1892

J. A. Gotch, *Architecture of the Renaissance in England: Illustrated by a Series of Views and Details from Buildings Erected between 1560–1635*, 2 vols, London, 1894

Country Life, published from 1897

J. Mackenzie, *The Castles of Great Britain*, 2 vols, London, 1897

The Victoria History of the Counties of England (*VCH*), published from 1900

J. A. Gotch, *Early Renaissance Architecture in England: A Historical and Descriptive Account of Tudor, Elizabethan, and Jacobean Periods, 1500–1625*, London, 1901

T. Garner and A. Stratton, *Domestic Architecture of England during the Tudor Period*, 2 vols, London, 1910

E. Armitage, *Early Norman Castles of the British Isles*, London, 1912

A. H. Thompson, *Military Architecture during the Middle Ages* Oxford, 1912

H. A. Tipping, *English Homes*, 8 vols, London, 1920–37

N. Curzon, *Bodiam Castle*, London, 1926

C. W. C. Oman, *Castles*, London, 1926

N. Curzon and H. A. Tipping, *Tattershall Castle, Lincolnshire*, London, 1929

H. Braun, *The English Castle*, New York and London, 1936

S. Toy, *A Short History of Fortifications from 1600 BC to 1600 AD*, London, 1939

H. C. Leask, *Irish Castles and Castellated Houses*, Dundalk, 1941

W. D. Simpson, *Castles from the Air*, London, 1949

N. Pevsner, *The Buildings of England*, Harmondsworth; London and New Haven, 1951–

S. Toy, *The Castles of Great Britain*, London, 1953

R. A. Brown, *English Castles*, London, 1954

B. H. St John O'Neil, *Castles and Canon: A Study of Early Artillery Fortifications in England*, Oxford, 1960

Château Gaillard Conference, European castle conference first held in 1962; transactions published from 1964

The History of the King's Works: The Middle Ages, ed. R. A. Brown, H. M. Colvin and A. J. Taylor, 2 vols, London, 1963

M. Wood, *The English Medieval House*, London, 1965

C. Hohler, 'Kings and Castles: Court Life in Peace and War', in *The Flowering of the Middle Ages*, ed. J. Evans, London, 1966, 125–46

W. D. Simpson, *Castles in Britain*, London, 1966

—, *Castles in England and Wales*, London, 1969

D. F. Renn, *Norman Castles in Britain*, London, 1969

W. Anderson and W. Swaan, *Castles of Europe from Charlemagne to the Renaissance*, London, 1970

A. Emery, *Dartington Hall*, Oxford, 1970

H. Turner, *Town Defences in England and Wales: An Architectural and Documentary Study, AD 900 to 1500*, London, 1970

R. A. Stalley, *Architecture and Sculpture in Ireland, 1150–1350*, Dublin, 1971

P. Warner, *The Medieval Castle*, London, 1971

The History of the King's Works, 1485–1660 (part 1), ed. H. M. Colvin, D. R. Ransome and J. Summerson, London, 1975 [cited here as *History of the King's Works*, vol. III]

W. Swaan, *Art and Architecture of the Late Middle Ages, 1350 to the Advent of the Renaissance*, London, 1977

J. Burke, *Life in the Castle in Medieval England*, London, 1978

M. Girouard, *Life in the English Country House*, New Haven and London, 1978

J. H. Harvey, *The Perpendicular Style*, London, 1978

C. Duffy, *Siege Warfare: The Fortress in the Early-Modern World, 1494–1660*, London, 1979

C. Kightly, *Strongholds of the Realm: Defences in Britain from Prehistory to the 20th Century*, London, 1979

R. A. Brown, C. Coulson and M. Prestwich, *Castles: A History and Guide*, Poole, 1980

C. Platt, *The Castle in Medieval England and Wales*, London, 1982

The History of the King's Works, 1485–1660 (part 2), ed. H. M. Colvin, J. Summerson, M. Biddle, J. R. Hale and M. Merriman,

London, 1982 [cited here as *History of the King's Works*, vol. IV]

D. J. C. King, *Castellarium Anglicanum: An Index and Bibliography of the Castles in England, Wales and the Islands*, 2 vols, New York, 1983

J. Holt, T. Holland and G. Zarnecki, *English Romanesque Art, 1066–1200*, exhibition catalogue, Hayward Gallery, London, 1984

J. Alexander and P. Binski, *The Age of Chivalry: Art in Plantagenet England, 1200–1400*, exhibition catalogue, Royal Academy, London, 1987

M. W. Thompson, *The Decline of the Castle*, Cambridge, 1987

D. J. C. King, *The Castle in England and Wales: An Interpretative History*, London and Sydney, 1988

Fortress, published from 1989 to 1993

A. Saunders, *Fortress Britain*, Liphook, 1989

T. B. James, *The Palaces of Medieval England, c.1050–1550*, London, 1990

J. R. Kenyon, *Medieval Fortifications*, Leicester, 1990

C. Platt, *The Architecture of Medieval Britain: A Social History*, London and New Haven, 1990

N. J. G. Pounds, *The Medieval Castle in England and Wales: A Social and Political History*, Cambridge, 1990

J. Mesqui, *Châteaux et enceintes de la France médiévale*, 2 vols, Paris, 1991

M. W. Thompson, *The Rise of the Castle*, Cambridge, 1991

J. Bradbury, *The Medieval Siege*, Woodbridge, 1992

P. Barker and R. Higham, *Timber Castles*, London, 1992

T. McNeill, *Castles*, London, 1992

R. Fawcett, *The Architectural History of Scotland: Scottish Architecture from the Accession of the Stewarts to the Reformation, 1371–1560*, Edinburgh, 1994

D. Howard, *The Architectural History of Scotland: Scottish Architecture from the Reformation to the Restoration, 1560–1660*, Edinburgh, 1995

P. M. Kerrigan, *Castles and Fortifications in Ireland, 1485–1945*, Cork, 1995

A. Emery, *Greater Medieval Houses of England and Wales*, 3 vols, Cambridge, 1996–2006

J. C. Grenville, *Medieval Housing*, London, 1997

T. McNeill, *Castles in Ireland: Feudal Power in a Gaelic World*, London and New York, 1997

J. Mesqui, *Châteaux forts et fortifications en France*, Paris, 1997

N. Cooper, *Houses of the Gentry*, New Haven and London, 1999

D. Sweetman, *The Medieval Castles of Ireland*, Cork, 1999; Woodbridge, 2000

E. Fernie, *The Architecture of Norman England*, Oxford, 2000

C. McKean, *The Scottish Château: The Country House of Renaissance Scotland*, Stroud, 2001

J. M. Steane, *The Archaeology of Power: England and Northern Europe, AD 800–1600*, Stroud, 2001

O. Creighton, *Castles and Landscapes: Power, Community and Fortification in Medieval England*, London, 2002

M. Johnson, *Behind the Castle Gate*, London and New York, 2002

J. Richard, *The Castle Community, 1272–1422*, Woodbridge, 2002

C. Coulson, *Castles in Medieval Society: Fortresses in England, France and Ireland in the Central Middle Ages*, Oxford, 2003

Gothic: Art for England, 1400–1547, ed. R. Marks and P. Williamson, exhibition catalogue, Victoria and Albert Museum, London, 2003

A. Wheatley, *The Idea of the Castle in Medieval England*, Woodbridge and York, 2004

O. Creighton and P. Higham, *Medieval Town Walls*, Stroud, 2005

R. Liddiard, *Castles in Context: Power, Symbolism and Landscape, 1066–1500*, Macclesfield, 2005

A. Gomme and A. Maguire, *Design and Plan in the Country House: From Castle Donjons to Palladian Boxes*, New Haven and London, 2008

J. R. Kenyon, *Castles, Town Defences and Artillery Fortifications in the United Kingdom and Ireland: A Bibliography, 1945–2006*, Donington, 2008

I THE ENGLISH CASTLE

J. Ayres, *Domestic Interiors: The British Tradition, 1500–1850*, New Haven and London, 2003

J. Blair, 'Hall and Chamber: English Domestic Planning, 1000–1250', in *Manorial Domestic Buildings in England and Northern France*, ed. G. Meirion-Jones and M. Jones, Occasional Papers from the Society of Antiquaries of London, new series, 15, London, 1993, 1–21

P. Brears, *All the King's Cooks*, London, 1999

—, *Cooking and Dining in Medieval England*, Totnes, 2007

T. Campbell, *Tapestry in the Renaissance: Art and Magnificence*, exhibition catalogue, Metropolitan Museum of Art, New York, 2002

D. Crouch, *The Image of Aristocracy in Britain, 1000–1300*, New York and London, 1992

P. Dixon and B. Lott, 'The Courtyard and the Tower: Contexts and Symbols in the Development of the Late Medieval Great House', *Journal of the British Archaeological Association*, 146 (1993), 93–101

G. Fairclough, 'Meaningful Constructions: Spatial and Functional Analysis of Medieval Buildings', *Antiquity*, 66 (1992), 348–66

P. A. Faulkner, 'Domestic Planning from the 12th to the 14th Century', *Archaeological Journal*, 115 (1958), 150–83

—, 'Castle Planning in the 14th Century', *Archaeological Journal*, 120 (1963), 215–35

—, 'Some Medieval Archiepiscopal Palaces', *Archaeological Journal*, 127 (1970), 130–46

B. Harvey, *Living and Dying in England, 1100–1540: The Monastic Experience*, Oxford, 1993

The Household of Edward IV: The Black Book and the Ordinance of 1478, ed. A. R. Myers, Oxford, 1959

E. Impey, 'Seigneurial Domestic Architecture in Normandy, 1050–1350', in *Manorial Domestic Buildings in England and Northern France*, ed. G. Meirion-Jones and M. Jones, Occasional Papers from the Society of Antiquaries of London, new series, 15, London, 1993, 82–120

M. W. Labarge, *A Baronial Household of the 13th Century*, London, 1965

S. McKendrick, 'Edward IV: An English Royal Collector of Netherlandish Tapestry', *Burlington Magazine*, 129 (1987), 521–4

—, 'Tapestries from the Low Countries in England during the 15th Century', in *England and the Low Countries in the Middle Ages*, ed. C. Barron and N. Saul, Stroud, 1995, 43–60

K. Mertes, *The English Noble Household, 1250–1600*, Oxford, 1988

B. M. Morley, 'Aspects of 14th-Century Castle Design', in *Collectanea Historica: Essays in Honour of Stuart Rigold*, ed. E. Detsicas, Maidstone, 1981, 104–13

I. Mortimer, *The Time Traveller's Guide to Medieval England*, London, 2009

'Ordinances for the Household Made at Eltham in the 17th year of King Henry VIII, AD 1526', in *Liber Niger*, ed. Anon., London, 1790, 109–61

A. Richardson, 'Gender and Space in English Royal Palaces, c.1160–1547', *Medieval Archaeology*, 47 (2003), 131–67

M. W. Thompson, *The Medieval Hall: The Basis of Secular Domestic Life, 600–1600 AD*, Aldershot, 1995

W. G. Thomson, *A History of Tapestry*, rev. edn, London, 1930

M. Wood, '13th-century Domestic Architecture in England', *Archaeological Journal*, 105 (1950), supplement

—, *Norman Domestic Architecture*, London, 1974

C. M. Woolgar, *The Great Household in Late Medieval England*, London and New Haven, 1999

G. Worsley, *The British Stable*, London and New Haven, 2004

2 THE CASTLES OF THE CONQUEST

J. Backhouse and L. Webster, eds, *The Making of England: Anglo-Saxon Art and Culture, AD 600–900*, exhibition catalogue, British Museum, London, 1991

F. Barlow, *Edward the Confessor*, second edn, New Haven and London, 1997

D. Bates, *Normandy before 1066*, London and New York, 1982

—, 'The Conqueror's Adolescence', *Anglo-Norman Studies*, 25 (2003), 1–18

R. A. Brown, 'The Norman Conquest and the Genesis of English Castle Building', *Château Gaillard*, 3 (1969), 1–14

—, *The Normans and the Norman Conquest*, London, 1969

—, 'An Historian's Approach to the Origins of the Castle in England', *Archaeological Journal*, 126 (1969), 131–46

—, *The Norman Conquest of England: Sources and Documents*, Woodbridge, 1984

W. J. Corbett, 'The Development of the Duchy of Normandy and the Norman Conquest of England', in *Cambridge Medieval History*, vol. v: *Contest of Empire and Papacy*, ed. J. R. Tanner et al., Cambridge, 1926, 507–20

R. H. C. Davis, 'William of Poitiers and his History', in *The Writing of History in the Middle Ages: Essays Presented to Richard William Southern*, ed. R. H. C. Davis and J. M. Wallace-Hadrill, Oxford, 1981, 71–100

B. Davison, 'Early Earthwork Castles: A New Model', *Château Gaillard*, 3 (1966), 37–46s

—, 'The Origins of the Castle in England: The Institute's Research Project', *Archaeological Journal*, 124 (1967), 202–211

—, 'Three Eleventh-Century Earthworks in England: Their Excavation and Implications', *Château Gaillard*, 2 (1967), 39–48

—, 'Reply . . . to Allen Brown', *Archaeological Journal*, 126 (1969), 146–8

D. C. Douglas, *William the Conqueror*, London, 1964

E. Fernie, *The Architecture of the Anglo-Saxons*, London, 1983

C. P. Lewis, 'The Early Earls of Norman England', *Anglo-Norman Studies*, 13 (1990), 207–23

J. O. Prestwich, 'The Military Household of the Norman Kings', *English Historical Review*, 96 (1981), 1–35

T. Purser, 'William Fitz Osbern, Earl of Hereford: Personality and Power on the Welsh Frontier, 1066–1071', in *Armies, Chivalry and Warfare in Medieval Britain and France: Proceedings of the 1995 Harlaxton Symposium*, ed. M. Strickland, Stamford, 1998, 133–46

D. F. Renn, 'The First Norman Castles in England, 1051–71', *Château Gaillard*, 1 (1964), 123–32

—, 'Burgheat and Gonfanon: Two Sidelights from the Bayeux Tapestry', *Anglo-Norman Studies*, 16 (1994), 177–98

W. H. St. John Hope, 'English Fortresses and Castles of the 11th and 12th Centuries', *Archaeological Journal*, 60 (1903), 72–90

A. Williams, *The English and the Norman Conquest*, Woodbridge, 1997

—, 'A Bell House and a Burh-Geat: Lordly Residences in England before the Conquest', in *Anglo-Norman Castles*, ed. R. Liddiard, Woodbridge, 2003, 23–40

3 THE CASTLES OF SETTLEMENT

W. M. Aird, *St Cuthbert and the Normans*, Woodbridge, 1998

F. H. Baring, *Domesday Tables*, London, 1909

F. Barlow, *The Feudal Kingdom of England*, London, 1961

—, *The English Church, 1066–1154: A History of the Anglo-Norman Church*, London, 1979

D. Bates, *William the Conqueror*, London, 1989

J. H. Beeler, *Warfare in England, 1066–1189*, New York, 1966

R. A. Brown, *The Normans and the Norman Conquest*, London, 1969

M. Chibnall, *Anglo-Norman England, 1066–1166*, Oxford, 1986

P. Dalton, *Conquest, Anarchy and Lordship: Yorkshire, 1066–1154*, Cambridge, 1994

D. C. Douglas, *William the Conqueror*, London, 1964

E. Fernie, *The Architecture of Norman England*, Oxford, 2000

J. Gillingham, 'The Introduction of Knight Service into England', *Anglo-Norman Studies*, 4 (1981), 53–64, 181–7

J. A. Green, *The Aristocracy of Norman England*, Cambridge, 1997

C. G. Harfield, 'A Hand-List of Castles Recorded in the Domesday Book', *English Historical Review*, 106 (1991), 371–92

J. C. Holt, 'The Introduction of Knight Service into England', *Anglo-Norman Studies*, 6 (1983), 89–106

W. E. Kapelle, *The Norman Conquest of the North: The Region and its Transformation, 1000–1135*, London, 1979

D. J. C. King, 'The Field Archaeology of Mottes in England and Wales', *Château Gaillard*, 5 (1972), 101–17

— and L. Alcock, 'Ringworks of England and Wales', *Château Gaillard*, 3 (1969), 90–127

W. Morris, *The Medieval English Sheriff to 1300* [1927], reprinted Manchester, 1968

J. O. Prestwich, 'The Military Household of the Norman Kings', *English Historical Review*, 96 (1981), 1–35

—, 'The Career of Ranulf Flambard', in *Anglo-Norman Durham, 1093–1193*, ed. D. Rollason, M. Harvey and M. Prestwich, Woodbridge, 1994, 299–310

R. A. Stalley, *Early Medieval Architecture*, Oxford, 1999

4 THE AGE OF MAGNIFICENCE

F. Barlow, *The Feudal Kingdom of England*, London, 1961

—, *The English Church, 1066–1154: A History of the Anglo-Norman Church*, London, 1979

—, *William Rufus*, London, 1983

G. Barrow, 'The Scots and the North of England', in *The Anarchy of King Stephen's Reign*, ed. E. King, Oxford, 1994, 231–53

R. Bartlett, *England under the Norman and Angevin Kings, 1075–1225*, Oxford, 2000

J. H. Beeler, *Warfare in England, 1066–1189*, New York, 1966

M. Chibnall, *The World of Orderic Vitalis*, Oxford, 1984

—, *Anglo-Norman England, 1066–1166*, Oxford and Cambridge, MA, 1986

—, 'Orderic Vitalis on Castles', in *Studies in Medieval History Presented to R. Allen Brown*, ed. C. Harper-Bill, C. Holdsworth and J. Nelson, Woodbridge, 1989, 43–56

—, *The Empress Matilda*, Oxford, 1993

H. A. Cronne, *The Reign of Stephen, 1135–54*, London, 1970

D. Crouch, *The Reign of King Stephen, 1135–1154*, Harlow, 2000

P. Dalton, *Conquest, Anarchy and Lordship: Yorkshire, 1066–1154*, Cambridge, 1994

E. Fernie, *The Architecture of Norman England*, Oxford, 2000

E. A. Freeman, *The Reign of William Rufus and the Accession of Henry I*, 2 vols, Oxford, 1882

J. A. Green, *The Government of England under Henry I*, Cambridge, 1986

—, *The Aristocracy of Norman England*, Cambridge, 1997

C. W. Hollister, *Monarchy, Magnates and Institutions in the Anglo-Norman World*, London, 1986

J. Holt, T. Holland and G. Zarnecki, *English Romanesque Art, 1066–1200*, exhibition catalogue, Hayward Gallery, London, 1984

E. King, 'King Stephen and the Anglo-Norman Aristocracy', *History*, 59 (1974), 180–94

J. Le Patourel, 'The Norman Succession, 996–1135', *English Historical Review*, 86 (1971), 225–50

S. Morillo, *Warfare under the Anglo-Norman Kings, 1066–1135*, Woodbridge, 1994

C. A. Newman, *The Anglo-Norman Nobility in the Reign of Henry I: The Second Generation*, Philadelphia, PA, 1988

J. H. Round, *Geoffrey de Mandeville: A Study of the Anarchy*, London, 1892

I. J. Sanders, *English Baronies: A Study of their Origin and Descent, 1086–1327*, Oxford, 1960

D. Walker, 'The Norman Settlement in Wales', *Anglo-Norman Studies*, 1 (1978), 131–43

G. H. White, 'King Stephen's Earldoms', *Transactions of the Royal Historical Society*, fourth series, 13 (1930), 51–82

5 THE EARLY ANGEVIN CASTLE

J. Baldwin, *Philip II Augustus: Foundations of French Royal Power in the Middle Ages*, Berkeley, CA, 1986

F. Barlow, *Thomas Becket*, London, 1986

R. Bartlett, *England under the Norman and Angevin Kings, 1075–1225*, Oxford, 2000

M.-P. Baudry, *Les Fortifications des Plantagênets en Poitou, 1154–1242*, Mémoires de la section d'archéologie et d'histoire de l'art, II, Paris, 2001

—, 'La Politique de fortification des Plantagênets en Poitou', *Anglo-Norman Studies*, 24 (2001), 43–68

J. H. Beeler, 'Castles and Strategy in Early Angevin England', *Speculum*, 31 (1956), 581–601

R. A. Brown, 'Royal Castle Building in England, 1154–1216', *English Historical Review*, 70 (1955), 353–98

—, 'A List of Castles, 1154–1216', *English Historical Review*, 74 (1959), 249–80

M. T. Clanchy, *England and its Rulers, 1066–1272*, London, 1983

D. Crouch, *William Marshal: Court, Career and Chivalry in the Angevin Empire, 1147–1219*, Harlow, 1990

R. H. C. Davis, *King Stephen*, London, 1967

R. W. Eyton, *Court, Household and Itinerary of Henry II*, London, 1878

M. T. Flanagan, *Irish Society, Anglo-Norman Settlers, Angevin Kingship: Interactions in Ireland in the Late 12th Century*, Oxford, 1989

R. Frame, *The Political Development of the British Isles, 1100–1400*, Oxford, 1990

J. Gillingham, *Richard the Lionheart*, Frome and London, 1978

—, *The Angevin Empire*, London, 1984

—, *Richard Coeur de Lion*, London and Rio Grande, 1994

L. Grant, 'Architectural Relationships between England and Normandy, 1100–1204', in *England and Normandy in the Middle Ages*, ed. D. Bates and A. Curry, London, 1994, 117–30

—, 'Le Patronage architectural d'Henri II et son entourage', *Cahiers de civilisation médiévale*, 37 (1994), 73–84

—, *Architecture and Society in Normandy, 1120–1270*, New Haven and London, 2005

J. E. A. Jollife, 'The Chamber and the Castle Treasuries under King John', in *Studies in Medieval History Presented to Frederick Maurice Powicke*, ed. R. W. Hunt, W. A. Pantin and R. W. Southern, Oxford, 1948, 117–42

J. S. Moore, 'Anglo-Norman Garrisons', *Anglo-Norman Studies*, 22 (1999), 205–59

R. Mortimer, *Angevin England, 1154–1258*, Oxford, 1994

W. L. Warren, *Henry II*, Berkeley and Los Angeles, 1973

—, *King John*, second edn, London, 1978

—, *The Governance of Norman and Angevin England*, London, 1987

6 THE GOTHIC CASTLE

M.-P. Baudry, *Les Fortifications des Plantagênets en Poitou, 1154–1242*, Mémoires de la section d'archéologie et d'histoire de l'art, 11, Paris, 2001

P. Binski, *The Painted Chamber at Westminster*, Occasional Papers of the Society of Antiquaries of London, new series, 9, London, 1986

—, *Westminster Abbey and the Plantagenets: Kingship and the Representation of Power, 1200–1400*, New Haven and London, 1995

J. Bony, *French Gothic Architecture of the 12th and 13th Centuries*, Berkeley, CA, and London, 1983

R. A. Brown, 'Royal Castle Building in England, 1154–1216', *English Historical Review*, 70 (1955), 353–98

—, 'A List of Castles, 1154–1216', *English Historical Review*, 74 (1959), 249–80

D. A. Carpenter, *The Minority of Henry III*, London, 1990

—, *The Reign of Henry III*, London, 1996

H. M. Colvin, ed., *Building Accounts of King Henry III*, Oxford, 1971

R. R. Davies, *Conquest, Coexistence and Change: Wales, 1063–1415*, Oxford, 1987

R. Eales, 'Castles and Politics in England, 1215–1224', *Thirteenth Century England*, 2 (1988), 23–43

R. F. Frame, *The Political Development of the British Isles, 1100–1400*, Oxford, 1990

P. Frankl, *Gothic Architecture*, second edn, revised by Paul Crossley, New Haven and London, 2000

L. Grant, *Architecture and Society in Normandy, 1120–1270*, New Haven and London, 2005

J. C. Holt, *The Northerners: A Study in the Reign of King John*, Oxford, 1961

W. Morris, *The Medieval English Sheriff to 1300* [1927], reprinted Manchester, 1968

F. M. Powicke, *The Loss of Normandy, 1189–1204*, second edn, Manchester, 1961

N. Vincent, *Peter des Roches: An Alien in English Politics, 1205–38*, Cambridge, 1996

N. D. Young, *Richard of Cornwall*, Oxford, 1947

7 THE KING'S WORKS AND WALES

J. Alexander and P. Binski, *The Age of Chivalry: Art in Plantagenet England, 1200–1400*, exhibition catalogue, Royal Academy, London, 1987

J. Bony, *The English Decorated Style*, Oxford, 1979

N. Coldstream, *The Decorated Style: Architecture and Ornament, 1240–1360*, Toronto and Bath, 1994

R. R. Davies, *Lordship and Society in the March of Wales, 1282–1400*, Oxford, 1978

J. G. Edwards, 'Edward I's Castle Building in Wales', *Proceedings of the British Academy*, 32 (1944), 15–81

R. M. Haines, *King Edward II*, Montreal, 2003

Knights of Edward I, ed. C. Moor, 5 vols, Harleian Society, 80–84, London, 1929–32

J. M. Hastings, *St Stephen's Chapel*, Cambridge, 1955

F. Mackenzie, *The Architectural Antiquities of the Collegiate Chapel of St Stephen*, London, 1844

J. E. Morris, *The Welsh Wars of Edward I*, Oxford, 1901

M. Morris, *A Great and Terrible King: Edward I and the Forging of Britain*, London, 2008

M. Prestwich, *War, Politics, and Finance under Edward I*, London, 1972

—, *The Three Edwards: War and State in England, 1272–1377*, London, 1980

—, *Edward I*, London, 1988

J. B. Smith, *Llywelyn ap Gruffudd, Prince of Wales*, Cardiff, 1998 edn

A. J. Taylor, *The King's Works in Wales, 1277–1330*, London, 1974 [reprinted section from *History of the King's Works*, vol. 1]

D. M. Williams and J. R. Kenyon, eds, *The Impact of the Edwardian Castles in Wales*, Oxford, 2010

8 THE KING'S SERVANTS AND THE ARCHITECTURE OF WAR

G. W. S. Barrow, *Robert Bruce and the Community of the Realm of Scotland*, third edn, Edinburgh, 1988

J. Bony, *The English Decorated Style*, Oxford, 1979

N. Coldstream, *The Decorated Style: Architecture and Ornament, 1240–1360*, Toronto and Bath, 1994

C. M. Fraser, *A History of Antony Bek, Bishop of Durham, 1283–1311*, Oxford, 1957

J. S. Hamilton, *Piers Gaveston, Earl of Cornwall, 1307–1312: Politics and Patronage in the Reign of Edward II*, Detroit, MI, 1988

Knights of Edward I, ed. C. Moor, 5 vols, Harleian Society, 80–84, London, 1929–32

J. R. Maddicott, *Thomas of Lancaster, 1307–1322: A Study in the Reign of Edward II*, Oxford, 1970

J. C. Parsons, *Eleanor of Castile: Queen and Society in 13th-century England*, Basingstoke, 1994

M. Prestwich, 'English Castles in the Reign of Edward II', *Journal of Medieval History*, 9 (1982), 159–78

M. G. A. Vale, *The Angevin Legacy and the Hundred Years War, 1250–1340*, Oxford, 1990

9 THE LION OF ENGLAND

J. Alexander and P. Binski, *The Age of Chivalry: Art in Plantagenet England, 1200–1400*, exhibition catalogue, Royal Academy, London, 1987

J. Bony, *The English Decorated Style*, Oxford, 1979

K. Fowler, *The King's Lieutenant: Henry of Grosmont, 1st Duke of Lancaster, 1310–1361*, London, 1969

C. Given-Wilson, *The English Nobility in the Late Middle Ages*, London, 1987

J. M. Hastings, *St Stephen's Chapel*, Cambridge, 1955

K. B. McFarlane, *The Nobility of Later Medieval England*, Oxford, 1973

I. Mortimer, *The Perfect King: The Life of Edward III*, London, 2006

M. Prestwich, *The Three Edwards: War and State in England, 1272–1377*, London, 1980

Register of Edward, the Black Prince, ed. M. C. B. Dawes, 4 vols, London, 1930–33

J. Vale, *Edward III and Chivalry: Chivalric Society and its Context, 1270–1350*, Woodbridge, 1982

M. Whiteley, 'The Courts of Edward III of England and Charles V of France: A Comparison of their Architectural Setting and Ceremonial Functions', in *Fourteenth Century England*, 1, ed. N. Saul, Woodbridge, 2000, 153–66

10 THE GENESIS OF THE PERPENDICULAR STYLE

J. Alexander and P. Binski, *The Age of Chivalry: Art in Plantagenet England, 1200–1400*, exhibition catalogue, Royal Academy, London, 1987

C. Allmand, *The Hundred Years War*, Cambridge, 1988

H. E. L. Collins, *The Order of the Garter, 1348–1461*, Oxford, 2000

A. Goodman, *John of Gaunt: The Exercise of Princely Power in 14th-century Europe*, London, 1992

J. H. Harvey, *The Perpendicular Style*, London, 1978

J. Munby, R. Barber and R. Brown, eds, *Edward III's Round Table at Windsor*, Woodbridge, 2007

W. M. Ormrod, *The Reign of Edward III*, London and New Haven, 1990

—, 'For Arthur and St George: Edward III, Windsor Castle and the Order of the Garter', in *St George's Chapel, Windsor, in the Fourteenth Century*, ed. N. Saul, Woodbridge, 2005, 13–50

C. Wilson, 'The Origins of the Perpendicular Style and its Development to c.1360', unpublished ph.d thesis, University of London, 1980

—, 'The Royal Lodgings of Edward III at Windsor Castle', in *Windsor: Medieval Archaeology, Art and Architecture of the Thames Valley*, ed. L. Keen and E. Scarff, British Archaeological Association Conference Transactions, 25, Leeds, 2002, 15–94

11 THE TRIUMPH OF THE PERPENDICULAR

C. Given-Wilson, *The Royal Household and the King's Affinity: Service, Politics and Finance in England, 1360–1413*, New Haven and London, 1986

A. Goodman, *The Loyal Conspiracy: The Lords Appellant under Richard II*, London, 1971

D. Gordon, L. Monnas and C. Elam, eds, *The Regal Image of Richard II and the Wilton Diptych*, London, 1997

J. H. Harvey, *Henry Yevele: The Life of an English Architect*, London, 1944

—, *The Perpendicular Style*, London, 1978

N. Saul, 'Richard II and the Vocabulary of Kingship', *English Historical Review*, 110 (1995), 854–77

—, *Richard II*, New Haven and London, 1997

—, 'Richard II, York and the Evidence of the King's Itinerary', in *The Age of Richard II*, ed. J. L. Gillespie, Stroud, 1997, 71–92

A. Tuck, *Richard II and the English Nobility*, London, 1973

R. S. Tuck, 'Richard II and the Border Magnates', *Northern History*, 3 (1968), 27–52

S. Walker, *The Lancastrian Affinity, 1361–99*, Oxford, 1990

12 THE LANCASTRIAN AGE

C. Allmand, *Henry V*, London and New Haven, 1997

C. Barron, 'England and the Low Countries, 1327–1477', in *England and the Low Countries in the Middle Ages*, ed. C. Barron and N. Saul, Stroud, 1995, 1–28

H. Castor, *The King, the Crown and the Duchy of Lancaster*, Oxford, 2000

R. R. Davies, *The Revolt of Owain Glyn Dŵr*, Oxford, 1995

V. Davis, *William Waynflete, Bishop and Educationalist*, Woodbridge, 1993

C. Given-Wilson, *The English Nobility in the Late Middle Ages*, London, 1987

Gothic: Art for England, 1400–1547, ed. R. Marks and P. Williamson, exhibition catalogue, Victoria and Albert Museum, London, 2003

R. A. Griffiths, *The Reign of King Henry VI: The Exercise of Royal Authority, 1422–1461*, London, 1981

—, *King and Country: England and Wales in the 15th Century*, London, 1991

G. L. Harriss, *Cardinal Beaufort: A Study in Lancastrian Ascendancy and Decline*, Oxford, 1988

J. H. Harvey, *The Perpendicular Style*, London, 1978

P. A. Johnson, *Duke Richard of York, 1411–1460*, Oxford, 1988

J. L. Kirby, *Henry IV of England: A Biography*, London, 1970

W. C. Leedy, *Fan Vaulting: A Study of Form, Technology and Meaning*, London, 1980

K. B. McFarlane, *The Nobility of Later Medieval England*, Oxford, 1973

L. Monckton, 'Late Gothic Architecture in South-West England: Four Major Centres of Building Activity at Wells, Bristol, Sherborne and Bath', unpublished ph.d thesis, University of Warwick, 1999

T. P. Smith, *The Medieval Brickmaking Industry in England, 1400–1450*, British Archaeological Reports, British Series, 138, Oxford, 1985

R. L. Storey, *Thomas Langley and the Bishopric of Durham, 1406–1437*, London, 1961

J. Stratford, ed., *The Bedford Inventories: The Worldly Goods of John, Duke of Bedford, Regent of France, 1389–1435*, London, 1993

K. H. Vickers, *Humphrey, Duke of Gloucester: A Biography*, London, 1907

J. Watts, *Henry VI and the Politics of Kingship*, Cambridge, 1996

B. P. Wolffe, *Henry VI*, London, 1981

F. Woodman, *The Architectural History of Kings College Chapel*, London, 1986

13 THE YORKIST AND EARLY TUDOR SETTLEMENT

A. Emery, 'The Development of Raglan Castle and Keeps in Late Medieval England', *Archaeological Journal*, 132 (1975), 151–86

Gothic: Art for England, 1400–1547, ed. R. Marks and P. Williamson, exhibition catalogue, Victoria and Albert Museum, London, 2003

J. H. Harvey, *An Introduction to Tudor Architecture*, London, 1949

M. Hicks, *False, Fleeting Perjur'd Clarence: George, Duke of Clarence, 1449–78*, rev. edn, Gloucester, 1992

—, *Edward IV*, London, 2004

M. Howard, *The Early Tudor Country House*, London, 1987

M. K. Jones and M. G. Underwood, *The King's Mother: Lady Margaret Beaufort, Countess of Richmond and Derby*, Cambridge, 1992

J. R. Lander, *Crown and Nobility, 1450–1509*, London, 1976

K. B. McFarlane, *The Nobility of Later Medieval England*, Oxford, 1973

J. Pollard, ed., *The North of England in the Age of Richard III*, Stroud, 1996

C. Ross, *Edward IV*, London, 1974

—, *Richard III*, London, 1981

S. Thurley, *The Royal Palaces of Tudor England*, New Haven and London, 1993

14 THE RENAISSANCE CASTLE

M. Airs, *The Making of the English Country House, 1500–1640*, London, 1975

—, *The Buildings of Britain: Tudor and Jacobean: A Guide and Gazetteer*, London, 1982

—, *The Tudor and Jacobean Country House*, Stroud, 1995

S. Anglo, *Spectacle, Pageantry and Early Tudor Policy*, Oxford, 1969

—, *Images of Tudor Kingship*, London, 1992

A. Blunt, *Art and Architecture in France, 1500–1700*, second edn, Harmondsworth, 1970

H. M. Colvin, 'Castles and Government in Tudor England', *English Historical Review*, 83 (1968), 225–34

G. Elton, *England under the Tudors*, London, 1956 edn

S. J. Gunn, *Charles Brandon, Duke of Suffolk, 1484–1545*, Oxford, 1988

M. Hayward, *Dress at the Court of Henry VIII*, Leeds, 2009

M. Howard, *The Early Tudor Country House*, London, 1987

The Inventory of King Henry VIII: The Transcript, ed. D. Starkey, London, 1998

G. Rimer, T. Richardson and J. Cooper, eds, *Henry VIII: Arms and the Man, 1509–2009*, exhibition catalogue, Tower of London, 2009

J. G. Russell, *The Field of Cloth of Gold*, New York, 1969

J. J. Scarisbrick, *Henry VIII*, London, 1981

D. Starkey, *The Reign of Henry VIII: Personalities and Politics*, London, 1985

—, *Henry: Virtuous Prince*, London, 2008

S. Thurley, 'The Domestic Building Works of Cardinal Wolsey', in *Cardinal Wolsey: Church State and Art*, ed. S. Gunn and P. Lindley, Cambridge, 1991, 76–102

—, *The Royal Palaces of Tudor England*, New Haven and London, 1993

—, *Whitehall Palace*, New Haven and London, 1999

15 THE CASTLE AND THE REFORMATION

M. Airs, *The Making of the English Country House, 1500–1640*, London, 1975

—, *The Buildings of Britain: Tudor and Jacobean: A Guide and Gazetteer*, London, 1982

—, *The Tudor and Jacobean Country House*, Stroud, 1995

R. Coope, 'The Long Gallery: Its Origins, Development, Use and Decoration', *Architectural History*, 29 (1986), 43–84

P. Croft, ed., *Patronage, Culture and Power: The Early Cecils*, New Haven and London, 2002

E. Duffy, *Fires of Faith: Catholic England under Mary Tudor*, New Haven and London, 2009

S. G. Ellis, *Tudor Ireland: Crown, Community and the Conflict of Cultures, 1470–1603*, Harlow, 1985

T. Garner and A. Stratton, *Domestic Architecture of England during the Tudor Period*, 2 vols, London, 1929

M. Girouard, 'The Smythson Collection of the Royal Institute of British Architects', *Architectural History*, 5 (1962), 23–184

—, *Robert Smythson and the Elizabethan Country House*, New Haven and London, 1983

—, *Elizabethan Architecture*, New Haven and London, 2009

P. D. A. Harvey, *Maps in Tudor England*, London, 1993

P. Henderson, *The Tudor House and Garden*, New Haven and London, 2005

D. E. Hoak, 'Rehabilitating the Duke of Northumberland: Politics and Political Control, 1549–1553', in *The Mid-Tudor Polity, c.1540–1560*, ed. J. Loach and R. Tittler, London, 1980, 29–51

J. Loach, *Edward VI*, New Haven and London, 1999

D. Loades, *The Reign of Mary Tudor: Politics, Government and Religion in England, 1553–58*, second edn, London, 1991

—, *John Dudley, Duke of Northumberland, 1504–1553*, Oxford, 1996

D. MacCulloch, *Thomas Cranmer: A Life*, New Haven and London, 1996

—, *Reformation: Europe's House Divided, 1490–1700*, London, 2004 edn

T. Mowl, *Elizabethan and Jacobean Style*, London, 1993

J. Newman, 'The Elizabethan and Jacobean Great House: A Review of Recent Research', *Archaeological Journal*, 145 (1988), 365–73

J. Nichols, *The Progresses and Public Processions of Queen Elizabeth*, 3 vols, London, 1823

A. Ricketts, *The English Household Chapel: Building a Protestant Tradition*, Reading, 2007

D. Starkey, *Elizabeth: Apprenticeship*, London, 2000

R. Strong, *The Cult of Elizabeth: Elizabethan Portraiture and Pageantry*, London, 1977

J. Summerson, *Architecture in Britain, 1530–1830*, Harmondsworth, 1950

A. Young, *Tudor and Jacobean Tournaments*, London, 1987

16 THE STUART CASTLE

M. Airs, *The Making of the English Country House, 1500–1640*, London, 1975

—, *The Buildings of Britain: Tudor and Jacobean: A Guide and Gazetteer*, London, 1982

—, *The Tudor and Jacobean Country House*, Stroud, 1995

J. Bardon, *A History of Ulster*, Belfast, 1992

N. Cooper, *The Jacobean Country House*, London, 2006

M. Girouard, 'The Smythson Collection of the Royal Institute of British Architects', *Architectural History*, 5 (1962), 23–184

—, *Robert Smythson and the Elizabethan Country House*, New Haven and London, 1983

M. Hall, ed., *Gothic Architecture and its Meanings, 1550–1830*, Reading, 2002

R. Lockyer, *Buckingham: The Life and Political Career of George Villiers, First Duke of Buckingham, 1592–1628*, London and New York, 1981

J. Maddison, ed., *The Jacobean Country House*, London, 1987

T. Mowl, *Elizabethan and Jacobean Style*, London, 1993

J. Nichols, *The Progresses, Processions and Magnificent Festivities of King James I, his Royal Consort, Family and Court*, 4 vols, London, 1828

S. Porter, *Destruction in the English Civil War*, Stroud, 1994

R. Strong, *Henry, Prince of Wales, and England's Lost Renaissance*, London, 1986

B. Worden, ed., *Stuart England*, London, 1986

G. Worsley, *Classical Architecture in Britain: The Heroic Age*, London and New Haven, 1995

PHOTOGRAPH CREDITS

INDEX

Index compiled by Meg Davies, Fellow of the Society of Indexers